Work, Family, Health,
and Well-Being

Work, Family, Health, and Well-Being

Edited by

SUZANNE M. BIANCHI
University of Maryland

LYNNE M. CASPER
ROSALIND BERKOWITZ KING
National Institute of Child Health and Human Development
National Institutes of Health

 LAWRENCE ERLBAUM ASSOCIATES, PUBLISHERS
2005   Mahwah, New Jersey   London

Lawrence Erlbaum Associates, Inc., Publishers
10 Industrial Avenue
Mahwah, New Jersey 07430
www.erlbaum.com

Cover design by Kathryn Houghtaling Lacey

Library of Congress Cataloging-in-Publication Data

Workforce/Workplace Mismatch: Work, Family, Health,
and Well-Being (2003 : Washington, D. C.)
     Work, family, health, and well-being / edited by Suzanne
M. Bianchi, Lynne M. Casper, Rosalind Berkowitz King.
       p.   cm.
     Includes bibliographical references and index.
     ISBN 0–8058–5254–9
     1. Family—United States. 2. Work and family—United States. 3. Social
change—United States. 4. Sex discrimination in employment—United
States. 5. Health—United States. I. Bianchi, Suzanne M. II. Casper,
Lynne M. III. King, Rosalind Berkowitz. IV. National Institute of
Child Health and Human Development (U.S.) V. Title.
HD4904.25.W77 2003
306.3'61'0973—dc22
                                                2004056394

Contents

Foreword

Kathleen E. Christensen

Alfred P. Sloan Foundation

The American way of life has undergone profound changes in the last 40 years. Nowhere has this been more evident than in American family life, as women, particularly mothers, have entered and stayed in the workplace. In this important volume, Suzanne Bianchi, Lynne Casper and Rosalind Berkowitz King take a comprehensive look at how today's working families cope with the competing demands of work and family and how these demands directly and indirectly affect a family's health and well-being.

This book and the chapters herein arose from a conference sponsored by NICHD, the Alfred P. Sloan Foundation, and several federal agencies in June 2003. Nearly 200 scholars, government officials, and advocates participated in this interdisciplinary meeting, which was framed around the theme of the "Workplace-Workforce Mismatch: Work, Family, Health, and Well-Being." Defining what we mean by *mismatch* is essential to understanding the significance of the research presented at the conference and in this book.

As early as 2002, we concluded that the most significant lesson learned from the 8 years of research sponsored by the Alfred P. Sloan Foundation on the "work-family" problem was that this issue is not any individual's personal problem. In fact, the problem is larger than any one occupation, profession, or industry. Indeed, if we are to understand this problem, we must enlarge our framing of the issue to reach beyond the individual; and if we are to solve this problem, we must adopt a broader societal approach to change. Based on this analytic review of the research, it is evident that a structural workplace/workforce mismatch exists in which the workplace itself no longer fits the needs of increasing numbers of workers.

For most of the 20th century, the American workplace fit the needs of most of its workers. At mid-century, the typical American worker was a male breadwinner who earned a family wage while his wife stayed home to care for the house, the family, and friends. His job required full-time, full-year work. It offered little to no time off from work, and provided maximum opportunities for overtime, thus enabling the male breadwinner to earn a family wage and to support his stay-at-home wife and children. Federal laws, particularly the Fair Labor Standards Act (FLSA) passed in the late 1930s, codified this workplace structure. It set the standard workweek at 40 hours and made provisions for overtime compensation.

But by the beginning of this new 21st century, this workplace that had once so well fulfilled the needs of the America worker has become profoundly *mismatched* to the needs of an increasingly diverse and varied workforce. In 2004, the typical worker is as apt to be female as male. He or she is likely a member of a dual-earner household and is likely unable to earn a family wage on his or her own. Today, over 70% of married couples are dual earners, and that has resulted in a profound change in the arithmetic of the family.

Traditionally, the American family had two adults and two jobs—breadwinner and homemaker. But in most families today, the same two adults share *three* jobs, that is, two breadwinners and one homemaker. In other words, while the number of adults has stayed constant—or even declined, with the growth in single-parent families—the overall workload has grown dramatically, with the demands of work outstripping the resources. This is particularly true for professionals, for whom paying jobs are demanding longer and longer hours. It is also true for low wage workers who often work over time or take on another job to earn a living wage.

For many "three jobs-two adult" and "two jobs-one adult" single-parent families, the solution to the family work overload has been to purchase or rely on *care replacement services*. These include child care and elder care services, as well as sick-child care back-up systems. Typically, families have to locate these services on their own; occasionally these services are provided by the employer. The basic reasoning behind these *care replacement services* is that they will free workers to work longer and harder. And while these services constitute a legitimate solution to the "three jobs-two adult" work overload, they are not the only solution. Another type of solution can be found by rethinking the structure of work in America.

The current rigid structure of full-time, full-year work, with minimal-to-no-flexibility subverts the needs of today's "three-two family" and "two-one" families. Few opportunities exist for high quality flexible work arrangements—including flexibility for full-time workers, flexibility for reduced hours, and career flexibility—and those that do often carry wage and advancement penalties. Quality workplace flexibility programs, offered without penalties, would free working parents to devote more time to their families. But working parents are not the only ones who would take advantage of this type of opportunity. Indeed, increasing evidence shows that while many older workers want and need to work beyond conventional ages of retirement, they do not necessarily want full-time, full-year work. Providing workplace flexibility constitutes a critical means of realigning the workplace to the needs of the changing workforce.

The compelling research reported in this volume documents the explosion of work that must be managed by the "three jobs-two adults" family. Bianchi, Casper, and King move the discussion of this issue forward by examining the effects of the mismatch on a number of dimensions of the health and well being of American employees, their spouses, children, and communities, as well. The strength of this volume rests in its comprehensiveness, and it will prove invaluable for those seeking to understand how we work and how we live in a new century.

Preface

This volume and the chapters in it grew out of a conference held in Washington, DC, in June 2003 on "Workforce/Workplace Mismatch: Work, Family, Health, and Well-Being," under the auspices of the National Institutes of Health (NIH) with a number of collaborative partnerships, including the Alfred P. Sloan Foundation. The purpose of the conference was to review the state of the science on different dimensions of work and family life and how these factors are interrelated with the health and well-being of workers, families, children, communities, and workplaces. The conference brought together an interdisciplinary group of stellar scholars to identify theories, methodologies, key concepts, and constructs and explore the existing research base pertaining to work, family, health, and well-being. Presenters and discussants were drawn from a wide range of disciplines, including anthropology, business and management, child development, demography, economics, epidemiology, occupational health, psychology, and sociology. Scholars brought a broad range of methodological approaches to the study of work, family, and health issues.

This conference launched a new research initiative led by Drs. Lynne M. Casper and Rosalind Berkowitz King of the National Institute of Child Health and Human Development (NICHD), which is aimed at identifying the best workplace policies and practices to reduce work-family conflict and improve health and well-being. It was supported by a number of U.S. Department of Health and Human Services agencies including the NICHD and the Office of Behavioral and Social Sciences Research (OBSSR; both of the NIH), the National Institute for Occupational Safety and Health (NIOSH) of the Centers for Disease Control and Prevention (CDC), and the Child Care Bureau of the Administration for Children and Families (ACF). Various agencies within the NIH and CDC have funded research on numerous topics relating to work, family, health and well-being for many years. The NIH has also supported large-scale nationally representative data sets on which much of the research reviewed in this volume is based. Investments by the NIH, CDC, and the Agency for Healthcare Research and Quality in a diverse set of work and family topics between 1998 and 2003 totaled nearly $200 million. In addition, the ACF supported studies assessing the effects of welfare reform and investigating child-care issues.

The Alfred P. Sloan Foundation's Workplace, Workforce and Working Families Program, founded in 1994 and under the direction of Dr. Kathleen Christensen, generously collaborated in the overall planning of the conference and provided financial support for the conference and the production of this volume. A decade of seminal research supported by the Alfred P. Sloan Foundation provided evidence of a workforce-workplace mismatch which helped to frame the June 2003 conference, as well as many of the chapters in this volume.[1] As one of the first funders of research on working families, the Sloan Foundation has supported six Sloan Centers on Working Families, one Workplace Center, a portfolio of over 200 projects, and has launched a national initiative on workplace flexibility.

Finally, under the direction of Dr. Suzanne Bianchi, the Maryland Population Research Center of the University of Maryland at College Park collaborated in organizing the conference, designing and hosting the Web site for the conference, and overseeing the production of this volume.

ACKNOWLEDGMENTS

Conferences and edited volumes do not just happen: They are the result of the support and efforts of many individuals. We would like to acknowledge Dr. Duane Alexander, Director of the NICHD, Dr. Yvonne Maddox, Deputy Director of the NICHD, and Dr. Christine Bachrach, Chief of the Demographic and Behavioral Sciences Branch, Center for Population Research, NICHD, for their involvement in the development of the Work, Family, Health, and Well-Being Initiative, their participation in the conferences of the Initiative, and their support of research at the NIH on the interrelations among work, family, health, and well-being.

A number of NICHD staff members, including Janice Wahlmann, Frank Avenilla, Erica Linden, and Jennifer Browning, handled the logistics for the conference. They were assisted by Sara Raley, Hoda Makar, Barbara Hillinger, and Sarbartha Bandyopadhay of the Maryland Population Research Center, as well as Pat Stanley from the Alfred P. Sloan Foundation.

The chapters in the volume benefited from review by scholars who critiqued sections of the book and made suggestions to authors for improvement in

---

[1] For more information on this program of research, see http://www.sloan.org.

their chapters. The chapters also benefited from presentations and discussion comments from a number of scholars beyond those whose chapters appear in the volume. We thank the following individuals for these intellectual contributions: Eileen Appelbaum, Rosalind Chait Barnett, Sherry Baron, Leslie Boden, Virginia Cain, Lindsay Chase-Lansdale, Andrew Cherlin, Kathleen Christensen, Shannon Christian, Sheldon Danziger, Barbara DeVinney, Paula England, Lawrence Fine, Diane Halpern, Leslie Hammer, Mona Harrington, Sandra Hofferth, Joseph Hurrell, Jr., Jerry Jacobs, Stanislav Kasl, Robert Lerman, Shelley MacDermid, Sharon McGroder, Phyllis Moen, Margaret Neal, Patricia Pastor, Anne Pebley, Marcie Pitt-Catsouphes, Kathy Salaita, Rona Schwarz, Pamela Smock, Jane Waldfogel, and David Wegman.

Finally, the editors are most indebted to two individuals, Sara Raley and Vanessa Wight, of the University of Maryland, who handled communications with the authors, shepherded the many drafts through the review process, and assisted with the final editing of each chapter. Without them and their consummate organizational skills and cheerfulness, this volume would never have been finished.

1

Complex Connections: A Multidisciplinary Look at Work, Family, Health, and Well-Being Research

Suzanne M. Bianchi
University of Maryland

Lynne M. Casper
National Institute of Child Health and Human Development

Rosalind Berkowitz King
National Institute of Child Health and Human Development

One cannot turn on the radio, pick up the newspaper, or sit before a TV news program, sitcom, or drama without soon being reminded of the frenetic pace of life and the constant challenges individuals face in allocating sufficient time to work and family life. Work and family constitute the two most important domains of adulthood. As Rosabeth Kanter (1977) reminded us three decades ago, despite the myth of the separate spheres of work and family, there are myriad ways in which work spills over and affects family life and vice versa. Occupations differ in the level of absorption—or commitment—they require on the part of the person who fills them. Some occupations require the unpaid assistance and cooperation of family members. Work hours, shifts,

1

and schedules tend to define the pace of family life and determine when family members can all be together. Work provides the income for the consumption that determines families' standard of living and the opportunities they can afford their members. Income can be variable, with some jobs providing access to security and high levels of economic well-being, whereas other jobs do not pay a living wage, are temporary, or do not come with steady, predictable hours. The nature of work—including work "cultures"—affects workers' physical health and social and psychological well-being. How successfully people organize their work lives can directly affect their health and well-being. Through the effects of workplaces on workers, job characteristics and work cultures can then spill over to affect the health and well-being of children and other family members as well as the communities in which workers live.

Yet family life also affects work. During periods of particularly intense family demands, such as after the birth of a child or during the illness of a family member, workers try to "scale back" their commitment to long work hours. They may have increased absences from work, and the quality and quantity of their output may slip. Increased home demands can also affect workers' physical health and social and psychological well-being. Thus, increasing family demands can affect employer well-being, along with the well-being of workers and their families, both directly and indirectly through feedback loops.

The effects of work and family life on health and well-being vary by gender and race/ethnicity. Women continue to shoulder a disproportionate amount of the burden of housework and child care even as their responsibilities in the labor market increase. A gender gap in wages persists for all but select sectors of the labor force, and women incur a wage penalty for motherhood that continues for years after childbirth (Budig & England, 2001). Non-White workers disproportionately occupy jobs with lower pay, fewer benefits, and less flexible working conditions. At the same time, minorities have larger families and thus greater levels of family responsibility. African-American women, in particular, spend less of their lifetimes within marriage than White women while having slightly higher fertility rates (Raley, 2000); thus, they tend to be particularly vulnerable as sole wage earners with multiple dependents. Health disparities exist in such areas as overall ratings of health, coronary heart disease, and hypertension, with African-American women generally fairing the worst. Given these striking differences in work, family, and health across race/ethnicity and gender, it is imperative to examine how they are all interrelated.

This volume considers multiple dimensions of health and well-being for workers, their families, their children, and their communities. For individuals, health includes physiological outcomes such as mortality, hypertension, diabetes, and lung cancer, as well as depression and other mental disorders. It also includes economic and social well-being. Research in the fields of occupational and public health has demonstrated that the settings for and activities engaged in during work hours have consequences for disease, injury, and disability among workers. Traditionally, occupational health researchers have focused on exposure to chemicals and the physical conditions under which labor is performed. As the nature and content of work has changed, the focus of research has shifted to the relationships between the psychosocial dimensions of work and worker health outcomes, including mental disorders and unhealthy habits. The health of the individual worker is intimately related to the health of the worker's family. Epidemiological investigations into the socioeconomic gradient in health within broad occupational categories have raised important questions about the role of specific psychosocial working conditions versus the role of conditions of employment, such as wages and level of job security afforded a worker and his or her family, in affecting health outcomes.

Social science research shows that work and family behaviors (e.g., how much time one devotes to work and family domains, how well work schedules interweave with family routines, and whether work and family experiences are positive or negative) affect not only physical and mental health, but also social and economic well-being. For families, work and family behaviors, the nature of the work being done, and the workplace environment can affect the health and well-being of spouses, children, and other family members, and how well the family functions. Stressful home conditions resulting from competing work and family demands, unfavorable work conditions, or the ill health of a parent can affect children's cognitive, social, and emotional development. For communities, work and family behaviors can cause adverse consequences by transferring more responsibilities to neighbors, schools, and community organizations. In addition, healthy individuals and families are the building blocks of healthy functioning communities.

Although research in work, family, health, and well-being spans many disciplines, researchers have typically used theories, methods, key concepts, and constructs from a single disciplinary perspective, limiting the types of questions they ask and the utility of the answers they provide. For example, labor economists and sociologists who study occupations tend to focus mainly on work and working conditions, family demographers focus mainly on family structure and behaviors, anthropologists study work culture and the everyday activities of individuals, occupational physicians focus on occupational health problems, psychologists focus on stress and mental health of the individual as they relate to either work or family, and management researchers assess the organization of work and production. As illustrated, these factors are all interrelated and need to be studied concurrently, applying a multidisciplinary approach. The first step in implementing a broader, more integrated approach, and the goal of this volume, is to bring together research that examines work, family, health, and well-being linkages from a variety of disciplinary perspectives. The volume draws together research exploring many dimensions of work and family life to assess the state of scientific knowledge and to provide directions for new areas of investigation.

The volume is organized into seven major sections: The first section provides an overview of changes in work and family time and time use, followed by a section focused on employers and workplaces. Next, the volume explores disciplinary perspectives on work, family, health, and well-being. This is followed by a section focused on the most studied work and family nexus, the interrelationship between parental employment, especially maternal employment, and child well-being. However, child well-being is but one important topic area in work and family research, and the remaining sections focus on additional family, work, and well-being interrelationships. A fifth section provides an examination of gender differences in the division of labor, the effect of marriage on health, the shifting nature of caregiving throughout life, and the role of work on various health and well-being outcomes. Next, the occupational health literature is explored. In the final section, the focus turns to the unique work-family issues faced by low-income families and workers in low-wage jobs. We now turn to a brief summary of the contents of the chapters in each section.

PART I: TIME, WORK, AND FAMILY

A unifying theme in the study of work and family change is the issue of time: time as a finite resource—time that may become increasingly scarce as families try to balance multiple work schedules with multiple family and life demands. Most work in this area has been done by sociologists and demographers. However, developmental psychologists have examined how time allocation affects children's outcomes. The chapters in this section form a unified whole, with each chapter discussing a different piece of the time-allocation issue in families. The purpose of this section is to paint a picture of the complexities involved in fulfilling the demands of work and family life given the limits of a 24-hour day and a 7-day week. Collectively, these chapters address one of the most important issues to consider in examining how work and family lives affect the health and well-being of workers and their families: time allocation.

In chapter 2, Suzanne M. Bianchi and Sara B. Raley describe the dilemma families face in deciding how to allocate time between market work and the home so that family members have the financial, emotional, and social resources they need to thrive and prosper. The authors trace how families have adapted over time to meet competing obligations, with women shedding time in housework and protecting time with children, as they add time in the labor force, and men increasing the time they spend doing housework and child care. They provide an intriguing picture of total (paid plus unpaid) work hours in married couple families, which suggests that fathers and mothers share workloads relatively equally and that workloads have increased for both parents. Yet gender specialization has not disappeared, with women devoting proportionately more of their total hours to housework and child care and men devoting far more of their time to market work.

Like Bianchi and Raley, Harriet B. Presser (chap. 3) is concerned with time in market activities, but her chapter goes beyond the number of hours worked per week and considers the time of day and days of the week on which this work occurs and the effects these schedules have on the health and well-being of workers. She points out that the consequences for family functioning are likely to depend on which hours and which days individuals work and which hours and which days their family members work. For example, working late at night or on a rotating shift appears to be more detrimental for individuals and their families than working on weekends. Additionally, evening work reduces the time parents spend with children, whereas night work may increase marital instability. Presser concludes by pointing out that the biggest growth in the economy is projected to be in service occupations, which have high levels of nonstandard work hours and shifts.

In chapter 4, Ann C. Crouter and Susan M. McHale acknowledge that the complexity of work time within and across families is important for family functioning and extend this notion to the study of children's outcomes. They argue that it is necessary to examine additional dimensions of time to understand how work and family considerations affect children. The chapter reviews the associations among parental work hours, schedules and shifts, the rhythms of family routines and family time, children's time use, and children's relationships, developmental outcomes, and psychosocial well-being. The research suggests that mothers' work hours are more weakly associated with child outcomes than fathers' work hours and that shift work scheduling can be problematic for children. Family time and family rituals are positively related to children's psychosocial functioning. Children's involvement in structured activities is associated with fewer behavior problems. The authors conclude that, although each of these time dimensions is important for children and youth outcomes, researchers have not adequately studied the interrelations among the different time dimensions and have not mapped the causal processes by which they affect child outcomes.

Finally, in chapter 5, Barbara Schneider and Linda Waite continue the focus on the dilemma of time allocation within families and how time allocation affects individuals and family members. They argue that it is important not only to know how people spend time throughout the day, but also how they "feel about it"—how they subjectively experience their activities. For example, what is it about long work hours that increases stress? Is it the number of work hours per se or is it how people feel about the type of activity they are doing or the coworkers with whom they are engaged when they work those long hours? The authors introduce the reader to the Experience Sampling Method (ESM) that can be used to collect the subjective information necessary to answer these questions. They also argue that, under certain circumstances, the ESM can provide better quality time use data than surveys or time diaries.

PART II: THE "WORK" IN WORK AND FAMILY

The second section of the volume focuses on the employer side of the work and family relationship, charting how workplaces have changed and how employers think about their responsibilities for meeting workers' family needs. Employers, consultants working with employers on workplace policies, and employees often see academic research in the work-family area—particularly studies that rely on secondary data analysis—as unrealistic in their assumptions and expectations. Employers have interests that do not always match those of employees, and organizational change can be difficult to accomplish especially in a short period of time. The chapters in this section seek to begin to bridge this gap between academic research and practices in work settings to make research in this area more applicable to real-world settings. Collectively, the authors bring perspectives from schools of business, social demography, economics, labor and industrial relations, management sciences, and public policy.

Beginning with the Holzer chapter and proceeding through each of the other chapters in turn, this section widens our perspective from a narrow, ground-level lens to a consideration of both broader and higher level contexts. All of the authors accept the health of the organization as a legitimate consideration. However, as the reader proceeds through the section, the primacy of that consideration is questioned on grounds that are relevant to employers, including productivity and community reputation.

In chapter 6, Harry J. Holzer presents an accessible discussion of the decision-making framework of employers with regard to work-family issues, laying out supply and demand processes. Holzer considers the factors that determine employers' choices about hiring, benefits, and workplace flexibility. He asks whether the mix of employer policies generated by the labor market is optimal from the point of view of workers, society, and employers. He argues that employers have an interest in assisting families in balancing work and family. By helping employees to manage the conflict between work and family, and subsequently minimizing the difficulties raised by absenteeism and turnover that are frequently associated with child care and increasingly elder care problems, employers can create a more stable and productive labor force. Employer size, industry, type of production, and target labor pool influence the level of workplace flexibility and family-related benefits offered. However, the labor market does not always distribute these benefits across workers equally. Holzer briefly considers the role of public policy advocating government mandates, tax subsidies, or credits as ways to correct for the inequitable distribution of benefits across workplaces.

Ellen Ernst Kossek (chap. 7) extends Holzer's economic viewpoint by reviewing the research on employer work-family policies and discussing the gaps in the literature. She identifies three types of studies on work-family policy: those that focus on how and whether policies are adopted, those that focus on who uses the policies (a demographic view), and those that focus on the effects of work-family policies on employees and employers. She then discusses the need to look at the different types of policies, the way they are implemented, whether employers support the policies, how individual supervisors and work groups affect the enactment of policies, how policies can be integrated into human resource strategies, and the difficulties with the "business case," which she argues overemphasizes the role of the shareholder in cost–benefit analyses.

In chapter 8, Cynthia A. Thompson, Jeanine K. Andreassi, and David J. Prottas build on Kossek's chapter and move further from the straightforward economic argument to a focus on workplace culture. First, the authors review the literature, noting that work-family culture is comprised of three parts: organizational time demands, career consequences for using work-family benefits, and managerial support. Research shows that a supportive work-family culture is related to a greater use of work-family policies. Extreme time demands have adverse effects on employees' health and well-being. In addition, these demands have implications for employees' use of family-friendly policies. A supportive relationship between employees and their manager has been shown to be a powerful predictor of use of work-family policies, greater work-family balance, and higher overall satisfaction with work. The authors also consider the antecedents to an unfriendly work culture and show that culture can vary across subunits of the same organization.

Lotte Bailyn, in chapter 9, shifts our perspective on the design and construction of the workplace in terms of both structures and mind-sets. She makes explicit the perspective in which the three previous chapters are grounded—that the organization is a given and workers' lives need to be adapted to it. She then discusses the implications of legitimating the workers' needs and placing that consideration above that of the already recognized legitimate needs of the workplace for policy and practice. Bailyn calls for realigning work and family to create an effective workforce, using two case studies to illustrate how workplaces might adapt to the family needs of workers.

In chapter 10, Ann Bookman moves the focus from the workplace out into the community in which workers and their employers are embedded.

She demonstrates how employer and worker decision-making processes do not occur in a vacuum, but rather within a web of community influences, and how the effects of these processes are felt beyond the boundaries of the individual employer, worker, or worker's family unit. She describes how the workplace–community link has changed over time largely as a result of industrialization and "separate spheres" thinking. Workplaces and communities are highly interdependent (e.g., employers rely on the local labor pool, and communities rely on employers to create jobs for their residents), but these connections are threatened by the fact that workers are no longer guaranteed job and income security simply by virtue of hard work and long service as well as increased economic inequality and urban sprawl. New approaches are needed to address this fragile link between workplaces and communities.

Finally, Richard Wertheimer, Susan Jekielek, Kristin A. Moore, and Zakia Redd (chap. 11) describe various work policies and governmental regulations, including the Fair Standards Labor Act, worker's compensation, social security, the FMLA, unemployment insurance, TANF, and child support enforcement, and comment that these programs affect families by offering them benefits and protecting them from harmful work circumstances. The chapter also focuses on more specific aspects of employment that affect families, such as work hours, and how work patterns affect the child care and preventive health care provided to children. The authors conclude with suggestions for additional research.

PART III: DISCIPLINARY PERSPECTIVES IN THE STUDY OF WORK AND FAMILY

Work and family research takes place in a number of academic disciplines. Part of the goal of this volume is to provide information on how work and family has been studied in different academic disciplines and how it is conceptualized within varying theoretical perspectives. The contributions in this section illustrate how work and family research has been theoretically developed and empirically studied in five academic disciplines: psychology, economics, anthropology, sociology, and public policy.

In chapter 12, Debra A. Major and Jeanette N. Cleveland provide a comprehensive view of the psychological theories that have been applied to work, family, health, and well-being research, including biological, cognitive, developmental, and social perspectives. These perspectives have been applied in several subdisciplines of psychology that study different aspects of the work-family interface, including developmental psychology, social psychology, clinical psychology, and industrial-organizational psychology. In psychology, particular attention has been paid to the multiple roles that individuals play in work and family domains and the effect of those roles on the individual's and family's health and well-being. The unique contribution of psychology to the study of work-family issues is the focus on the individual. Even when broader social and economic contexts are considered, the major focus of psychology is understanding the individual embedded in those contexts.

In chapter 13, Arleen A. Leibowitz introduces the reader to the economic perspective and explains that economics is first and foremost concerned with how families and firms decide on an optimal allocation of scarce resources. In the case of work and family research, time and money are most often the scarce resources of interest. Economists examine decisions regarding how these resources are marshaled and allocated within families and the consequences of those decisions for future earnings. Leibowitz also provides a discussion of how economists think about the effects of maternal employment on health outcomes for children and how they view the so-called *mismatch* between work at home and in the market. The unique contribution of economics to the study of work and family is that it provides a framework for understanding the decisions people make in the work and family spheres. Economists, like psychologists, are concerned with the individual; however, their primary focus is on individual decision making within the context of the family unit.

Charles N. Darrah (chap. 14) contributes a thought-provoking chapter on anthropological perspectives to the study of the workplace–workforce mismatch. The chapter introduces four fields within anthropology that are the cornerstones for understanding social phenomena: archaeology, linguistic anthropology, physical anthropology, and cultural anthropology. Darrah points out that cultural anthropology is at the center of the discipline's interest in work and family issues and is concerned with "practices that link social organization with cultural models and their material embodiments." Anthropology includes a holistic analysis of social systems, attention to the diverse understandings of cultural insiders, concern with the meaning of action to its participants, and relations between local settings and broader contexts. Perhaps the most important contribution of anthropology to this research area lies in conceptualizing work and family issues within the larger community and societal context while identifying the pathways through which work and family conflicts are manifested in the activities and interactions of everyday life.

Sociology, like psychology, has many theoretical perspectives that can be used to understand issues related to work and family. In chapter 15, Jennifer Glass provides a thoughtful overview of four major theoretical schools: symbolic interactionism, ecological systems theory, life course perspective, and conflict and exchange theories. The symbolic interactionist tradition shares some common ground with both psychological and anthropological perspectives: It emphasizes social roles and identity structures, and examines how behavioral expectations based on cultural norms and institutional practices are internalized. By contrast, systems theories share common ground with economic and anthropological perspectives, and focus on group needs and goals of families and workplaces, placing individual behavior within the group context. The life course perspective, also employed by economists and psychologists, emphasizes the timing of work and family involvements and how this timing affects future life events. Conflict and exchange theories focus on the role that differences in power and material wealth play in the social construction of work and family arrangements. This perspective has also been adopted by psychologists and some economists. Glass argues that the essential sociological insight is that the personal difficulties individuals face in trying to fulfill family and paid work responsibilities are socially patterned and somewhat predictable given the institutional friction generated by the competing social goals of industrial production and family reproduction.

Jane Waldfogel begins chapter 16 by synthesizing the unique contributions of each of the four disciplines just discussed to the study of work, family, health, and well-being. She then builds a case for why a public policy perspective is also needed and uses as examples two relevant bodies of research examining parental leave and child-care policies. The aim of the public policy perspective is to understand the effects of policies, document the potential of policies to produce desired outcomes, and inform future decisions about policies. Thus, the unique contribution of this perspective lies in the systematic evaluation of the tools societies can use to modify behavior.

PART IV: PARENTAL EMPLOYMENT
AND OUTCOMES FOR CHILDREN

Perhaps the most studied topic in the work and family arena is the interrelationship between parental employment, especially maternal employment, and family and child well-being. The chapters in this section summarize what we know about work, particularly maternal employment, care of children, and child health and well-being. Several also have a methodological focus. All review the existing literature. Two are from a psychological or developmental approach and two are from an economic approach. The final chapter discusses government and workplace family benefits, usage by working parents, and their potential to enhance child outcomes.

In chapter 17, Rena Repetti illustrates how the psychological perspective is useful for identifying, measuring, and evaluating the effects of parental employment on child and family well-being. Repetti discusses the challenge of detecting the effects of parental employment on health and well-being and the importance of considering family interaction as a health/well-being outcome, noting that social interaction often takes a central mediating role in the models that link work-family factors to child outcomes. She notes that because not all families respond to work-family stressors in the same way, it is important to consider moderating variables that distinguish family responses. Finally, Repetti considers the implications for research design and intervention implied by the psychological approach, calling attention to how health and well-being outcomes are conceptualized and how sampling strategies and experimental interventions are designed.

Following Repetti, Martha Zaslow, Susan Jekielek, and Megan Gallagher (chap. 18) ask whether maternal employment creates a mismatch with the developmental needs of children. They note evidence suggesting that maternal employment may conflict with the developmental needs at two particular stages in childhood: infancy and adolescence. Their approach to identify and understand the developmental mismatch requires one to identify a specific developmental task and the social contexts (such as home or work) that can affect a child's progress toward this task, and to document the links between aspects of the social environment and the child's progress. The authors note the need for better treatment of issues of selection; a greater consideration for low-income samples, as most of the original research was conducted on middle-income, dual-earner couples; a greater attention to processes that might mediate the relationship between maternal employment and child development; and an increasing consideration of both the home and child-care environments.

In chapter 19, Janet Currie discusses the methodological issues surrounding work-family research: specifically the problems with selection effect bias. First, she discusses the strengths and limitations of various approaches: employing an experimental design, controlling for confounding variables, using instrumental variables, and assigning propensity scores. Second, she reviews studies examining the relationship between maternal employment and child well-being and the relationship between child-care quality and child outcomes, paying attention to the various methodological strategies these studies employ to address selection bias. She concludes that what is needed in work-family research are results that can be replicated in a wide range of well-designed studies, and that currently the evidence on an effect of maternal employment on children's outcomes is greater than of child-care quality.

Currie's chapter is followed by Sanders Korenman and Robert Kaestner's (chap. 20) review of the economics literature on work-family trade-offs. The authors draw our attention to the difficulties and complexities associated with studying the effects of parental work on child development. They review 25 studies that directly test effects of parental employment on child health and development—providing a summary of the scope of the research as well as a general discussion of the ways economists have typically linked work-family mismatch to child development.

Finally, Christopher J. Ruhm (chap. 21) discusses government policies (or lack thereof) that help work-family balance. He shows the propensity with which small and large firms offer benefits like paid vacation and onsite child care. He also discusses the Family and Medical Leave Act (FMLA) and compares this legislation to that offered by European governments. Extended, paid parental leaves are common throughout Europe. Recent findings on the negative relationship between extensive maternal employment in the first year of a child's life and child well-being argue for much greater attention to the provision of paid leave for new U.S. parents. The chapter concludes with a commentary on private versus publicly negotiated labor market contracts and the pros and cons of relying on employers to offer family benefits such as parental leave.

PART V: GENDER AND EMPLOYMENT, CAREGIVING AND HEALTH

Gender is one of the most important factors relating to how individuals arrange their work and family lives. Some contributions to this section focus explicitly on gender differences in the work, family, health, and well-being literature, whereas others discuss topics such as caregiving that are inherently related to gender.

In chapter 22, Joyce K. Fletcher deconstructs the history and perceptions associated with the separate spheres of work and family framework. Specifically, she argues that (a) the public and private contexts associated with these spheres are assumed to be dichotomous, (b) the spheres are gendered, and (c) the spheres have an underlying set of rules that govern what is appropriate behavior to be successful in that sphere. With this in mind, Fletcher argues that research and policy initiatives need to explore (and, by implication, be wary of) work practices that maintain the separation of the two spheres as well as move away from a narrow focus on work cultures by directing attention toward norms and beliefs about caretaking as well as those associated with work cultures. The ultimate goal is to "create a framework that supports a new business model for integrating work and personal lives."

Pamela J. Smock and Mary Noonan (chap. 23) focus on the gendered division of domestic labor (considering housework and parenting separately) and the labor market implications of this unequal division of labor. First, they discuss three theoretical perspectives on domestic labor: time availability, relative resources, and doing gender, citing empirical research that supports all three perspectives. Then they focus more narrowly on parenting and discuss the trends over time in married parents' activities with children, single parenting, and nonresidential fathering. They also describe how marriage and parenting are associated with labor market outcomes. Specifically, marriage and motherhood are associated with a wage premium to men and a penalty to women. Finally, they discuss the psychological consequences of work-family issues and trade-offs for men and women.

In chapter 24, Ross M. Stolzenberg and Linda J. Waite focus on how the processes of working and maintaining relationships may interfere with each other and the effect this interference has on health and well-being. The authors consider two aspects of health: emotional well-being and physical health. They note that despite the issue of selection bias where healthy women and men may be more likely to marry than their nonhealthy counterparts, consensus exists that something about being married and unmarried affects health. For example, marriage provides men with someone to help monitor and encourage healthy behaviors, and both married men and women are less likely than their nonmarried counterparts to engage in risky behaviors. Stolzenberg and Waite advocate further research on how the economic and social changes over the last few decades influence spousal behavior in the labor market and in the home, how these changes influence marital relations, and the degree to which the benefits of marriage remain.

In chapter 25, Eliza Pavalko and Fang Gong examine three specific work-family issues faced by midlife women: caregiving (care work), age discrimination, and retirement. The aging of women's families creates caregiving responsibilities that present a unique challenge to balancing work and family. Age discrimination, which can result in the limiting of women's labor market opportunities, can have long-term financial, health, and well-being effects. Retirement issues demonstrate how structured benefit plans influence couples' decisions about whether and when to retire. The authors close by suggesting four directions for future research: more research on cohort variation in balancing work and family; better attention to issues of selection; more life course analysis of the interrelations of work, family, health, and well-being; and continued development of theoretical perspectives on midlife.

PART VI: OCCUPATIONS, WORKPLACE SETTINGS, AND HEALTH OF FAMILIES

A unique perspective on work and family arises from the occupational health literature. The chapters in this section review the theoretical perspectives and empirical research that connect workplaces with health outcomes and family stress and well-being. Together these chapters provide significant tools for future research into the interrelationships among work, family, health, and well-being. The chapters are connected to the anthropological, sociological, and psychological perspectives found elsewhere in the volume, and they provide a unique contribution, as perspectives of occupational health scientists have not often informed other social scientific research in the work and family area.

In chapter 26, Allard E. Dembe comprehensively covers the familial consequences of workplace-induced injuries and illness. The chapter is reminiscent of Darrah's (chap. 14) anthropological discussion of how families actually operate (i.e., the daily activities involved in the construction of family as a social phenomenon). First, Dembe considers how injury and illness can affect families through five pathways: medical care and recovery, psychological and behavioral, functional, economic, and vocational responses. Next, Dembe examines how *occupational* injuries and illnesses are distinct from other non-work-related injuries and illnesses in their effect on families. Examples of such complexities include navigating unfriendly workers' compensation systems, the burden to prove occupational causation, and possible litigation necessary to establish this proof, as well as issues surrounding the timing of return to work and loss of wages. A review of the literature reveals that much of what we know is limited to qualitative analysis with relatively few comparison groups. Dembe argues that key areas of additional research should include the nature of family caregiving when there is an occupational injury or illness; the effect these injuries have on educational, vocational, and recreational pursuits of children; how injury and illness affects alcohol and substance use among family members; and how workers' compensation representatives and families communicate and resolve claims.

Benjamin C. Amick and Cam Mustard (chap. 27) then move to a more abstract theoretical framework from which to approach the concrete analyses suggested by Dembe. They attempt to synthesize the perspectives of occupational health scientists in the discipline of epidemiology (where the focus is on exposure, health outcomes, and sources of illnesses, injuries, and disease) with those of social scientists focusing on the life course. The authors consider labor market exposure and experience, how it is measured over the working life course, and its relation to health. This chapter presents an important pioneering example of the research needed to bring the biomedical and social sciences perspectives together.

Finally, in chapter 28, Tage S. Kristensen, Lars Smith-Hansen, and Nicole Jansen identify work demands, the degree of influence and possibility of personal development, and the quality of interpersonal relations and leadership as three factors that influence outcomes in work-family conflict. They find that increasing work demands create time and energy conflict. The degree of freedom and influence that employees have at work is associated with their ability to control work hours, work breaks, and vacation time—important dimensions when faced with balancing family demands. Finally, positive relations between colleagues and supervisors, role clarity, and good quality of leadership reduce work-family conflict. The authors assess these dimensions of the work environment with an improved research instrument that is grounded in prior theoretical and empirical work. They provide a short, medium, and long version of the instrument for use in projects with different levels of resources and units of analysis, and they validate it empirically through analyses of results from multiple surveys in Denmark and the Netherlands.

PART VII: LOW-INCOME FAMILIES AND WORK, CARE, HEALTH, AND WELL-BEING

Much of the research on work and family has focused on the issues that middle-class families with young children face in negotiating work and family life. This final section of the book focuses on strains in low-income families and low-wage jobs. The goal of this section is to highlight the unique work and family challenges faced by the low-income population and employers who offer low-wage jobs.

In chapter 29, Maureen Perry-Jenkins highlights the work-family issues of working-class families using data from the Work and Family Transitions Project, a study of working-class adults transitioning into parenthood. Perry-Jenkins details the experiences of working-class parents, focusing on their unstable hours (including mandatory overtime), financial constraints, complex child-care arrangements, job satisfaction, and wide-ranging workplace benefits and resources (including health insurance coverage, leave-taking policies, and employer flexibility with regard to work schedules). Most of the couples' employers did not have extensive (or, in some cases, any) work-family policies and/or benefits, so most employees were at the mercy of their supervisor when they faced work-family conflicts. Perry-Jenkins concludes the chapter with four suggestions for future research: the need for "ecologically valid" approaches; greater attention to class, race, and family structure differences; a focus on subjective as well as objective dimensions of work-family mismatch; and more attention to change over the life course.

Julia R. Henly and Susan Lambert (chap. 30) outline the policies and practices that define the nature of the employment experience and shape the child-care needs of working parents in low-wage jobs. Two major issues confronting workers in low-wage jobs are: ambiguous employment statuses (e.g., a worker is employed on paper, but is not scheduled for any hours of work) and schedule instability (e.g., fluctuating and rotating shifts). Because their work hours fluctuate, parents in low-skilled jobs have multiple and complex child-care arrangements. To address the caregiving difficulties faced by these parents, policymakers need to move beyond efforts to extend hours, reduce costs, add services, and increase the availability of child care (although this is important) and address the nature of the jobs/workplaces. This would require changing both social policy and employer practices.

In chapter 31, Linda M. Burton, Laura Lein, and Amy Kolak discuss family health (the health of caregivers and children) in low-income families using data from Welfare, Children and Families: A Three-City Study. The chapter details the strikingly poor health of parents and children in low-income families: In most families, both parents and children have health problems, and many individuals (parents and children alike) have multiple afflictions. Families face tremendous and often insurmountable barriers to seeking treatment for their illnesses, holding onto jobs, and finding adequate child care. Hence, improved health and labor force policy must go hand in hand if the needs of low-income populations are to be met.

In chapter 32, Jody Heymann, Stephanie Simmons, and Alison Earle present findings from the Project on Global Working Families—the first global initiative to examine working conditions and family health and well-being. The authors discuss the global transformation in the composition of the labor force and urbanization and the effect this has on children and families. They compare the experiences of working parents and their children across six countries: Mexico, Vietnam, Botswana, the United States, Honduras, and Russia. Despite differences among the countries, the authors identify a number of common experiences, such as the negative effect of working conditions on child health outcomes, the impact of the lack of child care on educational and developmental outcomes of older children (who were often responsible for the care of younger siblings), and issues of insufficient parental availability. The authors discuss a number of policy issues such as maternity protection policies, human rights policies, and antidiscrimination legislation. They conclude that because the challenges of integrating work and family life are global, the solutions to these challenges need to be global as well.

PART VIII: CONCLUSION

In the final chapter, Lynne M. Casper, Suzanne M. Bianchi, and Rosalind Berkowitz King provide a conclusion to the volume. They reiterate the broad changes that have occurred in the arenas of family and work, and they discuss the importance of multidisciplinary work to understand the implications of these changes for health and well-being. They outline three crucial topic areas: the importance of including context in theory and analysis; the difficulty of establishing causal connections; and the necessity of considering the variability of families across socioeconomic status and life course stages. Rigorous research incorporating all of these elements is needed to form a foundation of knowledge to craft changes in workplaces and government policy.

In summary, a broad range of topics are covered in the chapters that follow. A number of disciplinary voices assess the state of work and family research and knowledge. The complexity of the issue is enormous. The chapters detail the wealth of information we have in hand as well as the large number of questions that remain to be answered.

REFERENCES

Budig, M. J., & England, P. (2001). The wage penalty for motherhood. *American Sociological Review*, 66(2), 204–225.

Kanter, R. M. (1977). *Work and family in the United States: A critical review and agenda for research and policy*. New York: Russell Sage Foundation.

Raley, R. K. (2000). Recent trends and differentials in marriage and cohabitation: The United States. In L. J. Waite (Ed.), *Ties that bind: Perspectives on marriage and cohabitation* (pp. 19–39). New York: Aldine de Gruyter.

PART I

Time, Work, and Family

2

Time Allocation in Families

Suzanne M. Bianchi
Sara B. Raley
University of Maryland

Families have long faced a dilemma in allocating time to work and family. Who will earn money to support the family financially and who will provide the caregiving children require and the physical and psychological support that the family earner(s) need? In post–World War II America, providing economically for a family largely took place within a two-parent context, and the economy was such that (White) men could often earn sufficient income from one job to support a wife and children. Following the Depression and World War II, there was little foreign competition as Europe and Japan rebuilt, and there was a sustained period of high productivity and strong wage growth for male earners (Levy, 1996). Further, discrimination against women in the workplace was legal and widespread—hence, opportunities for women outside the home were limited.

A high degree of specialization along gender lines solved the work-family time problem. Men did the paid work needed to support a family financially, and women did the unpaid work in the home needed to support children and a working husband. Family life in this era was unusual, with its early and nearly universal marriage, low divorce rates, and high Baby Boom fertility (Cherlin, 1992). Many Baby Boomers grew up under this "work and family" configuration, and nostalgia for the Ozzie and Harriet family of the 1950s and 1960s abounds (Coontz, 1992) as families forge new arrangements that include employed mothers and more single parenting.

In the latter half of the 20th century, the gender-specialized division of labor became less universal, less desirable, and perhaps less attainable as a solution to the work-family time-allocation problem. Women's educational and occupational opportunities expanded with the civil rights movement and renewed women's movements of the late 1960s and 1970s. More equal labor market opportunities between men and women called into question a division of labor that prescribed women's place in the home and men's in the market. At the same time, men's ability to earn a family wage diminished, particularly among those with a high school education or less. Beginning in the 1970s, workers and their families were buffeted by large-scale socioeconomic shifts: oil price shocks and high inflation, the onset of two decades of rising inequality in earnings and family income, and the decline in manufacturing and union strength.

Between 1970 and 1990, the dramatic increase in paid employment among mothers, particularly married mothers of young children, and the increase in single parenting heightened attention to the interplay and potential conflict between market work and family caregiving responsibilities. Changes in maternal employment and family living arrangements "quieted" in the 1990s, and some families still operate with a highly gender-specialized division of labor, particularly when there are two parents and very young children. Nonetheless, it is much more common for individuals to combine paid market work, unpaid domestic work, and family caregiving. This is especially true of women, who frequently combine work and family duties. Whether men have taken on significantly more domestic work is still being debated, although time diary research suggests some increase in housework and a sizable increase in child care among married fathers (Bianchi, 2000; Bianchi, Milkie, Sayer, & Robinson, 2000; Sandberg & Hofferth, 2001; Sayer, Cohen, & Casper, 2004).

A less gender-differentiated division of labor in the family means that each individual experiences firsthand the inevitable conflicts between allocating time to market activities and family caregiving. When each spouse (or partner) does some paid and unpaid work, each develops expertise in both domains, and perhaps also a sense of entitlement in "having a say" about how the work gets done and how the resources from paid work are allocated. The balance of power in the family also shifts when women's control of economic resources increases or approaches that of men. The limited empirical research suggests there is greater spending on children's and women's needs when women control a greater share of the family's income (e.g., Lundberg, Pollak, & Wales, 1997; Seltzer, 2002). Considerable empirical and theoretical attention has been given to whether relationships are destabilized as women's employment and earnings increase, with the dominant theory in economics predicting more marital discord under more egalitarian arrangements (Becker, 1991). Questions remain, however, about the strength of a causal connection between women's economic independence and marital disruption (Oppenheimer, 1997; Sayer & Bianchi, 2000).

When juggling paid work and unpaid caregiving, issues of coordination among family members become paramount. In married-couple families, one individual no longer controls one domain, the output of which can be exchanged for what the other individual controls. On the plus side, there is more redundancy in the married-couple family when time allocation is not so gender-specific. As such, some shocks to the system (e.g., the loss of one spouse's job) may be easier to absorb. However, the household may incur a cost in spending more time negotiating the inevitable time conflicts between work and family life. Families settle on routines, but whenever those routines are temporarily disrupted, say by a sick child, they must renegotiate who is to cover the home front when there is a conflict with market work (or vice versa when a paid work demand disrupts domestic routines).

Time-allocation issues are particularly complex in single-parent households. A quarter century ago, Vickery (1977) argued that not only were single mothers at heightened risk of financial poverty, but they also suffered a severe time deficit. A single parent's work and family negotiations may be particularly difficult, especially if they cross household boundaries. If a single mother is to balance work and childrearing with resources other than her own time and earnings (or welfare income), she must effectively obtain time and money (e.g., child support) from the child's other parent who resides elsewhere. Alternatively, she must negotiate assistance from extended kin or friends, either those who also live with her or those who live elsewhere.

In summary, in the United States (and elsewhere) today, time is allocated in a less gender-specific way. However, stresses and strains remain and vary by the number of adults and financial resources of the household, and the collective time availability and flexibility of family members, some of whom live together, some of whom do not. This general orientation to work and family provides the backdrop for an examination of trends in labor force participation and time use in families.

CHANGES IN MARKET AND NONMARKET TIME: A PORTRAIT

In 1950, for every 100 working adults there were 57 adults (ages 16–64) outside the labor force to (potentially) provide back-up services for them. By 2000, that number had dropped to 28 adults for every 100 adult workers, and it will likely remain near that level in the future (calculation based on Toosi, 2002). In other words, employed individuals likely have to do more of the support activities (run more of their own errands, pick up prepared meals on their way home from work, miss a day of work to care for a sick child) than they did in the past.

Time diary studies, done at roughly 10-year intervals in the United States beginning in 1965, allow us to assess how adults allocate time and how this changed between the mid-1960s and late 1990s.[1] On average, men ages 18 to 64 currently do less market work than they did in 1965 primarily because they retire earlier and enter the labor force later.[2] Meanwhile, they have increased their time doing household work, child care, and, somewhat surprisingly, leisure activities. During the same period (1965–1998), women increased the time they allocated to market work, decreased the time they spent in nonmarket work, especially housework, and decreased their leisure time as they took on a "second shift" of domestic work at the end of a work day.

Time allocation is greatly affected by one's stage in life. In young adulthood, few gender differences exist as both men and women increasingly allocate time to finishing school, often extending that schooling to include postsecondary education. Nearly two thirds of those who graduate from high school enroll in college, and college attendance and graduation rates are now higher for women than for men (Bianchi & Spain, 1996, Table 3; Newburger & Curry, 2000; Sayer, Cohen, & Casper, 2004). For young adults, the "work and family dilemma" increasingly focuses on work: how to become settled and secure in a job and prepared enough to take on the demands of family life.

Oppenheimer and her colleagues (Oppenheimer, 1997; Oppenheimer, Kalmijn, & Lim, 1997) found that it is taking young men, particularly those without a college education, several years to secure full-time employment. They argued that the difficulty young men have in securing a foothold in the U.S. labor market is one reason that other family formation behaviors are delayed. Rones, Gardner, and Ilg (1997) showed that among both male and female workers (ages 16–24), the percentage working full time decreased between the 1970s and 1990s, from 66% to 60% for men and from 56% to 49%

---

[1] These time diary studies include: the 1965–1966 Americans' Use of Time Study; Time Use in Economic and Social Accounts, 1975–1976; Americans' Use of Time, 1985; the 1988–1999 Family Interaction, Social Capital, and Trends in Time Use Study; and the 2000 National Survey of Parents.

[2] In the time use research, time is typically divided into contracted time (paid work), committed time (including housework and child care), personal time (self-care), and a residual category of discretionary time (free time; see Robinson & Godbey, 1999, for more detail). Free time captures all activities that are not included in the other three categories. Travel is generally included with the activity with which it is associated; hence, for example, commuting to work is considered with market time (Robinson & Godbey 1999, pp. 11–13). Because free time is a residual, it captures all activities in which individuals chose to engage during time other than that committed to paid work, domestic work and family care, and self-care or personal hygiene. Some of the activities coded as *free time* may not be considered truly elective uses of time.

for women. Therefore, young people in the United States are older when they enter the adult roles of full-time work, marriage, and parenting.

Delaying marriage and experimenting with other types of living arrangements, particularly cohabitation, is widespread and no doubt influenced by early experiences of becoming established in the labor market. For example, more than one half of U.S. marriages are preceded by cohabitation (Bumpass & Lu, 2000). Women still marry at a somewhat younger age than men, but the median age at first marriage for women rose from age 20 in 1960 to age 25 in 2000 and from age 23 to age 27 for men (Casper & Bianchi, 2002). The increase in age at marriage is sharpest among African-American women, who married earlier than White women at mid-century, but who now marry later. African-American women are less likely than White women to ever marry, stay married, and remarry (Cherlin, 1992).

Childbearing in the United States is also being delayed, but not as long as marriage, at least among some subgroups of the population. Almost one fourth of women have a child by age 20, and about one half of American women become mothers by age 25 (Casper & Bianchi, 2002, Table 3.1). African-American women, despite their greater propensity to delay marriage, are less likely to postpone childbearing. This has led to divergent racial trends in childbearing—far more African-American than White children are born to young, unmarried mothers (Cherlin, 1992).

Once adults become parents, a new array of potential work and family conflicts emerge. Some of the most time-squeezed individuals are those who are actively involved in day-to-day parenting of children. For this group, two trends are ratcheting up the work (over)load: (a) the growth in single-parent families, and (b) the dramatic increase in labor force participation among mothers in two-parent families.

MARKET WORK OF PARENTS

Table 2.1 shows shifts from 1965 to 2000 in the number and labor force status of parents with children. Even during the mid-1960s, when 90% of families with children included two parents, only about one half of all households with children fit the Ozzie and Harriet mold with a full-time, homemaker mother and bread-winning father. By 2000, this pattern characterized only one in five households with children. The most common family makeup was a dual-earner couple with children—41% of families fit this mold in 2000, up from about 24% in 1965.

In addition to the increase in dual-earner families, there has been a steady rise in single motherhood—particularly among African-American women. African-American women were more likely than White women to be single mothers in both 1965 and 2000, and this gap has widened over time. By 2000,

TABLE 2.1
Labor Force Status of Parents in Family Households
With Children under Age 18, 1965–2000

	1965	1970	1975	1980	1985	1990	1995	2000
Two Parent	**90.3**	**87.4**	**82.4**	**78.4**	**75.2**	**73.6**	**70.6**	**69.7**
Husband sole earner	57.0	49.4	41.4	32.9	27.9	23.7	20.7	20.7
Wife sole earner	2.4	2.9	4.4	4.5	4.3	5.0	4.9	4.2
Dual earner	23.9	28.3	27.4	34.3	36.3	39.4	40.0	40.9
Neither	6.9	6.8	9.3	6.8	6.6	5.4	5.1	3.8
Single Mother	**8.8**	**11.1**	**15.4**	**18.6**	**20.7**	**21.6**	**23.4**	**23.4**
Employed	4.4	5.5	7.5	10.3	11.2	12.5	13.8	16.1
Nonemployed	4.4	5.6	7.9	8.2	9.5	9.2	9.7	7.2
Single Father	**0.9**	**1.5**	**2.2**	**3.0**	**4.1**	**4.8**	**5.9**	**6.9**
Employed	0.7	1.2	1.5	2.2	3.0	3.7	4.4	5.4
Nonemployed	0.2	0.4	0.7	0.8	1.1	1.2	1.4	1.5
Sample size	11,048	21,790	19,496	27,102	23,521	22,621	21,705	19,013

Source. Authors' tabulations from the March Current Population Survey.

Note. Bolded categories add up to 100%. Universe is parents who maintain their own household. Employment defined as 1+ hours worked last week.

only 17% of White women and 25% of Hispanic women ages 25 to 54 were single mothers, compared with more than one half (52%) of all African-American women in the same age group (data not shown).

Table 2.2 shows changes in the labor force participation of all mothers (ages 25–54) based on Current Population Survey (CPS) data. The trends track the percent employed at least one week in the previous year, the average number of weeks worked, and the percent employed full time year round (i.e., those who report 35 or more hours of work per week and who were employed 50–52 weeks in the preceding year).[3] The trends also chronicle annual hours of employment by multiplying weeks worked in the last year by hours worked in the last week.

In 2000, 78% of mothers were employed—up from 45% in 1965. The trend characterizes all mothers regardless of race and educational attainment (data not shown for the latter two categories), although the rate of increase

---

[3]One of the reasons for uncertainty about the degree to which women's labor force participation has increased is because there are different ways to measure it and different universes that can be employed. In the March CPS, for example, one can ascertain whether an individual was in the labor force (which includes both the employed and those not employed, but who are actively looking for work) in the week before the survey and anytime in the preceding year. Respondents who are employed are also asked a "usual hours" question: how many hours they usually work per week and how many hours they worked in the week before the survey. In March, they are also asked how many weeks they worked in the preceding year. For a discussion of the effect of different universes, question wording, and reference periods on estimates of women's labor force participation, see Cohen and Bianchi (1999).

differs across groups. For example, the labor force participation rate of White mothers has increased more sharply than that of African-American mothers. Whereas African-American mothers had higher levels of employment in 1965 than White mothers, their employment levels converged by 2000. College-educated mothers had the highest levels of employment in both 1965 and 2000, and the gap in the labor force participation of college-educated mothers and those with only a high school education (or less) widened over time (authors' calculations, data not shown).

Over time the most significant change is that more mothers work for pay and work more weeks per year. They do not necessarily work more hours per week. Throughout the period, employed mothers worked between 33 and 36 hours per week on average. Hence, an employed mother in 1965 was juggling about as many hours of paid work per week as an employed mother in 2000.

TABLE 2.2

Hours Worked Per Week, Weeks Worked Per Year, and Estimated Annual Hours of Work for Mothers With Children under Age 18

	1965	1970	1975	1980	1985	1990	1995	2000
All mothers with children under age 18								
Percent employed previous year	44.7	52.2	56.1	65.7	68.7	73.8	75.1	78.1
Percent employed year round (50+ weeks)	19.1	25.5	29.6	35.6	41.8	47.2	51.9	56.5
Average hours worked per week	11	13	14	18	20	22	23	25
Average weeks worked per year	16	20	22	27	29	32	33	36
Estimated annual hours[a]	444	552	606	800	895	1,022	1,081	1,172
Sample size	9,382	17,984	16,007	22,200	19,502	19,097	18,286	15,633
Employed mothers with children under age 18[b]								
Percent employed year round (50+ weeks)	50.2	57.2	60.5	61.2	67.0	69.7	74.6	76.9
Average hours worked per week	34	33	33	34	35	35	35	36
Average weeks worked per year	38	41	42	42	44	45	46	47
Estimated annual hours	1,367	1,406	1,435	1,497	1,565	1,633	1,662	1,711
Sample size	3,106	7,055	6,784	11,791	11,185	11,939	11,830	10,679

Source. Authors' tabulations from the March Current Population Survey.

Note. Universe is mothers, ages 25–54, who are householders/spouses.

[a] The number of hours employed last week multiplied by the number of weeks employed last year.

[b] Women employed 1+ hours in the previous week.

However, as women's labor force attachment increased, employed mothers began working more weeks per year, rising from 38 to 47 weeks per year over the period. The increase in labor force participation and more continuous work patterns throughout the year has led to more than a doubling of the annual hours of employment for all mothers from 444 to 1,172. When averaged across employed women only, this translates to 344 hours more per year in 2000 than in 1965 (increasing from 1,367–1,711 hours).

Between 1970 and 1995, married mothers' employment rates increased more sharply than those of single mothers. After 1995, single mothers' employment rates jumped sharply as the economy boomed and welfare reform took hold (data not shown). Table 2.3 shows estimates of annual hours of employment for mothers by marital status. The top panel shows averages across all mothers, whereas the bottom panel is restricted to employed mothers. For all married mothers with children under age 18, on average, annual hours of employment more than doubled, and hours for those with children under

TABLE 2.3
Estimated Annual Hours of Employment of Married and Single Mothers, 1970–2000

	1970	1975	1980	1985	1990	1995	2000	1970–2000 % increase
				All Mothers				
Mothers with children under 18								
Married	512	561	739	850	984	1,060	1,114	117.6%
Single	901	871	1,078	1,078	1,171	1,155	1,372	52.4%
Sample size	17,984	16,007	22,200	19,502	19,097	18,286	15,633	
Mothers with children under 6								
Married	303	380	527	680	798	905	916	201.9%
Single	570	590	810	743	848	842	1,209	112.2%
Sample size	7,454	6,278	8,466	7,961	8,073	7,448	6,044	
				Employed Mothers				
Mothers with children under 18								
Married	1,367	1,390	1,432	1,509	1,578	1,622	1,672	22.3%
Single	1,634	1,637	1,749	1,775	1,842	1,802	1,832	12.1%
Sample size	7,055	6,784	11,791	11,185	11,939	11,830	10,679	
Mothers with children under 6								
Married	1,142	1,242	1,277	1,398	1,465	1,540	1,567	37.2%
Single	1,463	1,454	1,601	1,651	1,662	1,603	1,726	18.0%
Sample size	2,042	1,985	3,583	3,881	4,336	4,233	3,636	

Source. Authors' tabulations from the March Current Population Survey.
Note. Universe is all mothers, ages 25 to 54, who maintain their own household.

TABLE 2.4
Labor Market Hours by Age of Youngest and Number of Children
in Two-Parent Families, 2000

		Mother's Average Hours			Father's Average Hours			
	Sample Size	% With Any Hours	Avg. Per Worker	Avg. All Mothers	% With Any Hours	Avg. Per Worker	Avg. All Fathers	Parents' Combined Hours
Children								
Ages of Children								
All over age 6	6,781	72.8	36.0	26.2	89.4	45.8	40.9	67.1
At least one under age 6	5,109	58.4	33.6	19.6	90.8	45.6	41.4	61.1
At least one under age 4	3,671	56.0	32.8	18.3	91.1	45.7	41.7	60.1
At least one under age 1	918	46.3	31.3	14.5	91.0	46.6	42.4	56.8
Number of children								
One	4,249	72.1	36.5	26.3	89.4	45.2	40.4	66.7
Two	4,954	67.8	34.7	23.5	90.6	45.9	41.6	65.1
Three	2,116	60.1	33.9	20.4	89.9	46.3	41.6	62.0
Four+	896	47.4	32.4	15.3	85.9	45.3	38.9	54.2

Source. Authors' tabulations from the March Current Population Survey.

Note. Universe is all parents who maintain their own household where the mothers are ages 25 to 54.

age 6 tripled. Among employed married mothers with children under age 18, annual hours increased by about 22% over the period as they increased the number of weeks they worked per year.

Annual hours also jumped appreciably for single mothers—by 52% for all single mothers with children under age 18 and by more than double for single mothers with children under age 6. As with married mothers, the increases were much less sharp among employed single mothers at each point. Nonetheless, annual hours of employed single mothers rose by 12% for those with children under age 18 and by 18% for those with young children.

One final caveat on maternal employment: In 2000, it was still atypical for a married mother with preschool-age children to work full time or be employed full time year round. Although a growing percentage of couples with children are working long (combined) hours, a sizable minority of married couples continue to have one person in the home when children are young, and that person in the home is almost always the mother.

Table 2.4 shows that mothers' employment hours continue to be responsive to the number and ages of children, whereas fathers' work hours vary little by number of children and age of youngest child. Despite the media attention to

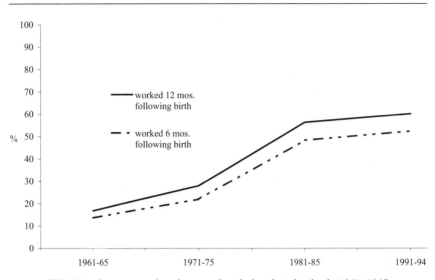

FIG. 2.1.   Percentage of mothers employed after their first birth: 1961–1965 to 1991–1994 (from Smith, Downs, & O'Connell, 2001).

stay-at-home dads, the CPS data suggest that about 90% of working-age fathers are employed, and they average 45 to 47 hours of market work per week no matter how many children they have or how young their children are. Married mothers' employment, in contrast, is highly responsive to the age of their youngest child. Only 46% of mothers with at least one child under age 1 are employed, and this rises to 73% when all children are over age 6.

The best available evidence suggests that, if anything, fathers tend to increase hours of employment after a birth of a child (Lundberg & Rose, 2000). Women, in contrast, tend to sort into at least two groups: Some return quickly to their employer, often to full-time work, but a sizable group curtail employment hours or take some time out of the labor force after the birth of a child. This sorting continues after the birth of the second child (Klerman & Leibowitz, 1999). An increasing proportion of employed women do not exit the labor force or change jobs as they transition to motherhood (Glass & Riley, 1998; Leibowitz & Klerman, 1994). Figure 2.1 shows the percentage of women working for pay at 6 and 12 months following the birth of their first child (calculations based on Smith, Downs, & O'Connell, 2001). At 6 months after childbirth, only 14% of mothers returned to work in the early 1960s, whereas by the early 1990s, this number had jumped to more than one half of mothers (52%). By the time their children were celebrating their first birthdays, only 17% of mothers were back at work in the early 1960s, compared with 60% in the early 1990s. The most rapid change occurred between the early 1970s and early 1980s.

Over the past 20 years in the United States, employer and public policies have made limited strides to ease the conflicts between family obligations and paid work, primarily by offering family benefits and (unpaid) parental leave (Hofferth, 2000; Smith et al., 2001). The Family and Medical Leave Act (FMLA) passed in 1993 requires employers with more than 50 employees to grant their workers up to 12 weeks of unpaid leave to care for a newborn child, a newly adopted child, or a sick family member. Some companies have taken additional measures to encourage mothers' return to work after childbirth, but substantial variation exists across employers in family benefits. Mother's own wage, liberal leave policies, and child care at the work site are the strongest predictors of maternal rates of return to paid work following childbirth (Hofferth, 2000). However, we still know relatively little about what workplace conditions keep new mothers in the labor force (Glass & Riley, 1998).

Whereas women's labor force participation no longer drops when they marry (Cohen & Bianchi, 1999), and women are much more likely to return to work within 6 months following a birth (Smith et al., 2001), young children continue to curtail mothers' hours of employment. Becker and Moen's (1999) findings from in-depth interviews with couples in upstate New York suggest that some "scaling back" of work effort (limiting time and devotion to work, characterizing work as a job rather than a career, and trading off between job and career over the life course) is common for both women and men during the early years of childrearing. Nonetheless, women scale back market work far more than men when children arrive despite egalitarian gender ideologies.

NONMARKET WORK OF PARENTS

Accompanying the dramatic changes in the time American parents spend at work are shifts in other aspects of time use, including time devoted to nonmarket work activities. As shown in Table 2.5, American mothers have dramatically curtailed the time they spend in housework tasks. Mothers' hours of housework (exclusive of child care) fell from an average of 32 hours per week in the mid-1960s to about 19 hours per week in 2000. Between 1965 and 1985, fathers' participation in housework chores increased from 4 hours to approximately 10 hours per week. However, their participation in household chores has remained relatively constant at this 1985 level. In 2000, mothers spent almost twice as many hours as fathers doing household chores. Although this ratio is dramatically lower than in 1965, when mothers did seven times as much housework as fathers, little change has occurred since 1985, and the ratio remains considerably above unity.

TABLE 2.5
Trends in Average Weekly Housework Hours of Parents by Sex, 1965–2000

	All Mothers					All Fathers					Ratio of Mother's Time to Father's Time				
	1965	1975	1985	1995	2000	1965	1975	1985	1995	2000	1965	1975	1985	1995	2000
Total housework	31.9	23.6	20.4	18.9	18.6	4.4	6.0	10.2	10.2	10.0	7.2	4.0	2.0	1.8	1.9
Core housework	29.0	21.6	17.6	14.9	15.1	1.6	1.8	3.9	3.3	4.9	18.6	12.1	4.5	4.6	3.1
Cooking meals	10.0	9.0	7.4	5.2	5.6	0.7	0.9	1.7	1.5	2.3	14.1	10.6	4.3	3.6	2.5
Meal cleanup	4.8	2.7	1.9	0.8	1.3	0.3	0.2	0.4	0.1	0.4	14.4	14.1	4.7	6.6	3.3
Housecleaning	8.0	6.2	5.5	6.6	4.9	0.3	0.5	1.5	1.4	1.9	23.1	11.6	3.7	4.8	2.6
Laundry and ironing	6.2	3.7	2.7	2.3	3.3	0.2	0.2	0.3	0.3	0.4	35.8	17.5	8.5	8.0	8.6
Other housework	2.9	2.0	2.9	3.9	3.5	2.8	4.2	6.2	6.9	5.1	1.0	0.5	0.5	0.6	0.7
Outdoor chores	0.3	0.4	0.4	0.8	0.7	0.6	1.0	1.3	2.3	2.0	0.5	0.4	0.3	0.3	0.3
Repairs	0.4	0.7	0.5	0.7	0.7	1.6	2.3	2.3	1.9	1.5	0.3	0.3	0.2	0.3	0.5
Garden and animal care	0.5	0.4	0.6	0.5	0.7	0.2	0.2	0.8	1.0	0.4	2.3	1.6	0.7	0.5	1.7
Bills, other financial	1.8	0.5	1.4	2.0	1.5	0.5	0.6	1.9	1.6	1.2	3.5	0.8	0.8	1.2	1.3
Sample size	417	369	903	307	999	343	251	693	180	632					

Source. Authors' tabulations from the 1965–1966 Americans' Use of Time Study; Time Use in Economic and Social Accounts, 1975–1976; Americans' Use of Time, 1985, 1995; the 1998–1999 Family Interaction, Social Capital, and Trends in Time Use Study; and the 2000 National Survey of Parents.

Note. Universe is all mothers and fathers ages 18–64.

32

TIME WITH CHILDREN

One of the biggest questions about the increase in parental work hours is what happens to parental time and supervision of children as more (parental) hours are committed to market work. Time diary data measure three aspects of mothers' and fathers' participation in childrearing: the time parents spend primarily engaged in a direct child-care activity, the time they spend either directly focusing on child care or doing a child-care activity in conjunction with something else, and the overall time they spend with their children whether engaged in child care or not (the most inclusive category). Table 2.6 shows estimates of married mothers' and married fathers' hours per day spent with children in 1975 and 2000 and the ratio of mothers' and fathers' time with children.

Despite the increase in maternal employment, on average mothers' overall time with children has remained at 1975 levels (at around 48 hours per week). Fathers (limited to those who live with their children) have significantly increased their time with children, from an average of about 26 hours in 1975 to 33 hours per week in 2000. Therefore, the gap between mothers' and fathers' time with children has declined. In 1975, fathers did slightly less than one third the primary child care that mothers did, and fathers spent a little more than half the time with their children as did mothers. By 2000, fathers were doing about half as much child care as mothers, and they were

TABLE 2.6
Change in Parents Weekly Hours
of Child Care and Time With Children

	1975	2000
Primary child-care activities		
Mothers	8.6	12.6
Fathers	2.6	6.8
Ratio	0.30	0.54
Primary or secondary activities		
Mothers	13.8	18.3
Fathers	4.7	8.8
Ratio	0.34	0.48
Any time with children		
Mothers	48.0	49.0
Fathers	25.8	32.6
Ratio	0.54	0.66

Source. Authors' tabulations from the Time Use in Economic and Social Accounts, 1975–1976 and the 2000 National Survey of Parents.
Note. Universe is all parents ages 18 to 64.

spending two thirds as much time as mothers with their children each week. Sandberg and Hofferth (2001) reported similar findings of increased father time with children, at least among married fathers, and no substantial decline in mothers' time with children on average. One caveat is that some of this time with children is "double counted," in that both mother and father can be present. Fathers remain much more likely to have their spouse present when spending time with their children, whereas mothers spend more solo time with children (Sayer, Bianchi, & Robinson, 2004).

Employed mothers spend less time with their children than nonemployed mothers. However, the differences may be minimized by the steps employed mothers can take to "protect" time with children: Mothers curtail hours of employment when children are young, try to synchronize employment hours with children's school schedules, "tag-team" work hours with a spouse to maximize parental availability to children, and curtail time spent in other activities such as housework outside of child care, volunteer work, personal care, and free-time pursuits (Bianchi, 2000).

A large gap in knowledge about fathers is the involvement of nonresidential fathers in their children's lives. There is evidence that stepfathers spend less time with children than biological fathers. Fathers who cohabit with a partner and her children spend more time with those children than stepfathers, on average, but still less than biological fathers (Hofferth & Anderson, 2003).

Another trend in the way mothers and fathers spend time with their children is multitasking. Both men and women have increased the amount of time they spend simultaneously caring for children while doing something else, most often a free-time activity (Sayer, 2001). Figure 2.2 shows that in 1975, child care was the sole activity for approximately 47% of the total time mothers cared for their children, whereas only 26% of mother's child-care time in 2000 was focused solely on providing care to her children. Similar trends characterize fathers' time. This trend may raise questions about the quality of time spent with children given that parents increasingly have other things on their mind during the time they devote to child care. It also raises questions about how "refreshing" free-time pursuits are for parents who spend more of them dealing with the demands of young children.

In addition to the permeation of parents' free time with childrearing, paid work and family caregiving may be curtailing time available for community involvement. Sayer (2001) classified free-time activities that constitute community and organizational involvement as *caring civic* leisure, and she labeled free-time activities that build informal social ties as *social leisure*. She estimated that the percentage of women who report a caring civic activity on the diary day decreased by one half between 1975 and 1998 (declining from 19%–9%). There was no change for men, with 12% reporting caring civic activities at both points. Although a majority of men (75%) and women (87%)

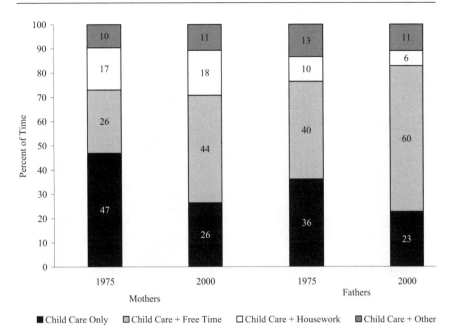

FIG. 2.2.   Multitasking among mothers and fathers while caring for children, 1975 and 2000 (from authors' tabulations from the Time Use in Economic and Social Accounts, 1975–1976 and the 2000 National Survey of Parents).

reported social leisure time in 1998, this had declined since 1975 especially for men; in 1975, 93% of men and 92% of women had reported social leisure time. This may be another reason that time pressures are so keenly felt by American working families today.

SUBJECTIVE FEELINGS ABOUT TIME

Changes such as delayed childbearing and increased labor force participation of mothers have dramatic implications for how daily life is lived. Not surprisingly, these changes affect public perceptions of family life and how parents feel about the adequacy of their time with family members. Despite increases in actual time with children, U.S. parents express strong feelings that they do not spend enough time with their children.

Figure 2.3 illustrates American parents' subjective feelings about their time with family members. Evidence of a "felt" time crunch is apparent given the large proportion of mothers and fathers reporting that they have too little time with their children and spouse and not enough time for themselves. Not surprisingly, more mothers than fathers report they have less than the ideal

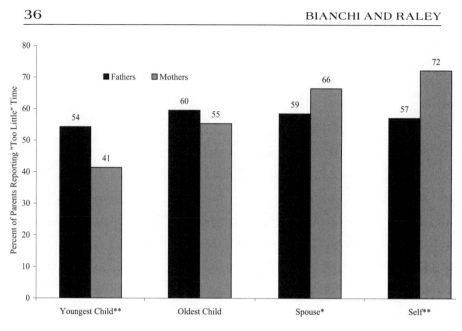

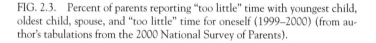

FIG. 2.3.   Percent of parents reporting "too little" time with youngest child, oldest child, spouse, and "too little" time for oneself (1999–2000) (from author's tabulations from the 2000 National Survey of Parents).

amount of time for themselves and their spouses. However, fathers more than mothers report they would like more time with their children. This gender difference is explained by the fact that mothers spend more time with their children, whereas longer work hours limit fathers' time with children. Indeed these subjective perceptions are highly correlated with parental work hours (Milkie, Mattingly, Nomaguchi, Bianchi, & Robinson, 2004). However, they may also signify the changing ideals of fatherhood. More men and women want fathers to be equally involved in child care, yet the division of labor is typically such that mothers shoulder a disproportionate share of the day-to-day child-care responsibilities (Milkie, Bianchi, Mattingly, & Robinson, 2002).

Another indicator of the heightened sense of time pressure among U.S. adults today is captured by a question asking how often they feel rushed. As shown in Table 2.7, in 1998, 39% of women reported always feeling rushed—a significant increase over the 28% who felt this way in 1975. The comparable percentages for men were 31% in 1998—up (although not significantly) from 26% in 1975. In both years, the vast majority of Americans reported either sometimes or always feeling rushed. Meanwhile, the proportion of adults reporting that they never felt rushed was cut in half between

TABLE 2.7
Women's and Men's Perceptions of Feeling Rushed,
1975 and 1998

	All		Women		Men	
	1975	1998	1975	1998	1975	1998
% Feeling rushed	100.0	54.5	100.0	53.3	100.0	55.9
Always	27.0	35.1[a]	27.8	39.1[a]	26.0	30.8[b]
Sometimes	52.6	54.5	51.3	53.3	54.3	55.9
Never	20.4	10.4[a]	20.9	7.7[a]	19.8	13.4[ab]
Mean	2.07	2.25[a]	2.07	2.31[a]	2.06	2.17[ab]
Sample size	751	964	456	547	295	417

Source. Mattingly and Sayer (2003).
[a]Change over time statistically significant.
[b]Gender difference is statistically significant.

the two years (from 20%–10%). The decline in those reporting never feeling rushed was much greater for women perhaps, not surprisingly, because women dramatically increased their labor force participation during this period, but also continued to be more likely than men to combine paid work with substantial amounts of unpaid family work and caregiving.

TOTAL WORK HOURS

Work-family stress, feeling rushed, and having too little time for children, spouse, or self reflects the double burden of combining paid work hours with unpaid family caregiving—termed the *second shift* by Arlie Hochschild in her book of the same title. A common claim is that mothers are working longer hours than fathers, an argument bolstered by statistics on women's greater hours of housework (Bianchi et al., 2000). There is no question that women do far more child care and housework than men, but relatively few studies compare the total workload of men and women or mothers and fathers. That is, women/mothers do more domestic work, but men/fathers continue to work more hours for pay. If one considers both unpaid, nonmarket work and paid, market work as necessary to the adequate support of American families, it would be helpful to know the total work effort expended by men and women.

Time diaries provide a 1-day snapshot that can be aggregated over individuals whose days represent all days of the week, all weeks of the year. The diaries provide estimates of total work hours of all adults and single and married parents. Past research has suggested that total hours may not be that different for men and women in the United States (Marini & Shelton, 1993; Robinson & Godbey, 1999; Zick & McCullough, 1991). Recent international comparisons suggest that gender differences in total work hours vary across countries. Bittman and Wajcman (2000) showed that total hours of work are lower for men than women in Italy, Canada, the United Kingdom, Finland, Norway, and Sweden (ranging from 5 fewer hours in Italy to 1 fewer hour per week in the United Kingdom). In contrast, women have a lighter total workload than men in Australia, Denmark, and the Netherlands (from a 25-minute difference to almost a 3-hour per week difference in the Netherlands).

Sayer (2001) offered the most recent and thorough examination of gender differences in time expenditures by calculating an index of dissimilarity in time expenditures. The index can be interpreted as showing the percentage of an average woman's (or man's) day that would have to be reallocated to other activities for the average man and woman to have the same time expenditures across categories of daily activities. Sayer (2001, Table 6.1) calculates that, among the total population of adults in 1965, one quarter of each day would have to be reallocated for women's time expenditures to match men's (or vice versa). In 1998 to 1999, this was cut in half—to 12%. In other words, men's and women's time allocation had become much more similar over the ensuing three decades.

Sayer (2001) showed that even in 1965, time allocation of single men and women was much more similar than that among married individuals or parents. Two things occurred in the intervening time span: The movement toward greater gender similarity in time allocation occurred among those who showed more divergence in 1965—married persons and parents. Also as marriage and children were delayed, the population began to shift toward statuses with less gender difference in time use (e.g., more single, childless adults).

Table 2.8 shows hours per week in market, nonmarket, and total work times for all men and women and for parents living with children under age 18 (including child-care time). Women's total workweek in 1998 to 1999 averaged 59 hours. This was up sharply from 1975 and also up slightly from 1965. Men's average workday in 1998 to 1999 was about 30 minutes shorter than women's, on average, for a workweek average of 56 hours.

At all points in time, women did more nonmarket work, whereas men did more market work. However, the ratio of women's market work to men's increased from only 30%, on average, in 1965 to 80% in 1998 to 1999. Women's nonmarket time was 3.7 times that of men in 1965, but decreased to about 1.6 times that of men by the end of the 1990s.

The picture is somewhat different for married parents. First, the total workload of married mothers and fathers is substantially greater in 2000 than at the earlier time points, it is similar for mothers and fathers, and it exceeds the average for all men and women by 8 hours a week for fathers and 6 hours

TABLE 2.8
Hours Per Week of Work (Market and Nonmarket / Paid and Unpaid)

	Total Adults					Married Parents					
	1965	1975	1985	1995	1998	1965	1975	1985	1995	1998	2000
Market work											
Women/mothers	15	19	22	29	30	6	15	20	25	25	23
Men/fathers	46	40	37	40	38	48	47	42	40	40	43
Ratio (women/men)	0.3	0.5	0.6	0.7	0.8	0.1	0.3	0.5	0.6	0.6	0.5
Nonmarket work											
Women/mothers	41	32	30	29	29	53	40	40	41	40	42
Men/fathers	11	11	16	16	18	12	12	19	21	23	21
Ratio (women/men)	3.7	2.9	1.9	1.8	1.6	4.4	3.3	2.1	2.0	1.7	2.0
Total work											
Women/mothers	56	50	53	58	59	59	55	59	65	65	65
Men/fathers	57	51	52	55	56	60	59	61	61	64	64
Ratio (women/men)	1.0	1.0	1.0	1.1	1.1	1.0	0.9	1.0	1.1	1.0	1.0
N women/mothers	700	689	2,383	573	556	358	278	673	198	194	506
N men/fathers	541	550	1,950	416	431	326	239	583	133	141	409

Source. Authors' tabulations from the 1965–1966 Americans' Use of Time Study; Time Use in Economic and Social Accounts, 1975–1976; Americans' Use of Time, 1985, 1995; the 1998–1999 Family Interaction, Social Capital, and Trends in Time Use Study; and the 2000 National Survey of Parents.
Note. Universe is all respondents ages 18 to 64.

for mothers. Therefore, a married father logs a 9-hour workday, 7 days a week, or about 64 hours per week. A married mother puts in a little more than a 9-hour work day, 7 days a week, or a nearly 65-hour workweek. The time spent in market work has risen for married mothers relative to fathers, but it is still about 50% of fathers', lower than the 80% for women in general. Mothers still do more nonmarket work, but the ratio has dropped substantially.

Sayer (2001, Fig. 6.2) found another group that stands out as having an unusually long (total) workday: married, childless women. Their market work hours are now similar to married, childless men, but they do an additional hour of nonmarket work per day than married, childless men. This is consistent with longitudinal evidence that suggests that marriage increases women's, but not men's, time in housework activities (Gupta, 1999).

CONCLUSION

We began this chapter with the dilemma families face: how to best allocate time to the market and the home so that children receive the nurturance they need and adults lead productive, healthy, and satisfying lives. We provided an overview of changes in family life, including the labor force participation and unpaid housework and child care of parents to illuminate the reallocation of time in the home during the past half century.

Time allocation of women and men has become much more similar, but gender specialization has not disappeared. Mothers' work hours remain responsive to the number and ages of their children, whereas fathers' paid work hours do not vary by age of youngest child. Mothers have accommodated their dramatically increased paid work hours by shedding housework, but, on average, they continue to spend as much time with children as mothers did in the past when labor force rates were lower. Married fathers have increased their time with children. Overall, workloads of mothers and fathers, when both market and nonmarket work are considered, are relatively equal and higher than in the past. Given this change, it is perhaps not surprising that many parents feel that they have too little time with family members. The proportion of women reporting that they always feel rushed is also higher today than in the past. In summary, achieving the right balance between work and family remains an elusive goal.

REFERENCES

Becker, G. (1991). *Treatise on the family.* Cambridge. MA: Harvard University Press.

Becker, P. E., & Moen, P. (1999). Scaling back: Dual-career couples' work-family strategies. *Journal of Marriage and Family, 61,* 995–1007.

Bianchi, S. M. (2000). Maternal employment and time with children: Dramatic change or surprising continuity? *Demography, 37,* 401–414.

Bianchi, S. M., Milkie, M. A., Sayer, L. C., & Robinson, J. P. (2000). Is anyone doing the housework? U.S. trends and gender differentials in domestic labor. *Social Forces, 79,* 191–228.

Bianchi, S. M., & Spain, D. (1996). *Balancing act: Motherhood, marriage, and employment among American women.* New York: Russell Sage Foundation.

Bittman, M., & Wajcman, J. (2000). The rush hour: The character of leisure time and gender equity. *Social Forces, 79,* 165–189.

Bumpass, L. L., & Lu, H. (2000). Trends in cohabitation and implications for children's family contexts in the United States. *Population Studies, 54,* 19–41.

Casper, L., & Bianchi, S. M. (2002). *Continuity and change in the American family.* Thousand Oaks, CA: Sage.

Cherlin, A. (1992). *Marriage, divorce, remarriage.* Cambridge, MA: Harvard University Press.

Cohen, P., & Bianchi, S. (1999). Marriage, children, and women's employment: What do we know? *Monthly Labor Review, 122,* 22–30.

Coontz, S. (1992). *The way we never were: American families and the nostalgia trap.* New York: Basic Books.

Glass, J., & Riley, L. (1998). Family responsive policies and employee retention following childbirth. *Social Forces, 76,* 1401–1435.

Gupta, S. (1999). The effects of marital status transitions on men's housework performance. *Journal of Marriage and the Family, 61,* 700–711.

Hofferth, S. (2000). Effects of public and private policies on working after childbirth. In T. L.

Parcel & D. B. Cornfield (Eds.), *Work and family: Research informing policy* (pp. 131–159). Thousand Oaks: Sage Publications.

Hofferth, S., & Anderson, K. G. (2003). Are all dads equal? Biology versus marriage as basis for paternal investment. *Journal of Marriage and Family, 65,* 213–232.

Klerman, J., & Leibowitz, A. (1999). Job continuity among new mothers. *Demography, 36,* 145–155.

Leibowitz, A., & Klerman, J. 1994. The work-employment distinction among new mothers. *Journal of Human Resources, 29,* 277–303.

Levy, F. (1996). *The new dollars and dreams.* New York: Russell Sage Foundation.

Lundberg, S., & Rose, E. (2000). Parenthood and the earnings of married men and women. *Labor Economics, 7,* 689–710.

Lundberg, S. J., Pollak, R. A., & Wales, T. J. (1997). Do husbands and wives pool their resources? Evidence from the United Kingdom child benefit. *Journal of Human Resources, 32,* 463–480.

Marini, M. M., & Shelton, B. A. (1993). Measuring household work: Recent experience in the United States. *Social Science Research, 22,* 361–382.

Mattingly, M., & Sayer, L. C. (2003, August). *Under pressure: Trends and gender differences in the relationship between free time and feeling rushed.* Paper presented at the annual meeting of the American Sociological Association, Atlanta, GA.

Milkie, M. A., Bianchi, S. M., Mattingly, M., & Robinson, J. P. (2002). The gendered division of childrearing: Ideals, realities, and the relationship to parental well-being. *Sex Roles, 47,* 21–38.

Milkie, M. A., Mattingly, M., Nomaguchi, N., Bianchi, S. M., & Robinson, J. P. (2004). Parents' feeling about time with children: The influence of employment, family structure, and gender. *Journal of Marriage and Family, 66,* 738–760.

Newburger, E. C., & Curry, A. (2000). Educational attainment in the United States: March 1999. *Current Population Reports* (P20–528). Washington, DC: U.S. Census Bureau.

Oppenheimer, V. K. (1997). Women's employment and the gain to marriage: The specialization and trading model. *Annual Review of Sociology, 23,* 431–453.

Oppenheimer, V. K., Kalmijn, M., & Lim, N. (1997). Men's career development and marriage timing during a period of rising inequality. *Demography, 34,* 311–330.

Robinson, J., & Godbey, G. (1999). *Time for life* (2nd ed.). State College, PA: Penn State Press.

Rones, P., Gardner, J., & Ilg, R. (1997). Trends in hours of work since the mid-1970s. *Monthly Labor Review, 120,* 3–14.

Sandberg, J. F., & Hofferth, S. L. (2001). Changes in children's time with parents: United States, 1981–1997. *Demography, 38,* 423–436.

Sayer, L. C. (2001). *Time use, gender, and inequality: Differences in men's and women's market, nonmarket and leisure time.* Unpublished doctoral dissertation, University of Maryland, College Park.

Sayer, L. C., & Bianchi, S. M. (2000). Women's economic independence and the probability of divorce: A review and reexamination. *Journal of Family Issues, 21,* 906–943.

Sayer, L. C., Bianchi, S. M., & Robinson, J. P. (2004). Are parents investing less in children? Trends in mothers' and fathers' time with children. *American Journal of Sociology, 110,* 1–43.

Sayer, L. C., Cohen, P. N., & Casper, L. M. (2004). *Women, men, and work. Census Bulletin.* Washington, DC: Population Reference Bureau.

Seltzer, J. (2002, July). *Income pooling and individual and family mobility.* Paper presented to the Research Committee on Social stratification, XV World Congress of Sociology, Brisbane, Australia.

Smith, K., Downs, B., & O'Connell, M. (2001). *Maternity leave and employment patterns: 1961–1995.* Washington, DC: U.S. Census Bureau.

Toosi, M. (2002). A century of change: U.S. labor force from 1950 to 2050. *Monthly Labor Review, 125*, 15–28.

Vickery, C. (1977). The time-poor: A new look at poverty. *Journal of Human Resources, 12*, 27–48.

Zick, C. D., & McCullough, J. L. (1991). Trends in married couples' time use: Evidence from 1977–78 and 1987–88. *Sex Roles, 24*, 459–487.

3

Embracing Complexity: Work Schedules and Family Life in a 24/7 Economy

Harriet B. Presser
University of Maryland

This chapter is entitled "Embracing Complexity" because I strongly believe that this is what we as researchers and policymakers must do, both to better understand the nature of work and family life at the start of the 21st century and to propose more effective solutions to existing problems. Yet acknowledging complexity is often antithetical to how we generally approach research and policy issues. There is elegance in analytic simplicity; moreover, the lack of data often forces us to research just a few aspects of a highly complex issue. In the policy arena, people often want short, bulleted suggestions on how to improve the situation at home or at the workplace without taking the complexities into account.

Just describing how work and family time are allocated among employed Americans is a challenge. Consider the following dimensions that affect the home-time structure of family life: the number of hours people work, which hours they work, whether they work weekends, the extent of flexibility in their work hours and workplace, and the extent of work-related travel. Choice also comes into play in the work-time arrangement, such as whether one is involuntarily working part time, overtime, or as a temporary worker; working late shifts and weekends while preferring a standard work schedule; or traveling away from home more days than desired. Job-related benefits may vary as well, such as vacation time and parental leave (paid and unpaid).

CLUSTERED WORK SCHEDULES

Researchers need to be mindful of several issues to accurately depict and understand the complexity of Americans' work and family lives. The first point I wish to stress is that in planning future research on the workplace–workforce mismatch, we must look simultaneously at many—if not all—of these work schedule patterns. Many individuals have what I call *clustered work schedules*, that is, combinations of two or more nonstandard work times that generate more work-time inequalities between individuals than is evident from looking at each work schedule characteristic of a job separately. Moreover, those with clustered schedules may find it difficult to synchronize their family activities with other family members more so than those with just one or no nonstandard work schedule. In other words, working more than 40 hours a week and working night shifts and weekends, along with minimal work hour flexibility and little vacation time, surely affects family functioning. The type of family may matter as well; traditional single-earner couples may be more adaptable to clustered work schedules than dual-earner couples or single mothers. Those in low-income occupations may be especially affected. Although those working long hours are more likely have good jobs (professionals and managers), it may be that those in low-income occupations experience the most clustering of different types of nonstandard work and family stress.

We have a limited body of research assessing the separate effects of different types of work schedules on children and adolescents (see chap. 4, this volume). This call for a clustered view asks that we take an even more multifaceted perspective and, as Crouter and McHale (chap. 4) suggest, do studies that cut across two or more levels of time organization.

THE FAMILY AS A UNIT

The second point I wish to stress is that, in addition to studying the individual, we must look at the family as a unit, and for married couples we must examine the pattern of work schedules for both spouses. This point is well made by Jacobs and Gerson (2001) with regard to the number of hours worked. They show that, although the average work week for Americans has not changed over the past 30 years, the average number of hours married couples jointly work has risen because of the substantial rise of dual-earner couples. Jacobs and Gerson also note that, although the average number of hours single mothers work has remained the same over the decades, there are now more single mothers, and thus now more in the labor force than ever before. In other words, it is the change in family types that is of central interest when studying trends in work hours for families.

Differences in work hours between spouses also affect family life, separate from the combined total number of work hours for both spouses. In other words, among couples with a combined total of 60 work hours, their home time and their perceived feelings of stress are undoubtedly different for families in which spouses split the 60 hours (e.g., each working 30 hours or one working 40 hours and the other 20) than for those in which one spouse works the entire 60 hours.

WORK SHIFTS AND WEEKEND EMPLOYMENT

Both perspectives—looking at the family as a unit of analysis and considering how spouses' work schedules vary within couples—have special relevance to the study of work shifts and weekend employment. Although we do not have reliable trend data over time, I have argued that we are moving to a 24/7 service economy (Presser, 1999, 2003). As of 1997, one fifth of all individuals did not work most of their hours in the daytime, and one third worked weekends. Together, two fifths of all employed Americans did not work mostly during the daytime or weekdays only.

This leads to a third point. We must address the issue of which hours and which days people work, from both a family and an individual perspective, if we are to adequately grasp the time diversity of family life in American society. In other words, there are many dual-earner couples in which spouses are on different work schedules, and there are many employed parents, both married and single, who may be at home but asleep during much of the day while their children are home and awake. Exactly who is working these schedules?

To address this question, I present a few findings from my book, *Working in a 24/7 Economy: Challenges for American Families* (Presser, 2003), based on analysis of data in the May 1997 Current Population Survey (CPS), a representative sample of about 50,000 American households. As noted earlier, one in five employed Americans works nontraditional hours (hours falling between 8 A.M. and 4 P.M.). The ratio would be higher if we included Americans who worked some of their hours in the evenings and nights—as many do—but here we are interested in those people who are primarily nondaytime workers.

When the couple is the unit of analysis, and specifically dual-earner couples (the predominant family type in the United States), more than one in four couples (27.8%) includes at least one spouse who works other than a regular daytime schedule. Among couples who have children under age 14, the ratio is nearer to one in three (31.1%). Among those with children under age 5, the ratio rises to more than one in three (34.4%). The ratio is even higher for couples of low income, for young couples, and for minorities, particularly African Americans.

Almost all of these dual-earner couples with a spouse working nontraditional shifts are split-shift couples, whereby one spouse works mostly during the day and the other mostly evenings, nights, or on highly variable or rotating shifts—that is, on shifts that change regularly from day to evening or night. Families with children may find economic and social advantages to this type of sequential parenting, but working different schedules clearly impinges on the time spouses have with one another.

Single mothers are more likely than married mothers to work late or rotating shifts. Among employed mothers with children under age 14, 20.8% of single mothers compared with 16.4% of married mothers work nonstandard hours. Weekend employment is particularly high for single mothers: 33.2% of single mothers work weekends compared with 23.9% of married mothers.

FAMILY FUNCTIONING IN A 24/7 WORKPLACE

The final point is that there are important consequences for family functioning when parents work late and rotating work shifts, and these consequences merit further research. Research suggests that the effects of weekend employment seem more benign than working late or rotating hours (Presser, 2003). In general, although some people may prefer to work nonstandard hours, such schedules are highly stressful for families with children, particularly dual-earner and single-mother families. When parents work late shifts, they have lower quality marriages, higher rates of separation and divorce, and more complex child-care arrangements for their children. Which late shift—evening, night, or rotating—also affects schedules and stress levels differently. For example, the extent to which parents eat dinner with their children is affected by working evening shifts, but marital instability is affected by night shifts. Among married couples, the gender of the parent working the particular shift also matters when assessing family outcomes.

On the positive side, compared with fathers who work the same shifts as their partners, fathers provide more child care when they work different shifts from mothers, and some might see this greater paternal time with children as beneficial. Also men do a greater share of the housework when their wives work different hours from them, compared with men whose wives share similar schedules. When they work late hours, parents are more likely to be home when children go to school and return, although we do not know whether the parents are awake or asleep at such times.

Another positive effect that might arise from nonstandard shifts when compared with standard shifts is greater parental child care. However, only a small minority of parents with preschool-age children who work nonday shifts report better child-care arrangements as their primary reason for working such shifts (Presser, 2003). In fact the majority of such parents say the primary reason is that it is a job requirement. These findings suggest that working different shifts to jointly manage child care when children are preschool age may be a purposeful strategy for some couples, but not for most. Fathers, in particular, rarely report choosing late work schedules for child-care reasons. However, when they work different hours from mothers and neither spouse has rotating schedules, fathers are almost always the primary caregivers for their preschool-age children. Others (primarily relatives) usually have to pitch in as well, given that among split-shift couples there are typically some hours in which both spouses are at work. The individuals pitching in, such as grandmothers, are also often employed. (Many grandmothers work split shifts and share child care with single mothers as well.)

Control over the conditions of work, such as autonomy and flexibility on the job, may be important for individual and family well-being. It may be especially important for shift workers—namely, having some control over which hours they work. Indeed research by Staines and Pleck (1983) suggested that having schedule control can reverse some of the negative effects of shift work on family life, even generating positive outcomes. Seniority is often relevant in attaining schedule control, but achieving seniority typically occurs after children are of school age.

In summary, we must alter our general conception of the home-time struc-ture of the American family to allow for its time diversity. The *togetherness* of the so-called *intact families* is not so together. Also with the high prevalence of nonstandard work schedules, nonstandard is not so nonstandard. There are millions of American households with young children whose parents are not home in the evenings or overnight and who often sleep during the day. We need much more information on how both the parents and children are coping with this time mismatch.

For those working night and rotating shifts, there is the additional consid-eration of how health risks associated with such employment interact with family functioning. These health risks stem from changes in the individual's circadian rhythms, which are linked to such biological functions as body tem-perature, hormone levels, and sleep. Evidence shows that those who work late and rotating schedules are at higher risk of cardiovascular disease, breast cancer, miscarriage, preterm birth, and low birthweight (Boggild & Knutsson, 1999; Schernhammer et al., 2001; U.S. Congress, 1991; Wedderburn, 2000). Moreover, evidence finds that chronic sleep deprivation and the resulting fatigue and stress reduce job productivity (Tepas & Price, 2001). An important question, therefore, is how these health considerations interact with family life.

Finally, it is critical that complex work schedules be considered when discussing such issues as moving mothers from welfare to work and keeping them on the job. Nearly one half of such mothers do not work traditional hours, yet the discourse on work and child care is almost always about *day* care.

If the Bureau of Labor Statistics' job growth projections for the current decade are realized, the largest job growth will be in service occupations with high degrees of shift work (see Presser, 2003). Such growth suggests that working in a 24/7 economy will only become more common in the years ahead. Let us, as researchers and policymakers, take a more realistic view and embrace this complexity when we think about how to help families cope with juggling work and family responsibilities.

REFERENCES

Boggild, H., & Knutsson, A. (1999). Shift work, risk factors, and cardiovascular disease. *Scandanavian Journal of Work and Environmental Health, 25*(2), 85–99.

Jacobs, J. A., & Gerson, K. (2001). Overworked individuals or overworked families? Explaining trends in work, leisure, and family time. *Work and Occupations, 28*(1), 40–63.

Presser, H. B. (1999). Toward a 24-hour economy. *Science, 284,* 1778–1779.

Presser, H. B. (2003). *Working in a 24/7 economy: Challenges for American families.* New York: Russell Sage Foundation.

Schernhammer, E. S., Laden, F., Speizer, F. E., Willett, W. C., Hunter, D. J., Kawachi, I., & Colditz, G. A. (2001). Rotating night shifts and risk of breast cancer in women participating in the Nurses Health Study. *Journal of the National Cancer Institute, 93*(20), 1563–1568.

Staines, G. L., & Pleck, J. H. (1983). *The impact of work schedules on the family.* Ann Arbor: University of Michigan, Institute for Social Research.

Tepas, D. I., & Price, J. M. (2001). What is stress and what is fatigue? In P. A. Hancock & P. A. Desmond (Eds.), *Stress, workload, and fatigue* (pp. 607–622). Mahwah, NJ: Lawrence Erlbaum Associates.

U.S. Congress, Office of Technology Assessment. (1991). *Biological rhythms: Implications for the worker* (OTA-BA-463). Washington, DC: U.S. Government Printing Office.

Wedderburn, A. (Ed.). (2000). *Shiftwork and health: Special issue of* Bulletin of European Studies on Time (BEST, Volume 1). Luxembourg: Office for Offical Publicatons of the European Communities. Available: http://www.eurofound.eu.int/themes/health/hwin4_3.html.

4

Work, Family, and Children's Time: Implications for Youth

Ann C. Crouter
Susan M. McHale
The Pennsylvania State University

The purpose of this chapter is to examine how children are affected by the way in which their parents spend time, the rhythms of family routines and family time, and the way they themselves spend time. We consider how each of these dimensions of time is related to the quality of youths' family relationships, developmental outcomes (including their social competence and school achievement), and psychosocial well-being. The review focuses primarily on school-age children and adolescents growing up in dual-earner families, which reflects a preoccupation in the field with middle-class and professional families and our own areas of expertise. Where possible, however, we review what is known about younger children, children growing up in single-parent families, and children in less economically advantaged family circumstances.

In conceptualizing how children are influenced by the way time is structured and organized, we consider three important factors, each of which plays a role in our understanding of the intersections between work and family life. First, children are influenced by their parents' work time, including how much time parents devote to employment, when that work takes place (e.g., shift work, weekend work), work-related travel, and the flexibility of work. Second, families as social groups vary in their orientation toward time, which has been studied primarily in the form of family routines and rituals and family time spent in shared activities. Third, the way that children and adolescents spend their discretionary time, including the nature of their activities and the people with whom they spend time, is another potentially important influence.

Before describing what we know about each of these areas of time organization, several caveats are in order. First, although we discuss them separately, the three levels are interrelated in complex ways. For example, in some families, parents' work schedules and the time demands of children's extracurricular activities may constrain opportunities for family routines and activities such as family dinners. Second, parents and children are not simply passive recipients of environmental influences; in the face of constraints, they actively make choices that define their life circumstances. Economists refer to this process as *selection*, whereas developmental scholars have used the term *niche picking* (Scarr & McCartney, 1983). The concept means that there are important, often unrecognized, confounds between family members' personal qualities and predispositions and their patterns of time use. A corollary is that children's relationships, development, and well-being—phenomena we treat as outcomes in this chapter—may influence time patterns at any of the three levels. A mother may cut back on her work hours, for example, if she believes that her child needs more supervision. Similarly, a child who is doing poorly in school may be ineligible to try out for the basketball team, which eliminates that time use choice.

Selection occurs at the level of the individual and the level of the environment. At the individual level, parents make decisions about how much education to get, what line of work to pursue, and how much time to devote to their jobs. They make choices about marriage and cohabitation, becoming parents, family size, neighborhood residence, and child-care arrangements. Likewise, children select their activities, and they gravitate to some peer groups and not others. In the early years, parents play a central role in managing their children's activities and choice of peers. For instance, some parents may steer children toward extracurricular activities that provide enrichment and cultivation of new skills—a parenting strategy that has become a hallmark of contemporary middle-class childrearing (Lareau, 2002). However, children play an increasingly active role in shaping their life circumstances as they move from childhood through adolescence.

The environment beyond the family also plays a sorting role. Workplaces make hiring, firing, and promotion decisions with an eye to attracting and retaining the most competent employees. The darker side of workplace selection involves discrimination based on sex, age, and race. Similarly, schools track children based on achievement—a process that exposes children to increasingly homogeneous peer groups as they move through school. Even so-called *free-time* activities may involve tryouts or auditions, as well as barriers such as financial costs, scheduling, and transportation, that make it easier for some children to participate than others.

A third and related caveat is that selection effects do not operate in a uniform way across individuals and families. Parents with high levels of education, skills, and social capital, such as middle-class and professional couples, have a wider range of options about how to structure work and family life than do parents with less human and social capital. Taken together, these caveats mean that the field must develop conceptual models and methodological approaches that consider the complexity implied by these interrelated and reciprocal influences on time and children's functioning, and by the multiple, layered sources of selection effects.

IMPLICATIONS OF PARENTS' WORK TIME FOR CHILDREN

More than 25 years ago, Kanter (1979) identified the time and timing of paid work as one of five key features of the workplace that have important implications for families. Since then, there has been a wealth of research on work time and timing, a small portion of which has focused on children. We focus on three dimensions of the time and timing of parents' work—work hours, shift work, and weekend work—making comparisons where possible between mothers and fathers.

Parents' Work Hours

The dimension of parents' work time that has received the most attention is how much time per week mothers and fathers devote to paid employment. From a developmental standpoint, long hours have been viewed as potentially risky for children because they imply that parents are less available for interaction, supervision, monitoring, and orchestrating children's activities. Moreover, if long hours are accompanied by stress and strain, parents may be less engaged with and responsive to their children. Barnett (1998) cautioned, however, that "Jobs with long hours tend to be 'good jobs,' that is, they are associated with high pay, good benefits, and more substantively complex work than are jobs with reduced hours" (p. 132). In other words, at least for some parents, there are trade-offs involved in working a long work week. A short work week, in contrast, may also be risky for children, at least indirectly, because it implies that parents are making limited wages and have a tentative foothold in the labor force. Moreover, a part-time schedule is not necessarily a flexible schedule. Barnett (1998) argued that the nature of the work that parents do (e.g., "more control and autonomy in a supportive environment") matters more than the number of hours worked.

Mothers' Work Hours. In an analysis of data from the National Longitudinal Survey of Youth (NLSY), Parcel and Menaghan (1994) concluded
that, holding a variety of possible confounding variables constant, mothers'
work hours have few consistent, direct effects on young children's cognitive
and social outcomes. Gottfried, Gottfried, and Bathurst (2002), reviewing
research from their Fullerton Longitudinal Study, reported no direct associations between mothers' work hours and child outcomes, but indicated that
the correlation between mothers' work hours and mothers' attitudes toward
the dual responsibilities of employment and parenting became stronger and
more negative as children moved through the school-age years. Having flexible schedules, in contrast, was consistently linked to less negative maternal attitudes, which in turn predicted lower levels of behavior problems in
children. Such findings suggest that mothers' work hours may have indirect
connections with child outcomes.

Other research documents that, at least in well-functioning, dual-earner
families, mothers' long work hours are not necessarily linked to mothers' own
parenting, but may have important implications for the roles that fathers play
in housework and childrearing (see Coltrane, 1996). Consider, for example,
the phenomenon of "parental knowledge"—that is, how informed parents
are about their children's daily activities, whereabouts, and companions. In
a study of working- and middle-class, dual-earner families with school-age
children, Crouter, Helms-Erikson, Updegraff, and McHale (1999) found that
mothers who worked longer hours knew as much about their children's daily
experiences as did mothers who worked fewer hours. In contrast, husbands
married to mothers who worked longer hours were significantly better informed than men whose wives worked fewer hours.

A similar finding emerged in a short-term, longitudinal analysis that examined seasonal changes in work hours. Using data collected on two-parent
families with school-age children during the academic year, the summer, and
the following academic year, Crouter and McHale (1993) compared outcomes
across three groups of families: (a) a "consistently single-earner group," in
which husbands were employed at all three time points and wives either were
homemakers or employed for pay few hours each week; (b) a "consistently
dual-earner" group, in which both spouses were employed at all three time
points; and (c) a group in which fathers were consistently employed and
mothers were employed in the academic year, but not during the summer.
The results show no between-group differences in knowledge among mothers. For fathers, however, the consistently dual-earner group maintained high
levels of knowledge of their children's activities at all three points of measurement, whereas those whose wives were employed in the school year but off
in the summer showed high levels of knowledge during the school year, a
pronounced drop over the summer, and then a sharp increase the following
school year when their wives had returned to work. Such findings suggest that

fathers may calibrate their attentiveness to their children's daily experiences depending on their wives' availability. In this way, the schedules of spouses' work and family activities are intertwined.

The same patterns held for parents' division of child care—specifically, the amount of time mothers and fathers spent in activities with their children (Crouter & McHale, 1993). When mothers cut back their paid work over the summer, the division of child care became markedly more traditional, with mothers doing proportionally more and fathers proportionally less child care. The division of parent–child activities reverted to less traditional forms again when mothers resumed paid work during the school year. Parent–child activities and knowledge about children's daily lives are interrelated phenomena because parents often learn about their children's experiences in the context of joint activities. Hence, it is not too surprising that these facets of parenting respond similarly to changes in mothers' work hours.

Fathers' Work Hours. In contrast to their null findings for mothers' work hours, Parcel and Menaghan (1994) found that a pattern of part-time, paternal work hours during children's early years was linked not only to lower levels of reading and math skills among children, but to higher rates of marital disruption among parents, which in turn had direct effects on children's subsequent behavior. Parcel and Menaghan (1994) also found a link between fathers' overtime schedules and lower achievement among their children in vocabulary and arithmetic.

Further, Parcel and Menaghan's (1994) findings also pointed to the importance of the patterning of spouses' work hours. When both parents had part-time work schedules, they provided their children with lower quality home environments than was the case when only one parent worked part time. Likewise, the combination of two parents working overtime was associated with higher levels of problem behavior in children and lower levels of verbal competence (i.e., vocabulary) than was the case when only one parent worked overtime.

Crouter et al. (1999) found no connection between fathers' work hours and either parent's knowledge of their children's daily experiences. However, research by Crouter, Bumpus, Head, and McHale (2001) underscored the importance of fathers' work hours for the quality of their relationships with their adolescent children. Whereas they found no associations between overwork (paid employment of more than 60 hours a week) or overload (fathers' subjective perceptions of being overwhelmed by having too much to do) and the amount of time fathers spent with their adolescents in daily activities, the combination of long paternal work hours and high paternal overload was consistently related to both fathers' and adolescents' reports of lower levels of acceptance and perspective-taking and greater conflict in their relationship. In other words, fathers' work hours, in and of themselves, were not related to the quality of father–adolescent relationships. Coupled with high levels of subjective strain, however, fathers' work hours were negatively linked to father–adolescent relationship quality from the perspective of both fathers and their adolescents. The research design made it impossible to discern whether fathers' hours exerted strain on the relationship or whether, in the face of less than positive father–adolescent relations, fathers increased their work hours. Both scenarios are possible.

Parents' Shift Work

As Presser (1999) argued, we are moving toward a 24-hour, 7-day-a-week economy. She noted that about 40% of employed Americans work a shift other than the standard day shift. Despite the widespread nature of shift work, however, surprisingly little is known about the implications for children and youth of when parents work. As with work hours, a concern is that parents who work nonstandard shifts may be less available to their children.

Using a 6-year span of data from the NLSY, Heymann (2000) reported that children with poor educational outcomes were significantly more likely to have had a parent who worked evenings or nights at least some of the time during the 6 years. The association was particularly strong for suspensions from school. These findings remained statistically significant after controlling for family income, parental education, marital status, child gender, and the total number of hours the parent worked. Whether the control variables accounted for all possible selection effects, however, is questionable. Moreover, these findings do not indicate the possible ways that nonstandard shifts influence children's outcomes or whether, as was the case for work hours, shift work has different implications for mothers and fathers.

Drawing on a national sample of married couples who were interviewed in 1980 and again in 1983, White and Keith (1990) found that, during the 3-year interval between interviews, couples who dropped shift work reported a marked decrease in child-related problems in their marriage—a construct that included a range of concerns such as spousal arguments about child care and experiencing time with children as irritating. Such changes presumably would have positive consequences, not only for the marriage, but for the quality of parent–child relationships and, in turn, for children's well-being.

Bogen and Joshi (2002) conducted the only large-scale study of the effects of mothers' nonstandard schedules on children in low-income, primarily single-mother households using data from the Welfare, Children, and Families: A Three-City Study. They find clear selection effects: Compared with mothers working day shifts, mothers working nonstandard shifts were more likely to receive welfare, work in the services sector, be members of unions, and receive lower health insurance coverage and less pay. Controlling for a variety of possible confounding variables, the authors found that the higher the propensity for nonstandard work, the more likely mothers were to report more problem behavior and less positive behavior among their 2- to 4-year-old children. In a noteworthy attempt to identify how nonstandard shifts make their mark, the investigators found that the associations between work shift and child functioning were in part mediated by mothers' perceived parenting challenges (e.g., low feelings of parenting competence and satisfaction; reports of irritability, anger, and impatience toward children). Thus, one way that nonstandard shifts might affect children is via their effects on parenting.

Recent research by Presser (2004) indicated some intriguingly complex associations between working a nonstandard shift and various parenting processes—associations that vary as a function of the parent's gender, nature of the shift, and family structure. For example, mothers in two-parent and single-parent families were less likely to help with homework when they worked rotating shifts. Fathers who worked nights, however, helped more with homework than other fathers. Interpreting these findings requires a nuanced understanding of mothers' and fathers' typical levels of involvement in their children's lives and how working a nonstandard shift tilts those patterns. In addition, in two-parent families, effects on children also undoubtedly depend on the patterning of the parents' shifts, as was the case for the patterning of parents' work hours.

Pioneering work by Presser (1989) underscored that many parents with young children work alternating shifts as a strategy to provide full-time parental care for their children. If one parent works days and the second parent works nights, for example, the child can remain at home under parental care—a convenient, inexpensive child-care arrangement. These arrangements may come with costs, however. Perry-Jenkins, Goldberg, Pierce, and Haley (under review) compared the mental health and marital quality of 46 same-shift couples and 45 alternating-shift couples across the first year of parenthood. During the prenatal period, they found no differences as a function of shift. Over time, however, wives in alternating shifts reported significant declines in both mental health and marital love. A year after the child's birth, alternating-shift husbands were also less in love with their wives than were husbands in same-shift couples. Perry-Jenkins and her colleagues explained:

> What is actually going on in alternating-shift households that influences marital discord and depression? It is not hard to imagine. Spouses have little time together and their days consist of working an eight-hour shift and then managing the second shift alone. While many of the couples in this study liked the idea of only using parental child care, it appears that this benefit may be outweighed by the costs of functioning like a single parent during much of the week. (p. 23)

It is unclear whether these declines in marital quality and psychological well-being have implications for the quality of care among alternating-shift couples, but it seems highly probable given that parental depression (Downey & Coyne, 1990) and marital tension and conflict (Grych, 2002) are correlates of less than optimal child well-being.

Working Weekends

Almeida (2004) recently conducted one of the few studies to examine the implications for children and families of parents' weekend work, using data from the National Study of Daily Experiences, part of the National Survey of Midlife in the United States (MIDUS). As was apparent in research on parents' work hours, there are interesting mother–father differences in the effects of weekend work. Working weekends was associated with fathers spending about 1 hour more per day at paid employment and about 30 minutes less per day with their children compared with fathers whose work schedules did not involve weekends. As Almeida noted, it is possible that working weekends cuts into the time when children are most available. In contrast, working weekends was not related to how much time mothers spent at work or with their children.

Comparing the Effects of Mothers' and Fathers' Work Time

Despite early concern about the effects of working mothers, the research generally suggests that it is the work hours, shift work, and weekend work of fathers, not mothers, that are related to parenting or child outcomes. An exception is the research by Bogen and Joshi (2002) on mothers working nonstandard shifts. Most of the mothers in their low-income sample, however, were single parents and, therefore, were, as are many fathers in two-parent families, the primary economic providers for their families. When fathers are present in families, we tend to find more systematic effects for fathers' work time than for mothers'.

One explanation for this is tied to men's and women's work and family roles. In dual-earner families, mothers typically work fewer hours than do fathers (Parcel & Menaghan, 1994). This pattern reflects widespread beliefs about the male provider role and women's responsibility for home and children, and it also may arise because men typically earn more than women. How fathers define their paternal role may be more varied than mothers, reflecting the more optional nature of father involvement. Presumably, this more varied script for fathers allows them greater variability in their parenting behavior (and, by implication, a narrower range of behavior for mothers). On a purely statistical level, more variability in measures of fathers' parenting and family roles provides for more predictive power in analyses linking fathers' family and parenting behaviors to contextual conditions, on the one hand, and youth outcomes on the other.

IMPLICATIONS OF FAMILY TIME
FOR CHILDREN

Families vary in the way they organize family time, and these variations may have important implications for children's relationships, development, and well-being. Family scholars have paid less attention to the family as a unit than one would expect. This somewhat sparse research falls into two areas: (a) investigations of family routines and rituals such as meal times, bedtime routines, weekend events, and holidays that give family life predictability and rhythm; and (b) studies of family time, which families spend together as a group. A theoretical root of this research is family systems theory—a perspective that holds that the family as a whole is not reducible to its component parts, its individual family members and relationships. Family units differ along multiple dimensions, one of which is their use of time.

Family Routines and Rituals

In a recent review of the research, Fiese et al. (2002) underscored the potentially positive implications of family routines and rituals for children, noting that children in families that sat down to dinner together three or four times a week and reported having weekend and holiday rituals tended to do well in school and report lower levels of anxiety compared with children in families without such routines. Family routines also appear to be protective for children experiencing stress, such as managing chronic asthma or living with an alcoholic parent (Fiese et al., 2002).

It is unclear how family rituals and routines are tied to children's psychosocial functioning. One possibility is that routines and rituals are a marker for family cohesion; the regularity and predictability of routines and rituals lend coherence and feelings of security and control to children's experiences of family life. Another explanation is that family rituals and routines signal closer and better functioning parent–child and marital relationships. Fiese, Hooker, Kotary, and Schwagler (1993) provided some evidence for the links between family rituals and marital quality in a study that compared couples whose first child was an infant and couples whose eldest child was of preschool age. More rituals were consistently linked to higher marital satisfaction for both mothers and fathers.

Although parents and children carve out family routines and rituals, developing and maintaining these family dynamics presumably are not immune to outside influences such as parents' employment. It may be more difficult for families to develop or maintain family routines and rituals when parents work long hours or have schedules that involve nonstandard shifts or weekend work. Following Rubin's (1976) claim that the inability to control the future sharply divides the experiences of poor and working-class families from those of the middle class, Roy, Tubbs, and Burton (2004), in an ethnography component of the Three-City Study, found that the ability of low-income mothers to create ongoing family routines was hampered by work schedules, long commute times, rigid social service schedules, and the inevitable curve-balls of illness and other family emergencies.

Family Time

Family time—how much time families spend together as a social unit—is another dimension of time use. Crouter, Tucker, Head, and McHale (2004) used daily family diaries to gauge the extent to which mother, father, and two adolescent siblings spent time together during 1 week. They found that family time was a scarce commodity. On average, the predominantly working- and middle-class, two-parent families spent about 4 hours a week in activities as a family. Much of their shared time involved eating meals together and watching TV. Despite the paucity of family time, however, adolescents who spent more time with their families at about age 14 tended to exhibit fewer conduct problems 2 years later, although overall the effects were modest. The association between family time and the oldest child's depressive symptoms was moderated by parents' education. The more time adolescents in better-educated families spent with their families, the less depressed they reported feeling 2 years later, yet this association was not significant for adolescents from less-educated families.

It is unclear why social class moderates the effects of family time, but recent qualitative research by Lareau (2002) suggests that contemporary middle-class families structure their children's time quite differently than working-class families. Specifically, middle-class and professional families use discretionary time to cultivate skills in their children and to expose them to new and enriching experiences, whereas working-class families tend to focus more on their children's naturally unfolding development, striving to provide a safe environment, but not going to great lengths to provide an elaborate array of lessons, sports, and other extracurricular activities for their children. Family time in a working-class household may be viewed as time to relax or time when there is nothing else to do (i.e., "default" time). Family time in a middle-class family, in contrast, may include planned, purposeful time use that carries positive implications for children.

Although the literature on routines, rituals, and family time suggests positive associations with children's psychosocial functioning, qualitative studies of family time suggest that families have a hard time living up to their idealized notions of family time. Using data from in-depth interviews and observations, Daly (2001) argued that employed parents think about family time in terms of a set of interrelated "oughts." Family time ought to be a source of memories for them and their children. Family time ought to be positive, and it ought to be spontaneous. In practice, however, family time was in short supply. Moreover, it frequently was accompanied not by joy and spontaneity, but by irritability, tension, and exhaustion. Daly suggested that the strong idealized flavor of contemporary notions about family time may create tensions for parents and should be reexamined.

THE IMPLICATIONS FOR DEVELOPMENT OF CHILDREN'S TIME USE

Having argued that children's psychosocial functioning is linked to the time commitments and organization of parents' work schedules and family involvement, we turn now to youths' own time use and its connection to development. Over the past two decades, researchers from a variety of disciplines have become interested in children and adolescents' time use. From an ecological perspective, the content and complexity of everyday activities index youths' psychological development (Bronfenbrenner, 1979); daily activities also serve as a forum for socialization (Rogoff, 1990; Weisner, 1989). As anthropologist Thomas Weisner (2002) argued,

> Activities crystallize culture directly in everyday experience, because they include values and goals, resources needed to make the activity happen, people in relationships, the tasks the activity is there to accomplish, emotions and motives of those engaged in the activity, and a script defining the appropriate, normative way to engage in that activity. (p. 275)

In short, an ecological perspective on children's time use points to the role of daily activities in distinguishing the lives of youth across time and place. Within such a framework, how children and youth spend their time reflects expectations about their future roles and provides opportunities for children to acquire particular skills and competencies and develop certain personal relationships. As such, time use should have significant implications for child and adolescent development.

Developmental Implications of Children's Work

As an example of an ecological approach to understanding the developmental implications of time use, Larson and Verma (1999) described differences in the work patterns of youth in different societies. In most societies, children become immersed in work during middle childhood. This is the period of industry according to Erikson (1959). In the United States, common wage-earning jobs for children in middle childhood are babysitting and newspaper routes, but elsewhere middle childhood is a time when children may begin to work for pay at factories, in the fields, or on the streets (Larson & Verma, 1999). In nonindustrial and transitional societies, children's work is economically productive to the family, including unpaid domestic work (household chores, sibling caregiving, agricultural labor) and wage earning. Youth in middle childhood (girls in particular) may spend half their waking hours doing domestic work. In postindustrial societies, in contrast, children's work centers around schooling and is designed to enhance children's own development and skills. In these societies, children spend less than a half hour per day in housework (Larson & Verma, 1999). Furthermore, societal differences in child's work reveal gender distinctions. Girls' activities tend to focus on domestic work, for example, whereas boys tend to be more involved in wage-earning activities. These distinctions often mirror the extent to which adult roles are gender-typed, and they suggest that children's daily activities have significant implications for their development.

Larson and Verma (1999) concluded that a key difference across social contexts lies in the work activities of children and youth, including the kinds of work they do, the developmental patterning of work, and the balance between work and leisure. More important, whether parents work in a postindustrial economy or a nonindustrial or transitional economy is central in defining the work patterns of youth.

By some accounts, the line between children's work and leisure is becoming blurred among more privileged families in contemporary U.S. society, where children's extracurricular activities are seen as an important way to foster children's future economic achievements (Lareau, 2002). For example, an 11-year-old boy recently explained to us that he was starting to take golf lessons because "golf is important in making business deals." In this way, subsistence demands and the material conditions surrounding them influence the everyday activities of youth, and activities, in turn, serve an important socialization function for future economic roles and activities in adulthood.

Developmental Implications of Children's Free Time

Most empirical research on the implications of time use among youth has focused on free time or leisure activities. This work is couched in several overlapping conceptual frameworks. Consistent with an ecological perspective, researchers have argued that free-time activities constitute important developmental opportunities (Larson & Verma, 1999; Silbereisen, Noack & Eyferth, 1986). The skills children learn in their activities during the industry period of middle childhood provide the foundation for a sense of identity that emerges in adolescence and thereby helps to shape decisions about education, career, and the like (McHale, Crouter, & Tucker, 2001). Research linking involvement in specific activities with specific developmental and adjustment outcomes is limited, with most available work examining links between activities and intellectual abilities. For instance, researchers have documented links between time children spend reading for pleasure and their school grades and test scores (Hofferth & Sandberg, 2001; McHale et al., 2001). Other studies have linked gender-specific play to stereotypical gender-specific cognitive skills, such as understanding spatial relations.

From a risk and resilience perspective, youths' everyday activities are also perceived as protections against or gateways into risky behaviors and problematic interpersonal relationships (e.g., Osgood, Wilson, O'Malley, Bachman, & Johnston, 1996; Werner, 1993). As a protective force, youth activities serve as contexts within which social bonds can be forged with peers who share similar interests or with adults who serve as mentors, confidantes, and role models and who foster youths' allegiance to social institutions (Eccles & Barber, 1999; Osgood et al., 1996). Hobbies, clubs, and sports can also be a source of pride and self-esteem as youth discover arenas in which they can excel, and such activities can serve as distractions or a place for escape in times of trouble and stress (Werner, 1993).

Studies of the adjustment correlates of free-time activities in middle childhood are limited, but available evidence suggests that, compared with time spent in unstructured and unsupervised activities, time spent in constructive and organized activities is associated with better school achievement and lower rates of internalizing and externalizing problems (McHale et al., 2001; Posner & Vandell, 1999). Other studies have examined the links between free-time activities and adjustment in adolescence, with findings again showing positive associations for organized and constructive activities (Eccles & Barber, 1999; Mahoney & Cairns, 1997; Marsh, 1992). This research also suggests that time spent in unsupervised and unstructured activities is linked to adjustment problems such as emotional difficulties, conduct problems, risky behavior, and poor school achievement (McHale, Crouter, & Tucker, 2001; Osgood et al., 1996; Posner & Vandell, 1999).

In considering the developmental implications of youths' time use, it is important to keep in mind that activities take place within a larger familial and social context that defines opportunities for how youth spend their time. For example, most studies document social class differences in time use, with youth from less advantaged backgrounds spending less time reading, more time watching TV, more time in unstructured outdoor play, and less time in sports (Bianchi & Robinson, 1997; Hofferth & Sandberg, 2001; Larson & Verma, 1999; McHale et al., 2001; Posner & Vandell, 1999). Several researchers have emphasized the importance of documenting whether the positive outcomes that have been ascribed to children's involvement in constructive activities stem from the nature of the activities per se or to selection effects—that is, more advantaged children have more opportunities for development-enhancing activities. For this reason, most studies attempt to control for the effects of factors such as parent income and education.

Also important with respect to selection effects, although less frequently examined, is children's own role in their activity patterns. A number of studies have raised the question of whether links between activity and adjustment are because better adjusted children and adolescents choose to become involved in more constructive and structured activities. To address this concern, investigators have used longitudinal data to determine whether links between time use and adjustment emerge over time, controlling for earlier adjustment. Such analyses document that involvement in constructive activities generally explains the change in individual differences in adjustment outcomes such as academic performance, conduct problems, and emotional well-being for adolescents (Marsh, 1992), working- and middle-class White children (McHale et al., 2001), and low-income, urban, White, and African-American children (Posner & Vandell, 1999).

However, two studies also found support for the notion that children play an active role in selecting their activity niches. Both Posner and Vandell (1999) and McHale and colleagues (2001) showed that children's positive adjustment predicted their involvement in constructive activities over time, controlling for initial activity involvement. For instance, low-income, urban, African-American children who did better in school in third grade were more likely to be involved in organized extracurricular activities and were less likely to be involved in unstructured activities 2 years later (Posner & Vandell, 1999). Further, low-income White children who had more behavior problems in the third grade spent relatively more time in unstructured outdoor play by the fifth grade (Posner & Vandell, 1999). McHale and colleagues (2001) reported similar findings with a slightly older sample: Better adjusted fourth and fifth graders (measured in terms of school grades, depression, and conduct problems) were relatively more likely to be involved in constructive activities and less likely to spend time in unstructured activities and in unsupervised settings 2 years later. These findings attest to the complexity of the processes underlying children's patterns of time use and the importance of understanding the confluence of factors that define opportunities and set constraints on children's everyday activities.

NEXT STEPS IN THE RESEARCH AGENDA

As we have suggested, children's unfolding relationships, development, and well-being are shaped in part by their parents' organization of time commitments, the rhythms of their family routines and family time, and the ways in which they spend their own discretionary time. Although each of these levels of time management is potentially important for children and youth, the research has rarely examined the interrelationships among the three areas. In the interest of encouraging greater integration of this research, we conclude with an agenda for future research, calling for studies that: (a) cut across two or more of the levels of time organization, (b) pay greater attention to selection effects and reciprocal connections between time management and children's outcomes, (c) effectively integrate qualitative methods with quantitative approaches to data collection, and (d) capitalize on intervention designs that manipulate one component of the work-family system and investigate its implications for children.

The field would benefit from research that examines the interplay between the levels of time organization that we have considered here, such as research on the implications of parents' shift work for family routines or for children's patterns of involvement in extracurricular activities. In such a study, it would be useful not only to assess the organization of parents' and children's lives, but also to measure parents' and children's attitudes, values, and beliefs about the time organization along the dimensions we have outlined. For example, how much stock do parents place in family routines? How do parents conceptualize the role of extracurricular activities in their children's development? What do children view as the trade-offs for them of parents' long work hours or nonstandard work shifts?

Understanding parents' and children's underlying attitudes and belief systems would also help us develop a more nuanced picture of selection effects. What choices do parents confront as they carve out a modus operandi of work and family life, and how do their choices vary as a function of socioeconomic status (SES), race and ethnicity, gender, and family structure? How do parents think about and explain their choices? To what extent are choices in one domain related to values, attitudes, and beliefs in another domain? For example, how are parents' ideas about the importance of extracurricular activities for their children related to the work arrangements they make for themselves?

As the field of work and family research becomes more integrated, it is useful not only to encourage interdisciplinary research, but to promote multimethod research, particularly research that combines in-depth qualitative approaches such as ethnography, with survey data and quantitative time use data. As we reviewed the state of knowledge, we were struck by the vividness of the ethnographic contributions (e.g., Daly, 2001; Lareau, 2002; Roy, Tubbs, & Burton, 2004; Weisner, 2002). Imagine the insights that could be generated by collaborative work in this area between, for example, ethnographers and demographers or ethnographers and developmental researchers.

In his book, *The Ecology of Human Development: Experiments by Nature and Design*, Urie Bronfenbrenner (1979) concluded that one of the most effective ways to understand the complex web of human development is to conduct intervention research. Citing an early mentor's advice to him, he noted, "If you want to understand something, try to change it" (Bronfen-brenner, 1979, p. 291). Not all of the levels of time organization that we have described here are amenable to intervention, but some are. Workplaces, for example, could be redesigned so that employees are given more control over the time and timing of work. Comparing employees in workplaces that institute such changes with matched workplaces that do not, one could trace who makes what choices (and why) and examine the short- and long-term effects for employees and their children. Similarly, communities could target children's extracurricular activities as a point of intervention, ensuring that they fit busy family schedules; reduce time, income, and transportation bar-riers to children's participation; and that they make efforts to find options that will appeal to boys and girls across wide age and socioeconomic ranges. Again, with an experimental design—one that perhaps compares communi-ties that are given funds to invest in this way with similar communities that are not—researchers could trace whether and how investments in youth programming pull children in, which children are pulled in, how children's involvement in such activities meshes or conflicts with their parents' work demands, what specific activities children choose, the nature of their interac-tions with peers and adults, and how involvement in these activities shapes subsequent development.

As we have suggested, this area of research is complex; it requires atten-tion to the dispositions and experiences of multiple family members, an un-derstanding of the larger ecology within which families are embedded, and an appreciation of the dynamic quality of time patterns as individuals, families, and social ecologies change over time As we pursue these important avenues of research, the boundaries among work time, family time, and children's time may become less defined, and the larger picture of the organization of time within family life may come into better focus.

REFERENCES

Almeida, D. M. (2004). Using daily diaries to assess temporal friction between work and family. In A. C. Crouter & A. Booth (Eds.), *Work-family challenges for low-income parents and their children*. Mahwah, NJ: Lawrence Erlbaum Associates.

Barnett, R. C. (1998). Toward a review and reconceptualization of the work/family literature. *Genetic, Social, and General Psychology Monographs, 124*, 125–182.

Bianchi, S. M., & Robinson, J. (1997). What did you do today? Children's use of time, family composition, and the acquisition of social capital. *Journal of Marriage and the Family, 59*, 332–344.

Bogen, K., & Joshi, P. (2002). *Bad work or good move: The relationship of part-time and nonstan-dard work schedules to parenting and child behavior in working poor families*. Paper presented at a conference entitled, "Working Poor Families: Coping as Parents and Workers," sponsored by the National Institute of Child Health and Human Development.

Bronfenbrenner, U. (1979). *The ecology of human development*. Cambridge, MA: Harvard University Press.

Coltrane, S. (1996). *Family man: Fatherhood, housework, and gender inequality*. New York: Oxford University Press.

Crouter, A. C., Bumpus, M. F., Head, M. R., & McHale, S. M. (2001). Implications of overwork and overload for the quality of men's family relationships. *Journal of Marriage and Family, 63*, 404–416.

Crouter, A. C., Helms-Erikson, H., Updegraff, K., & McHale, S. M. (1999). Conditions underlying parents' knowledge about children's daily lives in middle childhood: Between- and within-family comparisons. *Child Development, 70*, 246–259.

Crouter, A. C., & McHale, S. M. (1993). Temporal rhythms in family life: Seasonal variation in the relation between parental work and family processes. *Developmental Psychology, 29*, 198–205.

Crouter, A. C., Tucker, C. J., Head, M. R., & McHale, S. M. (2004). Family time and family members' psychosocial adjustment: A longitudinal study of adolescent siblings and their mothers and fathers. *Journal of Marriage and Family, 66*, 147–162.

Daly, K. J. (2001). Deconstructing family time: From ideology to lived experience. *Journal of Marriage and Family, 63*, 283–294.

Downey, G., & Coyne, J. C. (1990). Children of depressed parents: An integrative review. *Psychological Bulletin, 108*, 50–76.

Eccles, J. S., & Barber, B. L. (1999). Student council, volunteering, basketball, or marching band: What kind of extracurricular involvement matters? *Journal of Adolescent Research, 14*, 10–43.

Erikson, E. H. (1959). *Childhood and society*. New York: Norton.

Fiese, B. H., Hooker, K., Kotary, L., & Schwagler, J. (1993). Family rituals in the early stages of parenthood. *Journal of Marriage and the Family, 57*, 633–642.

Fiese, B. H., Tomcho, T. J., Douglas, M., Josephs, K., Poltrock, S., & Baker, T. (2002). A review of 50 years of research on naturally occurring family routines and rituals: Cause for celebration? *Journal of Family Psychology, 16*, 381–390.

Gottfried, A. E., Gottfried, A. W., & Bathurst, K. (2002). Maternal and dual-earner employment status and parenting. In M. H. Bornstein (Ed.), *Handbook of parenting* (Vol. 4, 2nd ed., pp. 207–229). Mahwah, NJ: Lawrence Erlbaum Associates.

Grych, J. H. (2002). Marital relationships and parenting. In M. H. Bornstein (Ed.), *Handbook of parenting* (Vol. 4, 2nd ed., pp. 203–226). Mahwah, NJ: Lawrence Erlbaum Associates.

Heymann, J. (2000). *The widening gap: Why American's working families are in jeopardy—and what can be done about it*. New York: Basic Books.

Hofferth, S. L., & Sandberg, J. F. (2001). How American children spend their time. *Journal of Marriage and Family, 63*, 295–308.

Kanter, R. M. (1979). *Work and family in the United States: A critical review and agenda for research and policy*. New York: Russell Sage Foundation.

Lareau, A. (2002). Invisible inequality: Social class and childrearing in black families and white families. *American Sociological Review, 67*, 747–776.

Larson, R., & Verma, S. (1999). How children and adolescents spend time across the world: Work, play and developmental opportunities. *Psychological Bulletin, 126*, 701–736.

Mahoney, J. L., & Cairns, R. B. (1997). Do extracurricular activities protect against early school dropout? *Developmental Psychology, 33*, 241–253.

Marsh, H. W. (1992). Extracurricular activities: Beneficial extension of the traditional curriculum or subversion of academic goals? *Journal of Educational Psychology, 84*, 553–562.

McHale, S. M., Crouter, A. C., & Tucker, C. J. (2001). Free-time activities in middle childhood: Links with adjustment in early adolescence. *Child Development, 72*, 1764–1778.

66   CROUTER AND McHALE

Osgood, D. W., Wilson, J. K., O'Malley, P. M., Bachman, J. G., & Johnston, L. D. (1996). Routine activities and individual deviant behavior. *American Sociological Review, 61*, 635–655.

Parcel, T. B., & Menaghan, E. G. (1994). *Parents' jobs and children's lives.* New York: Aldine de Gruyter.

Perry-Jenkins, M., Goldberg, A., Pierce, C., & Haley, H. (under review). Employment schedules and the transition to parenthood: Implications for mental health and marriage.

Posner, J. K., & Vandell, D. L. (1999). After school activities and the development of low-income children: A longitudinal study. *Developmental Psychology, 35*, 868–879.

Presser, H. B. (1989). Can we make time for children? The economy, work schedules, and child care. *Demography, 26*, 523–543.

Presser, H. B. (1999). Toward a 24-hour economy. *Science, 284*, 1778–1779.

Presser, H. B. (2004). Employment in a 24/7 economy: Challenges for the family. In A. C. Crouter & A. Booth (Eds.), *Work-family challenges for low-income parents and their children* (pp. 83–105). Mahwah, NJ: Lawrence Erlbaum Associates.

Rogoff, B. (1990). *Apprenticeship in thinking: Cognitive development in a social context.* New York: Oxford University Press.

Roy, K. M., Tubbs, C. Y., & Burton, L. M. (2004). Don't have no time: Daily rhythms and the organization of time for low-income families. *Family Relations, 53*, 168–178.

Rubin, L. B. (1976). *Worlds of pain: Life in the working-class family.* New York: Basic Books.

Scarr, S., & McCartney, K. (1983). How people make their own environments: A theory of genotype–environment effects. *Child Development, 54*, 424–435.

Silbereisen, R. K., Noack, P., & Eyferth, K. (1986). Place for development: Adolescents, leisure settings, and developmental tasks. In R. K. Silbereisen, K. Eyferth, & G. Rudinger (Eds.), *Development as action in context* (pp. 87–107). Heidelberg, Berlin: Springer-Verlag.

Weisner, T. S. (1989). Comparing sibling relationships across cultures. In P. Goldring-Zukow (Ed.), *Sibling interaction across cultures* (pp. 11–25). New York: Springer-Verlag.

Weisner, T. S. (2002). Ecocultural understanding of children's developmental pathways. *Human Development, 45*, 275–281.

Werner, E. E. (1993). Risk, resilience and recovery: Perspectives from the Kauai Longitudinal Study. *Development and Psychopathology, 5*, 503–515.

White, L., & Keith, B. (1990). Effect of shift work on quality and stability of marital relations. *Journal of Marriage and the Family, 52*, 453–462.

5

Timely and Timeless: Working Parents and Their Children

Barbara Schneider
Linda Waite
The University of Chicago

Instant messaging, 24-hour services, quick meals, and global interconnections are quickly erasing the boundaries between work and family life. As Presser (2003) noted in her recent book, *Working in a 24/7 Economy: Challenges for American Families*, the expansion of the service economy and the demand for around-the-clock services have been driven by changes in the organization of work by the composition of the workforce, which now includes a majority of working mothers, and by technological innovations that have made global communication an everyday occurrence. Such changes, and the time pressures they create for American families, have been the focus of several recent books, including *Time for Life* by Robinson and Godbey (1997), *The Time Bind* by Hochschild (1997), and *It's About Time* edited by Moen (2003). In addition to charting changes in the organization of work and family life, these books attempt to explain why American families perceive that they have too little time to deal with the daily demands they face at work and at home.

In *The Time Divide*, another recent book on this topic, Jacobs and Gerson (2004) identified those at risk of feeling time pressures and offered several explanations for why many Americans feel this way. First, they argued, it is professionals and managers who are working longer hours, not those with lower levels of education and less demanding jobs. It is this group of highly educated workers, who often write about their overscheduled lives, that has been receiving attention in the media and research circles. Second, it is dual-earner couples who are spending more time working. Over the past 30 years, the amount of time dual-career couples spend working has increased by about 3½ hours per week, most of which is a consequence of women spending more time in paid employment. Third, the nature of work has changed. Job pressures and responsibilities have increased, particularly for those in white-collar professions; nonstandard work shifts have expanded; and inequities in the workplace have grown, with women enjoying less job autonomy and flexibility while continuing to shoulder more of the burden of domestic work.

Part of the explanation for the time crunch can be traced to family demands and responsibilities. Concerns about children's safety and increased expectations of what it takes to raise a quality child may be extending the time parents spend with their children. However, it has been argued that the time set aside for leisure is now organized into highly structured activities, at least among middle-class parents and their children. The calendars of the middle class are now segmented beyond work and school into hours spent commuting to exercise classes, athletic games for parents and their children, and social activities that require a level of orchestration that challenges the limits of the palm pilot. Another source of pressure for working families, regardless of their financial means, is child care, which is often insufficient and costly for parents and exploitive of day-care workers, who are often underpaid and work in undesirable circumstances.

The topic of time allocation is timely; more women with children are in the labor force than in previous decades (see chap. 2, this volume). The demands and pressures of full-time work reduce the time that parents can spend with their children and on personal leisure. American families have limited time—they are literally timeless—and choices have to be made about how much time to spend on work and with their children. These choices about how to spend time are even more constrained for single parents. How people feel about what they are doing and how they are spending their time is also important for understanding the lives of working families.

THE IMPORTANCE OF SUBJECTIVE EXPERIENCE

Americans have a fascination with time, and this is perhaps most evident in the new American Time Use Survey (ATUS). In January 2003, the Bureau of Labor Statistics began the largest time use survey ever conducted in the United States or, for that matter, the world. Surveyors asked approximately

3,250 households, a subsample of the Current Population Survey (CPS), to recall their activities throughout a 24-hour period using time diaries. Of those asked, 1,800 respondents were expected to participate each month, yielding more than 21,000 time diaries each year. For each activity, sampled respondents identify where they are, whom they are with, and whether, in addition to the primary activity, they are engaged in a secondary activity. The question about secondary activities is asked to capture time spent on two activities at once, such as working on the computer and talking on the phone, or preparing dinner and watching TV.

What the ATUS does not explore is how individuals feel about how they spend their time and the complexities involved in defining and measuring these emotional experiences. How people make choices and decisions, however, continues to be a research focus of fields such as economics, organizational behavior, and others. Choice is important, but how individuals experience their daily activities seems critical for understanding time use and its consequences. The emotions experienced while working or spending time with one's family are subjective evaluations of these activities. Only the individual can express whether she or he is experiencing happiness, stress, or boredom (see Csikszentmihalyi, 1997, on this point). Stress experienced while working during the day, in the evenings, and on weekends is real to the person and captures more than a single global assessment of "how stressed I feel at work." With information on emotions experienced during daily life, it is possible to determine whether an individual feels more stressed if, for example, she or he works overtime at night and on the weekends. If such overtime activities raise one's subjective stress levels to the point that these negative emotions are transmitted to other family members, who in turn feel stressed, work stress becomes not just a worker, but also a family syndrome. In other words, simply measuring hours of overtime and its relation to an outcome variable overlooks individual motivations and personal understandings. By examining how a person feels throughout a day, it is possible to determine whether work is indeed more stressful than life at home. Analyses of subjective dimensions of time use can produce rich understandings of how people feel and the situations that make them feel that way. Examinations of subjective experiences in context can provide direction for changing the social systems that contribute to individual feelings and behaviors.

INTERTWINING TIME AND EMOTION: SOME EXAMPLES

In the late 1990s, Schneider and Waite began the 500 Family Study, a study of the work-life balance among American middle- and upper middle-class families; 200 of these families have kindergarten-age children and 300 have adolescents (Schneider & Waite, 2005). The typical family in this sample is a dual-career, married couple with children. Using a variety of methods, including interviews, surveys, and the Experience Sampling Method (ESM), the study examines the complex dynamics of today's families and the strategies they use to cope with the demands of work and family. Many of the items in the surveys have been used in other national studies, making it possible to compare responses of these families with those of other populations. The interviews were designed to complement the surveys and provide in-depth information on study participants, including personal histories.

The ESM is a unique method for examining how individuals spend their time and, much like traditional time diaries, includes questions on time spent with others and on the activities an individual does over the course of a typical week. Developed by Csikszentmihalyi and his colleagues (Csikszentmihalyi, 1997; Csikszentmihalyi, Hektner, & Schmidt, in press; Csikszentmihalyi & Larson, 1984; Prescott, Csikszentmihalyi, & Graef, 1981), the ESM is a week-long data collection in which participants wear a signaling device such as a beeper or watch and report on the activity they are doing when the beeper goes off. In the 500 Family Study, the participants wear wristwatches preprogrammed to beep eight times each day for 7 days. The watches randomly beep at some point every 2 hours, with no two beeps occurring less than 30 minutes apart. To the extent possible, mothers, fathers, and their adolescents have identical beeper schedules. The ESM differs from other time diaries because it also asks individuals what they are thinking at a particular moment and obtains detailed information about their subjective interpretations of various activities during daily life. In addition to estimating how much time a mother spends on housework, the ESM makes it possible to learn how she feels about doing various household chores and what she was thinking while cooking, cleaning, and so on.

Because the 500 Family Study involves both parents and children, it is possible to match ESM data from each family member and determine not only what a mother was doing and thinking, but also what her spouse and child were doing at the same time and how they felt about their activities. For example, Figs. 5.1 and 5.2 represent ESM data for 1 day for a husband and wife from the same family. Each time point represents when they were signaled and identifies where they were and their responses to the ESM item—for example, "felt happy [about the current activity]." With the ESM, each respondent has several data points, making it possible to standardize an individual "beep" with respect to the other "beeps" for one person. The responses in Figs. 5.1 and 5.2 are standardized, and thus reflect the individual's happiness at that particular point with respect to his or her own mean level of happiness for the week.[1]

---

[1] As with all standard scores, the mean is equal to zero with a standard deviation of 1. Therefore, if a value is greater than 0, the person is feeling happier than his or her overall mean.

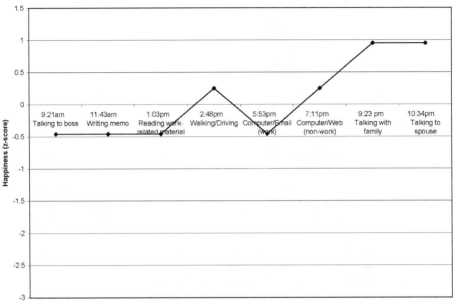

FIG. 5.1.   Variations in happiness over the course of a day (husband).

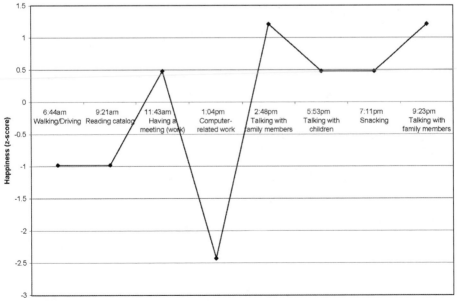

FIG. 5.2.   Variations in happiness over the course of a day (wife).

Figure 5.1 shows that the husband is below his average happiness during the morning hours when at work. In the early afternoon, when he is out walking and driving, his happiness increases to just above average. However, when returning to work, his happiness decreases to levels that are similar to those in the morning. The activities that provide him the most happiness are when he is engaged with his children and his spouse (one standard deviation above his average level of happiness).

The wife's initial value for happiness, when starting her work day, is lower than that of her husband (one standard deviation below her average). However, her mood becomes more positive when she engages with coworkers. Her low point occurs when she is doing computer-related activities. Similar to her husband, her happiness increases when with family members at home. Looking across the sample for all working mothers and fathers, happiness increases from work to home and decreases from home to work for both parents (see Fig. 5.3).

Combining the emotional experiences of working mothers and fathers using data from the ESM and other surveys with information on occupations obtained from the *Dictionary of Occupational Titles* makes it possible to identify how much time individuals spend on primary work tasks — tasks perceived as central to their occupation — and how they feel about that time. The occu-

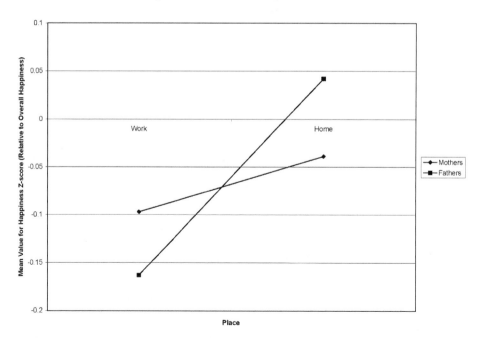

FIG. 5.3.   Happiness at work and at home relative to overall happiness for mothers and fathers.

pations of husbands and wives in the 500 Family Study range from high-level professions, such as physician, lawyer, and business executive, to low-level managerial jobs. Analyses of husbands and wives in 14 different occupations show that the number of hours spent working full time is fairly similar for men and women, although women spend slightly less time at work than men.

What is perhaps most interesting is that men and women across these occupations spend similar amounts of time on primary and secondary work tasks, but they feel more engaged and satisfied when doing the primary tasks (e.g., for a surgeon, operating on a patient) than secondary tasks (e.g., filling out hospital forms). The more time people spend doing primary work tasks, the more satisfied they are with their jobs and the less likely they are to bring negative feelings home, even if they work in jobs that are complex and demanding (Sexton, 2005). For many of these parents, work provides an environment of challenge and interest not found elsewhere, but home offers emotional benefits not found in the workplace. When parents are in occupations that allow them some autonomy and flexibility, they are more engaged at work and at home. These findings suggest that the emotional effects of being at work and at home are more complex than suggested by others (see e.g., Hochschild, 1997). Perhaps engagement in work tasks is essential to increasing both positive feelings and subsequent job satisfaction, but it is not a requirement for feeling positive at home. Sexton found that all parents feel more relaxed when at home, but feel much more engaged when at work. These findings suggest that sources of dissatisfaction among some employed parents may be associated with the type of work they perform, the control they can exercise in their jobs, and their general outlook.

Integrating survey and ESM data also allows for more direct evaluation of the effect that parents' emotions have on their children's emotions. As previously mentioned, if parents experience considerable stress at work, it is possible that their emotions will carry over to the home environment, thereby expanding a work phenomenon into a family one. Research with data from the 500 Family Study has identified characteristics associated with parents' work environments that influence the spillover of emotions from work to home and from parent to child. The findings suggest that fathers' work characteristics (e.g., work motivation, number of hours worked) are more likely than mothers' work characteristics to affect the transmission of emotions (specifically anxiety) from work to home. Conversely, mothers' emotions on first arriving home are more likely to cross over and affect adolescents' emotions at home than are fathers' (Matjasko & Feldman, 2005). Among the parents in the 500 Family Study, 88% reported experiencing work–family conflict sometimes, often, or almost always. A methodology such as the ESM clearly can help unravel the sources and influences of work–family conflict and is an important method of collecting specific data for both activities and emotions for multiple family members in various contexts.

Housework is another task that would benefit from further study with the ESM or similar methods. Several studies suggest that estimates of time spent on housework gathered from surveys may be inaccurate (see Lee, 2005, for a review). These inaccuracies can contribute to conflicts between spouses or between parents and children given that each family member incorrectly gauges their participation in household chores. The 500 Family Study suggests that estimates of time spent on housework vary according to who provides the information (wives, husbands, or adolescents), what definitions of housework are used, and whether secondary activities are taken into account. Retrospective survey estimates, when compared with ESM, substantially overestimate the time both husbands and wives spend on housework. This gap is reduced slightly if ESM estimates include time spent doing housework as either a primary or secondary activity. If time spent thinking about housework (which the ESM also captures) is included (what one might refer to as *household management*), the gap between reported time doing housework (from ESM estimates) and self-reported time doing housework (from the survey) is reduced even further. Findings also suggest that housework may be more pleasurable than previously assumed. When family members cooperatively engage in housework, even if they spend considerable time on it, they feel more positive. It is doing housework alone that seems to be most resented and undesirable (Lee, 2005). This is also the case for TV viewing, which is a more positive activity if the whole family watches together (Dempsey, 2005).

The 500 Family Study is predominately a middle- and upper middle-class sample in which the majority of parents have earned college or professional degrees. The findings, although robust and largely representative of U.S. upper middle-class families (see Hoogstra, 2005), do not necessarily reflect the objective and subjective experiences of parents in less skilled jobs with fewer economic resources. Many of the women in the 500 Family Study work by choice rather than necessity and have considerable flexibility in arranging their work hours. Parents in the 500 Family Study are also less likely to experience serious financial problems, sustained periods of unemployment, or difficulties in finding quality child care. They live in relatively safe neighborhoods, and their children attend local public schools with solid educational reputations. Nevertheless, these families represent a sizable portion of the working population and how they cope with work and family demands can inform family-friendly work policies.

The Sloan Study of Youth and Social Development offers additional evidence on the importance of studying both subjective and objective dimensions of time use. In this study, which focused on how adolescents form ideas about careers, the population is more diverse, and the study oversampled minorities and low-income adolescents. As with the 500 Family Study, the Sloan study used surveys, interviews, and the ESM. The sample included 1,221 adolescents who were followed for 5 years. Regardless of family background, the study found, these adolescents spent much of their time alone outside of school, and time spent alone increased from middle through high school. Findings from this study indicate that spending extensive time alone can be stressful, and young people who spend more than 40% of their time outside of school by themselves are more likely to have lower self-esteem, feel less happy and active, and are less likely to enjoy what they are doing (Schneider & Stevenson, 1999).

The Sloan Study of Youth and Social Development asked young people in middle and high school to categorize their experiences as work, play, both work and play, or neither (Csikszentmihalyi & Schneider, 2000). The work category, as might be expected, consisted primarily of school and home-work activities. Children from minority groups and those with fewer family resources were more likely to spend time in activities that they viewed as neither work nor play. On average, they spent approximately 10 hours each week in this purposeless state. Economically privileged children were more likely to perceive their activities, even those at school, as more like play.

When doing activities perceived of as neither work nor play, young people were less likely to enjoy what they were doing or to feel productive or happy (see Fig. 5.4). They were more likely to feel that they were not living up to their own or others' expectations, and they did not feel in control or good

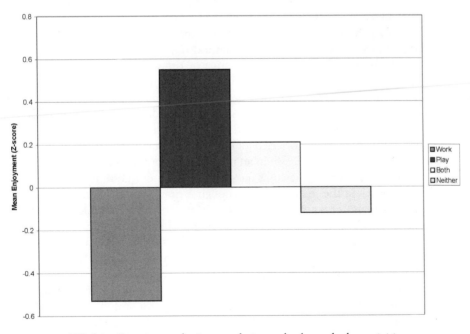

FIG. 5.4.   Experiences of enjoyment during work, play, and other activities.

about themselves. In addition, they felt less sociable, proud, and challenged, and the activities held little salience for them. Spending large amounts of time in this unpleasant, unfocused state is unlikely to promote positive development. These findings place concerns about the heavily scheduled, middle-class child in perspective. Soccer, tennis, piano lessons, and the other organized leisure activities that consume middle-class families may be positive alternatives to spending time alone or in purposeless activities.

MEASURING TIME USE

Regardless of how the study of time use is framed, a key concern is finding the most efficient and accurate method of measuring time allocation. This task is challenging because people tend to exaggerate time spent on socially desirable activities and underreport time spent on activities that most view as socially undesirable, such as fighting, gambling, and so on. How information on time use is obtained is subject to inherent sources of bias. Direct, unobtrusive observations of daily life, although certainly the most accurate, are clearly logistically problematic as well as costly—although this type of work is currently being conducted at the University of California, Los Angeles, under the direction of Elinor Ochs.

The most common way to measure time use is to ask respondents retrospective questions, such as those used by the Census Bureau. A typical survey question asks the respondent to report how many hours he or she worked in the previous week. Although this method has the advantage of brevity, it produces somewhat unreliable estimates of time use. An alternative to retrospective questions is, as noted previously, the time diary method, which requires individuals to record their activities and the times at which they occur. Perhaps the most well known is the full-day diary, used in a series of studies at the Universities of Maryland and Michigan.

Time diaries have been criticized for being burdensome and providing inaccurate estimates of time use. When an instrument is burdensome, people may choose not to answer a particular question or series of questions, or simply refuse to complete the instrument. Although a time diary may provide very accurate estimates of a person's day, it may not necessarily provide accurate estimates of a week or a month, thus creating problems of inference. Given that measuring time use is so important, researchers have conducted a series of methodological experiments in conjunction with the 500 Family Study to identify limitations of specific time use measures.

In two different studies, researchers compared time allocation estimates from the Sloan Study of Youth and Social Development and the 500 Family Study with estimates from other national studies. The researchers resolved sources of response and sampling bias using weighting and imputation techniques (Jeong, 2005; Mulligan, Schneider, & Wolfe, 2002). Results of these analyses suggest that some people are more compliant with study demands than others, and there are systematic differences in response rates by educational attainment, race, and gender.

In another study, researchers compared ESM and traditional time diary methods, such as those used by Robinson (1977, 1985, 1999; Robinson & Godbey, 1997) and Bianchi and Robinson (1997) for the same respondents over the same period of time. Results indicate that traditional time diaries are consistent with the ESM when measuring activities of long duration. However, the ESM is more accurate when measuring short activities—activities that often are excluded from traditional time diaries. The exclusion of these activities may bias estimates of time use. In work situations, for example, respondents may fail to mention short breaks that can constitute a significant proportion of time over the course of a week (Mulligan, Schneider, & Jeong, 2002). Measures of time use, much like other measures, should be carefully constructed and continually tested with different populations to ensure their validity and reliability. More studies are needed to ensure that what is counted and how it is counted produce accurate, unbiased estimates of how working families allocate their time.

INTERVENTION STRATEGIES FOR STUDYING WORK AND FAMILY

As we learn more about the complex pressures that families experience as a consequence of work–family conflict, a potential next step would be testing interventions designed to address this conflict, such as flexible work schedules, reduced hours, and compressed work weeks (Hart, 2003). How these interventions should be designed and implemented, however, must be carefully considered. In medicine, where the intervention is commonly a drug or regimented health routine, monitoring its implementation is relatively straightforward, although the medical research cites numerous instances where people fail to comply with treatment. Designing workplace, family, or community interventions is more much complex and problematic.

Interventions, much like other research methods, have their own inherent design problems. Before advocating their implementation, one would hope that more detailed discussions would take place regarding the benefits and liabilities of such an approach. In thinking about workplace interventions, one should consider their prevalence (e.g., the number of businesses that provide flexible work schedules), the population's characteristics (how many women would work part time if given realistic options), and the corporate culture (if workers are implicitly discouraged from working part time, few will choose to do so regardless of incentives offered by experimenters).

What types of incentives would encourage the participation of corporations, communities, and families in these studies? What procedures would ensure fidelity of implementation among those who agree to participate? Although intervention studies are promising approaches and are recognized as the most rigorous method for making causal inferences, effective strategies are difficult to design, and even the most well-designed experiments may encounter problems with selection bias, attrition, compliance, and other threats to validity.

Who are the overworked, time-deprived Americans? Jacobs and Gerson (2004) suggested it is dual-earner, professional couples. The 500 Family Study confirms their analyses. Many of these couples are working more hours per week than the national average, with 16% reporting working more than 50 hours per week. Forty percent of parents report arriving early to work or staying late in a given week; nearly 60% report that they work at home, with 54% indicating that they feel pressured to bring work home to keep up. Long hours appear to contribute to higher levels of stress, and children are not immune to their parents' work pressures. Time is a scarce commodity for dual-career families as they struggle to balance work and home life. Although the studies we discuss here cannot speak to the time pressures in single-parent families, single parents are sure to encounter similar challenges because there is only one parent to work both at home and in the workplace. Parents find themselves multitasking to meet job demands and ensure quality time at home. Through better time use studies that examine both objective and subjective dimensions of time allocation, it is possible to learn what is being sacrificed among these time-crunched families and how our social institutions can change to accommodate them.

REFERENCES

Bianchi, S. M., & Robinson , J. (1997). What did you do today? Children's use of time, family composition, and the acquisition of social capital. *Journal of Marriage and the Family, 59,* 332–344.

Csikszentmihalyi, M. (1997). *Finding flow: The psychology of engagement with everyday life.* New York: Basic Books.

Csikszentmihalyi, M., Hektner , J. M., & Schmidt, J. A. (in press). *Measuring the quality of everyday life: The experience sampling method handbook.*

Csikszentmihalyi, M., & Larson, R. (1984). *Being adolescent: Conflict and growth in the teenage years.* New York: Basic Books.

Csikszentmihalyi, M., & Schneider, B. (2000). *Becoming adult: How teenagers prepare for the world of work.* New York: Basic Books.

Dempsey, N. (2005). Television use and communication within families with adolescents. In B. Schneider & L. Waite (Eds.), *Being together, working apart: Dual-career families and the work-life balance* (pp. 277–296). Cambridge, England: Cambridge University Press.

Hart, P. (2003). *Imagining the future of work: A strategic research study conducted for the Alfred P. Sloan Center.* Washington, DC: Peter D. Hart Research Associates.

Hochschild, A. (1997). *The time bind: When work becomes home and home becomes work*. New York: Metropolitan Books.

Hoogstra, L. (2005). The design of the 500 Family Study. In B. Schneider & L. Waite (Eds.), *Being together, working apart: Dual-career families and the work-life balance* (pp. 18–38). Cambridge, England: Cambridge University Press.

Jacobs, J. A., & Gerson, K. (2004). *The time divide: Work, family, and gender inequality*. Cambridge, MA: Harvard University Press.

Jeong, J. (2005). Obtaining accurate measures of time use from the ESM. In B. Schneider & L. Waite (Eds.), *Being together, working apart: Dual-career families and the work-life balance* (pp. 461–482). Cambridge, England: Cambridge University Press.

Lee, Y.-S. (2005). Measuring the gender gap in household labor: Accurately estimating wives' and husbands' contributions. In B. Schneider & L. Waite (Eds.), *Being together, working apart: Dual-career families and the work-life balance* (pp. 229–247). Cambridge, England: Cambridge University Press.

Matjasko, J. L., & Feldman, A. F. (2005). Emotional transmission between parents and adolescents: The importance of work characteristics and relationship quality. In B. Schneider & L. Waite (Eds.), *Being together, working apart: Dual-career families and the work-life balance* (pp. 138–158). Cambridge, England: Cambridge University Press.

Moen, P. (Ed.). (2003). *It's about time: Couples and careers*. Ithaca and London: Cornell University Press.

Mulligan, C., Schneider, B., & Wolfe, R. (2002). *Non-response and population representation in studies of time use* (Sloan Working Paper 02-18). Chicago, IL: Alfred P. Sloan Center on Parents, Children, and Work, University of Chicago.

Prescott, S., Csikszentmihalyi, M., & Graef, R. (1981). Environmental effects on cognitive and affective states: The experiential time sampling approach. *Social Behavior and Personality, 9*, 23–32.

Presser, H. B. (2003). *Working in a 24/7 economy: Challenges for American families*. New York: Russell Sage Foundation.

Robinson, J. P. (1977). *How Americans use time: A social-psychological analysis of everyday behavior*. New York: Praeger.

Robinson, J. P. (1985). The validity and reliability of diaries versus alternative time use measures. In F. T. Juster & F. P. Stafford (Eds.), *Time, goods, and well-being* (pp. 33–62). Ann Arbor: University of Michigan, Survey Research Center, Institute for Social Research.

Robinson, J. P. (1999). The time-diary method. In W. E. Pentland, A. S. Harvey, M. P. Lawton, & M. A. McColl (Eds.), *Time use research in the social sciences* (pp. 47–89). New York: Kluwer Academic/Plenum Publishers.

Robinson, J. P., & Godbey, G. (1997). *Time for life: The surprising ways Americans use their time*. University Park, PA: The Pennsylvania State University Press.

Schneider, B., & Stevenson, D. (1999). *The ambitious generation: America's teenagers, motivated but directionless*. New Haven, CT: Yale University Press.

Schneider, B., & Waite, L. (Eds.). (2005). *Being together, working apart: Dual-career families and the work-life balance*. Cambridge, England: Cambridge University Press.

Sexton, H. (2005). Spending time at work and at home: What workers do, how they feel about it, and how these emotions affect family life. In B. Schneider & L. Waite (Eds.), *Being together, working apart: Dual-career families and the work-life balance* (pp. 47–71). Cambridge, England: Cambridge University Press.

PART II

The "Work" in Work and Family

6

Work and Family Life: The Perspective of Employers

Harry J. Holzer
Georgetown Public Policy Institute
The Urban Institute

Any discussion of balancing work and family ultimately leads to the work-place situation, and specifically to the wants or needs of their employers. Many workers would clearly prefer to have more family-related benefits and greater flexibility in their work schedules and arrangements. Of course these factors may conflict with the need of employers to limit compensation costs and have dependable workers. However, employers must also attract workers, many of whom need family-related benefits and flexibility before they can accept employment.

Employers' need for dependable and reliable workers influences whom they hire and how they recruit and screen job applicants. It also helps determine the compensation packages offered in terms of family-related benefits such as health care, child-care assistance, and the like. It influences the extent to which employers offer flexibility in hours on the job, as well as the ability of employees to work from home. The need for dependable workers may also affect employers' willingness to provide flexible contracting arrangements if that is what workers need.

Employers vary widely in their basic characteristics (such as their size, industry, and technologies used) and in their ability and willingness to create family-friendly workplaces. Given this variation, what factors determine their choices on hiring, benefits, and workplace flexibility to assist families? Is the mix of employer policies generated by the labor market optimal from the point of view of workers, society, and employers? If not, are there government policies that might induce employers to offer more family-friendly practices? Do these policies impose significant costs on employers, and are there unintended consequences on employment and earnings associated with these policies? If so, how can these be minimized? These are some of the issues covered in this chapter.

FAMILY-RELATED BENEFITS AND PRACTICES: WHAT EMPLOYERS WANT

A worker's family needs influence his or her choices and workplace behavior along a variety of dimensions. The same is true of employers regarding workers. The most basic decision that employers must make is whom to hire and how to recruit and screen job applicants. Employers clearly seek a wide range of general, as well as job-specific, skills, and they look to a variety of credentials to document these skills, such as educational degrees or other forms of skill certification, previous work experience, and references. They use written applications, personal interviews, and sometimes tests and background checks to screen their job applicants (Holzer, 1996; Moss & Tilly, 2001).

Among the general personal qualities that virtually every employer wants in a prospective employee are job readiness and reliability. Even in low-wage and low-skill labor markets, virtually all employers want workers who will show up on time, show up every day, and are personally reliable and trustworthy. In fact a number of studies of welfare recipients in the labor market indicate that these are the first, and often the most prominent, attributes that employers seek when hiring such workers (Holzer, 1999; Regenstein & Meyer, 1998). Likewise, the most common problem in hiring welfare recipients is frequent absenteeism. In a recent survey of more than 3,000 employers in several large metropolitan areas, about 700 of whom had hired current or former welfare recipients in the previous year, as many as 40% complain about absenteeism (Holzer & Stoll, 2001).

Furthermore, absenteeism figures prominently in employer evaluations of worker performance and in decisions on worker retention or turnover. In the survey noted earlier, employers regarded absenteeism as a problem for about three fourths of those who were no longer employed with the company. Absenteeism was also mentioned as a problem for more than 80% of those who were rated as performing worse than the average worker in that job. In contrast, it was mentioned as a problem among only about 20% of those rated better than average (see also Holzer, Stoll, & Wissoker, 2001).

The most common cause of absenteeism for the single mothers in the survey was difficulty associated with child care, which was reported in roughly 60% of the cases where absenteeism was mentioned as a problem. Health problems for either the worker or other family members were also a frequent cause of absences (in roughly 35% of these cases). Child-care needs thus affect not only whether employees show up every day and the extent to which they remain on the job, but also their job performance and suitability for future promotion. Of course we would expect child care and absenteeism to be relatively greater problems for low-income, single mothers than for others given that single mothers generally have less help within the nuclear family for child care and usually have more difficulty paying others for such care. Also, among jobs that require a greater degree of and a wider range of skills, absenteeism alone will no doubt figure less prominently in job performance and retention.

Still concerns over child care, and the associated problems of absenteeism and turnover, are not limited to the low-skill end of the labor market. Given that roughly 70% of mothers with young children now work outside the home (U.S. Department of Labor, 1999), child-care issues affect employees and employers across the skill spectrum. Child-care issues increasingly affect the labor market behaviors of men as well. In addition, now that more than 40% of the workforce provides some form of elder care to parents and other older family members (U.S. Department of Labor, 1999), elder care is added to child-care concerns.

Given the prevalence of child-care and elder-care issues, it is no longer possible for employers to simply avoid hiring workers with these needs.[1] However, it is also impossible for many employers to accept high rates of absenteeism and turnover among their workers. For some low-wage employers in the retail trade and service sectors, dead-end jobs associated with weak worker performance, high turnover, and few promotions are accepted facts of their workplace operations. However, where employer-provided training is necessary and where the costs of recruiting and screening new workers are not trivial, employers are not so sanguine about the prospects of worker turnover.

Thus, the fixed costs associated with hiring new employees will deter employers from accepting absenteeism or high turnover, and they will seek employees with at least some potential of being retained over a longer period of time.[2] Given the prevalence of family-related issues among prospective

---

[1] It would also be illegal to do so as the burdens of child and elder care continue to fall much more heavily on female than male workers, and to systematically avoid such workers would constitute gender discrimination in the workplace.

[2] The insight that the fixed costs of hiring and training workers with longer term potential is akin to an investment decision first appeared in Oi (1962). See also Becker (1975) and, for a more recent theoretical treatment of this issue, Jovanovic (1979).

members of their workforces, most employers will have difficulty attracting and retaining qualified employees unless they make at least some attempt to accommodate workers on family-related issues.

Employers have adopted various methods to attract and retain qualified workers. Benefits packages, for example, often recognize family issues by providing family health insurance coverage and child-care assistance. Employer-provided health insurance remains the norm in U.S. workplaces, although its incidence has been declining in recent years as health care costs have dramatically increased. According to Currie and Yelowitz (2000), roughly 70% of Americans have employer-sponsored health insurance, which has declined from about 76% in the late 1980s. Employer-provided child care is much less common, with only about 9% of employers providing care at or near the workplace, although many now offer information or assistance. The reasons that health care is more often a part of the benefits package are its preferential treatment by the federal tax code and the economies of scale that lower prices when employers choose a set of options on behalf of their workers. Many employees also may like the convenience of having employers choose among the myriad plans available instead of having to make these decisions on their own. Of course employees can pay for their own health insurance or child care if they do not obtain it directly from their employers. In fact most health care costs seem to be borne by the employees in the form of lower wages, rather than by their employers, as we note later.

When it comes to child care, many employees believe there is no substitute for a flexible schedule that enables them to be home to provide child (or elder) care. As a result, as many as two thirds of American employers allow employees some flexibility to periodically adjust their work schedules, and up to one quarter allow workers some degree of *flextime*, which enables them to adjust their starting and ending times on a daily basis (U.S. Department of Labor, 1999). More than 20 million Americans do at least some of their work at home, although they are not always directly compensated for this time (U.S. Department of Labor, 1999). These numbers are likely to rise over time as new technology makes it easier for workers to telecommute (Autor, 2001).

Employer flexibility also allows employees to work part time. Indeed nearly 20% of all workers now work fewer than 35 hours per week, although the overall fraction has leveled off somewhat in recent years as more women have chosen to work full time (Blank, 1998). Other kinds of flexible work arrangements include "contingent work," "temp" work arranged by agencies, and the use of independent contractors. Currently, roughly 10% of the U.S. labor force works in one or another of these arrangements (Autor & Houseman, 2002; Houseman, 1997; U.S. Department of Labor, 1999).

Of course, although these arrangements provide the flexibility that many workers seek to deal with their family responsibilities, employers might also use these arrangements to gain their own flexibility or to avoid paying for benefits. For example, employers may use part-time work or temporary workers to avoid paying benefits. Some employees might prefer full-time to part-time work, but accept the latter involuntarily (especially in slack labor markets). As Henly and Lambert point out (chap. 30, this volume), sometimes it is the employer who prefers irregular or off-shift hours, not the employee. Thus, the gains to American workers from the growing use of such arrangements, especially for those who seek more permanent forms of employment, continue to be heavily debated.

Why, then, do some employers offer more family-related benefits and flexible work schedules to their employees while others offer fewer? As indicated earlier, skill needs and training costs are one reason. In general, employers who pay higher wages also provide more fringe benefits. However, controlling for the overall level of compensation, factors such as employer size and industry are important determinants of employer willingness and ability to provide more benefits and flexible schedules. Larger employers often have greater expertise in and more professionalized human resources management, as well as potential "economies of scale" among their employees, all of which enable larger employers to provide a greater mix of benefits and wages to their workers (Brown, Hamilton, & Medoff, 1990). Further, at least some service industries require less group interaction at fixed production times than do construction or manufacturing, thereby leading to potentially greater flexibility in workplace scheduling. Depending on their need for direct contact with customers, and when such contact would occur, certain employers may be able to handle flexible hours and part-time work more easily as well.

The nature of the occupations matters as well. Highly skilled and high-paying occupations are generally much less amenable to part-time work, especially if employers have invested in significant training for these workers. (There are, however, some employers who allow their highly skilled employees to do part-time work, but without offering health insurance coverage and requiring them to work on an hourly basis.) However, some flexibility in scheduling may still be possible in these highly skilled occupational areas. Part-time employment in law firms and management positions, for example, seems to have grown more available in recent years, although the stigma associated with the *mommy track* remains.

The exact technologies used in the production of goods or services and the ways in which work is organized also help account for the varying willingness of employers to provide family-related benefits and flexibility. Whether workers are unionized (Freeman & Medoff, 1984) and other institutional or management characteristics (including their own personal attitudes and knowledge about this issue) also help explain variation across employers in this area.

Whether employers feel greater pressure to provide more benefits and flexibility to attract and retain married women or other providers of child or elder care also depends on the overall tightness of the labor market and the demographics of the groups that employers target. The extremely tight labor market of the late 1990s, for example, induced employers to offer a greater array of benefits and services than they had in previous years. As the economy recovers from the recent recession and "baby boomer" retirements approach at the end of this decade, those considerations will once again grow more salient. In addition, as more highly skilled women (as well as men) choose to juggle work and family, more employers will feel some pressure to accommodate them as a way to attract and retain them during tight markets.

EMPLOYER-PROVIDED BENEFITS AND FLEXIBILITY: IS THE MIX OPTIMAL?

The preceding discussion suggests that employers' own characteristics as well as those of their targeted workforce influence the extent to which they must provide workplace benefits and flexibility to those with family needs. Characteristics of both the demand (i.e., employer) and supply (i.e., worker) sides of the labor market will influence employer behavior and choices in this regard.

The forces of supply and demand in the overall labor market also balance these two sets of needs and interests. In the market, some workers and families, especially those with small children or elderly parents who need care, will need more of these services than do others. At the same time, some employers will be more able and willing than others to provide them for reasons noted before. Those workers who are most in need of family-related benefits and flexibility will sort or match themselves to those employers who can afford to provide more of these benefits (Rosen, 1986).

Beyond this matching process, some employers who need to attract workers with families, but who find it more difficult to provide these benefits and services, might have to pay a premium (or a *compensating differential* in economics jargon) in wages and salaries to continue to recruit such workers. However, families in greater need of workplace flexibility, health, or childcare services might have to accept lower wages or salaries than they otherwise would, thus providing a premium to employers. As more workers require family-related benefits and flexibility, the premiums that employers pay to avoid providing these benefits will rise, and more workers will be willing to forgo wages or salaries to obtain them.

Given these incentives, more employers will choose to provide these job characteristics over time. Thus, the forces of labor supply and demand will help balance the number of jobs with benefits and flexibility with the number of workers who need them. At the same time, market forces will help balance the employer costs of providing the benefits with the value placed on these characteristics by employees. The changing demographics of the workforce, in terms of rising numbers of workers juggling family and work responsibilities, will cause employers to offer a more family-friendly package of compensation and work arrangements.

Of course other forces will also affect the provision of benefits and workplace flexibility over time. On the one hand, new computer technologies will make working from home at odd hours more manageable for employers. On the other hand, the rising costs of health insurance will induce some employers to cease offering coverage. Expanded government provision of these benefits (through Medicaid, State Child Health Insurance Programs, etc.) may also reduce the pressure on employers to provide these benefits (Currie & Yelowitz, 2000).

An important question in this scenario is whether these market forces provide a socially optimal (or efficient) mix of family-related job attributes for those who need them. In general, the balancing of needs and values (in this case, on the supply side of the labor market) with costs (on the demand side) enables private markets to generate optimal mixes of goods or services, and optimal sets of characteristics for those goods and services generated. However, where market failure occurs, the resulting mix may not be optimal.

For instance, market forces will not provide for an optimum mix of job attributes or services that provide positive externalities or public goods, where the benefits extend beyond those who directly pay for them. In such a situation, too few of those services and attributes will be provided if employers and working parents do not fully value (and are not fully willing to pay for) the benefits provided to others in their families and communities by child care and workplace flexibility. Child- and elder-care benefits or flexible work schedules benefit children, the elderly, and the broader society in ways that may well extend beyond the benefits to working adults. Although these adults often try to incorporate the well-being of these other individuals into their decision making, whether they do so fully and in all cases remains in doubt.

The reliance on market forces to provide these job attributes might also create a problem economists call *adverse selection*, in which there are more workers who need these job attributes than employers who provide them realize. As workers who need these job attributes sort themselves exclusively into jobs providing them, the greater than anticipated costs to employers from this influx will result in undue hardship to those employers offering the benefits, perhaps driving some of them from the market (or away from providing the benefits) as a consequence.[3]

Finally, the market might generate a level of family-related benefits and workplace flexibility that is optimal in the aggregate, but these characteristics

---

[3] The adverse selection problem occurs because of imperfect (or asymmetric) information about the prevalence of worker interest in these benefits. See Akerlof (1970) for the original insights into this problem and Stiglitz (2000) for a more recent discussion.

may remain beyond the reach of lower income families, whose workers lack the skills or labor market networks to obtain the *good* jobs that provide them. In this case, the problem is not one of efficiency, but one of equity.

In all of these market scenarios, there are well-established economic arguments for policymakers to help the private sector achieve higher levels of family-related benefits and flexibility, as well as a more equitable distribution of these benefits and policies across workers. There are, however, several possible methods of doing so, each with its own costs and potential effects on employment and earnings. I turn to these policy approaches in the next section.

GOVERNMENT POLICY: MANDATES, SUBSIDIES, AND "UNINTENDED CONSEQUENCES"

The simplest way for government to raise the level of family-related benefits and workforce flexibility in private-sector labor markets is to mandate it—in other words, to require employers to provide health care benefits or flexible work schedules. This approach is used by federal and state governments on a variety of labor market issues. For instance, the Fair Labor Standards Act (FLSA) of 1938 mandates that all "covered" employees be paid a minimum wage, which is now $5.15 per hour. Over time both the statutory minimum rate and the coverage have risen considerably, even after allowing for inflation. States are allowed to impose minimum wage levels higher than the federal rate, and several states do so.

A number of mandates have been imposed on employers in areas that potentially affect family life. For instance, FLSA also mandates that employers pay overtime premiums for those working more than 40 hours per week. These higher wages likely deter many employers from requiring their employees to work long hours, although other possible approaches might generate even greater flexibility for families. For instance, some advocates (e.g., Marshall & Sawhill, 2002) argue that the federal rules should be amended to allow families the choice of taking comp time, or time off from work, in lieu of the higher wage. Also the Family and Medical Leave Act (FMLA) of 1993 requires that firms of 50 or more workers provide up to 3 months of unpaid leave for employees whose family members require care. Paid leave is, of course, not currently mandated by the federal government, although a few states are beginning to use their unemployment or disability insurance systems to help employers pay for it (Marshall & Sawhill, 2002).

In terms of health care, the United States does not mandate health insurance coverage by private employers, although this was the basis of President Clinton's proposals, which Congress refused to pass in 1994. When health

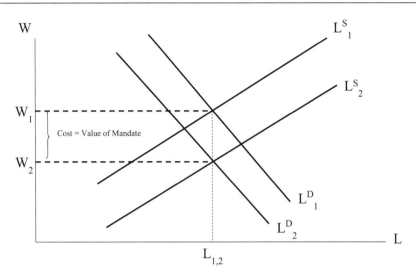

FIG. 6.1. Effects of government mandates on the demand for and supply of labor.

insurance is provided, the federal government does mandate certain kinds of coverage, such as for maternity (Gruber, 1994b).

Although mandated benefits and time off from work certainly generate more benefits and workplace flexibility for workers and their families, they come with some potentially serious economic costs. If the mandates impose higher costs on employers for every worker hired, employers might well choose to hire fewer workers. Any reduction in employer demand for labor would result in lower employment and earnings among American workers, as is evident from Fig. 6.1.

However, it is not obvious that the mandates would reduce employment. For instance, if workers happen to value the benefit or service that the government is mandating, they may be willing to accept lower wages. From a labor market perspective, this would constitute an outward shift of labor supply as seen in Fig. 6.1. Indeed if workers value the mandated benefits or flexibility as much as those benefits cost employers, the outward shift in labor supply would fully offset the inward shift in labor demand, resulting in no net loss of employment. Instead wages would be reduced by the full amount of the cost of the mandate, and employers would be no worse off from having provided them.

For this scenario to work, a number of assumptions would have to be met. First, employees must not only value the mandated conditions of work at the same level of cost to the employer, but they must also perceive that employers are saving them these costs and adjust their wage demands accordingly. Furthermore, there could be no wage rigidities limiting the downward adjustment of their wages, such as the minimum wage or union coverage might create (fewer than 5% of U.S. workers work for the minimum wage, whereas private-sector union coverage is about 9%). In addition, the benefits associated with the mandate must be provided only through employment, and not through a broader measure of universal coverage that extends to the nonemployed as well (as might be the case with health insurance).

Indeed, employer-provided health care costs seem to meet these conditions. In this case, total compensation of U.S. workers does not appear to have risen as health insurance costs have risen over time; the costs seem to be paid by workers in the form of lower take-home pay (Gruber, 1994a).

This, of course, may raise questions about whether workers are better off from having these benefits and whether the government should mandate them at all, instead of leaving the decision to workers and their employers. However, the arguments noted earlier regarding market failures (such as public goods or adverse selection) might still argue for mandates even under these circumstances.

Other market failures can create additional arguments for publicly mandated working conditions. For instance, imperfect information among workers about their own need for health coverage or flexible scheduling might be another rationale if workers tend to underestimate their future need for these policies. Economies of scale that help reduce the costs of providing certain benefits or working conditions might be yet another rationale for this approach if private-sector markets are imperfect. Finally, if employers earn above-normal profits in some sectors because of imperfect competition in that sector, it is possible that they can bear the increased costs of providing benefits. Imperfect competition creates less elastic demand for labor, which makes it easier for workers to pass on higher costs to employers without lowering their own employment.

The evidence to date whether such mandates imposed on employers have reduced employment or reduced wages suggests that, generally, employment incurs small negative effects when higher wages, benefits, or flexibility are mandated (Houseman, 1998), although the exact findings vary with the mandate being considered. In Europe, where many benefits are set at higher levels and mandated restrictions on employer freedom to hire and discharge at will are much greater, the costs (in terms of employment losses) seem more substantial, especially in more recent data (e.g., Bertola, Blau, & Kahn, 2001). Yet some of the mandates in those countries, such as those requiring maternity leave, might have positive effects on economic outcomes (Ruhm & Teague, 1993). Even in the United States, the provision of maternity leave by private employers seems to generate improved employment outcomes for the mothers of children in the labor market (Waldfogel, 1998). Thus, mandated family-related benefits or economic flexibility might well generate positive outcomes for those served by them at relatively modest cost to employment or the overall economy.

However, there might be other ways to provide these benefits and labor market flexibility without the government imposing potentially costly mandates on employers. Health benefits, for example, might be provided directly by the government and funded by taxes, either income taxes or some version of a payroll tax. Summers (1989) compared the economic effects of mandated employer benefits with those of government-provided benefits and generally found some economic benefit to employer-mandated approaches, such as greater choice when provision is private and fewer "distortions" on economic choices created by the tax system. Of course public provision can only be considered for benefits that impose an explicit upfront cost and not for benefits such as flexible work schedules or conditions.

Beyond these cases, one might consider less forceful methods of encouraging certain employer flexibility, perhaps through subsidies and tax credits. The tax system already subsidizes employer-provided health insurance, and it might be used to encourage other forms of family-friendly benefits that are considered socially beneficial. Tax credits to employees for child care exist as well, although these might be made more generous or progressive in a variety of ways (Marshall & Sawhill, 2002).

There are, however, limitations and costs to using tax credits or subsidies to encourage workplace changes. Credits and subsidies could become quite costly to the U.S. Treasury in a time of growing fiscal pressure generated by the upcoming retirements of baby boomers. To the extent that these tax credits and subsidies change employer behavior, rather than simply creating windfalls for those who provide benefits and flexibility anyway, is an open question. The use of the tax system for social policy is, after all, one that many public finance economists oppose on the grounds that it complicates the tax system and creates distortions in economic behavior.

Besides mandates and tax credits or subsidies, a variety of other methods might be used to encourage employer support for family-related benefits and workplace flexibility. These might include government grants to communities or employers who undertake innovative approaches to these issues, funding of pilot projects, dissemination of research results to employers, and a variety of other forms of technical assistance. In general, the benefits of using government mandates or the tax system to encourage greater employer flexibility, relative to other ways of promoting balance between work and family life, should be more thoroughly researched and debated.

CONCLUSION

Do U.S. employers have any interest in the family problems of their employees? The answer to that question is clearly yes. Most employers have an interest in minimizing absenteeism and turnover difficulties that are frequently associated with child-care problems, particularly among married women. As the number of women, and even men, in the labor market who have child- or elder-care responsibilities grows, employers have no choice but to help workers manage the conflict between their work and family lives. By providing health care and child-care assistance, as well as flexible working schedules and arrangements, employers can help employees become more stable and productive.

In this way, the forces of supply and demand in the U.S. labor market help balance the costs to employers of providing these benefits with the needs of workers. Some employers, depending on their size, industry, technology of production, and other institutional characteristics, will find it easier to provide family-related benefits and workplace flexibility than will others. Some employees, especially those with small children or elderly parents who need care, will need these benefits and flexibility more than others. Based on this equation, some natural sorting between employers and employees will take place, while wage adjustments will provide incentives for more employers to provide benefits as the prevalence of workers with these needs in the labor market grows.

The labor market, however, does not necessarily provide a socially optimal level of family-related benefits and workplace flexibility, and the distribution of these workplace attributes across workers is not necessarily equitable. Public policy can therefore play a role in encouraging the provision of these benefits and flexible workplaces. However, government mandates on employers can result in lower earnings and employment levels in the labor market, and government subsidies to encourage these practices have their own potential limitations.

Thus, we continue to face a challenge in learning how to encourage employers to provide family-related benefits and workplace flexibility while minimizing the economic costs to employers of doing so.

REFERENCES

Akerlof, G. (1970). The market for lemons: Quality uncertainty and the market mechanism. *Quarterly Journal of Economics, 84*, 488–500.

Autor, D. (2001). Wiring the labor market. *Journal of Economic Perspectives, 15*, 25–40.

Autor, D., & Houseman, S. (2002). *Do temporary help jobs improve labor market outcomes? A pilot analysis with welfare clients.* Unpublished, W. E. Upjohn Institute for Employment Research.

Becker, G. (1975). *Human capital* (2nd ed.). New York: National Bureau of Economic Research.

Bertola, G., Blau, F., & Kahn, L. (2001). Comparative analysis of labor market outcomes: Lessons for the United States from international long-run evidence. In A. Krueger & R. Solow (Eds.), *The roaring nineties* (pp. 159–218). New York: Russell Sage Foundation.

Blank, R. (1998). Contingent work in a changing labor market. In R. Freeman & P. Gottschalk (Eds.), *Generating jobs* (pp. 258–294). New York: Russell Sage Foundation.

Brown, C., Hamilton, J., & Medoff, J. (1990). *Employers large and small*. Cambridge MA: Harvard University Press.

Currie, J., & Yelowitz, A. (2000). Health insurance and less-skilled workers. In D. Card & R. Blank (Eds.), *Finding jobs* (pp. 233–261). New York: Russell Sage Foundation.

Freeman, R., & Medoff, J. (1984). *What do unions do?* New York: Basic Books.

Gruber, J. (1994a, November 18–19). *Payroll taxation, employer mandates, and the labor market: Theory, evidence and unanswered questions*. Prepared for the W. E. Upjohn Institute Conference on Employee Benefits, Labor Costs and Labor Markets, Kalamazoo, MI.

Gruber, J. (1994b). The incidence of mandated maternity benefits. *American Economic Review, 84*, 622–41.

Holzer, H. J. (1996). *What employers want: Job prospects for less-educated workers*. New York: Russell Sage Foundation.

Holzer, H. J. (1999). Will employers hire welfare recipients? New survey evidence from Michigan. *Journal of Policy Analysis and Management, 18*, 449–472.

Holzer, H. J., & Stoll, M. (2001). *Employers and welfare recipients: The effects of welfare reform in the workplace*. San Francisco: Public Policy Institute of California.

Holzer, H., Stoll, M., & Wissoker, D. (2001). *Job performance and retention among welfare recipients*. Discussion paper, Institute for Research on Poverty, University of Wisconsin-Madison.

Houseman, S. (1997). *Temporary, part-time and contract employment in the United States: A report on the Upjohn Institute's employer survey on flexible staffing practices*. Report prepared for the U.S. Department of Labor.

Houseman, S. (1998). The effects of employer mandates. In R. Freeman & P. Gottschalk (Eds.), *Generating jobs* (pp. 154–192). New York: Russell Sage Foundation.

Jovanovic, B. (1979). Job-matching and the theory of turnover. *Journal of Political Economy, 87*, 972–990.

Marshall, W., & Sawhill, I. (2002, October). *Progressive family policy in the 21st century*. Paper presented at the Maxwell School Conference on Public Policy and the Family, Syracuse University.

Moss, P., & Tilly, C. (2001). *Stories employers tell: Race, skill, and hiring in America*. New York: Russell Sage Foundation.

Oi, W. (1962). Labor as a quasi-fixed factor. *Journal of Political Economy, 70*, 538–555.

Regenstein, M., & Meyer, J. (1998). *Job prospects for welfare recipients: Employers speak out. Occasional papers, assessing the new federalism*. Washington, DC: The Urban Institute.

Rosen, S. (1986). The theory of equalizing differences. In O. Ashenfelter & R. Layard (Eds.), *The handbook of labor economics* (Vol. 1, pp. 641–692). Amsterdam: North Holland.

Ruhm, C., & Teague, J. (1993). *Parental leave policies in Europe and North America*. Working paper, University of North Carolina at Greensboro.

Stiglitz, J. (2000). The contributions of the economics of information to twentieth century economics. *Quarterly Journal of Economics, 115*, 1441–1478.

Summers, L. (1989). Some simple economics of mandated benefits. *American Economic Review, 79*, 177–183.

U.S. Department of Labor. (1999). *Futureworks: Trends and challenges for work in the 21st century*. Washington, DC: U.S. Government Printing Office.

Waldfogel, J. (1998). The family gap for young women in the United States and Britain: Can maternity leave make a difference? *Journal of Labor Economics, 15*, 505–545.

7

Workplace Policies and Practices to Support Work and Families

Ellen Ernst Kossek

Michigan State University

Today's employees differ dramatically from their counterparts even 50 years ago (Ozeki, 2003). Dual-earner families are the typical American family (Barnett, 2001), and women make up nearly one half of the U.S. workforce (Bond, Galinsky, & Swanberg, 1998). The burden of caring for dependents among working employees is only likely to increase in the next few decades. One half of all children will live with a single parent (often female) at some point in their childhood. Individuals over 65 are one of the fastest growing segments of the U.S. population and will likely add to the caregiving demands of the working population (Kossek, Colquitt, & Noe, 2001). In addition, many individuals are working into their late 60s and 70s, either delaying retirement or working part-time in a second career. Consequently, they are likely to be managing both their own and other family members' health while they are still employed.

A structural mismatch between labor force characteristics and employers' workforce demands has become a critical problem in society. *Structural mismatch* is the incongruence between the design of job demands and career systems and the caregiving demands of workers, which to be met require more flexibility and support at work. The ideal worker historically has been one who is rarely absent from or late to work and does not let family responsibilities encumber his or her work hours or commitment to the job (Williams, 1999). Many employers do not see work-family support as a legitimate human resource issue of critical concern; rather, they see it, if anything, as a fringe benefit offered as a piecemeal policy coerced by labor market shifts (e.g., nursing shortage) or legislation (Kossek, Dass, & DeMarr, 1994). Employer response to this shift in the demography of the workforce is not unlike the initial response of many employers in the 1960s to affirmative action and equal employment opportunity. Also with slowing gross national product (GNP) growth and increasing global market pressures, employers do not perceive an urgency, nor the resources, to act (Kossek et al., 1994).

In this chapter, I discuss what employers can do to assist workers in managing their multiple demands and how an organization is affected when employees have multiple competing demands. I also discuss trends and identify gaps to be addressed by future research. As the following review of research shows, more work is needed to fully answer these questions given that the work-family policy field is evolving in methodology and focus.

CURRENT STATE OF RESEARCH AND PRACTICE ON WORK-FAMILY POLICIES

Work-family policies, defined as employer policies and practices to support the integration of paid work with significant family demands, are increasingly linked, in theory, to recruitment and retention issues (Ryan & Kossek, 2003), individual and group performance (Van Dyne & Kossek, 2003), and greater employee commitment (Osterman, 1995). Consequently, over the past few decades, work-family policies have proliferated as a means to attract and retain employees (Kossek & Ozeki, 1999). Although employers often initially defined work-family integration as a parenting and dependent care issue, many firms eventually broadened policies and practices to support additional life roles such as community roles, elder care, teen supervision, personal health care, those related to personal values (e.g., political, religious), military service, domestic chores, or exercise. This trend reveals a growing recognition of the need to support not only those with visible family needs (e.g., child care), but all employees who may experience work-life stresses regardless of family status.

In practice, few employers have systematically evaluated the effectiveness of work-family policies, let alone linked them to business and human resource strategies. Employer interventions to help employees manage work and family are a form of workforce diversity management. Unfortunately, many organizations have adopted diversity interventions without effectively monitoring them, except only superficially (Comer & Soliman, 1996). Complicating matters more, the time lag between implementation and effects sometimes makes it difficult to identify clear relations between the adoption of work-family practices and productivity (Huselid & Becker, 1996). Work-life policies can also have group and organizational consequences, such as increased need for coordination or cross-training, which are sometimes difficult to disentangle (Van Dyne & Kossek, 2003). Further, successfully making major organizational change to support work-life integration for workers with heavy caregiving demands requires the company to transform the design of work and assumptions about the priority of work and family roles (Bailyn, 1993). Most jobs are currently designed without consideration of family needs. Workers are expected to reconfigure their family lives around work. The bottom line is that many jobs, at all ends of the pay scale, do not easily allow for work-life balance (Conlin, Merritt, & Himelstein, 2002).

Reflecting practice efforts, the research focus has broadened to include not only work-family policies, but also those related to work-life integration. However, far more research has focused on policies that help integrate the roles of child caregiver with work than on policies that address other family or life roles, or that address multiple roles simultaneously (e.g., elder and child caregiving) and, as my chapter shows, significant gaps in the research remain.

Although demographic shifts and the intensification of demands outside of work have spawned an explosion in general work and family research in the past decade, quality research on the effects of work-family policies is limited (Kossek & Ozeki, 1998, 1999). Recent meta-analyses of the individual and organizational outcomes of work and family policies (Kossek & Ozeki, 1998, 1999) and alternative work schedules (Baltes, Briggs, Huff, Wright, & Neuman, 1999) each found fewer than 30 articles reporting the statistical effects of policies on standard work outcomes such as absenteeism and job satisfaction (Ozeki, 2003). Although 30 is not necessarily a paltry number, the quality of these studies varies widely; many used skewed samples or only cross-sectional self-report data, and most did not use common measures that would allow for easier generalizability. This variation in quality makes it possible for some authors in this volume, such as Thompson and coauthors (see chap. 8, this volume) to highlight many studies that show positive effects, whereas others note the equivocation in the research. Yet both are accurate depending on which studies are chosen and the methodological lens used.

I organize this chapter into three categories: those that focus on how and whether policies are adopted and their availability and use, those that focus on who uses the policies (a demographic view), and those that focus on the effects of work-family policies.

Policy Adoption and Availability

The policy adoption branch of research examines which employer characteristics predict adoption of policies and responsiveness to employees' work-life
needs. This arm of research faces several limitations. Data on policy adoption
is focused at the organizational level of analysis despite that policy use is often
left to supervisor discretion and the needs of the business. Consequently,
policy adoption can vary widely in a single firm and across business units and
employee groups. As the following data show, some policies are only available
to employees in certain types of jobs and at certain levels, or they impose a
minimum tenure requirement, as is often the case, for example, with leaves
of absence or health care benefits. Such access rules may limit the availability
of many work-family policies, particularly for workers at the lower levels,
although they are often used to enhance a firm's public relations. Even the
federal Family and Medical Leave Act (FMLA), which was passed in 1993
and requires employers to provide leave for new parents and leave to care for
an ill family member or one's own illness, is more widely available to full-time
than part-time workers given that workers are required to have worked a
certain number of hours in the past year (Ferber & Waldfogel, 2000).

Furthermore, current research (and the media) may have overstated
the availability of policies given that much of the research involves larger
employers. Popular press reports in *Working Mother* and *Business Week* tend
to favor large employers as do surveys by the Alliance for Work-Life Progress (AWLP). Next I share results from two different surveys to illustrate
the wide variation in survey data on the purported availability of work-life
policies.

Table 7.1 shows results from two waves of an AWLP survey of policy adoption in 1999 and 2001 and offers an indication of the prevalence and range of
policies available as reported in surveys. The most commonly adopted policies, reported by three fourths of the organizations, were employee assistance
plans (where employees have access to mental health counseling and other
services, such as substance abuse rehabilitation) and flexible schedules. Paid
paternity leave and concierge services, which provide assistance with personal
domestic chores (e.g., dry cleaning, errands), were the least common policies.
A caveat, however, is that because many policies, such as flexible schedules,
are enacted at the work-group level by supervisors, there is no reliable way
to understand, based on these data, the actual use of these policies across an
organization.

Another gap requiring further attention is that available policies frequently go unused by employees owing to lack of publicity or other cultural
barriers (Eaton, 2003). As an example, new in 2001, AWLP required survey
respondents to report whether more than three fourths of their employees use
at least one work-life program. Only 26% of government agencies reported

TABLE 7.1
Summary of Alliance of Work Life
Professionals Surveys on Employer Adoption
of Work Life Policies by Program Type
and Industry

Policy Availability (%)	1999	2001
EAP services	77%	84%
Flexible schedules	77	83
Child-care referrals	83	75
Elder-care referrals	76	74
Tuition assistance	70	71
Work/family seminars	78	69
Wellness program	64	65
Telecommuting	70	64
Paid maternity leave	51	52
Medical services	38	40
Onsite child care	37	40
Backup child care	43	39
Child-care subsidy	29	35
Paid family leave	34	35
Concierge services	21	24
Paid paternity leave	27	21
Other programs (financial, personal assistance, education)	25	21

Percentage of 2001 respondents reporting that
over three-quarters of their employees use at least
one work-life program

Government agencies	26%
Corporations	15%
Consultants and service providers	13%
All other organizations	16%

*Respondents: 2001: N = 337; 1999: N =
104.
Source. Alliance of Work Life Progress
(http://www.awlp.org/Surveyreport.pdf).

that three fourths of their workers used at least one work–family program.
This figure dropped to only 15% among corporations and to 13% for service
providers. Thus, use of policies is much lower than their availability, and
future research must examine policy enactment that promotes use.

More representative data on the availability of policies among U.S. employers of all sizes are available from the Bureau of Labor Statistics (BLS),
National Compensation Survey (2000), which includes questions on work-
life benefits. Although this survey lacks the detail of those like the AWLP

survey, its strength is its truer representation of the range of U.S. employers. The BLS survey finds that the availability of work-life benefits is low and more prevalent in the service industry and for professional jobs. According to BLS survey data summarized in Table 7.2, only 4% of U.S. employers provided some sort of referral or other assistance for child care, 2% provided funds for child care, 2% provided onsite child care, and 1% provided off-site child care. Only 5% of employers provided adoption assistance, and 7% provided long-term care insurance. Finally, 5% provided flexible workplace schedules.

Policy adoption also varies by industry and job groups. The BLS National Compensation Survey also shows that in 2000, service-producing private employers were 2.5 times more likely to provide assistance for child care, one third more likely to provide long-term care insurance, and one third less likely to provide adoption assistance than goods-producing private employers. The BLS survey finds that access to policies varies widely by employee group, which casts doubt on whether firm-level adoption data are an accurate reflection of availability across a workforce. In 2000, professional and technical employees were twice as likely as clerical and sales employees and 5.5 times as likely as blue-collar and service employees to receive child-care assistance. Professional and technical employees were 2.5 times as likely as clerical and sales employees and 6 times as likely as blue-collar and service employees to receive adoption assistance. Professional and technical employees were twice

TABLE 7.2
Percent of Workers With Access to Selected Work-Family Benefits

	Total	Employer Provided Funds	On-Site Child Care	Off-Site Child Care	Adoption Assistance	Long-Term Care Insurance	Flexible Work Place
Total	4	2	2	1	5	7	5
Worker characteristics							
Professional, technical and related	11	4	6	3	12	14	12
Clerical and sales	5	3	1	2	5	7	4
Blue collar and service	2	1	1	—	2	4	1
Full-time	5	2	2	1	6	8	5
Part-time	3	1	1	1	2	2	2
Union	8	6	2	—	5	15	3
Nonunion	4	2	2	1	5	6	5
Establishment characteristics							
Goods-producing	2	1	—	—	6	5	4
Service-producing	5	2	3	1	4	8	5
1–99 workers	1	—	—	1	1	5	2
100 workers or more	9	4	4	2	9	10	7

Source. BLS, National Compensation Survey, Survey of Employee Benefits, 2000.

as likely as clerical and sales employees and 3.5 times as likely as blue-collar and service employees to receive long-term care insurance. Professional and technical employees were 3 times as likely as clerical and sales employees and 12 times as likely as blue-collar and service employees to have access to flexible schedules. Union employees were twice as likely as nonunion workers to have access to employer child-care assistance.

Most of the scholarly research does not reflect this within-firm variation in practice. Notwithstanding this, several studies offer additional insight into organizational characteristics that predict policy adoption. Goodstein's (1995) study on the adoption of elder-care policies shows that, regardless of industry or organizational size, employers are more likely to adopt policies when they have more female employees and are involved with other employer groups or professional organizations concerned about work-family issues. However, another study by Goodstein (1994) found that the proportion of parents in an organization did not predict responsiveness to institutional pressures for policy adoption. What mattered instead, and which was consistent with Morgan and Milliken (1993), was an employer perception that broadening work-family options would significantly influence productivity. The productivity link was echoed in Osterman's (1995) study showing that firms with high-commitment work systems, where clusters of human resource practices (e.g., self-managing teams, group-based pay, job security) are implemented to promote a high-involvement workplace, were more likely to adopt work-family programs.

Demographic Research

The second category of work-life research, exemplified by Kossek and Ozeki (1999), examines how employee personal and family backgrounds relate to work outcomes (e.g., absenteeism of women with young children) or the perceived attractiveness or use of various policies based on various demographic factors (e.g., women are more likely to prefer or use part-time work policies or parental leaves than men) (Grover & Crooker, 1995; Kossek, 1990). One problem with these studies is that they use demographic variables, such as number of children or elders in a family or being female, as proxies for work-family conflict, but until recently they rarely measured whether using available policies reduced work-family conflict (Kossek & Ozeki, 1998). Aside from discussions of gender and parental status differences (Blair-Loy & Wharton, 2002; Grover & Crooker, 1995), the management and psychological research does not devote much attention to how individual differences in personal values, goals, and life plans affect the role of work-life policies in job choice and turnover decisions (Ryan & Kossek, 2003). Yet it should be noted that economists such as Holzer (chap. 6, this volume) refer to the notion of *compensating differentials*; that is, the tendency of some employers to focus resources on benefits attractive to particular groups (e.g., working parents' interest in health care or flexibility) and less on compensation in the form of wages. Future work should not only measure demographics, but how these variables relate to the employee's level of involvement with caregiving, identification with work and family roles, and allocation of care demands across the family unit. Studies should also assess whether firms are allocating financial resources to the policies that are the most beneficial to employees with caregiving demands and whether the policies reduce conflict and stress.

The Effectiveness of Policy

The arm of research that focuses on policy effects examines how policy use predicts employee attitudes and behaviors (Kossek & Ozeki, 1999). These studies tend to use two main approaches. The most common approach uses same-source cross-sectional data to assess relations between program use and employee outcomes. Some of these studies confound results by not distinguishing between use and availability or make the assumption that the same variables correlated with favorable attitudes toward program availability also predict use and favorable outcomes from use. The reliance on same-source data for predictors and outcomes also makes causality difficult to disentangle. The second approach uses pre- and postmeasures (but not often control groups) to assess changes in employee attitudes and behaviors after introducing a single policy (Kossek & Ozeki, 1999).

   Given these methodological limitations, it is not surprising that the research shows mixed results that vary widely by employee samples, policy type, and outcomes assessed. Some research has found a positive relation between the presence or use of formal policies and employee loyalty (Roehling, Roehling, & Moen, 2001), individual performance and discretionary job behavior that goes above and beyond required job demands (Lambert, 2000), turnover intentions (Rothausen, 1994), absenteeism (Dalton & Mesch, 1990), commitment (Grover & Crooker, 1995), organizational productivity (Konrad & Mangel, 2000), and organizational performance (Perry-Smith & Blum, 2000). Yet just as many studies have found mixed or null results regardless of the type of employer support provided. For example, in a study of health care professionals with children at home, flexible scheduling and dependent care referral service use was not related to absenteeism (Thomas & Ganster, 1995). Wagner and Hunt (1994) found that users of an elder-care referral service missed more days of work for care than nonusers (these results may be confounded by the fact that heaver users were also the employees who were more involved in providing care). Hill, Miller, Weiner, and Colihan (1998) found no difference in work-family conflict between individuals working in the office and those who were required (nonvoluntarily owing to office restructuring) to work from home or elsewhere.

Null effects (possibly because they did not consider the time lag effect of policy use) were found in two quasi-experimental studies. One well-designed study that compared two different types of flexibility—a 4-day, 40-hour work week versus flextime—found that neither was significantly related to organizational effectiveness (Dunham, Pierce, & Casteneda, 1987). Another quasi-experimental study by Kossek and Nichols (1992) compared behaviors and attitudes of employees using an onsite child-care center with nonusers on the waiting list (a naturally occurring control group). The waiting list was a good comparison group, much better than comparing users to nonusers in the general population, because this employee group had a need for the employer intervention (child care). Another strength of the study was that it did not rely on same-source data for predictors and outcomes. The study noted employee perceptions and behaviors separately from outcome performance measures, which were collected from supervisors and company archives. The results show no relation between center use and supervisor measures of performance or absenteeism (Kossek & Nichols, 1992).

Lambert's (2000) study at Felpro was notable in that she measured benefit use at one time and then later measured outcomes. She found that the heaviest users of work and family policies made more suggestions—an indicator of higher discretionary performance. The main limitation of this study was that it was conducted in a single firm with a unique supportive culture. The firm has since been acquired by Federal Mogul, which may have a different culture, and it would be interesting to replicate the findings now or in a multiple-firm study.

EMERGING THEMES FOR FUTURE RESEARCH

For the remainder of the chapter, I discuss emerging themes that are promising for future research. These themes relate to types of policies, policy enactment, and employment decision making; work-family intensification; managing borders between work and home; voice and performance in the context of supervisors and work groups; program structure and links to human resource strategy; and legitimization and engagement.

Types of Policies, Policy Enactment, and Employment Decision Making

Ryan and Kossek (2003) argued that the research on employer policies to support work-life integration is simplistic in that many studies do not effectively differentiate between policy types nor do they recognize that the way in which policies are enacted may have different influences at various stages in one's career and employment decision making. With the exception of Perry-Smith and Blum (2000) and Eaton (2003), researchers have largely been silent on whether variation in the way work-life policies are enacted (e.g., whether they are universal, whether they are linked to human resource strategy) is relevant to how they are accepted and used.

Work-life policies may vary across and within organizations in how employees experience them depending on how the policies are designed and implemented in that organizational context. For example, two legal firms or two different departments of the same firm may state in recruiting materials that they offer reduced workload arrangements. However, in one firm, this option is unavailable in the more prestigious work units, or most career-oriented employees do not feel free to use the policy, whereas the other firm employs part-time workers throughout the organization in all sectors and at all levels. Note that it is not the written policy descriptions that are key, but how employees perceive the policy in their immediate work environment. In addition, individual differences matter—not all working women, for example, are alike—yet gross generalizations persist in the research.

Ryan and Kossek (2003) identified four policy attributes—universalism, cultural integration, negotiability, and boundary blurring—as important to future research on the role of work-life policies in job pursuit and turnover decisions. These implementation attributes move away from simply describing policy features and toward considering the social enactment or functioning of policies.

Universalism refers to whether policies are available for everyone in all levels and jobs and locations. *Work-life bundling* is the degree to which work-life policies have been communicated as part of an organizational strategy and as an employer of choice—that is, an employer that invests in and cares about all employees. Here work-life policies are not publicized as individual benefits only available to workers with salient work-family demands, but as a group of overlapping human resource policies that help employees of many different personal backgrounds and lifestyles manage work-life roles (for more on work-life bundling, see Perry-Smith & Blum, 2000).

Cultural integration is the extent to which the use of work-life policies is seen as being consistent with the core values of organizational members. Legge (1989) contended that a unitary approach to organizational culture may be too simplistic, given that organizations often have multiple cultures. Palthe and Kossek (2003) noted that subcultures may be particularly relevant in understanding how policies are practiced in organizations. With regard to work-life practices, cultural integration traditionally has been studied at the macro- or organizational level, but rarely at the work-group level where policies are typically enacted.

Negotiability, the third factor, reflects the degree to which the use of a policy must be negotiated with an organizational agent. Some work-life policies are available simply as a condition of employment (e.g., maternity leave). These policies may be enacted as a routine human resource transaction. For other benefits, such as the ability to work at home 1 day a week, a supervisor or the human resources department must approve use. Thus, whether and how the policy is invoked involves some negotiations. Evidence suggests that there is variation in whether and how policies are enacted given that the preferences of supervisors and employees on how to manage work-family roles are likely to differ (Kossek, Noe, & DeMarr, 1999).

Boundary blurring, the final attribute, refers to the degree to which work-life policies encourage individual and organizational boundary overlap and a mixing or blurring of work and nonwork roles (Kossek, Noe, & DeMarr, 1999). Some policies are designed and implemented to support high separation or segmentation between work and nonwork roles. For example, emergency well-child care (e.g., hiring backup care when a sitter fails to show up) includes policies that convey high boundary separation in that they imply that children should not interfere with one's ability to get to work (Kossek & Block, 2000). Integrative policies, such as flexible schedules, enable a worker to restructure work to mesh with family roles.

Ryan and Kossek (2003) believed work-life policies and their enactment may play a different role at different stages in the employment relationship, such as applicant recruitment compared with incumbent retention. Although it is a popular maxim that work-life policies affect "recruitment and retention," limited research has measured with precision whether and how these policies shape turnover and attraction and whether processes are similar at each employment and career stage. The reasons an individual joins a firm may differ from the reasons that an individual stays, and individuals' understanding and interest in how work-life policies are implemented may vary at these different stages. A *Business Week* report (Conlin, Merritt, & Himelstein, 2002) on high-achieving women highlights how the mismatch in their work-life needs changed from when they first left graduate school and when they had children. Although work-life balance issues were less of a concern when they first joined their firms, nearly all the women eventually quit their firms because the demanding nature of their jobs and the norms surrounding work-life policy use did not support their family needs. The role of individual differences, career stage, job design, and policy implementation characteristics on employment decisions merits future study.

Work-Life Intensification

Many employees today are experiencing a time compression at work and at home (Milliken & Dunn-Jensen, 2005). They simply feel they have too much to do in too little time. Along a similar vein, some research in Europe has focused on work intensification; although hours may be legally reduced in some countries, workers nevertheless feel they have to do the same full-time job in the reduced working time (P. Berg, personal communication, May 28, 2003). Work intensification is also caused by declining staffing levels, which increase current employees' workloads and the pace of work. These trends, coupled with the inability of many employees to manage family needs for flexibility during work hours, all contribute to rising stress. This intensification also applies to family life, when dual-earner or single-parent working families try to manage a demanding home life and their jobs with limited domestic help. The organization's role in exacerbating work-family intensification and encouraging overwork is a problem experienced at all economic levels and must be examined for policies to be effective. Interventions to develop new coping strategies and redesign work and norms, especially in high-commitment workplaces, merit future study.

Because many employees now juggle multiple and intensified life roles, and because it is important to society that employees not only care for families, but participate in other domains (e.g., elder care, exercise, etc.), future research should examine multiple policy use by employees both cross-sectionally and longitudinally given that employees often juggle many life roles at one time and needs for organizational support change over the life course. More studies using improved methodologies, such as a quasi-experimental design comparing types of interventions for treatment and control groups and multiple source data over time for predictors and outcomes, are sorely needed to add clarity to the research.

Managing Borders Between Work and Home

The world of work has increasingly blurred the boundaries between work and home. Approximately 15% of the workforce (mainly white collar) has experienced a fundamental transformation in how work is structured and organized. Because of new information technologies and a shift in job design and employee preferences toward greater self-management of where, when, and how work is done, work is increasingly portable and "on call" 24 hours a day, 7 days a week. Not only are companies contributing to this trend, with such functions as e-mail and other technology, but some employees desire a 24/7 flexibility to better mesh work and personal life (Kossek, Lautsch, & Eaton, 2005).

The work-family research often assumes that flexibility in time and place has mostly positive outcomes for the worker. The assumption is that flexibility enables workers to excel at both work and family or "have it all" (Kossek et al., 2005). Greater integration among work, family, and personal roles is seen as a way to balance work and family life and even to use one to effect positive change in the other (Friedman, Christensen, & DeGroot, 1998). Yet there may be times when setting boundaries between work and home are desirable. Few studies examine which types of flexibility lead to higher quality of life. Research is also limited on the trend among many white-collar workers (especially professionals) to have more informal flexibility in terms of how jobs are designed, instead of, or in addition to, existing human resource mediated policy. That is, some employees have increased access to autonomy and ability to control the timing and location of their jobs—not because of a formal policy (often overemphasized in the research), but because of the way their jobs are designed. More research is needed on how employees, particularly those in professional jobs, can influence the mental, physical, and time boundaries they establish between work and family domains and how the ability to control where and when one works affects effectiveness in work and life. Greater understanding is needed to identify predictors and outcomes about the different ways in which individuals manage the boundaries and borders between work and home. We also must better understand the enabling roles of job design and policies in supporting employee preferences for and outcomes of personal job autonomy (i.e., flexibility in where, when, and how one works).

Voice and Performance in the Context of Supervisors and Work Groups

Many studies have found that one of the most important factors in the success of work-life policies is a supportive boss, but few studies have focused on these managers, examining their actual experience over time and with more than one individual. Recent research has also indicated that many barriers remain in the successful implementation and management of alternative work arrangements. One of these barriers is that many corporate managers and clients still view "face time" as a measure of productivity; yet we still know little about how to change these perceptions. Although management training on how to support work-life needs is often cited as critical, few firms have effectively operationalized what it means to be a supportive supervisor, and more research is needed on the supervisor behaviors and attitudes that enable employees to feel free to voice and make work-life choices that are consistent with their needs and values.

The effects on work groups when employees use work-life policies, such as different types of alternative work arrangements (e.g., flextime, part-time work, telecommuting), have been overlooked (Van Dyne & Kossek, 2003). These flexibility policies are typically adopted at the organizational level, but the details of administration and daily management decisions are left to individual managers or groups. Cross-level research is needed that examines the group performance consequences of individual flexibility and that identifies effective ways for managers to manage flexibility within work groups and still meet client needs.

An individual's use of flexible policies should also be investigated in light of the characteristics of the work group and the nature of the client served (Blair-Loy & Wharton, 2002; Kossek, Barber, & Winters, 1999). Recent studies have shown that, although being female and having young children were predictors of use at the individual level of analysis, use also depended on the social context of work. Such findings underscore the importance of work-group characteristics in explaining the policy use. Blair-Loy and Wharton (2002), for example, found that although women in general are more likely than men to use family-care policies, employees in work groups with high percentages of women or with female supervisors report less family-care policy use. They also found having coworkers and supervisors with family responsibilities decreases, rather than increases, the use of flexibility policies. It seems flexibility is being allocated in work groups as a fixed and scarce resource.

Work-Life Program Structure and Links to Human Resources Strategy

One barrier to the effective implementation of work-life policies is that they are often not integrally tied to human resource strategies or business objectives. Work-life policies are often not viewed as central to the overarching human resource strategy. There are also few links between work-life policies and other human resource policies. Career development and training opportunities are sometimes lacking for those with significant family responsibilities or who work reduced loads (for background on reduced load, see http://flex-work.lir.msu.edu/). Bonuses and performance ratings are sometimes informally discounted to compensate for flexibility. Managers are also rarely evaluated on how well they manage the work-life balance.

More research is needed on the structure and formality of work-life strategies and factors determining links to human resource and business strategies. There is increasing variation in where the individual responsible for work and family policy is located within the organization and how work-life program structure is linked to effectiveness (i.e., the degree to which available policies are used, reduce work-family conflict, and support positive work behaviors such as lower absenteeism). In most firms, responsibility for work-life policy falls under human resource management. However, whether work-life policy should be a stand-alone entity is increasingly coming under review. In other words, rather than having a separate work-life department, some firms include their work-life policies in the workforce diversity office, the employee assistance plan office, benefits, wellness and fitness, and even quality. Some employers believe that housing the work-family agenda in a broad-standing unit of the firm will enable work-life policies to have longevity and more clout. However, some work-life professionals believe their policies will have greater long-term acceptance if they are not a separate unit. Still others believe that making work-family policy part of a diversity agenda will have greater line management acceptance given that workforce diversity management has a longer history and acceptance as a business issue in the firm. There are clearly tensions in this approach. Certainly, making work-life policy a critical management concern will increase effectiveness. However, if it is buried in another unit, there is a risk that the agenda will never be viewed as a legitimate business issue in it own right.

Organizations vary in their philosophy regarding work-life integration strategy. Some employers, for example, prefer to empower employees to manage their own work-life needs (respecting privacy) rather than interfere in the employees' lives through an active work-life department. Others are more actively involved in work-life issues, but this tends to stem less from formal policies than from CEO and top management commitment to supporting work-life integration. Starbucks is a good example of such a commitment; the CEO has a strong philosophy that employees should have work-life balance, and the organization provides full benefits for part-time workers. The informality of Starbucks shows that a firm can sometimes be family-friendly and effective without a lot of bureaucratic policies (www.fortune.com, 2005). What does seem important is true access. In some companies, mandates require that a certain percentage of employees have access to flexible working arrangements. More research is needed on best practices at companies of all sizes, how these practices are linked to the way work is done, and how the systems of managing employees are conducted.

Legitimization and Engagement

Cross-cultural research shows that work is defined and experienced differently in different societies; organizational and societal structures construct what individuals and families perceive as possible for work-life integration. Unlike other Western countries, in the United States, work-life integration issues are still largely viewed as an individual problem more than a business or societal problem. One study that examined how organizations overcome their resistance to adopting work-life policies found striking similarities between employers' resistance to such policies, as reflected in their discourse and language, and companies' early resistance to the Internet (Still, 2003). As they did during the Internet's early years, employers see work-life issues as unrelated to their core business and a matter on which they have little expertise. Study of how to overcome employer resistance to work-life assistance is clearly needed. Future research should examine how to promote employer support for work-life balance and effective policy use as an employer responsibility and a mainstream employment issue.

Although it is important to establish productivity links or the "business case" for work-life integration—which is often suggested as one way to promote increased employer involvement—there are cautions to overemphasizing the business case (i.e., showing the economic cost-benefit analysis of policies). The business case overemphasizes one stakeholder, the shareholder, over all over stakeholders (i.e., families, employees, society). Also the business case approach allows companies' commitment to work-life policies to wane in bad economic times, underestimates the long-term societal costs of noninvolvement, and holds work-life initiatives to a higher standard than many other organizational policies.

What might be more fruitful are stakeholder and criterion approaches, which could be developed in future research. A stakeholder approach would examine outcomes for the multiple constituencies served by the policies, such as employee outcomes, family outcomes, and community strength indicators. A criterion approach to evaluation might examine the goals of policies or practices and assess whether these goals are met.

A stakeholder approach must confront economic issues. If research shows that family-friendly policies raise productivity, there is no societal trade-off and everyone might gain from using such policies. However, if family-friendly policies cost money without raising productivity, then someone will bear the costs, such as nonusers in the firm. It may be that companies will only invest enough resources to attract financial investors. There remains, however, the possibility that innovation in work-life policies may increase productivity, which is an avenue policymakers should promote.

Beyond a focus on productivity, some employers believe it may be more beneficial to focus on employee engagement—that is, to show the link between effective work-life balance and being engaged at work. Work-life policies may help ensure employees are not stressed, have a higher job and life satisfaction (Kossek & Ozeki, 1998), a positive attitude, and arrive at work ready to fully concentrate on their jobs. Engagement may be an intermediate outcome that is necessary to ensure effectiveness at work and home.

ACKNOWLEDGMENTS

I wish to thank the School of Labor and Industrial Relations at Michigan State University for providing graduate assistantships to Casey Schurkamp and Chassidy Barton who helped with this research.

REFERENCES

Alliance for Work-Life Progress. Retrieved April 2003. 1999 and 2001 Annual Industry Survey of Members. Scottsdale, Arizona. www.awlp.org. Available: http://www.awlp.org/Survey report.pdf.

Bailyn, L. (1993). *Breaking the mold: Women, men and time in the new corporate world*. New York: The Free Press.

Baltes, B. B., Briggs, T. E., Huff, J. W., Wright, J. A., & Neuman, G. A. (1999). Flexible and compressed workweek schedules: A meta-analysis of their effects on work-related criteria. *Journal of Applied Psychology, 84*, 496–513.

Barnett, R. (2001). Women, men, work and family: An expansionist theory. *American Psychologist, 56*, 781–796.

Blair-Loy, M., & Wharton, A. S. (2002). Employees' use of work-family policies and the workplace social context, *Social Forces, 80*, 813–845.

Bond, J. T., Galinsky, E., & Swanberg, J. E. (1998). *The 1997 National Study of the Changing Workforce*. New York: Families and Work Institute.

Bureau of Labor Statistics. (2000). *National Compensation Survey, Survey of Employee Benefits, 2000* [On-line]. Available: www.bls.org.

Comer, D., & Soliman, C. (1996). Organizational efforts to manage diversity: Do they really work? *Journal of Managerial Issues, 8*, 470–483.

Conlin, M., Merritt, J., & Himelstein, L. (2002, November 25). Mommy is really home from work. *Business Week*, pp. 101–104.

Dalton, D. R., & Mesch, D. J. (1990). The impact of flexible scheduling on employee attendance and turnover. *Administrative Science Quarterly, 35*, 370–387.

Dunham, R. B., Pierce, J. L., & Castenada, M. B. (1987). Alternative work schedules: Two quasi-experiments. *Personnel Psychology, 40*, 215–242.

Eaton, S. (2003). If you can use them: Flexibility policies, organizational commitment and perceived performance. *Industrial Relations, 42*, 145–167.

Ferber, M., & Waldfogel, J. (2000). The effects of part time work and self-employment on wages and benefits: Differences by race/ethnicity and gender. In F. Carre, M. Ferber, L. Golden, & S. Herzenberg (Eds.), *Nonstandard Work: The nature and consequences of changing employment arrangements* (pp. 167–211). Urbana-Champaign, IL: Industrial Relations Research Association. Available: http://flex-work.lir.msu.edu/.

Friedman, S. D., Christensen, P., & DeGroot, J. (1998). Work and life: The end of the zero-sum game. *Harvard Business Review*, pp. 119–129.

Goodstein, J. (1994). Institutional pressures and strategic responsiveness: Employer involvement in work-family issues. *Academy of Management Journal, 37*, 350–382.

Goodstein, J. (1995). Employer involvement in elder care: An organizational adaptation perspective. *Academy of Management Journal, 38*, 1657–1671.

Grover, S., & Crooker, K. (1995). Who appreciates family-responsive human resource policies: The impact of family-friendly policies on the organizational attachment of parents and nonparents. *Personnel Psychology, 48*, 271–288.

Hill, J. E., Miller, B. C., Weiner, S. P., & Colihan, J. (1998). Influences of the virtual office on aspects of work and work/life balance. *Personnel Psychology, 41*, 667–683.

Huselid, M., & Becker, M. (1996). Methodological issues in cross-sectional and panel estimates of the human resource firm performance link. *Industrial Relations, 35*, 423–455.

Konrad, A., & Mangel, R. (2000). The impact of work-life programs on firm productivity. *Strategic Management Journal, 21*, 1225–1237.

Kossek, E. E. (1990). Diversity in child care assistance needs: Problems, preferences, and work-related outcomes. *Personnel Psychology, 43*, 769–791.

Kossek, E. E., Barber, A., & Winters, D. (1999). Managerial use of flexible work schedules: The power of peers. *Human Resource Management Journal, 38*, 33–46.

Kossek, E. E., & Block, K. (2000). *Managing human resources in the 21st century: From core concepts to strategic choice*. Cincinnati, OH: Southwestern College Publishing.

Kossek, E. E., Colquitt, J., & Noe, R. (2001). Caregiving decisions, well-being and performance: The effects of place and provider as a function of dependent type and work-family climates. *Academy of Management Journal, 44,* 29–44.

Kossek, E. E., Dass, P., & DeMarr, B. (1994). The dominant logic of employer-sponsored child-care: Human resource managers' institutional role. *Human Relations, 47,* 1121–1149.

Kossek, E., Lautsch, B., & Eaton, S. (2005). Flexibility enactment theory: Relationships between type, boundaries, control and work-family effectiveness. In E. E. Kossek & S. Lambert (Eds.), *Work and life integration: Organizational, cultural, and individual perspectives* (pp. 243–261). Mahwah, NJ: Lawrence Erlbaum Associates.

Kossek, E. E., & Nichols, V. (1992). The effects of employer-sponsored child care on employee attitudes and performance. *Personnel Psychology, 45,* 485–509.

Kossek, E. E., Noe, R., & DeMarr, B. (1999). Work-family role synthesis: Individual, family and organizational determinants. *International Journal of Conflict Resolution, 10,* 102–129.

Kossek, E. E., & Ozeki, C. (1998). Work-family conflict, policies, and the job-life satisfaction relationship: A review and directions for organizational behavior/human resources research. *Journal of Applied Psychology, 83,* 139–149.

Kossek, E. E., & Ozeki, C. (1999). Bridging the work-family policy and productivity gap: A literature review. *Community, Work, and Family, 2,* 7–32.

Lambert, S. J. (2000). Added benefits: The link between work-life benefits and organizational citizenship behavior. *Academy of Management Journal, 43,* 801–815.

Legge, K. (1989). Human resource management: A critical analysis. In J. Storey (Ed.), *New perspectives on human resource management* (pp. 19–40). London, England: Routledge.

Milliken, F., & Dunn-Jensen, L. (2005). The changing time demands of managerial and professional work: Implications for managing the work-life boundary. In E. E. Kossek & S. Lambert (Eds.), *Work and life integration: Organizational, cultural, and individual perspectives* (pp. 43–59). Mahwah, NJ: Lawrence Erlbaum Associates.

Morgan, H., & Milliken, F. (1993). Keys to action: Understanding differences in organization's responsiveness to work-and-family issues. *Human Resource Management Journal, 31,* 227–248.

Osterman, P. (1995). Work/family programs and the employment relationship. *Administrative Science Quarterly, 40,* 681–700.

Ozeki, C. (2003). *The effects of a family-supportive work environment on work-family conflict, family to work conflict, and emotional exhaustion.* Unpublished doctoral dissertation, Michigan State University, Ann Arbor.

Palthe, J., & Kossek, E. E. (2003). The role of organizational subcultures and employment modes in the translation of HR strategy into HR practice. *Journal of Organizational Change Management, 16,* 287–308.

Perry-Smith, J. E., & Blum, T. C. (2000). Work-family human resource bundles and perceived organizational performance. *Academy of Management Journal, 43,* 1107–1117.

Roehling, P. V., Roehling, M. V., & Moen, P. (2001). The relationship between work-life policies and practices and employee loyalty: A life course perspective. *Journal of Family and Economic Issues, 22,* 141–170.

Rothausen, T. (1994). Job satisfaction and the parent worker: The role of flexibility and rewards. *Journal of Vocational Behavior, 44,* 317–336.

Ryan, A. M., & Kossek, E. E. (2003). *Work-life policies, recruitment, and retention: The role of perceived implementation attributes in individual decision-making.* Unpublished manuscript, Michigan State University, East Lansing. (Portions of earlier paper presented at National Academy of Management meetings, Denver, August, 2002.)

Still, M. C. (2003). *Corporate response to divergent innovations: The Internet vs. work/life.* Unpublished manuscript, Cornell University, Ithaca, NY.

Thomas, L. T., & Ganster, D. C. (1995). Impact of family-supportive work variables on work-family conflict and strain: A control perspective. *Journal of Applied Psychology, 80,* 6–15.

Van Dyne, L., & Kossek, E. E. (2003). *Face-time matters: A cross level model of how work-life flexibility influences work performance of individuals and groups.* Unpublished manuscript, Michigan State University, East Lansing.

Wagner, D. L., & Hunt, G. G. (1994). The use of workplace eldercare programs by employed caregivers. *Research on Aging, 16,* 69–84.

Williams, J. (1999). *Unbending gender: Why work and family conflict and what to do about it.* New York: Oxford University Press.

www.fortune.com/fortune/bestcompanies. Retrieved February 5, 2005.

8

Work-Family Culture: Key to Reducing Workforce-Workplace Mismatch?

Cynthia A. Thompson
Jeanine K. Andreassi
David J. Prottas
Baruch College

Many organizations are interested in creating a family-friendly workplace for their employees. Motivations vary for implementing such policies; some organizations are truly concerned about the welfare of their employees, whereas some are interested in the public relations value of family-friendly policies. Regardless of their motivation, all organizations must think creatively about four interrelated components of family-friendliness (Pitt-Catsouphes, n.d.). They must design and implement benefits, practices, and policies to help their employees balance their work and nonwork lives. They must create workplace cultures that reflect a concern for employees' lives outside of work. They must encourage workplace relations that are respectful of employees' nonwork responsibilities, and they must revisit current work processes, systems, structures, and practices to determine which lead to unnecessary stress and overwork for employees.

This chapter focuses on what work-life experts consider to be a critical component for reducing workforce–workplace mismatch: workplace culture. We provide basic definitions of *work-family culture* and its many dimensions, describe current research on antecedents to and consequences of a supportive work-family culture, and conclude with directions for future research and practice.

Recent research suggests that family-friendly policies and practices alone will not create a supportive culture (Allen, 2001; Kossek, Noe, & DeMarr, 1999; Lewis, 1997; O'Driscoll et al., 2003). Employees are often reluctant to take advantage of work-life programs such as flextime or extended parental leave usually because of strong norms for *face time* (i.e., being physically present at the workplace) and long hours. Thompson, Beauvais, and Lyness (1999), for example, studied 276 professionals and managers and found that those who perceived less supportive cultures were less likely to use their employer's work-life programs. This and other research (e.g., Perlow, 1995) suggests that employees fear possible negative career consequences—and there is evidence their fears are not unfounded. In their study of more than 11,000 managers in a financial services organization, Judiesch and Lyness (1999) found that taking a leave of absence was associated with fewer subsequent promotions (the odds of promotion were 0.66 times less than those of their counterparts who had not taken a leave) and smaller salary increases (managers who took leaves received salary increases that were 1.4 percentage points smaller than their counterparts who did not take leaves). The findings support the notion of a "gendered organizational culture," which argues that managers who have multiple commitments, as evidenced by a leave of absence, do not conform to work expectations that place work over family and, therefore, they are less deserving of organizational rewards.

Together these findings suggest that work-life policies and programs alone do not go far enough in making a positive difference in employees' lives. Although organizations spend time, money, and energy developing and implementing these programs, low use suggests that either employees do not need the programs or they do not use them for fear of damaging their career or because their supervisor or manager does not support their use. Given the consistent finding that many employees experience work-life conflict at some point in their lives, is seems unlikely that the programs are unnecessary. What is more likely is that the organization's culture does not support their use. As a result, neither the organization nor the employee benefits from the much heralded work-life programs.

CONCEPTS AND DEFINITIONS

Work-family culture has been defined as the "shared assumptions, beliefs, and values regarding the extent to which an organization supports and values the integration of employees' work and family lives" (Thompson et al., 1999, p. 394). Similarly, Warren and Johnson (1995) defined a company with a family-friendly culture as one in which "the overarching philosophy or belief structure is sensitive to the family needs of its employees and is supportive of employees who are combining paid work and family roles" (p. 163). Allen (2001) described a related construct, family supportive organization perceptions, as the "global perceptions that employees form regarding the extent to which the organization is family supportive" (p. 414). Lewis (1997) used Schein's (1985) levels of organizational culture (i.e., artifacts, values, and assumptions) to describe aspects of culture that affect an employee's ability to balance work and family. She argued that work-life policies and programs are *artifacts* or surface-level indicators of an organization's intentions to be supportive. Values underlie artifacts and might include, for example, giving priority to work over family or family over work. Basic assumptions underlie values. For example, it is often assumed that time spent at work is equated with productivity, despite policies to the contrary (e.g., flexibility surrounding where one works). According to Lewis (1997), it is the values and assumptions that lie at the heart of workplace culture; unless they are examined, change toward a more family-friendly culture is impossible.

Although the definitions of work-family culture are quite similar, researchers differ greatly in how they operationalize them. Some have included both formal (e.g., benefits offered, degree of scheduling flexibility) and informal (e.g., perceptions of support) elements in their measures (e.g., Clark, 2001; Warren & Johnson, 1995). Others have included only informal or intangible aspects of culture (e.g., Allen, 2001; Jahn, Thompson, & Kopelman, 2003; Kossek, Colquitt, & Noe, 2001; Thompson et al., 1999). Because *organizational culture* has been defined in terms of employees' perceptions of expectations and norms for behavior at work, or what some authors have referred to as "the internal social psychological environment" (Denison, 1996), we focus in this chapter on employees' perceptions of the informal, intangible aspects of work-family culture, while recognizing that this culture is influenced, in part, by the formal benefits offered by the organization.

Dimensions of Work-Family Culture

Research by Thompson et al. (1999) suggested that work-family culture is composed of three parts: organizational time demands, career consequences for using work-family benefits, and managerial support. Organizational time demands is the extent to which long hours are expected at work and work is given priority over family. Corporate law firms and investment banks, for example, are known for excessive time demands. Perceived career consequences is the degree to which employees perceive positive or negative career consequences for using work-family benefits. The third component, managerial support, captures the extent to which individual managers are sensitive to and accommodating of employees' family needs.

Other researchers have also included managerial support as a component of a supportive culture. Galinsky and Stein (1990), for example, described a supportive supervisor as someone who believes that handling family issues is a legitimate part of their role, is knowledgeable about company policies, is flexible when family problems arise, and handles work-family problems fairly and without favoritism. Bailyn (1997) also argued that supervisor support for family needs is critical in establishing a family-friendly work culture. However, Allen (2001) found that perceptions of family-supportive work environments mediated the relation between supervisor support and work-family conflict, suggesting that supervisor support may be a precursor to a supportive work-family culture rather than an aspect of culture.

In addition to the dimensions described previously, there are most likely other relevant dimensions to be considered to fully understand the nature of work-family culture. For example, Kossek et al. (2001), who prefer the term *climate* to *culture*, proposed two dimensions of work climate that facilitate or inhibit an employee's ability to balance work and family. The first dimension, a work climate for sharing concerns, encourages employees to discuss family concerns with supervisors and coworkers, whereas the second, a work climate for sacrifices, entails making sacrifices in the family role to support work role performance. Kossek et al. (1999) proposed that organizations have a climate for boundary separation: Some have loose boundaries between work and family (e.g., employees can bring children to work) and some have tight boundaries (e.g., employees are not allowed to take personal calls at work). In addition, Kirchmeyer (1995) suggested that respect for an employee's nonwork life is an important component of a supportive organization. This area of research is ripe for investigation, especially given the lack of comprehensive studies to date that have investigated these multiple dimensions of work-family culture.

RESEARCH ON WORK-FAMILY CULTURE

Overall Supportiveness of the Culture

Although research investigating the effect of family-supportive policies on employee attitudes and behavior has found mixed results (see Kossek, chap. 7, this volume), research on the effect of supportive work-family cultures has been more consistently positive. For example, research has demonstrated that perceptions of a supportive work environment are related to greater use of work-family benefits (Allen, 2001; Thompson et al., 1999), and are associated with job satisfaction (Allen, 2001; Bond, Thompson, Galinsky, & Prottas, 2003) and commitment to the organization (Allen, 2001; Bond et al., 2003; Lyness, Thompson, Francesco, & Judiesch, 1999; Thompson et al.,

1999; Thompson, Jahn, Kopelman, & Prottas, 2004). In addition, perceptions of a supportive work-family culture are tied to less work strain (Warren & Johnson, 1995), work-family conflict (Allen, 2001; Anderson, Coffey, & Byerly, 2002), and fewer turnover intentions (Allen, 2001; Bond et al., 2003; Thompson et al., 1999). Both Allen (2001) and Thompson et al. (1999) found that these relations held after controlling for benefit availability, suggesting that a supportive culture has an influence on employee attitudes above and beyond simply offering work-life benefits. Similarly, O'Driscoll et al. (2003) studied 335 managers and found that neither availability nor use of work-family benefits was related to reduced work-family conflict or strain, but that perceptions of a family-supportive organization were linked to less work-family conflict.

Organizational Time Demands

A key component of work-family culture is the extent to which an organization requires long hours at work. Because the productivity of managerial and professional employees is often difficult to measure, the hours that an employee spends at work is often used as an indicator of both output and commitment to the organization (Bailyn, 1993; Blair-Loy & Wharton, 2002). Norms regarding face time create pressures for employees to work longer hours than are necessary just to prove their dedication and commitment (Bailyn, 1993; Fried, 1998). This creates a vicious cycle where long hours make work-family policies necessary, but employees are reluctant to use them out of fear that they may appear less productive or less committed to the organization (Blair-Loy & Wharton, 2002).

Researchers are only recently beginning to study the effect of time demands on blue-collar workers, who often work in tightly managed, low-control occupations and face the unique demand of mandatory overtime. Employees can be asked to work overtime with little warning, and the employer can fire or demote workers for refusing to do so under the Fair Labor Standards Act of 1938 (Perry-Jenkins, 2003).

Research suggests that working long hours has implications for employee health and well-being (Sparks, Cooper, Fried, & Shirom, 1997). For example, Major, Klein, and Ehrhart (2002) found that organizational norms for how much time should be spent at work were, in fact, predictive of hours worked, which, in turn, were related to work-family conflict. Work time was indirectly related to psychological distress (e.g., depression) through its effect on work-family conflict. Thompson et al. (1999) also found that employees who perceived heavy organizational time demands were more likely to report greater work-family conflict; this relation held even after controlling for hours worked. Finally, Brett and Stroh (2003) found that employees who worked the longest hours felt the most alienated from their families.

Perceived Negative Career Consequences

Perceived negative career consequences is another component of work-family culture identified by Thompson et al. (1999). They found that when employees perceived fewer negative career consequences from using work-family benefits, they were less likely to think about quitting and had less work-family conflict. Similarly, Anderson et al. (2002) found that employees who expected negative career consequences for putting their family first reported more work-family conflict, lower job satisfaction, and higher turnover intentions. Taken together, these results suggest that, although work-life programs may be enacted by organizations with the intent to help employees balance work and family, unsupportive cultures lead employees to fear their careers will be damaged if they participate in these programs or allow their family to be the top priority in their lives. These negative perceptions have consequences for the individual and the organization in terms of conflict experienced and intentions to quit.

Managerial and Supervisory Support

Researchers have found that an employee's relationship with his or her supervisor is a powerful predictor of work-family balance (Galinsky & Stein, 1990). Employees who have supportive supervisors report less work-family conflict (Anderson et al., 2002; Frone, Yardley, & Markel, 1997; Goff, Mount, & Jamison, 1990), less depression (Thomas & Ganster, 1995), less role strain, and fewer other health symptoms (Greenberger, Goldberg, Hamill, O'Neil, & Payne, 1989; O'Driscoll et al., 2003). Supportive supervision has also been linked to increased commitment (Allen, 2001; Greenberger et al., 1989; Thompson et al., in press), higher job satisfaction (Allen, 2001; Thomas & Ganster, 1995), higher career satisfaction (Aryee & Luk, 1996), less intention to quit (Allen, 2001; Thompson et al., 1999), and lower absenteeism (Goff et al., 1990).

Allen (2001) examined the process through which supervisor support lessens work-family conflict. She found that supervisor support directly affected the extent to which employees perceived the organization as supportive of family needs, which, in turn, was related to less work-family conflict. As Allen (2001) and others have noted, supervisors play a key role in determining whether employees are able to use work-life policies, and their willingness to be supportive influences employees' attitudes about their jobs and employer.

Additional Dimensions of Work-Family Culture

As noted earlier, Kossek et al. (2001) suggested a work climate that encourages sharing family concerns and one that encourages sacrificing family for work might be important dimensions that affect employee attitudes and decisions about how much time and energy to devote to work. They found that a climate for sharing family concerns at work was positively related to an employee's well-being and self-reports of work performance, whereas a climate of sacrificing family for work was associated with lower well-being and greater work-family conflict.

Kossek et al. (1999) proposed, but did not test, the idea that organizations might have a climate for boundary separation. Kirchmeyer (1995) examined a similar idea by investigating the effectiveness of three different organizational responses to managing work and nonwork roles: integration (organization supports combining work and family spheres), separation (the organization treats the domains as separate), and respect (the organization provides the support necessary for the individual to handle work-family demands). Among a sample of Canadian managers, researchers found that the most common policy was one of "separation," and it was associated with less organizational commitment. They found integration and respect policies, although less common, were associated with greater employee commitment (Kirchmeyer, 1995).

Culture and Benefit Use

Researchers have begun to investigate the relation between supportive work-family culture and the extent to which employees use the work-life benefits offered. As noted earlier, even if benefits are available, they often are unused in cultures that send mixed messages about their acceptance (Perlow, 1995). Two recent studies found that employees were more likely to use work-life benefits when they perceived their organizations and supervisors provided a family-supportive work environment (Allen, 2001; Thompson et al., 1999).

Blair-Loy and Wharton (2002) examined whether having powerful supervisors or coworkers would increase the use of family-care programs (e.g., day care and paid or unpaid leave) and flexible work policies. They argued that a social context with powerful individuals (e.g., with men being more powerful than women in the workplace) would provide the support necessary to reduce the potential negative career consequences of using work-family policies. They found that use of family-care policies was influenced solely by individual factors, with women, single individuals, and those with dependent care responsibilities more likely to use them. However, use of flexible policies (e.g., flextime, telecommuting) was affected by the amount of power that one's coworkers and supervisors had. For example, having a male, unmarried supervisor compared with a female, married supervisor increased the probability of using flexible policies by 50%.

ANTECEDENTS OF A
FAMILY-UNFRIENDLY CULTURE

In the preceding discussion, we argued that outcomes for both employees (e.g., job and life satisfaction, reduced stress and conflict) and organizations (e.g., less absenteeism, lower turnover, higher productivity) are enhanced when employees feel they work in a supportive culture that respects their lives outside of work. Indeed, there is a growing expectation that American organizations should help their employees manage work and family (Ingram & Simon, 1995). However, the media hype surrounding organizations that "make it" to the list of 100 Best Companies for Working Mothers suggests that family-responsive organizations are not yet the norm, and recent research by the Families and Work Institute bears this out. In a national sample of working adults, Galinsky, Kim, and Bond (1998) found that more than one fourth of the sample felt overworked or overwhelmed by how much work they did in the prior 3 months. Of those employees who worked in less supportive cultures, more than one half ranked their perception of overwork at the highest level. That these employees felt overworked suggests that there is still a large gap between what workers require to lead balanced lives and what organizations are offering. In fact, the Bureau of Labor Statistics found that few American employers offer work-life benefits (see Kossek, chap. 7, this volume).

The focus on work-family issues in academia and the enactment of work-family programs in the business world resulted from changes in the demographic composition of the American workforce in the final decades of the 20th century. Although unsupportive cultures might be dismissed as dysfunctional vestiges of a prior time, when the workforce consisted of married men with stay-at-home wives, the more complex and diverse workforce is no longer a recent development. Managers of private-sector, profit-oriented companies are paid to identify and respond to market trends and identify policies, practices, and cultural transformations that could promote a competitive advantage and improve firm performance. While acknowledging that managers are imperfect and some cultures may be maintained despite their dysfunction, it is imporant to ask why some organizations choose to be responsive to work-life needs by providing supportive programs and creating supportive cultures, whereas others do not. In fact, perhaps the question should be reframed as, under what constraints are family-*un*supportive organizations operating?

The analysis of organizational constraints must be concerned with the proper level of analysis for the organization. Prior research on the characteristics of organizations that adopted family-friendly practices focused on the organization at the firm and industry levels (Goodstein, 1994; Ingram & Simon, 1995; Osterman, 1995) and within the context of environmental forces that organizations faced (e.g., labor, competition, and sociopolitical). However, the analysis of possible antecedents of work-family culture likely needs to be finer-grained. For example, within organizations, there are wide discrepancies in who has access to work-life benefits and support and in who is penalized for taking advantage of such policies and programs. Professional and managerial employees appear to have greater access to flexible work schedules than lower level employees. In addition, in large organizations, the potential for wide discrepancies among divisions is great. A large financial service organization such as Citigroup employs such disparate work groups as employees in neighborhood retail branches and corporate bond traders on trading floors. Even a subcategory of *investment bank* includes disparate subunits, such as mergers and acquisitions advisors, floor traders, and back-office support staff. Such subunits face distinct labor markets for their employees, differing governance and control mechanisms, different customer segments with different expectations and demands, and dissimilar production technologies. It is likely that these subunits vary in the degree to which employees are allowed to have a life outside of work, although all employees have, at least in theory, access to identical corporate programs.

To begin to understand why some organizations are more supportive of work-life issues, and why some subunits within organizations are more supportive than others, researchers must identify factors that influence the extent to which an organization's culture (or a unit's subculture) supports work-life balance. Organizational cultures might be constrained by the technology used to produce goods and services. The technology, in turn, might influence the design of jobs. The culture might also be constrained by the demands and requirements of the external marketplace, both for its products and its inputs (e.g., its employees), as well as its customer requirements and expectations. Finally, the characteristics of the organization's technology and the requirements of its external markets might be constrained by the organization's strategy.

With respect to technology, one relevant taxonomy may be task interdependency. J. D. Thompson's (1967) forms of task interdependence (pooled, sequential, and reciprocal interdependence) may be relevant to analyzing the effect of supporting an individual employee's work-family preferences on his or her coworkers, the production process, and organizational outcomes. For example, the effect of allowing an individual person who has only occasional interactions with coworkers to work at home may be quite different from that of a person who constantly interacts with a large number of coworkers. Thus, an organization's tolerance for family-supportive norms might vary along these dimensions of task interdependence.

Perlow (1997) studied groups of software engineers whose tasks were reciprocally interdependent. She questioned whether the engineers' long hours were really necessary, or whether there was something about the way work was organized that contributed to the culture of long hours. Perlow (2001) found that type of coordination among group members affected the number of hours they worked and how much flexibility they had in choosing when and where they worked. Specifically, groups with manager-oriented coordination worked fewer hours with less weekend work and work outside of traditional business hours than did groups with either team- or expertise-oriented coordination.

In addition, workers in manager-oriented groups spent less time coordinating activities (13% of their time vs. 26%) and more of their time in task completion. She also found that team-oriented coordination affected the degree to which employees could substitute for one another, thus enhancing schedule flexibility. As such, type of coordination and interchangeability directly affect the culture of overwork and time use, thus affecting employees' ability to work the hours they need to lead balanced lives.

Woodward's (1958) distinction between small-batch and mass production technology may also be relevant. For example, Nollen (1982) found that manufacturing firms that used a batch process were better able to implement flextime than firms that used continuous-processing or assembly line technology. Although an organization's technology may constrain its ability to be supportive, we are not proposing a technological determinism that would prevent (or excuse) organizations from attempting to meet the needs of their employees. As with Perlow's work, we would argue that attempts to change an organizational culture may require some fundamental changes in how the organization performs its basic functions.

In addition to examining the influence of technology on work-family culture, it may be beneficial to evaluate jobs in terms of their task variety and task analyzability (Perrow, 1970). For example, Bailyn (1993) described the difficulty of measuring performance in managerial and professional jobs because of their open-ended nature and lack of clear boundaries. Because the performance criteria are often ambiguous, managers use face time or visibility at work as a measure of successful performance. This in turn "may induce behavior that responds less to the actual needs of the work than to stereotyped, habitual organizational expectations" (Bailyn, 1993, p. 45), which, in turn, creates a culture where "being there" is more important than actual work productivity.

Finally, an organization's basic business strategies have implications for task structure, customer segment expectations and requirements, and the labor market it must tap for the required skills and abilities. These ramifications, in turn, affect the ability of the organization to provide a family-supportive culture. For example, a firm with a global business strategy may require a high degree of task interdependence among geographically dispersed employees (as well as their external customers and suppliers), leading to greater amounts of business-related travel, which can have negative effects on the employee and family (Westman, 2003). Even if travel is avoided by using electronic media (e.g., telephone, video-conferencing, e-mail), the need to communicate across multiple time zones further blurs the boundary between work and family time. Multinational organizations commonly require conversations between employees whose normal "9 to 5" working hours never overlap. Thus, a global strategy may, by necessity, be less respectful of boundaries between home and office time than one that operates locally. However, firms that operate globally are likely to be larger—and the larger the firm, the greater the number and type of family-friendly policies (Goodstein, 1994; Ingram & Simon, 1995; Osterman, 1995). This wider selection may offset some of the negative effects of operating globally.

A "first mover" business strategy is often necessary to compete in a marketplace characterized by rapidly changing technology. Organizations that operate in these markets may perceive substantially greater costs involved in supporting its employees' attempts to balance work and family. In addition, when a strategy of getting to market first is critical for staying competitive, the perception that long hours of work—even if the employee must sacrifice family, friends, and hobbies—may be viewed as necessary for the survival of the company (Kidder, 1981; Perlow, 1997). For example, the assumption among engineers is that work will be all-consuming and that it must be all-consuming if their employers are to compete in the global market (Kunda, 1992; Perlow, 2001). Perlow's (1997) research showed that engineers who placed work in a different priority (e.g., having "hard stops" where they left at 5 P.M. every day) often suffered negative career consequences, further reinforcing the culture of work over family.

Finally, it is important to consider how top managers, especially CEOs, view work-life programs and policies. Do they consider them an important aspect of strategically managing the organization? Do they believe "family concerns can be treated at the margins, conceptually distinct from the primary goals of the organization?" (Bailyn, 1993, p. 68). Do they believe that work and nonwork should remain separate or fully integrated? (Kirchmeyer, 1995). Although CEO attitudes would not be considered a structural antecedent of work-family culture, their attitudes and beliefs surely affect the degree to which an organization has a supportive work-life culture. It is likely that CEO work-family attitudes serve as a moderator that influences the relation between structural antecedents and work-family culture. For example, two national accounting firms may operate in the same environment, offer the same policies, conduct work in basically the same way, but have different cultures due to the influence of the CEO and his or her support for work-life balance.

DIRECTIONS FOR FUTURE RESEARCH

Research suggests that a supportive work-family culture is related to important organizational outcomes, such as increased commitment, higher job satisfaction, lower absenteeism, less work-family conflict, less psychological distress, fewer somatic complaints, and less role strain. However, what is unclear is the relative importance of each of the various cultural dimensions (e.g., negative career consequences, climate for sacrifice) for predicting these outcomes. Knowing which dimension is most predictive of positive outcomes would enable organizations to focus their change efforts on dimensions that matter. Accordingly, developing an accurate and comprehensive measure of work-family culture—one that encompasses all relevant dimensions—should be a priority. A psychometrically sound instrument would enable employers to more accurately assess the state of work-family culture in their organization, and it would allow researchers to advance our understanding of the causes and consequences of an unsupportive culture.

We should also determine how perceptions of work-family culture vary within an organization, as well as by occupation, industry, organizational size, and business strategy. Recent research by the Families and Work Institute found that the extent to which an organization offered flexible work arrangements varied significantly by company size, industry, and percentage of executive positions held by women and minorities (Galinsky & Bond, 1998). Similar predictors of a supportive culture likely exist, as well as other factors such as job level, production technology, product life cycle, and level of client demand.

Finally, we should determine whether the importance of a supportive work-family culture varies across firms and across individuals. Given the considerable differences across firms in terms of worker demographics and career motivations, it is likely that some employees are happy with workaholic cultures. For example, it is possible that a "climate for sacrifice" is not problematic for a small software firm that employs mostly young singles. As noted by O'Driscoll et al. (2003), a one-size-fits-all approach to work-family balance will be ineffective, and researchers must determine which interventions and aspects of a family-friendly culture are important for particular firms and employees.

IMPLICATIONS FOR PRACTICE

Because workplace norms for long hours and sacrificing family for work often have deleterious consequences for individuals, their families, and the employers, some organizations have begun to consider strategies for supporting employees' well-being (Friedman & Johnson, 1996). In moving an organization from simple programs to culture change, work-life experts argue that efforts should be linked with an organization's strategy to ensure that work-life balance is considered essential to business success. More specifically, an organization should consider linking work-life efforts to strategic goals of increasing employee commitment and job and career satisfaction, as well as lowering employee turnover, absenteeism, job strain, and poor health.

Top-level support is crucial for any culture change to take place. Top managers must embrace a vision for the organization that supports work-life balance and then communicate this vision through the company's mission statement, intranet, newsletters, and e-mail announcements. Furthermore, top- and mid-level managers must model new behaviors. For example, in Ernst & Young's efforts to create a more balanced work-life culture, a managing partner on an assignment in Chicago flew home to New York midweek for his daughter's birthday, thereby demonstrating to other managers and his subordinates that certain family events have priority over work (Friedman, Thompson, Carpenter, & Marcel, 2001).

To reinforce the importance of a supportive work-family culture, Friedman and Johnson (1996) recommended that managers be held accountable. Some organizations reward managers via performance reviews for being supportive of their subordinates' efforts to combine work and family (*Working Mother*, October 2002). In addition, managers should be given the training needed to create a supportive culture and be taught to identify how they might be contributing to a culture of overwork. For example, managers should be encouraged to consider ways of measuring performance that do not include face time, the common practice of equating work hours with productivity and commitment to the organization.

At the most fundamental level, organizations should focus on work processes and consider the ways in which outdated assumptions influence the number of hours employees are expected to work, where they work, when they work, and how they work (Friedman & Johnson, 1996; Rapoport, Bailyn, Fletcher, & Pruitt, 2002). Ernst & Young, for example, addressed work redesign by implementing such practices as setting parameters around due dates, accessibility, and response time of employees so that clients have clear expectations about acceptable demands. In addition, deployment committees plan work assignments so that no one individual is overburdened, and team calendars mark personal commitments to help increase the organization's respect for nonwork obligations (Catalyst, 2003). Finally, Friedman, Christensen, and DeGroot (1998) proposed that managers "continually experiment with the way work gets done, looking for approaches that enhance the organization's performance and allow employees to pursue personal goals" (p. 120).

CONCLUSION

Because work-family culture is an important influence on the use of work-family benefits within an organization, and because use of benefits is related to job and life satisfaction (Judge, Boudreau, & Bretz, 1994; Kossek & Ozeki, 1998), it is essential that organizations understand the mechanisms through which work-family culture enhances or inhibits employees from achieving a balance between their work and nonwork lives. In addition, researchers have found that a supportive work-family culture is linked to employee health and well-being, and organizational productivity, by its influence on work-family conflict, turnover intentions, stress, absenteeism, and organizational commitment (Allen, 2001; Anderson et al., 2002; Thompson et al., 1999). Future researchers must now begin the process of determining the relative strength of individual and organizational forces that influence an organization's work-family culture. Only when we determine the root cause of the mismatch between employee and employer needs will we be able to develop solutions that satisfy both the individual and the organization.

REFERENCES

Allen, T. (2001). Family-supportive work environments: The role of organizational perceptions. *Journal of Vocational Behavior, 58*, 414–435.

Anderson, S., Coffey, B. S., & Byerly, R. T. (2002). Formal organizational initiatives and informal workplace practices: Links to work-family conflict and job-related outcomes. *Journal of Management, 28*(6), 787–810.

Aryee, S., & Luk, V. (1996). Work and nonwork influences on the career satisfaction of dual-earner couples. *Journal of Vocational Behavior, 49*, 38–52.

Bailyn, L. (1993). *Breaking the mold: Women, men, and time in the new corporate world.* New York: The Free Press.

Bailyn, L. (1997). The impact of corporate culture on work-family integration. In S. Parasuraman & J. H. Greenhaus (Eds.), *Integrating work and family: Challenges and choices for a changing world* (pp. 209–219). Westport, CT: Quorum Books.

Blair-Loy, M., & Wharton, A. (2002). Employees' use of work-family policies and the workplace social context. *Social Forces, 80*(3), 813–845.

Bond, T. J., Thompson, C. A., Galinsky, E., & Prottas, D. (2003). *Highlights of the 2002 National Study of the Changing Workforce.* New York: Families and Work Institute.

Brett, J. M., & Stroh, L. K. (2003). Working 61 plus hours a week: Why do managers do it? *Journal of Applied Psychology, 88*, 67–78.

Catalyst. (2003). http://www.catalystwomen.org/catalyst_award/overview.htm.

Clark, S. C. (2001). Work cultures and work/family balance. *Journal of Vocational Behavior, 58*, 348–365.

Denison, D. R. (1996). What is the difference between organizational culture and organizational climate? A native's point of view on a decade of paradigm wars. *Academy of Management Review, 21*(3), 619–654.

Fried, M. (1998). *Taking time: Parental leave policy and corporate culture.* Philadelphia: Temple University Press.

Friedman, D. E., Christensen, P., & DeGroot, J. (1998). Work and life: The end of the zero-sum game. *Harvard Business Review, 76*(6), 119–129.

Friedman, D. E., & Johnson, A. A. (1996). *Moving from programs to culture change: The next stage for the corporate work-family agenda.* New York: Families and Work Institute.

Friedman, S., Thompson, C., Carpenter, M., & Marcel, D. (2001). Proving Leo Durocher wrong: Driving work/life change at Ernst & Young. A Wharton Work/Life Integration Project (http://www.bc.edu/bc_org/avp/wfnetwork/loppr/cases.html).

Frone, M. R., Yardley, J. K., & Markel, K. (1997). Developing and testing an integrative model of the work-family interface. *Journal of Vocational Behavior, 50*, 145–167.

Galinsky, E., & Bond, T. (1998). *The 1998 business work-life study: A sourcebook.* New York: Families and Work Institute.

Galinsky, E., Kim, S., & Bond, J. T. (1998). *Feeling overworked: When work becomes too much.* New York: Families and Work Institute.

Galinsky, E., & Stein, P. J. (1990). The impact of human resource policies on employees. *Journal of Family Issues, 11*(4), 368–377.

Goff, S. J., Mount, M. K., & Jamison, R. L. (1990). Employer supported child care, work/family conflict and absenteeism: A field study. *Personnel Psychology, 43,* 793–809.

Goodstein, J. D. (1994). Institutional pressures and strategic responsiveness: Employer involvement in work-family issues. *Academy of Management Journal, 37,* 350–382.

Greenberger, E., Goldberg, W. A., Hamill, S., O'Neil, R., & Payne, C. K. (1989). Contributions of a supportive work environment to parents' well-being and orientation to work. *American Journal of Community Psychology, 17*(6), 755–783.

Ingram, P., & Simon, T. (1995). Institutional and resource dependence determinants of responsiveness to work-family issues. *Academy of Management Journal, 38,* 1466–1482.

Jahn, E. W., Thompson, C. A., & Kopelman, R. E. (2003). Rationale and construct validity evidence for a measure of perceived organizational family support (POFS): Because purported practices may not reflect reality. *Community, Work and Family, 6,* 123–140.

Judge, T. A., Boudreau, J. W., & Bretz, R. D. (1994). Job and life attitudes of male executives. *Journal of Applied Psychology, 79*(5), 767–782.

Judiesch, M., & Lyness, K. (1999). Left behind? The impact of leaves of absence on manager's career success. *Academy of Management Journal, 42*(6), 641–651.

Kidder, T. (1981). *The soul of a new machine.* New York: Avon.

Kirchmeyer, C. (1995). Managing the work-nonwork boundary: An assessment of organizational responses. *Human Relations, 48*(5), 515–536.

Kossek, E. E., Colquitt, J. A., & Noe, J. A. (2001). Caregiving decisions, well-being, and performance: The effects of place and provider as a function of dependent type and work-family climates. *Academy of Management Journal, 44*(1), 29–44.

Kossek, E. E., Noe, R. A., & DeMarr, B. J. (1999). Work-family role synthesis: Individual and organizational determinants. *International Journal of Conflict Management, 10*(2), 102–129.

Kossek, E. E., & Ozeki, C. (1998). Work-family conflict, policies, and the job-life satisfaction relationship: A review and directions for organizational behavior-human resources research. *Journal of Applied Psychology, 83*(2), 139–149.

Kunda, G. (1992). *Engineering culture: Control and commitment in a high-tech corporation.* Philadelphia: Temple University Press.

Lewis, S. (1997). Family friendly employment policies: A route to changing organizational culture or playing about the margins? *Gender, Work and Organization, 4,* 13–23.

Lyness, K., Thompson, C., Francesco, A. M., & Judiesch, M. K. (1999). Work and pregnancy: Individual and organizational factors influencing organizational commitment, timing of maternity leave, and return to work. *Sex Roles, 41*(7–8), 485–507.

Major, V. S., Klein, K. J., & Ehrhart, M. G. (2002). Work time, work interference with family, and psychological stress. *Journal of Applied Psychology, 87,* 427–436.

Nollen, S. D. (1982). *New work schedules in practice: Managing time in a changing society.* New York: Van Nostrand Reinhold.

O'Driscoll, M. P., Poelmans, S., Spector, P. E., Kalliath, T., Allen, T. D., Cooper, C. L., & Sanchez, J. I. (2003). Family-responsive interventions, perceived organizational and supervisor support, work-family conflict, and psychological strain. *International Journal of Stress Management, 10,* 326–344.

Osterman, P. (1995). Work/family programs and the employment relationship. *Administration Science Quarterly, 40,* 681–700.

Perlow, L. A. (1995). Putting the work back into work/family. *Group and Organization Management, 20,* 227–239.

Perlow, L. A. (1997). *Finding time: How corporations, individuals, and families can benefit from new work practices*. Ithaca, NY: Cornell University Press.

Perlow, L. A. (2001). Time to coordinate: Toward an understanding of work-time standards and norms in a multicountry study of software engineers. *Work & Occupations, 28*, 91–111.

Perrow, C. (1970). *Organizational analysis: A sociological view*. Belmont, CA: Wadsworth.

Perry-Jenkins, M. (2003). Dual-earner couples and the transition to parenthood: Study looks at challenges facing working class families. *Boston College Sloan Work and Family Research Network Newsletter, 5*, 4–6.

Pitt-Catsouphes, M. (n.d.). Family friendly-workplace. Sloan Work-Family Encyclopedia: http://www.bc.edu/bc_org/avp/wfnetwork/rft/wfpedia/wfpFFWent.html.

Rapoport, R., Bailyn, L., Fletcher, J. K., & Pruitt, B. H. (2002). *Beyond work-family balance: Advancing gender equity and workplace performance*. San Francisco: Jossey-Bass.

Schein, E. (1985). *Organizational culture and leadership*. San Francisco: Jossey-Bass.

Sparks, K., Cooper, C., Fried, Y., & Shirom, A. (1997). The effects of hours of work on health: A meta-analytic review. *Journal of Occupational and Organizational Psychology, 70*, 391–408.

Thomas, L. T., & Ganster, D. C. (1995). Impact of family-supportive work variables on work-family conflict and strain: A control perspective. *Journal of Applied Psychology, 80*, 6–15.

Thompson, C. A., Beauvais, L. L., & Lyness, K. S. (1999). When work-family benefits are not enough: The influence of work-family culture on benefit utilization, organizational attachment, and work-family conflict. *Journal of Vocational Behavior, 54*, 392–415.

Thompson, C. A., Jahn, E. W., Kopelman, R. E., & Prottas, D. J. (2004). The impact of perceived organizational and supervisory family support on affective commitment: A longitudinal and multi-level analysis. *Journal of Managerial Issues, 16*(4), 545–565.

Thompson, J. D. (1967). *Organizations in action*. New York: McGraw-Hill.

Warren, J., & Johnson, P. (1995). The impact of workplace support on work-family role strain. *Family Relations, 44*, 163–169.

Westman, M. (2003, August). *Impact of organizational support on travel stress*. Paper presented at the Academy of Management Meetings, Seattle.

Woodward, J. (1958). *Management and technology*. London: Her Majesty's Stationery Office.

9

Filling the Gap
by Redesigning Work

Lotte Bailyn
Massachusetts Institute of Technology

How do we bridge the gap between work and family particularly in a time of workforce and workplace mismatch? Presumably, the goal is to create a workplace where men and women, in different family structures and at different phases in life, can be as productive as possible. In other words, the goal is to combine issues of equity across groups with organizational effectiveness (Rapoport, Bailyn, Fletcher, & Pruitt, 2002). I suggest in this chapter that such an integration is possible, and I consider some of the conditions that would be necessary to bring it about. In general, it would require an institutional realignment and a reversal in thinking. In research, it would mean changing dependent variables to independent. In organizational practice, it would mean shifting marginal considerations to the center. Systemically, it would require moving from an individual to a collective view of the problem. My argument is not for simply creating a family-friendly workplace. Rather, it is for creating an *effective* workplace given the current workforce. I argue that we must devise policies and strategies that put family needs first and adapt working conditions to meet those needs. The result of this better family-work alignment, I suggest, will be a new commitment and effectiveness in the workplace (see Fig. 9.1).

Employers, in contrast, tend to think in exactly the reverse fashion; employees must first show commitment to the company before they are

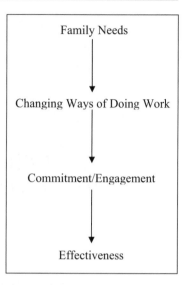

FIG. 9.1. Pathways to change (adapted from Bailyn, 1993, p. 137).

permitted any flexibility. Two things are lost in this characteristic thinking. First, it denies the possibility that problematic work behavior (e.g., tardiness, absences) may actually result from the conditions and practices dictated by the organization. Second, and most important, this way of thinking assumes that the way work is currently organized is the most effective, and that policies and programs are geared to helping people meet existing organizational expectations. Further, family policies are usually negotiated between a worker and manager and typically follow this traditional model. Such individual negotiation necessarily limits both the manager's willingness to grant flexibility and the employee's willingness to ask for and use it. It also limits the system from recognizing the structures, norms, and practices that have caused the problems in the first place.

Only by reversing this way of thinking and enacting the arrows as shown in Fig. 9.1 will employers and employees be open to alternative ways of meeting work goals—ways that meet the needs of both employer and employee. In other words, in this scenario, the organization of work shifts from an independent to a dependent variable, and family needs become the driving force.

My argument centers on the legitimacy of personal and family interests and responsibilities for all employees. To reach such a goal requires top-level support for conditions that help employees successfully integrate work and family, as well as the appropriate behavior of top-level management. If top managers say they support their employees in their quest to have integrated lives, but themselves work long hours, their actions speak louder than their words.

The realignment suggested here does not call for more family policies. Rather, it calls for family needs to be equally valued with organizational needs in the structure and culture of work. Without believing in the legitimacy and value of employees' personal, family, and community involvements, workplace effectiveness and equity cannot be achieved. My research has shown that recognizing the legitimacy of individual needs in workplace redesign not only promotes equity—because workers are no longer constrained by their outside responsibilities—but also improves the organization's effectiveness. Such a realignment is particularly important when the timing and scheduling of work are considered. True flexibility, the argument goes, will not work unless premised on this initial, fully embraced legitimacy of personal needs.

CASE EXAMPLES

Consider a Customer Administration Center of a large consumer products manufacturer, which we assessed in an earlier research project. The unit employed approximately 300 people under the direction of a controller. The employees were divided into groups, each with a supervisor, who reported to a mid-level manager before reaching the controller. The controller was a careful leader. He seldom embarked on changes until they had been shown to work elsewhere or unless they were handed down from corporate headquarters. And so he was waiting for company training before embarking on a corporate-mandated move to self-managed teams. Nonetheless, there were some problems in the unit. In particular, absenteeism was very high, with sanctions for lateness, which was always noted.

The company had progressive work-family policies. Every flexibility imaginable (e.g., job sharing, 4-day work weeks, flexible starting and ending times) was available. Yet few employees took advantage of them. An occasional employee was allowed slight deviation of starting and ending times, but no one utilized a compressed work week schedule or job sharing. The latter was not of great concern because few employees could have afforded less than full-time work given the low wages. Also because supervisors believed their presence was required when their subordinates were working, the limited deviation from the traditional 9 to 5 workday was not surprising. That is not to say that flexibility was not desired. The company was located in an urban area, and many employees had difficult commutes. Several also had children in day care or other responsibilities that could not always be met on weekends.

Our interviews revealed that employees would ask for flexibility and would often be turned down. Word would spread, and soon there were fewer and fewer requests. This only confirmed management's view that flexibility was unnecessary. It was when the controller realized that these self-reinforcing rigidities were rampant in his organization, and not only confined to family benefits, that he was willing to set up an experiment. In front of the entire group, he announced that he would let anyone take advantage of any of the flexibilities so long as the work got done. The experiment was to last 3 months, after which they would evaluate its success.

So what happened? First, almost everyone wanted a different schedule, and this applied not only to mothers with small children, but also to men and workers without children. Second, supervisors were no longer able to negotiate these changes one on one with their employees. They had no choice but to let the groups get together and figure out their schedules collectively to ensure that the work would get done. Finally, because schedules now roamed much more broadly over the day, supervisors were forced to allow their employees to work at times without supervisors present.

The result was that absenteeism dropped 30% and customer service, which had been a great concern owing to absenteeism, improved because longer hours were now being covered. Also once the groups found they could manage their own schedules, they began as well to assume some of the self-management tasks that the company wanted. The groups developed so well that when delayed corporate self-management training finally arrived, the workers sent it back, feeling that they were ahead of the game. Perhaps most important, the controller changed his image of himself. He no longer saw himself as conservative, but as innovative and experimental.

In this example, there was a willingness, mandated by top management, to put personal needs up front, although within a strict experimental framework and under the constraint that the work must get done. To meet this double goal of flexibility for employees and work effectiveness, several things happened. First, everyone was empowered to ask for the schedule they needed to get their work done, and hence absenteeism was dramatically reduced. Second, negotiation on schedules no longer could be done one on one between employee and supervisor, requiring the work groups to deal with schedules collectively. This enabled them, over time, to become the self-managed teams that had originally been envisioned for them, but that had been impossible to enact previously.

A key assumption about control was challenged by this change. Supervisors were forced to relinquish the notion that they had to be present whenever their subordinates were working, and they thus learned that surveillance may not be the best way to manage people. We found this same effect among a group of engineers whose supervisor had been monitoring them very closely. When a work design experiment was instigated that separated the day into times for independent work and interactive times (Perlow, 1997), the engineering supervisor realized that his engineers worked better when he was not looking over their shoulder. Both sets of supervisors, of course, could have been told this, but they had to experience it to change their assumptions about control.

This vignette exemplifies a positive, self-reinforcing cycle. Focusing first on workers' schedules leads to changes in the way the work is being done and managed, which has positive effects for the organization and the people involved. Because the flexibilities were available to everyone, both equity and effectiveness were served.

Consider another example — a small portfolio group of a large bank — with different issues. This group prepared financial reports for various divisions of the bank, including the vice president of finance and the board of directors. The work consisted of combining individual analyses into a coordinated report. The unit consisted of about six separate groups, each under a supervisor who nonetheless continued to do some of the analysis and who reported to one manager. There were about six people in each individual group.

The group had recently been formed by merging two existing groups and moving them to a new location. Hence, many of the workers now had long commutes. They reported feeling frenzied and harried, which was confirmed by others. Because their work was all computer based, they asked whether they could spend a day or so working from home, but this was not allowed. The manager also had some issues. She wanted to set up a coordination template, which would clearly indicate the status of all the parts of each report, with time goals for each part, leading to the final report. However, she had been unable to convince her staff that this template served a useful purpose. They believed they were in close enough contact with one another to coordinate without spending the time to develop a template and keep it current.

The company was worried about the stress on this group and decided to allow, for a limited period, employees to work from home for up to 2 days a week. Ordinarily, the group was connected by a local-area network (LAN), which stored all the data needed for their analyses. Although it was impossible to set this up in people's homes, the company agreed to provide connections to another location that also stored the necessary data.

One of the first reports from the employees was that they were now able to participate in family events that they never could have previously. They could go to a child's play and work in the evening, for example. Interacting groups reported that these workers were now much less frenzied and easier to work with. A dramatic event — the office LAN went down for a few days — helped put the experiment in a favorable light, and it also created some interesting learning opportunities; the only people who could get any work done were those working from home.

What about the work? How were the individual parts of these reports coordinated? It readily became apparent to the employees that the template their manager had devised was necessary under the new circumstances, and they quickly set it up. This so helped the manager oversee the work that she also began to work 1 day a week from home.

The division learned several lessons from this experiment. The first lesson involved technology. Even technology can benefit from redundancy (e.g., not depending on only one network), and that such redundancy fits well with flexibility in people's schedules. Another was that coordination does not necessarily require instant access to everyone involved. In fact it was only when the work became more distributed that the department established the coordination template. This is an important point. Continuous accessibility does not necessarily make a work group more efficient or effective. Another assumption was challenged. Because the expectation of continuous presence also imposes constraints on people's ability to integrate work with their personal lives, challenging this expectation may lead to workplace change that meets the personal needs of employees while also making the organization more effective.

The department did, however, encounter a problem during this experiment. The employees were so enthusiastic about their new-found flexibility that they had to be continuously reminded that their emphasis should be on the work, and that if they did not produce reports as quickly and with the same quality (or even better) than before, their new freedoms would disappear. This situation was similar to that in another financial analysis group we studied in a different company. There they had devised an intelligent way to coordinate people's flexibility needs with the needs of the work, but as time went on the flexibilities began to be viewed as entitlements, and the link to accomplishing the work was lost. As a result, when new management came in, the experiment ceased. In the cases reported here, however, the experiments became permanent, although there was a continuous need to monitor both sides of what we have called the *dual agenda* (Rapoport et al., 2002).

INTEGRATING WORKER NEEDS WITH WORKPLACE GOALS

These case examples show how putting family needs up front can lead to workplace changes that both help the employees and improve the effectiveness of a work unit. The examples locate the ultimate business case for legitimating employees' family and personal needs (which is different from family policies or a family-friendly work culture) in the effectiveness of the work itself.

In a larger institutional sense, this argument means constructing family, personal, and community needs as part of the basic business equation. Figure 9.2 illustrates this concept. The top section of Fig. 9.2 shows the usual concerns of business. The demands flowing from these concerns and their effect on employees (moving toward the middle of the figure) have led some companies to initiate policies that ease employees' lives—policies that are, however, frequently underused.

The lower portion of Fig. 9.2, in contrast, which also affects employees, seems to be below the radar in a strategic, systemic sense. If noticed at all,

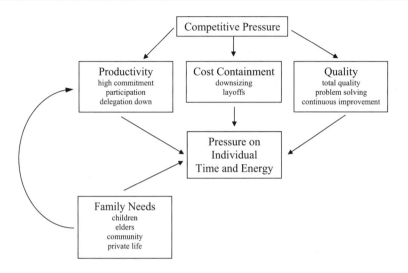

FIG. 9.2.   Incorporating family needs (adapted from Bailyn, 1993, p. 113).

this set of needs is viewed as individual issues for which occasional help is provided. Nor are businesses seemingly aware of the negative feedback loops that occur between this hidden part of employees' lives and the goals they cherish at the top of the figure. When family needs intrude, they affect workers' productivity (e.g., phone calls home when children arrive from school), the quality of their work (e.g., concentration wanes), and costs (e.g., Employee Assistance Program costs and health costs, as well as costs through absences, tardiness, and turnover). Schematically, what is being suggested by the sweeping arrow in Fig. 9.2 is that these family needs must move above the line to rest alongside the key business needs if institutional change is to work. Not only do people's lives and their communities depend on it, but so does business if it is to achieve its goals. That is what full legitimacy implies. Family policies and supportive work environments are clearly important, but they are premised on traditional assumptions about work and how it is best accomplished.

A final question, not addressed here, is what keeps this ineffective system in place and why is it so hard to change? I would suggest that the chapter by Joyce K. Fletcher (chap. 22, this volume) is the beginning of an answer to this question (see also Fletcher & Bailyn, 2005).

REFERENCES

Bailyn, L. (1993). *Breaking the mold: Women, men, and time in the new corporate world*. San Francisco: Jossey-Bass.

Fletcher, J. K., & Bailyn, L. (2005). *The equity imperative: Redesigning work for work-family integration*. In E. Kossek & S. Lambert (Eds.), *Work and life integration: Cultural and individual perspectives* (pp. 171–189). Mahwah, NJ: Lawrence Erlbaum Associates.

Perlow, L. (1997). *Finding time: How corporations, individuals, and families can benefit from new work practices*. Ithaca, NY: Cornell University Press.

Rapoport, R., Bailyn, L., Fletcher, J. K., & Pruitt, B. H. (2002). *Beyond work-family balance: Advancing gender equity and workplace performance*. San Francisco: Jossey-Bass.

10

Can Employers Be Good Neighbors? Redesigning the Workplace–Community Interface

Ann Bookman

Sloan School of Management
Massachusetts Institute of Technology

In 1992, Smith-Corona relocated a factory from a community in upstate New York to Tijuana, Mexico. All the American workers lost their jobs (Beneria, 1998). Despite retraining programs and other forms of assistance offered by the state and federal governments, most workers suffered economically. The plant was located in a rural community with a declining economy, and the only employment option for most of the laid-off workers was to take a new job in the service sector that paid less. For some, a lengthy period of unemployment resulted in physical and mental health problems, marital conflicts, and behavior problems among their children. Others were forced to sever ties with friends, neighbors, and coworkers when they had to leave their community to find a job. Although Smith-Corona may have gained greater flexibility in its operations and savings in its labor costs, the workers experienced a variety of social and economic losses, and the small, rural community lost its major employer and many skilled workers in the process.

Just before Christmas in December 1995, a large textile factory owned by Malden Mills burned to the ground. Most of the 3,000 workers expected to lose their jobs, but much to their surprise the owner of the company, Aaron Feuerstein, kept all the workers on the payroll with benefits and rebuilt the mill. Feuerstein said he considered the workers "an asset, not an expense" and recognized their work in the invention and production of the company's signature product, Polartec®. He also explained that, although he felt an obligation to the company shareholders, "I have an equal responsibility to the community. It would have been unconscionable to put 3,000 people in the streets and deliver a deathblow to the cities of Lawrence and Metheun" (Boulay, 1996). Although the company has been through some difficult economic times, ultimately Feuerstein's decision provided job and income security to thousands of working families and helped two struggling urban communities maintain their economic vitality.[1]

These stories reveal two different pictures of the workplace–community interface. Unfortunately, the former is much more common than the latter in the competitive world of the global economy. Many companies, such as Smith-Corona, have laid off workers in pursuit of low labor costs and higher profit margins, with little consideration of the consequences of their business decisions for families and communities. It does not, however, necessarily have to be that way. The need of companies to be lean and flexible and the need of families for job security and supportive communities do not have to be at odds. To explore the possibility of win-win solutions for both business and community life, I address four questions about the workplace–community interface:

1. How has the workplace-community interface evolved over time?
2. What do the connections between the workplace and the community look like today?
3. What kind of disconnects or disruptions currently characterize the relation between the workplace and the community?
4. What should the workplace–community interface look like in the future?

Although my focus is on two domains—work and community—I examine how changes in this interface have affected children, families, and family care. My ultimate concern is to lay the basis for redesigning this interface through private- and public-sector actions, with the goal of enhancing family health and well-being.

---

[1] Almost a decade after the fire, Malden Mills is fully operational, employs a significant number of workers, and even developed a cogeneration project in one of its new buildings that meets EPA standards. This not only saves Malden Mills $1 million a year, but benefits the community by reducing pollutant emissions (www.epa.gov/chp/chp_success.htm).

CONCEPTUAL AND METHODOLOGICAL PROBLEMS

The workplace–community interface has received little attention in the scholarship on work and family largely because community in general has been understudied. There are a wealth of community studies by sociologists and anthropologists, but for the most part they do not address workplace issues (Gans, 1962, 1967; Gregory, 1999; Lynd & Lynd, 1929, 1937; Mullings & Klumer, 2001; Myerhoff, 1978; Sanjek, 1998; Stack, 1974; Susser, 1982). Likewise, work-family researchers have paid extensive attention to workplaces, but they rarely address community issues and organizations (Voydanoff, 2001a, 2001b). Their focus has been on the changing demographics of the workforce, the rise of family-friendly policies among a segment of employers, the gap that often exists between policy and practice in constructing a family-friendly workplace culture, and, most recently, the organization of work. However, the communities where firms are located and the communities where employees live are rarely given in-depth attention.

Why is this? And what does it reveal about the conceptual challenges involved in linking the domains of work and community? I believe that a "separate spheres" model of social life still predominates public thinking. The most familiar use of the separate spheres model is the distinction that solidified during the period of industrialization between the male breadwinner in the workplace and the female caregiver in the home. The workplace was the sphere in which goods were produced and exchanged, ideas and inventions were generated, and from which all things of value emanated. The home was a retreat, even a haven, from the harsh world of work in which men were the major players. Women were assigned all family caregiving and household tasks and the moral teaching of children, and their role was idealized, although not fully valued in the same way that men's work was valued. In this paradigm, not only is family separate from work, but the communities where families live are also separate from work. A dualistic framework, with business and labor market institutions on one side and nonmarket institutions on the other, places community outside the sphere of the workplace and business concerns.

Although the separate spheres model did not reflect the reality of many people's lives during the era of industrialization, it came to represent a strongly held set of norms for White, middle-class families that permeated the entire culture. Despite the dramatic changes that have occurred in the composition of the labor force over the last 30 years, the separation of family and community from the world of work is still evident on practical, policy, and ideological levels. Workplaces are still organized, for the most part, as if each family is composed of one male breadwinner who is not "encumbered" with family responsibilities and one female family caregiver who does not work for pay, although that family type represents fewer than 20% of all families today. Workplace schedules and models for career advancement still reflect this "ideal worker norm" (Moen, 2003; Williams, 2000), and our public policies have also lagged behind new work-family realities.

Working families move seamlessly into and out of homes, communities, and workplaces in their daily routine, but these domains are not studied seamlessly by social scientists. We seem to prefer to divide things up into manageable "units of analysis" despite the fact that these units may not accurately reflect real-world experience. We also seem to hold onto a dualistic way of thinking about working families—they are either at home or at work—rather than seeing that both homes and workplaces are embedded in real geographic communities that shape family life and work. The next stage of work-family research must give community its rightful place in an understanding of work-family issues. By developing a concept of community and moving beyond dualistic modes of thinking, we can forge new solutions to work-family conflict.

BRIEF HISTORICAL OVERVIEW OF THE WORKPLACE–COMMUNITY INTERFACE

What has the workplace–community interface looked like in the past? Some of the early anthropologists, such as Lewis Henry Morgan and Franz Boas, provided a broad framework for understanding the changes that occurred over millennia from traditional societies, where there was little distinction between work, family, and community, to modern societies, where these spheres are highly differentiated (Leacock, 1981). Although a linear model of social evolution has been discredited for some time, it is still valuable to examine the overall movement from hunting-and-gathering societies to agrarian societies to industrial societies. In hunting-and-gathering societies, work either took place in extended family households, where food was prepared and clothing manufactured, or in collectively owned spaces, where multifamily groups fished and hunted for food (Briggs, 1970).

As people learned to domesticate plants and animals, sedentary agricultural societies began to develop. In agrarian systems, the home and workplace were still closely merged, but families began to claim particular areas as their own private property. This changed the configuration of community because families worked for their own members, rather than the band, tribe, or clan, and they passed land on to the next generation based on familial rather than communal rights. In recent agrarian societies, such as in colonial and postcolonial America, women, men, and children had different tasks, but they shared a common place of work—in some instances, these were slave plantations; in others, they were large family farms or small homesteading lots. Family care, especially the care of children, was the responsibility of mothers, fathers, extended family members, and even nonrelatives living in the households (Haraven, 1989). Community institutions were intertwined with the family-based agricultural enterprise, revolving around religious and civic associations.

As the industrial era unfolded, the distinction between the places where people worked for pay and the places where people performed unpaid work became sharply drawn for the first time. The workplace and home gradually became increasingly separate in terms of their physical location. In the United States, many people, including single and married women, left the family farm for factory jobs in rapidly growing urban areas. Although this was the first time significant numbers of women left their homes for paid employment, even larger numbers of married women remained in the countryside and "took work in," sewing clothes, shoes, and boots for their city-based employers in their homes (Kessler-Harris, 1982). The connections between work, family, and community were not irreversibly severed, but the nature of those connections changed. Workers belonged to multiple communities: communities in rural areas where they had been born and reared and where some still worked, and communities in the cities where they found jobs in new occupations unknown in the previous generation.

As industrialization expanded and cities became home to growing numbers of immigrant workers, many urban dwellers no longer had ties to the land. Community organizations grew up around types of employment and around ethnic neighborhoods with their own religious and cultural traditions. In urban areas, the relation between workplace and community took on a multiplicity of forms and meanings. Some working families lived in small company towns organized around textile and shoe production or mining. Although employers controlled virtually all aspects of employees' lives, running banks, stores, schools, and other community institutions, this did not mean there was no resistance to their control. In fact the rise of unionism in these cities was often a "community affair," bringing together men and women, workers, and neighbors (Dawley, 1977). Other workers lived in large cities with multiple employers, many of whom largely ignored the needs of poor immigrant workers. In this scenario, community associations run by workers struggled to provide social and financial support to working families.

As adult identities came to be shaped more by occupation than by kinship, the lives of children changed dramatically. Parents began to invest unprecedented resources and attention in their children, preparing them to be skilled workers through formal schooling rather than requiring that they join the family workforce at an early age (Levine & White, 1985). In the 19th century, children's attendance in school still rose and fell with the needs of domestic and agricultural production, whereas in the 20th century, school attendance became compulsory and attendance rose to unprecedented levels.

As public elementary and secondary schools grew in importance, their location in communities began to transform the cities and towns responsible for their funding and governance.

In the postindustrial era, the configuration of work, family, and community is still changing and varies depending on the nature of adult employment, family structure, and community environment. For workers in most industries, their workplaces and homes are in two separate locations. With the entrance of large numbers of women into the workforce, family life has both benefited and suffered. There are clear economic benefits to dual-earner families from two paychecks and access to health insurance and benefits, especially if one parent becomes unemployed. However, women's workforce participation has created significant challenges for the care of children and elders. Family care has become a commodity, and a very expensive one at that, and many families cannot afford the price of pre-school child care, afterschool programs, or adult day programs. Families can purchase care from community-based providers, but the quality of these services and the quality of public schools vary greatly, making some communities more desirable places to live than others.

A minority of workers, whose jobs have become mobile owing to information technology, are able to work from home. Although the ranks of those who can work from home have doubled in the last decade, they still represent only 3.3% of the workforce (U.S. Census Bureau, 2000). Some might argue that these families are witnessing a reconvergence of work, home, and community, but this phenomenon is quite different from our perhaps idealized notions of life in the preindustrial era, and working from home for pay dates back to the early period of industrialization (Christensen, 1988). The modern version of doing one's job from home, either full or part time, has both benefits and limitations. On the one hand, it can provide families the flexibility to meet family caregiving demands, making it possible for parents to care for preschool children and be home when children return from school. On the other hand, flexiplace arrangements make it difficult to create a firm boundary between work and home. Workers may feel that no time is exclusively reserved for family and community commitments, and that their days are shaped by continuous multitasking with little distinction between workdays and weekends.

DEFINING WORKPLACE–COMMUNITY CONNECTIONS

In contemporary American society, there are four major dimensions of connection between workplaces and communities—spatial, social, economic, and civic—and many definitions of *community* (Voydanoff, 2001a, 2001b). In this chapter, I use the term *community* to mean a physically bounded space—a neighborhood, city, town or suburb, or residential community. I also consider the concept of community as a shared feeling of social responsibility that can shape institutional policy and practice in ways that benefit the common good. This second type of community is often based on social networks that tie individuals together or connect individuals and institutions together. Thus, significant communities are formed among people who share common needs, goals, or values regardless of their physical location. Parents with children in the same school, congregants in the same faith-based institution, or friends often form complex reciprocal relationships that constitute a critical form of social support and a strong sense of belonging (Fischer, 1982; Wellman & Wortley, 1990).

The spatial dimension is a significant aspect of the workplace-community interface. Every day workers have to get from their homes and residential communities to their workplaces, and this experience affects the length of their workday and the level of daily stress. In 2000, workers reported that commutes take, on average, 25 minutes each way, up from 22 minutes in 1990 (U.S. Census Bureau, 2000). Over the last decade, the proportion of workers using private vehicles has risen, carpooling has declined, and the number of workers using public transit has declined to 4.6%. These trends largely stem from a major spatial realignment of workplaces and communities. In the 1960s and 1970s, suburbs were the communities for people who worked in the city. In the last 30 years, many jobs have moved from downtown areas to suburban "edge cities" (Garreau, 1991), and many homes have moved from inner-ring suburbs to outer-ring suburbs: employers move to save on space costs and families move farther from urban centers to find affordable housing and quality school systems. Despite the fact that suburb-to-suburb commuting has increased, commutes are no shorter. Part of the reason is the increase in rural-to-suburb commuting, and part of it is that suburb-to-suburb commuting may entail working in geographically distant parts of a large metropolitan area (U.S. Department of Transportation, 2003). In any case, if one measures commute time for households, rather than for individual workers, the increase in commute time for dual-earner families is dramatic.

These patterns—often referred to as *urban sprawl* and now *suburban sprawl*—have exacerbated the spatial distance between the workplace and residential communities for many workers, particularly those who live in outer-ring suburbs. Sprawl also increases economic segregation and exacerbates economic inequality (Dreier, Mollenkopf, & Swanstrom, 2001). Poverty remains concentrated in urban areas, where there are few employment opportunities for low-skilled workers (Wilson, 1996). This places at a disadvantage those families that do not have the means to live elsewhere, as well as families that do not have the means to move their homes to leafy suburban communities. The costs to poor families are obvious: lack of access to good jobs, quality health care, quality education, and even adequate stores. The costs to middle-class families are often hidden: long commutes, long work hours, increasing time pressure, and a culture driven by status concerns and consumerism (Schor, 1998).

On the social level, the relationship between employers and employees shapes the key elements of the workplace–community connection. Employers draw workers from multiple communities surrounding their offices and manufacturing plants, and the quality of community institutions, particularly the schools and institutions of higher education, affects the quality of the workforce. In addition, the community-based services and institutions that help working families care for their children and elders form another important connecting link. Without these community-based programs, employers could not rely on a stable workforce that comes to work regularly, and workers could not leave home regularly.

On an economic level, the wages and salaries that workers earn are directly fed into their communities. They patronize local restaurants and stores, pay local child-care workers and other service providers, and pay taxes to support public school systems and maintain the roads and bridges that connect work and home. With the rise of a highly competitive global economy, many have argued that the quality of the employer–employee relationship is changing and not necessarily for the better (Osterman, Kochan, Locke, & Piore, 2001). As the Smith-Corona example shows, some companies treat workers as expendable, which lowers employee loyalty and productivity. When workers cannot depend on their employers for job and income security, not to mention health insurance and pensions, both family and community life can be adversely affected.

On a civic level, workplaces and communities are connected by the involvement of some companies and some employees in building and sustaining community institutions. Many businesses are members of local chapters of the Chamber of Commerce and meet to discuss economic development strategies important to attracting new businesses, retaining established businesses, and creating jobs. Some employers make direct contributions to community services through the United Way or invest in workforce training by giving grants to schools and community colleges. At this point, only a minority of businesses have taken up the cause of community investment as part of their overall business strategy, and this growing trend is often referred to as *corporate citizenship* or *corporate social responsibility* (Reich, 2002). Employees may volunteer time to community programs, such as afterschool programs and homeless shelters, and in this way contribute to community life. A lack of widely available family-friendly policies, however, especially those allowing flexible work schedules and locations, make volunteering difficult for many workers.

In summary, the nature of the connections between workplaces and communities is contradictory. On the one hand, workplaces and communities are highly interdependent: Employers rely on the local labor pool, and communities rely on employers to create jobs for their residents, which in turn creates patrons for community businesses and taxes for community services. Employers and families both need strong educational and caregiving institutions. Schools, preschool child care, afterschool programs, elder-care programs, and other family support organizations are vital to both parties in creating the conditions that allow adults to leave home to earn a living and to spend the majority of their day outside their community of residence.

On the other hand, these connections are becoming fragile. In my view, the threads of connection are becoming increasingly frayed for two key reasons. First, the employer–employee relationship in the 21st-century workplace is being slowly degraded. Workers are no longer guaranteed job and income security simply by virtue of hard work and long service, and guaranteed pensions are fast becoming a relic of a bygone era, witness the Enron debacle. Although good wages and decent benefits have never been accessible to all workers, especially women, minority, and contingent workers, there is a sense today that employers have less control over the wages and benefits they offer because of the pressure to cut costs and stay competitive in a fierce global economy. This climate also negatively affects the extent to which communities can rely on local employers to maintain jobs and other investments they may have made to improve residents' standard of living.

Second, the patterns of economic growth and development in communities are characterized by sprawl and inequality, not integration and equality. This makes it increasingly difficult for working families to find jobs, family support services, and schools in one common place. Sprawl is also creating greater inequality between poor inner-city families and middle-class suburban families, lowering the quality of life for many families and the quality of education and employment opportunities for many children and young adults.

WORKPLACE–COMMUNITY DISRUPTIONS

The workplace–community interface cannot be characterized simply as a series of connections or even frayed connections. There are also major disconnects and disruptions in the relationship between these two domains that are important to understand. One of the main causes of disruption stems from companies downsizing or restructuring their firms to stay in business. This process often results in layoffs. Although one community's loss may be another community's gain, more often than not layoffs represent a harmful break in the relationship between workplaces and communities (Beneria, 1998). When workers involuntarily lose their jobs, they turn to a variety of services in their communities, yet they are no longer in a position to contribute to those communities as consumers or taxpayers. Unemployment has been shown to negatively affect mental and physical health (Leventman, 1981; Rubin, 1976). Job loss can also negatively affect marital and parental relationships when individuals lose the role of wage earner within their family. Unemployment has been shown to harm other social relationships with friends, neighbors, and coworkers, and many experience unemployment as a loss of status in one's community (Pappas, 1989). Although the unemployed may conceivably have more time to volunteer, the task of finding new employment constrains their time.

Another type of disruption stems from the decision of employers to relocate certain employees to offices or manufacturing facilities in other parts of the company—a trend that began in the 1950s and has continued to the present despite some difficulties in moving families with two wage earners. Although this affects a minority of workers each year, the number of families affected over a decade is worthy of note. Although the employee has continuity in their relationship with their employer in terms of pay, benefits, and seniority, they are forced to sever ties with friends and neighbors and build new social ties in their new community. This can cause multiple forms of stress on working families as spouses are forced to quit jobs and find new ones, and children leave their school and friends and try to make new friends and adjust to new schools. Beyond work and school, the family may experience isolation and lack of support as they struggle to put together the services they need—from child care and afterschool programs, to a new pediatrician and dentist, as well as build relationships with other families in their new community.

An additional disruption in the workplace–community interface occurs when a worker becomes seriously ill, takes a leave to care for a seriously ill relative, or takes a leave to care for a newborn or adopted child. If the employee works for a small firm not covered by the Family and Medical Leave Act (FMLA) or if the employee works for a company that has no family-friendly leave policies, he or she may be forced to quit a job to attend to family, causing a permanent disruption between work and community. The impact of taking a leave may be lessened if the employee is covered by existing public policies or the policies of their employer. In both cases, workers rely on their communities for both moral and material support, especially those who are forced to quit their jobs. The adequacy of community-based services to meet the needs of workers on leave for medical or family reasons is a significant issue for both employers and communities.

The spatial distance between the communities where workers live and the places where they work causes several problems for working families that go beyond the issue of long commutes. For example, this distance can complicate family care arrangements. It can make it difficult for working parents to transport children to afterschool programs when there are no local transportation services in their community, and it can make it difficult to take children and elders to doctors' appointments. More important to the quality of community life, the distance makes it difficult for working parents to volunteer in their children's child-care programs and schools and for all workers to volunteer in other community programs. This constraint on volunteerism can impede the ability of community institutions to grow and flourish, and it can affect the overall quality of civil society (Bookman, 2004).

Finally, the deficits that are currently plaguing so many state governments are creating further disruptions between workplaces and communities. State budget cuts are eroding the quality and sometimes existence of community-based support services. The inability of state government to provide adequate funding levels for these community-based services can have negative consequences on business performance, and it can make it difficult for families to shoulder both work and family responsibilities.

REDESIGNING THE WORKPLACE–COMMUNITY INTERFACE

What should the relationship between workplaces and communities look like to bring daily support to working families and enhance their lifelong health and well-being? A persistent assumption in most work-family research is that, to alleviate the conflict between work and family, policies and practices at the workplace must change. This has resulted in several important initiatives, including resource and referral services that help employees locate child care and elder care; flexible work hours and work location; and leave policies that enable workers to care for family members or recover from a serious illness. Although these policies are important, they are frequently, as others in this volume attest, underused, and those who do use them often suffer negative consequences, such as lack of advancement and promotion in their companies. There is still a culture in many workplaces that equates taking time for family with a lack of seriousness and commitment to job and career.

Although it would benefit many families if more employers adopted family-friendly policies, we also need to ask some difficult questions. New workplace policies are necessary to resolving work-family conflict, but are they sufficient? Given the decline in job security in many industries and the importance of community-based services in meeting the needs of working families, I believe we should reconsider whether family-friendly benefits should be delivered exclusively through the workplace. We should ask whether the labor force attachment of an individual worker to a specific company should be the only basis for access to family-friendly policies.

As I argue in my book, *Starting in Our Own Backyards: How Working Families Can Build Community and Survive the New Economy* (2004), we

need to change our approach to solving work-family issues and redesign the
workplace–community interface in three ways:

• First, employers must reach out beyond the walls of the workplace and
into the communities where they are located and into the communities where
their employees live. Employers must invest in the community institutions
their workers rely on for child care, elder care, education, and other forms of
family support. When a company adopts policies that build the capacity of
community services to meet the needs of working families, not only will its
workforce be well served, but its neighbors will also be well served.

• Second, we need multisector strategies to solve work-family problems.
We cannot expect employers to "do it all"; this is unrealistic and unfair
especially for small businesses. We must promote business–community partnerships to address work-family issues, such as the disconnect between work
hours and school hours. When companies partner with schools, faith-based
institutions, public safety officers, and family support professionals, community resources can be leveraged to expand support for working families. In
addition, costs can be shared by all parties in the partnership, and systemic,
rather than piecemeal, solutions can be created.

• Third, community organizations and community planning initiatives
must develop multi-issue agendas that integrate work-family issues with issues such as better public transportation systems, environmental protection,
and affordable housing. They must make quality of life for local residents
an issue for companies that do business in their communities, perhaps even
a condition for doing business. If these organizations can bring businesses
together with community service providers, city planners, and municipal
agencies, the process of designing family-friendly communities can begin to
move forward.

These three ideas are not utopian fantasies. In fact examples exist of
employers and communities that have begun to work together in innovative ways. For example, the American Business Collaboration for Quality
Dependent Care (ABC) has brought together 22 large companies to make
substantial investments in child care in the 65 communities where they
are located. These investments have been used to expand the availability
and quality of preschool care, upgrade the skills of child-care providers, and
build a community-based infrastructure of support that coordinates programs
for young children. By building the capacity of existing community-based
services, these employers serve the needs of their own employees and other
community residents, proving their commitment to being a good neighbor
and enhancing support for all families.

Another important example of business–community collaboration is the
labor-management partnership between the United Auto Workers (UAW)

union and the Ford Motor Company to build Family Service and Learning Centers in the communities where Ford's manufacturing facilities are located. This idea became a reality in the 1999 collective bargaining agreement between Ford and UAW. The two parties agreed to create centers that would provide a comprehensive set of services to working families, such as child care, afterschool programs, activities for teenagers, and classes for adult learners. The centers also organize Ford retirees to volunteer in these community programs so that a variety of programs can be sustained without raising staffing costs to an untenable level. Volunteers have conducted neighborhood clean-up campaigns, clothing and food drives, and mentoring programs for teens. By expanding the resources available to existing community-based programs, rather than creating new ones from scratch, this initiative is building the responsiveness of local institutions to serve their own residents and Ford employees.

Community organizations and urban planners are also creating innovative projects, reaching out to businesses with a new interest in dialogue and a new spirit of cooperation. For example, the Boston Society of Architects (BSA) has recently spearheaded the Civic Initiative for a Livable New England, which has convened business owners, developers, urban planners, government officials, and advocates for family support programs to create a new vision for community life and economic development. This multisector group has examined the problems with current models of economic development and community planning, conducted sessions to create a "regional civic vision," and moved to implement that vision in pilot communities with diverse populations. They have issued a final report to share with others the process of testing ideas for change, addressing resistance and solving problems, all while remaining attuned to the overarching vision of "livable communities" that inspired the initiative.

These are just three examples that illustrate a new relationship between employers and communities. Although each has a limited focus, they are replicable and share certain features that are applicable to many issues, industries, and regions of the United States. They all recognize the assets that exist in residential communities. Communities are not viewed as a drain on private-sector resources, but rather as a source of new resources that can be used to address work-family issues. They also show that by reaching outside the walls of a particular company or community organization, work-family issues can be addressed in a more holistic and comprehensive manner. The American Business Collaborative, for example, integrates and coordinates services for young children that are often fragmented; the UAW/Ford partnership address workers' needs across the life course; and the BSA's Civic Initiative links a wide variety of private, public, and nonprofit organizations around a strategic plan for "smart growth" that looks for common ground among often competing interests.

CONCLUSION

We must bring community from the margins into the center of the work-family conversation. It is my hope that by focusing on community needs and community resources—by exploring both the connections and disruptions between workplaces and communities—we can develop more effective ways to address the work-family issues affecting millions of American families.

Workplaces and communities are both part of a greater "community"—the community that crosses the boundaries between cities and suburbs, between regions and states, the community rearing the next generation of workers, parents, and citizens. Recognizing this larger community is essential to moving family care and family well-being out of private households and into the public domain. This expanded sense of community can be a catalyst for organizing workplaces and designing residential communities in new ways.

As the historical evolution of the relationship among work, family, and community shows, the workplace–community interface is not immutable. It has changed over time, reflecting different economic and social systems. Our current economic system, in which globalization is producing a new level of job insecurity and increasing income inequality, requires us to give greater consideration to the ways in which community institutions can support working families. The current nature of the employer–employee relationship is not durable enough to sustain families through the persistent cycles of restructuring and recession. However, with the scientific and technological advances of postindustrial society, the possible configurations of the workplace–community interface have expanded. We are in an optimal position today, with greater human and material resources than ever before, to redesign this interface in a way that will benefit the health and well-being of families, the effective performance of firms, and the vitality of our communities.

REFERENCES

Beneria, L. (1998). The impact of industrial relocation on displaced workers: A case study of Cortland, NY. *Community Development Reports, 6.*

Bookman, A. (2004). *Starting in our own backyards: How working families can build community and survive the new economy.* New York: Routledge.

Boulay, A. (1996). Malden mills: A study in leadership. *Quality Monitor Newsletter.* Portland, ME: Organizational Productivity Institute.

Briggs, J. (1970). *Never in anger: Portrait of an Eskimo family.* Cambridge, MA: Harvard University Press.

Christensen, K. (1988). *Women and home-based work: The unspoken contract.* New York: Henry Holt and Company.

Dawley, A. (1977). *Class and community: The industrial revolution in Lynn.* Cambridge, MA: Harvard University Press.

Dreier, P., Mollenkopf, J., & Swanstrom, T. (2001). *Place matters: Metropolitics for the twenty-first century.* Lawrence, KS: University Press of Kansas.

Fischer, C. S. (1982). *To dwell among friends: Personal networks in town and city.* Chicago, IL: University of Chicago Press.

Gans, H. (1962). *Urban villagers: Group and class in the life of Italian-Americans.* New York: The Free Press.

Gans, H. (1967). *The levittowners: The ways of life and politics in a new suburban community.* New York: Vintage Books.

Garreau, J. (1991). *Edge city: Life on the new frontier.* New York: Doubleday.

Gregory, S. (1999). *Black corona: Race and politics of place in an urban community.* Princeton, NJ: Princeton University Press.

Haraven, T. (1989). Historical changes in children's and networks in the family and community. In D. Belle (Ed.), *Children's social networks and social supports.* New York: Wiley.

Kessler-Harris, A. (1982). *Out to work: A history of wage earning women in the United States.* New York: Oxford University Press.

Leacock, E. (1981). *Myths of male dominance: Collected articles on women cross-culturally.* New York: Monthly Review Press.

Leventman, P. G. (1981). *Professionals out of work.* New York: The Free Press.

Levine, R. A., & White, M. (1985). Parenthood in social transformation. In J. B. Lancaster, J. Altmann, A. S. Rossi, & L. R. Sherrod (Eds.), *Parenting across the life span: Biosocial dimensions* (pp. 271–295). New York: Aldine DeGruyter.

Lynd, R. S., & Lynd, H. M. (1929). *Middletown: A study in modern American culture.* New York: Harcourt Brace.

Lynd, R. S., & Lynd, H. M. (1937). *Middletown in transition: A study in cultural conflicts.* New York: Harcourt Brace.

Moen, P. (Ed.). (2003). *It's about time: Couples and careers.* Ithaca, NY: Cornell University Press.

Mullings, L., & Klumer, A. W. (2001). *Stress and resilience: The social context of reproduction in central Harlem.* New York: Academic/Plenum.

Myerhoff, B. (1978). *Number our days.* New York: E. P. Dutton.

Osterman, P., Kochan, T., Locke, R. M., & Piore, M. J. (2001). *Working in America: A blueprint for the new labor market.* Cambridge, MA: MIT Press.

Pappas, G. (1989). *The magic city: Unemployment in a working-class community.* Ithaca, NY: Cornell University Press.

Reich, R. B. (2002). *I'll be short: Essentials for a decent working society.* Boston, MA: Beacon.

Rubin, L. (1976). *Worlds of pain.* New York: Basic Books.

Sanjek, R. (1998). *The future of us all: Race and neighborhood politics in New York City.* Ithaca, NY: Cornell University Press.

Schor, J. (1998). *The overspent American.* New York: Basic Books.

Stack, C. (1974). *All our kin: Strategies for survival in a Black community.* New York: Harper & Row.

Susser, I. (1982). *Norman street: Poverty and politics in an urban neighborhood.* New York: Oxford University Press.

U.S. Census Bureau. (2002). *Summary File 3, Journey to Work Characteristics, and DP-3, Profile of Selected Economic Characteristics.* Washington, DC: U.S. Government Printing Office.

U.S. Department of Transportation, Federal Highway Administration. (2003). *Journey to Work Trends in the U.S. and It Major Metropolitan Areas, 1960–2000* (Publication # FHWA EP-03-058). Washington, DC: U.S. Government Printing Office.

Voydanoff, P. (2001a). Conceptualizing community in the context of work and family. *Community, Work and Family, 4,* 133–156.

Voyandoff, P. (2001b). Incorporating community into work-family research: A review of the basic relationships. *Human Relations, 54,* 1609–1637.

Wellman, B., & Wortley, S. (1990). Different strokes for different folks: Community ties and social support. *American Journal of Sociology, 96,* 558–588.

Williams, J. (2000). *Unbending gender: Why family and work conflict and what to do about it.* New York: Oxford University Press.

Wilson, W. J. (1996). *When work disappears: The world of the new urban poor.* New York: Vintage Books.

11

Government Policies
as External Influences
on Work-Family Trade-Offs

Richard Wertheimer
Susan Jekielek
Kristin A. Moore
Zakia Redd
Child Trends

In this chapter, we identify factors in government policies that influence work-family trade-offs and mismatches for working families and identify some circumstances in which mismatches are particularly acute. Our review is based on an ecological model and a life course perspective. We presume that multiple influences affect people, ranging from societal forces to more immediate factors within the family (Bronfenbrenner, 1979). Workforce elements would fall in the middle of a theoretical or causal model, in that work is affected by macro-level social, economic, and cultural factors such as public policies, the economy, and cultural trends, and, in turn, work affects proximal factors such as family processes, which affect the well-being of adults and children. A life course perspective also underlies our discussion (see chapters 15 and 23, this volume). Specifically, we see the influence of work as distinctly different for families that do not yet have children, families with infants or young children, families with older children, and families whose children have grown up and moved out on their own.

We anchor this chapter in several research-based propositions. First, in general, paid work has many aspects that are beneficial. (We use the term *work* to refer to paid work for the sake of brevity, but we recognize that unpaid household and community activities are also work.) Employment provides income, fringe benefits, social resources such as friends and contacts, and a sense of purpose. Second, the implications of work for families are likely to vary across demographic and social groups (Kamerman & Hayes, 1982). Third, a given aspect of work may have positive, neutral, or negative implications, depending on the pathway and the person who is being examined. Finally, some elements of work-family conflict reflect a mismatch between the workplace and the family, but other elements reflect decisions that individuals and families make, and thus represent trade-offs (where optimal outcomes are maximized and negative outcomes are minimized) more than an inherent mismatch (see chapter 13, this volume).

We begin by describing government policies at the federal and state levels that affect the circumstances and rewards of work. We then consider policy-relevant work patterns that may influence children's outcomes, including child-care services and preventive health care practices. Finally, we identify issues that suggest new research topics, data collection needs, and intervention strategies that could be the focus of experimental research studies.

GOVERNMENT POLICIES

Because they provide benefits and regulate the terms of work, government programs and regulations have a substantial effect on how workplace requirements affect families. Governments regulate hours and wages, provide insurance coverage for certain work-related risks, and provide supports for persons who work. Governments also use tax subsidies to encourage employers to provide benefits not mandated by government, such as sick leave, health and disability insurance, life insurance, and pensions. This chapter summarizes some of the most important programs in the United States.

Government regulations on wages and hours impact a vast swath of employees. Passed by Congress in 1938, the Fair Labor Standards Act (FLSA) regulates the wages of more than 80 million workers who are paid by the hour, referred to as *nonexempt employees*. FLSA imposes a minimum wage of $5.15 per hour and mandates that workers receive 1½ times their regular hourly wage if they work more than 40 hours per week (U.S. Department of Labor, 2003).

Policies also impact other aspects of workplace relations. One key attempt to help families balance the demands of the workplace with the demands of family is the Family and Medical Leave Act (FMLA; Cantor et al., 2002). This federal law provides up to 12 weeks of unpaid, job-protected leave, with continued group health insurance benefits to eligible employees of covered employers for a set of family and medical reasons. Covered employers include public agencies and private firms with at least 50 employees. To be eligible, an employee must have worked for at least 12 months; worked at least 1,250 hours prior to the start of FMLA leave; and worked at a site with at least 50 employees onsite or within 75 miles of the work site. Benefits include up to 12 weeks of unpaid leave for the birth and care of a newborn child; placement and care of an adopted or foster child; care of a spouse, child, or parent with a serious health condition; and an employee's own serious health condition that prevents work. Also, a covered employer must maintain the employee's group health insurance (including family coverage).

Although the FMLA directly affects only a small percentage of all employees (only 12% of all establishments are covered by FMLA), more than one third of establishments not covered by FMLA offer full FMLA benefits, and most provide at least partial benefits. More than one half of employees taking leave for reasons covered under FMLA did so because of their own health problems. In addition, about 31% took leave to care for a seriously ill relative, and 26% took leave because of a maternity disability or to care for a newborn or an adopted or foster child.

Other government programs come into play when a health change negatively affects a worker's ability to perform physically or mentally in the workplace. As explored elsewhere in this volume (see chapters 26 and 31), becoming injured or disabled can temporarily or permanently reduce a worker's ability to make a living and provide for a family. Although Social Security is best known as a retirement program, it also provides benefits to families when a covered worker dies or becomes disabled. In 2001, more than 5 million children under age 18 received income from Social Security, about one third of whom were children in poor and near-poor families (i.e., those living at less than 125% of the official poverty threshold). African-American children are more likely than white children to receive Social Security because African Americans are more likely to die or become disabled, with dependent children for whom they are financially responsible. According to data from the 1996–1997 Survey of Income and Program Participation, for all children receiving Social Security benefits, the average amount received was more than $13,000, which amounted to 39% of family income. Additionally, Supplemental Security Income (SSI) is available to low-income families with a disabled worker or child. Disabled workers receive benefits if they are ineligible for Social Security or eligible for only low benefits. Disabled children are also eligible for benefits.

State governments also provide benefits. Workers' compensation is a set of state-level programs that provide monetary compensation for workers who are injured or disabled while at work. Programs typically provide partial reimbursement of an employee's salary (often two thirds) while an employee is recovering from a work-related disability or injury.

Unemployment Insurance (UI) is a social insurance program that provides cash payments to individuals with work experience who become unemployed involuntarily and who are actively seeking work. Although eligibility provisions vary by state, workers typically must have been "substantially attached" to the labor market, must have left their job involuntarily or quit for "good cause" (e.g., related to adverse conditions at work or in the relationship with the employer), and must be currently able and available for full-time work. Because of these requirements, low-wage unemployed workers are only half as likely as high-wage workers to receive UI, even though low-wage workers are twice as likely to be unemployed as high-wage workers. Employers pay the cost of UI benefits through a payroll tax applied to at least the first $7,000 of each employee's earnings. Tax rates vary by state and also by employer, depending on the employer's "experience rating"—that is, the amount of UI benefits collected by the firm's employees (U.S. General Accounting Office, 2000).

Several federally supported programs are not targeted directly at the relationship between workers and their workplaces but provide cash or other assistance to working parents, among other eligibles. Temporary Assistance for Needy Families (TANF), the successor program to Aid to Families with Dependent Children (AFDC), colloquially known as "welfare," has work requirements. The Earned Income Tax Credit (EITC) encourages work by effectively providing a wage subsidy to low-income working individuals and families. As of 2003, 17 states had also enacted their own EITC programs (Johnson, Llobrera, & Zahradnik, 2003).

Child-care subsidies, such as the Child Care and Development Fund (CCDF) and the TANF block grant, which are mostly federally funded, also provide family support, encourage work, and facilitate meeting the demands of work and family by covering work-related expenses. CCDF provided $4.8 billion to States, Territories, and Tribes in fiscal year 2004. The program, authorized as part of the 1996 welfare reform legislation, assists low-income families, families either receiving TANF benefits or transitioning from TANF by subsidizing child care so they can work or attend training. Subsidized child-care services are provided in the form of vouchers or contracts with child care providers (Administration for Children and Families, 2004). Food Stamps, Medicaid, and the State Child Health Insurance Program (SCHIP) provide noncash government benefits to low-income working families. By increasing family resources, these programs support families financially without reducing parental time at home.

Work Patterns, Child Well-Being and Government Policy: Contemporary Considerations

In this section, we focus on recent research on employment and child well-being and related government policies. We organize our discussion of these areas by the life course of childhood.

While the vast research on parental employment and child well-being does not find that parental employment is uniformly detrimental for children, one exception may be extensive maternal employment when children are very young (see summary by Zaslow et al., chap. 18, this volume). Further supporting this concern, research indicates that early maternal employment may limit the extent to which mothers breastfeed their infants, a practice which is important for the numerous health benefits that it provides to infants (U.S. Department of Health and Human Services, 2000). Specifically, longer maternity leaves are associated with longer periods of breastfeeding (Kurinij, Shiono, Ezrine, & Rhoads, 1989); part-time workers breastfeed to later ages than do full-time workers (Lindberg, 1996); and maternal hours per week are directly related to the number of breastfeedings per day (Roe, Whittington, & Fein, 1999). A potential resource for families with infants is the ability to make use of the FMLA. At the same time, however, it appears that many people who could benefit from FMLA aren't able to use this resource. Inability to afford the loss of income is the most common reason why eligible workers do not use FMLA.

Suggested revisions to PRWORA, which is up for reauthorization, should also be noted. The administration's proposal requires increasing participation in work-related activities to 40 hours per week for families receiving welfare. As with current law, states could exclude parents with children under 12 months of age from this participation rate calculation, if they choose. These decisions about parental work hours may have important implications for infant well-being.

Research on late infancy and the toddler years has generally focused on non-maternal child care. Although the effect sizes appear to be modest, the quality of child care is significantly associated with children's outcomes. Important aspects of care include the level of cognitive stimulation in the interactions between staff and children (NICHD Early Child Care Research Network, 2000) and the stability of child care. Experimental studies of high-quality early childhood programs have demonstrated positive cognitive and developmental impacts for children from disadvantaged backgrounds (Barnett, 1995; Campbell, Ramey, Pungello, Sparling, & Johnson, 2002; Peisner-Feinberg et al., 2001). Some job characteristics, particularly those attributed to low-wage work, make it more difficult for parents to find stable or quality care. For instance, mothers whose work hours vary are more likely to use multiple care arrangements (Folk & Yi, 1994); formal child care is rarely available for parents who work evenings, nights, or non-fixed schedules; and stable care has higher costs and is linked with higher maternal wages (Blau & Robins, 1998). Childcare subsidies have the potential to be helpful here, although childcare subsidies tend to be used for regulation-exempt care, including family and friends, and very little is known about the quality of care that children receive in these settings (Halle & Lavelle, 2004).

The needs for parental care and direct supervision change as children grow older. Work schedules do not completely overlap with school day schedules, and children typically are not enrolled in school during summer. Elementary-school-age children in families with two working parents or a single working parent are more likely to regularly be left to care for themselves for some part of the day than children in single-earner families (Smith, 2002). Particularly at risk of negative social, academic and health outcomes when in self-care are young school-age children (Belle, 1999; Kerrebrock & Lewitt, 1999), and children who live in disadvantaged or dangerous neighborhoods (National Research Council 2003). However, PRWORA legislation requires states to offer assistance to single, custodial parents who cannot obtain childcare for their children under age 6, but not necessarily for older children. Studies of families receiving welfare have found only limited evidence that employment mandates tied to cash assistance are associated with poor outcomes for children or for the mother (Zaslow, Moore, Tout, Scarpa, & Vandivere, 2002), although one recent study found that children's behavior problems worsened when low-income single mothers exit employment (Chase-Lansdale et al., 2003).

Research has also documented that child care centers that offer care before and after work vary widely in quality, and quality has been linked to children's outcomes at these ages (Belle, 1999; Rosenthal & Vandell, 1996). However, few rigorous studies have examined the effects of afterschool programs on children's outcomes, and more and higher quality research is needed to better understand the effects of program attendance on children's outcomes (Scott-Little, Hamann, & Jurs, 2002).

ISSUES FOR ADDITIONAL RESEARCH

After decades of research, there is still limited evidence about few clear causal effects of government policies and parents' employment on children's outcomes, net of the income it provides. Subgroups of parents who are already the focus of government policy in other areas may provide particularly interesting populations in which to look for influences of government policies directly related to the worker–workplace relationship. Although minimal research has been conducted with some potentially important subgroups—such as parents with disabled children and disabled parents—research on other subgroups has identified several factors connected to government policies that may be important moderators.

Despite substantial research on the preventive health practice of breast-feeding, important gaps remain in describing employment patterns for parents of infants and in examining the implications of these patterns for other preventive health care issues. Detailed studies of the timing of return to work after childbirth are needed. Given variation in state welfare reform laws, it would be possible to examine this issue among low-income mothers in a quasi-experimental study comparing differences across states under different program rules.

The implications of work have often been studied by comparing no employment or part-time employment with full-time employment. The lack of definitive differences across studies may reflect the possibility that part-time or no work versus full-time are not the contrasts that are important; what might truly matter is long work hours. Further work is needed to explore the implications of overtime work at a single job, particularly ongoing employment at very long hours, such as 50, 60, 70, or more hours of work each week. Although these work weeks characterize the traditional work patterns of many professional men, they may increasingly characterize the work life of professional women as well. In addition, because individuals often marry individuals who are similar to them, men and women who work long hours are likely to be paired, and the implications of this pattern for their relationship and for their parenting deserve study. Although, as noted earlier, the Fair Labor Standards Act regulates hours worked and requires pay at overtime rates for hours over 40 hours per week, these restrictions do not generally apply to the managers and professionals described here. France has restricted hours worked per week for salaried professionals and managers as well as hourly employees.

Long hours, possibly involving two or more jobs, are often required for low-wage workers to make ends meet. Indeed, single mothers seeking to leave or stay off welfare may find that they need to work very long hours to support their family. In particular, long hours in a low-wage job, perhaps with a long and difficult commute, may be a serious work-family mismatch (see chapter 31, this volume).

The current system of unemployment insurance is criticized by some for discouraging a rapid return to work and by others for not providing adequate benefits for low-wage workers and those seeking to work on a part-time basis. Using the welfare waivers experiments of the 1990s as a model, experimental research could be conducted in volunteering states to explore alternatives to the current system, including (a) individual unemployment insurance accounts with mandatory contributions by workers and owned by workers (analogous to 401-K accounts) and (b) eligibility for benefits for workers seeking part-time work.

The circumstances of employment and their connection to the health of adults and children would benefit from multidisciplinary study. As noted previously, an important area of concern is whether maternal employment restricts or facilitates access to preventive health care for children. More research is needed on how breastfeeding and other preventive health practices influence the relationship between maternal employment and children's outcomes. For example, type of employment before and during pregnancy and while breastfeeding has not been widely studied in large, representative samples. Another important area is how policy restricts or facilitates access to quality non-maternal child care. An important and understudied issue is that of the time and stress of commuting. A topic that may be related to commuting is that of residence. Persons who live in rural areas, small towns, medium-sized cities, and large cities experience very different environments and labor markets, yet place has not been systematically examined in studies of workforce issues. Environmental health researchers have examined the effects of specific toxins carried back to the home, but issues such as chemical exposure, hours of work, stress, parent health, and preventive health behaviors should be examined longitudinally and in interaction.

Finally, studies that examine elements of the workplace, including studies that experimentally vary workplace characteristics, are in short supply. Studies have identified a number of aspects of work that are associated with greater satisfaction and more positive outcomes, such as having more complex work and having greater autonomy on the job. Identifying ways to provide these positive elements in the workplace and then evaluating their implications for adults and for children might provide additional evidence for informing employment policies. It is interesting that, while mothers receiving welfare have been randomly assigned to work, working persons more generally have not been involved in random assignment studies that examine the implications of hours, schedules, job sharing, and shift work for their families and for themselves.

ACKNOWLEDGMENTS

The authors would like to acknowledge Sharon McGroder for her helpful input in the conceptualization and review of this chapter.

REFERENCES

Administration for Children and Families (2004). Child care and development fund. Child care bureau. Available on-line: http://www.acf.hhs.gov/programs/ccb/geninfo/ccdfdesc.htm.

Barnett, S. W. (1995). Long-term effects of early childhood programs on cognitive and school outcomes. *The Future of Children, 5*, 25–50.

Belle, D. (1999). *The after-school lives of children: Alone and with others while parents work.* Mahwah, NJ: Lawrence Erlbaum Associates.

Blau, D. M., & Robins, P. K. (1998). A dynamic analysis of turnover in employment and child care. *Demography, 35*, 83–96.

Bronfenbrenner, U. (1979). *The ecology of human development.* Cambridge, MA: Harvard University Press.

Campbell, F. A., Ramey, C. T., Pungello, E., Sparling, J., & Johnson, S. (2002). Early childhood education: Young adult outcomes from the Abecedarian Project. *Applied Developmental Science, 6*, 42–57.

Cantor, D., Waldfogel, J., Kerwin, J., McKinley-Wright, M., Levin, K., Rauch, J., Haggerty, T., & Stapleton-Kudela, M. (2002). *Balancing the needs of families and employers: Family and medical leave surveys.* Rockville, MD: Westat.

Chase-Lansdale, P. L., Moffitt, R. A., Lohman, B. J., Cherlin, A. J., Coley, R. L., Pittman, L. D., Roff, J., & Votruba-Drzal, E. (2003). Mothers' transitions from welfare to work and the well-being of preschoolers and adolescents. *Science, 299,* 1548–1552.

Folk, K. F., & Yi, Y. (1994). Piecing together child care with multiple arrangements: Crazy quilt or preferred pattern for employed parents of preschool children. *Journal of Marriage and Family, 56,* 669–680.

Halle, T., & Lavelle, B. (2004). Child care policies and practices: A review and synthesis of the reports of child care bureau funded studies. (Working paper.) Washington, DC: Child Trends.

Johnson, N., Llobrera, J., & Zahradnik, B. (2003). *A hand up: How state Earned Income Tax Credits help working families escape poverty in 2003.* Washington, DC: Center on Budget and Policy Priorities.

Kamerman, S. B., & Hayes, C. D. (Eds.). (1982). *Families that work: Children in a changing world.* Washington, DC: National Academy Press.

Kerrebrock, N., & Lewitt, E. M. (1999). Children in self care. *The Future of Children, 9,* 151–159.

Kurinij, N., Shiono, P. H., Ezrine, S. F., & Rhoads, G. G. (1989). Does maternal employment affect breast-feeding? *American Journal of Public Health, 79,* 1247–1250.

Lindberg, L. D. (1996). Women's decisions about breast-feeding and maternal employment. *Journal of Marriage and the Family, 58,* 239–251.

National Research Council. (2003). *Working families: Caring for children and adolescents.* Washington, DC: The National Academies Press.

NICHD Early Child Care Research Network. (2000). The relation of child care to cognitive and language development. *Child Development, 71,* 960–980.

Noble, S., & The Avon Longitudinal Study of Parents And Children Study Team. (2001). Maternal employment and the initiation of breast-feeding. *Acta Paediatrics,* 423–428.

Peisner-Feinberg, E. S., Burchinal, M. R., Clifford, R. M., Culkin, M. L., Howes, C., Kagan, S. L., & Yazejian, N. (2001). The relation of preschool child-care quality to children's cognitive and social developmental trajectories through second grade. *Child Development, 72,* 1534–1554.

Roe, B., Whittington, L., & Fein, S. B. (1999). Is there competition between breast-feeding and maternal employment? *Demography, 36,* 157–171.

Rosenthal, R., & Vandell, D. L. (1996). Quality of care at school-aged child-care programs: Regulatable features, observed experiences, child perspectives, and parent perspectives. *Child Development, 67,* 2434–2445.

Scott-Little, C., Hamann, M. S., & Jurs, S. G. (2002). Evaluations of after-school programs: A meta-analysis of methodologies and narrative synthesis of findings. *American Journal of Evaluation, 23,* 387–419.

Smith, K. (2002). *Who's minding the kids? Child care arrangements: Spring 1997.* Census Population Report No. P70–86. U.S. Department of Commerce, U.S. Census Bureau.

U.S. Department of Health and Human Services. (2000). *HHS Blueprint for Action on Breast-feeding.* Available on-line: http://www.cdc.gov/breastfeeding/00binaries/bluprntbk2.pdf.

U.S. Department of Labor. (2003). *Compliance assistance—Fair Labor Standards Act (FLSA).* Available on-line: http://www.dol.gov/esa/whd/flsa/.

Zaslow, M., Moore, K. A., Tout, K., Scarpa, J. P., & Vandivere, S. (2002). How are children faring under welfare reform? In A. Weil & K. Finegold (Eds.), *Welfare reform: The next act* (pp. 79–101). Washington, DC: The Urban Institute Press.

PART III

Disciplinary Perspectives in the Study of Work and Family

12

Psychological Perspectives on the Work-Family Interface

Debra A. Major
Old Dominion University

Jeanette N. Cleveland
Pennsylvania State University

Psychology is a discipline that is inherently multidisciplinary. Broadly defined as the scientific study of behavior and mental processes, psychology includes numerous subfields that differ markedly in terms of the specific behaviors and levels of analysis that are of interest. Our review focuses on those areas of psychology that investigate the experience or effects of the work-family interface—specifically the subfields of developmental, social, clinical, and industrial-organizational psychology. Despite varied outcomes of interest, these branches of psychology share a focus on the individual. Even when broader social systems (e.g., families or workplaces) are considered, the central interest in psychological research is understanding the individual embedded in that system. Psychology examines the behavior and attitudes of individuals embedded in both the work and family contexts, as well as the effects of spillover, integration, and synergy among the work and family domains.

FUNDAMENTAL PSYCHOLOGICAL PERSPECTIVES

Given that psychology is such a diverse discipline, there are no overarching theories of human attitudes and behavior that span subfields. Instead there are major psychological perspectives that cut across the subdisciplines of psychology—namely, the biological, cognitive, developmental, and social perspectives. The biological perspective focuses on basic physiological processes, especially those of the central and peripheral nervous systems. Research that examines the effects of work-family conflict on physical and mental health outcomes, such as depression and stress, emphasize the biological perspective (e.g., Frone, 2000; Frone, Russell, & Barnes, 1996; Frone, Russell, & Cooper, 1997). The cognitive perspective concentrates on information processing and higher order mental processes, especially those related to memory, learning, and reasoning. Research examining the roots of stereotypes encountered by women at home and in the workplace (e.g., Deaux, Winton, Crowley, & Lewis, 1985; Heilman, 1983) is an example of how the cognitive perspective is employed to understand aspects of the work-family interface. The developmental perspective emphasizes age-related physical, intellectual, and social changes that occur across the lifespan. Research that studies the effect of parents' work lives on children's adjustment (e.g., Crouter & Bumpus, 2001; Crouter, Bumpus, Head, & McHale, 2001; Crouter, Bumpus, Maguire, McHale, 1999; Harrison & Ungerer, 2002) and research that considers caregiving responsibilities across the lifespan (e.g., Barling, MacEwen, Kelloway, & Higginbottom, 1994; Hepburn & Barling, 1996) illustrate the developmental perspective. The social perspective focuses on ways in which individuals think about, influence, and relate to others. The influence of employment or family roles and relationships on the work-family interface is an example of the social perspective (e.g., Barnett, Brennan, & Marshall, 1994; Barnett, Brennan, Raudenbush, & Marshall, 1994; Bernas & Major, 2000; Gareis & Barnett, 2002).

SUBFIELDS OF PSYCHOLOGY THAT EXAMINE THE WORK-FAMILY INTERFACE

The major theoretical perspectives described earlier cut across subfields of psychology. Although psychology has many specialties, the most active subfields in the work-family interface include developmental, social, clinical, and industrial-organizational. We review the types of work-family outcomes most commonly studied in each of these subdisciplines.

Developmental Psychology

The developmental subdiscipline of psychology melds all four theoretical perspectives of psychology, relying most heavily on developmental, cognitive, and social. In terms of work-family research, this subfield shares interests with child development, social work, sociology, and many other disciplines interested in the well-being of children and families (e.g., education and public policy). Developmental work-family research is notably sensitive to demographic and social context factors such as age, race, gender, and socioeconomic status (SES).

In terms of children's outcomes, developmental stage is always a consideration. The primary developmental stages are, roughly, infancy, preschool to early childhood, school age, and adolescence. Generally, researchers are interested in both social and cognitive development across the child's entire developmental spectrum, but certain outcomes tend to be tied to particular stages. In terms of cognitive development, language development is a key issue in infancy. Reading readiness and kindergarten preparedness are important for early childhood, while academic achievement is important for school-age children and adolescents. Socioemotional development is important in each stage, but how it is manifested differs. For instance, attachment is important in infancy, friendship and play are relevant in early childhood, peer relationships are a focus for school-age children, and at-risk behaviors are a key focus for adolescents. Children's relationships with their parents are meaningful across the developmental spectrum.

As noted, work-family research influenced by developmental psychology focuses largely on links between parental employment and children's outcomes. The potentially negative effect of mothers' employment on children's development is the oldest research topic, spanning 50 years (see Gottfried, Gottfried, & Bathurst, 2002; Hoffman & Youngblade, 1999, for reviews). This issue is emotionally and politically charged and is still open to considerable debate given that some research has found no relation between maternal employment and children's developmental outcomes (e.g., Armistead, Wierson, & Forehand, 1990; Gottfried, Bathurst, & Gottfried, 1994), some studies report positive effects (e.g., Harrison & Ungerer, 2002; Vandell & Ramanan, 1992), and other work shows some negative effects under certain conditions (e.g., Baydar & Brooks-Gunn, 1991; Brooks-Gunn, Han, & Waldfogel, 2002; Han, Waldfogel, & Brooks-Gunn, 2001; Harvey, 1999; Hoffman & Youngblade, 1999). A tentative conclusion of the research is that when mothers engage in paid employment early in a child's life (i.e., before 9 months) and work more than 30 hours per week, children's cognitive and social development (e.g., school readiness, vocabulary, compliance) may be negatively affected, and some of these effects may persist into school-age years. Even this tentative conclusion, however, is subject to several qualifiers, including factors such as the child's gender and ethnicity, quality of child care, quality of the home environment, maternal sensitivity, and the family's SES (Brooks-Gunn et al., 2002; Han et al., 2001; Hoffman & Youngblade, 1999).

The developmental research lens extends beyond the effects of maternal employment into the effect of fathers' and dual earners' employment on children. Some of the best work-family research in the developmental arena is characterized by a richness not apparent in simple direct links between parental employment and children's outcomes. Instead developmental psychologists currently ask how the nature of work experiences might influence parents' well-being and the quality of parenting they deliver, with ultimate effects on children's development (e.g., Greenberger, O'Neil, & Nagel, 1994; Moorehouse, 1991; Perry-Jenkins & Gillman, 2000; Perry-Jenkins, Repetti, & Crouter, 2000). For example, one important body of research examines how work pressures and stressors influence parents' interactions with their children and children's outcomes (Crouter & Bumpus, 2001; Crouter, Bumpus et al., 1999; Crouter et al., 2001; Galambos, Sears, Almeida, & Kolaric, 1995; MacDermid & Williams, 1997; Repetti, 1994; Repetti & Wood, 1997). In general, these studies show that when work stressors result in feelings of overload for parents, their parenting is less effective, which in turn negatively affects the psychological adjustment and behavior of adolescents and younger children.

A related line of research examines the consequences of parental employment on supervision and monitoring (i.e., knowledge of children's activities and whereabouts) and, at least to some extent, on children's outcomes (Crouter, Helms-Erickson, et al., 1999; Crouter & McHale, 1993; Muller, 1995). This body of work is noteworthy both because it is another example of the complex and multiple links between parental employment and child outcomes and because it illustrates the importance of considering family context. For instance, Crouter, Helms-Erickson, and colleagues (1999) found that a mother's monitoring could not be predicted by her work hours, but that fathers were more knowledgeable about children when mothers worked longer hours. Moreover, a variety of family and child demographic variables had a stronger relationship to monitoring than hours worked.

Although much developmental work-family research focuses on children's outcomes, some also considers adult well-being, an interest developmental psychology shares with the other three subdisciplines of psychology reviewed here (i.e., social, clinical, and industrial-organizational). This type of developmental research examines the effects of work and family role attitudes and behaviors on psychological well-being (Klute, Crouter, Sayer, & McHale, 2001; O'Neil & Greenberger, 1994; Perry-Jenkins, Seery, & Crouter, 1992). For adults, well-being is manifested in a variety of ways, including marital, parental, and job satisfaction; stress; and numerous health-related outcomes (Galambos & Maggs, 1990; Perry-Jenkins & Crouter, 1990; Repetti, 1998).

Social Psychology

Social psychology is the subfield devoted to the study of individuals' thoughts, feelings, and behaviors in social situations, including the real or imagined presences of others (Allport, 1985). It is concerned with how individuals are influenced by their interpretation of their social environment. The field is grounded within the social and cognitive perspectives and increasingly includes both the biological and developmental perspectives.

Social psychology is not context specific, although it does examine individual-level behavior within social contexts. Therefore, it offers varied and rich contributions to understanding work and family issues (Crosby & Jaskar, 1993; Crosby & Sabattini, in press; Major, 1993, 1994). At least three research areas within social psychology have enhanced our understanding of the work-family interface: (a) attitudes, roles, and stereotyping; (b) power and social influence; and (c) group and cultural interactions.

Attitudes, Roles, and Stereotyping. Social psychology has a long history of research on attitude formation and stereotype processes (Brown, 1995; Fiske, 1998). Numerous social psychologists have articulated theories of discrimination, linking stereotyping, prejudicial attitudes, and discriminatory behaviors toward women (Deaux et al., 1985; Fiske, Cuddy, Glick, & Xu, 2002; Heilman, 1983; Major, 1994). Theoretical and empirical work has shown that stereotypes are an important way that individuals evaluate the behaviors of men and women at work and how women and men evaluate themselves. This research helps explain why women encounter more negative experiences at work and why the tasks women perform within the family are often less valued (Crosby & Sabattini, in press).

Fiske and colleagues (2002) showed that not all stereotypes are alike, and that it is important to understand the sources or origins of stereotype content. Their work demonstrates that two dimensions, warmth and competence, can explain stereotypes' content. The different combinations of stereotypic warmth and competence yield unique group emotion or prejudices aimed at various groups in society. For example, pity is associated with warm but incompetent subordinates, envy is associated with competent but not warm competitors, and contempt is saved for the outside groups seen as neither warm nor competent. Both Fiske's (see Fiske, 1998; Fiske et al., 2002) and Deaux's (see Deaux et al., 1985) work on stereotype content have been important in understanding the perception and value given to the role of caregiver within the family and work contexts.

Power and Social Influence. Social psychology has contributed extensively to our understanding of bases of personal power (French & Raven, 1959; Vescio, Snyder, & Butz, 2003) and the use of power in work settings.

Our understanding of gender variations in perceptions of effective leaders has been informed by work conducted by social psychologists in lab settings and by industrial-organizational psychologists in more applied settings. Although much social psychological theory and research has been applied to the work domain, Crosby and Sabattini (in press) recently discussed the division of family work within social psychological frameworks. Stereotypes and discrimination faced by women at work also affect what occurs within the family realm. Women's limited access to good jobs can increase their financial dependence on husbands and decrease their sense of entitlement or deservedness in family work. Lower opportunity for earnings can justify a division of labor at home that hampers women's financial and emotional independence (Steil, 1997).

Research in this area (e.g., Crosby & Jaskar, 1993; Steil, 1997) has shown that women often find themselves in the role of wanting to change the current situation, whereas men defend the status quo (Kluwer, Heesink, & Van de Vliert, 2000). In marital conflicts over the division of labor, husbands typically hold more power than wives. Wives may attempt to discuss the situation, but husbands retain a privileged power by avoiding such discussions and by stalling or blocking change by agreeing to participate in domestic labor but then forgetting to complete tasks or doing them incorrectly (Kluwer et al., 2000; Sagrestano, Christensen, & Heavey, 1998). Husbands do more domestic labor only when both they and their wives hold nontraditional beliefs about gender and marital roles (Greenstein, 1996).

Group and Cultural Interactions. Social psychologists have examined whether sources of conflict and work conditions have the same effects on both genders, across ethnic groups, and across various family structures (i.e., single- and two-parent families). In one example, Hegtvedt, Clay-Warner, and Ferrigno (2003) used a self-interest argument to examine backlash over the inequities that work-family policies may produce in the workplace. Specifically, they examined how self-interest (defined by parenthood and gender) affected resentment from inequitable benefit plans and workloads and how the context (i.e., supportive workplace, procedural justice) and liberal gender-role attitudes mitigated feelings of resentment. Although there was no evidence that parents were less resentful than nonparents, a supportive workplace consistently mitigated resentment levels. Resentment regarding extra work also depended on a worker's gender and gender-role attitudes.

Finally, social psychologists have examined work-family conflict among dual earners across various occupations within the United States and in other cultures (Izraeli, 1993). For example, among dual-career couples in Israel, stereotypical gender-role attitudes increased conflict for women but lessened conflict for men. Time spent in family work on weekends and being troubled about work performance had a greater effect on conflict for men than for women. Findings suggest that men and women who have similar occupational status and work in similar workplaces have similar sources of work-family conflict.

Clinical Psychology

Clinical psychology focuses on the assessment, treatment, and understanding of psychological and behavioral problems and disorders. Clinical psychologists use the principles of psychology to better understand, predict, and alleviate the relational, emotional, and physical troubles that people experience over the life course (Plante, 1999). This psychological subdiscipline offers an integrative and holistic approach to addressing human problems that considers biological, cognitive, and psychosocial factors.

Although *health psychology* could be legitimately labeled a subfield of psychology in its own right, it also fits nicely under the broader umbrella of *clinical psychology*. Health psychology has been instrumental in identifying correlates and causes of illness and dysfunction, particularly within the family, but increasingly in the workplace. One important research area focuses on health attitudes and behaviors, including substance abuse and work and family issues. Frone and colleagues (Frone, 2000; Frone, Barnes, & Farrell, 1994; Frone, Russell, & Cooper, 1991, 1993, 1997) have tested theoretical models that connect work-family conflict to heavy alcohol use, cigarette use, depression, and somatic symptoms among employed parents.

Research in health psychology has classified stressors that can cause illness, including major stressful life events, daily hassles, and chronic stresses (Taylor, 1999). Work and family interactions provide multiple sources of potential stressors that influence outcomes such as depression, anxiety, burnout, and role overload. Considerable research has been devoted to understanding the ways in which people attempt to manage or master stressful events (Lazarus & Folkman, 1984). Researchers have identified several coping strategies and their relative success in terms of physical, psychological, and behavioral outcomes (Taylor, 1999).

Beyond the broad category of health outcomes, clinical psychology can be divided into child and adult concentrations. Within the last 20 years, child clinical psychology has integrated developmental and clinical models to investigate the normal and pathological development of children. Increasing attention is being given to the role of the family as the primary context for children's development and pathology (Crnic & Harris, 1990). A critical family issue is the equality of the marital relationship. Marital dissatisfaction or disharmony can have implications for infants and young children. Major and minor stresses within the family, including work-family conflict, are important predictors of constructive child development. Often these stresses are believed to be indirectly mediated through the family or parenting system, rather than directly impinging on the child. Yet such stress has an adverse effect on parental attitudes and satisfaction, parent–child interaction behavior, and children's cognitive and behavioral development (Crnic & Greenberg, 1990).

Adult clinical psychology has focused extensively on the effects of maintaining multiple work and family roles on stress and well-being. Although some research has shown that the demands of multiple roles heighten stress and undermine well-being (e.g., O'Neil & Greenberger, 1994), most research demonstrates that having multiple roles per se is not detrimental. Further, even when one is affected negatively by multiple roles, there also tend to be numerous benefits. For example, Burden (1986) showed that working parents, particularly single mothers, are at risk for job-family role strain and threats to well-being. Despite this, single parents exhibited high levels of job satisfaction. Schwartzberg and Dytell (1996) found that in dual-earner families, both parents derived self-esteem from their accomplishments at work rather than accomplishments at home, whereas their emotional state of happiness or depression stemmed from their relationships within the family. On the one hand, the study found no support for the idea that men's sense of well-being is defined by their work experiences, whereas women's is defined by their experiences within the family. On the other hand, family stressors that result in depression were different for mothers and fathers; dual-earner fathers' depression arose from lack of spousal support or family role insignificance, whereas dual-earner mothers were sensitive to a lack of task sharing. These findings are consistent with previous studies indicating that working fathers seem more attuned to their emotional relationships with their spouses, whereas working mothers seem more attuned to the amount of actual assistance they receive around the house.

Current trends in clinical psychology emphasize the expansionist theory of multiple roles (Barnett & Hyde, 2001). This theory contends that multiple roles are generally beneficial for both women and men, and that several processes and contextual parameters contribute to these beneficial effects. On the one hand, role rewards associated with high-quality roles have positive implications for psychological well-being. On the other hand, multiple burdensome roles may have detrimental effects on well-being. In these respects, psychological gender differences are not large or immutable. Research also shows that the number of kin one helps is associated with depression for both women and men (Gerstel & Gallagher, 1993). The interference of such aid with both paid work and household obligations explains, in part, the relation between kin care and distress.

Research also suggests that role quality is better conceived of as an individual perception, rather than an objective characteristic of the role. For example, Barnett and colleagues demonstrated that long work hours per se are not predictive of psychological distress. Instead perceptual factors such as schedule fit, working one's preferred schedule, tasks with high-schedule control, and perceiving trade-offs as manageable are better predictors of distress (Barnett & Gareis, 2000; Barnett, Gareis, & Brennan, 1999; Barnett & Shen, 1997; Gareis & Barnett, 2002).

Industrial-Organizational Psychology

Industrial-organizational psychology studies human behavior and attitudes in the workplace. Theoretical paradigms draw most heavily from the social perspective, but biological, developmental, and cognitive perspectives are used as well. This branch of psychology is closely allied with the management disciplines, organizational behavior, and human resource management, and in terms of the work-family interface, these disciplines pursue similar and often indistinguishable topics (see Eby, Casper, Lockwood, Bordeaux, & Brinley, 2005).

The work side of the work-family interface has been more central in this branch of research. Research in this subfield also emphasizes the experiences of managers and professionals more so than other types of workers. In addition, the focus is typically the employee, and it is this individual's outcomes that are of particular interest, although a few studies examine outcomes for employed couples (e.g., Hammer, Allen, & Grigsby, 1997; Hammer, Bauer, & Grandey, 2003).

Over the past 25 years, the conflict perspective has dominated industrial-organizational psychology, with much of the research being influenced by Greenhaus and Beutell (1985). The fundamental premise of the conflict perspective is that work and family roles interfere with one another. In their recent review of the industrial-organizational psychology and organizational behavior work-family research, Eby and colleagues (in press) found that 63% of the studies they reviewed assumed unfavorable relations between work and family, whereas only 14% proposed favorable relations. Although the field once considered work-family conflict as a one-dimensional construct, it is now more common to consider reciprocal relations between the domains—work interference with family and family interference with work. Measurement has likewise evolved in an effort to capture the reciprocal influences across domains (e.g., Carlson, Kacmar, & Williams, 2000; Netemeyer, Boles, & McMurrian, 1996).

Industrial-organizational psychology researchers have been particularly interested in the effects of work-family conflict on job-related attitudes, and job satisfaction has received the most research attention (Allen, Herst, Bruck, & Sutton, 2000; Eby et al., 2005). Moreover, meta-analytic work has demonstrated a decidedly negative link between work-family conflict and job satisfaction (Allen et al., 2000; Kossek & Ozeki, 1998). Work-family conflict has likewise been linked to organizational commitment and turnover

TABLE 12.1
Weighted Average Correlations
Between Work-Family Conflict
and Work-Related Outcomes

Work-Related Outcomes	Mean r
Job satisfaction	−.24
Organizational commitment	−.23
Turnover intentions	.29
Work stress	.41
Job performance	−.12

intentions (e.g., Grandey & Cropanzano, 1999; Lyness & Thompson, 1997; Netemeyer et al., 1996) and actual turnover (Greenhaus, Collins, Singh, & Parasuraman, 1997). In addition, work-family conflict influences stress (e.g., Frone, Yardley, & Markel, 1997; Grandey & Cropanzano, 1999) and health (e.g., Frone, 2000; Frone et al., 1996). Finally, some research has found that work-family conflict is associated with poorer job performance (e.g., Frone, Yardley, & Markel, 1997). Table 12.1 shows the weighted average correlations between work-family conflict and these work-related outcomes as reported in the Allen et al. (2000) meta-analysis.

As an applied science, industrial-organizational psychology has a practical aim in studying the link between work-family conflict and various work outcomes. By demonstrating that conflict between work and family can affect work performance, this research highlights the vested interest employers have in considering their employees' nonwork lives. By revealing links to outcomes that matter to business (e.g., turnover), this research illustrates that attending to work-family is not simply a "moral imperative" or the right thing to do, but also makes good business sense.

Research in this field has examined the impact of employers' family-friendly initiatives on work-family conflict, job attitudes, and outcomes. In general, employees appreciate family-friendly benefits such as onsite child care (Kossek & Nichols, 1992; Rothausen, Gonzalez, Clarke, & O'Dell, 1998) and are attracted to employers that offer them (e.g., Allen, 2001; Grover & Crooker, 1995; Kossek & Ozeki, 1999). Family-supportive policies are associated with reduced work-family conflict, enhanced organizational commitment, and organizational citizenship (Lambert, 2000; Thomas & Ganster, 1995; Thompson, Beauvais, & Lyness, 1999). However, these positive results are only achieved when the workplace culture supports such programs and employees are encouraged to use their benefits (Thompson et al., 1999).

Although studied far less frequently than work-related outcomes, industrial-organizational research has not completely neglected outcomes in the family domain. For instance, one study found a negative relation between

TABLE 12.2
Weighted Average Correlations
Between Work-Family Conflict
and Family-Related Outcomes

Family-Related Outcomes	Mean r
Life satisfaction	−.28
Marital satisfaction	−.23
Family satisfaction	−.17
Family-related stress	.31

work-family conflict and family performance (Frone, Yardley, & Markel, 1997). Numerous empirical studies demonstrate a negative relation between work-family conflict and life satisfaction (e.g., Adams, King, & King, 1996; Judge, Boudreau, & Bretz, 1994; Netemeyer et al., 1996), as do the results of two recent meta-analyses (Allen et al., 2000; Kossek & Ozeki, 1998). The results are similar for work-family conflict, marital functioning or satisfaction (Duxbury, Higgins, & Thomas, 1996; MacEwen & Barling, 1994; Netemeyer et al., 1996), and family satisfaction (Parasuraman, Purohit, Godshalk, & Beutell, 1996; Rice, Frone, & McFarlin, 1992). Table 12.2 shows the weighted average correlations between work-family conflict and these family outcomes, as reported by Allen et al. (2000).

With a few exceptions (e.g., Barling, Dupre, & Hepburn, 1998), children are noticeably absent from industrial-organizational psychology research on the work-family interface, and when they are included it is typically as coarse representations (i.e., number of children, age of youngest child) of an employed parent's family demands (see Rothausen, 1999, for a review). Moreover, the research lacks a rich treatment of how children and other family variables influence employee behavior (Eby et al., 2005).

Although the conflict perspective has dominated the work-family research in industrial-organizational psychology, more positive conceptualizations of the work-family interface are emerging (e.g., Frone, 2003; Grzywacz & Marks, 2000). This trend is consistent with the more positive themes developing in other areas of psychology (Barnett & Hyde, 2001).

DIRECTIONS FOR FUTURE RESEARCH

Although our review of psychological research on the work-family interface distinguishes subfield specialties, the boundaries around subfields within psychology are often blurred and permeable. Indeed assigning some of the psychological research reviewed here to a particular subfield was a challenge especially when the topic, the background of the researcher, and the journal in which the work appeared all represent different subdisciplines. For instance, Frone, an industrial-organizational psychologist by training whose work-family research on substance abuse may be considered a clinical topic, has published in a variety of journals, including some multidisciplinary publications, some predominantly industrial-organizational outlets, and some with a health focus. Moreover, many work-family topics are of interest across psychological subdisciplines. For example, by virtue of their interest in the work-family interface, clinical, developmental, social, and industrial-organizational psychologists all study the effects of multiple roles. Likewise, although role quality may be operationalized differently across subfields, it is clearly a common theme. Finally, outcomes concerning individual health, well-being, and stress are evident, albeit to varying degrees, in each of the subdisciplines that study the work-family interface.

Yet despite the overlap, there remains a need for greater collaboration within psychology to better understand the work-family interface. For instance, the rich approaches to child outcomes used by developmental and clinical psychologists could be used in the industrial-organizational research to examine the outcomes of working parents and their employers (Major, Cardenas, & Allard, 2004). Similarly, industrial-organizational psychology has developed detailed, theory-based conceptualizations of the work domain and work experiences, at least for managers and professionals, that could expand methods used in the other psychological fields. Greater collaboration among the developmental, social, clinical, and industrial-organizational branches of psychology could also help improve our understanding of underrepresented groups in work-family research, including low- and middle-income employees and families (e.g., Perry-Jenkins & Gillman, 2000), ethnic minorities and multiracial families (Bigler, Averhart, & Liben, 2003), and families of varying structures (e.g., single-parent and extended family households).

Several examples exist of research in psychology that has effectively blended different psychology perspectives. For instance, the work of Barnett and colleagues is an exemplar of research incorporating the social, clinical, developmental, and industrial-organizational views. This breadth of perspective contributed to the seminal work on expansionist theory (Barnett & Hyde, 2001). This work, which advocates for considering the rewards and benefits of multiple roles across the work and family domains, encourages all psychological subdisciplines to expand beyond the conflict perspective and beyond the focus on negative consequences of the work-family interface.

Cross-disciplinary research also holds promise for advancing work-family research and practice. With its focus on individual outcomes, psychology demonstrates the consequences of the work-family interface at a human level. Collaborating with sociology places these psychological outcomes in a broader societal framework, both in terms of causes and social ramifications.

Add to this an anthropological perspective and the picture becomes richer, adding the cultural factors that influence the work-family interface. Economics is useful in that it provides a framework for understanding the decision making of individuals within the family context. Finally, integrating public policy research translates our understanding of individuals' work-family experiences into initiatives and programs that capitalize on the rewards and reduce the negative consequences of the work-family interface for individuals, organizations, and society.

REFERENCES

Adams, G. A., King, L. A., & King, D. W. (1996). Relationships of job and family involvement, family social support, and work-family conflict with job and life satisfaction. *Journal of Applied Psychology, 81*, 411–420.

Allen, T. D. (2001). Family-supportive work environments: The role of organizational perceptions. *Journal of Vocational Behavior, 58*, 414–435.

Allen, T. D., Herst, D. E., Bruck, C. S., & Sutton, M. (2000). Consequences associated with work-to-family conflict: A review and agenda for future research. *Journal of Occupational Health Psychology, 5*, 278–308.

Allport, G. W. (1985). The historical background of social psychology. In G. Lindzey & E. Aronson (Eds.), *The handbook of social psychology* (Vol. 1, pp. 1–46). Reading, MA: Addison-Wesley.

Armistead, L., Wierson, M., & Forehand, R. (1990). Adolescents and maternal employment: Is it harmful for a young adolescent to have an employed mother. *Journal of Early Adolescence, 10*, 260–278.

Barling, J., Dupre, K. E., & Hepburn, C. G. (1998). Effects of parents' job insecurity on children's work beliefs and attitudes. *Journal of Applied Psychology, 83*, 112–118.

Barling, J., MacEwen, K. E., Kelloway, E. K., & Higginbottom, S. F. (1994). Predictors and outcomes of elder-care-based inter-role conflict. *Psychology & Aging, 9*, 391–397.

Barnett, R. C., Brennan, R. T., & Marshall, N. L. (1994). Gender and the relationship between parent role quality and psychological distress: A study of men and women in dual-earner couples. *Journal of Family Issues, 15*, 229–252.

Barnett, R. C., Brennan, R. T., Raudenbush, S. W., & Marshall, N. L. (1994). Gender and the relationship between marital-role quality and psychological distress: A study of women and men in dual-earner couples. *Psychology of Women Quarterly, 18*, 105–127.

Barnett, R. C., & Gareis, K. C. (2000). Full-time and reduced-hours work schedules and marital quality: A study of female physicians with young children. *Work & Occupations, 29*, 364–379.

Barnett, R. C., Gareis, K. C., & Brennan, R. T. (1999). Fit as a mediator of the relationship between work hours and burnout. *Journal of Occupational Health Psychology, 4*, 307–317.

Barnett, R. C., & Hyde, J. S. (2001). Women, men, work, and family: An expansionist theory. *American Psychologist, 56*, 781–796.

Barnett, R. C., & Shen, Y. (1997). Gender, high- and low-schedule-control housework tasks, and psychological distress: A study of dual-earner couples. *Journal of Family Issues, 18*, 403–428.

Baydar, N., & Brooks-Gunn, J. (1991). Effects of maternal employment and child-care arrangements on preschoolers' cognitive and behavioral outcomes: Evidence from the children of the National Longitudinal Survey of Youth. *Developmental Psychology, 27*, 932–945.

Bernas, K. L., & Major, D. A. (2000). Contributors to stress resistance: A model of women's work-family conflict. *Psychology of Women Quarterly, 24,* 170–178.

Bigler, R. S., Averhart, C. J., & Liben, L. S. (2003). Race and the workforce: Occupational status, aspirations and stereotyping among African American children. *Developmental Psychology, 39,* 572–580.

Brooks-Gunn, J., Han, W., & Waldfogel, J. (2002). Maternal employment and child cognitive outcomes in the first three years of life: The NICHD study of early child care. *Child Development, 73,* 1052–1072.

Brown, R. (1995). *Prejudice: Its social psychology.* Oxford, England: Blackwell.

Burden, D. S. (1986). Single parents and the work setting: The impact of multiple job and homelife responsibilities. *Family Relations: Journal of Applied Family and Child Studies, 35,* 37–43.

Carlson, D. S., Kacmar, K. M., & Williams, L. J. (2000). Construction and initial validation of a multidimensional measure of work-family conflict. *Journal of Vocational Behavior, 56,* 249–276.

Crnic, K., & Greenberg, M. T. (1990). Minor parenting stresses with young children. *Child Development, 61,* 1628–1637.

Crnic, K., & Harris, V. (1990). Normal development in infancy and early childhood. In J. H. Johnson & J. Goldman (Eds.), *Developmental assessment in clinical child psychology: A handbook* (pp. 15–37). New York: Pergamon.

Crosby, F. J., & Jaskar, K. L. (1993). Women and men at home and at work: Realities and illusions. In S. Oskamp & M. Costanzo (Eds.), *Gender issues in social psychology* (pp. 143–171). Newbury Park, CA: Sage.

Crosby, F. J., & Sabattini, L. (in press). Family and work balance. In J. Worell & C. Goodheart (Eds.), *Handbook of girls' and women's psychological health.* New York: Oxford University Press.

Crouter, A. C., & Bumpus, M. F. (2001). Linking parents' work stress to children's and adolescents' psychological adjustment. *Current Directions in Psychological Science, 10,* 156–159.

Crouter, A. C., Bumpus, M. F., Head, M. R., & McHale, S. M. (2001). Implications of overwork and overload for the quality of men's family relationships. *Journal of Marriage and Family, 63,* 404–416.

Crouter, A. C., Bumpus, M. F., Maguire, M. C., & McHale, S. M. (1999). Linking parents' work pressure and adolescents' well being: Insights into dynamics in dual earner families. *Developmental Psychology, 35,* 1453–1461.

Crouter, A. C., Helms-Erickson, H., Updegraff, K., & McHale, S. M. (1999). Conditions underlying parents' knowledge about children's daily lives in middle childhood: Between- and within-family comparisons. *Child Development, 70,* 246–259.

Crouter, A. C., & McHale, S. M. (1993). Temporal rhythms in family life: Seasonal variation in the relation between parental work and family processes. *Developmental Psychology, 29,* 198–205.

Deaux, K., Winton, W., Crowley, M., & Lewis, L. L. (1985). Level of categorization and content of gender stereotypes. *Social Cognition, 3,* 145–167.

Duxbury, L. E., Higgins, C. A., & Thomas, D. R. (1996). Work and family environments and the adoption of computer-supported supplemental work-at-home. *Journal of Vocational Behavior, 49,* 1–23.

Eby, L. T., Casper, W. J., Lockwood, A., Bordeaux, C., & Brinley, A. (2005). Work and family research in IO/OB: Content analysis and review of the literature (1980–2002) [Monograph]. *Journal of Vocational Behavior, 66,* 124–197.

Fiske, S. T. (1998). Stereotyping, prejudice, and discrimination. In D. T. Gilbert, S. T. Fiske, & G. Lindsey (Eds.), *Handbook of social psychology* (Vol. 2, pp. 357–411). New York: Oxford University Press.

Fiske, S. T., Cuddy, A. J. C., Glick, P., & Xu, J. (2002). A model of (often mixed) stereotype content: Competence and warmth respectively follow from perceived status and competition. *Journal of Personality and Social Psychology, 82,* 878–902.

French, J., & Raven, B. H. (1959). The bases of social power. In D. Cartwright (Ed.), *Studies of social power* (pp. 150–165). Ann Arbor, MI: Institute for Social Research.

Frone, M. R. (2000). Work-family conflict and employee psychiatric disorders: The national comorbidity survey. *Journal of Applied Psychology, 85,* 888–895.

Frone, M. R. (2003). Work-family balance. In J. C. Quick & L. E. Tetrick (Eds.), *Handbook of occupational health psychology* (pp. 143–162). Washington, DC: American Psychological Association.

Frone, M. R., Barnes, G. M., & Farrell, M. P. (1994). Relationship of work-family conflict to substance use among employed mothers: The role of negative affect. *Journal of Marriage and the Family, 56,* 1019–1030.

Frone, M. R., Russell, M., & Barnes, G. M. (1996). Work-family conflict, gender, and health-related outcomes: A study of employed parents in two community samples. *Journal of Occupational Health Psychology, 1,* 57–69.

Frone, M. R., Russell, M., & Cooper, M. L. (1991). Relationship of work and family stressors to psychological distress: The independent moderating influence of social support, mastery, active coping and self-focused attention. *Journal of Social Behavior and Personality, 6,* 227–250.

Frone, M. R., Russell, M., & Cooper, M. L. (1993). Relationship of work family conflict, gender and alcohol expectancies to alcohol use/abuse. *Journal of Organizational Behavior, 14,* 545–558.

Frone, M. R., Russell, M., & Cooper, M. L. (1997). Relation of work-family conflict to health outcomes: A four-year longitudinal study of employed parents. *Journal of Occupational & Organizational Psychology, 70,* 325–335.

Frone, M. R., Yardley, J. K., & Markel, K. S. (1997). Developing and testing an integrative model of the work-family interface. *Journal of Vocational Behavior, 50,* 145–167.

Galambos, N., & Maggs, J. L. (1990). Putting mothers' work-related stress in perspective: Mothers and adolescents in dual-earner families. *Journal of Early Adolescence, 10,* 313–328.

Galambos, N. L., Sears, H. A., Almeida, D. M., & Kolaric, G. C. (1995). Parents' work overload and problem behavior in young adolescents. *Journal of Research on Adolescence, 5,* 201–223.

Gareis, K. C., & Barnett, R. C. (2002). Under what conditions do long work hours affect psychological distress: A study of full-time and reduced-hours female doctors. *Work & Occupations, 29,* 483–497.

Gerstel, N., & Gallagher, S. K. (1993). Kinkeeping and distress: Gender, recipients of care, and work-family conflict. *Journal of Marriage and the Family, 55,* 598–608.

Gottfried, A. E., Bathurst, K., & Gottfried, A. W. (1994). Role of maternal and dual-earner employment status in children's development: A longitudinal study from infancy through early adolescence. In A. E. Gottfried & A. W. Gottfried (Eds.), *Redefining families: Implications for children's development* (pp. 55–97). New York: Plenum.

Gottfried, A. E., Gottfried, A. W., & Bathurst, K. (2002). Maternal and dual-earner employment status and parenting. In M. H. Bornstein (Ed.), *Handbook of parenting: Vol. 2. Biology and ecology of parenting* (2nd ed., pp. 207–229). Mahwah, NJ: Lawrence Erlbaum Associates.

Grandey, A. A., & Cropanzano, R. (1999). The Conservation of Resources model applied to work-family conflict and strain. *Journal of Vocational Behavior, 54,* 350–370.

Greenberger, E., O'Neil, R., & Nagel, S. K. (1994). Linking workplace and homeplace: Relations between the nature of adults' work and their parenting behaviors. *Developmental Psychology, 30,* 990–1002.

Greenhaus, J. H., & Beutell, N. J. (1985). Sources of conflict between work and family roles. *Academy of Management Review, 10,* 76–88.

Greenhaus, J. H., Collins, K. M., Singh, R., & Parasuraman, S. (1997). Work and family influences on departure from public accounting. *Journal of Vocational Behavior, 50,* 249–270.

Greenstein, T. N. (1996). Husbands' participation in domestic labor: Interactive effects of wives' and husbands' gender ideologies. *Journal of Marriage and the Family, 58,* 585–595.

Grover, S. L., & Crooker, K. J. (1995). Who appreciates family-responsive human resource policies: The impact of family-friendly policies on the organizational attachment of parents and non-parents. *Personnel Psychology, 48,* 271–288.

Grzywacz, J. G., & Marks, N. F. (2000). Reconceptualizing the work-family interface: An ecological perspective on the correlates of positive and negative spillover between work and family. *Journal of Occupational Health Psychology, 5,* 111–126.

Hammer, L. B., Allen, E., & Grigsby, T. D. (1997). Work-family conflict in dual-earner couples: Within-individual and crossover effects of work and family. *Journal of Vocational Behavior, 50,* 185–203.

Hammer, L. B., Bauer, T. N., & Grandey, A. A. (2003). Work-family conflict and work-related withdrawal behaviors. *Journal of Business and Psychology, 17,* 419–436.

Han, W., Waldfogel, J., & Brooks-Gunn, J. (2001). The effects of early maternal employment on later cognitive and behavioral outcomes. *Journal of Marriage and Family, 63,* 336–354.

Harrison, L. J., & Ungerer, J. A. (2002). Maternal employment and infant-mother attachment security at 12 months postpartum. *Developmental Psychology, 38,* 758–773.

Harvey, E. (1999). Short-term and long-term effects of parental employment on children of the National Longitudinal Survey of Youth. *Developmental Psychology, 35,* 445–459.

Hegtvedt, K. A., Clay-Warner, W. J., & Ferrigno, E. D. (2003). Factors affecting workers' resentment toward family-friendly policies. *Social Psychology Quarterly, 65,* 386–400.

Heilman, M. E. (1983). Sex bias in work settings: The lack of fit model. In K. Rowland & G. Ferris (Eds.), *Research in organizational behavior* (Vol. 5, pp. 269–298). New York: Academic Press.

Hepburn, C. G., & Barling, J. (1996). Eldercare responsibilities, interrole conflict, and employee absence: A daily study. *Journal of Occupational Health Psychology, 1,* 311–318.

Hoffman, L. W., & Youngblade, L. M. (1999). *Mothers at work: Effects on children's well-being.* Cambridge, England: Cambridge University Press.

Izraeli, D. N. (1993). Work/family conflict among men and women managers in dual career couples in Israel. *Journal of Social Behavior and Personality, 8,* 371–385.

Judge, T. A., Boudreau, J. W., & Bretz, R. D. (1994). Job and life attitudes of male executives. *Journal of Applied Psychology, 79,* 767–782.

Klute, M. M., Crouter, A. C., Sayer, A. G., & McHale, S. M. (2001). Occupational self-direction, values, and egalitarian relationships: A study of dual-earner couples. *Journal of Marriage and Family, 64,* 139–151.

Kluwer, E. S., Heesink, J. S. M., & Van de Vliert, E. (2000). The division of household labor: An asymmetrical conflict issue. *Personal Relationships, 7,* 263–282.

Kossek, E. E., & Nichol, V. (1992). The effects of on-site child care on employee attitudes and performance. *Personnel Psychology, 45,* 485–509.

Kossek, E. E., & Ozeki, C. (1998). Work-family conflict, policies, and the job-life satisfaction relationship: A review and directions for organizational behavior-human resources research. *Journal of Applied Psychology, 83,* 139–149.

Kossek, E. E., & Ozeki, C. (1999). Bridging the work-family policy and productivity gap: A literature review. *Community, Work and Family, 2,* 7–32.

Lambert, S. J. (2000). Added benefits: The link between work-life benefits and organizational citizenship behavior. *Academy of Management Journal, 43,* 801–815.

Lazarus, R. S., & Folkman, S. (1984). *Stress, appraisal and coping.* New York: Springer-Verlag.

Lyness, K. S., & Thompson, D. E. (1997). Above the glass ceiling? A comparison of matched samples of female and male executives. *Journal of Applied Psychology, 82*, 359–375.

MacDermid, S. M., & Williams, M. L. (1997). A within-industry comparison of employed mothers' experiences in small and large workplaces. *Journal of Family Issues, 18*, 545–566.

MacEwen, K. E., & Barling, J. (1994). Daily consequences of work interference with family and family interference with work. *Work & Stress, 8*, 244–254.

Major, B. (1993). Gender, entitlement, and the distribution of family labor. *Journal of Social Issues, 49*, 141–159.

Major, B. (1994). From social inequality to personal entitlement: The role of social comparisons, legitimacy appraisals, and group membership. In M. Zanna (Ed.), *Advances in experimental social psychology* (pp. 293–355). New York: Academic Press.

Major, D. A., Cardenas, R. A., & Allard, C. (2004). Child health: A legitimate business concern. *Journal of Occupational Health Psychology, 9*, 306–321.

Moorehouse, M. J. (1991). Linking maternal employment patterns to mother-child activities and children's school competence. *Developmental Psychology, 27*, 295–303.

Muller, C. (1995). Maternal employment, parent involvement, and mathematics achievement among adolescents. *Journal of Marriage and the Family, 57*, 85–100.

Netemeyer, R. G., Boles, J. S., & McMurrian, R. (1996). Development and validation of work-family conflict and family-work conflict scales. *Journal of Applied Psychology, 81*, 400–410.

O'Neil, R., & Greenberger, E. (1994). Patterns of commitment to work and parenting: Implications for role strain. *Journal of Marriage and the Family, 56*, 101–118.

Parasuraman, S., Purohit, Y. S., Godshalk, V. M., & Beutell, N. J. (1996). Work and family variables, entrepreneurial career success and psychological well-being. *Journal of Vocational Behavior, 48*, 275–300.

Perry-Jenkins, M., & Crouter, A. C. (1990). Men's provider-role attitudes: Implications for housework and marital satisfaction. *Journal of Family Issues, 11*, 136–156.

Perry-Jenkins, M., & Gillman, S. (2000). Parental job experiences and children's well-being: The case of two-parent and single mother working-class families. *Journal of Family & Economic Issues, 21*, 123–145.

Perry-Jenkins, M., Repetti, R. L., & Crouter, A. C. (2000). Work and family in the 1990s. *Journal of Marriage and the Family, 62*, 981–998.

Perry-Jenkins, M., Seery, B., & Crouter, A. C. (1992). Linkages between women's provider-role attitudes, psychological well-being, and family relationships. *Psychology of Women Quarterly, 16*, 311–329.

Plante, T. G. (1999). *Contemporary clinical psychology.* New York: Wiley.

Repetti, R. L. (1994). Short-term and long-term processes linking job stressors to father-child interaction. *Social Development, 3*, 1–15.

Repetti, R. L. (1998). The promise of a multiple roles paradigm for women's health research. *Women's Health: Research on Gender, Behavior, and Policy, 4*, 273–280.

Repetti, R. L., & Wood, J. (1997). Effects of daily stress at work on mothers' interactions with preschoolers. *Journal of Family Psychology, 11*, 90–108.

Rice, R. W., Frone, M. R., & McFarlin, D. B. (1992). Work-nonwork conflict and the perceived quality of life. *Journal of Organizational Behavior, 13*, 155–168.

Rothausen, T. J. (1999). "Family" in organizational research: A review and comparison of definitions and measures. *Journal of Organizational Behavior, 20*, 817–836.

Rothausen, T. J., Gonzalez, J. A., Clarke, N. E., & O'Dell, L. L. (1998). Family-friendly backlash—fact or fiction? The case of organizations' on-site child care centers. *Personnel Psychology, 51*, 685–706.

Sagrestano, L. M., Christensen, A., & Heavey, C. L. (1998). Social influence techniques during marital conflict. *Personal Relationships, 5*, 75–89.

Schwartzberg, R., & Dytell, R. S. (1996). Dual-earner families: The importance of work stress and family stress for psychological well-being. *Journal of Occupational Health Psychology, 1,* 211–223.

Steil, J. (1997). *Marital equality: Its relationship to the well-being of husbands and wives.* Thousand Oaks, CA: Sage.

Taylor, S.E. (1999). *Health psychology* (4th ed.). New York: McGraw-Hill.

Thomas, L. T., & Ganster, D. C. (1995). Impact of family-supportive work variables on work-family conflict and strain: A control perspective. *Journal of Applied Psychology, 80,* 6–15.

Thompson, C. A., Beauvais, L. L., & Lyness, K. S. (1999). When work-family benefits are not enough: The influence of work-family culture on benefit utilization, organizational attachment, and work-family conflict. *Journal of Vocational Behavior, 54,* 392–415.

Vandell, D. L., & Ramanan, J. (1992). Effects of early and recent maternal employment on children from low-income families. *Child Development, 63,* 938–949.

Vescio, T. K., Snyder, M., & Butz, D. A. (2003). Power in stereotypically masculine domains: A social influence strategy × stereotype match model. *Journal of Personality and Social Psychology, 85,* 1062–1078.

13

An Economic Perspective on Work, Family, and Well-Being

Arleen A. Leibowitz
University of California, Los Angeles

The central concern of economics is the optimal allocation of scarce resources. Consumers decide how to spend their limited incomes on various goods and services to maximize their well-being. Firms decide how many and what types of goods to produce to maximize their profits. Men and women decide how to allocate their time between market work and time at home to maximize their family's well-being (see "Part I: Time, Work, and Family," this volume, for an in-depth discussion of time allocation). Because resources are limited, each choice means that other options are precluded. This concept of *opportunity cost* is particularly relevant in allocating time given that we all face limits on the number of hours available in a day. Additional time spent in one activity necessarily means reducing the time spent in another activity.

The economic model postulates that well-informed individuals or organizations maximize their utility by rationally weighing the costs and benefits of various alternatives. However, the usual assumptions in an economic model of perfect information and rationality are unlikely to apply when deciding how to allocate time between family and career. The extensive debate about the effect of market work on children reflects the significant uncertainty surrounding different time allocations between work and family. In such a scenario, it may be extremely difficult to gather all the information relevant to the specific decision at hand, and decisions must be made with incomplete information. Economists argue that because it is costly to acquire information, it is rarely optimal to gather all the facts relevant to a given decision. Rather, decision makers rely on "bounded rationality" and gather information to the point at which the costs of gathering additional information exceed its potential. One way to learn about likely consequences of a decision when there is little opportunity to learn from one's prior choices (such as taking a short maternity leave) is to observe patterns of behavior that others have adopted.

Decisions about such emotion-laden issues as child care, work, and family responsibilities may also fail to satisfy the axioms of strict rationality. Behavioral economics has documented several ways in which decision makers fail to behave in a manner that can be fully predicted by a simple expected utility model (Kahneman, 2003; Kahneman & Snell, 1990; Kahneman & Varey, 1991).

Despite these well-documented departures from perfect information and rational decision making, the economic model does provide a theoretically grounded explanation of family and work choices that finds empirical support in both longitudinal and cross-sectional analyses. The economic model, for example, is broadly consistent with changes in work and family size both over time and at points in time (e.g., cross-section; Pencavel, 1998; Rindfuss, Morgan, & Offutt, 1996). Thus, it seems worthwhile to first examine the basic economic model of household production before describing the model's application to family formation and work decisions. The chapter concludes by exploring the implications of the economic model for family health and well-being and for the mismatch between home and the workplace.

ECONOMIC MODELS
AND WOMEN'S MARKET WORK

The concept of well-being is central to economic analysis (Frey & Stutzer, 2002). Economists call it *utility* and postulate that all individuals are *utility maximizers*—that is, they choose how to allocate their time and resources to maximize their well-being or utility given their endowments. These allocation choices involve not only which goods to consume, but also the fundamental choices of whether to marry, how many children to have, whether to work in the labor market, and how much time and money to invest in one's health and well-being and the health of one's children.

Becker (1965) conceptualized utility in a way that is particularly useful for considering allocations of time to home and work. He argued that utility or well-being depends on consumption of leisure time and commodities that are produced at home by combining purchased goods and one's own time. The family has fixed budgets of time, but can increase money income by supplying more time to the labor market. This greater money income can be spent on purchased goods, which are used to enhance utility. However, by working more hours in the labor market, the family has fewer hours to spend at home and may have less leisure time.

An important component of this model is that adult members of the family make collective decisions about maximizing the family's welfare. Thus, their goal is to maximize the (agreed-on) family utility subject to an overall budget constraint that is the sum of the value of time in all its uses for each family member, plus unearned income. An important implication that follows from placing a value on both time spent outside the labor market and in the labor market is the recognition that unpaid labor in the home is also valuable for the family.

To maximize utility, each adult in the family must equate the marginal increment to well-being (the marginal utility) of an additional hour spent in the labor market to that of an additional hour spent in nonmarket activity. For example, if the last hour spent at work yields less utility than the last hour spent in leisure, total utility or satisfaction could be increased by transferring an hour from work time to leisure time.

The home production framework has an immediate application to choices about market work. Although utility cannot be directly measured, we can measure the wage rates and prices of contributions to household production and predict the effect of price changes for these contributions. Women offered higher wages in the labor market have greater opportunity costs of time and find time-intensive home production more costly than goods-intensive production. The economic model predicts that they would rationally work more outside the home and use less of their own time to produce commodities at home. Thus, it is important to recognize that family members are not solely choosing between work and leisure, but are choosing among market work, work in the home, and leisure (Mincer, 1962).

Consider the example of preparing dinner. A home cook could make dinner by spending a considerable amount of time transforming low-cost ingredients into a delicious stew. Alternatively, having a pizza delivered would minimize the cook's time, but require spending more money. The time and money cost of the stew is lower if the opportunity cost of the cook's time is low rather than high (e.g., low- vs. high-market wages). Thus, if the stew and the pizza contribute equal amounts of satisfaction to the family, the model predicts that, because families seek to minimize the costs of providing dinner, otherwise identical families in which the cook has high opportunity cost of time are more likely to choose pizza for dinner. This occurs because the wages earned during the additional hours worked easily cover the cost of the pizza and leave extra money for other sources of satisfaction. The opposite may be true for the low-wage cook, whose time cost in making a stew produces more satisfaction for the family than spending those hours in market work.

Economists use the wage rate as the measure of the opportunity cost of spending time outside the labor market. However, men still have a comparative advantage in the labor force over women—they tend to make more money, and their opportunity costs of spending time outside of work are higher. Hence, in married-couple families, couples will typically allocate more of the husband's time to market work and more of the wife's time to nonmarket activities (see Smock & Noonan, chap. 23, this volume). As women's wages have risen relative to men's, women's optimal allocation of time between market and nonmarket activities has changed as has that between men and women within the family. The growth in the opportunity cost of a woman's time has also increased the relative cost of time-intensive activities such as childrearing. Although individual women may not explicitly make these economic calculations, the economic model does have strong predictive power for the population as a whole. The historical decline in number of births has proceeded in tandem with the growth in women's wages (Rindfuss, Morgan, & Offutt, 1996). The negative correlation between potential wages and number of children ever born also explains cross-sectional variation in family size (Martin, 2000). The strength of this price effect is so strong that it dominates the income effect, which would otherwise lead higher income families to have more children (Mincer, 1963).

Growth in women's wages, which affects choices about labor supply both directly and indirectly through choices about family size, can explain a large share of the changes in women's labor force participation over time (Heckman, 1993; Killingsworth & Heckman, 1986). Smaller family size and changes in other demographic characteristics (maternal education and age, paternal age) accounted for about 20% of the observed growth in women's labor force participation between 1971 and 1990 (Leibowitz & Klerman, 1995). More important, the husband's and wife's opportunity costs (predicted wages based on individual characteristics and local market conditions) explained an additional 25% of the increased participation over the period. Thus, it is clear that the increasing rewards for women in the labor market drew them to work outside of the home. At the same time, higher wages made it more costly to spend time at home. In addition, the rising labor force participation of women is also connected to changing attitudes about the acceptability of employment for women and their role in the home (Pencavel, 1998).

The most dramatic increase in labor supply has been among mothers of the youngest children. Although mothers of infants less than 1 year old are still less likely to be in the labor force than mothers of older children, this trend eroded significantly during the two decades (Leibowitz & Klerman, 1995).

FAMILIES AS PRODUCERS
OF HUMAN CAPITAL

One of the major activities that families undertake is nurturing children. I noted earlier that the growth in women's wages has led to smaller families. A further question is whether it has also changed women's childrearing inputs, and, if so, what the effect is on children. Adapting the economic model to understand childrearing choices is straightforward if one recognizes that child health and human capital are two of the primary commodities that provide utility to families. Following Grossman (1972), the utility framework can be expanded to include child health and human capital (H) as arguments in the utility function, along with the consumption of household-produced commodities (Z) and leisure (L):

$$U = U(Z,L,H)$$

Although higher levels of child human capital would yield greater utility, the family is constrained by limited resources with which to produce that human capital and by competing sources of satisfaction (e.g., other consumption and leisure).

Adapting the household-production framework to child human capital requires defining children's physical and emotional health and cognitive growth as outputs. Inputs to child human capital are parental and child time and purchased goods (such as child care). In the production context, it is important to recognize that a parent's use of time and goods can have positive or negative effects on the child. For example, the time a parent spends reading to a child may increase the child's language skills. Alternatively, the parent could prepare fatty, high-cholesterol foods that increase the child's risk of heart disease in the future or use harsh discipline that undermines a child's emotional health. Because nurturing children is one of the family's most important activities, economists use the development of a child's human capital as a lens through with to examine the consequences of parental time-allocation decisions. The following sections discuss the role of parents' time, purchased inputs (commodities), and the child's time as contributors to children's well-being.

Parent Time

The economic model recognizes the importance of parental time in child health and development (Steinberg, Lamborn, Dornbusch, & Darling, 1992). It treats a family's decision about which parent assumes most of the child-care duties as a choice determined by the relative wages of mother and father. In practice, time diary data reveal that mothers provide a preponderance of the parental time with children (Bailey, 1995; Bianchi, 2000; Bianchi & Raley, chap. 2, this volume; Sandberg & Hofferth, 2001). As a consequence, most analyses have focused on mothers, with much of the work examining the effect of maternal work on child outcomes.

It is also important to consider the full range of effects, including changes in both time and goods inputs that result from a mother's participation in the labor force. On the one hand, maternal work reduces time spent with children and alters the way that home commodities are produced. On the other hand, it increases income and access to health insurance. In addition, maternal work generally means that young children will experience some nonparental child care, and it may alter the other activities (and the time spent doing them) that children do as well.

Working mothers necessarily spend fewer hours at home (except for the small minority who work at home). How does the time devoted to work affect children? Evidence from nonexperimental studies is difficult to interpret given that those mothers who feel most able to manage both job and family duties may be the most likely to work outside the home (Currie, chap. 19, this volume). However, a dramatic policy change in 1996 offered an opportunity to more precisely study the effects of mother's work on children. Beginning in 1996, the Temporary Assistance for Needy Families (TANF) program instituted new work mandates for welfare recipients and also limited the number of years that families could receive assistance. The implementation of TANF and the welfare experiments that preceded it provide an opportunity to observe the effects on children of a not altogether voluntary entry into market work by mothers. Because several of the welfare studies incorporated experimental designs that stimulated work to different extents, it is possible to draw some causal inferences about the effect of work on children, particularly children from disadvantaged families.

Evaluations of welfare reform focused particularly on outcomes for preschool children, for whom the change in time with the mother would be greatest. They found little evidence of either harm or benefit to preschool children whose mothers went to work outside the home (Stagner, Kortenkamp, & Reardon-Anderson, 2002). Results for older children, however, conflict. Some studies have found poorer school performance among older adolescents (ages 12–18), whereas others found improved mental health among younger adolescents (ages 11.5–15.5; Kalil, Dunifon, & Danziger, 2001; Chase-Lansdale et al., 2003).

These equivocal results may reflect that mothers do not necessarily have to reduce their time with children by 1 hour for each hour worked outside the home given that they can reduce time spent in other activities. Even if she is not working, a mother still must choose how to spend her time at home. Will she spend time with children (e.g., read to the child), produce other goods at home (e.g., prepare gourmet meals), or spend time in her own consumption (e.g., read a novel or watch a soap opera on TV)?

Time diary studies indicate that mothers working outside the home try to preserve the amount of time they spend with children—spending, on average, nearly as many hours in direct child interaction as nonemployed mothers (27 vs. 31 hours per week; Leibowitz, 1975; Sandberg & Hofferth, 2001). Reductions in leisure time, sleep, and time spent in other household chores allow mothers to maintain time with children that is nearly comparable to that spent by nonworking mothers (Bianchi, 2000). In studies of time use by women leaving welfare for work, Chase-Lansdale and colleagues (2003) found that mothers had 2.1 fewer hours per day with preschoolers. Fuller, Kagan, and Loeb (2002) reported that twice as many working mothers (50%) as nonemployed mothers (25%) report spending less time with preschool-age children on weekdays than they did 1.5 to 2 years previously.

In contrast, the amount of time mothers and their adolescents spent together fell by only 45 minutes per day when mothers transitioned from welfare to work. Mothers of these older children decreased their time in social and personal activities by 2.8 hours each day, which nearly offset the additional 3.7 hours per day that they were working outside the home (Chase-Lansdale et al., 2003). As the economic model suggests, fathers spend more time with children when mothers work (Bailey, 1995; Bianchi, 2000; Sandberg & Hofferth, 2001).

Although the child outcome studies and the levels of time inputs suggest children may not be adversely affected when mothers work outside the home, there has been little research on the effect of that work on mothers' health. The reduction in personal time, leisure, and sleep may extract a large toll on women's physical and emotional health.

Household Commodities

Child-relevant commodities that families purchase range from developmental nursery schools or health care, which may enhance child human capital, to those that may be detrimental to child health and human capital, such as second-hand smoke or foods high in saturated fats.

A mother who works in the labor force directly affects her family's well-being by increasing family income. Many studies document the positive relation between income and health (Case, Lubotsky, & Paxson, 2002; Deaton, 2003; Ettner, 1996). This relation is more evident in poor countries than in developed countries (Pritchett & Summers, 1996), although it is also evident in developed countries (van Doorslaer et al., 1997). Greater access to medical care in developed countries is an insufficient explanation for the relation between income and health because the relation exists even in countries, such as the United Kingdom, that provide free access to medical care (Currie & Hyson, 1999; Marmot et al., 1991). Although sufficient quantities of food may be available to all in developed countries, housing in neighborhoods with clean air is costly, and healthy foods are expensive. Thus, we would expect higher income families to consume more of these goods and to produce better health. Of course higher income may also lead families to consume food that is tasty and expensive, but not healthy.

It is difficult to interpret the meaning of the positive relation between income and health for adults given that the pathway from poor health to low income is as plausible as the pathway from low income to poor health (Smith, 1999). However, it is easier to make the case that, for children, the causal relation runs from income to health. Case, Lubotsky, and Paxson (2002) found higher family income is associated with better health for children, and lower income is associated with measures of poor health, such as restricted activity days, hospital episodes, and chronic conditions.

The studies of welfare reform confirm similar findings for children. Higher family income leads to improved child well-being. Apparently, the increased income that working mothers provide for their families offsets any negative effects of their reduced time with preschoolers. For adolescents of former welfare recipients, the net effect of working mothers may be positive given that teens did not lose much time with mothers, and there is evidence that maternal work reduces a teenager's level of anxiety by easing concerns about financial insecurity (Chase-Lansdale et al., 2003). This argument is consistent with the finding of better behavioral health outcomes for children whose mothers earned higher wages than others in a sample of women with welfare experience (Moore & Driscoll, 1997). Conversely, job loss is associated with increases in behavioral problems among adolescents (Chase-Lansdale et al., 2003). Despite these improvements in health outcomes with increased income, the earning gains among women transitioning from welfare to work were modest (Fuller et al., 2002).

Market work may also provide access to certain benefits—such as health insurance—that are more costly to obtain by other means. Most American families with health insurance have an employer-provided policy (National Center for Health Statistics, 2002) because privately purchased policies are more expensive and often have preexisting conditions exclusions (Pauly & Nichols, 2002). Health insurance reduces the cost of obtaining medical care and, in the economic model, reduces the cost of producing health. However, increasing use of medical care at the margin has been shown in a randomized treatment study to have only a small effect on health for nonelderly Americans (Newhouse & the Insurance Experiment Group, 1993).

Market work also affects how household commodities are produced at home, which may affect the health of both adults and children. The growth in women's opportunity costs has increased the costs of commodities that are relatively time-intensive (such as the home-cooked stew) relative to those that are less time-intensive (delivered pizzas). These changes in relative prices can have indirect effects on health. The obesity epidemic among U.S.

children may, in fact, relate to working women's incentives to substitute fast (and often high-calorie and high-fat) foods for more nutritious, but more time-consuming, meals. Adults as well as children may suffer the effects of economizing on time but not on money.

Child Time

Mothers working outside the home may call on their children to substitute for them in producing household commodities, thereby reducing the time the child has to develop his or her own human capital. The negative education effects for adolescents whose mothers have left welfare for work (e.g., Tout, Scarpa, & Zaslow, 2002) appear to be localized among teenagers with younger siblings (Duncan, 2003). It has been hypothesized that these adolescents are providing child care at the expense of their own development and school success.

Another aspect of child time is that spent in nonparental care. For example, research has found that preschool children cared for in child-care centers have a greater incidence of communicable diseases (Silverstein, Sales, & Koepsell, 2003), and the incidence increases with the size of the child-care group (Johansen, Leibowitz, & Waite, 1988). In terms of cognitive and social development, child-care centers appear to be as or more productive than mothers in developing a child's human capital between ages 2 and 4. The evidence indicates that toddlers in day-care settings develop better than children reared entirely at home (Clarke-Stewart, 1991; Harvey, 1999; Hill, Waldfogel, & Brooks-Gunn, 2002). The positive effect of high-quality child care on cognitive development is most evident for children from disadvantaged backgrounds (Campbell & Ramey, 1994; NICHD Early Child Care Research Network, 2000).

However, the findings on substitution are less positive for children younger than 1 year, the group for whom maternal employment has been growing most rapidly. Several studies find that mothers' long work hours negatively affect children's outcomes in the first year of life (Baum, 2003; Baydar & Brooks-Gunn, 1991; Belsky & Eggebeen, 1991; Blau & Grossberg, 1992; Brooks-Gunn, Han, & Waldfogel, 2002; Desai, Chase-Lansdale, & Michael, 1989; Waldfogel, Han, & Brooks-Gunn, 2002). Ruhm (2000) found that child health improved in European countries that extended maternity leave, which allows new parents to spend more time away from work in a child's first year of life. In the United States, the Family and Medical Leave Act (FMLA) of 1993 only guarantees up to 12 weeks of unpaid leave for individuals who work in the private sector in companies with more than 50 employees. This short duration may induce many new mothers to return to work at an earlier date than they would have preferred (Klerman & Leibowitz, 1999).

MISMATCH BETWEEN WORK AT HOME
AND IN THE MARKET?

The economic model predicts that family members choose the amount of time they spend in the market and in the home to maximize their well-being. If that is a good representation of decision making, why is it that so many parents report experiencing the stress of the competing demands of home and employment? It is important to recognize that some family heads do not freely choose to work. Rather, they are constrained to do so. For example, parents who reach time limits under TANF can remain out of the labor force only by accepting low family income, which may be inadequate to support their children. Borrowing against future earnings may not be a realistic option for low-income individuals with limited assets and without solid credit histories. Thus, TANF recipients may be unable to substitute money for time because they have so little of each. They will feel the work-family conflicts most acutely.

The economic model postulates that a worker can adjust hours of work along a continuum to equate the marginal utility of the last hour at work with that of the last hour spent at home. Although it may be possible to alter the number of hours worked by changing jobs, many workers will find it difficult to fine-tune their work hours in the short run. There is also a large wage penalty in choosing part-time work.

Some new mothers change employers or reduce their hours with the same employer in anticipation of an increased demand for their time at home after giving birth to a child. In 1990, 53% of the women who had worked part time while pregnant were not employed in the first 18 months after giving birth. Thirty-nine percent of these workers returned to employment at a different job, and 8% worked at the same job either part or full time. Among women who had been employed full time during pregnancy, only 28.2% did not return to work in the first 18 months, and many more (61%) returned to the same job. Of these, three quarters were working full time (Klerman & Leibowitz, 1999). The higher rate of returning to the same job and the greater rates of full-time work by women who had worked full time during pregnancy reflect the higher levels of training and a better job match between these women and their employers. Although women may have returned to the job held during pregnancy because they believed the job represented their best opportunity over the longer term, this does not preclude them from experiencing stress and pressures from the competing demands in the short run, particularly for mothers of newborns.

Some of the causes of mismatch between work and home responsibilities are less predictable than being a new parent and result from short-term surges in the demands for time either in the home or in the workplace. Even if workers optimally allocated their time between home and work based on the expected level of effort required in each sector, there will be times when temporary variation in those needs causes stress. Examples of these short-term demands include a family illness, a child-care disruption, or a fast-track project at work. As Holzer discusses (chap. 6, this volume), both employers and employees find it worthwhile to maintain the employment relationship when they can gain the benefits of investments already made in training or a good job match.

Imperfect and incomplete information at the time decisions must be made limits the ability of most workers facing family changes to make realistic decisions about work commitments. When family members experience the actual amount of conflict engendered by their work and family roles, they may reevaluate their situation and alter their decision in light of increased information. When the difficulty of pursuing the initial allocation of time between work and home becomes great enough, it may become worthwhile to bear the costs of changing their time commitments. Work and family pressures may be alleviated by negotiating different work schedules, changing employers, or temporarily dropping out of the labor force. Alternatively, the demands of home time may be reduced through bargaining between spouses to reallocate home responsibilities or hire additional household help (Lundberg & Pollak, 1996). The stronger the mismatch between work and home time and the longer it is expected to persist, the greater the incentive to make a permanent change in time allocations. For short-duration surges in time demands, employer policies such as maternity leave, sick leave, or family leave can help to relieve the stress. Policies to deal with unanticipated surges in demand for work time are much less developed.

CONCLUSION

The fact that working parents, particularly highly educated working mothers, significantly reduce the time they devote to leisure and other types of home production to preserve their time with children illustrates and validates the home-production framework. It also points to the underlying causes of stress among those who combine work and family careers. Although children may be protected from adverse effects of their mothers' work, we have yet to fully assess the health effects on adults, both mothers and fathers. Short-term reductions to sleep and leisure may be readily accommodated, but we know little about the health effects on parents who experience chronic, long-term deficits in the time they can devote to their own health.

The economic framework presented here also draws attention to some of the second-order health problems that may develop as a result of parents substituting other inputs for their own efforts. For example, the emerging epidemic of obesity among children and adults may be attributable, in part, to the substitution of prepared food for home-cooked meals. Children may be putting their own developmental tasks at risk if they are called on to substitute too much of their time for their parents' time in producing commodities for family consumption.

We do not yet have a complete understanding of which substitutions for parents' increasingly scarce time will prove benign. Recent research in psychology and neurobiology suggests that parental time, particularly in the first year of a child's life, is an important input to children's social, emotional, and physical development. We must cast the net broadly to fully understand the effect on parents and children of combining sometimes conflicting roles. Thus, it is a particular concern that workplaces make only minimal accommodations to the competing needs of work and families.

REFERENCES

Bailey, W. T. (1995). A longitudinal study of fathers' involvement with young children: Infancy to age 5 years. *Journal of Genetic Psychology, 155*, 331–339.

Baum, C. L. (2003). Does early maternal employment harm child development? An analysis of the potential benefits of leave taking. *Journal of Labor Economics, 21*, 409–448.

Baydar, N., & Brooks-Gunn, J. (1991). Effects of maternal employment and child care arrangement in infancy on preschoolers' cognitive and behavioral outcomes: Evidence from the children of the NLSY. *Developmental Psychology, 27*, 918–931.

Becker, G. S. (1965). A theory of the allocation of time. *Economic Journal, 75*, 493–517.

Belsky, J., & Eggebeen, D. (1991). Early and extensive maternal employment and young children's socioemotional development: Children of the National Longitudinal Survey of Youth. *Journal of Marriage and the Family, 53*, 1083–1110.

Bianchi, S. M. (2000). Maternal employment and time with children: Dramatic change or surprising continuity? *Demography, 37*, 401–414.

Blau, F. D., & Grossberg, A. J. (1992). Maternal labor supply and children's cognitive development. *Review of Economics and Statistics, 74*, 474–481.

Brooks-Gunn, J., Han, W. J., & Waldfogel, J. (2002). Maternal employment and child cognitive outcomes in the first three years of life: The NICHD Study of Early Child Care. *Child Development, 73*, 1052–1072.

Campbell, F. A., & Ramey, C. T. (1994). Effects of early intervention on intellectual and academic achievement: A follow-up study of children from low-income families. *Child Development, 65*, 684–698.

Case, A., Lubotsky, D., & Paxson, C. (2002). Economic status and health in childhood: The origins of the gradient. *American Economic Review, 92*, 1308–1334.

Chase-Lansdale, P. L., Moffitt, R. A., Lohman, B. J., Cherlin, A. J., Coley, R. L., Pittman, L. D., Roff, J., & Votruba-Drzal, E. (2003). Mothers' transitions from welfare to work and the well-being of preschoolers and adolescents. *Science, 299*, 1548–1552.

Clarke-Stewart, A. (1991). A home is not a school: The effects of child care on children's development. *Journal of Social Issues, 47*, 105–123.

Currie, J., & Hyson, R. (1999). Is the impact of health shocks cushioned by socioeconomic status? The case of low birthweight. *American Economic Review, 89*, 245–250.

Deaton, A. (2003). Health, inequality, and economic development. *Journal of Economic Literature, 41*, 113–158.

Desai, S., Chase-Lansdale, P. L., & Michael, R. (1989). Mother or market? Effects of maternal employment on cognitive development of four-year-old children. *Demography, 26*, 545–561.

Duncan, G. J. (2003, January). *Welfare reform and child and adolescent well-being.* Paper presented at the American Economics Association annual meeting, Washington, DC.

Ettner, S. L. (1996). New evidence on the relationship between income and health. *Journal of Health Economics, 15*, 67–85.

Frey, B. S., & Stutzer, A. (2002). What can economists learn from happiness research? *Journal of Economic Literature, 40*, 402–435.

Fuller, B., Kagan, S. L., & Loeb, S. (2002). *New lives for poor families? Mothers and young children move through welfare reform* (Wave 2 Technical Report). Available: www.gse.berkeley.edu/research/PACE/gup_tech_rpt.pdf.

Grossman, M. (1972). *The demand for health: A theoretical and empirical investigaton* (National Bureau of Economic Research Occasional Paper 119). New York: Columbia University Press.

Harvey, E. (1999). Short-term and long-term effects of early parental employment on children of the National Longitudinal Survey of Youth. *Developmental Psychology, 35*, 445–459.

Heckman, J. J. (1993). What has been learned about labor supply in the past twenty years? *American Economic Review, 83*, 116–121.

Hill, J., Waldfogel, J., & Brooks-Gunn, J. (2002). Assessing the differential effects of high quality child care: A new approach for exploiting post-treatment variables. *Journal of Policy Analysis and Management, 20*, 601–627.

Johansen, A., Leibowitz, A., & Waite, L. (1988). Child care and children's illness. *American Journal of Public Health, 78*, 1175–1177.

Kahneman, D. (2003). Maps of bounded rationality: Psychology for behavioral economics. *American Economic Review, 93*, 1449–1475.

Kahneman, D., & Snell, J. (1990). Predicting utility. In R. Hogarth (Ed.), *Insights in decision making* (pp. 295–310). Chicago, IL: University of Chicago Press.

Kahneman, D., & Varey, C. (1991). Notes on the psychology of utility. In J. Romer & J. Elser (Eds.), *Interpersonal comparisons of well-being* (pp. 127–163). Cambridge, MA: Cambridge University Press.

Kalil, A., Dunifon, R. E., & Danziger, S. K. (2001). In G. J. Duncan & P. L. Chase-Lansdale (Eds.), *For better and for worse: Welfare reform and the well-being of children and families* (pp. 154–178). New York: Russell Sage Foundation.

Killingsworth, M. R., & Heckman, J. J. (1986). Female labor supply: A survey. In O. C. Ashenfelter & R. Layard (Eds.), *Handbook of labor economics* (Vol. 1, pp. 103–144). Amsterdam: North-Holland.

Klerman, J. A., & Leibowitz, A. (1999). Job continuity among new mothers. *Demography, 36*,145–155.

Leibowitz, A. (1975). Education and the allocation of women's time. In F. Juster (Ed.), *Education, income, and human behavior* (pp. 171–197). New York: National Bureau of Economic Research and Carnegie Commission.

Leibowitz, A., & Klerman, J. A. (1995). Explaining changes in married mothers' employment over time. *Demography, 32*, 365–378.

Lundberg, S., & Pollak, R. A. (1996). Bargaining and distribution in marriage. *Journal of Economic Perspectives, 10*, 139–158.

Marmot, M. G., Smith, G. D., Stansfeld, S., Patel, C., North, F., Head, J., White, I., Brunner, E., & Feeney, A. (1991). Health inequalities among British civil servants (The Whitehall II Study). *Lancet, 8*, 1387–1393.

Martin, S. P. (2000). Diverging fertility among U.S. women who delay childbearing past age 30. *Demography, 37*, 523–533.

Mincer, J. (1962). Labor force participation of married women: A study in labor supply. In H. G. Lewis (Ed.), *Aspects of labor economics* (pp. 63–97). Princeton, NJ: Princeton University Press.

Mincer, J. (1963). Market prices, opportunity costs, and income effects. In C. F. Christ (Ed.), *Measurement in economics: Studies in mathematical economics and econometrics in memory of Yehuda Grunfeld* (pp. 67–82). Stanford, CA: University Press.

Moore, K. A., & Driscoll, A. K. (1997). Low-wage maternal employment and outcomes for children: A study. *The Future of Children, 7,* 122–127.

National Center for Health Statistics. (2002). *Health, United States, 2002* (With Chartbook on Trends in the Health of Americans). Hyattsville, MD: Author.

NICHD Early Child Care Research Network. (2000). The relation of child care to cognitive and language development. *Child Development, 71,* 960–980.

Newhouse, J. P., & the Insurance Experiment Group. (1993). *Free for all? Lessons from the RAND Health Insurance Experiment.* Cambridge, MA: Harvard University Press.

Pauly, M. V., & Nichols, L. M. (2002). *The nongroup health insurance market: Short on facts, long on opinions and policy disputes. Health affairs.* Available: <healthaffairs.org/WebExclusives/ 2106.Pauly.pdf>. Accessed January 7, 2003.

Pencavel, J. H. (1998). The market work behavior and wages of women: 1975–94. *Journal of Human Resources, 33,* 771–804.

Pritchett, L., & Summers, L. H. (1996). Wealthier is healthier. *Journal of Human Resources, 31,* 841–868.

Rindfuss, R. R., Morgan, S. P., & Offutt, K. (1996). Education and the changing age pattern of American fertility: 1963–1989. *Demography, 33,* 277–290.

Ruhm, C. J. (2000). Parental leave and child health. *Journal of Health Economics, 19,* 931–960.

Sandberg, J. F., & Hofferth, S. L. (2001). Changes in children's time with parents: United States, 1981–1997. *Demography, 38,* 423–436.

Silverstein, M., Sales, A. E., & Koepsell, T. D. (2003). Health care utilization and expenditures associated with child care attendance: a nationally representative sample. *Pediatrics, 111,* 371–375.

Smith, J. P. (1999). Healthy bodies and thick wallets: The dual relation between health and economic status. *Journal of Economic Perspectives, 13,* 145–166.

Stagner, M., Kortenkamp, K., & Reardon-Anderson, J. (2002). *Work, income, and well-being among long-term welfare recipients.* Urban Institute. Available: www.urban.org/template .cfm?NavMenuID.../ViewPublication.cfm&Publication ID=785. Accessed September 24, 2002.

Steinberg, L., Lamborn, S. D., Dornbusch, S. M., & Darling, N. (1992). Impact of parenting practices on adolescent achievement: Authoritative parenting, school involvement, and encouragement to succeed. *Child Development, 63,* 1266–1281.

Tout, K., Scarpa, J., & Zaslow, M. J. (2002). *Children of current and former welfare recipients: Similarly at risk.* Washington, DC: Child Trends Research Brief.

van Doorslaer, E., Wagstaff, A., Bleichrodt, H., Calonge, S., Gerdtham, U.-G., Gerfin, M., et al. (1997). Income-related inequalities in health: Some international comparisons. *Journal of Health Economics, 16,* 93–112.

Waldfogel, J., Han, W. J., & Brooks-Gunn, J. (2002). The effects of early maternal employment on child cognitive development. *Demography, 39,* 369–392.

14

Anthropology and the Workplace-Workforce Mismatch

Charles N. Darrah

San Jose State University

The mismatch between workplace and workforce is manifested in ways both large and small. On the grand scale, there are changes in the nature of work and employment arrangements, new technologies that seemingly erode the limitations of space and time, increased participation of women in the workforce, and the often demanding dictates of global competition (Osterman, Kochan, Locke, & Piore, 2001). These transformations become especially real for families when they alter the fabric of everyday life. Such alterations can seem trite or merely difficult to see, but they are redefining the familiar landmarks of daily life.

Consider, for example, Humberto and Suzanne's (pseudonyms) recently remodeled kitchen. Humberto is a fire captain who also responds to hazardous materials incidents and performs arson investigations for both his department and insurance companies. Suzanne is a job-sharing, high-tech marketer who also cares for two preschool-age daughters. Humberto proudly gestures to a blank wall and announces the plumbing and electrical "rough in" for his *next* kitchen remodeling concealed within it. The design was inspired by a kitchen he spotted while responding to a medical emergency in his capacity as firefighter. Later, he was able to look at the grateful homeowner's blueprints. The refrigerator sits against the opposite wall, its door a billboard for the family calendar and mission statement. The latter is also stored in Suzanne's Palm Pilot, along with other information about work and family. The impetus for the statement comes from Steven Covey's book, *The Seven Habits of Highly Effective People*. Suzanne was part of an informal network of coworkers who discussed and followed Covey's advice, and her employer provided support for seminars and materials. Spouse, coworkers, management guru, and employer were thus implicated in defining the family as one with a specific mission. The statement was even prepared on a laptop computer purchased by Suzanne for work and then reimbursed by her employer.

Just as work penetrates the home through Suzanne's actions, so too does family migrate to the workplace, where she manages her retirement portfolio, asssembled incrementally at previous employers, or gives and takes advice about parenting from a corporate listserv. Of course, she says, you must be careful about what advice to share: She would *never* reveal that her children have not been vaccinated because the outcry could damage her reputation at work.

Humberto is a little skeptical about the mission statement, but he too integrates work into his life in subtle ways. He has found most of the sub-contractors for his home through the fire department, and he organizes them using his department's Incident Command System (ICS). The system was de-veloped in Los Angeles County to coordinate operations, planning, logistics, and finances at wildfires, and it has been adopted by many other fire depart-ments. Humberto has internalized ICS and even defined himself in terms of operations, planning, logistics, and finances during a recent job interview.

Suzanne and Humberto's family is experiencing the mismatch between workplace and workforce in their own distinct way. They are but one among myriad other families, and the constraints they operate within are undoubtedly distinct even among job-sharing, high-tech marketer–fire captain couples. The challenge is to use these distinct family sagas to find ways to ameliorate the collective difficulties of meeting competing obligations under new re-alities. For example, Humberto and Suzanne's situation allows a glimpse of a broader social change. The interpenetration of work and family blurs the boundary between these familiar domains, turning each into a simultaneously exotic realm. What constitutes work becomes ambiguous. The workplace, too, becomes a site for exploring family issues, and although it is sometimes a source of strain, the workplace is also where the resources used to cope with those strains originate. Although the couple's daily life is hectic and ordinary, through it they engage a larger moral universe, one that often fails to provide clear guideposts. Their mission statement, for example, is as contested as it is shared, and it is also a way to work through conflicts between culturally shaped obligations and the exigencies of daily life. Although much about their lives is rationalized by the rubric of efficiency, they are also creating new stories and rituals that mediate the ambiguities of work and family. Finally, as Suzanne and Humberto engage the mismatch, they also redefine the category of the person and the desirable qualities of personal character. They live grounded in traditional religious faith, yet their daily lives compel them to ask, Who are we and who should we be?

Stories such as those of Humberto and Suzanne remind us that the mismatch is more complex than simply trying to optimize the relation between workplaces and workforce. It entails understanding a broader set of factors that play out in the lives of real people in different ways. Understanding both the mismatch and its broader context is a prelude to developing responsive, effective policy.

ANTHROPOLOGY AND THE STUDY OF THE AMERICAN MAINSTREAM

Anthropology is popularly associated with studies of the exotic, and such studies arguably define the discipline for many of its practitioners. Nonetheless, the history of ethnographic and anthropological studies of the American mainstream is lengthy. Ethnography and anthropology are closely related, but they are worth distinguishing. *Ethnography* refers to a methodology (Bernard, 2002) characterized by extended fieldwork in the everyday settings of people's lives. It involves a varied set of methods, such as participant observation, open and closed interviewing techniques, and systematic observation. Although it is most associated with cultural anthropology, its methods have long been used in sociology and, more recently, in fields such as education, health care, and organizational behavior. *Anthropology* refers to a discipline characterized by its theoretical perspectives, which include commitments to cross-cultural comparison and a holistic understanding of the human species.

The ethnographic tradition of U.S. community studies began with the "Middletown" studies by sociologists Robert and Helen Lynd (Lynd & Lynd, 1929, 1937) and continued with anthropologist W. Lloyd Warner in his studies of "Yankee City" (Warner 1949; Warner & Lunt, 1941, 1942). (The reader is referred to Mary Margaret Overbey and Kathryn Marie Dudley's [2000] discussion of history, tradition, and methods in *Anthropology and Middle Class Working Families* for a full discussion of anthropological-ethnographic studies of the U.S. mainstream. This account is largely based on their discussion.) Other studies by anthropologists varied the forms of community by using regions, ethnic populations, and industries. The works of Davis, Gardner, and Gardner (1941) in the southern United States, and Drake and Clayton (1945), Powdermaker (1939), and Goldschmidt (1947, 1978) are representative.

Community studies conducted after World War II challenged the assumption of cultural homogeneity and conformity popular at the time. The 1967 study by Herbert Gans of Levittown, a planned community typically portrayed as blandly conformist, drew attention to its diversity of behaviors and beliefs (Gans, 1967). Anthropologist Varenne (1977) explored the typically American values of individualism and community participation in a midwestern town, documenting tension and conflict as well as conformity and integration.

Anthropologists also documented the place of work in people's lives and in the very nature of community. Lamphere (1987) traced the participation of generations of immigrant women in the New England textile industry. Newman's *Falling From Grace* (1988) and *Declining Fortunes* (1993) focused specifically on middle-class families and communities caught in the spiral of de-industrialization, downward mobility, and falling expectations. This research was extended by Dudley (1994, 2000) in the midwest. Other ethnographers are contributing to a nascent comparative research agenda on middle-class families. Gullestad's (1984) *Kitchen Table Society*, for example, explored how the lives of young Norwegian mothers unfold in their homes and neighborhoods. Other studies, such as Weston's (1991) study of lesbian families, expanded our definition of family.

Although much of anthropology's work is relevant to issues of work and family, it is only recently that some anthropologists have focused explicitly on work and family in the U.S. mainstream. Three of the Alfred P. Sloan Foundation Centers on Working Families are broadly anthropological and ethnographic in focus, and their agendas and projects are especially relevant to the mismatch thesis, although they pursue distinct research agendas (Fricke, 1998). The Sloan Foundation Centers are interdisciplinary at the core, and they are organized around research questions, not anthropological identity. Their projects explore the everyday lives of family members as they navigate domains including, but not limited to, work and family. The socialization of children into the changing realities of work and family is a common concern, as is the role of stress in the lives of families.

The Four Fields of Anthropology

Anthropology clearly cannot claim a privileged role in understanding the mismatch; the contributions of other disciplines and fields are noteworthy. Thus, we may fairly ask, What role remains for anthropology to play? I argue that it is anthropology's tradition of integrating different perspectives on complex, emerging phenomena that makes it essential. The idea of a mismatch is shorthand for a larger and multidimensional cultural shift with important features that are only beginning to emerge. It represents the intersection of structural changes in the lives of families, as conceptualized in a way that is culturally familiar and comforting. What anthropology offers is an integrative perspective on the mismatch, as well as a way to contextualize it in a particular historical moment.

It does so through its four-field approach to understanding social phenomena, reflecting the discipline's constituent fields of archaeology, linguistic anthropology, physical anthropology, and cultural anthropology. The latter field, and its associated methodology of ethnography, is at the center of the discipline's interest in work and family. Cultural anthropologists are especially concerned with practices that link social organization with cultural models and their material embodiments. They are sensitive to inconsistencies or contradictions between structural constraints, lived experience, and familiar cultural assumption, values, and norms. Distinctive characteristics of cultural anthropology include a holistic analysis of social systems, attention to the often divergent understandings of cultural insiders, concern with the meaning of action to its participants, and the relations between local settings and larger systems.

Linguistic anthropology focuses both on the primary means by which children are socialized into practices and the categories by which cultural models are organized. The language socialization paradigm, for example, assumes that "language is a form of social action, as well as a critical means of social reproduction and transformation across generations" (Paugh, 2002, p. 2). It focuses on the activities and interactions of everyday life in which children participate and observe, and it is especially valuable for understanding how children gain working knowledge of adult worlds. The paradigm provides a tool for understanding how a family is created and maintained through talk, such as personal narratives, directions or instructions, expressions of emotion, and topics of conversation. It allows comparable analyses of how children learn about work and how knowledge about the mismatch is being transmitted from parents to children (Paugh, 2002).

Physical anthropology draws our attention to the interplay of cultural practices and meanings and human biology. Thomas (1998), in his discussion of the biology of poverty, presents a model that incorporates environmental stressors and their impact on human biology, as well as biological and psychological adjustments, social inequalities, and access to essential resources. Worthman, DeCaro, and Brown (2002) created a model that incorporates concepts of cultural consensus modeling, status incongruity, and the analysis of cultural models, with psychobiological models of stress, affective regulation, and reactivity.

Archaeology, long associated in the popular imagination with the monumental remains of past cultures, is useful for understanding the everyday lives of household members. Archeological methods can be used to analyze the architecture of houses, the organization and use of spaces within them, and their provisioning with artifacts (Arnold & Graesch, 2002).

As different as the fields of anthropology are, they share characteristics that make them relevant to the mismatch thesis. First, the different fields permit exploratory research where the existence and nature of a phenomenon is uncertain and where familiar measures and indicators may be misleading. Second, they document processes and systems that can shape decisions on which dimensions of a phenomenon to measure. Third, they question the categories they seek to explore. Rather than simply accept assumed categories, the fields allow us to confront our own, often culture-bound, assumptions about that which we seek to explain. The fields of anthropology are thus well matched to the challenges posed by the mismatch thesis.

ANTHROPOLOGY, ETHNOGRAPHY, AND THE MISMATCH THESIS

The anthropological research program on U.S. families and work is still in its early stages, and it is premature to speak of consensus among its practitioners. Nonetheless, I can offer several generalizations—not as a definitive summary of the field, but rather for their salience to the mismatch thesis.

The Field of Obligations

Ethnographic research demonstrates that people engage in obligations that cut across work, family, and other familiar cultural domains, such as recreation, religion, and civic involvement. These obligations are often discharged independent of particular places, so that different domains influence the meanings and practices of the others. Driving these obligations are structural changes that have left individuals increasingly empowered to assume more responsibilities, such as managing their children's educations and their own retirement portfolios, shopping for the best deals on everything from airline tickets to utilities, and becoming experts on health and medical information. The tasks associated with these obligations are performed opportunistically, and they far exceed any simple distinction between work and family. Yet they are not merely externally imposed; they also reflect decisions about lifestyles, status, and a bias toward activity and doing more.

Several implications follow. One is that we cannot assume work to be simply a source of stress given that it can also be a source of the resources people use to manage their obligations. Another implication is that families may be less a refuge from an often hostile or indifferent world than sources of stress for their members; the workplace may provide that respite. A deeper issue is that the interface of work and family may simply be the visible arena where problems are expressed even if their causes lie elsewhere. Finally, by breaking down familiar categorizations, the web of obligations may be driving the need to create personal and family narratives that provide people with meaningful identities and coherent trajectories through life. The ethnographic record suggests that people do not organize their lives along discrete variables, but through narratives that connect disparate elements and weave them together. In doing so, they provide us with windows onto the strains and tensions with which people grapple daily. None of this is to minimize the impact of jobs and work on families, but instead to caution against narrow formulations of the relationships and normative assumptions regarding good or bad outcomes.

It's in the Details

The ethnographic record shows that specific conditions affect how work and family play out. People do not work or have families in general, but they work in particular ways and have particular families; they face specific opportunities and constraints. They want to be workers and family members and people in specific ways, and the details of their lives, such as how they define being a good person, worker, parent, child, and neighbor, have consequences.

Assumptions about prototypical workers, jobs, homes, and families are misleading, and responsive policy must be based on assumed variability. For example, we cannot simply juxtapose the workplace as the location for work and the home as the place for leisure. The former is indeed the site of leisure for many workers, and accounts of hours spent with nose to grindstone often exaggerate hours spent working. Furthermore, we cannot assume that the tasks performed at work are necessary, especially when workers have learned the necessity of appearing busy to protect their jobs. There is a performance or theatrical aspect of work, one in which people signal to one another that they are indeed hard pressed to meet the demands of their jobs. At the same time, households have taken on many workplace characteristics as the requirements of maintaining homes have become another job. Yet allocating tasks at home may be less well defined than at work, and the tasks can be less predictable, stable, or sequential. A child's sudden need to construct a model of the earth from familiar kitchen goods or to investigate the history of the Greek alphabet can upset evening plans, but so too can cancelled insurance policies, demands for medical information, and troubleshooting defunct Palm Pilots or personal computers. The home can be the site of multitasking and real work precisely because the stakes are higher and slack is nonexistent.

Family as Code

We speak comfortably of work and family, often assuming that the former is robbing us of time to meet the obligations of the latter. Yet family, or "doing family," has become a code for many obligations the family has assumed after those obligations are shed by other institutions. The result is a burgeoning collection of activities that are designated as "family," but that could be (and has been) performed elsewhere. When parents share information about the variety of teams, courses, and clubs that they can potentially patch together to provide after-school care, it is simultaneously a commentary on family and the absence of safe neighborhoods and unavailable adult supervision. When they devote evenings to investigate college opportunities for their children, it is a commentary on the lack of such services in cash-strapped schools. When they become one another's medical experts, it is a commentary on the availability of medical advice. Ethnography shows us the results of these proliferating choices and responsibilities in so many domains of life that ultimately play out in the family.

A corollary to this scenario is that providing families with more time may not be beneficial, but rather just be absorbed by more of this type of work. The mismatch thesis is thus situated in a much larger sociocultural shift that is largely playing out in the intimate realm of family and household. An implication is that policy experiments cannot simply be bounded by the parameters of work and family. Any gains for the family would likely soon be absorbed by the relentless incursion of obligations from elsewhere, further transforming the family into a site for production and consumption, rather than for intimacy, refuge, and simply being.

Time Management

Becoming better at managing time, working smarter, and being more efficient have become middle-class mantras for the new century, as indicated by the steady stream of self-improvement books and workshops, the quest for technology that enhances our ability to communicate and keep track of our lives, and the importation of management techniques from workplace to home. Yet the emphasis on time management poses the question, What precisely is being managed? It deflects attention from the activities being performed and somehow managed without asking why those activities are necessary in the first place. It is a question of content, not just creating more time or better ways to manage it.

Ethnographic research (Darrah, English-Lueck, & Freeman, 2001) documents both the proliferation of obligations and the creation of a social and technological infrastructure to cope with them. Creating plans and their backups, collecting intelligence about threats to busy schedules, providing and maintaining efficiency enhancing devices, and building social networks that can buffer uncertainty are time-consuming. It is not enough to simply improve time management skills or even give people more time; it is also necessary to address the underlying necessity for activities that consume the time.

Talk about time and its management is at best distracting, diverting us from the sources of our busyness and seeking to enable us to take on more. A more sinister view is that the apparent time bind is a function of the notion of efficient management that creates or enacts it. There is a growing sense that we can and should do more, and the notion of productivity has pervaded many families that emphasize constant activity and the increased status that busyness and participation brings. In this way, the logic of the workplace has pervaded home, and we must question the sense in which family and work are mismatched.

Agency and Best Practices

Ethnography documents people's creative efforts to develop practices to cope with the demands of work and family. Regardless of what researchers, policymakers, or employers expect or think is reasonable, families are not simply passive responders to external changes, but rather they exert agency to control their lives. They do so by colonizing their homes with offices that mirror what they have at work, just as they colonize workplaces to fulfill the obligations of other domains of life. From their perspectives, these practices make sense and are usually the best they can do under the existing constraints. Just as researchers look to best practices, so too do ordinary people watch and query others for best practices and experiment with their everyday lives.

This is neither to argue that folk wisdom should trump empirical research nor that the practices people use are optimal. Indeed the quest for best practices is embedded in a larger worldview in which there is a status value to activities. Parents may well enact their own lives in those of their children through overscheduling, thus creating a demonstrable act of devotion. Middle-class status, once simply a function of consumption, may now be equally defined by activities—the more we do, the higher our status. This value of busyness is not only imposed on us, it also results from internal drives toward status. That said, we must not once again assume the need for new solutions to the mismatch: American families are already conducting their own experiments.

Individuals, Together and Apart

Finally, ethnographic fieldwork documents the impact of broader social change in the lives of ordinary people. These changes also provide the context for the mismatch thesis, and they reveal an individualism that is both typically American and strikingly new (Hall & Lindholm, 1999). American individualism has been long noted and variously defined, and much of the phenomena subsumed by the mismatch thesis reflect the rhetoric of the empowered individual, free to assume responsibilities and navigate routes in perilous waters. Attachments to particular employers can be brief, and jobs can suddenly disappear. Anticipating unpredictability is both oxymoronic and ubiquitous.

Building a career that spans different organizations is increasingly the norm, and those careers are ultimately the responsibilities of virtuous individuals.

At the heart of the mismatch thesis is a dissonance between structural necessities and the space for alternative conceptualizations of the self. If the mismatch can be viewed more broadly as one between workplace and workforce, then more narrowly the mismatch is between culturally variable notions of character and moral virtue, and the ability to act in ways that realize those virtues (Sennett, 1998). The resulting dilemmas cannot be resolved by individual efficiency or productivity alone.

Ethnography suggests that different implications follow from these macro- and microlevel views. The former leads to experiments with workplace arrangements that take for granted a flexible, malleable self that can be engineered to fit the new, inevitable specifications of work. The latter suggests experiments that respect variable conceptions of the self and that enable people to live consistently with them. The macro thus focuses on remaking the self to fit new realities, and the micro focuses on remaking our institutions, including workplaces, in ways that respect different notions of character. These perspectives can be viewed as conflicting or just as easily as complementary: How can we have productive workplaces in which qualities of character are assets and are not diminished?

IMPLICATIONS

Several implications follow from the analysis presented in this chapter. First, the analysis suggests conceptualizing the mismatch thesis in a larger context while tracing its impacts on the minutiae of everyday life. The view from the larger context calls for us to examine the relationships of work and family to larger systems. We cannot understand the causes and consequences of the mismatch between work and family without also understanding, for example, the ramifications for community, consumption, and health care. The view from the microcosm of everyday life calls for a focus on the specific pathways by which the mismatch is manifested in the lives of diverse families. In this way, we can capture how the mismatch is remaking the definitions of family and character, and how these changes are affecting health and well-being of workers and their children.

Second, the analysis suggests a research design in which ethnography is combined with other methods, such as survey research. Ethnography can inform survey design and construction by pointing to measures closer to empirical data and providing contextual data that can shed further light on empirical findings by explicating potential causal relationships. The breadth of anthropological data-collection strategies and techniques is well suited to this challenge.

Relatedly, surveys and other quantitative methods can enhance the rigor of ethnographic findings by testing relationships and measuring the extent of phenomena described through field research. Integrating the methods of linguistic anthropology, physical anthropology, and archaeology with ethnography and survey methods can contribute to the theoretical integration demanded by the mismatch thesis.

Third, anthropology can inform us about the domains in which we should experiment. It suggests an approach that binds analyses of body and ritual, technology and household economics, and artifacts and meaning. Above all, it suggests experiments that build on the extant practices people are using to cope with the mismatch in their own lives.

Finally, ethnography can capture the impact of experiments on both workplaces and families, including their costs and benefits from the perspectives of different stakeholders. Addressing the mismatch requires research to go beyond familiar assumptions that equate family with goodness and respite, work with badness and stress. Teasing apart the complex sentiments surrounding both work and family is a critical step in addressing the mismatch, one to which anthropology is well suited.

ACKNOWLEDGMENTS

The author thanks Tom Fricke and Bradd Shore for their generous contributions to this chapter. Jim Freeman graciously provided editorial comments on short notice. Responsibility for the content, of course, rests solely with the author. The fieldwork on which parts of this chapter are based was sponsored by the Alfred P. Sloan Foundation (Darrah, English-Lueck, & Freeman, 2001). The author acknowledges the support of the Foundation and program officer Kathleen Christensen, as well as the contributions of co-principal investigators Jan English-Lueck and Jim Freeman. The author also acknowledges the assistance of Sloan Foundation Centers on Work and Family directors Tom Fricke (Center for the Ethnography of Everyday Life, University of Michigan), Elinor Ochs (UCLA Center on Everyday Lives of Families, University of California, Los Angeles), and Bradd Shore (The Emory Center for Myth and Ritual in American Life, Emory University) in preparing the section on the explicit anthropological focus on work and family in the U.S. mainstream.

REFERENCES

Arnold, J., & Graesch, A. (2002). *Space, time and activities in the everyday lives of working families: An ethnoarchaeological approach* (Working Paper No. 2). Los Angeles: UCLA Center on Everyday Lives of Families.

Bernard, H. R. (2002). *Research methods in anthropology: Qualitative and quantitative approaches* (3rd ed.). Walnut Creek, CA: AltaMira Press.

Darrah, C. N., English-Lueck, J. A., & Freeman, J. M. (2001). *Ethnography of dual career middle class families* (Final report to the Alfred P. Sloan Foundation).

Davis, A., Gardner, B. B., & Gardner, M. R. (1941). *Deep south: A social anthropological study of caste and class.* Chicago: University of Chicago Press.

Drake, S. C., & Clayton, H. R. (1945). *Black metropolis: A study of Negro life in a northern city.* New York: Harcourt, Brace.

Dudley, K. M. (1994). *The end of the line: Lost jobs, new lives in postindustrial America.* Chicago: University of Chicago Press.

Dudley, K. M. (2000). Debt and dispossession: *Farm loss in America's heartland.* Chicago: University of Chicago Press.

Fricke, T. (1998). *Changing cultures of family and work: Background document for the Center for the Ethnography of Everyday Life* (Working Paper No. 001-98). Ann Arbor, MI: University of Michigan Center for the Ethnography of Everyday Life.

Gans, H. (1967). *The Levittowners: Ways of life and politics in a new community.* New York: Pantheon.

Goldschmidt, W. (1947). *As you sow.* New York: Harcourt, Brace.

Goldschmidt, W. (1978). *As you sow: Three essays in the social consequences of agribusiness.* Montclair, NJ: Allenheld Osmun.

Gullestad, M. (1984). *Kitchen-table society: A case study of the family life and friendships of young working-class mothers in urban Norway.* Oslo: Universitetsforlaget.

Hall, J. A., & Lindholm, C. (1999). *Is America falling apart?* Princeton, NJ: Princeton University Press.

Lamphere, L. (1987). *From working daughters to working mothers: Immigrant women in a New England industrial community.* Ithaca, NY: Cornell University Press.

Lynd, R., & Lynd, H. (1929). *Middletown: A study in American culture.* New York: Harcourt, Brace, Jovanovich.

Lynd, R., & Lynd, H. (1937). *Middletown in transition: A study in cultural conflict.* New York: Harcourt, Brace, Jovanovich.

Newman, K. (1988). *Falling from grace: The experience of downward mobility in the American middle class.* New York: The Free Press.

Newman, K. (1993). *Declining fortunes: The withering of the American dream.* New York: Basic Books.

Osterman, P., Kochan, T. A., Locke, R. M., & Piore, M. (2001). *Working in America: A blueprint for the new labor market.* Cambridge, MA: MIT Press.

Overbey, M. M., & Dudley, K. M. (2000). *Anthropology and middle class working families: A research agenda.* Arlington, VA: American Anthropological Association.

Paugh, A. (2002). *Child language socialization in working families* (Working Paper No. 6). Los Angeles: UCLA Center on Everyday Lives of Families.

Powdermaker, H. (1939). *After freedom: A cultural study in the deep south.* New York: Viking.

Sennett, R. (1998). *The corrosion of character: The personal consequences of work in the new capitalism.* New York: W. W. Norton.

Thomas, R. B. (1998). The evolution of human adaptability paradigms: Toward a biology of poverty. In A. Goodman & T. Leatherman (Eds.), *Building a new biocultural synthesis: Political-economic perspectives on human biology* (pp. 43–73). Ann Arbor: University of Michigan Press.

Varenne, H. (1977). *Americans together.* New York: Teachers College Press.

Warner, W. L. (1949). *Social class in America.* New Haven, CT: Yale University Press.

Warner, W. L., & Lunt, P. S. (1941). *The social life of a modern community.* New Haven, CT: Yale University Press.

Warner, W. L., & Lunt, P. S. (1942). *The status system of a modern community*. New Haven, CT: Yale University Press.

Weston, K. (1991). *Families we choose: Lesbians, gays, kinship*. New York: Columbia University Press.

Worthman, C., DeCaro, J., & Brown, R. (2002). *Cultural consensus approaches to the study of American family life* (Working Paper No. 13). Atlanta, GA: The Emory Center for Myth and Ritual in American Life.

15

Sociological Perspectives on Work and Family

Jennifer Glass
University of Iowa

Sociologists have been concerned with institutional friction between work and family systems in the industrialized West as far back as the 1960s, when Lewis and Rose Laub Coser (1974) first labeled both the family and workplace *greedy institutions* that monopolized individuals' time and energy. Although the problem has been framed in different ways at different times, the essential sociological insight that ties their different perspectives together is that the personal difficulties individuals face in trying to fulfill both family and paid work responsibilities are socially patterned and somewhat predictable given the competing goals of industrial production and family reproduction.

Sociological research has addressed many facets of this mismatch: the consequences of a mother's employment for herself, her family, and her employers; the growth of solo parents in the labor force; the time squeeze in middle-class, dual-earner families; the decline of organized labor and labor laws; the child-care "crisis"; and the effects of globalization on workers, to name just a few. Two questions, however, have dominated the work-family mismatch research in sociology: (a) Who does the housework and child care in American families, and why have men not assumed more responsibility as women's employment has grown? and (b) What causes the gender wage gap, and why does it continue to exist? The persistence of a strong gender division of labor in both families and workplaces has significant consequences for the material wealth and well-being of women and children. The different sociological approaches to these problems range from social-psychological concepts of identity formation and role commitment to macrotheories that emphasize conflict between social groups and institutional inertia. In this chapter, I explore how each of the four frameworks—symbolic interactionism, ecological systems, life course, and conflict theories—has been used to identify and explain friction between work and family systems. Symbolic interactionism is the natural place to begin given that it is the intellectual precursor of theories of role enactment and role commitment that have dominated work and family research across multiple disciplines.

THE SYMBOLIC INTERACTIONIST TRADITION

Symbolic interactionism is rooted in the notion that social order is accomplished by the routine enactment of social roles (Goffman, 1959; McCall & Simmons, 1978). Adhering to social roles makes interaction orderly and predictable, simplifying the accomplishment of routine tasks. Because social roles are typically taken for granted, they are only thrown into relief when deviations occur (public discomfort with house husbands is an example). The responses to this deviation can range from mild confusion to extreme social ostracism or economic ruin. Prominent among social roles are those involving gender, marriage, and parenthood. Roles within work organizations include worker, supervisor, manager, or owner. The appropriate behavior in these roles is determined culturally and learned through childhood socialization.

During the course of 19th-century industrialization, the needs of a new capitalist system of production dramatically transformed social roles of men and women. Masculinity was recast as the pursuit of money outside the home, whereas responsibility for the education and moral development of children was relinquished to mothers. Wage labor became the province of men, whereas the role of *housewife* was created and defined as most suitable for women. This redefinition of gender roles was in response to the removal of productive labor from the home and the emergence of mass commercial production in large, hierarchical factories. Social institutions (educational systems, businesses, political and judicial systems, health care systems, etc.) adapted their operations around these new definitions of masculine and feminine roles, although large segments of the population (immigrants, African Americans, and poor Whites) could not organize their lives around these roles. This latter point is extremely important in understanding the effect of gender roles. Institutions became embedded with gendered codes of behavior based on the roles of middle-class women and men in the larger society—or as Acker (1990) stated, institutions became *gendered*.

As a result, by the beginning of the 20th century, the contradictory social roles of employee and homemaker were difficult to simultaneously fulfill. Employees were forced to devote long hours and much energy to jobs in a location often distant from home and neighborhood. At work interruptions were not tolerated, tardiness and absences were discouraged, and rules limited employee autonomy over the schedule of work shifts. The tasks of daily reproduction (being fed, housed, clothed, and cared for) were to occur off-site in the home. The role of homemakers, in essence, was to provide such family care for workers and future workers (children). However, as rising divorce rates, declining male wages, smaller family sizes, increases in nonmarital childbearing, longer life spans, and feminism began to erode the viability of traditional gender roles (Davis, 1989) during the 20th century, these contradictions in the expectations of worker and homemaker could no longer be ignored.

Many concepts from symbolic interactionism have filtered into popular discourse about work-family issues, including role conflict, role strain, role overload, and role scripts, to name just a few. An employee who should attend an important meeting at the same time as a daughter's birthday party experiences role conflict; a breastfeeding mother who must use her 15-minute breaks at work to pump breast milk in an unheated closet experiences role strain; a single parent who must work overtime to provide for two children and still perform all the domestic labor experiences role overload; while a father who provides primary care for his infant while his wife works violates a role script. Much research on employed parents' mental health, happiness, and effectiveness has been based on theories of role performance (Lennon, 1987; Thoits, 1983) and the twin notions that successful role enactment produces positive mental and physical health benefits for individuals while deviance or role failure produces stress and social censure.

More sophisticated renditions of role theory have posited both positive and negative health consequences for successful role performance, pointing out that some social roles (e.g., professional worker) provide more opportunities for material and social reward than others (e.g., housewife; see Bernard, 1981; Gove & Tudor, 1973). Theorists have also recognized that role performances always occur in a particular context. Sometimes those circumstances are conducive to success, but often they are not, leading to what researchers labeled poor *role quality*. A hostile supervisor or noxious working conditions may limit the positive effect of employment on health, just as a temperamental or disabled child or a distant, cold spouse might limit the positive effect of caregiving roles (Barnett, Brennan, & Marshall, 1994; Lennon, 1994). Additional work has focused on role constellations (particular combinations of roles), arguing, in contrast to the theorized negative outcomes of role overload or conflict, that multiple roles can both provide multiple opportunities for self-enhancement and act as buffers to offset the inadequacies of any single role performance (Barnett & Baruch, 1985; Marks, 1977). Finally, theorists note that social roles differ in their salience or the level of commitment an individual brings to a particular social role. Stronger role commitments produce stronger effects on well-being.

Applying symbolic interactionism to the division of domestic labor and the gender wage gap has focused on the primacy of the work role for men and the primacy of family roles for women. If women are sanctioned for failing to perform domestic roles and men are sanctioned for failing to provide materially as workers, then each gender, the theory presumes, will focus more energy and commitment on the roles that provide the most rewards. Hence, men will only reluctantly engage in domestic labor, although they may love their children, and women will commit less time to career enhancement, although they earn wages and enjoy their jobs.

Role theory has been criticized on numerous fronts, but mainly for its failure to produce clear hypotheses about the sources of continuity and change in the behaviors associated with social roles, its inability to predict either individual or aggregate role behavior as social conditions change, and its focus on a reflexive performance motivation (i.e., people act to avoid social censure and receive social rewards). It does not, for example, explain why individuals continue to adhere to social roles that are obsolete or do not meet their needs or goals. Nor does it address whether pressures to conform truly explain gendered roles in both work and family that result in less material wealth and worse health for women and men.

For these reasons, symbolic interactionism has shifted its focus to the social psychology of role commitments. Newer work in self-identity theory attempts to explain how individuals internalize role prescriptions so that social control is unnecessary. In self-identity theory (Burke, 1991; Stryker & Burke, 2000), individuals, through both social learning and direct experience, develop commitments to core identities, which then direct and control behavior in situations that activate those identities. Core identities might include occupation or profession, motherhood or fatherhood, religious affiliation, and so forth. Successful role performance can help develop meaningful identities, but it is not always necessary for strong role commitments to develop. Cultural ideologies can also stimulate commitment to core identities. Being a good mother, for example, can be important to a childless woman who aspires to motherhood.

Several prominent scholars of work-family issues have used these notions of core identities and ideological commitments to explain the seemingly intractable nature of the gender division of labor. For example, Hochschild (1989) used the notion of "deep ideologies" of gender to explain why women continue to perform the vast majority of housework and child care despite economic independence or their own exhaustion from the "second shift" of domestic labor at the end of their paid workday. Similarly, the notion of core identities can explain why men may limit their involvement in family life despite supporting feminism and a belief in equally sharing domestic labor and child care. Brines (1994) used such notions to explain why un- or underemployed men are particularly likely to eschew housework and child care despite their availability to do these tasks. Hays (1996) used the idea of dominant ideological commitments to explain why both employed and nonemployed mothers adhere to a single standard of deeply "involved motherhood" and try to justify their employment, or lack thereof, within the framework of children's best interests. Deutsch (1999) used a similar framework of ideological commitments to explain why many couples at some point make life choices that result in stronger work involvement for husbands and stronger domestic involvement for wives and then justify that choice post hoc as economically rational.

Self-identity theory is also evident in the numerous studies that find that the greatest psychological and health benefits of work and family roles accrue when behavioral preferences and practices match, regardless of what those preferences might be (traditional or egalitarian: see, e.g., Burke & Greenglass, 2000; Ross, Mirowsky, & Huber, 1983). Within this framework, it is not the roles that individuals fill that enhance or detract from well-being; rather, it is the congruence between the core identities that form a sense of self and the roles routinely enacted in everyday life. Thus, the mere fact of a mother's employment says little about how it will affect her own or her family's well-being, but the ability of a given job to facilitate the level of work and family involvement that a mother desires is quite important.

The twin notions that cultural ideologies are important in shaping individual identities and that, once formed, identities structure behavior even when it can lead to deprivation, are still widely used to explain work-family behavior and its effect on health and well-being (Simon, 1995; Tang & Tang, 2001).

ECOLOGICAL SYSTEMS THEORY

Although symbolic interactionism is useful for understanding tensions between work and family life, it focuses on individuals rather than systems of cooperating individuals. Ecological systems theory (Bronfenbrenner, 1989) and family systems theory (Broderick, 1993) broaden the focus to the larger context in which individuals operate—a systemic division of labor among families, workplaces, and communities. Ecological systems theory is based on the idea that individual development, including health and well-being, is determined by the interplay of systems within which individuals reside.

Such systems have both temporal and spatial dimensions. For example, families are systems within which individuals both receive and provide care at different points in time. Mothers may provide care and social support for young children to the detriment of their own physical and mental health, yet find that their children are social supports in later life, which fathers may lack. Communities are locations within which certain amenities (e.g., jobs and schools, child care, and shops) are either easily available and high quality or not. Communities either provide the opportunities to improve health and well-being and reduce conflict and strain across social roles or they exacerbate these issues. The roles that individuals assume, their level of commitment, and their performance are all explained, in large part, by the context in which they find themselves. For example, a single mother in an urban, low-income community would have a much more difficult time finding a high-paying job and reasonably priced, high-quality child care than a well-educated, married, suburban mother. Committing to a job and basing one's identity on success in that job is, therefore, less likely for the urban mother than the suburban mother.

According to ecological systems theory, individual characteristics can either create opportunities for role involvement or foreclose them. Some characteristics are internally determined (such as temperament), but many are socially derived (e.g., level of education, wealth). Others are ascribed characteristics (age, race, class, and gender) that vary in their meaning by culture, but are almost invariably used either directly or indirectly to structure opportunities in work, family, and community systems. For example, social class and ethnicity in the United States often determine access to safe neighborhoods with good schools and jobs.

Family systems theory focuses specifically on the interplay among the activities of family members. Rarely can the actions of individuals be explained or their effects on well-being understood without determining how the actions fit within the larger family system. For example, the effects of a mother's employment on the well-being of family members depend as well on the work activities of other household members. Is the mother employed because her partner cannot find work or cannot find enough work to support the family? When the mother is at work, are children in high-quality care or are they left to their own devices? Are domestic tasks shared by a spouse, children, or paid help, or does the mother perform a second shift of housework and home management after work? Is the mother's work schedule compatible with the children's schedules or does it interfere with family time together?

By understanding the family context, analysts can better understand some of the contradictory or ambiguous findings of research on work and family. For example, early research showed that wives' employment enhanced their own but reduced their husbands' mental health. Later work showed that this result occurred only for husbands who failed to help with any of the housework and child-care chores (Ross, Mirowsky, & Huber, 1983). Husbands who failed to perform any domestic labor may have had wives who were tired or resentful, which lowered husbands' quality of life.

Systems theories have provided analytic concepts such as work-family balance and work-family fit to describe the homeostatic nature of work-family systems. In systems theories, the behavior of individuals is often motivated by system goals, and maintaining smoothly functioning systems determines the activities of system members. Individuals seek the quantity and type of roles that mesh with the actions of other family members in achieving family goals. Individuals avoid, whenever possible, activities that destabilize the smooth operation of daily life within work, family, and community systems. When these destabilizing activities cannot be avoided, they produce conflict and lessen the well-being of system members.

It is easy to envision from a systems perspective why work and family became different and gendered realms of behavior that have proved resistant to change. The breadwinner–housewife system emerged from pressure on an earlier agrarian system of household production. With fathers out of the house and into the factory, mothers assumed a stronger management role in child care and housework. This complementary system enabled families to efficiently generate revenue and produce healthy, educated children. So long as the breadwinner–housewife system solves the quandary of caring for dependent children in an economy organized around adult wage labor, the gendered division of labor within families will prove stubbornly resilient. The wage gap between men and women will also persist and appear to be the result of rational choices to maximize the family's material wealth by employing the person with the highest wage-earning potential (husband) and sheltering him from housework and child care that might hinder career growth.

Although change in work, family, and community systems can be cataclysmic (e.g., in response to the death of a family member or a political revolution), systems theories tend to view change as evolutionary, occurring in response to historical changes in major social institutions. Hence, information technology, the rise of the knowledge worker, the globalization of economic production, and the lengthening human life span are all modern external forces that will slowly alter work arrangements, the timing of marriage and fertility, and the division of domestic labor within households (Moen & Wethington, 1992). This "accommodationist" approach to social change suggests that current work-family conflicts and mismatch will gradually result in system changes within both work and family that lead to homeostasis once again, whether that be increases in part-time employment, increased male caregiving for family members, or increased numbers of work-life programs in business organizations.

The problems with system theories are those of evolutionary or functionalist explanation more generally. Systems theories tend to ignore resource differences among individuals and power dynamics as explanations of the gendered division of labor, assuming that individual and group interests are usually one in the same. The emphasis on system maintenance and homeostasis as explanations for behavior misses the complexities of individual negotiations in families and workplaces, and the hidden costs of compliance with systems arrangements that benefit certain individuals more than others.

Although fewer empirical studies explicitly use a systems framework (see, e.g., Grzywacz & Marks, 2000), systems concepts are frequently invoked in empirical research on work-family issues. Coverman and Sheley (1986) used a systems-based "time demands and time availability" hypothesis to explain variation in child care and housework performed by husbands and wives in dual-earner households. Becker and Moen (1999) used a family systems approach to examine joint work-family strategies among married couples, and Pittman (1994) viewed "work-family fit" as the mediator between work conditions and marital quality. Systems theories point out the effect of sociocultural contexts on behavior and encourage causal models that move beyond individuals as the unit of analysis.

THE LIFE COURSE PERSPECTIVE

The life course perspective expands on systems theories by paying particular attention to time variations in individuals' activities over their life, individual changes over time, and connections between early life events and later life outcomes (Cooksey, Menaghan, & Jekielek, 1997). Life course dynamics became important within sociology when studying family life cycles and individual work careers. Life course patterns have revealed the cumulative effects of early adult decisions and actions regarding work, marriage, and fertility on long-term material and emotional well-being (Marini, Shin, & Raymond, 1989). For example, leaving the labor force early to rear children may result in cumulative disadvantages for both the labor market and family. These mothers may fail to garner the work experience and backstage family support necessary for career success later in life. Moreover, most young mothers withdraw from the labor force during their prime career-building years; as a result, they may miss out on tremendous earnings growth or face age discrimination when they reenter the labor market later in their lives. Because of these timing issues, the wage and earnings gap between genders becomes larger over the life course, leaving more women than men facing poverty in old age.

Because early decisions can profoundly shape life outcomes, research has paid particular attention to the transition to adulthood. Many empirical studies focus on education, entrance into the labor market, first unions or marriages, and the timing of first births, as well as the interrelationships among these transitions (Rindfuss, 1991; Upchurch & McCarthy, 1990). Life course research has also focused on the changing nature of family priorities and needs as families age. Young couples with no children have a less pronounced division of labor, more time and energy for paid work and community pursuits, and fewer obligations to kin. As children arrive, these families must both generate more income and devote more time to caregiving, often resulting in a more extreme division of labor, in which mothers reduce employment to attend to young children while fathers accelerate their work effort to make up for lost income. When children get older, the need for additional income often outweighs the need for caregiving, and mothers intensify their paid-work effort. In later life, after children have left home, couples may experience a renewal of intimacy and greater sharing of domestic tasks. The important insight here is that individual behavior changes across the life course as family needs change, and static, cross-sectional research may miss this distinction.

Life course researchers also concentrate on how period-specific events affect individuals differently at different life stages (Elder, 1974). Unemployment or layoffs from periodic economic crises or long-term industrial transformation affect young, unattached workers differently than they affect families rearing young children. Although the former may postpone or avoid marriage and parenthood during bad economic times (Oppenheimer, Kalmijn, & Lim, 1997), the children in families facing the same economic crisis may suffer cumulative disadvantages because of their parents' increased risk for poverty, divorce, and mental health problems (Duncan, Yeung, Brooks-Gunn, & Smith, 1998; Yeung & Hofferth, 1998).

The life course perspective is as much a sensitizing framework as a theory. Although life course analysis explicitly models the development and persistence of inequality by race, class, and gender, it does not address why social institutions (principally work organizations, schools, and families) are constructed in ways that create these inequalities.

CONFLICT THEORIES

Social exchange and conflict theories explicitly focus on the resource and power differences actors face when interacting with others (Blau, 1964). Social exchange theories focus on strategic action by individuals within social structures, whereas conflict theories focus on how social institutions become structured in ways that favor dominant classes of actors. For conflict theorists, existing institutional arrangements are seldom the only alternatives for meeting social needs. Rather social institutions become structured with certain rules and procedures as a result of struggles between competing interest groups with different sources of power and influence.

Social exchange theory has been widely used to explain why people do (or do not) marry, have children, and establish a particular division of housework and child care. The principles of social exchange mimic those of market exchange, except that transactions are not limited to goods and services. Social exchange can cover intimacy, sexual gratification, prestige, emotional or physical care, and companionship. Actors will exchange resources whenever they need or desire something that others can provide and when they can arrange satisfactory terms of exchange. Note that satisfactory does not mean fair or equal; as with market exchanges, actors seek the best terms from the available alternatives with no guarantee that the best terms are not exploitive. Efficiency, rather than fairness, largely determines whether actors will exchange with others. Social exchange theorists have gone beyond economic models of behavior, however, in understanding how resource preferences are formed, as well as how resource exchanges are patterned.

The tenets of social exchange theory can easily be seen in theories of women's labor force participation, marriage, and divorce. As male wages and job stability decline, as divorce becomes more available, and as children become increasingly expensive to rear, more women prefer to delay marriage, delay and limit childbearing, share domestic labor, gain education, and increase labor force participation (South, 1992). Men are also affected, with their preferences switching to cohabitation or later marriage, limited responsibility for children, dual-earner marriages, and better educated partners. Men and women negotiate their different preferences for cohabitation, shared housework, and child care based on the resources and available alternatives each partner possesses.

The persistence of the sexual division of housework and child care occurs in a marriage market in which women outnumber men and divorce is readily available, and in a labor market in which many men outearn women. Women are at a disadvantage when trying to negotiate more domestic work from their partners. Some research supports the hypothesis that husbands do more housework when wives are relatively more powerful (earn more or have more education; Brines, 1994; South & Spitze, 1994).

Researchers have explained the continued gender gap in earnings in similar terms. If women's preferences (and standards) for providing care to their children are stronger than men's, they are more likely to make career sacrifices to organize and provide care for their children. Research has shown that the gender gap in earnings stems more from the effect of marital status and children on women's earnings than from deficiencies in women's training, effort, or direct employment discrimination (Waldfogel, 1997). There is, in essence, a motherhood wage gap that could be avoided by remaining single and childless. Mothers have relatively little bargaining power in negotiations with employers over the hours and conditions of work when fathers and childless workers are readily available substitutes. Thus, workplace accommodations that reduce work hours, create flexibility, and allow leaves for family care are likely to be only weakly institutionalized within workplaces and fraught with ambiguity over their long-term career consequences.

Social exchange theory is also evident in explanations of change in work rules and work-family policies. The labor market is structured around exchanges and implicit contracts between employers and employees. As a market, it operates based on efficiency considerations. For employers that means getting the most and best work for the lowest cost, whereas for employees it means earning the highest wages under the best working conditions. Although neoclassical economic theory has much to say about the wage and productivity side of this exchange, less has been said about working conditions, particularly managerial prerogatives to set hours, schedules, work rules, and leave policies. Such negotiations were of limited importance when workers paid for children, but did not have to care for them directly. However, the rise in women's labor force participation, dual-earner marriages, and single mothers has created new pressures on employers to accommodate family needs. In the absence of coercion from unions or the government, exchange theory suggests that employers would first provide accommodations to those workers with the most bargaining power (those most valuable to the firm and least replaceable), not necessarily those with the greatest need for family accommodations. Research on workplace policies has supported this prediction, showing that men without dependent children and higher wage professionals have more access to workplace flexibility than mothers in clerical or service jobs (Dietch & Huffman, 2003; Glass & Fujimoto, 1995; Golden, 2001).

Although social exchange theory attends to the microsociological exchanges in everyday life, conflict theory more generally tries to explain the origin of social structures that create inequality in resources and that define possible exchanges. Conflict theories eschew notions of system equilibrium and evolutionary change, viewing social change as the outcome of competing social groups with varying degrees of political and economic power. Work and family conflict from this perspective is neither natural nor unchangeable, but the result of socially constructed decisions about how to organize economic production and social reproduction, educate future workers, and care for dependent elderly and disabled family members (England & Folbre, 1999; Skocpol, 1996). For example, policies of taxation and redistribution can either lessen the costs of caring for families or exacerbate them, encourage mothers to work for pay or discourage it, stimulate new forms of workplace flexibility or deter them (Gornick & Meyers, 2003). Inequality between husbands and wives is not inevitable, but rather the result of legal, cultural, and institutional restrictions on how work gets done, how schools are organized, and how health care is distributed.

From a conflict perspective, the important goal for work-family research is to explain why the separation between paid work and family responsibilities persists in the face of large-scale transformations in family and economic systems, and why certain forms of "work" are still materially rewarded and privileged (e.g., wage labor), whereas other forms (e.g., family care and domestic work) are minimally rewarded and ignored. Many conflict theorists have focused on the decay of the breadwinner–housewife system during the 20th century (Bernard, 1981; Davis, 1989; Ehrenreich, 1983), leaving both women and men increasingly dependent on wage labor for their subsistence and resulting in declining fertility and marriage. Research has documented how conflicts over this slow erosion of family stability have played out in controversies over welfare state spending, abortion, the public provision of day care, and no-fault divorce (Burstein, Bricher, & Einwholer, 1995) and in legislation covering pregnancy discrimination by employers, employer-provided child-care assistance, and the Family and Medical Leave Act (Kelly, 2003; Kelly & Dobbin, 1999). Conflict theorists have also explored why some industrialized countries have intervened to socialize the costs of rearing the next generation while the United States has not (Gornick & Meyers, 2003; Skocpol, 1996).

CONCLUSION

I have reviewed four sociological approaches to the study of work-family issues: symbolic interactionism, ecological systems theory, life course analysis, and conflict theory. Each approach brings its own strengths and weaknesses to the study of contemporary work and family life. The symbolic interactionist tradition, with its emphasis on social roles and identity structures, examines how behavioral expectations based on cultural norms and institutional practices are internalized. This approach highlights the role of cultural definitions of appropriate work and family roles for men and women even in the face of rapidly changing material realities. In contrast, systems theories draw attention to the group needs and goals of families and workplaces, viewing individual behavior in its group context as a product of both internal motives and contextual factors relating to the resources and constraints of other group members. Life course analysis draws attention to the timing of work and family involvements, showing how early life course decisions about education, work, marriage, and fertility either permit or constrain future activities. Social exchange/conflict theories underscore the role that differences in power and material wealth play in the social construction of work and family arrangements.

Given the routine, everyday conflicts between paid work and family caregiving, conflict theories seem best poised to answer the challenging questions of how these institutional arrangements came into being, why they seem so resistant to change, and which policy options might best relieve work-family stress. Yet the social-psychological approaches perhaps do more to help us understand how larger institutional realities are experienced by individuals who almost daily must decide how much to invest in paid and care work in the face of these institutionally structured opportunities and constraints.

Research that addresses the interface between institutional structures and individual action is needed, particularly research that can shed light on how working families adapt and conform to existing institutions and the conditions that encourage mobilization and resistance. Political and cultural struggles over who should care for children and who should bear the costs of producing the next generation are likely to intensify as globalization proceeds and more nations are incorporated into a global wage labor market. The costs to health and well-being of conforming to existing institutional arrangements must be carefully monitored to develop a more coherent sense of when intervention is likely to be politically supported and effective in reducing work-family stress.

REFERENCES

Acker, J. (1990). Hierarchies, jobs, bodies: A theory of gendered organizations. *Gender and Society, 4*, 139–158.

Barnett, R. C., & Baruch, G. K. (1985). Women's involvement in multiple roles and psychological distress. *Journal of Personality and Social Psychology, 49*, 135–145.

Barnett, R. C., Brennan, R. T., & Marshall, N. L. (1994). Gender and the relationship between parent role quality and psychological distress: A study of men and women in dual-earner couples. *Journal of Family Issues, 15*, 229–252.

Becker, P. E., & Moen, P. (1999). Scaling back: Dual-earner couples' work-family strategies. *Journal of Marriage and the Family, 61*, 995–1007.

Bernard, J. (1981). The good-provider role: Its rise and fall. *American Psychologist, 36*, 1–12.

Blau, P. (1964). *Exchange and power in social life.* New York: Wiley.

Brines, J. (1994). Economic dependency, gender, and the division-of-labor at home. *American Journal of Sociology, 100*, 652–688.

Broderick, C. B. (1993). *Understanding family process: Basics of family systems theory.* Newbury Park, CA: Sage.

Bronfenbrenner, U. (1989). Ecological systems theory. *Annals of Child Development, 6*, 187–249.

Burke, P. J. (1991). Identity processes and social stress. *American Sociological Review, 56*, 836–849.

Burke, R. J., & Greenglass, E. R. (2002). Work status congruence, work outcomes, and psychological well-being. *Stress Medicine, 16*, 91–99.

Burstein, P., Bricher, M. R., & Einwholer, R. (1995). Policy alternatives and political change: Work, family and gender on the congressional agenda. *American Journal of Sociology, 60*, 67–83.

Cooksey, E. C., Menaghan, E. G., & Jekielek, S. M. (1997). Life course effects of work and family circumstances on children. *Social Forces, 76*, 637–667.

Coser, L. A., & Coser, R. L. (1974). *Greedy institutions.* New York: The Free Press.

Coverman, S., & Sheley, J. (1986). Change in men's housework and child-care time, 1965–1975. *Journal of Marriage and the Family, 48*, 413–422.

Davis, K. (1989). Wives and work: A theory of the sex-role revolution and its consequences. In S. Dornbusch & M. Strober (Eds.), *Feminism, children, and the new families* (pp. 67–85). New York: Guilford.

Dietch, C., & Huffman, M. (2003). Family responsive benefits and the two-tiered labor market. In R. Hertz & N. Marshall (Eds.), *Work and family.* Berkeley: University of California Press.

Deutsch, F. (1999). *Halving it all: How equally shared parenting works.* Cambridge, MA: Harvard University Press.

Duncan, G. J., Yeung, W. J., Brooks-Gunn, J., & Smith, J. R. (1998). How much does childhood poverty affect the life chances of children? *American Sociological Review, 63,* 801–817.

Ehrenreich, B. (1983). *The hearts of men: American dreams and the flight from commitment.* Garden City, NY: Anchor Press/Doubleday.

Elder, G. (1974). *Children of the Great Depression.* Chicago: University of Chicago Press.

England, P., & Folbre, N. (1999). Who should pay for the kids? *Annals of the American Academy of Political and Social Science, 563,* 194–207.

Glass, J., & Fujimoto, T. (1995). Organizational characteristics and the provision of family benefits. *Work and Occupations, 22,* 380–411.

Goffman, E. (1959). *The presentation of self in everyday life.* Garden City, NY: Doubleday.

Golden, L. (2001). Flexible work schedules: Which workers get them? *American Behavioral Scientist, 44,* 1157–1178.

Gornick, J. C., & Meyers, M. K. (2003). *Families that work: Policies for reconciling parenthood and employment.* New York: Russell Sage.

Gove, W. R., & Tudor, J. F. (1973). Adult sex roles and mental illness. *American Journal of Sociology, 82,* 1327–1336.

Grzywacz, J. G., & Marks, N. F. (2000). Reconceptualizing the work-family interface: An ecological perspective on the correlates of positive and negative spillover between work and family. *Journal of Occupational Health Psychology, 5,* 111–126.

Hays, S. (1996). *The cultural contradictions of motherhood.* New Haven, CT: Yale University Press.

Hochschild, A., with Machung, A. (1989). *The second shift.* New York: Avon Books.

Kelly, E. L. (2003). The strange history of employer sponsored child care: Interested actors, uncertainty, and the transformation of law in organizational fields. *American Journal of Sociology, 109,* 606–649.

Kelly, E. L., & Dobbin, F. (1999). Civil rights law at work: Sex discrimination and the rise of maternity leave policies. *American Journal of Sociology, 105,* 455–492.

Lennon, M. C. (1987). Sex differences in distress: The impact of gender and work roles. *Journal of Health and Social Behavior, 28,* 290–305.

Lennon, M. C. (1994). Women, work, and well-being: The importance of work conditions. *Journal of Health and Social Behavior, 35,* 235–247.

Marini, M. M., Shin, H., & Raymond, J. (1989). Socioeconomic consequences of the process of transition to adulthood. *Social Science Research, 18,* 89–135.

Marks, S. R. (1977). Multiple roles and role strain: Some notes on human energy, time, and commitment. *American Sociological Review, 41,* 921–936.

McCall, G. J., & Simmons, J. L. (1978). *Identities and interactions: an examination of human associations in everyday life.* New York: The Free Press.

Moen, P., & Wethington, E. (1992). The concept of family adaptive strategies. *Annual Review of Sociology, 18,* 223–251.

Oppenheimer, V. K., Kalmijn, M., & Lim, N. (1997). Men's career development and marriage timing during a period of rising inequality. *Demography, 34,* 311–330.

Pittman, J. F. (1994). Work/family fit as a mediator of work factors on marital tension: Evidence from the interface of greedy institutions. *Human Relations, 47,* 183–209.

Rindfuss, R. (1991). The young adult years: Diversity, structural change and fertility. *Demography, 28,* 493–512.

Ross, C., Mirowsky, J., & Huber, J. (1983). Dividing work, sharing work, and in-between: Marriage patterns and depression. *American Sociological Review, 48,* 809–823.

Simon, R. W. (1995). Gender, multiple roles, role meaning and mental health. *Journal of Health and Social Behavior, 36,* 82–194.

Skocpol, T. (1996). *States, social knowledge, and the origins of modern social policies*. Princeton, NJ: Princeton University Press.

South, S. J. (1992). For love or money? Sociodemographic determinants of the expected benefits from marriage. In S. South & S. E. Tolnay (Eds.), *The changing American family* (pp. 171–194). Boulder, CO: Westview.

South, S. J., & Spitze, G. (1994). Housework in marital and nonmarital households. *American Sociological Review, 59*, 327–347.

Stryker, S., & Burke, P. J. (2000). The past, present, and future of an identity theory. *Social Psychology Quarterly, 63*, 284–297.

Tang, T. N., & Tang, C. S. (2001). Gender role internalization, multiple roles, and Chinese women's mental health. *Psychology of Women Quarterly, 25*, 181–196.

Thoits, P. (1983). Multiple identities and psychological well-being: A reformulation and test of the social isolation hypothesis. *American Sociological Review, 48*, 174–187.

Upchurch, D., & McCarthy, J. (1990). The timing of a first birth and high school completion. *American Sociological Review, 55*, 224–234.

Waldfogel, J. (1997). Working mothers then and now: A cross-cohort analysis of the effects of maternity leave on women's pay. In F. Blau & R. Ehrenberg (Eds.), *Gender and family issues in the workplace* (pp. 92–126). New York: Russell Sage.

Yeung, W. J., & Hofferth, S. (1998). Family adaptations to income and job loss in the United States. *Journal of Family and Economic Issues, 19*, 255–283.

16

Work and Family Research: A Public Policy Perspective

Jane Waldfogel
Columbia University

With the rising labor force participation of women, and particularly women with young children, comes an increasing interest in family-friendly policies that might address the links among work, family, health, and well-being. Two thirds of U.S. children now live in families where every adult is working—up from only one third in 1975 (Smolensky & Gootman, 2003; Waldfogel, 2001a). Thus, the issues of workforce–workplace mismatch, and how work and care arrangements affect child and family well-being, now touch a majority of American families.

The chapters in this section examine these issues from the vantage point of four different perspectives: psychology, anthropology, sociology, and economics. This chapter considers two questions: What lessons can we draw from these four perspectives? What is the contribution of public policy research?

LESSONS FROM THE FOUR PERSPECTIVES

The psychological perspective, presented by Debra Major and Jeanette Cleveland, is helpful in setting the context for research and policy. This perspective focuses our attention on the individual and the many ways that work and family issues affect individual development and well-being. Particular attention has been paid to the multiple roles that individuals play in the work and family arena and the effect of those roles on the individual's and family's well-being (see, e.g., Barnett & Hyde, 2001). Psychological research has also studied how parents' employment affects their children. For instance, one line of research has studied how work influences parents' interactions with their children, while another has studied parents' supervision and monitoring.

Anthropology, and especially studies using ethnographic methods, also helps set the context for work in this area. As Charles Darrah (chap. 14, this volume) points out, work and family issues have been at the heart of many of the classic studies in anthropology. Such studies are helpful in highlighting the importance of the meaning of work and family and the complex roles these play in individuals' lives and the importance of taking into account individual differences and the specific opportunities and constraints that individuals face.

The two other disciplines represented in this section—sociology and economics—have also long studied issues of work and family and have contributed both theoretical insights and empirical findings. A rich literature in sociology has used qualitative and ethnographic methods to shed light on work and family issues (see, e.g., the Lynds' [1929] classic *Middletown* and more recent studies that specifically focus on work and family issues, such as Arlie Hochschild's [1989] *The Second Shift* and *The Time Bind* [1997]). Sociologists have also developed theories about work and family issues, as Jennifer Glass (chap. 15, this volume) documents. Consistent with feminist and legal perspectives (see chap. 22 by Joyce Fletcher, this volume, and work by legal scholars Rhode [1989, 1997] and Williams [2000]), sociologists have emphasized the importance of gendered roles and separate spheres—that is, the different sectors of the world to which men and women belong. These concepts play a key role in the sociological theories in the work-family arena, and they are particularly relevant to the two specific questions that Glass discusses in her chapter: What are the reasons for the male–female division of labor in couples? What are the reasons for the male–female wage gap?

Economists, too, have paid considerable attention to the issues of separate spheres and gendered roles, although they tend to use different terminology (e.g., comparative advantage) to refer to them. There is considerable research in economics on women's and men's decisions on allocating time to work in the labor market and in the home, and the consequences of those decisions for future earnings. Classic works include Gary Becker's (1981) *A Treatise on the Family* (see also Becker, 1965) and articles by Mincer and coauthors (Mincer, 1962; Mincer & Ofek, 1982; Mincer & Polachek, 1974; for an excellent overview, see Blau, Ferber, & Winkler, 1998). Somewhat more recently, economists have addressed child health and family decisions about investments in children. Arleen Leibowitz (chap. 13, this volume) provides an accessible introduction to this research and works through an example—how economists would think about the effects of maternal employment on health outcomes for children. As Leibowitz illustrates, the net effects of maternal employment on child health are not clear a priori because effects are likely to be both negative and positive (see also Duncan & Chase-Lansdale, 2002). This example highlights the complexities of issues in this area, but also the usefulness of economic models in structuring analyses of such issues.

THE CONTRIBUTION
OF PUBLIC POLICY RESEARCH

Many of the studies discussed in the four chapters in this section have implications for public policy. For example, the studies reviewed by Leibowitz on maternal employment and child outcomes have implications for public policy, as do the studies reviewed by Glass on the wage gap. However, studies usually focus on something other than policy and draw policy implications only as an afterthought.

The field of public policy differs from other disciplines in that its primary purpose is to understand the effects of policies and inform future decisions about policies. As such the target audience for public policy research is policy-makers. The focus of public policy research tends to be on analyses of specific policy issues, such as the extent to which families have access to particular policies, the effects of particular policies on outcomes, or the likely effects of future policy decisions. Public policy is a relatively new field (its professional organization, the Association of Public Policy Analysis and Management, is only 25 years old). Its origins are in economics and other quantitatively oriented disciplines (such as operations research), but the field now draws on theory and methods from many disciplines, although it is fair to say that economics still plays a dominant role. In some areas of work and family, public policy research is fairly well developed. Here I review two bodies of work: studies of parental leave policies, and studies of child care.

Parental Leave

Parental leave policies, which provide a period of job-protected leave and usually some income replacement for mothers and fathers around the time of childbirth, vary greatly across countries and have also changed within countries over time (Kamerman, 2000a, 2000b; Waldfogel, 2001b). Analysts have taken advantage of these differences across countries and over time to estimate effects of parental leave policies on child and family outcomes. This research includes several cross-national studies of the effect of parental leave policies on health outcomes for women and children. These studies find that when leave policies are more generous, health outcomes for women and children improve (Core & Koutsegeorgopoulou, 1995; Ruhm, 2000; Tanaka, in press; Winegarden & Bracy, 1995). Cross-national research has also examined the effects of parental leave policies on fertility, finding that more generous policies increase fertility, but also have indirect effects that reduce fertility (Winegarden & Bracy, 1995). Another cross-national study has examined the effect of parental leave policies on employment and wages for women, finding that more generous policies are accompanied by higher rates of employment, but somewhat lower wages (Ruhm, 1998).

Because the United States has less developed parental leave policies, a question of primary interest in the U.S. context is the extent to which employees are covered by parental leave policies and the effect of legislation on coverage. Studies have documented that the Family and Medical Leave Act (FMLA) of 1993 raised coverage rates (Commission on Family and Medical Leave, 1996; Waldfogel, 1999a, 1999b). Nevertheless, coverage remains incomplete, with the FMLA missing roughly one half of the private-sector workforce because it is limited to firms with 50 or more employees and because to qualify employees must have worked 1,250 hours for the employer in the prior year (Cantor et al., 2001; Waldfogel, 2001c).

Also of interest has been the effect of parental leave policies such as the FMLA on women's labor supply postbirth. The likely effect on labor supply is unclear a priori. On the one hand, the FMLA, which offers unpaid leave extensions, allows those women who prefer a long leave to remain at home longer even though they may have returned to work at the end of their paid leave. On the other hand, these leave extensions may allow other women, who would have quit their jobs rather than return to work after a short maternity leave, to return to work (Blau & Ehrenberg, 1997; Klerman & Leibowitz, 1995). Another factor in the U.S. context is that the FMLA and most state laws that exist provide *unpaid* leave, which some new parents may not be able to afford (for evidence on this point, see Commission on Family and Medical Leave, 1996; Cantor et al., 2001; Waldfogel, 2001c). Empirical studies of the FMLA and state leave laws have found generally neutral or small positive effects of leave extensions on leave taking and leave duration (Berger & Waldfogel, 2004; Han & Waldfogel, 2003; Klerman & Leibowitz, 1998; Ross, 1998; Waldfogel, 1999b). Given the generally weak effects of the laws on leave taking, it is perhaps not surprising that few effects on wages have been found (see, e.g., Waldfogel, 1999b).

In the United States, where most states do not have parental leave laws and where the federal law only covers about one half of private-sector workers, laws are not the only determinants of leave coverage. Some employers implement leave policies as part of union contracts, whereas others implement them voluntarily. As a result, a larger share of employees is covered by leave policies than is covered by state or federal laws mandating such policies. There is also considerable variation among firms in the generosity of their parental leave coverage, although most tends to be unpaid (Smolensky & Gootman, 2003). Less research has been done on the effects of such employer policies on employee leave taking and job retention. This research finds, as expected, that when employers offer parental leave, women are more likely to take a leave, but they are also more likely to return to work at their prebirth place of employment (see, e.g., Glass & Riley, 1998; Hofferth, 1996; Waldfogel, 1998). One study also finds that when U.S. firms offer more generous parental leave policies, fertility rates are higher (Averett & Whittington, 2002).

Although the research is extensive, large gaps in our knowledge about parental leave policies remain. We know very little about the effect of public or employer policies on men's parental leave taking. It is thought that most men are taking some leave with the birth of a child, although typically for fairly short durations (Hyde, Essex, & Horton, 1993; Malin, 1994, 1998; Pleck, 1993). However, the few studies that have examined men's parental leave taking have been hampered by small sample sizes (see, e.g., Han & Waldfogel, 2003). We also know relatively little about the effect of family leave policies on employees' leave taking for other family and medical reasons (although see evidence in Cantor et al., 2001).

Child Care

Child care, for both preschool and school-age children, is another policy area that has been extensively studied. Studies have documented families' access to various types of child care and the effects of various types of child care on child outcomes (see Blau, 2001; Helburn & Bergmann, 2002; Vandell & Wolfe, 2000).

Many studies have examined the effects of child care on child health. Child care in group settings has been found to pose some health risks to young children (see review in Meyers, Rosenbaum, Ruhm, & Waldfogel, 2004), although high-quality child-care programs can potentially improve child health if they offer preventive health care services such as screening or immunization. There is also a large, multidisciplinary research base on the links among maternal employment, child care, and other child outcomes, such as cognitive development and socioemotional adjustment. Policy-oriented work by economists builds on a large and important body of work by developmental psychologists, but differs in its more careful attention to issues of selection bias (see Currie, chap. 19, this volume). Recent work in this vein includes studies by James-Burdumy (2000), Neidell (2000), and Ruhm (2004), as well as collaborative studies by policy-oriented economists and psychologists (see, e.g., a study of child care and child outcomes by the

NICHD Early Childhood Research Network and Duncan, 2003; and studies of early maternal employment and child outcomes by Brooks-Gunn, Han, & Waldfogel, 2002; Waldfogel, Han, & Brooks-Gunn, 2002). Such studies have shed light on how early maternal employment and child care affect child outcomes and for which children.

As in the parental leave arena, countries vary considerably in the nature, scope, and generosity of child-care policies (see Kamerman & Kahn, 1995; Waldfogel, 2001b). However, there have been no studies that assess the effect of this cross-country variation in child-care policies on child outcomes. Child-care policies within the United States also vary extensively. Although most U.S. child care is paid for privately, the federal government's investments in child care have grown rapidly in recent years, both as a way of supporting mothers' work and as a way of promoting child development, particularly for disadvantaged children (see recent reviews by Kamerman & Waldfogel, in press; Meyers et al., 2004). States, too, are major funders of child care, and they are playing an increasingly important role as their own funds increase and also as recent changes in federal policy give states more flexibility in spending federal funds (Meyers et al., 2004). In addition, states set regulations for child care, specifying health and safety standards, group size, teacher training, and so forth (Gormley, 1995).

Studies have documented the share of families participating in various types of child care and the share receiving support from various publicly funded child care programs (see, e.g., the recent report of the National Academy of Sciences in Smolensky & Gootman, 2003). However, relatively few studies have examined the effect of child-care policies on child or family outcomes. A few studies examine the effect of child-care subsidies on women's labor supply (Bainbridge, Meyers, & Waldfogel, 2003; Meyers, Heintze, & Wolf, 2002), building on a much larger body of work on the effects of child-care costs on women's labor supply (see reviews in Anderson & Levine, 2000; Han & Waldfogel, 2002). A few studies also examine the effect of public child-care expenditures on child-care arrangements (see, e.g., Meyers & Durfee, 2004; Meyers & Jeong, 2003). Finally, a few studies examine the effect of regulations on child outcomes. Currie and Hotz (2001), for example, found that tougher regulations reduce accidents, but also raise the cost of care, thus pricing some families out of the child-care market.

Thus, in the child-care policy area, substantial gaps in our knowledge remain. Work in this area is hampered by the lack of nationally representative data on the quality of child care. In fact a recent National Academy of Sciences panel identified this as the first priority for future research in the work-family area (Smolensky & Gootman, 2003). Other priorities are for experimental data with which to assess the effect of child care on child outcomes, and sufficient quantitative data to fully analyze both the costs and benefits of alternative child-care options.

Linking Policies, Family Arrangements, and Child Outcomes

A common shortcoming of research in both parental leave and child care is that few studies document the links among public policies, the arrangements families make, and child and family outcomes. For example, studies link parental leave policies with families' work and care arrangements, and other studies link those arrangements with child outcomes, but no studies link the three pieces together.

As an example of what such work might look like, Berger, Hill, and Waldfogel (2003) looked at the effects of parental leave policies on the timing of women's return to work after childbirth and on child health outcomes. We estimated two-stage, least-squares (instrumental variables) models, in which we first estimated the effect of policy-related variables on the timing of women's return to work after childbirth, and then we estimated the effect of the returns to work predicted by those policies on child outcomes. We found that the absence of parental leave laws and low levels of unionization led women to return to work earlier, which in turn was associated with poorer health outcomes for their children. For instance, women who were not covered by parental leave laws at the time of the birth were more likely than women who were covered to return within the first 6 weeks after birth, and their children received fewer well-baby visits in the first year. Women who lived in states with low levels of unionization (and thus were least likely to have parental leave coverage at work) were more likely than comparable women to return within the first 12 weeks postbirth, their children received fewer well-baby visits, and their children were less likely to be fully immunized at 18 months.

Our approach in this study is potentially important because it ties policies to behaviors and outcomes, and because it addresses some of the problems of selection bias that might otherwise confound estimates of the effects of parental choices on child outcomes. Nevertheless, it is always a challenge to estimate effects precisely using instrumental variables models. In other work, we used a different method—propensity score matching—as a further way to control for selection bias (Berger, Hill, & Waldfogel, in press).

In studying child care, an analogous approach would examine the effect of child-care policies on child-care arrangements and, in turn, the effect of those arrangements on child outcomes. As an example, Magnuson, Ruhm, and Waldfogel (2004) estimated the effect of public child-care expenditures on families' care arrangements for preschool children, and the effect of those arrangements on children's school-readiness. The results help us understand the extent to which policies can improve child outcomes and also whether the effects that have been found between arrangements and child outcomes are truly causal, or whether they are biased by unmeasured selection factors.

CONCLUSION

My review of the work in the public policy arena suggests two potentially important contributions that public policy research can make above and beyond the contributions of other disciplines represented in this section of the volume. One contribution is the explicit focus on public policies, their scope, and their effects. Documenting who is covered by existing policies and who is not can be helpful in pointing the way to future policy initiatives. So too can estimating the effects of policies on the outcomes we care about. If policymakers are to invest more in parental leave benefits or child-care programs, they need to know what effects these policies have and how the benefits compare with the costs. Public policy research can clearly play an important role in answering those questions.

The second contribution that public policy research can make is to demonstrate the use of methods that distinguish between the effects of choices that families make on their own and choices that are influenced by public policy. Families' choices about work and family arrangements are highly personal, and many of the determinants of those choices cannot be observed or measured by researchers. As a result, selection bias is a constant threat to research in this area (see also Currie, chap. 19, this volume). Carefully documenting public policies, and showing how those policies affect families' decisions, is thus of interest not just in its own right, but also as a means to address selection bias in estimating the effects of those choices on child and family outcomes. Public policy researchers, who are at the forefront in using such methods, are thus well positioned to make a contribution to knowledge in this area.

ACKNOWLEDGMENTS

I am grateful for funding from NICHD and the William T. Grant Foundation, and for helpful comments from the volume editors and an anonymous referee.

REFERENCES

Anderson, P., & Levine, P. (2000). Child care and mothers' employment decisions. In D. Card & R. Blank (Eds.), *Finding jobs: Work and welfare reform* (pp. 420–462). New York: Russell Sage Foundation.

Averett, S., & Whittington, L. (2002). Does maternity leave induce births? *Southern Economic Journal, 68*, 403–417.

Bainbridge, J., Meyers, M., & Waldfogel, J. (2003). Child care reform and the employment of single mothers. *Social Science Quarterly, 84*, 771–791.

Barnett, R. C., & Hyde, J. S. (2001). Women, men, work, and family: An expansionist theory. *American Psychologist, 56*, 781–796.

Becker, G. (1965). A theory of the allocation of time. *Economic Journal, 75*, 493–517.

Becker, G. (1981). *A treatise on the family.* Cambridge, MA: Harvard University Press.

Berger, L., Hill, J., & Waldfogel, J. (2003, June). *Parental leave policies, early maternal employment, and child outcomes.* Paper presented at the annual meeting of the European Society of Population Economics, New York.

Berger, L., Hill, J., & Waldfogel, J. (in press). Maternity leave, early maternal employment, and child outcomes in the U.S. *The Economic Journal.*

Berger, L., & Waldfogel, J. (2004). Maternity leave and the employment of new mothers in the United States. *Journal of Population Economics, 17*, 331–349.

Blau, D. (2001). *The child care problem: An economic analysis.* New York: Russell Sage Foundation.

Blau, F., & Ehrenberg, R. (1997). Introduction. In F. Blau & R. Ehrenberg (Eds.), *Gender and family issues in the workplace* (pp. 1–19). New York: Russell Sage Foundation.

Blau, F., Ferber, M., & Winkler, A. (1998). *The economics of women, men, and work.* Upper Saddle River, NJ: Prentice-Hall.

Brooks-Gunn, J., Han, W., & Waldfogel, J. (2002). Maternal employment and child cognitive outcomes in the first three years of life: The NICHD study of early child care. *Child Development, 73*, 1052–1072.

Cantor, D., Waldfogel, J., Kerwin, J., McKinley Wright, M., Levin, K., Rauch, J., Hagerty, T., & Stapleton Kudela, M. (2001). *Balancing the needs of families and employers: Family and medical leave surveys, 2000 Update.* Rockville, MD: Westat.

Commission on Family and Medical Leave. (1996). *A workable balance: Report to the Congress on family and medical leave policies.* Washington, DC: Women's Bureau, U.S. Department of Labor.

Core, F., & Koutsegeorgopoulou, V. (1995, August/September). Parental leave: What and where? *The OECD Observer, 195*, 15–21.

Currie, J., & Hotz, J. (2001). *Accidents will happen? Unintentional childhood injuries and child care policy.* University of California at Los Angeles mimeo.

Duncan, G., & Chase-Lansdale, L. (2002). Welfare reform and child well-being. In G. Duncan & L. Chase-Lansdale (Eds.), *For better and for worse: Welfare reform and the well-being of children and families* (pp. 1–21). New York: Russell Sage Foundation.

Glass, J., & Riley, L. (1998). Family responsive policies and employee retention following childbirth. *Social Forces, 76*, 1401–1435.

Gormley, W. (1995). *Everybody's children: Child care as a public problem.* Washington, DC: Brookings Institution.

Han, W., & Waldfogel, J. (2002). The effect of child care costs on the employment of single and married mothers. *Social Science Quarterly, 82*, 552–568.

Han, W., & Waldfogel, J. (2003). Parental leave: The effect of recent legislation on parents' leave-taking. *Demography, 40*, 191–200.

Helburn, S., & Bergmann, B. (2002). *America's child care problem: The way out.* New York: Palgrave/St. Martin's.

Hochschild, A. (1989). *The second shift: Working parents and the revolution at home.* New York: Avon.

Hochschild, A. (1997). *The time bind: When work becomes home and home becomes work.* New York: Metropolitan Books.

Hofferth, S. (1996). Effects of public and private policies on working after childbirth. *Work and Occupations, 23*, 378–404.

Hyde, J., Essex, M., & Horton, F. (1993). Fathers and parental leave: Attitudes and experiences. *Journal of Family Issues, 14*, 616–641.

James-Burdumy, S. (2000, November). *The effect of maternal labor force participation on child development*. Paper presented at the Association for Public Policy Analysis and Management Fall Research Conference, Seattle, WA.

Kamerman, S. (2000a). From maternity to parenting policies: Women's health, employment, and child and family well-being. *Journal of the American Women's Medical Association, 55,* 1–4.

Kamerman, S. (2000b). Parental leave policies: An essential ingredient in early childhood education and care policies. *Social Policy Report, 14,* 3–15.

Kamerman, S., & Kahn, A. (1995). *Starting right: How America neglects its youngest children and what we can do about it.* Oxford: Oxford University Press.

Kamerman, S., & Waldfogel, J. (in press). Market and non-market institutions in early childhood education and care. In R. Nelson (Ed.), *Market and non-market institutions.* New York: Russell Sage Foundation.

Klerman, J., & Leibowitz, A. (1995). *Labor supply effects of state maternity leave legislation.* Santa Monica, CA: RAND.

Klerman, J., & Leibowitz, A. (1998, April). *FMLA and the labor supply of new mothers: Evidence from the June CPS.* Paper presented at the annual meeting of the Population Association of America, Chicago, IL.

Lynd, R., & Lynd, H. (1929). *Middletown: A study in contemporary American culture.* New York: Harcourt, Brace.

Magnuson, K., Ruhm, C., & Waldfogel, J. (2004). *Does prekindergarten improve school preparation and performance?* (NBER Working Paper No. 10452). Cambridge, MA: National Bureau of Economic Research.

Malin, M. (1994). Fathers and parental leave. *Texas Law Review, 72,* 1047–1095.

Malin, M. (1998). Fathers and parental leave revisited. *Northern University Law Review, 19,* 25–56.

Meyers, M., & Durfee, A. (2004). *Child care policy and child care mode choice.* University of Washington mimeo.

Meyers, M., Heintze, T., & Wolf, D. (2002). Child care subsidies and the employment of welfare recipients. *Demography, 39,* 165–179.

Meyers, M., & Jeong, S. (2003, April). *The effect of government child care subsidy programs on child care choice among low-income families.* Paper presented at the annual meeting of the Population Association of American, Minneapolis, MN.

Meyers, M., Rosenbaum, D., Ruhm, C., & Waldfogel, J. (2004). Inequality in early childhood education and care: What do we know? In K. Neckerman (Ed.), *Social inequality* (pp. 223–270). New York: Russell Sage Foundation.

Mincer, J. (1962). Labor force participation of married women. In H. Greg Lewis (Ed.), *Aspects of labor economics* (Universities National Bureau of Economic Research Conference Series, No. 14). Princeton, NJ: Princeton University Press.

Mincer, J., & Ofek, H. (1982). Interrupted work careers, depreciation, and restoration of human capital. *Journal of Human Resources, 17,* 3–24.

Mincer, J., & Polachek, S. (1974). Family investments in human capital: Earnings of women. *Journal of Political Economy, 82,* S76–S108.

Neidell, M. (2000). *Early parental time investments in children's human capital development: Effects of time in the first year on cognitive and non-cognitive outcomes* (Working Paper No. 806). Los Angeles, CA: University of California.

NICHD Early Childhood Research Network and Duncan, G. (2003). Modelling the effects of child care quality on children's preschool cognitive development. *Child Development, 74,* 1454–1475.

Pleck, J. (1993). Are "family-supportive" employment policies relevant to men? In J. C. Hood (Ed.), *Men, work, and family.* Newbury Park, CA: Sage.

Rhode, D. (1989). *Justice and gender: Sex discrimination and the law*. Cambridge, MA: Harvard University Press.

Rhode, D. (1997). *Speaking of sex: The denial of gender inequality*. Cambridge, MA: Harvard University Press.

Ross, K. (1998, April). *Labor pains: The effects of the Family and Medical Leave Act on recent mothers' returns to work after childbirth*. Paper presented at the annual meeting of the Population Association of America Annual Meeting, Chicago, IL.

Ruhm, C. (1998). The economic consequences of parental leave mandates: Lessons from Europe. *Quarterly Journal of Economics, 113*, 285–318.

Ruhm, C. (2000). Parental leave and child health. *Journal of Health Economics, 19*, 931–960.

Ruhm, C. (2004). Parental employment and child cognitive development. *Journal of Human Resources, 39*, 155–192.

Smolensky, E., & Gootman, J. (Eds.). (2003). *Working families and growing kids: Caring for children and adolescents*. Washington, DC: The National Academies Press.

Tanaka, S. (in press). Parental leave and child health across OECD countries. *The Economic Journal*.

Vandell, D., & Wolfe, B. (2000). *Child care quality: Does it matter and does it need to be improved?* Report prepared for the Office of the Assistant Secretary for Planning and Evaluation, U.S. Department of Health and Human Services. Available from http://aspe.hhs.gov/hsp/ccquality00/index.htm.

Waldfogel, J. (1998). The family gap for young women in the United States and Britain: Can maternity leave make a difference? *Journal of Labor Economics, 16*, 505–545.

Waldfogel, J. (1999a). Family leave coverage in the 1990s. *Monthly Labor Review, 122*, 13–21.

Waldfogel, J. (1999b). The effect of the Family and Medical Leave Act. *Journal of Policy Analysis and Management, 18*, 281–302.

Waldfogel, J. (2001a). Family-friendly policies for families with young children. *Employee Rights and Employment Policy Journal, 5*, 273–296.

Waldfogel, J. (2001b). What other nations do: International policies toward parental leave and child care. *The Future of Children: Caring for Infants and Toddlers, 11*, 99–111.

Waldfogel, J. (2001c). Family and medical leave: Evidence from the 2000 surveys. *Monthly Labor Review, 124*, 17–23.

Waldfogel, J., Han, W., & Brooks-Gunn, J. (2002). The effects of early maternal employment on child cognitive development. *Demography, 39*, 369–392.

Williams, J. (2000). *Unbending gender: Why work and family conflict and what to do about it*. New York: Oxford University Press.

Winegarden, C. R., & Bracy, P. (1995). Demographic consequences of maternal-leave programs in industrial countries: Evidence from fixed-effects models. *Southern Economic Journal, 61*, 1020–1035.

PART IV

Parental Employment and Outcomes for Children

17

A Psychological Perspective on the Health and Well-Being Consequences of Parental Employment

Rena Repetti

University of California, Los Angeles

Psychologists study emotional, behavioral, cognitive, and biological processes. For instance, a psychologist asks questions such as, How do individuals react to employment experiences, and why do they react that way? How do those behavioral and emotional reactions influence other family members and their behavior? These questions lead to an analytic approach; an outcome is no longer a single measurable variable, but a series of steps in a process. This often entails an examination of more minute processes, which consist of small, intermediary consequences. Therefore, the study of intermediary outcomes and short-term effects that can cumulate over time are natural avenues for psychologists to pursue. This chapter shows how a psychological perspective can guide the identification, measurement, and evaluation of the effects that parental employment experiences have on children and families.

IDENTIFYING HEALTH AND WELL-BEING OUTCOMES

It may seem pessimistic to assert at the outset that psychologists expect the health and well-being consequences of parent employment to be difficult to detect. However, as discussed below, those effects can be much stronger than they appear because small effects cumulate over time and the effect of employment varies among individuals and groups. If we consider typical health endpoints, such as individual psychological functioning, social adjustment, and physical health, the consequences for individual family members often appear small. The primary reason is obvious: Work and work-family conflict are but one small component of a daily life that is filled with many direct influences on physical and emotional well-being. With respect to children's well-being, in particular, parents' occupations would have, at best, an indirect influence—one that is mediated through work's effect on parents and the parent–child relationship.

Several investigations have examined correlations between parents' work and work-family experiences and various measures of child well-being. Different characteristics of parents' occupations have been examined, such as decision latitude at work, job demands, job insecurity, job tension (Stewart & Barling, 1996), job satisfaction (Stewart & Barling, 1996; Voydanoff, 2004), work pressure (Crouter, Bumpas, Maguire, & McHale, 1999), work stress (Galambos & Maggs, 1990), and hours spent at work (Greenberger & Goldberg, 1989; Harvey, 1998; Voydanoff, 2004). Some researchers have also considered parents' subjective experience of work-family conflict as measured by their reports of interrole conflict (MacEwen & Barling, 1991; Stewart & Barling, 1996), role overload (Crouter et al., 1999; Galambos, Sears, Almeida, & Kolaric, 1995), mood at home after work (Voydanoff, 2004), and satisfaction with the role of employed mother (MacEwen & Barling, 1991).

These studies have also cast a wide net when assessing the well-being of offspring as possible correlates of parental job characteristics. Teens' feelings of self-worth (Crouter et al., 1999), their academic competence (Voydanoff, 2004), their involvement in social activities with friends (Galambos et al., 1995), their positive mood, their feelings of mastery, and their confidence in their ability to cope (Galambos & Maggs, 1990) have all been examined as possible correlates of parents' work-related experiences. Various indicators of maladjustment in adolescent offspring have also been considered, including both internalizing problems, such as depression and symptoms of anxiety (Crouter et al., 1999; Voydanoff, 2004), and externalizing problems, such as difficulty with impulse control (Galambos & Maggs, 1990), problem behaviors, and association with deviant peers (Galambos et al., 1995; Voydanoff, 2004). Researchers have also assessed both externalizing and internalizing problems in school-age and younger children, as well as motivation and performance in school (Greenberger & Goldberg, 1989; Harvey, 1998; MacEwen & Barling, 1991; Stewart & Barling, 1996). Despite some significant correlations, there is no consistent evidence across the multiple samples and different measures cited here of a direct association between parent job characteristics and child well-being. Having a parent who works in a noxious or stressful job, or one who reports considerable work-family conflict, does not appear to be directly linked to any of these indicators of adjustment or maladjustment of children in the family.

These results suggest a possible misspecification of the consequences of parental work. Psychologists often conceptualize health and well-being in terms of biological, social, emotional, and behavioral processes that are linked to one another in a cascading flow. Disruptions in these processes can have long-term, cumulative effects, such that symptoms may be observed in the future (Repetti, Taylor, & Seeman, 2002). For example, in job stress research, working in a high-strain occupation (i.e., a job with high demands and low control) is associated with an elevated risk of coronary artery disease (Schnall, Belkic, Landsbergis, & Baker, 2000). However, scientists are often more interested in examining how chronic exposure to certain job characteristics, such as low control or high demands, might be linked to precursors of coronary artery disease, such as high blood pressure, dysregulated stress hormones, or smoking and alcohol consumption (Repetti & Mittman, 2004). Not everyone in a high-strain occupation advances to coronary artery disease. However, many show evidence of behavioral and physiological disruptions that occur earlier in the cascade and that can lead to coronary artery disease. The effects of job strain on these precursors are, therefore, stronger than the effect on a definitive health endpoint such as coronary artery disease. Because of limitations of measurement error and small sample sizes, which can limit the power to detect small effects, it is much easier to observe an association between a stressful occupational characteristic and one of these precursors than to detect the link to actual cases of coronary artery disease.

Just as in occupational stress research, the consequences of work may be most clearly observed early in the health cascade, not at the endpoints. Studies of the immediate effects of work are well suited to an approach that focuses on health processes, rather than health endpoints. Daily diary studies, in which participants record information one or more times each day, have been used to examine the short-term effects of day-to-day changes in work. These studies suggest that adults' daily experiences of overload and distressing social interactions at work are associated with immediate increases in negative mood, minor health complaints, and indicators of physiological arousal, such as blood pressure and heart rate (Barling & Macintyre, 1993; Jamner, Shapiro, Goldstein & Hug, 1991; MacEwen, Barling, & Kelloway, 1992; Repetti, 1993). Although there are fewer studies of the short-term outcomes associated with work-family conflict, at least one study found that descriptions of work interfering with family or family interfering with work correlated with an increase in reports of negative mood that day (MacEwen & Barling, 1994). Physiological arousal, mood disturbance, and minor physical symptoms are precisely the types of short-term outcomes that one would seek as evidence of a psychological and biological system responding to stress. These short-term responses to work and work-family stressors are evident among employed individuals. If the stressor is chronic and the biological stress response systems are repeatedly activated, these short-term reactions may act as precursors to more significant health problems.

A search for the consequences of parental work experiences early in the cascade process may be especially appropriate for studies of the health and well-being of offspring. According to a *risky families* model of child health and development presented next, the effect of parents' jobs on health endpoints would not become evident until adolescence or adulthood. During childhood, the consequences would instead be most likely observed in the intermediate pathways or the precursors to physical and mental health. As discussed in the next section, the family environment is an important early component of the cascade that contributes to long-term physical and mental health outcomes.

FAMILY INTERACTION AS A HEALTH AND WELL-BEING OUTCOME

Parents' experiences at work and of a mismatch between their work and family lives appear to shape the way they interact with other family members (Perry-Jenkins, Repetti, & Crouter, 2000). The functioning and well-being of families, as reflected in the quality of parent–child interactions, can certainly stand alone as important outcomes in their own right. However, a focus on the family is also essential to any understanding of the consequences of work-family stress for child well-being. Conceptual models linking work-family factors to child outcomes all place some form of family social interaction in the central mediating role (e.g., Crouter & Bumpus, 2001). Whether through socialization or spillover, the connection from parental work to child outcome is always assumed to be indirect, with behaviors, events, and emotions that take place within the family playing the central linking role.

There are strong theoretical and empirical rationales for placing family social interaction in this key role, particularly when the outcome of interest is the health of offspring. The social environment in which a child is reared is an integral part of his or her health and development. A risky families model of family characteristics associated with poor long-term health in offspring identified high levels of conflict and aggression, and relationships that are cold, unsupportive, and neglectful as the key pernicious aspects of family social life (Repetti et al., 2002). Research suggests that these qualities of family relationships, in particular parent–child relationships, help shape the development of stress-responsive biological regulatory systems, emotion regulation processes, social competence, and health behaviors during childhood and adolescence. Taken together, these biological, emotional, and behavioral consequences of early environments, in combination with genetic predispositions, represent an integrated profile of risk for mental and physical health in adulthood.

It is perhaps not surprising that, in contrast to measures of child adjustment and maladjustment, studies that include parent–child and parenting outcomes provide more reliable evidence of an association with employment, including work-family conflict. For example, in one study, both mothers and fathers who were employed in jobs that required more complex interactions with people described their approach to controlling their 5- to 7-year-old children as less harsh, and independent observers also rated those parents as warm and responsive during interactions with their children (Greenberger, O'Neil, & Nagel, 1994). Another investigation found that fathers who were more satisfied with their careers showed greater warmth, attentiveness, and responsiveness with their 5-year-old children as rated by independent observers (Grossman, Pollack, & Golding, 1988). In a study of air traffic controllers, fathers whose work teams had a negative social climate (described by coworkers as unsupportive, unpleasant, or conflictive) described their interactions with their children over 3 days as being less positive and more negative in emotional tone (e.g., fewer expressions of affection and more anger; Repetti, 1994). In a recent longitudinal study, mothers' social climate at work was associated with changes in parent–infant interactions 3 months later (Costigan, Cox, & Cauce, 2003). Observers' ratings indicated that both mothers' and fathers' interactions with their 1-year-old child became less child-centered, and parents expressed more negative affect when mothers perceived a more negative social atmosphere at work (e.g., lower morale and less cohesion among coworkers). However, the work social climate of fathers was not associated with changes in parent–child interactions.

Investigations relying solely on parent self-report data have also uncovered significant correlations between parents' descriptions of their jobs and their parenting style or the quality of their interactions with their children (Galambos et al., 1995; Stewart & Barling, 1996). The pattern of significant associations is not replicated in every study (e.g., Crouter et al., 1999; Galambos & Maggs, 1990), nor is it consistently found in studies with multiple measures of work and parenting (e.g., Greenberger et al., 1994; Repetti, 1994). However, there is a trend that suggests an association between parents' work experiences and the quality of the parent–child relationship.

That trend has been replicated in tests of the short-term effect of parents' work experiences on parent–child interaction. One daily diary study of two-parent families compared mothers who were employed full time with those who were either not employed or who worked fewer than 30 hours each week (Almeida, Wethington, & Chandler, 1999). This investigation focused on the ways in which daily stressors in parents' lives might be linked to tensions in the parent–child relationship, such as disagreements, arguments, or discipline problems. Families with a mother employed full time appeared to be more reactive, at least in the short term, to daily stressors. Experiences such as a marital argument or work overload were more likely to be associated with a short-term increase in parent–child tensions in the families with full-time employed mothers.

In the study of air traffic controllers mentioned earlier, increases in workload and distressing social interactions during the workday were associated with paternal withdrawal later that day, as well as greater use of discipline and a more negative emotional tone during interactions with children (Repetti, 1994). In another study, both mothers and independent observers described mothers as more withdrawn with their preschoolers (e.g., less speaking, fewer expressions of affection) on days when the mothers experienced increases in the same two job stressors (i.e., greater workloads or more negative social interactions with coworkers and supervisors; Repetti & Wood, 1997). Short-term effects are not always observed. An analysis of data from the daily diary study of full- and part-time married mothers noted previously (Almeida et al., 1999) did not reveal a same-day association between self-reports of stressful experiences at work and a single-item measure of tensions or arguments with children at home (Bolger, DeLongis, Kessler, & Wethington, 1989).

Experiences such as role overload in dual-earner couples (i.e., feeling overwhelmed by multiple commitments) and interrole conflict (i.e., the extent to which work interferes with family demands) appear to have similar effects on the parent–child relationship. A sense of greater mismatch between the needs of family and work has been linked to parent reports of more punishment and rejection (Stewart & Barling, 1996), more parent–child conflict (Crouter et al., 1999), and less parental acceptance (Crouter, Bumpus, Head, & McHale, 2001). Employment conditions that directly affect work-family conflict have also been associated with the quality of parent–child interaction. For example, one investigation found that mothers who took shorter leaves following the birth of their child displayed more negative maternal affect and behavior (e.g., insensitivity, expressions of anger or displeasure) during an infant-feeding session (Clark, Hyde, Essex, & Klein, 1997).

The characteristics of the parent–child relationship that appear to be shaped by parents' experiences at work—the amount of warmth and responsiveness, on the one hand, and harshness, punishment, rejection, and conflict, on the other—are the types of interactions that modulate children's risk for poor health (Repetti et al., 2002). This is precisely the type of process model at the core of most of the research described here: Parental employment experiences are linked to a child well-being outcome through a parenting or parent–child-mediating variable (Crouter et al., 1999; Galambos & Maggs, 1990; Galambos et al., 1995; Harvey, 1998; MacEwen & Barling, 1991; Stewart & Barling, 1996). In most cases, a direct link from the work role variable to the child well-being endpoint was not established. However, the evidence typically supported a series of connections along a chain of variables that connected a work or work-family experience with a child health or adjustment outcome.

THE ROLE OF MODERATOR VARIABLES

There is no reason to expect all families to respond to job stressors and work-family conflict in the same manner. The characteristics or qualities that distinguish families that respond in one way from families that respond in another way are referred to as *moderator variables*. Some studies have tested characteristics of families and individual family members as possible moderators of the health and well-being consequences of parents' employment experiences. The research discussed next indicates that the quality of family relationships, as well as the gender, personality, psychological adjustment, and attitudes of individual family members, may all act as moderators.

At least two investigations into the effects of mothers' employment on child development have identified parenting characteristics as important moderator variables. A study of 9- to 12-year-old children's school performance and conduct examined the role of parental monitoring—that is, parents' daily knowledge of their children's companions, activities, and whereabouts—in dual- and single-earner families (Crouter, MacDermid, McHale, & Perry-Jenkins, 1990). (The mothers in single-earner families worked fewer than 15 hours per week.) Consistent with other research cited here, there was no pattern of across-the-board differences between the children growing up in single-earner families and those growing up in dual-earner families. However, child gender and parental monitoring acted as significant moderator variables; although there were no average differences between children in the two family types, there were subgroup differences. Sons, but not daughters, in dual-earner families were more likely than other children to get into trouble, quarrel, and fight, but only if their parents were not keeping track of their daily activities and experiences. The conduct of sons in dual-earner families who were well monitored did not differ from that of other children.

Moorehouse (1991) found similar results between changes in mothers' employment and children's social and cognitive competence as indicated by first-grade teachers' ratings and school grades. In this case, Moorehouse found that the consequences of changes in maternal employment were moderated by the mothers' parenting styles. When mothers frequently shared activities with their children, such as reading books and telling stories, any potentially disruptive effects of changes in employment on children's social and cognitive competence seemed to be mitigated. The evidence suggested that both cognitive and social outcomes suffered when two conditions were met: a mother had either increased or decreased her hours at work during the previous 3-year period and she relatively infrequently spent time in shared child activities. Among families whose mothers frequently engaged in shared child activities, there were no differences between the children whose mothers changed their employment situation and those whose mothers remained stably employed or stably nonemployed. In both of these studies, aspects of maternal employment were associated with child well-being outcomes, but only for a portion of the families. Mothers' employment seemed to matter only in families with less parental monitoring or less intensive parent–child involvement.

Moderators and Parenting

It is not surprising that the effects that parental employment experiences have on the parent–child relationship also vary for different families. For example, in two of the studies mentioned before, the association between parenting style and parents' job characteristics differed for mothers and fathers (Costigan et al., 2003; Greenberger et al., 1994). In one investigation, the link between work and parenting also varied depending on whether the child in the family was a son or daughter (Greenberger et al., 1994). A study examining the association between a short maternity leave and mother–child interactions indicated that the quality of the mother's interactions with her infant was affected only when the mother showed fairly high levels of postpartum depressive symptoms or when her infant had a difficult or fussy temperament (Clark et al., 1997). There was no association between a relatively quick return to work (a maternity leave of 6 or fewer weeks) and the amount of positive maternal affect and behavior with the baby (e.g., warm tone of voice, cheerful mood, expressions of pleasure and enjoyment) for the other mothers in the study.

A study of parental monitoring in dual-earner families compared three groups: a "high mother demands" group (in which mothers experienced long work hours, intense work pressure, and considerable role overload), a "high father demands" group (in which the fathers experienced long work hours, intense work pressure, and considerable role overload), and a "low demands" group (Bumpus, Crouter, & McHale, 1999). On average, there were no differences in the degree to which parents in these three groups kept aware of their children's daily experiences, activities, and whereabouts. However, parental monitoring differences appeared when the gender of offspring and the quality of the parents' marital relationship were taken into account. Parents in the "high father demands" group were less knowledgeable about their children's daily lives only if there were young boys in the family and they reported a less happy marriage. Under any other family circumstances, the authors found no differences in parental monitoring among the three groups. The research discussed here indicates that the effect of parents' work and work-family experiences on the parent–child relationship depends on any number of moderator variables: characteristics of the child, such as gender and temperament; characteristics of the parent, such as psychological functioning; and the quality of other relationships within the family, such as the parents' marital relationship.

The short-term effect of work experiences on parent–child interaction also appears to vary across families. In the daily report study of mothers and their preschoolers noted earlier, daily job stressors had a stronger effect on the parenting behavior of mothers with lower psychological well-being scores (more symptoms of depression and anxiety) and those who reported engaging in more of the classic Type A behaviors (feeling pressed for time, getting upset at having to wait for anything; Repetti & Wood, 1997). These mothers not only were more socially withdrawn on higher job-stress days, but also had more aversive interactions with their preschool-age children on those days. However, among the mothers who reported high levels of psychological well-being and little Type A behavior, day-to-day variation in parent–child interaction did not correlate with experiences at work. Findings such as these indicate that a weak or nonsignificant correlation between parents' employment experiences and individual or family well-being may not always reflect a uniformly weak effect. Depending on a family's circumstances, the effect of job characteristics and work-family stressors on health and well-being can range widely.

IMPLICATIONS FOR RESEARCH AND INTERVENTION

A psychological approach in examining the consequences of parental employment has implications for research design and intervention. The choice of health outcomes and sampling strategies are discussed within the context of the small effect sizes typical in this field. In this section, I discuss how a psychological perspective influences the design of effective interventions.

Conceptualizing Health and Well-Being Outcomes

A psychological perspective as described here regards health as a cumulative process. Some steps occur early in the health process, perhaps within minutes, hours, or days of a precipitating event. Over time and with repeated exposure, the small steps may accumulate, functioning as stages in a health process. These stages may be reached only over relatively long time spans, perhaps months or years. However, each step, whether short or long, is an intermediate outcome critical to the process. In any research study or intervention, the choice of outcome must be consistent with the time frame of the study or intervention. With respect to the health consequences for children of parental employment, particularly when the children are young, research and theory point to emotion regulation and social competence as parts of a cascade of influence (Repetti et al., 2002). Early disruptions in these processes continue to have an effect on development in future stages. The health and well-being consequences of parents' work and work-family stress for children would be most easily detected in intermediate developmental processes that act as precursors to later physical and mental health.

The consequences of parental employment for health endpoints, such as psychopathology and illness, may exist in childhood, but the effect sizes appear to be quite small. Perhaps health endpoints are reached only among children and families with certain vulnerabilities or perhaps only among children whose parents work in unusually stressful occupations. Either way the overall effects in a random sample would be so small that a very large study would be required to observe them. An alternative would be to follow children and families over longer spans of time in longitudinal studies. At later stages in development, the effects of parental work would have accumulated, causing the effects on health endpoints to be stronger and easier to detect. Therefore, the conceptualization of health and well-being—whether as an immediate reaction to an event, a developmental deficit that acts as a precursor, or a hard health endpoint—determines when effects will be observed and their magnitude.

Choosing a Sampling Strategy

One reason that effect sizes in work-family research can be small is because of the role played by moderator variables. The effect of employment-related stress on health and well-being varies by group differences, such as gender, family characteristics, and individual differences. Consider the research discussed previously indicating that sons in dual-earner families that do not monitor their children's activities well are more likely to get into trouble (Crouter et al., 1990). In that study, the average difference between the children in single- and dual-earner families was too small to be detected at the aggregate level. However, once the analysis accounted for group differences based on child gender and parental monitoring, associations between parent earner status and child behavior were detected. The effect was substantial enough within a certain subgroup of children, yet too weak to be detected in the random sample.

The important role of moderator variables suggests that investigations of the health consequences of employment adopt one of two sampling strategies.

Very large, diverse samples can detect small effects and the types of group differences that moderator variables reflect. An alternative approach, involving carefully selected, more homogeneous samples, offers two advantages. First, although this strategy may limit the generalizability of the findings, it allows researchers with a relatively small study size to detect effects that are small in the general population. That is because health and well-being processes are influenced by many factors. Selecting more homogeneous samples reduces variance in health processes owing to factors extraneous to the main focus of the research study, thereby increasing the chances of detecting a relatively small effect with a relatively small sample. Second, moderator effects found in large-sample studies can be further investigated in samples that are selected to reflect the subgroups of interest. For example, the finding that sons of dual-earner parents who do not monitor their children well are at increased risk of getting into trouble is intriguing, but that finding alone does not reveal what is happening in those families or, if the goal is to reduce child behavior problems, how to intervene. One could address those issues in a follow-up study of dual-earner families who vary on parental monitoring and who have 9- to 12-year-old sons. Of course the findings from such a study may not generalize to sons who are older than age 12 or younger than age 9 or to daughters in dual-earner families. However, intensive measurement procedures, such as observations or repeated measures, are more feasible in studies with fewer participants. Limited generalizability can be offset by more dense information and greater precision of measurement.

The Design of Experimental Interventions

Experiments are essential for testing causal models. An experiment with random assignment and meaningful control conditions is the only way to determine whether an employment-related experience affects health and well-being. The design of any experiment, including an experimental intervention, requires a clear conceptual base to guide the choice of variables to manipulate and those to target for change. Psychological interventions typically do not target the ultimate outcome—the health endpoint—directly. Instead the intervention is designed to change a variable earlier in the cascade—one that precedes the health endpoint, such as cognitions, motivations, behaviors, or feelings.

A process approach to defining health and well-being facilitates the design of effective interventions. Knowing that parental employment experiences are associated with particular health endpoints does not necessarily convey any information about the processes that connect work to health. It is only through an understanding of the intermediate steps linking a work or work-family variable to a health outcome that we can begin to design interventions that have a desired outcome. The work of social-developmental psychologist

Daphne Bugental illustrates this point. Bugental identified a cognitive bias in some individuals that results in certain beliefs about children and their behavior, which in turn increases the likelihood that the parents will maltreat their children. From this theoretical and empirical base, she developed a cognitively based prevention program for parents who were at risk for child maltreatment and abuse. The intervention was tested in a random-assignment, experimental design, including a support-based comparison condition. The program achieved its goal to reduce child abuse by fostering parents' ability to view problems as controllable, solvable challenges with a remarkable level of success (Bugental et al., 2002). Note that the intervention did not directly target the abusive behavior. Instead it was aimed at changing parents' cognitions. By construing the family well-being outcome as a process consisting of a mix of behaviors, emotions, motivations, and cognitions, Bugental was able to pinpoint a step in the process at which she could intervene and effect real change. The intervention research not only provided the strongest possible test of Bugental's model of the role that parent attributions play in child maltreatment, it also showed how and why strong psychological theory and empirical findings provide the power to design highly effective interventions.

CONCLUSION

Psychologists approach the study of health, well-being, and employment by thinking about processes composed of multiple, intermediary steps that unfold over time and the role moderator variables play in shaping the effects at each stage. This perspective helps explain why effects sizes in this area of research are often small, and it has important implications for research design and the development of effective interventions.

ACKNOWLEDGMENTS

This chapter was supported by the UCLA Center on the Everyday Lives of Families, which is funded by a grant (2000-12-13) from the Alfred P. Sloan Foundation.

REFERENCES

Almeida, D. M., Wethington, E., & Chandler, A. L. (1999). Daily transmission of tensions between marital dyads and parent-child dyads. *Journal of Marriage and the Family, 61*, 49–61.

Barling, J., & Macintyre, A. T. (1993). Daily work role stressors, mood and emotional exhaustion. *Work and Stress, 7*, 315–325.

Bolger, N., DeLongis, A., Kessler, R. C., & Wethington, E. (1989). The contagion of stress across multiple roles. *Journal of Marriage and the Family, 51*, 175–183.

Bugental, D. B., Ellerson, P. C., Lin, E. K., Rainey, B., Kokotovic, A., & O'Hara, N. (2002). A cognitive approach to child abuse prevention. *Journal of Family Psychology, 16*, 243–258.

Bumpus, M. E., Crouter, A. C., & McHale, S. M. (1999). Work demands of dual-earner couples: Implications for parents' knowledge about children's daily lives in middle childhood. *Journal of Marriage and the Family, 61*, 465–475.

Clark, R., Hyde, J. S., Essex, M. J., & Klein, M. H. (1997). Length of maternity leave and quality of mother-infant interactions. *Child Development, 68*, 364–383.

Costigan, C. L., Cox, M. J., & Cauce, A. M. (2003). Work-parenting linkages among dual-earner couples at the transition to parenthood. *Journal of Family Psychology, 17*, 397–408.

Crouter, A. C., & Bumpus, M. F. (2001). Linking parents' work stress to children's and adolescents' psychological adjustment. *Current Directions in Psychological Science, 10*, 156–159.

Crouter, A. C., Bumpus, M. F., Head, M. R., & McHale, S. M. (2001). Implications of overwork and overload for the quality of men's family relationships. *Journal of Marriage and the Family, 63*, 404–416.

Crouter, A. C., Bumpus, M. F., Maguire, M.C., & McHale, S. M. (1999). Linking parents' work pressure and adolescnets' well-being: Insights into dynamics in dual-earner families. *Developmental Psychology, 35*, 1453–1461.

Crouter, A. C., MacDermid, S. M., McHale, S. M., & Perry-Jenkins, M. (1990). Parental monitoring and perceptions of children's school performance and conduct in dual- and single-earner families. *Developmental Psychology, 26*, 649–657.

Galambos, N. L., & Maggs, J. L. (1990). Putting mothers' work-related stress in perspective: Mothers and adolescents in dual-earner families. *Journal of Early Adolescence, 10*, 313–328.

Galambos, N. L., Sears, H. A., Almeida, D. M., & Kolaric, G. C. (1995). Parents' work overload and problem behavior in young adolescents. *Journal of Research on Adolescence, 5*, 201–223.

Greenberger, E., & Goldberg, W. A. (1989). Work, parenting, and the socialization of children. Work, parenting, and the socialization of children. *Developmental Psychology, 25*, 22–35.

Greenberger, E., O'Neil, R., & Nagel, S. K. (1994). Linking workplace and homeplace: Relations between the nature of adults' work and their parenting behaviors. *Developmental Psychology, 30*, 990–1002.

Grossman, F. K., Pollack, W. S., & Golding, E. (1988). Fathers and children: Predicting the quality and quantity of fathering. *Developmental Psychology, 24*, 82–91.

Harvey, E. (1998). Parental employment and conduct problems among children with attention deficit/hyperactivity disorder: An examination of child care workload and parenting well-being as mediating variables. *Journal of Social and Clinical Psychology, 17*, 476–490.

Jamner, L. D., Shapiro, D., Goldstein, I. B., & Hug, R. (1991). Ambulatory blood pressure and heart rate in paramedics: Effects of cynical hostility and defensiveness. *Psychosomatic Medicine, 53*, 393–406.

MacEwan, K. E., & Barling, J. (1991). Effects of maternal employment experiences on children's behavior via mood, cognitive difficulties, and parenting behavior. *Journal of Marriage and the Family, 53*, 635–644.

MacEwan, K. E., & Barling, J. (1994). Daily consequences of work interference with family and family interference with work. *Work and Stress, 8*, 244–254.

MacEwan, K. E., Barling, J., & Kelloway, E. K. (1992). Effects of short-term role overload on marital interactions. *Work and Stress, 6*, 117–126.

Moorehouse, M. J. (1991). Linking maternal employment patterns to mother-child activities and children's school competence. *Developmental Psychology, 27*, 295–303.

Perry-Jenkins, M., Repetti, R. L., & Crouter, A. C. (2000). Work and family in the 1990s. *Journal of Marriage and the Family, 62*, 981–998.

Repetti, R. L. (1993). Short-term effects of occupational stressors on daily mood and health complaints. *Health Psychology, 12*, 125–131.

Repetti, R. L. (1994). Short-term and long-term processes linking job stressors to father-child interaction. *Social Development, 3*, 1–15.

Repetti, R. L., & Mittman, A. (2004). Workplace stress. In A. Christensen, R. Martin, & J. Smyth (Eds.), *Encyclopedia of health psychology* (pp. 342–344). New York: Kluwer Academic/ Plenum.

Repetti, R. L., Taylor, S. E., & Seeman, T. (2002). Risky families: Family social environments and the mental and physical health of offspring. *Psychological Bulletin, 128*, 330–366.

Repetti, R. L., & Wood, J. (1997). The effects of daily stress at work on mothers' interactions with preschoolers. *Journal of Family Psychology, 11*, 90–108.

Schnall, P. L., Belkic, K., Landsbergis, P., & Baker, D. (2000). The workplace and cardiovascular disease. *Occupational Medicine: State of the Art Reviews, 15*(1). Beverly Farms, MA: OEM Press.

Stewart, W., & Barling, J. (1996). Fathers' work experiences effect children's behaviors via job-related affect and parenting behaviors. *Journal of Organizational Behavior 17*, 221–232.

Voydanoff, P. (2004). Work, community, and parenting resources and demands as predictors of adolescent problems and grades. *Journal of Adolescent Research, 19*, 155–173.

18

Work-Family Mismatch Through a Child Developmental Lens

Martha Zaslow
Susan Jekielek
Megan Gallagher
Child Trends

In this chapter, we shift the focus from workers to workers' children. We further narrow the focus to workers who are mothers. We explore whether maternal employment creates a mismatch with the developmental needs of children. We use the term *mismatch* to refer to the degree of correspondence between demands of the workplace and needs of workers—and in this case the children as well. Although the research on maternal employment has found no widespread negative implications for children's development, and indeed finds effects ranging from negative to neutral to positive, recent research has indicated that maternal employment may pose a mismatch with developmental needs at two ends of the age continuum—infancy and adolescence—although only for specific groups of families.

The particular focus on maternal employment and children, in part, reflects demographic changes in recent decades. A report of the Committee on Family and Work Policies of the National Research Council and Institute of Medicine (Smolensky & Gootman, 2003), which includes national data from

1970 through 2000, notes that although the employment rates of fathers have remained high and stable, the employment rates of mothers of children under age 18 have changed markedly. Overall, from 1970 to 2000, the workforce participation rate of mothers with children under age 18 increased from 38% to 68%; the rate for mothers of children between birth and age 3 increased from 24% to 58%.

Although these increases occurred primarily before 1990 among married mothers, single mothers saw a substantial rise in workforce participation during the latter half of the 1990s. Nearly two thirds (65%) of married women with children under age 18 were in the workforce in 1995, and nearly the same percentage, 66% were working in 2000. The parallel figures for single mothers were 63% in 1995 and 75% in 2000. This recent increase among single mothers is assumed to reflect the combined influence of welfare reform, the Earned Income Tax Credit, and a strong economy in the latter half of the 1990s. Total weekly hours of employment during this time span increased only from 33 to 36 hours per week among all mothers with children under age 18. However, an increasing proportion of the U.S. workforce is employed during nonstandard hours, and this shift disproportionately affects parents and low-income workers (Presser & Cox, 1997).

With these changes in employment patterns, the daily childrearing context for large numbers of children has changed. The recent shifts suggest a need to focus especially on the children of single and low-income mothers. Although acknowledging that the work circumstances of both parents matter to children's development, we focus on whether changes in work and caregiving for mothers create a match or mismatch with the developmental needs of children at different ages.

The match–mismatch conceptualization is used in developmental psychology to refer to the fit of the social environment and children's developmental needs at a particular stage (stage-environment fit). As a noteworthy example, Eccles and her colleagues (1993) used this conceptualization to help explain a troubling decline in developmental status (a "downward spiral") that affects some young adolescents. Research indicates a decline in school grades, motivation, and self-concept and an increase in conflict with parents for some young adolescents, coinciding approximately with the transition to middle or junior high school.

Eccles and colleagues (1993) noted that although young adolescents experience a need for greater participation in decision making, many actually experience a decline in self-determination. When this occurs in the classroom, it may have implications for their academic engagement. For example, Eccles and colleagues summarized findings from research by Mac Iver and Reuman (1988) showing that those students who "perceived their seventh-grade math classrooms as putting greater constraints on their preferred level of participation in classroom decision making than their sixth-grade math classrooms . . .

evidenced the largest and most consistent declines in their intrinsic interest in math as they moved from the sixth grade into the seventh grade" (Eccles et al., 1993, p. 96). Similarly, in the home, when adolescents press for greater autonomy, some parents respond with greater restrictiveness rather than allowing them more voice in decision making, creating a mismatch in the home environment.

Building on the work of Eccles and colleagues (1993), we propose that the developmental mismatch approach requires that one specify a developmental goal or task that characterizes a particular age range; consider both the home and other environments as contexts that can affect progress toward the developmental task or goal; and document a link between specific features of the social environment and children's progress toward the task or goal.

At the outset, we underscore that the body of research on maternal employment does not predict widespread patterns of developmental mismatch. The earliest research on maternal employment expressed alarm at the growing rates of employment and focused on whether employment would harm children. The model was a main effects model with a unidirectional prediction: Maternal employment would be associated with negative effects across population groups (Bronfenbrenner & Crouter, 1982). However, the accumulating evidence has not indicated widespread harm among children of employed mothers. Indeed, there is evidence that maternal employment can be associated with a range of outcomes, from negative to neutral to positive, and that many of the findings fall in the neutral range (Smolensky & Gootman, 2003). Further, findings tend to differ across subgroups (Zaslow, Rabinovich, & Suwalsky, 1991).

The report of the Committee on Family and Work Policies (Smolensky & Gootman, 2003) noted several reasons that help explain why the associations of maternal employment to child outcomes do not follow a simple pattern. First, families actively adapt to maternal employment by compensating for a mother's time away. For example, studies of dual-earner families show greater father involvement with children, making overall time with parents more comparable to families with a nonemployed mother (e.g., Hoffman, Youngblade, Coley, Fuligni, & Kovacs, 1999). Employed mothers allocate their hours to maximize their time available to children, cutting their time spent in leisure activities and on household tasks not involving child care (Bianchi, 2000). Mothers with young children tend to work fewer hours, and parents in dual-earner families may work schedules that allow one parent to be available to the child(ren). There may be more constraints, however, on the degree to which low-income and single mothers can adapt in these ways.

The report also found that the implications of employment for children are influenced by mothers' employment circumstances, rather than employment status per se (employed or not employed). Features of the employment, such as extent, timing of employment after a birth, occupational complexity, wages, and the contribution to overall family income, are important factors in understanding implications for children's development (e.g., Jekielek & McGroder, 2003; Menaghan & Parcel, 1991; Parcel & Menaghan, 1994a, 1994b).

A third reason for the complexity in employment effects is that multiple aspects of family life can be influenced simultaneously by maternal employment. For example, employed mothers may simultaneously experience increased self-esteem and increased role strain or time stress. Employment may increase overall family income, but decrease maternal availability. Children may be affected in light of the net or balance of these positive and negative influences (Desai, Chase-Lansdale, & Michael, 1989; Greenstein, 1995; McGroder, Zaslow, Papillo, Ahluwalia, & Brooks, in press). A developmental mismatch thus reflects a tipping of the multidetermined balance toward the unfavorable, rather than the presence of a single influential factor or process.

Earlier reviews have considered whether maternal employment has different effects for children of different ages (e.g., Zaslow et al., 1991), but it is helpful to reexamine these findings in light of several advances.

Better Treatment of Selection

Most of the research on maternal employment and children involves self-selection by mothers into an employment status. It is clear from this research that there are differences between families in which the mothers are and are not employed that may have implications for children's development, such as marital status and maternal education. Recent studies of maternal employment and children have been grappling with selection issues, using more rigorous statistical approaches to isolate effects of employment on children, such as expanded sets of control variables, family fixed effects models, and instrumental variable approaches. In addition, studies focusing on welfare reform and children have used experimental designs (see overview in Zaslow et al., 2002). These studies do not involve random assignment to work per se, but they do permit researchers to consider what happens to children's development in low-income samples when mothers are or are not randomly assigned to a program requiring and encouraging work.

Much Greater Consideration of Maternal Employment in Low-Income Samples

Although early research on maternal employment focused heavily on middle-income, dual-earner families, recent research focuses on families from a range of socioeconomic backgrounds, including families making the transition from welfare to work. The inclusion of families from a wide socioeconomic range is particularly important when considering the mismatch issue. As mentioned, strategies for adapting to maternal employment, with mothers compensating for time away from the child, may be more difficult in single-parent or low-income families. Distinct challenges faced by low-income families in particular settings, such as inner city neighborhoods, may increase the risk of a mismatch (Jarrett, 1998). At the same time, employment may be a source of income and, as such may allow low-income families to better meet the needs of children (Desai et al., 1989). The greater attention to low-income families in the research makes it possible to explore these possibilities.

Much Greater Consideration of Mediating Processes

As we have noted, the match–mismatch conceptualization requires that a process be identified through which a goal or task specific to a particular stage of development is fostered or frustrated. Recent research on maternal employment has focused much more on the explanatory processes. As one example, Hoffman and colleagues (1999) examined the role of father involvement, maternal psychological well-being, and parenting in explaining associations between maternal employment and more positive achievement and adjustment in a sample of third-grade children whose mothers had been consistently employed over a 3-year period.

Increasing Consideration of Both the Home and Child-Care Environment

As illustrated in the research by Eccles and colleagues (1993), mismatch may occur both in and beyond the home environment. The research on maternal employment is increasingly acknowledging the simultaneous influence of the home and child-care environments on children, and several recent papers consider their joint influence. Although not all children in child care have employed mothers (Tout, Papillo, Zaslow, & Vandivere, 2001), a high enough proportion do to examine the research on child care for issues of stage-environment fit in relation to maternal employment.

Given these developments, recent evidence on maternal employment across a range of ages indicates that at certain points, for certain subgroups, and on specific outcomes, maternal employment may be a worse match with children's developmental needs. Identifying instances of mismatch in this review should not be construed as a typical pattern of association of maternal employment and child outcomes overall, but as red (or green) flags for the effects of maternal employment on children's development in specific circumstances.

This chapter points to emerging data suggesting the presence of mismatch with developmental needs early and late in children's development. It is particularly noteworthy that certain patterns occur only during infancy or when approaching and reaching adolescence. Within particular studies, there are developmental borders in the sense that unfavorable results occur in association with maternal employment only for children of particular age ranges. For example, there may be unfavorable outcomes of maternal employment in the first year of life, but not in the second or third. Participation in welfare reform programs that increase family income may benefit young school-age children, but do not appear to consistently do so for adolescents, and indeed adolescents may experience negative effects.

EARLY CHILDHOOD: EARLY AND EXTENSIVE EMPLOYMENT, SENSITIVE INTERACTION BETWEEN MOTHER AND CHILD, AND QUALITY OF CHILD CARE

A series of recent studies suggests negative implications for child development in some families when a mother resumes employment during a child's first year of life, particularly when the employment is greater than part time and begins earlier in the first year. Although not every recent study has reported this pattern, unfavorable outcomes have been found using several different data sets, with some reports involving particularly rigorous attempts to account for selection effects.

Han and colleagues (2001) and, more recently, Waldfogel, Han, and Brooks-Gunn (2002) reported on analyses using the National Longitudinal Survey of Youth–Child Supplement (NLSY–CS). Although earlier studies with this data set reported mixed findings for children whose mothers were employed in their first year, more recent studies follow children for a longer period (through ages 7–8) and include women who had given birth over a wider age span and whose employment occurred in years representing a wide variety of economic climates.

Waldfogel and colleagues (2002) considered five cognitive outcomes: receptive vocabulary at age 3 to 4, and math and reading achievement at both ages 5 to 6 and 7 to 8. Regression analyses indicate that all five measures were significantly lower for children in White non-Hispanic families when the mother resumed work in the first year of the child's life. No such pattern was found for children in African-American or Hispanic families. For White children, working more than 21 hours was the point at which employment began to affect outcomes unfavorably. Negative outcomes were largest for children in the lowest income group and for girls. Controlling for scores on the HOME-Short Form (a measure of stimulation and support in the home environment) reduced, but did not eliminate, the associations between early maternal employment and each of the five child outcomes. Whether mothers had breastfed their children did not help explain the findings. The pattern held most consistently for children who had been cared for in home-based care by nonrelatives and, to a lesser extent, by fathers in the first year.

Sibling analyses considered the effects of employment when mothers resumed work early for one sibling but not the other. Even when controlling for HOME scores, regression analyses indicated small, but significant, negative associations of early maternal employment for four of the five outcomes. Further analyses with the sibling sample (using random effects and family fixed effects approaches) suggest that unobserved differences between employed and nonemployed mothers may lead to overestimates of the strength of the pattern, but these analyses also indicate that the pattern cannot be dismissed.

Although the study following children through age 8 by Waldfogel and colleagues (2002) did not consider behavioral outcomes, research by Han and colleagues (2001) indicates that for children in White non-Hispanic families (albeit with a somewhat different sample), any maternal employment before the fourth quarter of the first year of life was associated with greater externalizing behavior problems at age 4 and again at ages 7 and 8.

Brooks-Gunn, Han, and Waldfogel (2002) recently examined this issue using data from the National Institute of Child Health and Human Development (NICHD) Study of Early Child Care. They focused only on the children in the sample from White non-Hispanic families and looked at Bayley Mental Development Index scores at 15 months, the revised version of the Bayley at 24 months, and Bracken school-readiness scores at 36 months. Any employment before the child was 9 months old and employment for 30 or more hours a week by either the sixth or ninth month were associated with significantly lower Bracken, although not Bayley, scores. The researchers found the strongest pattern for boys (rather than girls as discussed earlier) whose mothers resumed employment 30 or more hours a week before the child was 9 months old. They found stronger negative associations with early maternal employment for children whose parents had been married at the time of their birth.

This study found that those mothers who were employed 30 or more hours a week by the child's 9th month were less sensitive in interactions with their children at 36 months, controlling for early levels of maternal sensitivity. Further, children of mothers who worked 30 or more hours a week by the 9th month were in child care of lower quality at 36 months. Quality of parenting and the home environment (maternal sensitivity and HOME scores considered together) and child-care quality helped explain the negative association between early extensive maternal employment and lower Bracken scores.

Youngblade (2003) studied the implications of early maternal employment in a sample of third-grade children from White and African-American two-parent families of varying socioeconomic backgrounds. Early maternal employment was defined as consistent employment for 10 or more hours a week throughout the child's first year beginning within 3 months of the child's birth. When compared with children whose mothers had not been employed in the first year, those whose mothers had been employed were more often nominated by their peers in third grade as hitting and being mean and by their teachers as having more externalizing behavior problems and less frustration tolerance. Differences, although statistically significant, were not large in magnitude and did not generally place children in the range indicating dysfunctional outcomes. Interactions of early employment with child gender and social class indicated that boys and working-class children with mothers who were employed early were seen as hitting more. The number of different types of child care used during the first year, a measure of child-care stability, helped explain the association between early employment and peer ratings of hitting.

Earlier we noted that, to claim developmental mismatch from a pattern of unfavorable outcomes, it is necessary to identify the developmental task or goal and provide evidence that an aspect of the social context (in the home or outside of the home) is detracting from progress toward that goal. A primary developmental task of infancy is establishing reciprocally responsive patterns of communication with primary caregivers. An extensive body of research indicates that a mother's sensitive reading of and responsiveness to her infant's cues are predictive of the development of secure infant–mother attachment (Ainsworth, Blehar, Waters, & Wall, 1978; Bowlby, 1969).

The results from the study by Brooks-Gunn and colleagues (2002) suggest that, in White families, maternal employment of 30 or more hours per week by the child's 9th month is associated with a decline in maternal sensitivity by 36 months. In other results from the NICHD study (Early Child Care Research Network, 1999), which focused on extent of child care received in the first 3 years rather than on maternal employment specifically, more hours in child care predicted less maternal sensitivity and less child engagement with the mother. According to the researchers in the NICHD Early Child Care Research Network (1999), "the findings are consistent with the hypothesis that the amount of time that mothers and children spend together is associated with the ease of their interactions and communication" (p. 1410). The effects, however, were small, and the decreases in sensitivity were not of sufficient magnitude to result in differences in security of attachment in light of the extent of early child care. Perhaps the decrease in sensitivity identified with early maternal employment and the decrease in both sensitivity and positive child engagement with more extensive early child care indicate that the child is receiving slightly, but steadily, less input from the mother that is important to early cognitive and social development. Although quality of interaction may be essential to type of attachment, these findings may reflect small declines in quantity as well as quality of interaction because of less mutual engagement. The pathway of influence on the child of early maternal employment would not be through security of attachment, but through the extent of reciprocal, positive engagement.

Recent work by Belsky (1999) was consistent with this possibility. This work focused on nonmaternal care during a child's first 5 years in White, two-parent families with first-born sons, although without differentiating resumption of employment in the first versus subsequent preschool years. Results indicate that more extensive child care in the first 3 years was associated with more negative observed mothering behavior and less positive fathering during the second and third years. Children who had experienced more extensive nonmaternal care in their first 3 years and their first 5 years were reported by their mothers to have more externalizing behavior problems. Amount of nonmaternal care through age 5 also predicted more negative adjustment in a laboratory observation at 5 years. Parenting behavior as observed in the home at the end of the day (around dinnertime) during the second and third year was found to mediate the findings for externalizing behavior and the lab-based adjustment measure. Belsky suggested that having less time with the child may undermine mothers' development of interaction skills with their children, or that employed mothers may not be less skillful overall, but may be tired and less energetic or patient at the end of a workday. With either possibility, less positive parenting appears to contribute to the child outcomes.

Child care is also implicated as a possible mediator in several studies. Type of care was found to play a role in the results reported by Waldfogel and colleagues, with less favorable outcomes associated with the use of home-based, nonrelative care. Quality of child care helped explain the results in the work reported by Brooks-Gunn and colleagues (2002), and quality of care was found to be lower at age 3 for children of mothers who had resumed employment early. Stability of care helped to explain one of the outcomes reported by Youngblade (2003) in her study of third-grade children from White and African-American two-parent families of varying socioeconomic backgrounds. The less favorable behavioral outcomes noted by Belsky (1999) were associated with extent of care received in the first years of life.

The findings regarding extent, quality, and type of care noted are especially interesting in light of findings from the NICHD Early Child Care Research Network (2002) regarding children's development at age 4½ years. All three seem to matter for children's development even when all are considered simultaneously (for example, quality is considered net of quantity and type). In these analyses, children with greater overall exposure to child care showed more problem behaviors than children who experienced less care according to their caregivers. More exposure to center-based care was associated with better scores on measures of language and memory development. Exposure to care of higher quality and care that increased in quality over time during the early years was associated with better pre-academic skills and language development.

An earlier NICHD (1999) study also suggested that there may be links across parent–child interactions and characteristics of child care. In the sample as a whole, fewer hours in care were related to greater maternal sensitivity and more positive child engagement. Among those participating in child care, child engagement was related to fewer hours in child care, whereas maternal sensitivity was related to higher quality care. The fact that both parenting and child-care characteristics appear to help explain the findings for early and extensive maternal employment may thus be a reflection not only of their cumulative influence, but also of their interrelatedness.

In summary, there is an emerging hypothesis of developmental mismatch suggesting that an early and extensive resumption of employment, for some groups of families, provides a social context in which: (a) it is slightly harder for mothers and infants in some groups to become attuned to each other and may potentially lead to less mutual engagement when they are together, and (b) children are exposed to care of lower quality and to more home-based nonfamilial care (which is not as positively related to language and pre-academic outcomes as center-based care). Even if differences in environment are small and do not result in less secure attachment, a decline in quantity, quality, or both, of mother–child interaction (and perhaps also father–child interaction) and differences in type and quality of child care may be sufficient to contribute to less positive cognitive and social development.

Further work is needed to help explain why the pattern appears to occur in some groups of families, but not others. For example, it is unclear why early maternal employment might affect children in White but not minority families or children of one gender but not another. A better understanding is needed of the circumstances surrounding early maternal employment (e.g., why the pattern is stronger in two-parent families). Is it the case that in these families fathers are facing employment difficulties and mothers resuming employment in the first year would prefer to be at home and, as such, are experiencing role conflict? Research should explicitly examine stress surrounding the return to employment in the child's first year to explore whether it alone helps to explain the decline in sensitivity and the lower quality of care. Recent work carried out in Australia (Harrison & Ungerer, 2002) suggests that early maternal employment there, which is most often part time and widely accepted socially, may be associated with greater rather than less maternal sensitivity. Thus, the social context of employment may be important to consider as well.

APPROACHING AND ENTERING ADOLESCENCE: THE PACING OF AUTONOMY

Middle childhood and adolescence mark an expansion in children's social worlds, as children increasingly participate in settings beyond the immediate supervision of parents and other caregivers (Collins, Harris, & Susman, 1995). Entry into school and participation in out-of-school activities confront the child with a range of different tasks and relationships. Peer relations become much more central, and social competence with peers during middle childhood predicts sense of self-worth, achievement, and later social competence with peers (Masten & Coatsworth, 1998).

The increasing engagement of children in out-of-home activities and with peers poses challenges for the parent–child relationship. Maccoby (1984) described the transition beginning in middle childhood as movement toward coregulation or development of mutually acceptable plans. There is a gradual shift from parental control and decision making to child assumption of responsibility for decisions. With the child functioning more often beyond immediate parental supervision, the parent takes on the key task of monitoring or keeping informed about the child's companions, whereabouts, and activities (Dishion & McMahon, 1998). The negotiation of a different parent–child balance in terms of autonomy and participation in decision making is an ongoing process entering and traversing adolescence (Collins et al., 1995).

Parenting always involves both direct interaction with the child and managerial or gatekeeping components (Chase-Lansdale & Pittman, 2002; Hartup, 1992), such as deciding on the child's pediatrician and which child care or school the child will attend. However, during middle childhood and adolescence, a shift occurs in the balance of these aspects of parenting, with the managerial role becoming relatively more important. Monitoring becomes an important predictor of development during middle childhood and remains so into adolescence (Dishion & McMahon, 1998).

The evidence suggests that maternal employment can provide a match with these developmental tasks of the parent–child relationship if the employment yields resources that augment the managerial role, for example, enabling the mother to afford a quality after-school program. In balance with this, however, Brooks and colleagues (2001) hypothesized that maternal employment can be a source of difficulty if it results in an accelerated granting of autonomy, such that the child or adolescent is overburdened with responsibility or given too much of a role in decision making. Such an accelerated timetable could occur if the mother is weary from stressful or extensive employment and *gives up* rather than calibrates each new step toward autonomy, or if the mother urgently needs assistance from an older child in managing a household.

Work by Jarrett (1998) cautioned that there may be particular challenges in inner-city neighborhoods that require more active, even strenuous efforts to monitor older children to keep them off the "street pathway of development" and within the conventional path. Jarrett noted the special challenges of balancing employment with this heightened vigilance. If employment compromises monitoring in such a context, youth can experience particularly problematic outcomes.

Regarding the role of employment in this match, Chase-Lansdale and Pittman (2002) found that participation in welfare-to-work programs can enhance the gate-keeping function, with children of mothers in some of the programs more likely to participate in formal child-care arrangements and afterschool activities. One particularly interesting example from middle childhood is reported in the New Hope evaluation (Bos et al., 1999; Huston et al., 2001). This intervention provided financial supports to low-income families, ensuring income above the poverty line, health insurance, and child-care subsidies for full-time workers. A rigorous experimental evaluation found that the sons of mothers assigned to New Hope had higher teacher ratings of positive social behavior, lower ratings of behavior problems, and disciplinary action.

Mothers in New Hope were encouraged by caseworkers to use licensed child care and formal afterschool care, and they were given a subsidy to help pay for such care. As a result, children in middle childhood participated more often in organized activities and afterschool care, especially boys. The researchers hypothesized that the mothers were particularly concerned about the possibility of their sons' exposure to neighborhood influences, and when resources became available mothers made use of organized care and activities. The more favorable outcomes for boys in middle childhood may be attributable, in part, the researchers surmise, to their participation in formal afterschool programs and activities. Thus, employment within New Hope appeared to augment mothers' managerial role.

A recent study of low-income families found that mothers did not spend substantially less time with their adolescents (ages 11½–15½ years) when the mothers moved into employment—about 45 fewer minutes a day—and that employment significantly increased family income (Chase-Lansdale et al., 2003). This same study found no negative effects of employment or of leaving welfare, and even found improvements in adolescent mental health when mothers moved into employment, suggesting that adolescents may benefit from maternal employment when it leads to greater income and does not result in substantially less time in parent–child interactions. A limitation of this study is that the authors were unable to differentiate effects for mothers who made transitions owing to welfare reform, as is possible in experimental evaluations of welfare-to-work programs.

Researchers who consider the link between mothers' job characteristics and their children's development have hypothesized that features of the work environment lead mothers (and also fathers) to emphasize certain behavior in their children (see overview of this research in Menaghan & Parcel, 1995). Mothers in jobs higher in occupational complexity tend to encourage greater independence and self-regulation in their children (paralleling the greater autonomy in decision making in their own job). This may complement the developmental tasks of middle childhood and adolescence so long as offspring are not pushed prematurely toward autonomous roles or required to assume too much responsibility. Thus, employment in jobs with higher complexity may also provide a match with developmental needs in later childhood.

Recent research supports the notion that the occupational complexity of parental work is important in middle childhood (Cooksey, Menaghan, & Jekielek, 1997) and into adolescence (Menaghan, Kowaleski-Jones, & Mott, 1997). Higher job complexity for mothers was associated with fewer behavior problems of early adolescents in single-mother families, controlling for earlier levels of these same behaviors. Further, in families with 10- to 14-year-olds, Menaghan and colleagues (Menaghan, Kowaleski-Jones, & Mott, 1997) found that maternal occupational complexity has modest positive associations with active structuring, cognitive stimulation, and warmth. These results are in line with the hypothesis that the benefits of maternal job complexity may operate, in part, by encouraging appropriate levels of autonomy through active structuring of time and activities.

Evidence supporting the contrasting hypothesis—that maternal employment can accelerate progress toward autonomy sometimes too quickly, with potential negative effects—has been found in welfare-to-work evaluations. Across several different evaluations, even those that increased overall family income and benefited younger children, effects on adolescents (when reported) have been largely unfavorable. A meta-analysis by Gennetian and colleagues (2004) indicated that the overall pattern involves small but significantly negative effects on school outcomes for adolescents. In addition, individual studies, such as the Canadian Self-Sufficiency Project (Morris & Michalopoulos, 2000), reported unfavorable program effects on adolescents' behavioral outcomes, including risk-taking behavior.

Brooks and colleagues (2001) noted that three quite different possibilities for negative outcomes are all reasonable to consider, although direct evidence is limited. A first hypothesis is that adolescents in these low-income families are being called on to help the family function and are being overburdened with responsibilities. In the Florida's Family Transition Program (Bloom et al., 2000), one of the welfare-to-work programs evaluated, mothers in the program group more often reported that they relied on their older children to care for younger children. Further, adolescents in the Canadian Self-Sufficiency Project were more likely to be working 20 or more hours a week and performed household chores more frequently (Morris & Michalopoulos, 2000).

A second hypothesis suggested by Brooks and colleagues (2001) is that parental monitoring is being impeded (rather than enhanced, as found in studies of higher complexity jobs) when mothers work. No findings are available on mothers' monitoring of the adolescents in the welfare-to-work evaluations, and the findings that are available on monitoring of younger children are mixed. Results suggest less monitoring of younger children in the Family Transition Program (Bloom et al., 2000), but the opposite pattern was found in the Minnesota Family Investment Program (Gennetian & Miller, 2000).

Finally, Brooks and colleagues (2001) suggested that the unfavorable effects for adolescents may be related to greater friction in the parent–adolescent relationship. This might occur, for example, if the adolescents are "wrestling" with their mothers on the extent of autonomy and decision making, particularly when the mother is away. In the Canadian Self-Sufficiency Project, mothers in the program group reported increased harsh parenting. The ethnographic work by Jarrett underscores the potential for parent–adolescent conflict around participation in the "street developmental pathway."

Secondary analyses of the National Longitudinal Survey of Youth (1997 cohort) also inform the latter two possibilities. Among families with 12- to 14-year-olds, all with incomes below 200% of the federal poverty level, maternal employment was related to lower maternal monitoring and lower perceived quality of the relationship with the mother, but only among families with prior (not current or recent) welfare receipt (Brooks et al., 2003). The researchers noted that access to resources and information through caseworkers may help explain why findings differ for current and recent welfare recipients. For example, caseworkers may help guide mothers to jobs that match better with their adolescents' schedules or may provide the mothers with information about appropriate afterschool activities for adolescents or how to combine employment with monitoring.

These results suggest that maternal employment can enhance the gatekeeping function of parenting during middle childhood by providing information or work-related benefits that result in the use of structured afterschool care or activities. In addition, indications emerge that maternal employment can facilitate the transition to appropriate autonomy within the context of greater structuring (as in the findings regarding greater occupational complexity) or, to the contrary, possibly overburden an adolescent with too much autonomy and responsibility. Thus, balancing match and mismatch hypotheses exist regarding maternal employment and key tasks of parenting prior to and during adolescence.

Recent research complements these hypotheses with a growing understanding of how specific characteristics of the out-of-home care and activities for teens of working mothers may affect their development. The research on the characteristics and quality of child care and activities for younger children is far more extensive than that for school-age children and adolescents. However, recent work is beginning to yield important, and sometimes unexpected, insights into the contexts tied to developmental outcomes. This work is an important complement to the hypotheses regarding parenting and maternal employment at older ages.

The recent report of the Committee on Family and Work Policies found that the quality of afterschool programs is associated with middle childhood development. For example, Pierce, Hamm, and Vandell (1999) found that boys participating in programs with a positive emotional climate were reported by their first-grade teachers to have fewer problem behaviors than boys in programs with a less positive climate. Although having a greater variety of available activities was not associated with more favorable outcomes, allowing children flexibility in choosing among the available activities was linked with teacher perception of greater social skills in boys. This finding is in keeping with the developmental research that suggests the need for a growing role in decision making.

Some school-age children are not in supervised settings, but are home alone caring for themselves, and this proportion grows with age. Vandivere and colleagues (2003) reported that in 1999, 7% of U.S. children between ages 6 and 9 and 26% of those between ages 10 and 12 stayed on their own or alone with a sibling age 12 or younger on a regular basis during the last month, even for a small amount of time. Research is beginning to examine the implications of self-care more closely according to the specific context (Smolensky & Gootman, 2003). For example, two recent studies suggest that self-care may be particularly problematic for child outcomes when it involves unsupervised time with peers (McHale, Crouter, & Tucker, 2001; Pettit, Laird, Bates, & Dodge, 1997). Pettit and colleagues also found more negative implications of self-care when parental monitoring (e.g., calls to check on the child) was low and the family lived in a dangerous neighborhood. These findings again underscore the importance of proper levels of autonomy (something that may vary with the characteristics of the broader social environment).

While their mothers are employed, adolescents may participate in activities that are not labeled child care or afterschool care. Recent work is beginning to identify the features of youth activities that can support or undermine adolescent development. Mahoney and Stattin (2000) noted that "youth leisure pursuits can range from having virtually no structure to being highly complex, solitary/non-cooperative pursuits to collaborative group engagement, and societal condemnation to public and financial support by the community" (p. 114).

A study of eighth graders in Sweden found no difference in rates of antisocial behavior by participation in activities, but rather by the nature of the activities. Participation in structured activities (activities that were regularly scheduled, guided by rules, supervised by one or more adult, and emphasized skill building) was associated with less antisocial behavior, especially among boys. Participation in youth recreation centers that provide a place to hang out and are low in structure, skill-building activities, and supervision was found, over time, to be associated with increased risk of antisocial behavior (Mahoney, Stattin, & Magnusson, 2001).

In summary, the findings for children in middle childhood and adolescence point to a need to consider maternal employment in relation to children's experiences, both with parents and beyond the home. For these older children, how much autonomy and responsibility are granted and how parents handle monitoring seem particularly salient. There is a potential for work-developmental match when maternal employment results in older children and adolescents participating in structured afterschool activities that provide opportunities for choice or when autonomy is granted within a context of overall structuring and monitoring. An emerging hypothesis suggests that there is a mismatch when maternal employment results in too much autonomy or responsibility, and when older children and youth regularly spend time in unstructured activities or are unsupervised (especially when with peers).

CONCLUSION

We have argued that maternal employment can provide a match or mismatch with key developmental tasks of childhood. Both home and child-care environments are important to consider, and both can either hinder or foster progress toward key developmental goals. We have offered examples of how maternal employment may provide a mismatch by inhibiting reciprocal mother–child responsiveness in infancy, and how maternal employment can help or hinder the careful calibration of autonomy and responsibility in middle childhood and adolescence.

We contend that viewing the findings on maternal employment through a developmental lens can help clarify them. Yet we sound some caution. First, because we are seeking to explain findings (reports of statistical effects of maternal employment on child outcomes), we focus on instances of favorable or unfavorable implications of maternal employment. However, in this research as a whole, many studies show weak or no associations of child outcomes with maternal employment. Further, we have emphasized that many of the findings only pertain to subgroups. Interestingly, the patterns we have highlighted often involve low-income families, a subgroup for whom it may be harder to muster resources to adapt flexibly to employment and, at the same time, for whom additional resources derived from employment may be particularly important to the child.

Gaps in our knowledge are also quite apparent from this review. For example, our understanding of the characteristics of child care that foster positive outcomes is greater for younger than for older children. We are at the earliest stages of research on the characteristics of school-age child care and of activities for adolescents that do (and do not) support development. Yet recent findings suggest that just as the specific characteristics of child care for infants and preschool-age children are related to their developmental outcomes, it is important to focus on the specific features of care and activities for older children. Future work linking care and activities to the outcomes of maternal employment for children of older ages is clearly needed. Further, it is only in the infancy and early childhood periods that research has considered the joint role of parenting and child care in mediating the effects of maternal employment on children. It would be extremely productive to incorporate such an approach in research on out-of-school care and activities for older children and adolescents.

We must better understand how far we can generalize the findings for children of different ages in welfare-to-work programs to broader populations. Are these findings specific to those making a move into employment from welfare that is accelerated by program incentives or requirements? In this chapter, we have grouped together middle childhood and adolescence as periods across which the regulation of increasing child autonomy is a central task for parents and children to negotiate. Yet there are many ways in which these developmental periods differ. If developmental match–mismatch theory is to progress beyond the rough outlines provided here, further developmental differentiations should be made. Finally, across developmental periods, we need a much greater understanding of why findings pertain to particular groups but not others. Such features as unpredictable daily schedules among low-income families have not yet been studied in relation to child outcomes. It may be that more finely specifying and examining the characteristics of low-wage employment will provide a base for understanding subgroup findings, and especially why some of the patterns discussed here pertain particularly to low-income families.

ACKNOWLEDGMENTS

The authors gratefully acknowledge funding from NICHD (#R01 HD38762-02) for the preparation of this chapter. The authors thank Sharon McGroder and Kristin Moore for their helpful feedback on drafts of this chapter.

REFERENCES

Ainsworth, M. D. S., Blehar, M. C., Waters, E., & Wall, S. (1978). *Patterns of attachment*. Hillsdale, NJ: Lawrence Erlbaum Associates.
Belsky, J. (1999). Quantity of nonmaternal care and boys' problem behavior/adjustment at ages 3 and 5: Exploring the mediating role of parenting. *Psychiatry, 62*, 1–20.

Bianchi, S. M. (2000). Maternal employment and time with children: Dramatic change or surprising continuity? *Demography, 37,* 401–414.

Bloom, D., Kemple, J. J., Morris, P. A., Scrivener, S., Verma, N., & Hendra, R. (2000). *The Family Transition Program: Final report on Florida's initial time-limited welfare program.* New York: Manpower Demonstration Research Corporation.

Bos, J. M., Huston, A.C., Granger, R., Duncan, G. J., Brock, T. W., & McLoyd, V. C. (1999). *New Hope for people with low incomes: Two-year results of a program to reduce poverty and reform welfare.* New York: Manpower Demonstration Research Corporation.

Bowlby, J. (1969). *Attachment and loss.* New York: Basic Books.

Bronfenbrenner, U., & Crouter, A. C. (1982). Work and family through time and space. In S. B. Kamerman & C. D. Hayes (Eds.), *Families that work: Children in a changing world* (pp. 29–83). Washington, DC: National Academy Press.

Brooks, J. L., Hair, E. C., & Zaslow, M. J. (2001). *Welfare reform's impacts on adolescents: Early warning signs* (Child Trends Research Brief). Washington, DC: Child Trends.

Brooks, J. L., Kinukawa, A., McGarvey, A., McGroder, S., Zaslow, M., & Hair, E. (2003). *The relationship between maternal employment and adolescent well-being among families with different histories of welfare receipt.* Manuscript submitted for publication.

Brooks-Gunn, J., Han, W., & Waldfogel, J. (2002). Maternal employment and child cognitive outcomes in the first three years of life: The NICHD study of early child care. *Child Development, 67,* 396–408.

Chase-Lansdale, P. L, Moffitt, R. A., Lohman, B. J., Cherlin, A. J., Coley, R. L., Pittman, L. D., et al. (2003). Mothers' transitions from welfare to work and the well-being of preschoolers and adolescents. *Science, 299,* 1548–1553.

Chase-Lansdale, P. L., & Pittman, L. D. (2002). Welfare reform and parenting: Reasonable expectations. *Future of Children: Children and Welfare Reform, 12,* 167–183.

Collins, W. A., Harris, M. L., & Susman, A. (1995). Parenting during middle childhood. In M. Bornstein (Ed.), *Handbook of parenting: Vol. VI. Children and parenting* (pp. 65–89). Mahwah, NJ: Lawrence Erlbaum Associates.

Cooksey, E. C., Menaghan, E. G., & Jekielek, S. M. (1997). Life course effect of work and family circumstances on children. *Social Forces, 76,* 637–667.

Desai, S., Chase-Lansdale, P. L., & Michael, R. T. (1989). Mother or market? Effects of maternal employment on the intellectual ability of 4 year old children. *Demography, 26,* 545–561.

Dishion, T. J., & McMahon, R. J. (1998). Parental monitoring and the prevention of child and adolescent problem behavior: A conceptual and empirical foundation. *Family Psychology Review, 1,* 61–75.

Eccles, J. S., Midgley, C., Wigfield, A., Buchanan, C. M., Reuman, D., Flanagan, C., et al. (1993). Development during adolescence: The impact of stage-environment fit on adolescents' experiences in schools and families. *American Psychologist, 48,* 90–101.

Gennetian, L. A., Duncan, G. J., Knox, V., Vargas, W., Clark-Kauffman, E., & London, A. S. (2004). How welfare policies affect adolescents' school outcomes: A synthesis from experimental studies. *Journal of Research on Adolescence, 14,* 399–423.

Gennetian, L. A., & Miller, C. (2000). *Reforming welfare and rewarding work: Final report on the Minnesota Family Investment Program: Volume 2. Effects on children.* New York: MDRC.

Greenstein, T. (1995). Are the most advantaged children truly disadvantaged by maternal employment? Effects on child cognitive outcomes. *Journal of Family Issues, 16,* 149–169.

Han, W., Waldfogel, J., & Brooks-Gunn, J. (2001). The effects of early maternal employment on later cognitive and behavioral outcomes. *Journal of Marriage and Family, 63,* 336–354.

Harrison, L. J., & Ungerer, J. A. (2002). Maternal employment and infant-mother attachment security at 12 months postpartum. *Developmental Psychology, 38,* 758–773.

Hartup, W. N. (1992). Peer relations in early and middle childhood. In V. B. Van Hasselt (Ed.), *Handbook of social development: A lifespan perspective* (pp. 257–281). New York: Plenum.

Hoffman, L., Youngblade, L. M., Coley, R. L., Fuligni, A. S., & Kovacs, D. D. (1999). *Mothers at work: Effects on children's well being.* New York: Cambridge University Press.

Huston, A. C., Duncan, G. J., Granger, R., Bos, J., McLoyd, V., Mistry, R., et al. (2001). Work-based antipoverty programs for parents can enhance the school performance and social behavior of children. *Child Development, 72,* 318–336.

Jarrett, R.L. (1998). African American children, families and neighborhoods: Qualitative contributions to understanding developmental pathways. *Applied Developmental Science, 2,* 2–16.

Jekielek, S., & McGroder, S. M. (2003). *Welfare to working: Does the quality and timing of mother's employment matter?* Paper presented at the From 9-to-5 to 24/7: How Workplace Changes Impacts Families, Work and Communities, Orlando, FL.

Mac Iver, D., & Reuman, D. A. (1988, April). *Decision-making in the classroom and early adolescents' valuing of mathematics.* Paper presented at the annual meeting of the American Educational Research Association, New Orleans, LA.

Maccoby, E. F. (1984). Middle childhood in the context of the family. In W. A. Collins (Ed.), *Development during middle childhood* (pp. 184–239). Washington, DC: National Academy Press.

Mahoney, J. L., & Stattin, H. (2000). Leisure activities and adolescent antisocial behavior: The role of structure and social context. *Journal of Adolescence, 23,* 113–127.

Mahoney, J. L., Stattin, H., & Magnusson, D. (2001). Youth recreation center participation and criminal offending: A 20-year longitudinal study of Swedish boys. *International Journal of Behavioral Development, 25,* 509–520.

Masten, A. S., & Coatsworth, J. D. (1998). The development of competence in favorable and unfavorable environments. *American Psychologist, 53,* 205–220.

McGroder, S. M., Zaslow, M. J., Papillo, A. R., Ahluwalia, S. K., & Brooks, J. (in press). The estimated effect of maternal employment under mandatory and non-mandatory employment circumstances. *Community, Work and Family.*

McHale, S. M., Crouter, A. C., & Tucker, C. J. (2001). Free-time activities in middle childhood: Links with adjustment in early adolescence. *Child Development, 72,* 1764–1778.

Menaghan, E. G., Kowaleski-Jones, L., & Mott, F. L. (1997). The intergenerational costs of parental social stressors: Academic and social difficulties in early adolescence for children of young mothers. *Journal of Health and Social Behavior, 38,* 72–86.

Menaghan, E. G., & Parcel, T. L. (1991). Determining children's home environments: The impact of maternal characteristics and current occupational and family conditions. *Journal of Marriage and the Family, 53,* 417–431.

Menaghan, E. G., & Parcel, T. L. (1995). Social sources of change in children's home environments: The effects of parental occupational experiences and family conditions. *Journal of Marriage and Family, 57,* 69–84.

Morris, P. A., & Michalopoulos, C. (2000). *The Self-Sufficiency Project at 36 months: Effects on children of a program that increased parental employment and income.* Ottawa, Ontario: Social Research and Demonstration Corporation.

NICHD Early Child Care Research Network. (1999). Child care and mother-child interaction in the first 3 years of life. *Developmental Psychology, 35,* 1399–1413.

NICHD Early Child Care Research Network. (2002). Early child care and children's development prior to school entry: Results from the NICHD Study of Early Child Care. *American Educational Research Journal, 39,* 133–164.

Parcel, T. L., & Menaghan, E. G. (1994a). *Parents' jobs and children's lives.* New York: Aldine De Gruyter.

Parcel, T. L., & Menaghan, E. G. (1994b). Early parental work, family social capital, and early childhood outcomes. *American Journal of Sociology, 99,* 972–1009.

Pettit, G. S., Laird, R. D., Bates, J. E., & Dodge, K. A. (1997). Patterns of after-school care in middle childhood: Risk factors and developmental outcomes. *Merrill-Palmer Quarterly, 43,* 535–538.

Pierce, K. M., Hamm, J. V., & Vandell, D. L. (1999). Experiences in after-school programs and children's adjustment in first-grade classrooms. *Child Development, 70,* 756–767.

Presser, H. B., & Cox, A. G. (1997). The work schedules of low-educated American women and welfare reform. *Monthly Labor Review, 120,* 25–34.

Smolensky, E., & Gootman, J. (Eds.). (2003). *Working families and growing kids: Caring for children and adolescents.* National Research Council and Institute of Medicine, Committee on Family and Work Policies. Washington, DC: The National Academies Press.

Tout, K., Papillo, A. R., Zaslow, M. J., & Vandivere, S. R. (2001). *Early care and education: Work support for families and developmental opportunity for young children.* (Assessing the New Federalism Occasional Paper No. 51). Washington, DC: Urban Institute.

Vandivere, S. R., Tout, K., Capizzano, J., & Zaslow, M. J. (2003). *Left unsupervised: A look at the most vulnerable children* (Child Trends Research Brief). Washington, DC: Child Trends.

Waldfogel, J., Han, W., & Brooks-Gunn, J. (2002). The effects of early maternal employment on child cognitive development. *Demography, 39,* 369–392.

Youngblade, L. M. (2003). Peer and teacher ratings of third- and fourth-grade children's social behavior as a function of early maternal employment. *Journal of Child Psychology & Psychiatry & Allied Disciplines, 44,* 477–488.

Zaslow, M. J., Moore, K. A., Brooks, J. L., Morris, P. A., Tout, K., Redd, Z. A., & Emig, C. A. (2002). Experimental studies of welfare reform and children. *Future of Children: Children and Welfare Reform, 12,* 79–98.

Zaslow, M., Rabinovich, B., & Suwalsky, J. (1991). From maternal employment to child outcomes: Preexisting group differences and moderating variables. In J. V. Lerner & N. L. Galambos (Eds.), *Employed mothers and their children* (pp. 237–282). New York, London: Garland.

19

When Do We Know What
We Think We Know?
Determining Causality

Janet Currie
University of California, Los Angeles

Social scientists are often asked to determine whether one thing causes another. The answer to this question of causality may have important implications for public policy. However, it is generally difficult to establish that "A causes B" beyond a shadow of a doubt, and researchers often arrive at conflicting conclusions depending on their data sources and methods. This conundrum is, of course, not confined to the social sciences. Researchers in the hard sciences often come to conflicting conclusions regarding questions such as what killed the dinosaurs, the existence of global warming, and the safety and effectiveness of hormone replacement therapy for older women.

This chapter considers some of the methods that social scientists who study work and family use to get at the question of causality. It provides a general overview of some of the issues and problems, and it discusses these issues in the context of two specific examples: (a) the effect of maternal employment on child well-being, and (b) the effect of child-care quality on children's outcomes. In both cases, studies have arrived at different conclusions. In the first case, a range of studies using different data sets and techniques provides the basis for an emerging consensus, whereas in the second case, the issue of selection has not yet been satisfactorily addressed.

I conclude with the reminder that replication is at the heart of science, and findings must be reproducible before they can provide a reliable basis for policy. Moreover, given the ubiquity of the sample selection problem in social science, the issue must be addressed preferably using a number of techniques.

THE PROBLEM OF SELECTION AND POTENTIAL RESPONSES

In social science, questions about causality are clouded by the problem of sample selection. For example, mothers who work tend to be healthier and better educated, on average, than those who do not. Hence, it would not be surprising to find that their children did better than those of nonworking mothers, on average, even if there were no causal relation at all between maternal employment and child outcomes. Similarly, children from more advantaged backgrounds are likely to be in better child care, making it difficult to distinguish between the effects of child-care quality and the effects of family background.

Using Experimental Methods to Address Selection

In principle, the problem of sample selection can be solved using experimental methods. For example, if it were possible to randomly assign women to the *working* and *nonworking* groups, we could compare the outcomes of the children of the two groups to determine the causal effect of maternal employment. So long as the sample size is large enough, there will be no difference in the other observed or unobserved characteristics of the women, on average, because the assignment to the two groups is randomly determined. This approach suggests that it is possible to check that the random assignment worked by comparing mean values of the observable characteristics of the two groups. If there are no statistically significant differences between the means, we can assume that the unobservables are also similar across the two groups.

However, the sheer ridiculousness of this example highlights one of the main problems with relying on experiments in social science. Women are not plots of land to be randomly assigned different fertilizer treatments. Experiments with human subjects often run into several difficulties. First, individuals who are dissatisfied with their group assignment may take measures to change groups. For example, Heckman, Hohmann, and Smith (2000) discussed experimental evaluations of job training programs in which individuals assigned to the *no training* control groups often enrolled in training programs at their own expense. Individuals in the control group may also be more likely than those in the treatment group to leave the study. Such varying attrition threatens the validity of the experiment by making it less likely that the mean characteristics of the controls will be equal to the mean characteristics of the treatment group.

Conversely, not everyone assigned to the treatment group may show up for treatment. It is important to keep in mind that what is randomly assigned is one's initial allocation to either the treatment or control group (this is sometimes called the *intent to treat*), not necessarily their participation. Hence, considering outcomes only among those who were assigned to the treatment group and who showed up for training would partially nullify the benefit of the random assignment, given that individuals who choose to take the training course are a self-selected subsample of the treatment group, and this subsample likely does not have the same average characteristics as the controls.[1]

Experiments in social science are not a panacea to all methodological issues. In addition to problems in implementing random assignment and attrition, social experiments are sometimes objectionable on ethical grounds. For example, it may be objectionable to some that a potentially beneficial treatment would be withheld from controls. However, if we knew for certain that the treatment was indeed beneficial, there would be no need to conduct an experiment. Also treatments are often rationed regardless, owing to insufficient funding. Where funding is limited, random assignment can replace administrator discretion in deciding who gets access to the treatment without violating any ethical principle.

Heckman and Smith (1995) raised two additional objections to experiments. First, such methods are often costly, especially relative to analysis of existing data sets. Second, it may be difficult to generalize the results from an experiment to the wider population. Experimental evaluations of Head Start, for example, tend to show that the initial effects on children's cognitive test scores fade over time. Based on those evaluations, which focused on inner-city, African-American children, critics of Head Start concluded that the program had no long-term effect on children. However, other studies (Currie & Thomas, 1995; Currie & Thomas, 1999; Garces, Thomas, & Currie, 2002) of national populations of Head Start children show that effects tend to be more long-lived among Hispanic and non-Hispanic White children.

Addressing Selection by Controlling for Confounding Variables

One potential response to the selection problem in nonexperimental data is to control for the confounding variables directly. For example, if a spurious

---

[1] One way to avert this problem is to use the random assignment as an instrumental variable for whether the person was treated. See Katz, Kling, and Leibman (2001) for an example of this approach in the context of a public housing mobility experiment.

correlation between maternal employment and child outcomes were driven by maternal health and education, imposing adequate controls for these two variables would eliminate the selection problem. Of course it is always possible that there are other, unobserved confounders, and researchers have investigated this possibility by progressively adding variables to regression models. That, too, poses complications. If the parameter of interest does not vary when controls are progressively added, and if unobservable variables are likely to be correlated with the observables, it may be that adding further controls would also have little effect.

A second approach to sample selection is to use fixed effects to control for permanent, unobservable characteristics that may be associated with both selection into the sample and outcomes. For example, suppose that women with a certain personality type (e.g., very nurturing) are both less likely to work and more likely to have children with positive outcomes. Researchers can regard the personality as a fixed characteristic that is unobserved, but correlated with both the probability of employment and child outcomes. Estimates that do not take account of differences in personality type across the population will produce biased estimates of the effects of employment; it will appear that employment causes poor child outcomes, when in reality it is the less nurturing personalities of the employed women that cause these outcomes.

A possible solution to this dilemma is to compare siblings' outcomes. If a mother works during the childhood of one sibling but not during the childhood of the other, researchers can obtain an alternative estimate of the effect of maternal employment. This estimate will not be affected by personality type (so long as both children respond to personality type in the same way, which is a strong assumption) because both children are exposed to the same type of personality. That is, by differencing the observations on the siblings, one can difference out the effect of the omitted variable. In other contexts, we might wish to include child-specific fixed effects (e.g., to look at changes in children's outcomes with changes in their circumstances) or child-care center fixed effects depending on the type of unobserved variables one is attempting to control.

Fixed effects estimates are subject to several potential problems. First and most obvious, the relevant omitted variable may not be fixed over time. In the prior example, a mother might become more nurturing between children or might be more nurturing with one child (a girl) than with the other (a boy). Second, the fixed effects strategy often significantly reduces the effective sample size. In the previous example, the effect of employment is identified only for women who change employment status between children. Mothers who are either always employed or always unemployed are not counted when identifying the effects of employment. Third, the mothers who change status may not be representative of the initial population of mothers. Ideally, we would like to know why some mothers changed employment status between the births. Suppose, for example, that a major economic downturn led many women to lose their jobs. One might expect this crisis to have its own negative effect on child outcomes. Alternatively, a woman who worked while one child was an infant might not work during the infancy of a child with health or developmental problems (Powers, 2001). In this case, there would be a spurious positive correlation between maternal employment and child outcomes in the fixed effects models.

A fourth problem with using fixed effects is that, in the presence of random measurement error, fixed effects estimates are generally biased toward zero. Intuitively, we can divide a measured variable such as a test score into a true signal and a random noise component. The true signal may be persistent between siblings (e.g., if both children have high IQ), whereas the noise component may be more random (e.g., one child has a bad day on the day of the test). As a result, when examining the difference between siblings, researchers can ultimately difference out much of the true signal (given that the true signal is similar for both siblings) and be left only with the noise.

Although it is important to keep these potential problems in mind, fixed effects do offer a powerful way to control for constant, unobserved background characteristics. The Head Start studies discussed before typically find that, in ordinary least squares (OLS) models, child outcomes are not influenced by Head Start participation, and in fact these children often do worse than other children on average. However, Head Start children come from very poor backgrounds relative to all children. When this background is controlled by including household fixed effects, positive effects of Head Start become apparent. In other words, Head Start children do systematically better than siblings who did not attend Head Start, although they do worse than other children on average.

Addressing Selection Using Instrumental Variables

A third way to deal with selection is to use an instrumental variable. An instrument is something that is correlated with the endogenous variable of interest, but that is not correlated with the omitted variables, and therefore is not correlated with the outcome variable (except through its effects on the endogenous variable). In a model in which child outcomes depend on maternal employment, maternal employment is the endogenous variable. It is chosen by the mother and may be affected by other unmeasured variables, which are in turn also related to child outcomes. To implement instrumental variables, one can estimate a two-stage least squares model, in which the endogenous variable is first regressed on the instrument (and all the other exogenous variables in the model). In the second stage, the model of interest is estimated, including the predicted value of the endogenous variable derived from the first stage and adjusting the standard errors appropriately (standard statistical packages do this automatically). Given that the instrument is uncorrelated with the omitted variables, the predicted value of the endogenous variable will also be uncorrelated with them so that the estimation is purged of the bias that results from these omitted variables.

In the prior maternal employment example, the instrument should be something that predicts maternal employment, but that is uncorrelated with the other omitted variables and has no independent effect on outcomes (once its effect through maternal employment is taken into account). To continue with the example, an economic downturn might influence maternal employment, but it probably would not be a valid instrument because it can also affect child outcomes through other pathways, such as reductions in father's employment and reductions in school spending and other social services.

It is generally difficult to find valid instruments, although several studies in recent years have used changes in laws as instruments for measuring involvement in various social programs (these studies are often referred to as *natural experiments*). Moreover, it is impossible to test the validity of one's assumptions about the instruments, although it is possible to determine whether different instrumental variables yield consistent results (this is the essence of an overidentification test). An additional instrument problem is that, even when valid (in the sense that they are uncorrelated with other omitted variables), instruments may be "weak," in that they explain little of the variation in the endogenous variable. Weak instruments often lead to large standard errors in the second-stage regression and may also lead to biased and misleadingly precise estimates (see Bound, Jaeger, & Baker, 1995; Staiger & Stock, 1997, for further discussion of the problem of weak instruments and some diagnostic tests).

Instrumental variables estimation is closely related to Heckman's (1979) selection-correction method. In this procedure, researchers first estimate a probit model predicting the probability that an individual is selected into the sample. This model is used to construct a control for the probability of selection (the inverse Mill's ratio). This term is then included in the model of interest to correct for selection bias. In principle, there should be variables (akin to instruments) that predict the probability of being selected into the sample, but do not have any independent effect on outcomes. However, because the selection correction term is a nonlinear function of the data, it is possible in practice to estimate Heckman's selection-correction models without these exclusion restrictions. Such a model is estimable only because the selection-correction term is assumed to be a nonlinear function of the data, whereas the main equation of interest is assumed to be linear (or to have nonlinearities of some other known form). Because these functional form assumptions seldom have any basis in theory, they form a tenuous basis for identification. Many standard econometrics textbooks now recommend that the Heckman correction method be used only if there are credible exclusion restrictions (Johnston & DiNardo, 1997), in which case one could also use instrumental variables.

Addressing Selection Using Propensity Scores

More recently, social scientists are turning to propensity scores as a way to address selection bias, following Rosenbaum and Rubin (1983). Propensity scoring posits that treatments and controls should be matched. That is, the preferred comparison is between child outcomes of employed and nonemployed mothers who have the same characteristics. As in the Heckman method, the first step is to estimate a probit model of the probability of selection into the treatment (in this example, employment). A predicted propensity of being in the treatment group is then assigned to each person in the data set. Generally, no variables are excluded from the main model and included in the selection equation, unlike in the Heckman selection procedure.

There are several ways to use these scores to construct the match between treatments and controls. By far the most common is to divide people into a number of *bins* (often starting with five) based on propensity scores. Within each bin, the average observable characteristics of those who participate and do not participate in the treatment should be equal (just as they are in an experiment with random assignment). It is then possible to obtain the effect of the treatment on the treated by finding the weighted sum of the differences between the treatments and the controls in each bin.

If the average characteristics are not equal within bins, it is necessary to develop a more refined model of the propensity to be in the treatment group. Also it is often helpful to exclude treatments and controls who do not overlap at all in terms of their observable characteristics. For instance, if all women with doctorate degrees worked and all women with less than an eighth-grade education did not work, one might wish to exclude these two categories from the analysis given that these women are sufficiently different and comparing them would shed no light on the effect of maternal employment per se.

The propensity score approach does not rely on distributional assumptions (in contrast to the Heckman correction) or exclusion restrictions (in contrast to instrumental variables analysis). As in the fixed effects method, a limitation of propensity scoring is the requirement that there be both treatments and controls within a bin for the observations in the bin to reveal anything about the effect of interest. If, for example, the top and bottom quintile of the propensity score distribution held only nonemployed and employed women, respectively, the effect would be to ignore 40% of the observations in the propensity score analysis. However, if these women have little in common, comparing the outcomes of their children is likely not a meaningful way to assess the effects of maternal employment. The propensity score method does make it clear what part of the data is providing the comparison.

The main limitation of the propensity score method is that it fails to truly address the question of selection on unobservable variables. Treatment and controls are ultimately balanced within bins on the basis of observables, but this does not rule out the possibility that they are systematically different in terms of unobserved characteristics. This brief overview suggests that all the methods for dealing with selection bias have pros and cons. In the next two sections, I consider what can be learned from a comparison of studies using different methods in the context of two specific examples.

ASSESSING THE ASSESSMENTS: MATERNAL EMPLOYMENT AND CHILD OUTCOMES

Concern about the effects of maternal employment on child well-being has been spurred by dramatic changes in the labor force participation rates of mothers with young children. Studies have caused concern that children will suffer harmful effects from being separated from a primary caregiver (usually the mother) at too early an age (Ainsworth, Blehar, Waters, & Wall, 1978; Bowlby, 1969). In addition to potentially reducing the time a mother spends with her child, maternal employment might reduce the quality of interaction by increasing a mother's stress levels. However, mothers presumably work to earn income, and there are many studies that point to a positive association between income and child well-being. The effects of nonmaternal care are also likely to be mediated by the quality of that care. For example, Bianchi (2000) suggested that the time mothers spend in employment may be offset by increasing the time fathers spend with their children. Given these varied theories and studies, it is not surprising that numerous studies have found evidence of positive, zero, and negative effects of maternal employment on young children.

This section attempts to classify studies by methodology, both to highlight the ways in which the conclusions vary and to detect whether a consensus is emerging. This survey is not intended to be comprehensive. More comprehensive recent surveys on the effects of maternal employment are Hoffman and Youngblade (1999) and Zaslow and Emig (1997). This survey also limits itself to the effects of maternal employment on young children (for a discussion of effects on adolescents, see Zaslow et al., chap. 18, this volume).

There are several recent welfare-to-work experimental studies on the effects of maternal employment among welfare recipients. Surveys of these experiments in Grogger, Karoly, and Klerman (2002); Morris, Know, and

Gennetian (2002); and Zaslow et al. (2002) conclude that increasing household income is associated with small, positive effects on cognitive and behavioral outcomes of young children, but reducing maternal time with children without increasing household income is sometimes associated with negative effects. These welfare-to-work experiments are well executed, with careful attention to randomization and minimizing attrition. Thus, they provide compelling evidence for the subset of the population they examine.

However, the effects of maternal employment might be substantially different in this population of welfare recipients than in the population at large. Higher maternal employment income may have larger, positive effects in poor households, but the loss of maternal time may also be more important in single-parent households. Thus, these studies illustrate the general point that experiments can yield credible evidence regarding specific questions and subpopulations, but it may be difficult to generalize their results to larger populations.

Many studies attempt, with mixed results, to control for observable variables that may be correlated both with maternal employment and outcomes using nonexperimental, observational data. In one of the earliest studies of this issue, Leibowitz (1977) used data from 1969 and found no effect of maternal employment on Peabody Picture Vocabulary Test (PPVT) scores. More recently, many studies examine data from the children in the National Longitudinal Survey of Youth (NLSY).[2] To use two relatively recent examples, Greenstein (1995) found no significant effect on PPVT scores, while Harvey (1999) found initially negative effects on PPVT and Peabody Individual Achievement Tests in Mathematics and Reading (PIAT) scores, which dissipate with age. Two studies of more disadvantaged children (welfare mothers and low-income children, respectively) also found evidence of positive effects on test scores (Moore & Driscoll, 1997; Vandell & Ramanan, 1992), which is consistent with the experimental evidence cited earlier for poor women. Han, Waldfogel, and Brooks-Gunn (2001) examined 7- and 8-year-old children and found that the negative effects of maternal employment in the first year persisted for White children, but not for African-American children.

In a thorough exploration addressing selection by controlling for a wide range of observables, Ruhm (2000) showed how estimates of the effects of maternal employment change when adding covariates to the ordinary least squares regression model. As he showed, the correlation between test scores and maternal employment is initially positive. Including controls for a standard set of covariates, such as mother's age, education, and race, generally

---

[2] The NLSY79 began with a sample of 12,652 individuals ages 14 to 21 in 1979. They have been surveyed regularly since then. Beginning in 1986, the children of female sample members have been given a battery of developmental assessments every other year. In addition, mothers are asked a series of questions about the home environment and home inputs to child development as well as about child care.

reduces this correlation to zero, although there is still a positive effect of maternal employment on PPVT scores in the second and third years of a child's life. Adding more variables to the model causes the effects to become negative (although not generally statistically significant). Adding measures of the mother's previous and subsequent employment probabilities causes some estimated effects to become significantly negative. In further analyses of this last specification, Ruhm found that maternal employment is associated with negative effects only in households where the father is present.

Variables measuring the mother's past and future employment may be one way to capture the unobserved maternal characteristics that are correlated with employment in the child's early years. However, past, present, and future employment are likely to be highly correlated, which complicates the interpretation of each single coefficient. Perhaps the safest conclusion to be drawn from this suite of studies is that, because the results are extremely sensitive to which observable variables are included in the models, the results may be sensitive to omitted, unmeasured variables.

A few recent studies employ a fixed effects strategy to examine the effects of maternal employment, controlling for unobservable variables. Waldfogel, Han, and Brooks-Gunn (2002), based on NLSY data, reported that in OLS models, maternal employment in the first year had a negative effect on some outcomes within different age groups for White children, but not for Hispanic or African-American children. The fixed effects models yielded similar point estimates, but larger standard errors; therefore, the researchers could not reject the hypothesis that the OLS and fixed effects estimates are the same. Yet they also could not reject the hypothesis that there is no effect of maternal employment in the fixed effects models. Similarly, Neidell (2002) found little evidence of an effect of maternal employment in household fixed effects models. As discussed, fixed effects estimates may be biased toward zero if measurement error exists in test scores, and these estimates often rely on relatively small subsets of the data (which helps explain the increase in standard errors when researchers move to a fixed effects design).

Several studies address the endogeneity of maternal employment using instrumental variables methods. For example, James-Burdumy (1999) and Baum (2003) used local labor market conditions as an instrument for whether a woman worked after her child was born. The identifying assumption underlying this specification is that local labor market conditions affect child outcomes only through the mother's probability of employment, and not, for example, through effects on the husband's income. These estimates have fairly large standard errors, with the result that none of the estimated effects is statistically significant.

Baum also employed a crude form of matching by restricting the analysis only to women who worked in the quarter before the birth. His rationale was that women who were working in the quarter before they gave birth are all relatively strongly attached to the labor market and may be more homogeneous than other groups of women. In this subsample, he found some significant negative effects of maternal employment in the first year on child well-being. These effects, however, were offset by increases in family income. Baum surmised that the effect of maternal employment on child PIAT-mathematics scores was neutral in households where the mother's employment added $40,000 to the household income.

Hill, Waldfogel, Brooks-Gunn, and Han (2003), using propensity scores, found small, negative effects of maternal employment in the child's first year on PPVT and PIAT scores. Interestingly, these effects occurred for Whites, African Americans, and Hispanics and were stronger for married women in higher income households. This suggests that it may be more difficult to find an adequate substitute for high-skilled women's time spent caring for their children.

What can we learn from all of this? First, crude estimates of the relation between maternal employment and child outcomes are contaminated by selection bias. Mothers who are employed have characteristics that would cause their children to do well in any case. After controlling for observed and unobserved characteristics in a variety of ways, the findings suggest that maternal employment may negatively affect children in their first year, but the effects are generally negligible thereafter. The findings also suggest that the effects may be more negative for children of mothers who have greater socioeconomic status (SES). For disadvantaged children, there is relatively strong evidence that maternal employment may even be beneficial so long as it raises family income.

These conclusions can be drawn because numerous studies report generally similar findings using different methods and identifying assumptions. A key point is that, given the limitations inherent in each method, we should avoid drawing strong conclusions from a single method and place more weight on conclusions that can be replicated across studies.

ASSESSING THE ASSESSMENTS: CHILD-CARE QUALITY AND CHILD OUTCOMES

The increase in labor force participation of mothers has focused more attention on the quality of child care. The National Institute of Child Health and Human Development (NICHD) Early Child Care Study found that most infants were placed in some sort of nonmaternal care by 4 months of age (NICHD Early Child Care Research Network, 1997). Studies of the effects of the inputs on child-care quality and child development and the effects of quality on child outcomes are reviewed in Smolensky and Gootman (2003),

Shonkoff and Phillips (2000), Love, Achochet, and Meckstroth (1996), and Lamb (1998). As the surveys reveal, many studies use small convenience samples that are not randomly selected, they use few or no measures of family and child characteristics, and few address the issue of selection into child-care arrangements. Some do not use any type of control group. As discussed, if children who have other advantages also get better child care (Meyers, Rosenbaum, Ruhm, & Waldfogel, 2004), those in higher quality care will have better outcomes. However, it is difficult to attribute the better outcomes to the causal effects of child-care quality.

There is at least one experimental evaluation of child-care quality. The National Day Care Study (NDCS; Ruopp, Travers, Glantz, & Coelen, 1979) closely monitored a sample of 1,600 children for 9 months in 64 day-care centers serving low-income children. The children were given baseline developmental assessments and were assessed again at the end of the 9-month period. The study design included two experiments in which children were randomly assigned to classrooms with different staff–child ratios and teachers with different levels of training. They found that preschool children whose teachers had training in early childhood education made greater gains on tests of language receptivity and general knowledge and showed more cooperative behavior than other children. Staff–child ratio was not associated with child development for preschoolers, but was for toddlers (ages 1–2). As discussed previously, one of the main limitations of experiments is generalizability. Although this study suggests that higher quality care benefits low-income children, its effects on other children remain unclear.

The effects of quality care can also be ascertained from early intervention programs for disadvantaged children. Currie (2001) and Currie and Blau (in press) provided surveys of this research. Briefly, evidence from experimental interventions such as the Perry Preschool Project, the Carolina Abcedarian project, and the Infant Health and Development Program, as well as current evaluations of Early Head Start (Head Start from children at birth to 3 years old) all show that quality preschool programs can have positive effects on disadvantaged children, although they do not identify which factors are critical to producing quality.

Several large-scale, observational studies have attempted to examine child-care quality in more representative groups of children. The Cost, Quality, and Child Outcomes Study (CQOS) Team, (1999; Helburn, 1995) collected data from 400 day-care centers in four states in 1993. Controlling for maternal education, child gender, ethnicity, and the teacher's rating of her relationship with the child, Peisner-Feinberg et al. (2001) found a positive association between child-care quality at age 4 and subsequent mental development, math achievement, and behavior in kindergarten and second grade. These are suggestive findings, but the absence of information on the home environment and baseline development assessment leaves considerable uncertainty about whether these findings represent causal effects.

Mocan, Burchinal, Morris, and Helburn (1995) used the CQOS data to estimate a model of classroom quality as a function of child-care inputs. This study included more control variables than do many others. The researchers found positive effects on quality of staff–child ratios, teacher wages, and the fraction of the staff with a college degree, and they found a negative effect on quality of teacher turnover. However, Blau (2000) re-analyzed these data using a center-based fixed effects approach to control for unobserved fixed characteristics of the centers that might affect child outcomes. Within centers, he found that only workshop training for teachers affected quality. Blau (1997) used data from the National Child Care Staffing Study (NCCSS) in a similar analysis of the effects of various factors on classroom quality with similar results. These studies illustrate that the fixed effects method can be used to control for a variety of potentially omitted variables, although for reasons discussed earlier, these estimates may be the lower bounds on the true effects.

The NICHD Study of Early Child Care (SECC; U.S. Department of Health and Human Services, 1998) followed more than 1,300 children from their birth in 1991 to the present, closely monitoring their home and child-care environments and their development. The study used hospital birth records in 10 sites in the United States during 1991 to select a sample of healthy births to English-speaking mothers over age 18 who planned to remain in the site during the next year. Researchers visited families at regular intervals to assess the home environment, and they visited children in their child-care arrangements. Through direct measurement and observation, the researchers measured the quality of the arrangement with a variety of assessment instruments. A novel feature of the study was the inclusion and assessment of all types of nonmaternal child-care arrangements, not just centers and family day-care homes. They also followed children as they changed child-care arrangements.

Several researchers in the NICHD Early Child Care Research Network (ECCRN; 1998, 2000a, 2000b) analyzed the data collected in this study, finding generally positive effects. Most of these studies address selection by controlling for some subset of observable variables in OLS models. The results are more credible than most because of the longitudinal design of the NICHD study, the inclusion of children in all types of child care (in some, but not all, of the studies), and the availability of extensive information on nonchild-care factors. However, the richness of the data has not been fully exploited in most of the studies. For example, baseline measures of outcomes are seldom included, and most studies exclude children who were not in child care at the time of observation. This could lead to biased estimates if such children are different from the included children in unobserved ways.

A recent analysis of the data by NICHD ECCRN and Duncan (2002) makes an effort to overcome some of these problems. This study controls for more home and child characteristics than the other studies, and it also estimates models of changes in test scores. Focusing on changes in test scores is akin to estimating models with child-specific fixed effects because factors that affected the base score are implicitly controlled. The results indicate that a 2 standard deviation (SD) improvement in child-care quality in early childhood is associated with .20 SD increase in cognitive functioning at age 54 months in a standard regression model with extensive controls. It is also associated with a ⅙ to ⅐ of an SD increase in cognitive functioning in a change score model that controls for the level of cognitive functioning at age 2.

Few studies of child-care quality have attempted to further control for the possibility of nonrandom selection on unobservable characteristics. Blau (1999) used data from the NLSY in models that controlled for numerous family and child characteristics. He found mainly small and insignificant effects of structural measures of child-care quality, such as group size, staff–child ratios, and teacher training, both in OLS and family fixed effects analyses. In contrast, he found that measures of the home environment were all significant, and the effects were three to five times larger than those of any of the child-care effects.

I am unaware of studies that use instrumental variables to address the selection problem in child-care quality studies. One possibility for instrumental variables analysis would be to use changes in child-care regulations as instruments for observed changes in child-care inputs. The Florida Child Care Quality Improvement Study (FCCQIS; Howes et al., 1998) does something akin to this by exploiting changes in day-care center regulations that occurred in Florida in 1992. The study interviewed teachers and children in a stratified random sample of 150 day-care centers in four Florida counties before and after the new regulations went into effect. The study found that the regulations appeared to bind (i.e., be enforced), but that there was no significant change in classroom quality. In terms of child outcomes, the only significant finding was that child attachment security increased. Although it is striking that attachment improved coincident with a change in regulation, the absence of any control group makes it difficult to further assess. Ideally, one should compare the changes among children in child-care centers affected by the legislation with changes in similar centers that were not affected by the regulations. It is also possible that changes in regulation affect the pool of children using centers so that the gains in attachment security could reflect compositional, rather than causal, effects.

Hill, Waldfogel, and Brooks-Gunn (2002) used propensity scores to determine whether children who participated in the Infant Health and Development Program (IHDP) might have otherwise used different types of care. In the absence of the IHDP, they could have used maternal care; nonmaternal, home-based care; or center-based care. The authors find that the effects of the intervention were largest for children who would not have used center-based care in the absence of the intervention and smallest for those who would have used center-based care in any case.

This brief overview suggests that the research on the effects of child-care quality is less developed than that on the effects of maternal employment. Although there are many studies, comparatively few pay any attention to the selection issue. Because the quality of child care is a choice that is likely to be correlated with many other characteristics of children and families, it is necessary to conduct studies that account for selection before research and policy can draw strong conclusions about the effects of child-care quality on child development, although the experimental evidence certainly suggests that high-quality care may benefit low-income children.

CONCLUSION

At this point, it is appropriate to return the question posed in the title: "How do we know what we think we know?" The answer is familiar to all scientists: We can be reasonably confident of our results if they can be replicated in a wide range of well-designed studies. In the social sciences, well-designed studies should attempt to deal with the ubiquitous problem of sample selection. Studies that compare results using a number of different methodologies and/or data sets are also more informative.

ACKNOWLEDGMENTS

I would like to thank Diane Halpern for helpful comments.

REFERENCES

Ainsworth, M. D. S., Blehar, M. D., Waters, E., & Wall, S. (1978). *Patterns of attachment: A psychological study of the strange situation*. Hillsdale, NJ: Lawrence Erlbaum Associates.

Baum, C. L. (2003). Does early maternal employment harm child development? An analysis of the potential benefits of leave taking. *Journal of Labor Economics, 21*, 409–448.

Bianchi, S. M. (2000). Maternal employment and time with children: Dramatic change or surprising continuity? *Demography, 37*, 401–414.

Blau, D. M. (1997). The production of quality in child care centers. *Journal of Human Resources, 32*, 354–387.

Blau, D. M. (1999). The effect of child care characteristics on child development. *Journal of Human Resources, 34*, 786–822.

Blau, D. M. (2000). The production of quality in child care centers: Another look. *Applied Developmental Science, 4*, 136–148.

Bound, J., Jaeger, D. A., & Baker, R. M. (1995). Problems with instrumental variables estimation when the correlation between the instruments and the exogenous explanatory variable is weak. *Journal of the American Statistical Association, 90*, 443–450.

Bowlby, J. (1969). *Attachment and loss*. New York: Basic Books.

Cost, Quality, and Child Outcomes Study Team. (1999). *The children on the cost, quality, and outcomes study go to school, executive summary* [online]. Available: www.fpg.unc.edu/~NCEDL/PAGES/eqes.htm.

Currie, J. (2001). Early childhood intervention programs: What do we know? *Journal of Economic Perspectives, 15*, 213–238.

Currie, J., & Blau, D. (in press). Who's minding the kids?: Preschool, day care, and after school care. In F. Welch & E. Hanushek (Eds.), *Handbook of education economics*. New York: North Holland.

Currie, J., & Thomas, D. (1995). Does Head Start make a difference? *American Economic Review, 85*, 341–364.

Currie, J., & Thomas, D. (1999). Does Head Start help Hispanic children? *Journal of Public Economics, 74*, 235–262.

Garces, E., Thomas, D., & Currie, J. (2002) Longer-term effects of Head Start. *American Economic Review, 92*, 999–1012.

Greenstein, T. N. (1995). Are the "most advantaged" children truly disadvantaged by early maternal empoyment? Effects on child cognitive outcomes. *Journal of Family Issues, 16*, 149–169.

Grogger, J., Karoly, L. A., & Klerman, J. A. (2002). *Consequences of welfare reform: A research synthesis*. Santa Monica, CA: RAND.

Han, W., Waldfogel, J., & Brooks-Gunn, J. (2001). The effects of maternal employment on children of the National Longitudinal Survey of Youth. *Developmental Psychology, 35*, 445–459.

Harvey, E. (1999). Short-term and long-term effects of early parental employment on children of the National Longituidnal Survey of Youth. *Developmental Psychology, 35*, 445–459.

Heckman, J. J. (1979). Sample selection bias as a specification error. *Econometrica, 47*, 153–161.

Heckman, J. J., Hohmann, N., & Smith, J. A. (2000). Substitution and dropout bias in social experiments: A study of an influential social experiment. *The Quarterly Journal of Economics, 115*, 651–694.

Heckman, J. J., & Smith, J. A. (1995). Assessing the case for social experiments. *Journal of Economic Perspectives, 9*, 85–110.

Helburn, S. W. (Ed.). (1995). *Cost, quality, and child outcomes in child care centers technical report*. Denver CO: Center for Research in Economic and Social Policy, University of Colorado at Denver.

Hill, J., Waldfogel, J., & Brooks-Gunn, J. (2002). Differential effects of high quality child care. *Journal of Policy Analysis and Management, 21*, 601–627.

Hill, J., Waldfogel, J., Brooks-Gunn, J. & Han, W. J. (2003). *Towards a better estimate of causal links in child policy: The case of maternal employment on child outcomes*. Unpublished paper, Columbia University School of International and Public Affairs.

Hoffman, L., & Youngblade, L. (1999). *Mothers at work: Effects on children's well being*. New York: Cambridge University Press.

Howes, C., Galinsky, E., Shinn, M., Gulcur, L., Clements, M., Sibley, A., Abbott-Shim, M., & McCarthy, J. (1998). *The Florida child care quality improvement study*. New York: Families and Work Institute.

James-Burdumy, S. (1999). *The effect of maternal labor force participation on child development*. Washington, DC: Mathematica Policy Research.

Johnston, J., & DiNardo, J. (1997). *Econometric methods* (4th ed.). New York: McGraw-Hill.

Katz, L. F., Kling, J., & Leibman, J. B. (2001). Moving to opportunity in Boston: Early results of a randomized mobility experiment. *The Quarterly Journal of Economics, 116*, 607–654.

Lamb, M. E. (1998). Nonparental child care: Context, quality, correlates, and consequences. In

W. Damon (Ed.), *Handbook of child psychology: Vol. 4. Child psychology in practice* (5th ed., pp. 73–133). New York: Wiley.

Leibowitz, A. (1977). Parental inputs and children's achievement. *Journal of Human Resources, 12*, 242–251.

Love, J. M., Achochet, P. Z., & Meckstroth, A. (1996). *Are they in any real danger? What reserach does and doesn't tell us about child care quality and children's wellbeing.* Princeton, NJ: Mathematica Policy Research.

Meyers, M., Rosenbaum, D., Ruhm, C., & Waldfogel, J. (2004). Inequality in early childhood education and care: What do we know? In K. Neckerman (Ed.), *Social inequality.* New York: Russell Sage Foundation.

Mocan, N., Burchinal, M., Morris, J. R., & Helburn, S. (1995). Models of quality in center child care. In S. Helburn (Ed.), *Cost, quality, and child outcomes.* Denver: Center for Research on Economic and Social Policy, University of Colorado at Denver.

Moore, K. A., & Driscoll, A. K. (1997). Low-wage maternal employment and outcomes for children: A study. *The Future of Children, 7*, 122–127.

Morris, P., Know, V., & Gennetian, L. A. (2002). *Welfare policies matter for children and youth: Lessons for TANF reauthorization.* Manpower Demonstration Research Corporation [online]. Available: http://www.mdrc.org/Reports2002/NG_PolicyBrief/NG_PolicyBrief.htm[2002].

Neidell, M. (2002). *Early time investments in children's human capital development: Effects of time in the first year on cognitive and non-cognitive outcomes.* Chicago: University of Chicago Press.

NICHD Early Child Care Research Network. (1997). Child care during the first year of life. *Merrill-Palmer Quarterly, 43*, 340–360.

NICHD Early Child Care Research Network. (1998). Early child care and self-control, compliance, and problem behavior at twenty-four and thirty-six months. *Child Development, 69*, 1145–1170.

NICHD Early Child Care Research Network. (2000a). Characteristics and quality of child care for toddlers and preschoolers. *Applied Developmental Science, 4*, 116–135.

NICHD Early Child Care Research Network. (2000b). The relation of child care to cognitive and language development. *Child Development, 71*, 960–980.

NICHD Early Child Care Research Network, & Duncan, G.J. (2001, April). *Modeling the impacts of child care quality on children's preschool cognitive development.* Paper presented at Society for Research on Child Development, Minneapolis, MN.

Peisner-Feinberg, E. S., Burchinal, M. R., Clifford, R. M., Culkin, M. L., Howes, C., Kagan, S. L., & Yazejian, N. (2001). The relation of preschool child-care quality to children's cognitive and social development trajectories through second grade. *Child Development, 72*, 1534–1553.

Powers, E. (2001). New estimates of the impact of child disability on maternal employment. *American Economic Review, 91*, 135–140.

Rosenbaum, P. R., & Rubin, D. B. (1983). The central role of the propensity score in observational studies for causal effects. *Biometrika, 70*, 41–55.

Ruhm, C. (2000) *Parental employment and child cognitive development working paper #7666.* Cambridge, MA: National Bureau of Economic Research.

Ruopp, R., Travers, J., Glantz, F., & Coelen, C. (1979). *Children at the center.* Cambridge: ABT Books.

Shonkoff, J., & Phillips, D. (Eds.). (2000). *From neurons to neighborhoods: The science of early childhood development.* Washington, DC: National Academy Press.

Smolensky, E., & Gootman, J. A. (Eds.). (2003). *Working families and growing kids: Caring for children and adolescents.* Washington, DC: National Academy Press.

Staiger, D., & Stock, J. (1997). Instrumental variables regression with weak instruments. *Econometrika, 65*, 557–587.

U.S. Department of Health and Human Services. (1998). *The NICHD study of early child care*. Washington, DC: National Institute of Child Health and Human Development.

Vandell, D. L., & Ramanan, J. (1992). Effects of early and recent maternal employment on children from low-income families. *Child Development, 63*, 938–949.

Waldfogel, J., Han, W. J., & Brooks-Gunn, J. (2002). Early maternal employment and child cognitive development. *Demography, 39*, 369–392.

Zaslow, M. J., & Emig, C. A. (1997). When low-income mothers go to work: Implications for children. *Future of Children, 7*, 1001–1115.

Zaslow, M. J., Moore, K. A., Brooks, J. L., Toot, K., Redd, Z. A., & Emig, C. A. (2002). Experimental studies of weflare reform and children. *Future of Children, 23*, 79–98.

20

Work-Family Mismatch and Child Health and Well-Being: A Review of the Economics Research

Sanders Korenman

School of Public Affairs, Baruch College, CUNY

Robert Kaestner

University of Illinois, Chicago

Economists, especially health and labor economists, have long studied trade-offs that families face in the decisions they make about childbearing and working. Therefore, they are quite used to thinking about work-family mismatch, a theme of this volume, as work-family trade-offs. Nearly all economic studies of the implications of family-work trade-offs for child health refer to the Grossman/Becker model of child health, child development, or, more generally, child quality (Becker, 1981; Grossman, 1972a, 1972b). Their central premise is that families produce child and adult health as part of a process of maximizing the welfare of the family. Families desire consumer goods and leisure, but they also care about the health of their members. Family members' health is produced according to a production technology (production function) in which the outcome is health—broadly defined to encompass all aspects of development—and the inputs include purchased goods and services such as medical care and family members' time. The Grossman/Becker model also recognizes that health evolves over time: Individuals begin life with a health endowment that is partly genetic in origin, and health at any age has a random component. Therefore, when modeling health and development at any age, it may be necessary to measure health status at earlier ages or lifetime environmental conditions.

Family-work trade-offs stem from the dual role that family members' time plays in achieving family objectives. The family earns income needed to buy goods by supplying the time of its members to the labor market. The inescapable fact that time is required both to earn income and to produce health creates potential trade-offs (or mismatches) between work and health. If both purchased goods and services and family members' time are important for health, at the margin, families can increase one input only by reducing the other.

We say trade-offs are potential because inputs such as child care may be purchased or may be available "free" to the family, as when a grandparent provides care at no charge. These services may be good substitutes for, or even superior to, parental time in producing child health. In this case, parents may work without diminishing their children's health if some of the extra income from working is used to purchase inputs that completely compensate for the reduction in parental time. However, there may be no entirely adequate substitutes for some parental inputs. Furthermore, at some point, additional purchased resources may be unable to compensate for reduced parental time, and greater work effort will adversely affect health. This apparently simple theoretical framework can generate complex relations among family responsibilities, work, and members' health. As a result, interpreting empirical associations among family responsibilities, work, and health is not always straightforward.

FAMILY RESPONSIBILITIES, WORK, AND HEALTH: ESTIMATION CHALLENGES

Empirically, it is difficult to identify the consequences of parental work. If parents were randomly assigned to either care for children or work in the labor market, researchers could estimate the average effect of parental work on child health and development simply by examining differences in the averages of health and developmental indicators between children whose parents work more and those whose parents work less. Random assignment, however, is not possible. This presents an empirical challenge because many factors that affect child health, some of which are difficult to measure, also influence families' choices about living arrangements and how much each parent (or potential caregiver) works or invests in producing child health. Therefore, the observed associations between family responsibilities and work and child health will reflect the direct effects of these variables on health and the indirect effects of the confounding, unmeasured factors. For example, the decision about whether a mother works shortly after the birth of a child is influenced by her marital status, her productivity in the labor market (i.e., wages), her productivity in caring for children, and the health of the child. All else the same, a mother who is more productive in the labor market is more likely to work or to work soon after the birth of a child; if she does, her children may be adversely affected by reduced maternal time inputs.

All else, however, is not the same. Mothers who have skills that are highly valued in the labor market may also tend to be skilled caregivers of children or to be otherwise advantaged. Their children might be expected to be healthier or more developmentally advantaged regardless of whether their mother worked. Unless the mother's skills are carefully controlled in the analysis, estimates of the effects of mother's work on child development will be biased by unmeasured human capital and other attributes of the mother. Therefore, the economics research has stressed the importance of research designs (e.g., fixed effects) and model specifications that control for mother's education and cognitive skills.

The most natural economic interpretation of empirical studies of family-work mismatches is that they attempt to estimate the parameters of the health production function, which is the technical relationship that determines the effects of inputs in producing family members' health. Family responsibilities and work are used as proxy measures for the amount of time the family invests in producing health. These are crude proxy variables. For example, greater work effort by the mother does not necessarily imply less time spent caring for and nurturing children, because there are other uses of time (e.g., Bianchi, 2000). In addition, the production function is a technical relationship between quantities of physical inputs (time inputs, food, medical care) and the quantity of output (health). Financial variables per se do not enter the production function. However, most researchers who study work-family trade-offs include family income or family structure controls as proxy variables for inputs of goods and services. Including income in the production function is problematic because income is directly (negatively) affected by the amount of time spent caring for one's children (Rosenzweig & Schultz, 1983). In addition, given that it is unlikely that all the (physical) inputs of the production function will be measured, estimates of the association between child health and inputs that are included in the analysis, say family members' time, are likely to be biased.

These considerations have implications for the empirical estimates of production function parameters. Not only do the associations among family responsibilities, work, and health reflect the technical relationships that govern the production of health, but they also reflect differences in preferences, intellectual ability, genetic makeup, physical environment, and geographic area because all of these factors may affect the costs and benefits of obtaining the things people want (goods, inputs into child health). In other words, focusing on differences in family responsibilities and work to explain differences in health ignores the importance of these underlying causes. Only if all the inputs of the production function were accurately measured and included in the analysis would such associations provide evidence of the effect of, say, greater maternal work effort on child health.

To illustrate this problem, let us consider more closely how one potentially unmeasured factor, an adult's intellectual ability, may affect his or her choices related to family, children, work, and health. Intellectual ability appears to be rewarded by labor markets; those with more ability earn higher wages. The price of goods in terms of work effort is relatively low for a person with a high hourly wage, and the price of leisure time (or work outside the paid labor market) is relatively high for such a person given that reducing hours at work has a higher opportunity cost in forgone consumption. This implies that more able persons would work more, have greater levels of consumption, and have less leisure (nonmarket time) than less able persons. More able persons would also produce fewer goods that require time inputs, such as rearing children.

One way to reduce the relatively high cost of time and time-intensive goods (e.g., children) is to marry. A more able person who likes children may find it more worthwhile to marry because a spouse's time may be a substitute for this person's time in child development, particularly if the high-ability person marries a person of somewhat lower ability. Because his or her reward for market work is relatively low, the lower-ability spouse may choose nonmarket work over market work, and therefore spend more time producing goods, such as child development, that require nonmarket time. Indeed this type of specialization within marriage may reinforce differences in the amount of time high- and low-ability persons spend working and can lead to greater gains to marriage that encourage and prolong marriages. A higher ability person, however, may still have fewer children than a lower ability person, depending on whether greater productivity afforded by specialization within marriage can offset the relatively high opportunity cost of children.

As for health, a high-ability person may be more motivated to stay healthy than a person of lesser ability because the cost of missing work for health reasons is high. Yet investing in health (e.g., exercise) takes time, and time is relatively costly to a high-ability person. Therefore, their health may be better or worse than that of lower ability persons depending on which of these effects dominates.

The example implies that intellectual ability would be positively correlated with earnings, hours of work, consumption, and marriage. It would be negatively correlated with work outside the paid labor force. The theory does not offer a clear prediction of whether intellectual ability raises the desired number of children and adult health.

Even this example, however, is too simple. It ignores important decisions, such as the timing of marriage, work, and childbearing. Similarly, the simple model ignores the possibility that intellectual ability may increase the productivity of nonmarket time. If it does, then more able persons may be healthier and have healthier children than less able persons even when the former invest less time than the latter in their health and the health of their children. The simple model also ignores the presence of market substitutes for nonmarket time that may offset some of their disadvantage in obtaining goods that require nonmarket time. For example, more able persons may be able to purchase high-quality child care or better medical services. Finally, the simple model ignores possible genetic correlations among ability, health, and children's health.

In summary, the theoretical causal pathways underlying the relation among family responsibilities, work, and health are complex. For many purposes, particularly understanding the effects on child health of policies that might ease the work-family conflict, we would like to know the relationship between parental time inputs and child health. As the prior example illustrates, however, it is difficult to uncover these causal pathways in an empirical analysis. Specifically, observed quantities of work and family responsibilities and child health are associated not only because there is a relationship between parental time inputs and child health, but also because both time inputs and health are the outcomes of complex choice processes. Therefore, nonexperimental studies of the relation among family responsibilities, work, and health can provide only limited guidance to policymakers interested in improving the health of working families. With this cautionary note in mind, we proceed with a review of the economics research on the family-work mismatch.

ECONOMICS RESEARCH
ON THE FAMILY-WORK TRADE-OFF

A feature that distinguishes many economic studies of health and development from those in other fields is the centrality of the idea that health and development are both influenced by economic status and are one of its key determinants. Economists are naturally concerned with the determinants of the level and distribution of economic well-being. The conceptual treatment of health as a form of human capital has clearly influenced the choice of health outcomes and the specification of statistical models in economic studies. For example, economists are attracted to the study of those aspects of health most closely linked with economic status, such as cognitive development, and particularly those that might be amenable to intervention or manipulation by social policies.

Depending on how one defines work-family conflict and how one circumscribes the field of economics, the research is either vast or fairly manageable. To make our task more manageable and to focus our efforts on a topic that we believe is both of great social importance and in need of additional research, we focus mainly on studies that investigate the possible implications of parents' employment, especially mothers, on the health and development of children. Although not exhaustive, this review includes 25 studies that directly test effects of parental employment on child health and development. It also includes a selection of papers more loosely related to this narrower topic. The focus on studies that test directly for parental employment effects on child health excludes a good deal of related economics research, such as studies of whether child health affects parents' work participation (Norberg, 1998; Salkever, 1990; Vistnes, 1997), whether poor child health reduces family stability (Corman & Kaestner, 1992), whether higher family income improves child health and development (although we do touch briefly on this important question), whether child responsibilities affect occupational choice, especially exposure to health risks (DeLeire & Levy, 2001), whether female labor force participation reduces family stability, and whether family instability harms children (e.g., Cherlin, 1999; Cutler, Glaeser, & Norberg, 2000; Gruber, 2000).

Our review suggests that some generalizations are possible about the economics research on the effects of parental employment on child health. We first offer a summary discussion regarding the scope of this research, and then we discuss generalizations about the way economists have linked family-work trade-offs to child health and development, with reference to two broad categories: (a) outcome measures, and (b) specification of employment-related variables. We conclude with some suggestions for further investigation.

Scope

Studies of effects of maternal employment on child health and development have been particularly concerned with the effects of early return to employment after birth. At what age of the child is it safe or optimal for the mother to return to work (see e.g., Neidell, 2000)? A few studies have questioned whether the duration or intensity of work among mothers with young children might be related to child health (e.g., Ruhm, 2003b, 2004). Fewer still have questioned whether children of parents who work irregular hours (split shifts, nights and weekends) might suffer health or developmental effects (Han, 2004).

Others have posited that the effects of parental work vary by context. For example, if the family is able to use good quality day care, because they can purchase such care, are eligible for subsidized care, or have a good source of family care, then employment might be developmentally beneficial or at least not harmful to children. A few economists have studied the effects of child-care quality (e.g., Blau, 2001; Vandell & Wolfe, 2000, provide a cross-disciplinary review), although there are numerous studies outside of economics that consider child-care quantity, quality, and timing (see e.g., Currie, chap. 19, this volume for further discussion; see also NICHD Early Child Care Research Network, 1998, 2003a, 2003b). As we noted, relatively few studies explicitly model child-care quantity or quality as a mediator of the relation between parental work and child development. Among those that do, neither Baum (2003) nor Ruhm (2004) found an important role for the mode or type of child care (center, family care, etc.) in the relation between maternal employment and child development. Brooks-Gunn, Han, and Waldfogel (2002) found that child-care quality does not account for the relation between long hours of maternal work and child outcomes (30+ hours per week vs. no work), but could account for some of the differences between children whose mothers work part time and full time. Currie and Hotz (2001) found that child-care regulations—in particular, caregiver education requirements—in part mediate the relation between work-oriented welfare reform and child maltreatment. Hill and O'Neill (1994) found no evidence that preschool mediates the statistical relation between maternal employment and child outcomes. Datcher-Loury (1988) found that educational attainment or children's years of schooling is increased by time spent in child care, controlling for maternal labor supply in two periods. Han (2004) found that child-care quality in part mediates the adverse relation between nonstandard hours of parental work (specifically night shifts) and child outcomes.

Another overlooked issue in the economics research is the effect of fathers' employment or time input (Waldfogel, Han, & Brooks-Gunn, 2002; Ruhm, 2004, are exceptions; Ruhm, 2003a, provided additional references outside the economics research). Direct study of maternal or parental time or health inputs as mediating paths for parental employment is also rare. Studies of conflicts between employment during a child's infancy and breastfeeding, such as that by Chatterji and Frick (2003), are the exception. Although many studies estimate the effects of a mother smoking, using drugs or alcohol, and her prenatal care on infant health, they are not often treated as mediating variables in the relation between work and infant or child health.

Many studies estimate effects of family income on child health and development (see Blau, 1999; Duncan & Brooks-Gunn, 1997; Korenman & Miller, 1997; Korenman, Miller, & Sjaastad, 1995; Mayer, 1995; Meara, 2001; Miller & Korenman, 1994; Shea, 2000; Wilcox-Gock, 1985). These studies are obviously relevant to determining the potentially offsetting effects of income and parental time inputs. Although results are mixed, the evidence generally points to no more than a small positive effect of income on child health and development.

Although education and parental academic ability are controlled in nearly all studies, and economic theory since Grossman (1972a) has stressed the role of education in transforming information into child health, economists have not often examined directly whether effects of education are mediated by health knowledge (Glied, 1999; Kenkel, 1991, are exceptions). Finally, more researchers are studying effects of policies such as welfare reform, parental leave policies, and child-care regulations (Paxson & Waldfogel, 1999, 2003). This is a welcome development if the purpose of the analysis is to draw inferences about effects of specific policies (NRC 1991, 2003).

LINKING WORK-FAMILY ISSUES CONCEPTUALLY AND OPERATIONALLY TO HEALTH AND WELL-BEING

As noted, human capital theory makes a fairly direct link between work-family issues and child health because parents' time is used both for work and to produce child health, creating trade-offs. The theory also notes that, because health capital is a stock, analysts must consider lifetime behaviors, histories of parental labor force participation, and long-term (i.e., permanent) income in studying these relations. For example, economists have studied whether adolescents' risky behaviors are related to family income and parental employment in early childhood. Considering early conditions is particularly important if early childhood is a critical time for developmental investments (National Research Council, 2000). Operationally, the typical empirical economic study in this area regresses one or more health or developmental outcomes on measures of maternal employment or labor supply.

Outcomes

Economists have considered a wide range of outcomes in the work-family arena. Table 20.1 lists 11 categories of outcomes that appear frequently, with the corresponding child ages. Listing outcomes in this way might suggest that all outcomes are studied with equal frequency. In fact our survey of the research suggests that, beyond infant health, developmental outcomes have been emphasized relative to health outcomes, although recently, obesity as a child health concern is gaining interest (Anderson, Butcher, & Levine 2002; Ruhm, 2003b). Among the most common developmental outcomes studied is cognitive development. As we noted, one explanation for this emphasis is economists' long-standing interest in factors that determine economic status and economic inequality and the established importance of education

TABLE 20.1
Common Child Health Outcomes of Interest
by Economists Studying Work and Family Issues

Outcome	Ages (years)
1. Birth weight, and infant, neonatal, postneonatal mortality	birth
2. Breastfeeding initiation and duration	0
3. Cognitive development as measured by achievement test scores: Peabody Picture Vocabulary Test (PPVT), Peabody Individual Achievement Test in Reading and Math (PIAT–R and PIAT–M); Bracken, Bayley Mental Development Indexes	0–8
4. Maternal reports of behavior problems	4+
5. Accidental injuries (mortality rates; medical attention, hospitalization, total mortality, auto, pedestrian, fire, mortality, drowning)	1–5, 6–12
6. Child reported self-esteem indicators	8+
7. Never/ever repeated a grade in school; ever suspended from school	10+
8. Obesity and overweight	0–15
9. Abuse and neglect (reported & substantiated cases; out-of-home care)	0–17
10. Risky behaviors: cigarettes, alcohol, marijuana, sex without birth control, crimes	15–17
11. Suicide attempts and suicide death rates	15–24

and cognitive development in determining economic status (e.g., Arrow, Bowles, & Durlauf, 2000). Another reason for the focus on developmental outcomes such as cognitive development is that human capital investments are also a primary policy target for promoting economic welfare, and cognitive development is an important component of human capital. Although this emphasis is understandable, economists may have neglected other health outcomes that are less obviously tied to cognitive development or academic success.

In examining the effects of parental employment on children, economists have studied infancy and young childhood more often than middle childhood or teenagers. Although random assignment evaluations are available to examine children at these later ages (see National Research Council, 2003), they have been limited to low-income or welfare populations. This limitation may be consequential because nonexperimental studies that test for differences in effects of maternal employment between less advantaged and more advantaged families generally find smaller adverse effects (or no effects or even beneficial effects) of employment in lower income families (e.g., Ruhm, 2003b). Economists have also more often studied the effects of maternal employment rather than the mediating effects of child care, either quantity or quality (Currie, chap. 19, this volume).

Finally, in studies of the effects of maternal employment on child cognitive development, researchers have relied heavily on a single source of data, the National Longitudinal Survey of Youth (NLSY79). Although an excellent source of data on employment and child development, it is unclear that the results of many of the studies (especially those based entirely on the early waves of 1986 or 1988) can be generalized to larger populations because the mothers were fairly young. More recent studies using the NLSY79 cover a wider span of maternal ages; hence, broader generalizations are more appropriate so long as the upper age limit for inclusion of children in the sample is not too high (e.g., Aughinbaugh & Gittleman, 2003, study of 15- to 17-year-old children of the NLSY respondents).

Key Explanatory Variables

Researchers have used a wide assortment of employment measures in their work. Key labor supply variables in the studies include:

1. Number of hours per week and number of weeks per year worked by the mother in the year prior to the assessment of the child's life or over the life of the child (e.g., average over the life of the child);
2. Annual hours worked when the child was age 1 or ages 0 to 2, or in the 3 years prior to the assessment;
3. Hours per week worked and not on leave from a job; labor force participation in each of the first four quarters of a child's life or in each of the first 3 years;
4. Child care and quality: both process and structural/caregiver measures have been used. Structural/caregiver measures include group size, teacher–pupil ratios, and caregivers' education and specialized training. Process measures are more difficult to collect, and generally involve a sustained period of observation by a trained observer; several measures are used heavily in studies of family leave.
5. Mother ever worked full time by the time the child was 9 months old;
6. Whether the mother returned to work before the children was 3 months old and whether she worked full time;
7. Female (mother) labor force participation rates (aggregate or cross-national);
8. Mother employed in quarter or other employed;
9. Welfare reform components: benefits, family cap, sanctions, and work requirements;
10. Average weekly work hours during the year, or during the first year of child's life and ages 2 and 3 combined, or between ages 1 and 9; percent of weeks worked in year.
11. Father's employment or high hours of work.

Clearly, a wide variety of employment measures are in use, and there is little apparent consensus as to the correct specification. Researchers have also defined part- and full-time work in a variety of ways.

Some studies report little sensitivity to alternative variable specifications. Ruhm (2003a, 2004) noted substantial heaping of work hours at zero and full time, especially when children are young. Therefore, in practice, there may be little advantage to specifications that indicate hours worked compared with those that simply use indicators of employed or not employed. This observation also suggests that, for example, it may be difficult to reach firm conclusions regarding the recommended number of hours mothers should work conditional on participating in the labor market. If researchers are interested in hypotheses regarding effects of different number of hours of work, it is critical to check the sensitivity of results to different characterizations of the number of hours of work, and confidence intervals should be reported.

RESEARCH ON THE EFFECT
OF EMPLOYMENT ON ADULT HEALTH

Although effects on children are the focus of this chapter, we briefly summarize the relatively small body of economics research on the effects of employment and unemployment on adult health. Because employment status is endogenous (jointly determined with health), most studies of the effect of employment on health have examined the relation between rates of unemployment and health. The rationale for this choice is that macroeconomic effects that result in unemployment are not under the influence of the individual. Therefore, changes in aggregate economic activity will alter the probability of employment, and this externally generated variation in employment is used to identify the effect of employment on health. Of course changes in aggregate economic activity may also have direct effects on health.

Ruhm (2000, 2003a) provided a concise review of the research and the most thorough analyses. Ruhm (2000) found that unemployment is associated with improved health, in contrast to some earlier studies. This finding is, in part, explained by changes in health behaviors; he (2000, 2003a) showed that smoking and obesity decrease during economic recessions. Ruhm (2003a) also showed that recession-induced reductions in work hours explain part of the relation between macroeconomic conditions and health. In summary, employment provides income that can, over a long period, improve health, but may have detrimental health effects by increasing stress and reducing time constraints that affect health behaviors.

Case and Deaton (2003) made a similar point when they examined whether the type of work affects health. They hypothesized that the physical demands of manual labor adversely affect health. This raises another trade-off; not only may work adversely affect health indirectly because it limits time to invest in health, but work may directly affect health. Case and Deaton found that health deteriorates with age much more rapidly for those in manual occupations than in other occupations, which supports their hypothesis.

Kaestner and Tarlov (2003) and Bitler, Gelbach, and Hoynes (2004) investigated how low-educated single mothers' health and health behaviors were affected by changes in the welfare caseload that resulted from welfare reform. As with changes in unemployment studied by Ruhm, change in welfare caseloads represents plausibly exogenously induced transitions between work and nonwork. Both Kaestner and Tarlov and Bitler et al. found that decreases in welfare caseloads had little effect on measures of health status. Kaestner and Tarlov found that changes in caseload were associated with statistically significant decreases in binge drinking and increases in physical activity.

ISSUES FOR FURTHER CONSIDERATION

Although the economics research on the relation between maternal employment and child health has reached varied conclusions, some interpretation issues are underappreciated. Clearly, the question of whether study designs and estimation procedures support causal inferences is paramount (Currie, chap. 19, this volume). Also our review has highlighted that the research has focused on the relation between work-family trade-offs and the health and development of young children, and it has somewhat neglected the health of older children and adult family members.

Turning now to challenges to causal inference, we first note problems associated with a high correlation in labor force participation across periods. For example, Ruhm (2003a) reported a year-to-year correlation in labor force participation of 0.70 or higher among new mothers. This high correlation makes detection of effects of work's timing over a child's early life difficult. The high correlation means we should expect multicollinearity problems when a set of controls that measure employment in adjacent periods is included in the same regressions. For example, estimates of timing effects are sometimes based on regression models that include indicators for whether mothers worked in the first year following birth and in the second year following birth. These specifications often result in coefficient estimates that are roughly equal in size and of opposite signs, where the effect of work in the first year is negative and the effect in the second year is positive. The interpretation offered is that it may be harmful to the child for mothers to work in the first year after the birth of the child (e.g., Blau & Grossberg, 1992). The results also indicate, however, a near-zero effect of working during the first 2 years (relative to not working). Others have noted that the effects of timing of maternal work in early childhood are usually not significantly different from one another.

One solution to this problem is to form four distinct categories of work in the first 2 years. In some studies, work in the second year appears more protective than work in both the first and second years (combined), although the difference is most often not statistically significant. Work in the first year only, however, is often no different from work in the second year only, which seems contrary to the conclusion that work in the first year may be harmful to children. However, relatively few mothers work in the first year of a child's life and not the second.

A second repeated finding is a strong (large and significant) partial correlation between maternal academic ability or cognitive achievement and both child development and maternal labor market outcomes. This correlation is treated prominently in the theory. However, few data sources contain adequate information on mothers' cognitive abilities, labor market outcomes, and child health and development to study these issues. The NLSY is an exception, which explains the field's heavy reliance on it. Not having controls for maternal cognitive ability or achievement is an important source of (generally positive) omitted variable bias in estimates of employment effects on child development or health.

A final comment pertains to another fairly common result in the research—the apparently substantial differences by race, education, and marital status in the effects of maternal employment on child health. In particular, stronger adverse effects are typically found for children of married women and children of non-Hispanic White women (Anderson et al., 2002; Baydar & Brooks-Gunn, 1991; Desai, Chase-Lansdale, & Michael, 1989; Ruhm, 2003a, 2003b, 2004; National Research Council, 2003). This pattern is sometimes overlooked in policy discussion that, for example, might criticize welfare-to-work programs based on evidence of adverse effects on average for early resumption of employment after birth. In fact, however, there is little evidence of adverse effects for low-income, minority, or single women who, historically, have been the most likely recipients of welfare. There are many plausible explanations for this finding, including the developmental quality of child care compared with the home environment, better social support among the poor, or the greater benefit of earned income at lower income levels (diminishing returns to higher income in child development). However, all of these explanations remain in the realm of speculation and should be a priority for further investigation.

REFERENCES

Anderson, P. M., Butcher, K. F., & Levine, P. B. (2002, February). *Maternal employment and overweight children* (NBER WP No. 8770). Cambridge, MA: National Bureau of Economic Research.

Arrow, K., Bowles, S., & Durlauf, S. (Eds.). (2000). *Meritocracy and economic inequality*. Princeton, NJ: Princeton University Press.

Aughinbaugh, A., & Gittleman, M. (2003, February). *Maternal employment and adolescent risky behavior* (BLS WP No. 366). Washington, DC: U.S. Bureau of Labor Statistics.

Baum, C. L. (2003). Does early maternal employment harm child development? An analysis of the potential benefits of leave taking. *Journal of Labor Economics, 21*, 409–448.

Baydar, N., & Brooks-Gunn, J. (1991). Effects of maternal employment and child-care arrangements on preschoolers' cognitive and behavioral outcomes: Evidence from the children of the National Longitudinal Survey of Youth. *Developmental Psychology, 27*, 932–945.

Becker, G. (1981). *A treatise on the family*. Cambridge, MA: Harvard University Press.

Bianchi, S. (2000). Maternal employment and time with children: Dramatic change or surprising continuity? *Demography, 37*, 401–414.

Bitler, M., Gelbach, J., & Hoynes, H. (2004, March). *Welfare reform and health*. Santa Monica, CA: Rand Corporation.

Blau, D. M. (1999). The effect of income on child development. *The Review of Economics and Statistics, 8*, 261–276.

Blau, D. M. (2001). *The child care problem: An economic analysis*. New York: Russell Sage Foundation.

Blau, F. D., & Grossberg, A. J. (1992). Maternal labor supply and children's cognitive development. *Review of Economics and Statistics, 74*, 474–481.

Brooks-Gunn, J., Han, W., & Waldfogel, J. (2002). The effects of early maternal employment on child cognitive development. *Demography, 39*, 369–392.

Case, A., & Deaton, A. (2003). *Broken down by work and sex; How our health declines* (NBER WP No. 9821). Cambridge, MA: National Bureau of Economic Research.

Chatterji, P., & Frick, K. (2003, April). *Does returning to work after childbirth affect breastfeeding practices?* (NBER WP No. 9630). Cambridge, MA: National Bureau of Economic Research.

Cherlin, A. J. (1999). Going to extremes. *Demography, 36*, 421–428.

Corman, H., & Kaestner, R. (1992). The effects of child health on marital status and family structure. *Demography, 29*, 389–408.

Currie, J., & Hotz, V. J. (2001, January). *Accidents Will Happen? Unintentional Injury, Maternal Employment, and Child Care Policy* (NBER WP No. 8090). Cambridge, MA: National Bureau of Economic Research.

Cutler, D. M., Glaeser, E. L., & Norberg, K. E. (2000, May). *Explaining the rise in youth suicide* (NBER WP No. 7713). Cambridge, MA: National Bureau of Economic Research.

Datcher-Loury, L. (1988). Effects of mother's home time on children's schooling. *Review of Economics and Statistics, 70*, 367–373.

DeLeire, T., & Levy, H. (2001, November). *Gender, occupation choice and the risk of death at work* (NBER WP No. 8574). Cambridge, MA: National Bureau of Economic Research.

Desai, S. P., Chase-Landsdale, L., & Michael, R. T. (1989). Mother or market? Effects of maternal employment on the intellectual ability of four year old children. *Demography, 26*, 545–561.

Duncan, G. J., & Brooks-Gunn, J. (Eds.). (1997). *Consequences of growing up poor*. New York: Russell Sage Foundation.

Glied, S. (1999, July). *The value of reductions in child injury mortality in the US* (NBER WP No. 7204). Cambridge, MA: National Bureau of Economic Research.

Grossman, M. (1972a). *The demand for health: A theoretical and empirical investigation*. New York: Columbia/NBER.

Grossman, M. (1972b). On the concept of health capital and the demand for health. *Journal of Political Economy, 80*, 223–255.

Gruber, J. (2000). *Is making divorce easier bad for children? The long run implications of unilateral divorce* (NBER WP No. 7968). Cambridge, MA: National Bureau of Economic Research.

Han, W. (2004, April). *Nonstandard work schedules and child cognitive outcomes*. Paper presented at the meeting of the Population Asociation of American, Boston, MA.

Hill, M. A., & O'Neill, J. (1994). Family endowments and the achievement of young children with special reference to the underclass. *Journal of Human Resources, 29*, 1064–1100.

Kaestner, R., & Tarlov, E. (2003). *Changes in the welfare caseload and the health of low-educated mothers*. Chicago, IL: University of Illinois at Chicago.

Kenkel, D. (1991). Health behavior, health knowledge and schooling. *Journal of Political Economy, 99*, 287–305.

Korenman, S. D., & Miller J. E. (1994). Poverty children's nutritional status in the United States. *American Journal of Epidemiology, 140*, 233–243.

Korenman, S. D., & Miller, J. E. (1997). Effects of long-term poverty on physical health of children in the National Longitudinal Survey of Youth. In G. J. Duncan & J. Brooks-Gunn (Eds.), *Consequences of growing up poor* (pp. 70–100). New York: Russell Sage Foundation.

Korenman, S. D., Miller, J. E., & Sjaastad, J. (1995). Long-term poverty and child development in the United States. *Children and Youth Services Review, 17*, 127–155.

Leibowitz, A. (1977). Parental inputs and children's achievement. *Journal of Human Resources, 12*, 242–51.

Mayer, S. (1995). *What money can't buy*. Cambridge, MA: Harvard University Press.

Meara, E. (2001, April). *Why is health related to socioeconomic status? The case of pregnancy and low birth weight* (NBER WP No. 8231). Cambridge, MA: National Bureau of Economic Research.

Miller, J. E., & Korenman, S. (1994). Poverty and children's nutritional status in the United States. *American Journal of Epidemiology, 140*(3), 233–243.

National Research Council, Committee on Family and Work Policies. (2003). *Working families and growing kids: Caring for children and adolescents*. Washington, DC: National Academy Press.

National Research Council, Committee on Integrating the Science of Early Childhood Development. (2000). *From neurons to neighborhoods: The science of early childhood development*. Washington, DC: National Academy Press.

National Research Council, Panel on Employer Policies and Working Families, Committee on Women's Employment and Related Social Issues. (1991). *Work and family: Policies for a changing work force*. Washington, DC: National Academy Press.

Neidell, M. J. (2000). *Early parental time investments in children's human capital development: Effects of time in the first year on cognitive and non-cognitive outcomes*. Los Angeles, CA: UCLA Department of Economics.

NICHD Early Child Care Research Network. (1998). Early child care and self-control, compliance and problem behavior at 24 and 36 months. *Child Development, 69*, 1145–1170.

NICHD Early Child Care Research Network. (2003a). Does quality of care affect child outcomes at age 4½? *Developmental Psychology, 39*, 451–469.

NICHD Early Child Care Research Network. (2003b). Does amount of time spent in child care predict socioemotional adjustment during the transition to kindergarten? *Child Development, 74*, 976–1005.

Norberg, K. (1998, October). *The effects of daycare reconsidered* (NBER WP No. 6769). Cambridge, MA: National Bureau of Economic Research.

Paxson, C., & Waldfogel, J. (1999, September). *Work, welfare and child maltreatment* (NBER WP No. 7343). Cambridge, MA: National Bureau of Economic Research.

Paxson, C., & Waldfogel, J. (2003). Welfare reforms, family resources and child maltreatment. *Journal of Policy Analysis and Management, 22*, 85–113.

Rosenzweig, M., & Schultz, T. P. (1983). Estimation of a household production function: Heterogeneity, the demand for health inputs, and their effects on birthweight. *Journal of Political Economy, 92*, 723–746.

Ruhm, C. J. (2000). Are recessions good for your health? *Quarterly Journal of Economics, 115*, 617–650.

Ruhm, C. J. (2003a). *Healthy living in hard times* (NBER WP No. 9468). Cambridge, MA: National Bureau of Economic Research.

Ruhm, C. J. (2003b, November). *Maternal employment and adolescent development.* Greensboro, NC: University of North Carolina Press.

Ruhm, C. J. (2004). Parental employment and child cognitive development. *Journal of Human Resources, 39*, 155–192.

Salkever, D. S. (1990). Child health and other determinants of single mothers' labor supply and earnings. In R. Frank, I. Sivageldin, & A. Sorkin (Eds.), *Research in human capital and development* (pp. 147–181). London: JAI Press.

Shea, J. (2000). Does parent's money matter? *Journal of Public Economics, 77*, 155–184.

Vandell, D. L., & Wolfe, B. (2000, November). *Child care quality: Does it matter and does it need to be improved?* (Institute for Research on Poverty Special Report No. 78). Madison, WI: University of Wisconsin.

Vistnes, J. P. (1997). Gender differences in days lost from work due to illness. *Industrial and Labor Relations Review, 50*, 304–323.

Waldfogel, J., Han, W., & Brooks-Gunn, J. (2002, May). The effects of early maternal employment on child cognitive development. *Demography, 39*, 369–392.

Wilcox-Goek, V. L. (1985). Mother's education, health practices, and children's health needs: A variance components model. *Review of Economics and Statistics, 67*, 706–710.

21

How Well Do Government and Employer Policies Support Working Parents?

Christopher J. Ruhm
University of North Carolina at Greensboro

The first years of life are a particularly important period for children (Carnegie Task Force on Meeting the Needs of Young Children, 1994; Council of Economic Advisers, 1997). Recent research emphasizes the effects of early influences on brain development (Shore, 1997), and investments during young childhood are likely to be significant for learning skills, gaining self-esteem, and emotional security (Heckman, 2000), although the mechanisms for these effects are poorly understood and the relation between early brain development and future outcomes remains controversial (Bruer, 1999). Many parents face particular demands in the workplace during these critical years of their children's lives as parents attempt to establish or advance in careers and meet the financial needs of their growing families. These pressures may be aggravated by job insecurity, increased pace of work, and other burdens such as the need to care for aging relatives.

This chapter examines whether employer policies mitigate or exacerbate these difficulties. Because the policies adopted in the United States diverge dramatically from those in many other industrialized countries, I provide

TABLE 21.1

Percent of Full-Time Employees Receiving or Eligible for Benefits in Medium and Large Private Firms (Various Years)

Benefit	1980	1981	1982	1983	1984	1985	1986	1988	1989	1991	1993	1995	1997	1999	2000
Paid															
Holidays	99	99	99	99	99	98	99	96	97	92	91	89	89	90	92
Vacations	100	99	99	100	99	99	100	98	97	96	97	96	95	93	95
Sick leave	62	65	67	67	67	67	70	69	68	67	65	58	56	67	—
Personal leave	20	23	24	25	23	26	25	24	22	21	21	22	20	—	—
Maternity leave	—	—	—	—	—	—	—	2	3	2	3	—	—	—	—
Paternity leave	—	—	—	—	—	—	—	1	1	1	1	—	—	—	—
Family leave	—	—	—	—	—	—	—	—	—	—	—	2	2	—	—
Unpaid															
Maternity leave	—	—	—	—	—	—	—	33	37	37	60	—	—	—	—
Paternity leave	—	—	—	—	—	—	—	16	18	26	53	—	—	—	—
Family leave	—	—	—	—	—	—	—	—	—	—	—	84	93	—	—
Child Care															
Any employer assistance	—	—	—	—	—	—	—	4	5	8	7	8	10	9	9
Provided funds	—	—	—	—	—	—	—	—	—	—	—	4	6	5	4
Onsite child care	—	—	—	—	—	—	—	—	—	—	—	3	3	4	4
Offsite child care	—	—	—	—	—	—	—	—	—	—	—	1	1	3	2

Note. Until 1986, *small* establishments were those with less than 50 or 250 employees, where the threshold varied by industry. (Thus, those with ≥ 250 employees were medium/large in all cases; those with 50 to 250 were small in some industries and medium/large in others; those with < 50 employees were always small.) After 1986, the same standard was used across all industries: Those with 0 to 99 employees were small, and those with 100+ were medium/large. After the 1993 survey, maternity and paternity leave are combined and reported as family leave. Personal leave is not reported after 1997.

Sources. U.S. Census Bureau; *Statistical Abstract of the United States*, various years (1981–1988, 1990, 1991, 1993, 1995, 1998, 1999); U.S. Department of Labor, Bureau of Labor Statistics (1999, 2003).

some international comparisons before speculating on possible sources and effects of the differences.

EMPLOYER BENEFITS

Are private employers in the United States family-friendly? Although there are many dimensions to this question, one obvious aspect to consider is the benefits offered by companies. Toward this end, Tables 21.1 and 21.2 document the availability of employer-provided benefits to full-time workers that might help with balancing responsibilities at home and in the workplace. Table 21.1 provides information on medium and large establishments, and Table 21.2 offers corresponding data for small employers.

More than 90% of full-time employees in medium and large companies receive (often brief) paid holidays and vacation. However, even these have become somewhat more limited over time; the share of full-time workers who receive holiday and vacation time has drifted from 96% and 98%, respectively, in 1988 to 92% and 95%, respectively, in 2000. The majority of full-time employees can also take paid sick leave, although there are again hints

TABLE 21.2
Percent of Full-Time Employee Receiving Benefits
in Small Private Firms

Benefit	1990	1992	1994	1996	1999	2000
Paid holidays	84	82	82	80	84	83
Paid vacations	88	88	88	86	87	87
Paid sick leave	47	53	50	50	59	—
Paid personal leave	11	12	13	14	—	—
Paid maternity leave	2	2	—	—	—	—
Paid paternity leave	<.5	1	—	—	—	—
Paid family leave	—	—	2	2	—	—
Unpaid maternity leave	17	18	—	—	—	—
Unpaid paternity leave	8	8	—	—	—	—
Unpaid family leave	—	—	47	48	—	—
Child Care						
Any employer assistance	1	2	1	2	2	1
Provided funds	—	—	1	1	2	<.5
Onsite child care	—	—	1	1	1	<.5
Off-site child care	—	—	<.5	1	<.5	1

See note to Table 21.1 for explanations for missing data. Small establishments include those with fewer than 100 employees.

Sources. U.S. Census Bureau; *Statistical Abstract of the United States*, various years (1992, 1994, 1997, 1998); U.S. Department of Labor, Bureau of Labor Statistics (2001, 2003).

of a declining trend. Other paid benefits are rare. Between 20% and 25% of workers receive paid personal leave, fewer than one tenth receive employer assistance for child care, and fewer than 1 in 20 works for an employer that offers either on-site or off-site child care. By contrast, unpaid family leave is more common. It was available to one third of women and one sixth of men working full time for medium or large employers in 1988, and it was almost universally offered by the late 1990s. This change reflects the enactment of federal legislation (discussed later).

Although corresponding information for small employers has been available for a shorter period, 1990 to 2000, it is clear that such companies supply family-friendly benefits less often than their larger counterparts (although they may be more likely to make accommodations on an informal basis). Between 80% and 88% of full-time employees at small firms received paid holidays or paid vacations, and roughly half received sick leave. Paid personal leave was available to just one in eight full-time employees in the early and mid-1990s, and paid family leave or child care was rare. Unpaid family leave increased sharply over time, just as for larger companies, but was still offered to fewer than one half of full-time employees in 1996.

Firms are even less likely to offer the aforementioned benefits to part-time and less-skilled workers, who often have the fewest resources available to mitigate work-family conflicts. For instance, 90% of full-time employees of private firms (of all sizes) received paid vacations, and 87% received holidays in 1999, compared with 43% and 36%, respectively, of part-time workers (U.S. Department of Labor, Bureau of Labor Statistics, 2001). Similarly, among managerial, technical, and professional employees, employers offered 88% paid vacations, 89% paid holidays, and 12% child-care assistance. Among blue-collar service employees, the corresponding figures were 75%, 69%, and 4%.

FAMILY LEAVE POLICIES

As noted, one benefit that has expanded markedly in recent years is unpaid family leave. Where just one third of females and one sixth of males employed full time at medium or large establishments were able to take unpaid family leave in 1990, more than 90% of both sexes could do so in 1997. This is largely the result of the 1993 Family and Medical Leave Act (FMLA).

Key provisions of the FMLA are detailed in Table 21.3. Briefly, the law requires public agencies and sufficiently large private establishments to offer 12 weeks of unpaid leave during a 1-year period to employees caring for newborn or adopted children, relatives with serious medical conditions, or for their own health problems. The entitlement is limited in several ways. Most important, the leave is unpaid, and workers may be required to first use ac-

TABLE 21.3
Key Features of Family and Medical Leave Act (FMLA)

Variable	Description
Effective date	August 5, 1993
Benefit	12 weeks of unpaid leave in 12-month period. Health insurance continued and employee may be required to use accrued sick leave or vacation.
Uses	Care of newborn or adopted children, relatives with serious medical conditions, own health problems.
Coverage	Private establishments employing 50 or more persons within 75 miles of worksite during at least 20 weeks of current or previous year. All public agencies covered.
Eligibility	Worked for covered employer for at least 1,250 hours in previous 12 months.
Job security	Reinstatement into original or equivalent job guaranteed, except for key employees (salaried and among the highest paid 10% of employees within 75 miles of worksite).

Source. U.S. Department of Labor, Employment Standards Administration (2003).

crued sick leave or vacation time. However, health insurance continues during leave. Small employers (those with fewer than 50 employees in a 75-mile radius) are exempt, and, under specified conditions, firms are not required to offer job reinstatement (at the end of the leave) to certain key employees.

The exemption of small firms, exclusion of key employees, and work history requirements limit the scope of FMLA coverage. In earlier work (Ruhm, 1997), I estimated that approximately one half of all workers are covered by the law. Although this legislation is often viewed as providing parental leave to care for newborns, the FMLA is primarily used for other purposes. For instance, in 1995, just 14.3% of employees taking FMLA leave did so to care for a newborn or newly adopted child; in 2000, 17.9% of leaves were for this purpose (Waldfogel, 2001). By far the most common reason for taking leave is for one's own health problem, accounting for 61.4% of FMLA absences in 1995 and 47.2% in 2000. As I discussed in detail in a prior study (Ruhm, 1997), one reason for this is that many women eligible for maternity leave under the FMLA already had the rights to job absences under the Pregnancy Discrimination Act (PDA) of 1978, temporary disability insurance programs in some states (that extend beyond the PDA), and state leave laws covering private and public employees.

The situation in the United States contrasts sharply with that in most other nations. In 1999, more than 125 countries, including virtually all industrialized nations, provided some form of paid job-protected maternity leave, most entitling women to at least 2 or 3 months of paid leave during the period surrounding childbirth (Kamerman, 2000). To illustrate, Table 21.4 details the paid leave entitlements, rate of pay, source of funds, and conditions for

TABLE 21.4
Paid Parental Leave in 2002, Various Countries

Country	Leave Entitlement	Rate of Pay	Source of Funds	Qualification Conditions
Austria	16 weeks	100% with maximum	Payroll taxes, government	In covered employment
Belgium	15 weeks	82% in first month, 75% thereafter with maximum	Payroll taxes, government	Insured 6 months before leave
Denmark	30 weeks	100% with maximum	Employers, government	74 hours of employment in preceding 8 weeks
Finland	53 weeks	70% with minimum; lower rate at high incomes	Payroll taxes, government	Residence in country
France	16 weeks	100% with maximum	Payroll and dedicated taxes	200 hours of paid employment in 3 months before pregnancy
Germany	14 weeks	100% with minimum and maximum	Payroll taxes, government	Residence in country
Greece	17 weeks	50% with minimum + 10% for each dependent	Payroll taxes, government	200 days of contributions during last 2 years
Ireland	18 weeks	70% with maximum	Payroll taxes, government	39 weeks of contributions in previous year or 52 weeks in prior 2 years.
Italy	48 weeks	80% first 5 months, 30% next 6 months	Employers, government	Employed and insured at start of pregnancy
Netherlands	12 weeks	100% with maximum	Payroll taxes, government	Employed or unemployed
Norway	42 weeks	100% with maximum	Payroll taxes, government	Employed in 6 of last 10 months
Portugal	30 weeks	100% with minimum	Payroll taxes, government	Employed with 6 months of insurance contributions
Sweden	76 weeks	80%, 63 weeks; flat rate, 13 weeks	Payroll taxes	Insured 240 days before childbirth
Switzerland	16 weeks	Varies with type of insurance fund	Social insurance premiums	9 months of insurance contributions
United Kingdom	18 weeks	90% with maximum	Payroll taxes, employers, government	6 months employment in previous 15 months, with minimum earnings

Sources. Ruhm (2000); Social Security Administration, Office of Research, Evaluation and Statistics (2002).

eligibility in 2002 for 15 European nations. Each provides at least 12 weeks of leave, usually between 50% and 100% of pay, and many provide rights to much longer job absences. Moreover, the leave durations are often extended in cases of complicated pregnancy or childbirth, sick children, or other reasons (such as multiple births). A portion of the leave is sometimes available to fathers, and additional lengthy unpaid job absences with guaranteed re-employment are frequently permitted after the end of the paid leave period.

MATERNAL EMPLOYMENT AND CHILD CARE

Owing, in part, to the limited paid parental leave, most women in the United States quickly return to work after giving birth. For instance, evidence from the 1979 cohort of the National Longitudinal Survey of Youth (NLSY) indicates that one fourth of mothers who had babies during the early 1980s through the mid-1990s were back at work less than 1 week after delivery, although a small fraction of these may have initially been on brief maternity leaves (Ruhm, 2004a). In addition, 65% of women returned to jobs prior to their child's first birthday, 77% before the second birthday, and 84% before the child's third birthday, as did 53%, 70%, and 79%, respectively, of those taking some time off work after delivery.

Because most mothers work in their children's early years, the majority of families use nonparental child care. The cost of this care sometimes presents difficulties and necessitates a variety of adjustments. In recent research, Rosenbaum and I (2003) attempted to measure the *cost burden* of child care, defined as day-care expenses for children ages 5 and under divided by disposable income (earnings plus nonearned income minus taxes). Table 21.5 summarizes some of our estimates. The average preschool-age child lives in a family spending 4.9% of its disposable income on child care. This average, however, conceals enormous diversity. Fully 63% of children live in families with no child-care costs. Conversely, families at the 75th, 90th, and 95th percentiles of the cost burden distribution spend 5.9%, 16.3%, and 25.3% of disposable income on child care, respectively.

The concentration of child-care costs is remarkable. Families in the top decile of the cost burden distribution average $624 per month for child care versus only $80 per month for the other 90% of families, yet the group in the top decile of the cost burden distribution has monthly disposable incomes averaging only $2,268, which is less than the $3,150 mean monthly income of the other 90%. One reason is that working single parents account for 40% of the highest cost burden group. However, zero costs need not imply an absence of nonparental child care given that 23% of young children are in families that use only free sources of care. These households are disproportionately disadvantaged, as measured by the predicted earnings of the primary caregiver based on characteristics such as education, age of the parent, and race or ethnicity.

Table 21.6 provides information on the sources and costs of child care. Children under age 6 reside in families in which individuals other than parents or siblings provide an average of 25 hours per week of care. Of these children, 60% are in families that use an external source of care, two fifths of which is provided free of charge (mostly by grandparents and other relatives). The quantity and cost of care vary substantially across types of families. Rosenbaum and Ruhm (2003) estimated that single-parent families use 50% more child-care hours than married parents (33 vs. 22 hours per week),

TABLE 21.5
Child Care Cost Burden and Its Components

Cost Burden Component	Sample Mean	Cost Burden Percentile			
		0–63	63–75	75–90	90–100
Child-care cost burden	4.9%	0%	3.1%	10.1%	29.7%
	(0.1%)	(0%)	(0.1%)	(0.1%)	(0.5%)
Monthly child-care costs	$135	$0	$145	$365	$624
	($4)	($0)	($6)	($7)	($20)
Weekly child-care hours	25.0	12.5	29.1	47.5	65.1
	(0.5)	(0.5)	(1.1)	(1.0)	(1.8)
Monthly family income	$3,060	$2,708	$4,757	$3,706	$2,268
	($39)	($47)	($156)	($65)	($84)

Note. The child-care cost burden is defined as the cost of nonimmediate family child care for children ages 5 and under divided by total family income after subtracting taxes and adding transfer payments. Standard errors are in parentheses. From Rosenbaum and Ruhm (2003).

TABLE 21.6
Sources and Costs of Care for Preschool-age Children

Mode of Child Care	Hours per Week	Percent Using	Dollars per Hour	Dollars per Month	Percent Receiving Free Care
All nonimmediate family care	25.0	60.2	$1.24	$135	39.0
Relative or grandparent	10.0	29.8	$0.31	$ 13	76.3
Nonrelative	3.4	11.4	$1.77	$ 26	18.0
Family child care	3.4	8.4	$1.77	$ 26	10.1
Center based or preschool	7.9	22.7	$2.01	$ 69	12.4
Head Start	0.3	1.2	$0.13	$ 0	82.3

Note. This table excludes child care provided by parents and siblings. From Rosenbaum and Ruhm (2003).

but also use cheaper sources ($0.80 vs. $1.50 per hour on average) and, as a result, spend 20% less on child care ($114 vs. $143 per week). Families whose primary caregiver is a non-Hispanic White use slightly fewer hours of outside child care than minority families (24 vs. 27 hours per week), but pay more per hour ($1.49 vs. $0.87) and per month ($155 vs. $100) for these services. Highly educated parents use large amounts and expensive sources of child care, resulting in relatively high expenditures.

IMPLICATIONS

Balancing employer and family responsibilities presents particular challenges to parents with young children in the United States, probably more so than in most other industrialized countries. The U.S. labor market can reasonably be characterized as one with long work hours, short vacations, limited availability of parental leave, and restricted state or employer support for child care. For example, Altonji and Oldham (2003) provided evidence linking long annual work hours in the United States to the absence of legislation mandating minimum paid time off work, in sharp contrast to all Western European countries (other than the United Kingdom), where employees are generally entitled to lengthy vacations.

That said, considerable caution is needed before assuming that the more family-friendly institutional arrangements in other nations would be desirable for the United States. There is good reason to believe that many Americans willingly trade off higher labor supply and reduced workplace flexibility for increased incomes. The United States is also characterized by a particularly high reliance on market-based solutions and distrust of government regulations or interventions. In the absence of significant sources of market failure, public goods, or externalities, privately negotiated labor market arrangements lead to economically efficient (although not necessarily equitable) solutions, and regulations impose net costs on society. Thus, one interpretation of the findings is that employers provide and the government mandates few family-friendly benefits because the public prefers it that way.

These points notwithstanding, my suspicion is that the work-family arrangements common in the United States are suboptimal. There is increasing evidence that paid parental leave that is not too lengthy improves the labor market outcomes of women (Baum, 2003a; Ruhm, 1998), enhances child health (Ruhm, 2000), and raises the quality of mother–infant interactions (Clark, Hyde, Essex, & Klein, 1997). Recent research on maternal employment, which contains better controls and more sophisticated strategies for accounting for heterogeneity than earlier studies, finds that labor supply during the child's infancy has a deleterious effect on cognitive development (e.g. Baum, 2003b; Brooks-Gunn, Han, & Waldfogel, 2002; Han, Waldfogel,

& Brooks-Gunn, 2001; Ruhm, 2004a, 2004b). Evidence also suggests that high-quality formal child care in the year prior to kindergarten increases school-readiness (Magnuson, Meyers, Ruhm, & Waldfogel, 2004; Shonkoff & Phillips, 2000). Taken as a group, these results seem at odds with limited rights to parental leave, greater market employment by parents with young children, and the high cost (and frequently poor quality) of formal child-care arrangements.

Moreover, voluntarily negotiated private arrangements may fail to yield efficient or desirable solutions for several reasons. Adverse selection under asymmetric information provides a potential source of market failure. For example, companies that voluntarily offer extensive paid parental leave may attract a disproportionate number of employees likely to use the costly benefit. If these expenses are financed by lower earnings, individuals less likely to use leave will avoid such firms because they do not wish to have their wages reduced to reflect the average rates of taking leave. This is likely to occur even if they would have been willing to accept the (smaller) earnings decreases required to finance their own leaves, had they not been pooled with the persons with the higher expected rates of taking leave. This is analogous to Rothschild and Stiglitz's (1976) argument for market failure in insurance markets. Aghion and Hermalin (1990) suggested that, in some situations, socially optimal parental leave might not be voluntarily provided to any workers. This might occur because low-risk individuals signal their status to employers by agreeing to contracts providing for little or no leave. High-risk workers sometimes do better mimicking their counterparts by taking positions without leave than by revealing their propensity for absenteeism.

Privately negotiated arrangements might also fail to provide socially desirable outcomes if parents lack information on the results of their decisions. For instance, they may be insufficiently informed about the quality of alternative child-care options or the consequences of different choices. Similarly, if parents' liquidity is constrained and capital markets are imperfect, they may be unable to finance desired high-quality, but costly, child care. Another reason families might underinvest in children is if some of the benefits represent public goods. For instance, high-quality child care could increase school-readiness, which in turn could lead to lower crime rates during adolescence. Certain types of medical care may similarly reduce health risks to other children (e.g., by decreasing communicable diseases). However, many of these benefits will not be directly observed by the parents (or employers) paying the additional costs, reducing incentives to undertake the expenditures.

The inefficiency of privately negotiated labor contracts under asymmetric information has been demonstrated across a variety of contexts, raising the possibility of benefits from well-designed public policies. For example, if employers are unable to sufficiently reduce wages to offset the costs of leave, profits will fall and economic viability may be threatened. A government mandate eliminates the incentive for this type of sorting behavior and has the potential to raise welfare. That said, it is often not obvious how (if at all) these sources of market failure can best be remedied.

Government policies that have desirable aims may nevertheless make it more difficult for parents with young children to balance their joint work-family responsibilities. Most obviously, reforms to the welfare system have placed pressure on recipients (particularly single mothers) to quickly enter or resume employment, possibly increasing time constraints and the difficulties in caring for children. More generous tax treatment under the EITC has similarly encouraged more single mothers with young children to enter the workforce. Even with greater returns to work, some families may nevertheless incur stress. The proposed elimination of the *marriage penalty* could also create incentives for married individuals (especially mothers) with young children to increase employment, again highlighting issues of work-family balance.

The government policies just mentioned all operate to raise employment, earnings, and presumably national income. However, they generally have not been accompanied by aggressive efforts to balance the increasing job responsibilities with the needs of families. As discussed, paid parental leave is a rarity in the United States, child-care options are limited, and vacations are short. Changing these or related family-friendly policies through government programs, regulations, or direct employer actions is likely to be expensive and controversial. Discussion of what courses of action might best assist families with young children is worthy of future debate.

ACKNOWLEDGMENTS

Research assistance from Stuart Spencer and financial support from the National Institute of Child Health and Human Development (HD38521-01A1), the National Science Foundation (SES-9876511), and the Russell Sage Foundation Program on the Social Dimensions of Inequality is gratefully acknowledged. All opinions, findings, conclusions, and recommendations are those of the author and do not necessarily reflect the views of the funding agencies.

REFERENCES

Aghion, P., & Hermalin B. (1990). Legal restrictions on private contracts can enhance efficiency. *Journal of Law, Economics, and Organization, 6,* 381–409.

Altonji, J. G., & Oldham, J. (2003). Vacation laws and work hours. *Federal Reserve Bank of Chicago: Economic Perspectives, 27,* 19–29.

Baum, C. L. (2003a). The effects of maternity leave legislation on mothers' labor supply after childbirth. *Southern Economic Journal, 69,* 772–799.

Baum, C. L. (2003b). Does early maternal employment harm child development? An analysis of the benefits of leave taking. *Journal of Labor Economics*, *21*, 409–448.

Brooks-Gunn, J., Han, W., & Waldfogel J. (2002). Maternal employment and child cognitive outcomes in the first three years of life: The NICHD Study of Early Child Care. *Child Development*, *73*, 1052–1072.

Bruer, J. T. (1999). *The myth of the first three years: A new understanding of early brain development and lifelong learning.* New York: The Free Press.

Carnegie Task Force on Meeting the Needs of Young Children. (1994). *Starting points: Meeting the needs of our youngest children.* New York: Carnegie Corporation of New York.

Clark, R., Hyde, J. S., Essex, M. J., & Klein, M. H. (1997). Length of maternity leave and quality of mother-infant interactions. *Child Development*, *68*, 364–383.

Council of Economic Advisers. (1997). *The first three years: Investments that pay.* Washington, DC: Author.

Han, W., Waldfogel, J., & Brooks-Gunn, J. (2001). The effects of early maternal employment on later cognitive and behavioral outcomes. *Journal of Family and Marriage*, *63*, 336–354.

Heckman, J. J. (2000). Policies to foster human capital. *Research in Economics*, *54*, 3–56.

Kamerman, S. B. (2000). Parental leave policies: An essential ingredient in early childhood education and care policies. *Social Policy Report*, *14*, 3–15.

Magnuson, K. A., Meyers, M., Ruhm, C. J., & Waldfogel, J. (2004). Inequality in pre-school education and school readiness. *American Education Research Journal*, *41*, 115–137.

Rosenbaum, D. T., & Ruhm, C. J. (2003). *Caring for young children: Inequality in the cost burden of child care.* Mimeo, University of North Carolina at Greensboro.

Rothschild, M., & Stiglitz, J. (1976). Equilibrium in competitive insurance markets: An essay on the economics of imperfect information. *Quarterly Journal of Economics*, *90*, 629–649.

Ruhm, C. J. (1997). Policy watch: The Family and Medical Leave Act. *Journal of Economic Perspectives*, *11*, 175–186.

Ruhm, C. J. (1998). The economic consequences of parental leave mandates: Lessons from Europe. *Quarterly Journal of Economics*, *113*, 285–317.

Ruhm, C. J. (2000). Parental leave and child health. *Journal of Health Economics*, *19*, 931–960.

Ruhm, C. J. (2004a). Parental employment and child cognitive development. *Journal of Human Resources*, *39*, 155–192.

Ruhm, C. J. (2004b). *Parental employment and adolescent development.* National Bureau of Economic Research Working Paper No. 10691, August.

Shonkoff, J. P., & Phillips, D. A. (Eds.). (2000). *From neurons to neighborhoods: The science of early childhood development.* Washington, DC: National Academy Press.

Shore, R. (1997). *Rethinking the brain: New insights into early development.* New York: Families and Work Institute.

Social Security Administration, Office of Research, Evaluation and Statistics. (2002). *Social security programs throughout the world: Europe, 2002.* Washington, DC: U.S. Government Printing Office. Accessed on June 11, 2003. Available: http://www.ssa.gov/policy/docs/progdesc/ssptw/2002/europe/ssptw02euro.pdf.

U.S. Bureau of the Census. (Various Years). *Statistical Abstract of the United States: 1981–1988, 1990, 1991, 1993, 1995, 1998, 1999* (101–108, 110, 111, 113, 115, 118, 119th eds.). Washington, DC: U.S. Government Printing Office.

U.S. Department of Labor, Bureau of Labor Statistics. (1999). *Employee Benefits in Medium and Large Private Establishments, 1997, Bulletin 2517* (Table 3). Accessed on June 6, 2003. Available: http://www.bls.gov/ncs/ebs/sp/ebbl0017.pdf.

U.S. Department of Labor, Bureau of Labor Statistics. (2001). *National Compensation Survey: Employee benefits in private industry in the United States, 1999 supplementary tables.* Accessed on June 5, 2003. Available: http://www.bls.gov/ncs/ebs/sp/ebtb0001.pdf.

U.S. Department of Labor, Bureau of Labor Statistics. (2003). *Employee Benefits in Private Industry in the United States, Supplementary Tables, Bulletin 2555* (Table 1). Accessed on June 5, 2003. Available: http://www.bls.gov/ncs/ebs/sp/ebtb0002.pdf.

U.S. Department of Labor, Employment Standards Administration. (2003). Fact Sheet No. 28: *The Family and Medical Leave Act of 1993.* Accessed on June 10, 2003. Available: http://www.dol.gov/esa/regs/compliance/whd/whdfs28.htm.

Waldfogel, J. (2001). Family and Medical Leave Act: Evidence from the 2000 Surveys. *Monthly Labor Review, 124,* 17–23.

PART V

Gender and Empoyment, Caregiving and Health

22

Gender Perspectives on Work and Personal Life Research

Joyce K. Fletcher

Simmons School of Management

One of the bedrock assumptions of Western society is that there is a division of labor between the masculine sphere of paid work and the feminine sphere of domestic life (Acker, 1990; Bellah, Madsen, Sullivan, Swidler, & Tipton, 1985; Bradley, 1989; Parsons & Bales, 1955). In this chapter, I offer a theoretical perspective that uncovers some of the less visible assumptions underlying this historic separation of spheres and explore why integrating the two spheres would be beneficial not only for families and communities, but also for the quality and effectiveness of the workplace.

GENDERED DIVISION OF LABOR: THE TWO SPHERES OF WORK AND HOME

The belief that men and women have distinct roles to play in society has a long history.[1] Agrarian and preindustrial societies used the differences between men's and women's musculature and reproductive organs to explain and justify this division of labor. Social norms supporting separate spheres

---

[1] For a more comprehensive analysis of the underpinnings of the separate spheres phenomenon, see Rapoport, Bailyn, Fletcher, and Pruitt in chapter 2 of *Beyond Work Family Balance: Advancing Gender Equity and Workplace Performance*, New York: Jossey Bass, 2002.

became more clearly defined and more prescriptive in the context of industrialization in the Western world. The life situation of White, middle- and upper class women and men was idealized and, at least in theory, generalized to the entire population, resulting in a division of labor linked directly to definitions of *masculinity* and *femininity*. In today's industrialized society, we tend to conceptualize the world as being divided into two spheres of activity—a public arena dedicated to producing things, and a private one dedicated to producing people.

Although the separation of these spheres may not reflect the actual life situations of many, the belief in separate spheres as an ideal is quite powerful and exerts significant, albeit often unacknowledged, influence in our lives. If we reveal the underpinnings of this phenomenon, we can uncover a useful perspective to inform future research in the field of work and personal life as well as proposed solutions to the issue of mismatch between the two spheres. I focus on three such characteristics relevant to this discussion of mismatch. The first is that the two spheres are perceived as a dichotomy, the second is that they are sex-linked and gendered, and the third is that there is an underlying body of knowledge or a "logic of effectiveness" about what it means to do good work in each sphere.

Dichotomy

The first characteristic relevant to a discussion of mismatch is that the spheres are constructed as a dichotomy. As with all dichotomies (such as "good" and "evil," "culture" and "nature," or "reason" and "emotion"), the spheres are socially constructed as separate and discrete, are assumed to be adversarial, and are valued unequally (Calás & Smircich, 1991; Diamond & Quinby, 1988; Flax, 1990). In this case, these features interact and reinforce one another to produce several corollary assumptions about the primary actor in each sphere. For example, the separation and adversarial relationship of the spheres leads to a view of an ideal worker (Acker, 1990; Bailyn, 1993; Kanter, 1977) as someone who can afford the luxury of being primarily involved in only one sphere. Thus, ideal workers in the occupational arena are assumed to have someone in the domestic sphere who handles family and community responsibilities. Likewise, in the domestic realm, the ideal caregiver—the one who would achieve the best outcomes—is one who can focus exclusively on that realm without other responsibilities in the paid-work sphere. Work practices in each sphere are designed with this ideal worker in mind; the best business practices and the best parenting practices, for example, reflect this assumption that the "actors" will have unlimited time and energy to devote to their activity.

That the spheres are assumed to be at odds with each other means that the skills and attributes associated with each are set in opposition, and they are deemed inappropriate when practiced in the opposing sphere. Skills valued in the domestic realm not only are devalued in the occupational realm, but conventional wisdom holds that having skills in one sphere can disqualify an individual from being good in the other. For example, one might assume that a caring, sensitive person might have a difficult time succeeding in the workplace. Likewise, it would be assumed that a hard-driving, bottom-line thinker might not be the best at parenting. It is assumed that the spheres are fundamentally different, and that what it takes to be good in one is different, or even opposite, from what it takes to be good in the other.

The last feature of dichotomies, that the entities are unequally valued in the dominant discourse, places the issue in a larger societal context of power and privilege and underscores the fact that, although the phenomenon of separate spheres might seem like a power-neutral concept, it is not. As anthropologists, sociologists, economists, and feminists have noted, in virtually every society, caretaking in the sphere of family and community is consistently devalued in relation to paid work in the public arena. Although the phenomenon of separate spheres is often described as a complementary dynamic, where two separate domains function together for the good of society, it is far more complex than that in its effect. Dichotomies are not power neutral. Through common usage in everyday discourse, the value assigned to each side becomes so embedded in society's understanding of what is "natural" or "right" that the dichotomy itself is an "unobtrusive exercise of power" (Lukes, 1974) that maintains economic and political systems of oppression (Clegg, 1989; Diamond & Quinby, 1988; Flax, 1990). Thus, from a poststructuralist point of view, the devaluing of caretaking is not simply a "natural" phenomenon, but serves a larger purpose: It preserves inequitable systems, structures, and relationships of power and privilege in society.

Sex-Linked and Gendered

The second characteristic of dual spheres relevant to this discussion of work and personal life is that the spheres are constructed as both sex-linked and gendered. Men and idealized[2] masculinity are associated with the public arena of the workplace where things are produced, and women and idealized femininity are associated with the private arena of family and community where people are nurtured (Acker, 1990; Kanter, 1977). In our mind's eye, we tend to associate men with producing things and women with "growing" people. Again, the fact that this is not true for much of the population does not diminish, and may even enhance, the power of this assumption.

---

[2] By "idealized" I mean to convey that these notions of masculinity and femininity are based on attributes and life situations that reflect White, Western, heterosexual notions of ideal men and women of the middle and upper classes.

In addition to being sex-linked, the spheres are gendered. It is not only the biologically determined categories of "man" and "woman" that are aligned with each sphere, but also a set of attributes and skills socially constructed to align with our very definitions of masculinity and femininity. Doing good work in the occupational realm is associated with traditionally masculine characteristics. Both men and women can display these characteristics, but the characteristics themselves, such as linear thinking, rationality, assertiveness, and competitiveness, are typically thought of as masculine. Doing good work in the domestic sphere is associated with traditionally feminine characteristics such as empathy, listening, and sensitivity.

This association of each sphere with appropriate gender roles works in reverse as well, serving to define notions of masculinity and femininity as well as reflect them. Doing work in the occupational arena is conflated with "doing masculinity" (Martin, 1996) while doing work in the domestic arena is conflated with "doing femininity" (Fletcher, 1999b). This association is so pervasive that were it not for the gendered division of labor, it would be difficult to imagine what other criteria we might use to define, separate, and distinguish masculinity from femininity.

Logic of Effectiveness

The third characteristic of the spheres, related to the first two but worthy of its own discussion because of its importance in understanding workplace culture, is that there is an implicit body of knowledge, or "logic of effectiveness," underlying each sphere (Calás & Smircich, 1991; Calás, Jacobson, Jacques, & Smircich, 1991; Fletcher, 1994). Each sphere has a separate and distinct set of rules and principles that define what it means to do good work in that sphere and, as such, what leads to successful, effective outcomes. Just as with the spheres themselves, these logics of effectiveness are constructed in the dominant discourse as dichotomies. Not only are they assumed to be separate and distinct, but they are also at odds, such that rules deemed appropriate in one sphere will be deemed inappropriate in the other (e.g., encouraging competition or pay for service among family members). As with all dichotomies, this construction serves to maintain and re-create the separation. The result is that these two, distinct bodies of knowledge, summarized in Table 22.1, rarely inform each other in meaningful ways.

IMPLICATIONS OF A
SEPARATE-SPHERES PERSPECTIVE

This discussion of separate spheres provides an interesting terrain on which to explore work and personal life. It helps makes visible some aspects of the landscape that may not have received much attention in the past but are

TABLE 22.1
Separate Spheres Perspectives

Occupational Sphere	Domestic Sphere
Work is something you have to do.	Work is something you want to do.
Money is the motivator.	Love is the motivator.
Work is paid.	Work is unpaid.
Rationality reified.	Emotionality reified.
Abstract.	Concrete, situated.
Time span defined.	Time span ambiguous.
Output: marketable goods, services, money.	Output: people, social relations, creation of community.
Context of differential reward leads to focus on individuality.	Context of creating a collective leads to focus on community.
Skills needed are taught; work is considered complex.	Skills needed are thought to be innate; work is considered not complex.

Note. Adapted from Fletcher, 1999b.

important to note as the field moves forward into the next generation of research and action.

The first thing this framework makes visible is the existence of an "ideal worker" in each sphere, not just in the occupational realm. This may seem obvious, but the work and family literature has rarely taken it into account in its vision of the future. Indeed, the fact that there are two images of excellence that must be challenged in order to change the entire system suggests that the notion of "balance" itself might have outlived its usefulness. Balance implies that the two spheres will remain separate and that the goal of research and action is to help individuals balance their involvement in each as a way to reduce negative "spillover" between the two (Barnett, 1994; Edwards & Rothbard, 2000; Kirchmeyer, 1993). Rather than balance, my coauthors and I, in our book *Beyond Balance: Advancing Gender Equity and Workplace Performance* (Rapoport, Bailyn, Fletcher, & Pruitt, 2002), suggest that a better goal is integration.

Renaming the research and policy goals as *integration* rather than *balance* is not a trivial change. It reframes the task at hand and defines it as a more systemic issue. The task from an integration perspective is to relax the separation of the two spheres in a way that allows everyone (men and women) to be involved in both, and allows the images of excellence underlying each sphere to be informed—and improved—by the other. Two implications of this observation are worth noting. First, it sheds light on why the recent move in the field to focus research and action on work culture—on the subtle, system-level factors that make integration difficult—is so important. Only by exploring those work practices that intentionally or unintentionally maintain or strengthen the separation of the two spheres will the occupational sphere itself be changed. A single-minded focus on policies, programs, and benefits that promote balance, as important as these are, will only perpetuate the assumption that the spheres are separate and that actors in the occupational realm who have personal lives are an aberrant subset who require special accommodation.

The second implication of an integration approach is that looking at work cultures is not enough. To change both spheres we also must examine work practices, norms, and beliefs about caretaking. DeGroot and colleagues at the Third Path (www.thirdpath.org) are making important headway in this area. They suggest that ideal images of parenting, which assign one parent to family and the other to career, should be challenged at a fundamental level. They offer a "third path" that is neither primarily a family nor career life focus, but rather an integration of both. They propose a model of parenting called "shared care" and offer couples help in implementing this model in both the family and work realms. Rewriting child-rearing manuals; bringing together marriage counselors, family therapists, and career counselors to suggest techniques that would help people integrate their lives rather than segment them; bringing couples together to re-envision their life together; and finally, thinking about how to redesign their work are important steps in moving beyond balance toward integration. By re-envisioning family, the Third Path approach creates "pull" in the workplace for culture change and identifies specific work practices on which to focus.

Examining the assumptions that underlie separate spheres also helps to highlight the fact that the monolithic view of men and women (their skills, attributes, and life situations) is based on the idealization of White, Western, heterosexual, middle- and upper-class values, gender roles, and social identity. It does not—and perhaps never did—reflect the experience of much of the population. Whereas recent research in the area of work and personal life often addresses this concern through the inclusion of nonprofessionals, other aspects of social identity have received less attention. The concept of "simultaneity" (Foldy, 2002; Holvino, 2001; Proudford, 2003) is one promising way to address this gap. Simultaneity refers to the fact that the multiple threads that make up our social identity—race, sex, class, sexual identity, and so forth—interact and are experienced simultaneously as we respond to and interact with the material and social conditions around us. Rather than proposing an overarching framework to address the intersection of race, gender, and class, the construct of simultaneity offers a way of working with the issue in its complexity, recognizing that the goal of organizational change is to relax interacting systems of all oppression, and not just the oppression of one nondominant group. Operationalizing this construct, for example, would require the inclusion of what Holvino (2001) calls "hidden stories" at the intersection of multiple social identities rather than the more common practice of separating and universalizing groups based on one characteristic such as race or gender. For example it is often noted that establishing an on-site child care center advances the interests of professional women but does so at the expense of working-class women who provide the care at wages so low they cannot afford to use the center themselves (Fletcher, 1999a). Working class women of color, however, who are subject to racism as well as class constraints, might have a different perspective and favor child-care jobs as an alternative to the dangerous or demeaning jobs they are often forced to take. The point is that an approach which allows the effects of social identity characteristics to be voiced leads to a richer dialogue and a more comprehensive search for solutions. Although a deeper discussion of simultaneity is beyond the scope of this chapter,[3] it is one example of how research in the arena of work and personal life can benefit from new ways of conceptualzing the material effects of social identity.

A final contribution of uncovering the assumptions that underlie separate spheres is a new business rationale for work–personal life integration. As noted, the driving logic of effectiveness in each sphere is assumed to be distinct and at odds with principles of the other sphere. This means that each body of knowledge is in some sense closed to wisdom from the other because association with that other sphere taints it as inappropriate.

There is a growing recognition that this separation is problematic for work organizations. In today's knowledge-intensive world, where the importance of teamwork and collaboration is increasing, wisdom about people is critical to business success. Indeed, many of the strategic initiatives in large companies, from a focus on teamwork and collaboration, to Six Sigma quality initiatives, to kaizen process improvements, rely on relational skills, competencies, and models of effectiveness that are more aligned with feminine than masculine stereotypes. The proliferation of books and articles about relational and emotional intelligence and leadership in the workplace (Fletcher & Kaeufer, 2003; Gardner, 1990; Goleman, 1998) indicates that feminine, historically undervalued skills in "growing people" are what organizations need to compete in today's knowledge-intensive world. This suggests that in addition to a workforce–workplace mismatch between "ideal" and "real" workers, there is another, more powerful mismatch at play. Old, industrial-era definitions of effectiveness do not match the requirements of today's knowledge-intensive workplace (Jacques, 1996). In other words, integration of the two spheres not only can foster gender equity, it is essential to effectiveness in the new economy.

---

[3] For one perpective on the guidelines, principles, and strategies for working with the concept of simultaneity in organizational change efforts, see E. Holvino (2000), *Complicating gender: The simultaneity of race, gender and class in organization change(ing)* (Working Paper No. 14). Boston, MA: Simmons School of Management, Center for Gender in Organizations.

A Dual Agenda: Linking Equity and Effectiveness

The requirements of knowledge work set the stage for what my colleagues and I call "dual agenda" outcomes, or the linking of equity and effectiveness (Rapoport et al., 2002). Conflating idealized masculinity with doing work creates equity issues for women. Not only might women find it more difficult to pretend they do not have a personal life or family responsibilities, but they might find it more difficult to display stereotypically masculine characteristics without negative consequences.[4] However, conflating idealized masculine attributes and life situations with implicit definitions of good work is also problematic for the work itself. Work practices based on these norms are out of line with what is needed in the new economy. Thus, equity *and* effectiveness can be achieved through integration.

Unpacking the dichotomy of separate spheres not only offers a new way of making the business case for integration, it also offers guidelines on where to look and how to identify the specific work practices that can serve as leverage points for achieving what is increasingly recognized as the preeminent challenge in the field: changing work culture. In other words, it helps us see how dysfunctional work practices are rooted in separate-spheres thinking, where to look for them, and how to understand the forces that are holding them in place.

Methods to ferret out the work practices that would be good leverage points for change is the subject of the book *Beyond Work-Family Balance* (Rapoport et al., 2002) and in it the authors outline a full range of problematic work practices and their experience in helping organizations effect change. Here, I include a few examples to illustrate the power of this lens.

Use and Politics of Time.   The separate spheres belief that the best workers are those who are willing and able to devote as much time to work as it demands has led to work practices based on an assumption that "time is cheap." This often leads to crisis-driven work cultures, where people routinely put in excessive overtime, or have their days interrupted by countless emergency meetings and consultations. Lack of planning and coordination is so rampant in some cases that a 24-hour rule prevails: if it's not due in the next 24 hours, it isn't worth talking about because no one will be able to focus on it. Work norms that support these crisis-driven cultures can appear to be based on the needs of the work alone (responding to client demands for last-minute changes or breakdowns that demand immediate work-arounds in software

---

[4]As an aside, it is interesting to note that of course the opposite equity issue would be true of men in the domestic sphere. Although this is not something we focus on much, it is the flip side of the work–personal life issue at work and something that would be interesting to explore further.

code). However, on closer inspection, often these practices are held in place by another dynamic. They give people an opportunity to demonstrate that time is no obstacle to their commitment to work. Work comes first, before all else. Thus, there is little incentive to change crisis-driven work cultures when, in a sense, one needs these crises to demonstrate commitment.

The Use and Politics of Time

A marketing department in a high tech company on the West Coast is a classic example of this time equals commitment work practice. The department often worked in crisis mode and rarely planned ahead. As a result, the group responsible for client presentations was constantly pulling all-nighters. When the other workers would arrive the next morning, people would applaud the extraordinary effort of those who had worked all night. The managers would give them kudos, holding them up as examples of dedication and "doing whatever it takes." Of course, there were costs to their work and personal lives in having to pull all-nighters. But ironically, it was the fact that it *was* a cost to their personal lives that showed they were truly committed. Hidden, however, was the cost to the work. Those who pulled all-nighters had enough energy to make it to the client presentation the next day and were even able to go out for lunch to celebrate. Afterward, however, they went home to rest and often failed to show up the next day, forcing others on the team to put their own projects on hold. The effectiveness implications and costs of this work norm, although obvious in retrospect, were rarely noted or discussed, and the practice itself was not questioned. At some level, it seemed like this was just the nature of the job and the price one had to pay for being in this line of work. There was little incentive within the system itself to change. Pressures of deadlines, the attention one got when meeting the expectation, and the desire not to be seen as someone who was unwilling to "do whatever it takes" all made it highly unlikely that anyone would voice concern about the norm or suggest that it was ineffective.

—Reprinted with permission from L. Bailyn and J. K. Fletcher,
Work Redesign: Theory, Practice and Possibility, working paper,
MIT Workplace Project, Cambridge, MA, 2002

Work practices that contribute to the mismatch are not limited to the use of time. The politics of time also matter, such as when and where decisions are made and important information is shared. Norms such as 7 A.M. "voluntary" meetings to discuss problems and work flow before the start of the workday, or the practice of making decisions during informal, after-hours discussions between decision makers and those who stay late, reveal that certain hours of the day are more valuable than others in terms of influence and effect. Early morning and late evening have the most political capital, not only in terms of impression management but also in terms of personal power, influence, and effectiveness. That these practices have negative consequences for the work itself (decisions made without key input often result in costly errors or have ripple effects that need to be reversed) is often invisible.

A separate-spheres framework allows researchers to highlight not only the unintended costs of these work practices on the work itself, but also the underlying dynamic that keeps the norm so firmly in place. It allows research, for example, to reveal the insidious underbelly of "face time" as an exercise of power that has negative consequences for workers who have outside commitments, as well as for the work itself.

Implicit Definition of "Real" Work. Many invisible, dysfunctional, or simply out-of-date work practices reside in the implicit definition of "real" work as operationalized in an organization's work culture. The separate-spheres perspective can uncover work practices that are, or could be, valuable in the occupational sphere but that are undervalued or devalued because of their unconscious association with the domestic sphere. As researchers in the field of comparable worth note (England, 1992; Steinberg, 1999), many assumptions about competence and "real" work overemphasize technical capability and individual achievement, and de-emphasize other, equally important skills, such as facilitating collective achievement, team building, or the ability to relate to peers and customers. Although most managers would say that both sets of skills are important, in practice they typically give technical skills precedence. That people with highly technical skills may be deficient in relational skills is often overlooked. Indeed, the lack of relational skills, especially in men, is rarely seen as a problem. Instead, it is often assumed that these skills will somehow be gained on the job.

Definition of "Real" Work

In a financial services department, we noticed a difference between the attributes and abilities it took to get an analyst's job and those it took to do the job well. In responding to questions about what it took to get ahead and be promoted into their high-level positions, analysts talked about quantitative and analytical skills as the basic requirements, with actuarial backgrounds being the most highly valued. Doing the job well, however, did not depend on that set of skills alone. The ability to do good work also required acquiring good, timely, accurate data from other departments. People who really contributed to the overall effort were those who also had relational skills, such as the ability to understand, empathize, and offer help. As one female analyst noted, "What you need to do is call down and instead of hassling people, ask them 'What can I do to help you get the numbers?' and then actually *doing* it. I've done things like get people lunch or even gone down there and crunched some numbers for them while they worked on pulling it all together." The willingness to do some lower status work such as getting someone lunch or crunching numbers, the ability to understand a situation and the pressures someone else is under and to create an appropriate response, were not skills viewed as crucial to the job. More often, people who interacted with others in this way were regarded as especially "nice" or "thoughtful" rather than especially competent. Viewed as personal attributes rather than skills, these abilities were not mentioned in the job description and people who possessed them, and especially women, rarely thought of themselves as particularly qualified for the job and rarely considered emphasizing these relational skills during an interview. As a result, some people who might have applied did not, and those who were hired often lacked the relational skills to be effective, despite their technical ability.

Another workplace phenomenon that the separate-spheres perspective can help highlight is why some work practices, even when widely acknowledged as ineffective, are so resilient. For example, recent emphasis on listening and responding to customer needs notwithstanding, many companies find that sales agents continue to act as if customers are barriers to overcome or obstacles between them and the sale. The separate-spheres perspective shows that one reason an aggressive sales style might be so resilient is that it is linked to images of (idealized) masculine identity. Because of the sex- and gender-linked nature of separate spheres, work becomes an opportunity to enact masculinity, a task that has different consequences for men and for women, but that is traditionally required of each. Thus, requiring change of people who have been trained to eschew the softer, relational skills (such as listening and inquiry) in favor of more stereotypically masculine skills (such as persuasion and advocacy), will be fraught with problems. Understanding how relational skills and attributes are unconsciously linked to femininity, powerlessness, and a devalued activity associated with the domestic sphere (Fletcher, 2003) helps us see why it is risky to practice the "new" behavior, even, or maybe especially, for women, even when it is outwardly verbalized as a value.

SUMMING UP

Revealing the assumptions embedded in the mythical construct of separate spheres offers a powerful theoretical perspective from which to effect workplace change. It highlights the need to broaden the field to engage in research and action that would foster increased integration between the spheres rather than a continued separation. More specifically, it puts the focus on systemic issues, such as changing work practices and work cultures, rather than on individual-level issues, such as helping people and workplaces to cope with things the way they are. More specifically, it highlights the need to diminish the separation between these two spheres of life in ways that will *change both,* rather than merely reallocating, or "balancing," time between them as they currently exist.

Second, unpacking the origins of the idealized images within each sphere and each sphere's assumptions about the sex, race, class, ethnicity, and sexual orientation of the "ideal worker" highlights the fact that social identity matters. Once we begin to take social identity seriously (e.g., listening for its effect), it becomes obvious that solutions and actions are going to be experienced by real people who live at the intersection of multiple social identities (i.e., race *and* class *and* sex, etc.). In other words, the power this construct of separate spheres exerts on the material circumstances of people's lives may be ubiquitous, but it is not uniform even within social identity groups. In thinking about solutions, policies, and practices that would enhance equity between those who have family and community responsibilities and those who can "hide" or otherwise absolve their responsibilities in these areas, it is important to take into account the fact that taking action to foster "integration" will be experienced differently and have a different effect on the material circumstances of people depending on how different aspects of their social identities interact. This highlights the importance of taking the simultaneity of social identity into account not only in understanding the issues, but in devising solutions and remedies.

Finally, understanding the underpinnings of sex- and gender-linked images of "good" work, competence, and commitment serves as a guide in looking for those particular work practices that might not, on the surface, appear to be linked to work and personal life integration but that, if addressed, can begin to change a work culture in ways that both integrate the separate spheres and allow a multiplicity of work practices and diverse perspectives.

REFERENCES

Acker, J. (1990). Hierarchies, jobs, bodies: A theory of gendered organizations. *Gender & Society, 4,* 139–158.

Bailyn, L. (1993). *Breaking the mold: Women, men and time in the new corporate world.* New York: The Free Press.

Bailyn, L., & Fletcher, J. K. (2002). *Work redesign: Theory, practice and possibility.* Working Paper, MIT Workplace Project, Cambridge, MA.

Barnett, R. (1994). Home to work spillover revisited: A study of full-time employed women in dual earner couples. *Journal of Marriage and the Family, 56,* 647–656.

Bellah, R., Madsen, R., Sullivan, W., Swidler, A., & Tipton, S. (1985). *Habits of the heart.* Berkeley: University of California Press.

Bradley, H. (1989). *Men's work, women's work.* Minneapolis: University of Minnesota Press.

Calás, M. B., & Smircich, L. (1991). Using the "F" Word: Feminist theories and the social consequences of organizational research. In A. J. Mills & P. Tancred (Eds.), *Gendering organizational analysis* (pp. 222–234). London: Sage.

Calás, M., Jacobson, S., Jacques, R., & Smircich, L. (1991). *Is a woman centered theory of man-*

agement dangerous? Paper presented at the meeting of the Academy of Management, Miami, FL.

Clegg, S. (1989). *Frameworks of power.* Newbury Park, CA: Sage.

Diamond, I., & Quinby, L. (1988). *Feminism and Foucault.* Boston: Northeastern University Press.

Edwards, J., & Rothbard, N. (2000). Mechanisms linking work and family: Clarifying the relationship between work and family constructs. *Academy of Management Review, 25*(1), 178–199.

England, P. (1992). *Comparable worth: Theories and evidence.* New York: Aldine de Gruyter.

Flax, J. (1990). *Thinking fragments.* Berkeley: University of California Press.

Fletcher, J. K. (1994). Castrating the female advantage: Feminist standpoint research and management science. *Journal of Management Inquiry, 3*(1), 74–82.

Fletcher, J. K. (1999a). *A radical perspective on power* (CGO Insight No. 5). Boston, MA: Simmons School of Management, Center for Gender in Organizations.

Fletcher, J. K. (1999b). *Disappearing acts: Gender, power and relational practice at work.* Cambridge, MA: MIT Press.

Fletcher, J. K. (2003). *The paradox of post heroic leadership: Gender matters* (CGO Working Paper No. 17). Boston, MA: Simmons School of Management, Center for Gender in Organizations.

Fletcher, J. K., & Kaeufer, K. (2003). Shared leadership: Paradox and possibility. In C. Pearce & J. Conger (Eds.), *Shared leadership* (pp. 21–47). London: Sage.

Foldy, E. (2002). *Be all that you can be.* Unpublished doctoral dissertation, Boston College, Boston, MA.

Gardner, H. (1990). *Leading minds.* New York: Basic Books.

Goleman, D. (1998). *Working with emotional intelligence.* New York: Bantam Books.

Holvino, E. (2001). *Complicating gender: The simultaneity of race, gender and class in organization change(ing)* (Working Paper No. 14). Boston, MA: Simmons School of Management, Center for Gender in Organizations.

Jacques, R. (1996). *Manufacturing the employee: Management knowledge from the 19th to the 21st century.* London: Sage.

Kanter, R. M. (1977). *Men and women of the corporation.* New York: Basic Books.

Kirchmeyer, C. (1993). Nonwork-to-work spillover: A more balanced view of the experiences and coping of professional women and men. *Sex Roles 28,* 531–552.

Lukes, S. (1974). *Power.* London: Macmillan.

Martin, P. Y. (1996). Gendering and evaluating dynamics: Men, masculinities and managements. In D. Collinson & J. Hearn (Eds.), *Men as managers, managers as men* (pp. 186–209). London: Sage.

Parsons, T., & Bales, R. F. (1955). *Family, socialization and interaction process.* New York: The Free Press.

Proudford, K. (2003). *Viewing dyads in triadic terms: Toward a conceptualization of the in/visible third in relationships across difference* (CGO Working Paper No. 16). Boston, MA: Simmons School of Management, Center for Gender in Organizations.

Rapoport, R., Bailyn, L., Fletcher, J., & Pruitt, B. (2002). *Beyond work–family balance.* San Francisco, CA: Jossey Bass.

Steinberg, R. (1999). Emotional labor in the service economy. In R. J. Steinberg & D. M. Figart (Eds.), *Annals of the American Academy of Political and Social Science* (Bol. 561). Thousand Oaks, CA: Sage Publications.

23

Gender, Work, and Family Well-Being in the United States

Pamela J. Smock
The University of Michigan

Mary Noonan
The University of Iowa

Work, family, and gender is a currently popular topic in the social sciences, although its roots go back for quite some time. Demographers, for example, have for decades been interested in the interrelationships between work and family and the conflict between the two for women. The flagship population journal *Demography* has published numerous articles on this topic since its inception in 1966. Early examples include "Mobility, Non-familial Activity, and Fertility" (Tien, 1967), "Family Composition and the Labor Force Activity of American Wives" (Sweet, 1970), and "Women's Work Participation and Fertility in Metropolitan Areas" (Collver, 1968).

Our specific task in this chapter is to review and synthesize social science research on aspects of the intersection of work and family that are relevant to gender (see Perry-Jenkins, Repetti, & Crouter, 2000, for a review of the work-family literature in the 1990s). We emphasize quantitative studies based on nationally representative survey data, although we also interweave insights drawn from qualitative studies and nonrepresentative samples. Gender is clearly one of the driving themes of social science research on work and family. In fact one of the conclusions emerging from our review is that gender is arguably the central characteristic that structures workers' experiences of work and family conflicts.

We first consider the issue that has arguably received the most attention: the domestic division of labor. We discuss housework, other forms of domestic labor, and parenting in turn. We then examine the labor market consequences of the division of domestic labor for men and women. Finally, we discuss the implications of the intersection of work and family for the well-being of men and women.

THE DOMESTIC DIVISION OF LABOR

By domestic labor, we refer to labor (typically unpaid) that is undertaken to maintain the well-being of families and households. Although housework has by far received the most attention in the research, there are other, more subtle types of domestic labor as well. According to our definition, parenting is also a form of domestic labor, but we treat this topic separately in this chapter.

The central theme of housework research is that, despite the substantial rise in women's employment during the past three decades, domestic labor has remained primarily women's work. This large and growing body of research has consistently arrived at three major findings (see Coltrane, 2000; Shelton & John, 1996, for reviews).

First, women do substantially more housework than men, and this is especially true for married men and women. Although estimates vary based on data, sample, and how housework is measured, there is consensus about this basic pattern. For example, South and Spitze (1994), using data from the first wave (1987–1988) of the National Survey of Families and Households (NSFH), reported that married men do about 18 hours of housework per week and women do about 37 hours (see also Bianchi, Milkie, Sayer, & Robinson, 2000). Although the gender gap is smaller for unmarried men and women (e.g., those who are cohabiting, divorced, or single), unmarried women still perform more domestic labor than their male counterparts.

Second, married women's movement into paid employment has not been accompanied by an equally dramatic increase in the amount of housework done by husbands. Thus, scholars suggest that responsibility for the *second shift* of housework has fallen primarily on women (Hochschild, 1989). Although gender differences in unpaid housework have narrowed somewhat over time, studies show that this is primarily a result of a decline in women's housework rather than a substantial increase in men's housework. One study, drawing on data from time diaries, found that married women's time spent doing housework declined from about 34 hours per week in 1965 to 19.4 hours in 1995. Married men's time spent doing housework, meanwhile, doubled from 1965 to 1995, but only from 4.7 to 10.4 hours (Bianchi et al., 2000).

A third important research finding is that not only do women perform significantly more housework than do men, but they also perform different types of household tasks (Blair & Lichter, 1991; Meissner, 1977; Twiggs, McQuillan, & Ferree, 1999). Women tend to perform chores that take place inside the home and are routine, daily, and closely associated with child care (e.g., meal preparation, housecleaning, laundry, and cleaning up after meals). These tasks are often termed *female* or *feminine* because women more often perform them. Offering little discretion as to when they are performed, they bind one into a fixed, even rigid, daily schedule. In contrast, traditional male tasks (e.g., household repairs, automobile maintenance) tend to have a well-defined beginning and end, are more likely to take place outside the home, offer discretion as to when the task is performed, and may even be experienced as leisure. *Neutral* tasks, including driving, paying bills, and shopping, tend to be shared more equally between men and women (e.g., Bianchi et al., 2000; Blair & Lichter, 1991; Noonan 2001b).

Measurement Issues

Several measurement issues arise when interpreting research on housework. First, data sources vary in their definition of *housework*. In some studies, time spent caring for children is included as housework, although most focus on the accomplishment of specific household tasks (e.g., laundry, meals). For example, the NSFH, the most popular source of data for recent studies on housework in the United States, asks respondents how much time they spend in a series of activities, but excludes child care.

A second important issue is that studies vary in terms of how the data are collected. In the NSFH, for example, the respondent is asked to provide an absolute number of hours spent doing specific tasks. Time diaries, in contrast, are based on logs that account for time spent on various activities, usually for a 24-hour period. This method is thought to result in the most accurate estimates, and it produces much lower estimates of time spent on activities than does the NSFH (Bianchi et al., 2000). It may, however, underestimate simultaneous activities (e.g., doing the laundry and feeding the baby).

Nonetheless, although reporting hours as a measure may inflate time spent on housework, estimates from different methods are highly correlated. Moreover, if one is interested in differences between men and women, this inflation is not terribly problematic because evidence suggests that both men and women tend to overestimate their contributions and double-count time in simultaneous activities (see Coltrane, 2000; Robinson & Godbey, 1997).

Other Domestic Labor:
Emotion, Kin, and Caring Labor

Conventional measures of housework are arguably missing some important domains of domestic labor that qualitative studies suggest are more commonly performed by women. For example, the behind-the-scenes responsibility for household management usually appears to be performed by women (Hochschild, 1989). This may include a range of tasks such as thinking through menus that will please the tastes of various family members, arranging doctors' appointments for children, buying birthday presents, arranging for repairs or deliveries, and a host of other activities (DeVault, 1991; Hochschild, 1989; Mederer, 1993).

Two specific kinds of such work have been termed *emotion work* and *kin work*. Erickson (1993) defined *emotion work* as that which "tends to involve the enhancement of others' emotional well-being and provision of emotional support" (p. 888). Erickson found, albeit among a nonrepresentative sample, that wives perform more emotion work than husbands. *Kin work*, sometimes termed *kinkeeping*, is usually defined as the work required to sustain ties with relatives and care for them (e.g., staying in touch, sending out holiday cards, organizing family gatherings). Gerstel and Gallagher (1993) used a measure of kinkeeping that includes the practical (e.g., giving a ride, preparing a meal, helping with repairs, etc.), the material (e.g., lending or giving money, giving a gift), and personal support (e.g., talking through personal problems, providing advice). They found that wives help a significantly larger number of kin and spend nearly three times as many hours per month as their husbands helping kin.

What Accounts for Gender Differences
in Domestic Labor?

Why, in the face of dramatic increases in women's employment and earnings, has housework seemed to largely remain women's work? In assessing the forces behind the gender gap, research has developed three theoretical perspectives: time availability, relative resources, and doing gender.

Time Availability. This perspective suggests that the division of household labor is rationally allocated based on the availability of household personnel in relation to the amount of housework to be done (Coverman, 1983). Time availability is typically operationalized with variables such as employment status or hours worked. Individuals who work more in the labor market are expected to do less housework. More recently, studies have operationalized availability with additional measures such as employment schedules and the use of flexible work-family policies because these variables are thought to more precisely identify availability to do housework (Presser, 1994; Silver & Goldscheider, 1994).

This perspective has generally received considerable support. Findings from many studies show that wives' employment hours are a statistically significant predictor of husbands' and wives' housework time. When women work more hours in the labor market, they do less housework and their husbands do more (Barnett & Baruch, 1987; Blair & Lichter, 1991; Coltrane & Ishii-Kuntz, 1992; Coverman, 1985; Greenstein, 1996b; Hiller & Philliber, 1986; Kamo, 1988; Shelton & John, 1993). Research has also found that housework is shared more equitably in couples that work nonoverlapping shifts (Presser, 1994).

At the same time, the direction of causality is not resolved in this perspective. It is quite likely that domestic responsibilities affect employment and employment hours especially for women. As we discuss in a later section, women still often reduce their employment when they become parents.

Relative Resources. This perspective is based on the notion that the resources (such as wages, education, or occupation) individuals bring to a relationship determine how much housework they do. This is thought to stem from a quest to maximize efficiency (Becker, 1991) or as the outcome of power dynamics (Blood & Wolfe, 1960). The efficiency perspective assumes that the division of labor is consensual and that the partner doing more housework will have less leisure; the perspective focusing on power dynamics makes neither assumption. In housework studies, resources are typically measured as earnings, with the theory predicting that individuals with higher wages do less housework. As with the time availability perspective, the direction of causality is at issue: Earnings are likely to be, in part, a result of the domestic division of labor and not simply a cause.

Many studies find that as wives earn more money or as their relative contribution to couple income increases, they do less housework (Bianchi et al., 2000; Blair & Lichter, 1991; Brayfield, 1992; Hersch & Stratton, 1997; Kamo, 1988; Orbuch & Eyster, 1997; Presser, 1994; Shelton & John, 1993; Silver & Goldscheider, 1994; South & Spitze, 1994). Other studies find that highly educated women do less housework (Bianchi et al., 2000; Greenstein, 2000; Hersch & Stratton, 1997; Orbuch & Eyster, 1997; Sanchez & Thompson, 1997; Shelton & John, 1993; South & Spitze, 1994).

Doing Gender. Increasingly, researchers are drawing on a *doing gender* perspective to explain why gender remains the most important predictor of housework time, even after including variables representing time availability and relative resources. This perspective argues that domestic labor is a symbolic enactment of gender relations (West & Zimmerman, 1987). That is, women and men perform different tasks "because such practices affirm and reproduce gendered selves, thus reproducing a gendered interaction order" (Coltrane, 2000, p. 1213). By performing housework or doing various types of housework, a woman or man demonstrates his or her gender and reinforces a gendered division of labor.

One frequently cited example of this perspective is Brines (1994). Contrary to predictions from the relative resources perspective, Brines found that men who are more economically dependent on their wives do less housework than average (see also Bittman, England, Folbre, Sayer, & Matheson, 2003; Greenstein, 2000). Other studies have tried to examine the doing gender theory by examining time spent in housework across various marital statuses. The idea is that the gender divide should be most marked when men and women are doing their performances in front of one another. Consistent with this, South and Spitze (1994) found that the largest gender gap in housework occurs among married persons compared with those of other marital statuses (see also Gupta, 1999, for a longitudinal analysis that lends even greater support to the doing gender perspective).

Housework studies vary considerably in focus, operationalization of concepts, data employed, and dependent measures, making comparisons across studies difficult. Despite this variation, the evidence suggests that time availability and resources matter for the gender gap in housework. The *doing gender* approach, although difficult, if not impossible, to falsify, adds a compelling dimension of explanation for observed patterns. Many studies include attitudinal measures and generally show that men and women with traditional gender attitudes share less housework than men and women with more egalitarian attitudes (Blair & Lichter, 1991; Coltrane & Ishii-Kuntz, 1992; Greenstein, 1996b; Kamo, 1988; Presser, 1994; Sanchez, 1994; Twiggs, McQuillan, & Ferree, 1999). However, similar to the causality issues raised by the other perspectives, it may well be that attitudes follow behavior.

GENDER AND PARENTING

Also important is the intersection of paid work and parenting. Our focus is on parental involvement with children in married and single-parent families. Given that most children living with only one biological parent live with their mothers, we also touch on the issue of nonresidential parenting—a form of parenting much more common for men than for women.

Married Parents' Time and Activities With Children

Two of the most important patterns in terms of time with children echo those found for housework. First, fathers devote less time to childrearing than mothers regardless of whether mothers are in the labor force (Pleck, 1985;

Sandberg & Hofferth, 2001; Yeung et al., 2001). Using time diary data from the 1997 Panel Study of Income Dynamics, Yeung et al. (2001) reported that, on weekdays, children spend 67% as much time with fathers as with mothers; on weekends, the comparable figure is 87%. Second, the amount of time married fathers devote to childrearing has increased substantially over recent decades. Based on time diary data (Americans' Use of Time), Bianchi (2000) reported that, in 1965, fathers spent approximately 25% of the time that mothers spent in child care. By 1998, the ratio had risen to 56% of mother's time (see also Sandberg & Hofferth, 2001).

A few variables seem to exert more consistent effects than others in predicting the time fathers will spend with their children. First, studies show that fathers spend more time with their children when the children are young (Barnett & Baruch, 1987; Marsiglio, 1991; Pleck, 1985). Second, the longer hours fathers work, the less time they spend with children (Glass, 1998; Marsiglio, 1991; Nock & Kingston, 1988; Pleck, 1985; Yeung et al., 2001). Third, employment schedules matter. Studies show that fathers are most likely to care for their children when they work different hours than their wives (Brayfield, 1995; Presser, 1988), and that fathers' time with children is maximized when couples' work schedules do not overlap (Casper & O'Connell, 1998; see also Estes, Noonan, & Glass, 2003; Presser, 1988).

Finally, gender differences are evident in the types of activities mothers and fathers do with their children. For instance, research shows that more of men's time with their children is in the form of interactive activities, such as playing or helping with homework, rather than in custodial activities, such as bathing and feeding (McBride & Mills, 1993; Robinson & Godbey, 1997).

Single Parenting

Trends in marriage, divorce, and nonmarital childbearing have led to sharp increases in single-parent households. In these cases, the residential parent usually has the double responsibility of domestic duties and market work. Perhaps the most important fact relating to gender is that the vast majority of single-parent households are led by women. There are roughly 11.7 million single parents in the United States. Of these 82.5% are female (Fields & Casper, 2001). In addition, female single-parent households include more children, on average, than that of their male counterparts. Of all children living with a single parent, only about 10% are living with their father (Fields, 2001). Furthermore, although employment rates are relatively high for female single parents, they are still lower than those among male single parents (77% vs. 84%; Fields & Casper, 2001). Female single parents are also twice as likely to be poor as their male counterparts (34% vs. 17%).

There has been little research devoted to understanding domestic labor in single-parent homes. One study suggests that, although the patterns of interaction and housework of single mothers and single fathers are more similar than those of married mothers and fathers, gendered patterns remain. Hall, Walker, and Acock (1995) found that single mothers spend substantially more time on feminine household tasks per week, whereas single fathers spend about twice as much time as single mothers on masculine tasks. Also single fathers spend less time in private talk and more time playing with children than single mothers.

Nonresidential Parenting

Married fathers have become more involved in childrearing, but another less optimistic picture (that of nonresidential fatherhood) has emerged. Nonresidential fatherhood is on the rise, and it is well known that many children have limited contact with their biological fathers (Furstenberg, 1988). At the same time, recent research shows that many men who live apart from one set of biological children ultimately assume paternal responsibility for new biological or stepchildren through cohabitation or remarriage; this pattern has been termed *child swapping* or *serial parenting* (Furstenberg, 1988; Manning & Smock, 2000). For example, Manning, Stewart, and Smock (2003) found that one half of all nonresident fathers have parenting responsibilities beyond a single set of children, and that nearly three fourths of those who are remarried or cohabiting have responsibilities for other children.

These findings highlight the challenges in accurately identifying and defining what an *involved father* is in a society in which nonmarital childbearing, cohabitation, divorce, and remarriage are commonplace. Although some men may be less involved with some children, many men may be forging new ties to the children with whom they live.

LABOR MARKET IMPLICATIONS
OF THE DOMESTIC DIVISION OF LABOR

A relatively long history of social science research, dating back 30 years or so, has focused on the labor market consequences for women of marriage and parenthood (Cramer, 1980; Hanson, 1983; Hudis, 1976; Mincer & Ofek, 1982; Mott & Shapiro, 1978; Presser & Baldwin, 1980; Stolzenberg & Waite, 1984). A key finding, and one continuing to the present, is that marriage and parenthood directly or indirectly decrease women's earnings and earnings potential. As discussed next, this is not typically the case for men.

Marriage

Married men experience a boost to their wages when they marry. Even after accounting for selection processes into marriage and other characteristics (e.g., jobs and human capital), estimates suggest that married men receive a wage premium of between 5% and 30% (Daniel, 1995; Hersch & Stratton, 2000; Korenman & Neumark, 1991; Loh, 1996; Waite, 1995). Findings, however, are more mixed for women (e.g., Waite, 1995). One study suggested that African-American women experience a 2.8% marriage premium, but White women are penalized with a 4.4% reduction in wages (Daniel, 1995), the net effect being no overall premium for women.

Although difficult to disentangle and not mutually exclusive, the most common explanations posed for this phenomenon are that more productive men marry (a selection effect), and marriage makes men more productive (causation). The latter could occur because of the division of labor between husbands and wives. That is, married men are able to spend more time and energy in the labor market than unmarried men because wives assume much of the responsibility for housework and childrearing. A third possible explanation, potentially in combination with the first two, is employer discrimination in favor of married men. For example, employers may treat married men better than unmarried men, offering them wage-enhancing promotions or additional training.

A few studies have suggested that the male marriage premium has declined over time (Blackburn & Korenman, 1994; Gray, 1997; Loh, 1996) possibly because of less traditional gender role specialization within marriage. However, Cohen (2002) showed that the decline in the premium is overstated when, as done in earlier studies, cohabitors are included in the never-married group (Cohen, 2002).

Parenthood

How does parenthood affect men's and women's labor market outcomes? First, women have typically reduced their labor market involvement to absorb childbirth and child-care responsibilities, whereas men have not. That is, parenthood has asymmetrical effects for men and women in terms of employment. Drawing on nationally representative panel data of young men and women spanning more than 30 years (1966–1998), Noonan (2001a) examined the behavior of two birth cohorts of married men and women to identify employment responses to first-time parenthood. Figure 23.1 shows patterns of employment around the time of childbirth for the two cohorts of married women. Clearly, women's responses are changing: The more recent cohort has higher levels of employment at all months. However, they still reduce employment near the time of childbirth. Figure 23.2 shows the identical data for married men. The figure is striking in underscoring the stability of men's employment in response to parenthood (see also Lundberg & Rose, 2000). Similarly, other studies (and data by Bianchi and Raley, chap. 2, this volume) showed that men are likely to increase their work hours and women to decrease theirs when they have a child (Jacobs & Gerson, 2001; Kaufman & Uhlenberg, 2000; Moen, 1985).

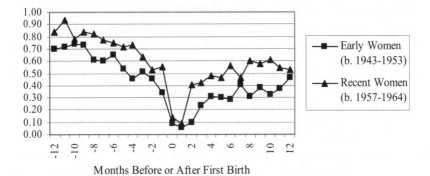

FIG. 23.1.   Proportion of married women employed and at work, before and after first birth, by cohort (NLS data).

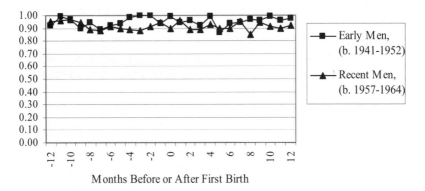

FIG. 23.2.   Proportion of married men employed and at work, before and after first birth, by cohort (NLS data).

Second, studies that have explicitly examined trade-offs between work and family document that women are much more likely to report trade-offs that inhibit earnings or earnings potential. Carr (2002) found that, overall, two thirds of women report having made a trade-off to accommodate children compared with less than one fifth of men. The study defined *trade-offs* as stopping work, cutting back on hours of employment, or taking a less demanding or more flexible job. Another study shows that the types of trade-offs differ by gender, with men substantially more likely to report that they took on more work to meet family responsibilities and that they miss family occasions owing to work demands (62% vs. 37% for women; Milkie & Peltola, 1999).

A third key finding is that there appears to be a wage penalty to motherhood, net of the effects of children on work experience, with several studies showing that mothers earn less than women without children. Studies that control for a wide array of human capital (e.g., work experience, education, etc.) and job characteristics report that women experience wage penalties ranging from 2% to 10% for one child and from 5% to 13% for two or more children (Anderson, Binder, & Krause, 2003; Avellar & Smock, 2003; Budig & England, 2001; Hill, 1979; Korenman & Neumark, 1991; Lundberg & Rose, 2000; Taniguchi, 1999; Waldfogel, 1997, 1998). Further, the penalty has endured over several decades (Avellar & Smock, 2003).

Fourth, unlike for women, men appear to experience an earnings premium with children. Depending on model specification and the age and number of children, studies show that children increase men's wages by between 3% and 5% (Cohen, 2002; Daniel, 1995; Hersch & Stratton, 2000).

WORK, FAMILY, AND WELL-BEING

Social scientists have also examined links between a couple's division of labor and various aspects of well-being, including mental health and marital quality and stability. We briefly discuss each in turn.

In terms of mental health, several studies find that time spent doing housework is associated with increased depression for women (Glass & Fujimoto, 1994). If husbands help with the housework, wives are less depressed (Ross, Mirowsky, & Huber, 1983). In addition, one study indicates that only hours spent in low-schedule-control tasks (i.e., feminine tasks) lead to more psychological distress (Barnett & Shen, 1997; see also Lennon, 1994). Although this relationship exists for both men and women, its consequences are greater for women because they disproportionately perform such tasks. Wives may also be affected by perceived equity in performance of housework. Bird (1999), using longitudinal data with a control group for prior mental health status, found that men's lower housework contribution accounts, in part, for wives' higher depression levels.

Trade-offs made between work and family have subtler psychological consequences as well, and this appears true for both men and women. Carr (2002) found that Baby Boom (born 1944–1959) and Baby Bust (born 1960–1970) women who cut back on employment hours had lower levels of self-acceptance (i.e., self-esteem). In a qualitative portion of the study, however, Carr found compelling evidence that mid-life men (age 59) experience feelings of regret connected with the pressures they felt to be a "good provider," which, they perceived, limited their ability to choose professions they found personally rewarding or to take career risks (Carr, in press). Most also regretted that their jobs constrained their involvement as parents, saying they wished they had spent more time with their children when they were young.

Several studies link satisfaction with the division of domestic labor to marital quality and marital stability (Erickson, 1993; Frisco & Williams, 2003; Voydanoff & Donnelly, 1999). Suitor (1991), for example, found that satisfaction with the division of housework is moderately related to both wives' and husbands' marital quality across almost all life stages. Studies also attempt to elucidate the mechanisms by which inequality in housework translates into a sense of unfairness and marital dissatisfaction (Baxter & Western, 1998; Greenstein, 1996a; Pleck, 1985; Sanchez & Kane, 1996).

The few studies that directly measure marital instability, rather than satisfaction or perceptions of instability, come to similar conclusions. Frisco and Williams (2003) examined the relation among perceived fairness in the division of housework, marital happiness, and divorce in dual-earner marriages (see also Greenstein 1995, 1996b). They found that perceived inequity in the division of household labor impinges on both husbands' and wives' reported marital happiness and increases the odds of divorce among wives.

Finally, the structure of employment can affect marital quality, but it is not an inherently gendered effect. One example is the timing of work. Presser (1999) reported that only 30% of employed people work a standard workweek. Twenty-eight percent of dual-earner couples include at least one spouse who works other than a fixed daytime schedule, and 55% have one spouse who works weekends. In a related study, Presser (2000) found rather substantial negative effects of nonstandard work schedules on union stability; night and rotating shifts, for example, substantially increase the odds of instability for couples with children (see also White & Keith, 1990). Although the causal mechanisms are not yet well understood, certainly a portion of the effect stems from the stress of little leisure time together.

DISCUSSION

We conclude with a few broad observations. The first is rather commonplace, and that is the co-occurrence of stability and change. On the one hand, the bulk of childrearing and domestic labor continues to be borne by women. This has critical ramifications for women's strides toward equality in the labor market, and thus their economic status and that of their children should these women become single parents (Holden & Smock, 1991).

On the other hand, although the pace of change in men's contributions to domestic labor has been slower than women's contributions to paid labor, leading many to speak of a *stalled revolution*, the direction of change seems clear to us. During the past few decades, married men have increased their domestic labor, both absolutely and relatively, and they are increasingly involved in child care and likely to espouse egalitarian gender role attitudes. These are substantial shifts. We would also point to Carr's (2002) findings of cohort change in reported work-family trade-offs among men. Only 10% of the oldest men (b. 1931–1943), but 20% of the Baby Boom men and one fourth of Baby Bust men made a work-family trade-off.

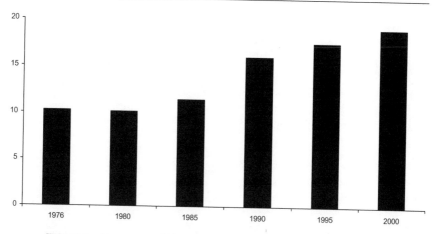

FIG. 23.3.   Percentage of U.S. women 40 to 44 years old who are childless (Bachu & O'Connell, 2001).

Second, it seems to us that there is another trade-off that some women have been making—and one that is important to recognize for its implications for the continuing difficulty among women juggling work and family. Childlessness is a growing phenomenon in the United States, perhaps the ultimate balancing being done. In 2000, almost 20% of women were childless at ages 40 to 44 (by these ages, women are nearing the end of their childbearing years). As shown in Fig. 23.3, the proportion is nearly double that in 1976.

Moreover, childlessness varies in a way that suggests women with greater human capital are most likely to forgo childbearing. For example, in 1998, roughly 29% of 40- to 44-year-old women with bachelor's degrees had no children compared with about 14% of those with high school degrees or less. Similar differences occur within occupations. Among those with professional and managerial occupations, more than 26% were childless in 1998 compared with 17% of women in other occupations (Bachu & O'Connell, 2001). Other evidence indicates that women with the most extreme demands from employment (executives at corporations, etc.) have much higher rates of childlessness—in some subgroups nearing 50% (see e.g., Crittenden, 2001; Hewlett, 2002).

As stated in our introduction, demographers have been wrestling with the relation between women's employment and fertility for some time. In the classic 1959 Hauser and Duncan volume, *The Study of Population*, the author of the chapter on work identifies the most critical questions for demographers to ask about working behavior. Listed first is the following:

Just how is the fertility pattern of a woman related to her participation (or non-participation) in the working force? Does one "cause" the other, is there a feedback interrelationship, or are both phenomena manifestations of an underlying factor? Under what conditions will more or fewer women be in the working force, and how will such behavior seem to affect the birth rate . . . ? (Jaffe, 1959, p. 608)

The answer to the last question, we think, varies historically and by nation, and it depends on the structures in the workplace, families, and government to support the tasks of parenthood.

REFERENCES

Anderson, D. J., Binder, M., & Krause, K. (2003). The motherhood wage penalty revisited: Experience, heterogeneity, work effort, and work schedule flexibility. *Industrial and Labor Relations Review, 56,* 273–294.

Avellar, S., & Smock, P. J. (2003). Has the price of motherhood declined over time? A cross-cohort comparison of the motherhood wage penalty. *Journal of Marriage and the Family, 65,* 597–607.

Bachu, A., & O'Connell, M. (2001). *Fertility of American women: June 2000* (Current Population Reports, Series P20-543RV). Washington, DC: U.S. Census Bureau.

Barnett, R. C., & Baruch, G. B. (1987). Determinants of father's participation in family work. *Journal of Marriage and the Family, 49,* 29–40.

Barnett, R. C., & Shen, Y. (1997). Gender, high- and low-schedule-control housework tasks, and psychological distress. *Journal of Family Issues, 18,* 403–428.

Baxter J., & Western, M. (1998). Satisfaction with housework: Examining the paradox. *Sociology: The Journal of the British Sociological Association, 32,* 101–120.

Becker, G. S. (1991). *A treatise on the family.* Cambridge, MA: Harvard University Press.

Bianchi, S. (2000). Maternal employment and time with children: Dramatic change or surprising continuity? *Demography, 37,* 401–414.

Bianchi, S. M., Milkie, M. A., Sayer, L. C., & Robinson, J. P. (2000). Is anyone doing the housework? *Social Forces, 79,* 191–228.

Bird, C. (1999). Gender, household labor, and psychological distress: The impact of the amount and division of housework. *Journal of Health and Social Behavior, 40,* 32–45.

Bittman, M., England, P., Folbre, N., Sayer, L., & Matheson, G. (2003). When does gender trump money? Bargaining and time in household work. *American Journal of Sociology, 109,* 186–214.

Blackburn, M., & Korenman, S. (1994). The declining marital status earnings differential. *Journal of Population Economics, 7,* 249–270.

Blair, S. L., & Lichter, D. T. (1991). Measuring the division of household labor: Gender segregation of housework among American couples. *Journal of Family Issues, 12,* 91–113.

Blood, R. O., & Wolfe, D. M. (1960). *Husbands and wives: The dynamics of married living.* New York: The Free Press.

Brayfield, A. (1992). Employment resources and housework in Canada. *Journal of Marriage and the Family, 54,* 19–30.

Brayfield, A. (1995). Juggling jobs and kids: The impact of employment schedules on fathers' caring for children. *Journal of Marriage and Family, 57,* 321–332.

Brines, J. (1994). Economic dependency, gender, and the division of labor at home. *American Journal of Sociology, 100,* 652–688.

Budig, M. J., & England, P. (2001). The wage penalty for motherhood. *American Sociological Review, 66,* 204–225.

Carr, D. S. (2002). The psychological consequences of work-family trade-offs for three cohorts of men and women. *Social Psychological Quarterly, 65*, 103–124.

Carr, D. S. (in press). The psychological consequences of midlife men's social comparisons with their young adult sons. *Journal Marriage and the Family*.

Casper, L. M., & O'Connell, M. (1998). Work, income, the economy, and married fathers as child-care providers. *Demography, 35*, 243–250.

Cohen, P. N. (2002). Cohabitation and the declining marriage premium for men. *Work and Occupations, 29*, 346–363.

Collver, O. A. (1968). Women's work participation and fertility in metropolitan areas. *Demography, 5*, 55–60.

Coltrane, S. (2000). Research on household labor: Modeling and measuring the social embeddedness of routine family work. *Journal of Marriage and the Family, 62*, 1208–1233.

Coltrane, S., & Ishii-Kuntz, M. (1992). Men's housework: A life-course perspective. *Journal of Marriage and the Family, 54*, 43–57.

Coverman, S. (1983). Gender, domestic labor time, and wage inequality. *American Sociological Review, 48*, 623–637.

Coverman, S. (1985). Explaining husbands' participation in domestic labor. *The Sociological Quarterly, 26*, 81–97.

Cramer, J. C. (1980). Fertility and female employment. *American Sociological Review, 45*, 167–190.

Crittenden, A. (2001). *The price of motherhood*. New York: Metropolitan Books.

Daniel, K. (1995). The marriage premium. In M. Tommasi & K. Ierulli (Eds.), *The new economics of human behavior* (pp. 113–125). Cambridge, MA: Cambridge University Press.

DeVault, M. (1991). *Feeding the family: The social organization of caring as gendered work*. Chicago: University of Chicago Press.

Erickson, R. J. (1993). Reconceptualizing family work: The effect of emotion work on perceptions of marital quality. *Journal of Marriage and the Family, 55*, 888–900.

Estes, S. B., Noonan, M., & Glass, J. (2003, May). *Does the use of work-family policies influence time spent in domestic labor?* Paper presented to the Population Association of America, Minneapolis, MN.

Fields, J. (2001). *Living arrangements of children: Household economic studies* (Current Population Reports, Series P70-74). Washington, DC: U.S. Bureau of the Census.

Fields, J., & Casper, L. (2001). *America's families and living arrangements: Population characteristics* (Current Population Reports, Series P20-537). Washington, DC: U.S. Bureau of the Census.

Frisco, M., & Williams, K. (2003). Perceived housework equity, marital happiness, and divorce in dual-earner households. *Journal of Family Issues, 24*, 51–73.

Furstenberg, F. F. (1988). Good dads–bad dads: Two faces of fatherhood. In A. J. Cherlin (Ed.), *The changing American family and public policy* (pp. 193–218). Washington, DC: Urban Institute Press.

Gerstel, N., & Gallagher, S. K. (1993). Kinkeeping and distress: Gender, recipients of care, and work-family conflict. *Journal of Marriage and the Family, 55*, 598–607.

Glass, J. L. (1998). Gender liberation, economic squeeze, or fear of strangers: Why fathers provide infant care in dual-earner families. *Journal of Marriage and the Family, 60*, 821–834.

Glass, J. L., & Fujimoto, T. (1994). Housework, paid work, and depression among husbands and wives. *Journal of Health and Social Behavior, 35*, 179–191.

Gray, J. S. (1997). The fall in men's return to marriage: Declining productivity effects or changing selection? *Journal of Human Resources, 32*, 481–504.

Greenstein, T. N. (1995). Gender ideology, marital disruption, and the employment of women. *Journal of Marriage and the Family, 57*, 31–42.

Greenstein, T. N. (1996a). Gender ideology and perceptions of the fairness of the division of household labor: Effects on marital quality. *Social Forces, 74*, 1029–1042.

Greenstein, T. N. (1996b). Husbands' participation in domestic labor: Interactive effects of wives' and husbands' gender ideologies. *Journal of Marriage and the Family, 58*, 585–595.

Greenstein, T. N. (2000). Economic dependence, gender, and the division of labor in the home: A replication and extension. *Journal of Marriage and the Family, 62*, 322–335.

Gupta, S. (1999). The effects of transition in marital status on men's performance of housework. *Journal of Marriage and the Family, 61*, 700–711.

Hall, L. D., Walker, A. J., & Acock, A. C. (1995). Gender and family work in one-parent households. *Journal of Marriage and the Family, 57*, 685–692.

Hanson, S. L. (1983). A family life-cycle approach to the socioeconomic attainment of working women. *Journal of Marriage and the Family, 45*, 323–338.

Hauser, P., & Duncan, O. D. (1959). *The study of population: An inventory and appraisal.* Chicago: University of Chicago Press.

Hersch, J., & Stratton, L. S. (1997). Housework, fixed effects, and wages of married workers. *The Journal of Human Resources, 32*, 285–307.

Hersch, J., & Stratton, L. S. (2000). Household specialization and the male marriage wage premium. *Industrial and Labor Relations Review, 54*, 78–94.

Hewlett, S. A. (2002). *Creating a life: Professional women and the quest for children.* New York: Hyperion.

Hill, M. (1979). Wage effects of marital status and children. *Journal of Human Resources, 14*, 579–594.

Hiller, D. V., & Philliber, W. M. (1986). The division of labor in contemporary marriage: Expectations, perceptions, and performance. *Social Problems, 33*, 191–201.

Hochschild, A. (1989). *The second shift: Working parents and the revolution at home.* New York: Viking.

Holden, K. C., & Smock, P. J. (1991). The economic costs of marital dissolution: Why do women bear a disproportionate cost? *Annual Review of Sociology, 17*, 51–78.

Hudis, P. M. (1976). Commitment to work and to family: Marital-status differences in women's earnings. *Journal of Marriage and the Family, 38*, 267–278.

Jacobs, J. A., & Gerson, K. (2001). Overworked individuals or overworked families? Explaining trends in work, leisure, and family time. *Work and Occupations, 28*, 40–63.

Jaffe, A. J. (1959). Working force. In P. Hauser & O. D. Duncan (Eds.), *The study of population: An inventory and appraisal* (pp. 604–620). Chicago: University of Chicago Press.

Kamo, Y. (1988). Determinants of household division of labor: Resources, power, and ideology. *Journal of Family Issues, 9*, 177–200.

Kaufman, G., & Uhlenberg, P. (2000). The influence of parenthood on the work effort of married men and women. *Social Forces, 78*, 931–941.

Korenman, S., & Neumark, D. (1991). Does marriage really make men more productive? *Journal of Human Resources, 26*, 282–307.

Lennon, M. C. (1994). Women, work, and well-being: The importance of work conditions. *Journal of Health and Social Behavior, 35*, 235–247.

Loh, E. S. (1996). Productivity differences and the marriage wage premium for white males. *Journal of Human Resources, 3*, 566–589.

Lundberg, S., & Rose, E. (2000). Parenthood and the earnings of married men and women. *Labor Economics, 7*, 689–710.

Manning, W. D., & Smock, P. J. (2000). Swapping families? Serial parenting and economic support for children. *Journal of Marriage and the Family, 62*, 111–122.

Manning, W. D., Stewart, S., & Smock, P. J. (2003). The complexity of fathers' parenting responsibilities and involvement with nonresident children. *Journal of Family Issues, 24*, 645–667.

Marsiglio, W. (1991). Paternal engagement activities with minor children. *Journal of Marriage and the Family, 53*, 973–986.

McBride, B. A., & Mills, G. (1993). A comparison of mother and father involvement with their preschool age children. *Early Childhood Research Quarterly, 8,* 457–477.

Mederer, H. J. (1993). Division of labor in two earner homes: Task accomplishment versus household management as critical variables in perceptions about family work. *Journal of Marriage and the Family, 55,* 133–145.

Meissner, M. (1977). Sexual division of labor and inequality: Labor and leisure. In M. Stevenson (Ed.), *Women in Canada* (pp. 160–180). Toronto: Women's Educational Press.

Milkie, M. A., & Peltola, P. (1999). Playing all the roles: Gender and the work-family balancing act. *Journal of Marriage and the Family, 61,* 476–490.

Mincer, J., & Ofek, H. (1982). Interrupted work careers: Depreciation and restoration of human capital. *Journal of Human Resources, 17,* 3–24.

Moen, P. (1985). Continuities and discontinuities in women's labor force activity. In G. H. Elder (Ed.), *Life course dynamics: Trajectories and transitions, 1968–1980* (pp. 113–155). Ithaca, NY: Cornell University Press.

Mott, F. L., & Shapiro, D. (1978). Pregnancy, motherhood, and work activity. In F. Mott (Ed.), *Women, work, and family* (pp. 29–56). Lexington, MA: Lexington Books.

Nock, S. L., & Kingston, P. W. (1988). Time with children: The impact of couples' work-time commitments. *Social Forces, 67,* 59–85.

Noonan, M. (2001a). *The changing effects of parenthood on men's and women's employment.* Unpublished doctoral dissertation, University of Michigan, Ann Arbor, MI.

Noonan, M. (2001b). The impact of domestic work on men's and women's wages. *Journal of Marriage and the Family, 63,* 1134–1145.

Orbuch, T. L., & Eyster, S. L. (1997). Division of household labor among black couples and white couples. *Social Forces, 76,* 301–332.

Perry-Jenkins, M., Repetti, R. L., & Crouter, A. C. (2000). Work and family in the 1990s. *Journal of Marriage and the Family, 62,* 981–998.

Pleck, J. H. (1985). *Working wives, working husbands.* Beverly Hills, CA: Sage.

Presser, H. B. (1988). Shift work and child care among young dual-earner American parents. *Journal of Marriage and the Family, 50,* 133–148.

Presser, H. B. (1994). Employment schedules, gender, and household labor. *American Sociological Review, 59,* 348–364.

Presser, H. B. (1999). Toward a 24-hour economy. *Science, 284,* 1778–1779.

Presser, H. B. (2000). Nonstandard work schedules and marital instability. *Journal of Marriage and the Family, 62,* 93–110.

Presser, H., & Baldwin, W. (1980). Childcare as a constraint on employment: Prevalence, correlates and bearing on the work and fertility nexus. *American Journal of Sociology, 85,* 1202–1213.

Robinson, J. P., & Godbey, G. (1997). *Time for life: The surprising ways Americans use their time.* University Park, PA: Pennsylvania State University Press.

Ross, C. E., Mirowsky, J., & Huber, J. (1983). Dividing work, sharing work, and in-between: Marriage patterns and depression. *American Sociological Review, 48,* 809–823.

Sanchez, L. (1994). Gender, labor allocations, and the psychology of entitlement within the home. *Social Forces, 73,* 533–553.

Sanchez, L., & Kane, E. L. (1996). Women's and men's constructions of perceptions of housework fairness. *Journal of Family Issues, 17,* 358–387.

Sanchez, L., & Thompson, E. (1997). Becoming mothers and fathers: Parenthood, gender, and the division of labor. *Gender and Society, 11,* 747–772.

Sandberg, J. F., & Hofferth, S. L. (2001). Changes in children's time with parents, U.S. 1981–1997. *Demography, 38,* 423–436.

Shelton, B. A., & John, D. (1993). Does marital status make a difference? Housework among married and cohabiting men and women. *Journal of Family Issues, 14,* 401–420.

Shelton, B. A., & John, D. (1996). The division of household labor. *Annual Review of Sociology*, *22*, 299–322.

Silver, H., & Goldscheider, F. (1994). Flexible work and housework-work and family constraints on women's domestic labor. *Social Forces*, *72*, 1103–1119.

South, S. J., & Spitze, G. (1994). Housework in marital and nonmarital households. *American Sociological Review*, *59*, 327–347.

Stolzenberg, R., & Waite, L. (1984). Local labor markets, children and labor force participation of wives. *Demography*, *21*, 157–170.

Suitor, J. J. (1991). Marital quality and satisfaction with the division of household labor across the family life cycle. *Journal of Marriage and the Family*, *53*, 221–230.

Sweet, J. A. (1970). Family composition and the labor force activity of American wives. *Demography*, *7*, 195–209.

Taniguchi, H. (1999). The timing of childbearing and women's wages. *Journal of Marriage and the Family*, *61*, 1008–1019.

Tien, H. Y. (1967). Mobility, non-familial activity, and fertility. *Demography*, *4*, 218–227.

Twiggs, J. E., McQuillan, J., & Ferree, M. M. (1999). Meaning and measurement: Reconceptualizing measures of the division of household labor. *Journal of Marriage and the Family*, *61*, 712–724.

Voydanoff, P., & Donnelly, B. W. (1999). The intersection of time in activities and perceived unfairness in relation to psychological distress and marital quality. *Journal of Marriage and the Family*, *61*, 739–751.

Waite, L. (1995). Does marriage matter? *Demography*, *32*, 483–507.

Waldfogel, J. (1997). The effect of children on women's wages. *American Sociological Review*, *62*, 209–217.

Waldfogel, J. (1998). Understanding the family gap in pay for women with children. *Journal of Economic Perspectives*, *12*, 137–156.

West, C., & Zimmerman, D. H. (1987). Doing gender. *Gender and Society*, *1*, 125–151.

White, L., & Keith, B. (1990). The effect of shift work on the quality and stability of marital relations. *Journal of Marriage and the Family*, *52*, 453–462.

Yeung, J., Sandberg, J., Davis-Kean, P., & Hofferth, S. (2001). Children's time with fathers in intact families. *Journal of Marriage and the Family*, *63*, 136–154.

24

Effects of Marriage, Divorce, and Widowhood on Health

Ross M. Stolzenberg
Linda J. Waite
University of Chicago

In his celebrated response to an inquiry about the benefits of psychological adjustment, Sigmund Freud noted just two things that a well-adjusted person should be able to do well: loving and working. Freud seemed to have expected that others already understood and agreed that success in work or success in love might be common accomplishments, even if difficult to achieve, but that the combination of successful work and successful love was an exceedingly lofty and difficult goal. That was a lot to communicate in three words, so we can hardly complain that the father of psychotherapy did not also say in the same answer just how mental health alone could secure simultaneous success in both love and work.

Nevertheless, it would have been nice if Freud had explained it all. Even a long, unpoetic answer would be useful. After all these years, questions still linger. For example: Does loving interfere with working? Does working interfere with loving? If so, how do working and loving get in each other's way? What are some of the consequences of that interference? Are mutual effects of love and work, if they do indeed exist, really an entirely psychological problem for individuals, or do they have something to do with the ways in which work is institutionalized in the occupational structure and the labor market, and the ways in which love is institutionalized in marriage? These are the questions that occupy us in this chapter, albeit less poetically, less concisely, and with less certainty in our answers than Freud had in his.

We first present short working definitions of two key dimensions of health: emotional well-being and physical health and longevity. Next, we review some findings on the effects of marriage on the emotional well-being and physical health of adults. Then we discuss research on the effect on health of marital dissolution through divorce and widowhood. We discuss the mechanisms through which marriage may improve and marital disruption may damage emotional and physical health. We consider challenges to the argument that marriage and marital disruption cause these changes. We discuss the mechanisms through which work by one spouse affects his or her own health and the health of the other spouse. Finally, we draw some conclusions about some useful next steps for future research and theory building on this topic.

EMOTIONAL HEALTH

For our purposes, emotional well-being consists of feeling hopeful, happy, and good about oneself. Those in good emotional health feel energetic, eager to get going, and connected to others (Ross, Mirowksy, & Goldsteen, 1990). The absence of well-being is manifested in various syndromes. Psychological distress may come in the form of depression, with symptoms of sadness, loneliness, and hopelessness. Depending on the severity of their condition, individuals suffering from depression may feel demoralized and worthless, wish they were dead, have trouble concentrating, have trouble sleeping, not feel like eating, cry at things that would not ordinarily bother them, and feel rundown and unable to get going. Psychological distress may also appear as anxiety, with symptoms of tenseness or restlessness. People who are anxious feel worried, afraid, or irritable, perhaps with the acid stomach, sweaty palms, cold sweats associated with the fight-or-flight response, shortness of breath, and a hard, rapid heartbeat. Depression and anxiety constitute the two biggest threats to emotional well-being. As the descriptions make clear, emotional distress may produce physical symptoms, linking psychological to physical health. Anxiety and depression often appear together, and they afflict everyone occasionally. Depressed and anxious individuals are also more likely than others to drink alcohol heavily and to suffer from affective difficulties such as problematic anger and cognitive problems such as paranoia (Mirowsky & Ross, 1989, 2003). Although rates of mental illness are quite similar for men and women in the United States today, women show higher rates of affective and anxiety disorders, with symptoms of nonspecific anxiety, distress, and depression. Men have higher rates of antisocial personality and substance abuse-dependence disorders that manifest themselves in antisocial behavior and drug and alcohol problems (Kessler et al., 1994).

PHYSICAL HEALTH

People in good physical health tend to feel fit and energetic, without pain, disability, or symptoms of disease compared with others their own age. Good health means more than just the absence of disease or its symptoms; it means feeling robust and strong (Ross et al., 1990). Feeling fit and energetic may persist in the early stages of declining health, and feelings of poor health may persist after underlying conditions or illnesses are cured. The association, however, is very strong between actual health and feelings of vitality.

If one of the hallmarks of good health is energy or vitality, one of the primary characteristics of poor health is its opposite; those in poor health are often tired, rundown, fatigued, and unable to accomplish the basic physical tasks of living, such as walking from their car to a store, lifting groceries or a vacuum, bending to tie shoes or pick up a dropped glove, or even getting out of bed and dressing (Ross et al., 1990; Waldron, 1988). Poor health may limit what people can do, but leave them able to function fairly well within those limits. For example, a person with a bad back might avoid pain and function well if he does prescribed exercises and is careful to observe prescribed limitations. Someone with diabetes might function well if she is strict about her diet, monitors her blood insulin carefully, and administers appropriate medication. Poor physical health can interfere with employment, causing people to miss work, get less done at work, or limit the hours they can work or the types of work they can do. Those in the poorest health may be unable to hold a job at all.

MARRIAGE AND PHYSICAL HEALTH

Marriage is one of the most basic human relationships and is the foundation of family life. Both men and women enjoy a range of benefits from marriage, including better physical health, mental health, and financial well-being (see Waite & Gallagher, 2000, for a summary). For example, Waite and Hughes (1999) found that among men and women at midlife, those who were married and living only with a spouse (and, perhaps, children) reported significantly better physical health and were less likely to have a condition that limited their mobility than unmarried adults or those in more complicated living arrangements. A recent article by Williams and Umberson (2004), however, suggested that the health benefits of marriage depend on both gender and stage in life. They found that men who married for the first time and those who remarried showed improved health compared with their nonmarried counterparts, but that women experienced either no improvement (for first marriage) or small improvements (for remarriage).

Ross and colleagues (1990) summed up the evidence on the relation between marital status and health and longevity: "Compared to married people, the nonmarried . . . have higher rates of mortality than the married: about 50% higher among women and 250% higher among men" (p. 1061). The unmarried face especially high mortality rates from causes of death that have a large behavioral component, such as suicide (Smith, Mercy, & Conn, 1988), accidents, lung cancer, and cirrhosis (Ross et al., 1990).

All marriages, however, are not equal, and the quality of the relationship influences the effect of being married on physical health. One study showed that couples whose marriages improved, as rated by the spouses, showed gains in the physical health for both spouses primarily through the improvements in psychological well-being that accompany better marriage quality (Wickrama, Lorenz, Conger, & Elder, 1997).

MARRIAGE AND EMOTIONAL WELL-BEING

Mental and emotional well-being tend to accrue more often to married adults than to those who are single. Married men and women report less depression, less anxiety, and less psychological distress than those who are single, divorced, or widowed (Mirowksy & Ross, 2003). According to some researchers, marriage protects the emotional health of men more than that of women. These researchers pointed to the larger gap in well-being between married and unmarried men than between married and unmarried women (Bernard, 1972). They also argued that marriage brings both benefits and strains, including those from rearing children and balancing work and family, but that the strains are felt more strongly by wives than husbands. The balance of benefits and strains, then, is more positive for men than for women, which may account for the smaller net gain in emotional well-being for women than for men (see also Logan & Spitze, 1996).

The psychological benefits of marriage, however, come only from good marriages—those rated by the individual as *happy*. Men and women in the relatively small number of unhappy marriages—who say that their relationships are unhappy, that they would like to change many aspects of their relationship, and that they often consider leaving their spouse or partner—show more psychological distress than single men and women (Ross, 1995). In short, a good marriage is a source of emotional support, but an unhappy marriage is a source of emotional uncertainty.

DIVORCE, WIDOWHOOD, HEALTH, AND WELL-BEING

The end of a marriage through either death or divorce effectively stops the flow of marital health benefits to the former spouse(s). One reason that unmarried (in this case, formerly married) men and women lead less healthy lives than the married is that the dissolution of a marriage causes tremendous strain (Williams & Umberson, 2004). Losing a spouse to death is a wrenching experience with profound emotional consequences. Widowhood, although extremely difficult, is the usual endpoint of an intact marriage, embodied in the common ceremonial promise, "till death us do part." Widows and widowers tend to receive both social and financial support unavailable to the divorced. For example, in the United States, widows and widowers with dependent children receive Social Security payments for those children until they are 18. Life insurance, pension benefits, and inheritance of shared assets, especially a house, all cushion the financial blow for many of the widowed, but fewer of the divorced. Thus, widows and widowers tend to have substantially greater assets than divorced or separated people of the same age (Lupton & Smith, 2003). Financial well-being seems to be an important mechanism through which marriage improves women's health and longevity, and being unmarried tends to damages health and well-being (Lillard & Waite, 1995). Men and women whose spouse has died also tend to receive emotional support from their children, families, and communities to a much greater extent than divorcing people do (Lye, Klepinger, Hyle, & Nelson, 1995).

Nevertheless, widowhood can affect health. Although widows and widowers face a less severe financial blow than divorced couples, they often experience a decline in their financial resources, and widowed men lose the intimacy, health monitoring, and household management that their wives often provide (Holden & Smock, 1991). During bereavement, the newly widowed face dramatically increased chances of dying themselves—from everything from heart disease to suicide and auto accidents. Death of a spouse poses a danger to both widows and widowers, but the danger is greater for men (Kaprio, Koskenvuo, & Rita, 1987). Williams and Umberson (2004) found that widowhood is associated with declines in self-rated health among men, but not women. They also found that these negative effects of widowhood on men's health become stronger with age, but are confined to those whose wife died recently. On average, the financial losses that often accompany widowhood apparently are not as problematic for women as the loss of intimacy, health monitoring, and household management is to men.

Divorce differs from widowhood in key ways. Divorce marks the failure of the marriage relationship. (Marital separation and divorce differ primarily in their legal status, rather than in their consequences for the health of the individual; therefore, we include both in our discussion.) Marital dissolution by divorce brings all of the negative emotions of widowhood, but also tends to include hostility and aggressive behavior between former spouses (Mazur & Michalek, 1998), a sense of guilt or disappointment over the failure of the marriage (Hopper, 2000), and reductions in socioemotional support (Mirowksy & Ross, 2003). In addition, divorce is often costly, consuming assets in the legal process and leaving each former spouse with less. The need to support two separate households on the same income that formerly supported one—with the loss of the economies of scale of marriage—tends to reduce the disposable money income of both former spouses (McLanahan, Casper, & Sorensen, 1995; Sorensen, 1992). All of these changes are associated with reduced physical and emotional health.

Women suffer a more substantial decline in income—between 25% and 33%—following divorce than men, on average, even when taking into account the fact that their household includes one fewer adult. Men's per capita household income rises by about 10%, on average, after divorce (Peterson, 1996) mainly because children tend to remain with their mothers and the mother's needs remain high. Child-care responsibilities limit women's hours of work, the types of jobs they can take, and their earnings (Waldfogel, 1997). Men tend to earn substantially more money than women even before they have children; parenthood widens the divide. Men generally take their higher earning power with them when the family dissolves (Smock, Manning, & Gupta, 1999). Child support awards and payments do not equalize the financial situation of men and women following divorce, at least on average (Beller & Graham, 1993). In short, husbands do better financially than their wives and children following divorce—although everyone has less money on average—but lose the socioemotional supports that marriage provides (Braver & O'Connell, 1998).

The acrimony and emotional strain of the breakdown of the marriage and the divorce process, the need to give up one lifestyle and rebuild, and the financial devastation of divorce all cause stress. Kiecolt-Glaser and her colleagues examined differences in immune function for married women, women who had divorced in the past year, and women who had been divorced for several years (Kiecolt-Glaser et al., 1987). They found that women whose marriage had ended within the last year had poorer immune function than a matched sample of married women. So, however, did women who had been divorced for some time, suggesting that something about being married improves immune function (or that something about being divorced depresses it even years after the divorce occurred).

People who divorce or separate also tend to move toward worse health behaviors. Men who divorce or separate smoke and drink more on average than they did when they were married (Bachman, Wadsworth, O'Malley, Johnson, & Schulenberg, 1997). Simon (2002) found that both men and women who divorce report a significant increase in the probability of alcohol abuse. Both men and women who were underweight during marriage tend to lose more weight, and women tend to get less sleep after divorce (Umberson, 1992). For women, loss of income, and for men, loss of emotional support, tend to increase psychological distress for the separated and divorced (Gerstel, Reissman, & Rosenfield, 1985). Simon (2002) found that divorce increases average symptoms of emotional distress among both women and men, but women tend to show greater increases than men in depressive symptoms following divorce.

SELECTION INTO AND OUT OF MARRIAGE AND HEALTH

Cross-sectional differences in both emotional and physical health between the married and divorced are sizable, but the differences may result from selection bias; because healthy men and women might be more likely to marry and the unhealthy less likely to marry, results from studies examining the effects of marriage on health might be biased. Many recent studies have addressed possible selection bias by following individuals over time to assess the relation between changes in marital status and changes in physical or mental health. Consistently, analysts conclude, on average, marrying improves mental health for both men and women and marriage breakdowns decrease it (Horwitz, White, & Howell-White, 1996; Marks & Lambert, 1998; Simon, 2002), with the single exception that very young adults who marry do not show improvements in emotional well-being compared with those who remain single (Horwitz & White, 1991). Simon (2002) found that, on average, men and women who divorced reported more depression and more alcohol problems earlier than those who remained married, and increases in both following divorce, which she interpreted as evidence that low levels of emotional well-being are both a cause and consequence of disruption. Less is known about selection into marriage by physical health, although Lillard and Panis (1996) found that among older men, those in poor health are more likely to marry than those in better health. A consensus exists that something about being married and unmarried affects health (Mirowsky & Ross, 2003), but the causal mechanism is yet to be understood fully.

HOW DOES MARRIAGE IMPROVE HEALTH?

How does marriage improve health? For one thing, marriage provides individuals, especially men, with someone who monitors their health and keeps track of such things as diet, smoking, and exercise, and who encourages them to take care of themselves (Ross, 1995; Umberson, 1987, 1992). This tends to improve these health behaviors.

Married people, again especially married men, have better health behaviors than those who are not married. One out of four young single men reported in a recent national survey that they drink enough to cause them problems at work or problems with aggression. Young married men the same age—who were also similar in level of education and race—reported substantially fewer problems with alcohol. Single men probably see more problems from drinking because they drink more—almost twice as much as married men. One out of four married men drink so little alcohol that they qualify as *abstainers*; only one out of six or seven single men drink this little (Miller-Tutzauer, Leonard, & Windle, 1991). Divorced and widowed men also have substantially more problems with alcohol than married men (Umberson, 1987).

Single men do not just drink more, on average, than married men. They are also more likely to drink and drive, more likely to get into fights, and more likely to take risks that increase the chances of accidents and injuries (Bachman et al., 1997; Ross et al., 1990; Umberson, 1987). Alcohol often plays a role in many of these behaviors (Parker, Parker, Harford, & Farmer, 1987).

Marriage tends to discourage these unhealthy behaviors. Among single men who are heading toward marriage, average alcohol consumption starts to decline up to a year before the wedding. At the same time, the alcohol consumption of young men who stay single remains high, and they continue to experience problems from drinking. Further, young men who were light drinkers, moderate drinkers, and heavy drinkers prior to marrying all drink less after they marry (Bachman et al., 1997; Miller-Tutzauer et al., 1991).

Marriage also seems to benefit women during their young adult years, when they are most likely to smoke, drink heavily, and use drugs. Although young women less often drink or drink heavily than young men, and less often use cocaine or marijuana, female drug and alcohol users who marry tend to reduce these negative behaviors dramatically compared with those who stay single (Bachman et al., 1997).

Marriage seems to provide somewhat different health benefits to husbands and wives, probably because husbands and wives tend to specialize in different health-promoting activities, both for themselves and their spouses. The extent and nature of this gender division appears to be shaped by cultural traditionalism. In the most traditional pattern, the husband directs the great bulk of his attention to earning money at a job outside the home while the wife does nearly everything else (Berk, 1985; Goldscheider & Waite, 1991; Nock, 1998; Oakley, 1974; Orbuch & Eyster, 1997; Spitze, 1986). The most traditional wife is responsible for managing the health and socioemotional condition of family members, including her husband and herself (Caldwell, 1993; Christakis, Ware, & Kleinman, 1994; Harris & Guten, 1979; Harrison, 1978; Nathanson, 1977; Waldron, 1988).

This aspect of traditional roles appears to be fully institutionalized. From early ages, girls tend to be socialized and trained to perform the traditional wife's tasks, including health, emotional management, and organization of social contacts (Baker, 1984; Blair & Lichter, 1991; Hochschild, 1983; White & Brinkerhoff, 1981). Further, the traditional wife's locus of activity is in the home, which gives her a continuous flow of incidental opportunities to monitor and influence her husband's health, social contacts, and emotional state. In contrast, husbands tend to be socialized to not monitor or manage health and socioemotional issues for anyone at all, not even themselves, and boys may even be socialized to place themselves in harm's way and ignore their own health, safety, and stress (Harris & Guten, 1979; Harrison, 1978; Nathanson, 1977; Waldron, 1988). Put another way, husbands are socialized to promote their own health and their wife's health by earning money and leaving other activities to their wife.

Although there are exceptions to the general pattern, these institutionalized patterns make the average wife far better trained and socialized than her husband to manage her own and her husband's health. Thus, the husband tends to depend on the wife for these services, and the wife tends not to depend on the husband for similar services (Umberson, 1992). This is likely why research finds that the average health of married men suffers greatly when they lose a wife through divorce, and the average health and survival probability of divorced men improves considerably if they remarry (Berardo, 1985; Lillard & Waite, 1995; Williams & Umberson, 2004).

Marriage, and the parenthood that often accompanies it, also seems to provide individuals with a sense of meaning in their lives (Mirowsky & Ross, 2003). Husbands and wives in good marriages realize that their partners' well-being depends on them. They recognize how devastated their family would be by their illness, injury, or death, and this realization makes them more cautious and careful. The obligation that married people feel to their partner inhibits them from driving dangerously, drinking excessively, or failing to take their medication. It gives them the incentive to take care of their health so they can meet their obligations to those who are counting on them (Gove, 1973; Umberson, 1987).

A good marriage also gives individuals someone they can rely upon for help, encouragement, advice, and sympathy. This social support helps individuals avoid and ameliorate stress, thereby bolstering their physical and emotional health (Mirowsky & Ross, 2003).

In addition to general social support, marriage provides access to support from an intimate relationship. Intimacy fosters feelings of self-esteem and mastery (see Pearlin & Johnson, 1977). In a study of depression, Kessler and Essex (1982) found that the intimacy of relationships with spouses and other important confidants is such an important resource that in its absence almost nothing else alleviates depressive symptoms, and in its presence almost nothing else exacerbates them. Thus, the resource of intimacy is one of the most important benefits of marriage.

Feeling that one is loved and cared for improves emotional well-being, decreasing depression and anxiety and increasing psychological resources such as self-esteem, mastery, and confidence. Intimacy and emotional support that are ordinary components of marriage can also affect physical health and, consequentially, perceptions of one's own health. Emotional health seems to help in maintaining proper neuroendocrine reactivity. Emotional health also improves immune function, especially cellular immunity. For example, people with strong networks of social support are less likely than those with weak networks to contract upper repiratory infections after exposure to the common cold virus (Cohen, Doyle, Skoner, Rabin, & Gwaltney, 1997; Herbert & Cohen, 1993). Further, emotional health provides resources necessary for a healthy lifestyle, which directly improves their physical health (Duncan & McAuley, 1993).

Spouses can also promote each other's health by providing each with income, and they can help each other manage money effectively. Money does not buy health directly, but it can be used to purchase goods and services that make good health more likely. These goods and services include nutritious food, a hygienic and safe environment, medical care, and amenities that reduce psychological stress (Feinstein, 1993; Preston & Taubman, 1994; Rosenzweig & Schultz, 1983; Taubman & Rosen, 1982; Williams & Collins, 1995). Unless estranged or unusually wealthy, husbands and wives almost always share their financial resources and purchase and consume many of these health-promoting goods and services jointly.

The added money income that marriage provides seems to be especially salubrious for women (Mirowsky & Ross, 2003). Women with income in excess of their own earnings tend to rate their health as better than women without these financial resources (Hahn, 1993). Married women's longer lives seem to result, in large part, from the greater financial resources that husbands bring (Lillard & Waite, 1995).

Marriage also gives women access to private health insurance—an increasingly precious commodity in the contemporary United States. Hahn (1993) showed that just over one half of divorced, widowed, and never-married women had private health insurance compared with 83% of married women. Women with private health insurance rate their health significantly higher than women without private health insurance. Insurance coverage improves health directly by giving women access to health care services, and it improves psychological health by giving people a sense of security about their health care (Hahn, 1993).

WIFE'S EMPLOYMENT AND HUSBAND'S HEALTH

Promoting the health of a spouse appears to consume significant amounts of a caregiver's time. For example, it takes time to monitor the well-being of another person, to diagnose the ways in which his or her behavior might be modified to better promote health, and to motivate and direct efforts to produce change. When combined with her other role requirements, the traditional wife's health-monitoring and health-promotion responsibilities leave her little free time, as reflected by the traditional dictum, "a woman's work is never done" (see Hochschild, 1989, for a description of the time constraints of married women who work full time). If a married woman holds a job outside her household, she must further allocate her time at home. When a woman works, some of her traditional tasks must be assumed by her husband, children, or other unpaid workers; be replaced by purchased goods and services; be done by her during time that she otherwise would use for rest or leisure; or be left undone.

The pressure on an employed wife to leave some things undone appears to be strong. Although some husbands share equally in household labor and others do more of it than their wife, research suggests that it is rare for husbands of employed wives to take over more than a small part of the traditional wife's task set (Goldscheider & Waite, 1991; Presser, 1994; Ross, 1987; Shelton & John, 1996; Spitze, 1986). Evidence also suggests that purchased goods and services usually cannot replace the household labor of a working wife, in part because gender differences in pay keep women's earnings low enough that women's pay is rarely sufficient to offset the cost of such purchases despite considerable job effort by women workers (Bielby & Bielby, 1988). Finally, because traditional wives' tasks leave them little leisure time originally, they seem unlikely to be able to simply reduce their leisure in response to make time for additional duties. Thus, Stolzenberg (2001) argued that the more time a wife spends at a paid job, the less time she is likely to have available for her traditional household duties, including those activities that supply her with information about, and opportunities to, influence her husband's health and emotional states. On average and over time, then, a husband who is subjected to less of this management and influence will become less healthy than a husband who is subjected to more of this management and influence. Indeed Stolzenberg (2001) found that if a wife worked fewer than 40 hours a week, her paid work had neither significant nor substantial effect on her husband's health during a 3-year period. However, if she worked more than 40 hours a week, her paid work had substantial, statistically significant, negative effects on her husband's health.

HUSBAND'S EMPLOYMENT AND WIFE'S HEALTH

As described earlier, the traditional husband holds a job to supply money income for himself, his wife, and other members of their household. Money buys many things that are necessary or useful to maintaining health. The traditional husband's role, however, does not include much management of health behavior, social contacts, and emotional well-being for anyone, including his wife. Further, his early socialization provides him with little training for these tasks. Thus, the diversion of a married man's time from the home to a paying job provides his wife with substantial financial resources (which have strong health benefits) and does not deprive her of many, if any, other health-promoting services. Further, the husband's involuntary unemployment is usually stressful for both husband and wife, with consequent strong negative effects on health for both (Brenner & Mooney, 1983; Madge & Marmot, 1987; Moser, Fox, & Jones, 1987; Ross & Wu, 1995). Of course the employment of both husbands and wives may affect their own health as well as that of their spouse. Several researchers argue that paid employment has positive, nonpecuniary health effects for all adult men and women (Ross & Mirowsky, 1995). Stolzenberg (2001) found virtually no effect of a wife's employment or hours of work on her own health, but a husband's employment has substantial positive effects on his own health. The beneficial effect of the husband's job on his own health is not mediated by the purchasing power that his earnings provide.

CONCLUSION

For most adults, work and family choices are intertwined, perhaps even made as one decision rather than two. We have outlined several keys aspects of these choices: the consequences of marriage and marital disruption on the emotional and physical health of adults, and the consequences of employment on spouses' health. We lack sufficient space to discuss several related and important topics: research on the effect of marriage and marital disruption on the employment, hours of work, and earnings of men and women; research on the effect of men's and women's employment, hours of work, and job demands on their own physical and emotional health; research on the effects of parenthood; and research on effects of nontraditional family forms, such as cohabiting couples and gay and lesbian couples.

Couples tend to make decisions together about the ways in which each spouse will allocate time and effort between work and family (Goldscheider & Waite, 1991; Orrange, Firebaugh, & Heck, 2003). These decisions, however, are made within constraints imposed by culture, the law, social norms, public policies, the economy, organizational practices, and each spouse's personal tastes and abilities (Hakim, 2000). In most couples, the work that wives do and the work that husbands do are not interchangeable; each gender brings unique abilities, tastes, perspectives, and socialization to the tasks that keep the family functioning. Men and women face a different set of choices and constraints outside of marriage (England, 2000). To make matters more complicated, husbands and wives often renegotiate their arrangements with the arrival of children (Altucher & Williams, 2003; Waite, Haggstrom, & Kanouse, 1985, 1986), with changes in health, and as they plan for retirement (Hutchens & Dentinger, 2003).

Over the past several decades, men and women have responded differently to the social and economic shifts that have occurred; women have increased their paid employment at the same time that men have done the opposite. These changes have led to shifts in the division of effort devoted to supporting the family financially and to somewhat more modest changes in the division of labor at home (Bianchi, Milkie, Sayer, & Robinson, 2000). Further, conflict between spouses about work-family issues seems to have negatively affected marital quality among young couples (Rogers & Amato, 1997), perhaps reducing the benefits of marriage and increasing the risk of divorce. Clearly these issues deserve the attention of scholars and policymakers if we are to help men and women reap the benefits of marriage for health in the age of the all-worker family.

REFERENCES

Altucher, K. A., & Williams, L. B. (2003). Family clocks: Timing parenthood. In P. Moen (Ed.), *It's about time: Couples and careers* (pp. 49–59). Ithaca, NY: Cornell University Press.

Bachman, J. G., Wadsworth, K. N., O'Malley, P. M., Johnson, L. D., & Schulenberg, J. E. (1997). *Smoking, drinking, and drug use in young adulthood*. Mahwah, NJ: Lawrence Erlbaum Associates.

Baker, P. M. (1984). Age differences and age changes in the division of labor by sex: Reanalysis of White and Brinkerhoff. *Social Forces, 62*, 808–814.

Beller, A. H., & Graham, J. W. (1993). *Small change: The economics of child support*. New Haven, CT: Yale University Press.

Berardo, F. M. (1985). Social networks and life preservation. *Death Studies, 9*, 37–50.

Berk, S. F. (1985). *The gender factory: The apportionment of work in American households*. New York: Plenum.

Bernard, J. (1972). *The future of marriage*. New York: Bantam.

Bianchi, S. M., Milkie, M. A., Sayer, L. C., & Robinson, J. P. (2000). Is anyone doing the housework? Trends in the gender division of household labor. *Social Forces, 79*, 191–228.

Bielby, D. D., & Bielby, W. T. (1988). She works hard for the money: Household responsibilities and the allocation of effort. *American Journal of Sociology, 93*, 1031–1059.

Blair, S., & Lichter, D. (1991). Measuring the division of household labor: Gender segregation of housework among American couples. *Journal of Family Issues, 12*, 91–113.

Braver, S. L., & O'Connell, D. (1998). *Divorced dads: Shattering the myths*. New York: Jeremy P. Tarcher/Putnam.

Brenner, M. H., & Mooney, A. (1983). Unemployment and health in the context of economic change. *Social Science and Medicine, 17*, 1125–1138.

Caldwell, J. C. (1993). Health transition: The cultural, social, and behavioural determinants of health in the Third World. *Social Science and Medicine, 36*, 125–135.

Christakis, N., Ware, N., & Kleinman, A. (1994). Illness behavior and health transition in the developing world. In L. C. Chan, A. Kleinman, & N. Ware (Eds.), *Health and social change in international perspective* (pp. 275–302). Cambridge, MA: Harvard University Press.

Cohen, S., Doyle, W. J., Skoner, D. P., Rabin, B. S., & Gwaltney, J. M., Jr. (1997). Social ties and susceptibility to the common cold. *Journal of the American Medical Association, 227,* 1940–1944.

Duncan, T. E., & McAuley, E. (1993). Social support and efficacy cognitions in exercise adherence: A latent growth curve analysis. *Journal of Behavioral Medicine, 16,* 199–218.

England, P. (2000). Marriage, the costs of children, and gender inequality. In L. Waite, C. Bachrach, M. Hindin, E. Thomson, & A. Thornton (Eds.), *The ties that bind: Perspectives on marriage and cohabitation* (pp. 320–342). New York: Aldine deGruyter.

Feinstein, J. (1993). The relationship between socioeconomic status and health. *The Milbank Quarterly, 71,* 279–322.

Gerstel, N., Reissman, C. K., & Rosenfield, S. (1985). Explaining the symptomatology of separated and divorced women and men: The role of material conditions and social networks. *Social Forces, 64,* 84–101.

Goldscheider, F. K., & Waite, L. J. (1991). *New families, no families? The transformation of the American home.* Berkeley: University of California.

Gove, W. (1973). Sex, marital status, and mortality. *American Journal of Sociology, 75,* 45–67.

Hahn, B. A. (1993). Marital status and women's health: The effect of economic marital acquisitions. *Journal of Marriage and the Family, 55,* 495–504.

Hakim, C. (2000). *Work-lifestyle choices in the 21st century: Preference theory.* Oxford, England: Oxford University Press.

Harris, D., & Guten, S. (1979). Health-protective behavior: An exploratory study. *Journal of Health and Social Behavior, 20,* 17–19.

Harrison, J. (1978). Warning: The male sex role may be dangerous to your health. *Journal of Social Issues, 34,* 65–86.

Herbert, T. B., & Cohen, S. (1993). Depression and immunity: A meta-analytic review. *Psychological Bulletin, 113,* 472–486.

Hochschild, A. (1983). *The managed heart: Commercialization of human feeling.* Berkeley: University of California Press.

Hochschild, A. (1989). *The second shift: Working parents and the revolution at home.* New York: Viking.

Holden, K. C., & Smock, P. J. (1991). The economic costs of marital dissolution: Why do women bear a disproportionate cost? *Annual Review of Sociology, 17,* 51–78.

Hopper, J. (2000). The symbolic origins of conflict in divorce. *Journal of Marriage and the Family, 63,* 430–445.

Horwitz, A. V., & White, H. R. (1991). Becoming married, depression, and alcohol problems among young adults. *Journal of Health and Social Behavior, 32,* 221–237.

Horwitz, A. V., White, H. R., & Howell-White, S. (1996). Becoming married and mental health: A longitudinal study of a cohort of young adults. *Journal of Marriage and the Family, 58,* 895–907.

Hutchens, R. M., & Dentinger, E. (2003). Moving toward retirement. In P. Moen (Ed.), *It's about time: Couples and careers* (pp. 259–274). Ithaca, NY: Cornell University Press.

Kaprio, J., Koskenvuo, M., & Rita, H. (1987). Mortality after bereavement: A prospective study of widowed persons. *American Journal of Public Health, 77,* 283–287.

Kessler, R. C., & Essex, M. (1982). Marital status and depression: The importance of coping resources. *Social Forces, 61,* 484–507.

Kessler, R. C., McGonagle, K. A., Zhao, S., Nelson, C. B., Hughes, M., Eshleman, S., et al. (1994). Lifetime and 12-month prevalence of *DSM–III–R* psychiatric disorders in the United States. *Archives of General Psychiatry, 51,* 8–19.

Kiecolt-Glaser, J. K., Fisher, L. D., Ogrocki, P., Stout, J. C., Speicher, C. E., & Glaser, R. (1987). Marital quality, marital disruption, and immune function. *Psychosomatic Medicine, 49,* 13–34.

Lillard, L. A., & Panis, C. (1996, August). Marital status and mortality: The role of health. *Demography, 33*, 313–327.

Lillard, L. A., & Waite, L. J. (1995). Til death do us part: Marital disruption and mortality. *American Journal of Sociology, 100*, 1131–1156.

Logan, J. R., & Spitze, G. D. (1996). *Family ties: Enduring relations between parents and their grown children.* Philadelphia: Temple University Press.

Lupton, J., & Smith, J. P. (2003). Marriage, assets, and savings. In S. Grossbard-Shechtman (Ed.), *Marriage and the economy.* Cambridge: Cambridge University Press.

Lye, D. N., Klepinger, D. H., Hyle, P. D., & Nelson, A. (1995). Childhood living arrangements and adult children's relations with their parents. *Demography, 32*, 261–280.

Madge, N., & Marmot, M. (1987). Psychosocial factors in health. *Quarterly Journal of Social Affairs, 3*, 81–134.

Marks, N. F., & Lambert, J. D. (1998). Marital status continuity and change among young and midlife adults: Longitudinal effects on psychological well-being. *Journal of Family Issues, 19*, 652–686.

Mazur, A., & Michalek, J. (1998). Marriage, divorce and male testosterone. *Social Forces, 77*, 315–330.

McLanahan, S. S., Casper, L. M., & Sorensen, A. (1995). Women's roles and women's poverty. In K. O. Mason & A.-M. Jensen (Eds.), *Gender and family change in industrialized countries* (pp. 258–278). Oxford: Clarendon.

Miller-Tutzauer, C., Leonard, K. E., & Windle, M. (1991). Marriage and alcohol use: A longitudinal study of "maturing out." *Journal of Studies on Alcohol, 52*, 434–440.

Mirowsky, J., & Ross, C. E. (1989). *Social causes of psychological distress* (1st ed.). New York: Aldine de Gruyter.

Mirowsky, J., & Ross, C. E. (2003). *Social causes of psychological distress* (2nd ed.). New York: Aldine De Gruyter.

Moser, K. A., Fox, J., & Jones, D. R. (1987). Unemployment and mortality in the OPCS longitudinal study. In R. G. Wilkinson (Ed.), *Class and health: Research and longitudinal data* (pp. 75–87). London: Tavistock.

Nathanson, C. A. (1977). Sex roles as variables in preventative health behavior. *Journal of Community Health, 3*, 142–155.

Nock, S. J. (1998). The consequences of premarital fatherhood. *American Sociological Review, 63*, 250–263.

Oakley, A. (1974). *The sociology of housework.* New York: Oxford University Press.

Orbuch, T. L., & Eyster, S. L. (1997). Division of household labor among black couples and white couples. *Social Forces, 76*, 301–332.

Orrange, R. M., Firebaugh, F. M., & Heck, R. K. Z. (2003). Managing households. In P. Moen (Ed.), *It's about time: Couples and careers* (pp. 153–167). Ithaca, NY: Cornell University Press.

Parker, D. A., Parker, E. S., Harford, T. C., & Farmer, G. C. (1987). Alcohol use and depression symptoms among employed men and women. *American Journal of Public Health, 77*, 704–707.

Pearlin, L. I., & Johnson, J. S. (1977). Marital status, life strains and depression. *American Sociological Review, 42*, 704–715.

Peterson, R. R. (1996). A re-evaluation of the economic consequences of divorce. *American Sociological Review, 61*, 528–536.

Presser, H. B. (1994). Employment schedules among dual earner spouses and the division of household labor by gender. *American Sociological Review, 59*, 348–364.

Preston, S. H., & Taubman, P. (1994). Socioeconomic differences in adult mortality and health status. In L. G. Martin & S. H. Preston (Eds.), *Demography of aging* (pp. 279–318). Washington, DC: National Academy Press.

Rogers, S. J., & Amato, P. R. (1997). Is marital quality declining? The evidence from two generations. *Social Forces, 75,* 1089–1100.

Rosenzweig, M., & Schultz, T. P. (1983). Estimating a household production function: Heterogeneity, the demand for health inputs and their effect on birth weight. *Journal of Political Economy, 91,* 723–746.

Ross, C. E. (1987). The division of labor at home. *Social Forces, 65,* 816–833.

Ross, C. E. (1995). Reconceptualizing marital status as a continuum of social attachment. *Journal of Marriage and the Family, 57,* 129–140.

Ross, C. E., & Mirowksy, J. (1995). Does employment affect health? *Journal of Health and Social Behavior, 36,* 230–243.

Ross, C. E., Mirowksy, J., & Goldsteen, K. (1990). The impact of the family on health: Decade in review. *Journal of Marriage and the Family, 52,* 1059–1078.

Ross, C. E., & Wu, C. (1995). The links between education and health. *American Sociological Review, 60,* 719–745.

Shelton, B. A., & John, D. (1996). The division of household labor. *Annual Review of Sociology, 22,* 299–322.

Simon, R. W. (2002). Revisiting the relationship among gender, marital status, and mental health. *American Journal of Sociology, 107,* 1065–1096.

Smith, J. C., Mercy, J. A., & Conn, J. M. (1988). Marital status and the risk of suicide. *American Journal of Public Health, 78,* 78–80.

Smock, P. J., Manning, W. D., & Gupta, S. (1999). The effect of marriage and divorce on women's economic well-being. *American Sociological Review, 64,* 794–812.

Sorensen, A. (1992). Estimating the economic consequences of separation and divorce: A cautionary tale from the United States. In L. J. Weitzman & M. MacLean (Eds.), *Economic consequences of divorce: The international perspective* (pp. 263–282). Oxford: Clarendon.

Spitze, G. (1986). The division of task responsibility in U.S. households: Longitudinal adjustments to change. *Social Forces, 64,* 689–701.

Stolzenberg, R. M. (2001). It's about time and gender: Spousal employment and health. *American Journal of Sociology, 107,* 61–100.

Taubman, P., & Rosen, S. (1982). Healthiness, education, and marital status. In V. R. Fuchs (Ed.), *Economic aspects of health* (pp. 121–142). Chicago: University of Chicago Press.

Umberson, D. (1987). Family status and health behaviors: Social control as a dimension of social integration. *Journal of Health and Social Behavior, 28,* 306–319.

Umberson, D. (1992). Gender, marital status and the social control of health behavior. *Social Science and Medicine, 34,* 907–917.

Waite, L. J., & Gallagher, M. (2000). *The case for marriage: Why married people are happier, healthier and better off financially.* New York: Doubleday.

Waite, L. J., Haggstrom, G. W., & Kanouse, D. E. (1985). Changes in the employment activities of new parents. *American Sociological Review, 50,* 263–272.

Waite, L. J., Haggstrom, G. W., & Kanouse, D. E. (1986). The effects of parenthood on the career orientation and job characteristics of young adults. *Social Forces, 65,* 43–73.

Waite, L. J., & Hughes, M. E. (1999). At risk on the cusp of old age: Living arrangements and functional status among black, white, and Hispanic adults. *Journal of Gerontology: Social Sciences, 54B,* S136–S144.

Waldfogel, J. (1997). The effect of children on women's wages. *American Sociological Review, 62,* 209–217.

Waldron, I. (1988). Gender and health-related behaviors. In D. S. Gochman (Ed.), *Health behavior: Emerging research perspectives* (pp. 193–208). New York: Plenum.

White, L. K., & Brinkerhoff, D. B. (1981). The sexual division of labor: Evidence from childhood. *Social Forces, 60,* 170–181.

Wickrama, K. A. S., Lorenz, F. O., Conger, R. D., & Elder, G. H. J. (1997). Marital quality and physical illness: A latent growth curve analysis. *Journal of Marriage and the Family, 59*, 143–155.

Williams, D., & Collins, C. (1995). U.S. socioeconomic and racial differences in health: Patterns and explanations. *Annual Review of Sociology, 21*, 349–86.

Williams, K., & Umberson, D. (2004). Marital status, marital transitions, and health: A gendered life course perspective. *Journal of Health and Social Behavior, 45*, 81–98.

25

Work and Family Issues
for Midlife Women

Eliza K. Pavalko
Fang Gong
Indiana University, Bloomington

Discussions of work-family conflict often focus on the challenges faced by young families (particularly young women) when establishing work careers as they rear children. However, a life course perspective challenges us to broaden our understanding of work-family conflict beyond its application to young adults. Work-family issues do not disappear as children grow up and move out of the home or as careers become more established, but they do change. These changes stem from both changes that occur as women age and changes associated with the aging of the women's families. Our focus is on midlife, which we define as between the ages of 40 and 70 (Lachman, 2001), and our emphasis is on the social dimensions associated with midlife for women. Thus, we view work-family issues for midlife women as unique not only because of biological changes that occur with age, but because women move through the life course within institutions, cultures, and family relationships that also change with age.

Employers and government policies structure the working life by imposing age-based eligibility rules for public and private pension policies (Han & Moen, 1999). Within this institutional context, a woman's age becomes highly relevant in decisions about how work and family are combined, and the cost of interruptions from work for family care may become increasingly salient as women approach retirement. Culturally, perceptions of age, and especially aging women, may also affect how women are perceived in the workforce, and women are at increasing risk for age discrimination as they move through midlife (Gee, Pavalko, & Long, 2002).

The age structure of families also influences the challenges (and benefits) of combining work and family. The demands and rewards of caring for young children are likely to be different from those presented by teenagers, and they differ still from caring for elderly parents or an ill spouse. Most important, caring for an ill or disabled family member is strongly associated with increases in depression and distress and declines in well-being (Schulz, O'Brien, Bookwala, & Fleissner, 1995; Schulz, Vistintainer, & Williamson, 1990), whereas caring for young children may have both positive and negative health effects. The timing of these types of care also differ; caring for children tends to span many years, have a fairly predictable duration, and change slowly with time, whereas caring for elderly parents or an ill spouse is less predictable and varies more widely in its duration (Moen, Robison, & Fields, 1994). Many women also approach retirement within a family structure that may shape their retirement decisions. Most notably, the age and retirement plans of a spouse or partner tend to shape women's own retirement decisions (Szinovacz & Ekerdt, 1995).

In this chapter, we examine three specific issues that are direct manifestations of these institutional, cultural, and family contexts. First, we examine caregiving to illustrate how the aging of women's families presents unique work-family challenges to midlife women. Second, age discrimination serves as an example of how cultural views of age may limit women's labor market opportunities and affect their health and well-being. Finally, retirement illustrates how institutionally defined pension policies intersect with family dynamics as husbands and wives coordinate retirement decisions, and pension income is based on the cumulative work-family decisions women make during their adult lives.

Our focus is on women because of their continued responsibility for managing much of work and family life, but we concur with Moen (2001) that the work and family careers of these women are intricately coupled with their spouses, partners, and other family members, and we consider these relationships where possible. Even as we discuss midlife women as if they are a uniform group, we recognize that doing so ignores the broad variation in women's experiences in midlife. Indeed this variation is so great that it is difficult to characterize midlife by any single set of transitions or experiences. This variation is further complicated by the vast differences in experiences of midlife by race and class. Finally, the rapid changes in women's work and family roles during the past half century mean that different cohorts of midlife women are likely to enter midlife with dramatically different patterns of work and family careers, job characteristics, and occupational opportunities.

CAREGIVING

One of the most direct sources of work-family conflict for mature families and middle-age women is caring for an ill or disabled family member. (We concur with Harrington-Meyer's [2000] assertion that *care work* is a more appropriate term than *caregiving* because it more accurately reflects the lack of choice and degree of labor involved in providing care. However, given the widespread use of the term *caregiving* in the literature, we use these two terms interchangeably.) There is growing evidence that women *pay* for the care work they do through gaps in labor force participation, by forgoing promotions and other work opportunities, and through lower wages for those doing paid work in the caring professions (England, Budig, & Folbre, 2002; Folbre, 2001; National Family Caregivers Association, 1997; Pavalko & Artis, 1997). Furthermore, these costs are incurred in both the short and long term as income penalties incurred during women's work lives affect their Social Security and pension income (Harrington-Meyer, 1996; Kingson & O'Grady-LeShane, 1993). In this section, we first review broad trends in care work and examine the relation between caregiving and employment. We conclude by reviewing research assessing workplace policies and its effect on care work.

Trends and Prevalence of Caregiving

Recent national studies estimate that roughly one in five adults ages 35 to 64 provides care to an ill or disabled family member either inside or outside the home (Marks, 1996). Furthermore, as the population ages, the demand for informal caregiving is likely to grow. The growth in caregiving demands has led to an explosion of research on the topic in recent decades. Although findings vary because of inconsistent definitions of caregiving (Dentinger & Clarkberg, 2002; Walker, Pratt, & Eddy, 1995), several consistent conclusions can be drawn from the caregiving research. First, it comes as little surprise that women are more likely than men to provide care, and they often care for persons with higher levels of impairment than do men. When men do provide care, they are more likely to be secondary providers (Fredriksen, 1996; Marks, 1998; Neal, Ingersoll-Dayton, & Starrels, 1997). The gender differences in care work are particularly striking when comparing parental care by sons and daughters (Brody, Hoffman, Kleban, & Schoonover, 1989).

Second, providing care appears to affect the health of the caregiver. Caregivers consistently have higher rates of depression than noncaregivers, and depression is particularly likely among spousal caregivers and for those caring for someone with behavioral problems (for reviews, see Schulz et al., 1990, 1995). The effect of caregiving on the physical health of caregivers is less conclusive, but several studies have found that caregivers have more disease symptoms, physical limitations, chronic conditions, or poorer immune function (Kiecolt-Glaser, Dura, Speicher, Trask, & Glaser, 1991; Pavalko & Woodbury, 2000).

Third, although estimates indicate that only a small percentage of U.S. adults are caring for someone at any given time, adults, and especially women, are more likely than not to provide care at some point in their life (Marks, 1998; Robison, Moen, & Dempster-McClain, 1995). The greatest proportion of caregiving occurs in midlife (Marks, 1996; Moen et al., 1994), which is when many families are juggling demands of work and other family responsibilities. Evidence is emerging of an increase in full-time workers who have the responsibility of caring for both elderly parents and minor children (Spillman & Pezzin, 2000), often referred to as the *sandwiched generation* (Brody, 1981; Ingersoll-Dayton, Neal, & Hammer, 2001).

The Relation Between Employment and Caregiving

Recent estimates find that 52% of caregivers are employed full time and another 12% are employed part time (Fredriksen & Scharlach, 1999; NAC/AARP, 1997), suggesting that balancing employment and caregiving presents a challenge to many women at some time in midlife. Early research on employment and caregiving noted that, compared with nonemployed women, employed women were less likely to be providing care (Gerstel & Gallagher, 1994; Matthews, Werkner, & Delaney, 1989; Moen et al., 1994; Stone, Cafferata, & Sangl, 1987; Wolf & Soldo, 1994), leading some to question whether increases in women's labor force participation were generating a crisis in care (Gerstel & Gallagher, 1994). However, this concern assumes a causal direction to this relation—that employment reduces women's ability to provide care. An alternative hypothesis is that employed women may reduce or stop employment when faced with heavy caregiving demands. Studies using longitudinal designs and statistical controls to separate these causal relations have generally found that women continue to provide care, but that they do so at risk of reducing their labor force participation, thus compromising their economic security. Whether women are employed has little influence on whether they subsequently assume the responsibilities of care (Pavalko & Artis, 1997), but the initiation of caregiving does increase the likelihood of reducing employment, leaving the labor force, or retiring (Dentinger & Clarkberg, 2002; Ettner, 1996; Pavalko & Artis, 1997; but see O'Rand & Farkas, 2002). Even among those providing care, the labor force behaviors associated with care work appear to differ for men and women.

Although providing care to a spouse increases the likelihood that women will retire, some evidence suggests that it delays retirement for men (Dentinger & Clarkberg, 2002). We return to this issue in our section on retirement.

Although women caregivers are more likely to reduce hours or stop work than noncaregivers, as indicated earlier, more than one half of those providing care are employed, and a growing body of research suggests that the negative health effects of caregiving are reduced by working (Hong & Seltzer, 1995; Martire, Stephens, & Atienza, 1997; Pavalko & Woodbury, 2000; Spitze, Logan, Joseph, & Lee, 1994). Several studies have suggested that flexible work schedules and family illness leave are especially helpful in managing work and family care and differentiate between caregivers who remain in the labor force and those who exit (Pavalko & Woodbury, 2000; Scharlach & Boyd, 1989). Given the importance of workplace policies for how women manage care work and paid employment, we briefly review what we know about workplace polices.

Workplace Policies Relevant to Caregivers

The bulk of research on family-relevant workplace policies has focused on those designed to help families balance employment with the care of young children, but many of these same policies are relevant to workers involved in other types of care work. One clear finding from recent research on workplace policies is that the availability of some of the most basic policies has increased in recent years (Golden, 2001; Waldfogel, 2001). Most notably, the 1993 Family and Medical Leave Act (FMLA) requires establishments with 50 or more employees to provide up to 12 weeks of unpaid, job-protected leave per year to eligible employees for leaves to care for a child, spouse, or parent who has a serious health condition. However, the availability of paid leave is far less common, and thus the option of family leave remains realistic for only a small subset of workers.

The FMLA has clearly had some effect on the availability of leave policies. For example, a parallel set of national surveys of private firms and employees conducted in 2000 found that 83.7% of firms covered by the FMLA offered all of the benefits mandated by the law, but that only one third of firms not covered by the law offered these benefits (Waldfogel, 2001). However, employee use of these plans remains limited. The median length of employee leave was only 10 days, and 90% of leaves lasted 12 weeks or fewer. Although employees who took leaves reported being generally satisfied with the amount of time they took off, the lack of pay during the leave was problematic. More important, it was cited as a major factor in the decisions to not take a leave even when needed (Waldfogel, 2001).

Access to flexible work schedules is another resource that workers could potentially draw on to help manage the demands of work and family care.

This flexibility may be particularly important for caregiving because of the unpredictable nature of this work (e.g., an unexpected change in the care recipient's health may require an abrupt change in the caregiver's work schedule). Estimates of the percentage of workers who have access to flexible schedules vary widely. Data from the 1997 Current Population Surveys suggest that 27% of workers report they can make changes in the time they begin or end work, and these percentages are highest among part-time workers and workers who work more than 50 hours per week (Golden, 2001). However, this greater access to flexibility coincides with an increase in unpredictable work hours and average hours worked per week (Golden, 2001). A more limited definition of a *flexible workplace* in the 2000 National Compensation Survey estimates that only 5% of private industry workers have access to a flexible workplace as a specific employee benefit (U.S. Bureau of Labor Statistics, 2002).

We now know much about the importance and implications of this unpaid work of caregiving. Most notably, the costs and benefits—to women, family members, and society—of providing this care are clear. What remains less clear are the structural conditions that can reduce the burdens faced by those providing care (but see Gerstel & Gallagher, 1994; Harrington-Meyer, 2000). Potential solutions such as workplace policies are often framed as less viable solutions because they are costly to employers. However, this might not be the case. For example, a recent study by Ruhm (1998) found that paid leave for the care of young children was associated with better labor force outcomes for women. Clearly, more research is needed to assess which policies are most helpful to those caring for an ill or disabled family member and whether those policies may provide other types of benefits for employers and caregivers.

DISCRIMINATION

Anecdotal evidence suggests that another issue particularly salient to late midlife workers is discrimination. A growing body of research has documented that perceptions of discrimination are relatively common, and that they have consequences for health, well-being, and job outcomes (see e.g., Gee, 2002; Johnson & Neumark, 1997; Kessler, Mickelson, & Williams, 1999; Neumark & McLennan, 1995; Pavalko, Mossakowski, & Hamilton, 2003). For example, more than one half of the respondents (61%) in a nationally representative sample of U.S. adults reported experiencing some type of day-to-day discrimination, and 34% reported a major discriminatory event in their lifetime, such as not being hired for a job, denied a bank loan, being hassled by police, or receiving inferior service (Kessler et al., 1999). After documenting the high frequency of perceptions of discrimination and the mental health consequences of these perceptions, Kessler and his colleagues (1999) speculated that discrimination is one of the most important stressors identified as causing mental health problems. The workplace appears to be one of the most risky places for discriminatory experiences (Kessler et al., 1999; Pavalko et al., 2003).

Is Age Discrimination a Problem?

Although women are at risk of gender discrimination and women of color are at risk of multiple forms of discrimination throughout life, as women move through midlife, their risk of age discrimination grows. Research has paid far less attention to the prevalence and effect of age discrimination than of forms of unfair treatment, particularly gender and racial discrimination. In this section, we first review the available evidence on the prevalence of age discrimination and then turn to what we know about how it may affect health and well-being. Although some patterns are emerging that suggest age discrimination is a problem, more research on age discrimination and how it may intersect with other forms of discrimination is clearly needed.

A sizable number of adults report age as a reason for their discriminatory experiences. For example, in the Kessler et al. (1999) study, the two most common reasons cited for discrimination were race or ethnicity (37%) and gender (33%), but 24% identified being discriminated against because of their age. Other studies have suggested that age discrimination may be more prominent than other types of discrimination possibly because this form of discrimination is viewed less negatively and is less likely to be reported. College students were more likely to discriminate by age in voting for a hypothetical mayoral candidate than by race or gender (Sigelman & Sigelman, 1982), and several studies have documented negative perceptions of older workers (Kalavar, 2001; Perry, Kulik, & Bourhis, 1996). In 2001, individuals filed more than 17,400 age discrimination charges with the Equal Employment Opportunity Commission, composing 22% of all charges filed in that year. Reports of age discrimination peak between ages 50 and 55, but they are also relatively high in early adulthood (20s and 30s; Gee et al., 2002).

Age discrimination, as with other forms of perceived discrimination, has implications for health and well-being. Although the health effects of age discrimination per se have not been thoroughly investigated, one study of workplace discrimination among women found that health effects of discrimination persisted even when analyses were restricted to the subsample of Whites, the group most likely to report age discrimination in this study and even after controlling for prior health (Pavalko et al., 2003). Among men, reports of age discrimination have been linked to increased risk of job separation and labor force exit (Johnson & Neumark, 1997).

RETIREMENT

Retirement is the most clearly defined event of midlife—that which marks the transition from midlife to later life. It is also the culmination of an individual's work life. Because of the structure of pensions, opportunities and constraints in retirement reflect the cumulative effect of work-family decisions made earlier. Work and family decisions during the life course are thus central to retirement experiences. In this section, we review two issues—the coupling of retirement decisions and the cumulative effects of care work on retirement income—both of which illustrate the centrality of work-family decisions to retirement.

The Coupling of Retirement Decisions

Numerous studies have documented the unprecedented increase in women's labor force participation in recent years, and this trend has had a profound impact on the coupling of retirement decisions, as working husbands and working wives coordinate the timing of retirement and pool their resources. Recent cohorts of women are more likely to retire as "pension-covered and health-insurance-covered workers ... instead of as dependent spouses" (O'Rand & Farkas, 2002, p. 15). According to the 2000 Social Security Administration reports, the ratio of women entitled to Social Security as workers (instead of as dependent spouses) changed from two in five women in 1960 to two in three women in 1999 (O'Rand & Farkas, 2002).

Research examining coupled retirement has demonstrated that, among dual-earner couples, retirement timing often requires coordination and compromises that are contingent on both early work and family trajectories and later work and family characteristics (Henretta & O'Rand, 1983; Henretta, O'Rand, & Chan, 1993; O'Rand & Farkas, 2002). Couples tend to coordinate their retirements if possible. For example, findings from a study of 1,409 retired couples (ages 62–72) showed a tendency for sequential synchronizing, which means that the exit rates were higher after one's spouse retired (Henretta et al., 1993). In a recent study using data from the National Longitudinal Survey of Labor Market Experiences, O'Rand and Farkas (2002) reported that joint career exits are most likely among older couples who are old enough to be eligible for Social Security and Medicare benefits.

Despite synchronizing their career exits, women's primary responsibility for family makes this joint process a gendered process, with a wife's retirement often affected and determined by her husband's retirement (Moen, Kim, & Hofmeister, 2001). The way in which a wife combines career and family early in life affects her retirement decisions and timing. For example, a wife's discontinuous employment during childbearing years is associated with early retirement (Henretta et al., 1993). Han and Moen's (1999) sequence analysis of life-history data suggested that women's traditional career pathways—delayed entry, intermittent, and steady part time—all affect their planned and actual retirement timing.

As mentioned earlier, caregiving can also influence retirement planning. Studies show that women may opt for early retirement when faced with caregiving responsibilities (Pavalko & Artis, 1997; Szinovacz & Ekerdt, 1995). For example, Dentinger and Clarkberg (2002) found that wives caring for their husbands were five times more likely to retire than wives who were not caregivers. In contrast, caregiving had a much less significant effect on a husband's retirement. However, these findings do vary across studies and may partially reflect variation in how the studies measured caregiving. For example, O'Rand and Farkas (2002) found that wives caring for husbands continued to work in paid labor to maintain earnings and/or health insurance for their husbands.

The Cumulative Effect of Care Work on Retirement Income

The potential effect of family care on retirement is not limited to the years immediately prior to or during retirement. Several studies have shown that women face a cumulative disadvantage in both paid and unpaid labor over their lives, and this affects their economic circumstances in their retirement (Harrington-Meyer, 1990; Harrington-Meyer & Bellas, 1995; O'Rand, 1996; Quadagno, 1988; Willson & Hardy, 2002). Female employees and retirees are more likely to have had delayed or interrupted employment because of childbearing and other domestic responsibilities, they tend to be excluded from occupational and industrial sectors with highest retirement income and benefits, and they tend to have worked part time and received low wages (Han & Moen, 1999; Kim & Moen, 2001). As a result, the gender wage gap reproduces a gender pension gap. O'Rand and Henretta (1999) documented that the wage gap between women and men ages 55 to 64 is 0.62 (female–male wage ratio), whereas the pension income gap is about 0.60. Furthermore, gender inequality in pension income between men and women has increased in the past decades (O'Rand, 2001).

One reason for the wage-pension gap is that exits from the labor force to provide care, regardless of where they occur in the life course, affect women's long- and short-term income. For example, analyses of Social Security primary insurance amounts (PIAs), which serve as the basis for Social Security benefits, indicate that both early (primarily to rear children) and later labor force exits to provide care depress the PIAs of recently retired women (Kingson & O'Grady-LeShane, 1993). Because most old-age income programs do not recognize or compensate for women's family roles (O'Grady-LeShane & Williamson, 1992; Street & Wilmoth, 2001), they are "penalized for conforming to a role that they are strongly encouraged to assume—unpaid household worker—and their disadvantaged economic position carries into old age" (Harrington-Meyer & Bellas, 1995, p. 266).

Some argue that spouse-widow benefits are rewards for unpaid domestic labor. However, Harrington-Meyer and her colleagues found that these benefits are based on family status rather than financial rewards to unpaid domestic labor (Harrington-Meyer, 1990, 1996; Harrington-Meyer & Bellas, 1995; Street & Wilmoth, 2001). Women are at greater risk if their marital status is unstable. Along with the demographic trend showing an increase in divorce rates and shortened length of marriages, more divorced women become ineligible for spousal benefits, which require at least 10 years of marriage (Harrington-Meyer, 1996). Although widow benefits are available, they are often limited, and they only apply to survivors older than age 60 unless they have dependent children (Szinovacz & Ekerdt, 1995). Thus, divorce and widowhood are often associated with women's insecure financial situations in retirement. Similarly, Willson and Hardy (2002) showed that, especially for African Americans, women's own employment provided greater income security in later life than did marriage.

In summary, it is clear that the workforce–workplace mismatch and women's greater responsibility for unpaid family labor raise challenges for women throughout their adult lives, but it is also becoming clear that the lack of workplace and public supports for family care creates a cumulative disadvantage for women. However, it is during retirement that the full effect of women's life-long responsibility for family care becomes most marked.

NEW RESEARCH DIRECTIONS

A life course perspective provides a valuable lens for viewing midlife women, both as individuals moving through their life course and as members of families that are also aging. Our focus on caregiving, age discrimination, and retirement highlights three issues that arise from these intersecting paths. Although we have learned much about these specific issues in recent decades, there is much we still do not know about the broader experiences of women, families, and work in midlife.

First, despite widespread documentation that work and family roles have changed dramatically during the past half century, we know surprisingly little about how or even whether relations among domains such as work, family, health, and leisure differ by birth cohorts (but see Moen, Dempster-McClain, & Williams, 1992; Rexroat, 1992). For example, numerous studies have identified the benefits of multiple roles for health (Moen et al., 1992; Pavalko & Smith, 1999), but do these benefits vary across cohorts? Given changes in the types of jobs women hold, the division of labor in the household, and family structures, it seems likely that the strains and benefits of combining these roles may differ across cohorts. Attention to cohort variation may shed light on processes of change, but also provides another tool for understanding how combining roles affects health and well-being. The growing availability of longitudinal archives makes it increasingly possible to examine cohort variation in these relationships.

Second, future work on effects of work and family roles would benefit from closer attention to processes of selection into or out of roles. We know, for example, that some of the health advantage observed among those who are employed reflects a healthy worker effect, rather than an actual benefit stemming from employment (Adelmann, Antonucci, Crohan, & Coleman, 1990; Pavalko & Smith, 1999; Waldron & Jacobs, 1988), but attention to this effect has been viewed more as a process to be ruled out than a theoretically informative process. However, if we view individuals as agents who select themselves into or out of roles given certain constraints and opportunities, the selection of individuals into or out of roles is theoretically important and interesting (Pavalko & Woodbury, 2000; Thoits & Hewitt, 2001). When examining the health effects of employment, the removal of less healthy women from the labor force will clearly make those who are employed a more select group, but do similar processes apply when we consider other reasons women may not be in the labor force? For example, does the extent of choice that individuals have in adopting or discarding a role factor into its health benefits? A more dynamic view of selection into and out of roles has the potential to consider the relevance of agency in various social roles.

Third, we know little about whether relations among employment, family, and health change as women and men age. For example, although job satisfaction and job tenure increase with age (Rosenfeld, 1992; Warr, 1998), it remains unclear whether these age-related changes affect health and well-being or how they compare with other workplace changes such as technological innovations (Schaie & Schooler, 1998). For example, does employment have an increasingly protective (or disadvantageous) effect on health as workers age? Is the trend more pronounced for physical health, which tends to worsen with age, than for emotional health, which is more likely to remain stable or improve with age? Do workplace innovations affect the health or job opportunities of workers differently as they age?

Finally, research on midlife women and their families would benefit from the continued development of a variety of theoretical perspectives on midlife. Despite general agreement about the importance of midlife (Lachman, 2001), we still lack the broad range of perspectives on midlife roles and transitions that we have for childhood, adolescence, young adulthood, and later life (for an exception, see Staudinger & Bluck, 2001). The difficulty many researchers have in defining *midlife* (Lachman, 2001), particularly in terms other than age, highlights the challenges of studying this varied phase of life. One avenue for future research will be to explore how individuals define midlife and how they view it as distinctive from other points in the life.

A life course perspective reminds us that even as work-family challenges continue across one's life, their form and meaning may shift with age. Although linked to age, many of these changes have little to do with the biological changes that occur as people grow older. Instead they reflect the social dimensions of aging, including the age-graded structures and cultures in which we live, and the location of individuals within networks of friends and family that are also aging. Attention to shifting work and family challenges across the life course can thus offer unique insights into the changing structural and cultural dimensions of the life course.

ACKNOWLEDGMENTS

This research is supported by grant R01-AG11564 from the National Institute on Aging, Eliza K. Pavalko, P.I.

REFERENCES

Adelmann, P. K., Antonucci, T., Crohan, S. E., & Coleman, L. M. (1990). A causal analysis of employment and health in midlife women. *Women and Health, 16*, 5–20.

Brody, E. M. (1981). Women in the middle and family help to older people. *The Gerontologist, 21*, 471–480.

Brody, E. M., Hoffman, C., Kleban, M. H., & Schoonover, C. J. (1989). Caregiving daughters and their local siblings: Perceptions, strains, and interactions. *The Gerontologist, 29*, 529–538.

Dentinger, E., & Clarkberg, M. (2002). Informal caregiving and retirement timing among men and women: Gender and caregiving relationships in late midlife. *Journal of Family Issues, 23*, 857–879.

England, P., Budig, M., & Folbre, N. (2002). Wages of virtue: The relative pay of care work. *Social Problems, 49*, 455–473.

Ettner, S. L. (1996). The opportunity costs of elder care. *The Journal of Human Resources, 31*, 189–205.

Folbre, N. (2001). *The invisible heart: Economics and family values*. New York: New Press.

Fredriksen, K. I. (1996). Gender differences in employment and the informal care of adults. *Journal of Women and Aging, 8*, 35–53.

Fredriksen, K. I., & Scharlach, A. E. (1999). Employee family care responsibilities. *Family Relations, 48*, 189–196.

Gee, G. C. (2002). A multilevel analysis of the relationship between institutional and individual racial discrimination and health status. *American Journal of Public Health, 92*, 615–623.

Gee, G. C., Pavalko, E., & Long, J. S. (2002). *Age discrimination over the life course*. Paper presented at the annual meetings of the Gerontological Association of America, Boston, MA.

Gerstel, N., & Gallagher, S. K. (1994). Caring for kith and kin: Gender, employment, and the privatization of care. *Social Problems, 41*, 519–538.

Golden, L. (2001). Flexible work schedules: What are we trading off to get them? *Monthly Labor Review, 124*, 50–67.

Han, S. K., & Moen, P. (1999). Clocking out: Temporal patterning of retirement. *American Journal of Sociology, 105*, 191–236.

Harrington-Meyer, M. (1990). Family status and poverty among older women: The gendered distribution of retirement income in the United States. *Social Problems, 37*, 1101–1113.

Harrington-Meyer, M. (1996). Making claims as workers or wives: The distribution of social security benefits. *American Sociological Review, 61*, 449–465.

Harrington-Meyer, M. (Ed.). (2000). *Care work: Gender, class, and the welfare states.* New York: Routledge.

Harrington-Meyer, M., & Bellas, M. (1995). U.S. old age policy and the family. In V. Bedford & R. Blieszner (Eds.), *Handbook on aging and the family* (pp. 263–283). New York: Academic Press.

Henretta, J. C., & O'Rand, A. M. (1983). Joint retirement in the dual worker family. *Social Forces, 62*, 504–520.

Henretta, J. C., O'Rand, A. M., & Chan, C. G. (1993). Joint role investments and synchronization of retirement: A sequential approach to couples' retirement timing. *Social Forces, 71*, 981–1000.

Hong, J., & Seltzer, M. M. (1995). The psychological consequences of multiple roles: The nonnormative case. *Journal of Health and Social Behavior, 36*, 386–398.

Ingersoll-Dayton, B., Neal, M. B., & Hammer, L. B. (2001). Aging parents helping adult children: The experience of the sandwiched generation. *Family Relations, 50*, 262–271.

Johnson, R. W., & Neumark, D. B. (1997). Age discrimination, job separations, and employment status of older workers: Evidence from self-reports. *The Journal of Human Resources, 32*, 779–811.

Kalavar, J. M. (2001). Examining ageism: Do male and female college students differ? *Educational Gerontology, 27*, 507–513.

Kessler, R. C., Mickelson, K. D., & Williams, D. R. (1999). The prevalence, distribution, and mental health correlates of perceived discrimination in the United States. *Journal of Health and Social Behavior, 40*, 208–230.

Kiecolt-Glaser, J. K., Dura, J. R., Speicher, C. E., Trask, O. J., & Glaser, R. (1991). Spousal caregivers of dementia victims: Longitudinal changes in immunity and health. *Psychosomatic Medicine, 53*, 345–362.

Kim, J. E., & Moen, P. (2001). Moving into retirement: Preparation and transitions in late midlife. In M. E. Lachman (Ed.), *Handbook of midlife development* (pp. 487–527). New York: Wiley.

Kingson, E. R., & O'Grady-LeShane, R. (1993). The effects of caregiving on women's Social Security benefits. *The Gerontologist, 33*, 230–239.

Lachman, M. E. (Ed.). (2001). *Handbook of midlife development.* New York: Wiley.

Marks, N. F. (1996). Caregiving across the lifespan: National prevalence and predictors. *Family Relations, 45*, 27–36.

Marks, N. F. (1998). Does it hurt to care? Caregiving, work-family conflict, and midlife well-being. *Journal of Marriage and the Family, 60*, 951–966.

Martire, L. M., Stephens, M. A. P., & Atienza, A. A. (1997). The interplay between work and caregiving: Relationships between role satisfaction, role involvement, and caregivers' well-being. *Journal of Gerontology, Social Sciences, 52B*, S279-S289.

Matthews, S., Werkner, J., & Delaney, P. (1989). Relative contributions of help by employed and nonemployed sisters to their elderly parents. *Journal of Gerontology, Social Sciences, 44*, S36-S44.

Moen, P. (2001). The gendered life course. In R. H. Binstock & L. K. George (Eds.), *Handbook of aging and the social sciences* (5th ed., pp. 179–196). San Diego, CA: Academic Press.

Moen, P., Dempster-McClain, D., & Williams, R. M. J. (1992). Successful aging: A life-course perspective on women's multiple roles and health. *American Journal of Sociology, 97,* 1612–1638.

Moen, P., & Han, S.-K. (2001). Reframing careers: Work, family, and gender. In V. W. Marshall, W. R. Heinz, H. Kruger, & A. Verma (Eds.), *Restructuring work and the life course* (pp. 424–445). Toronto, Ontario: University of Toronto Press.

Moen, P., Kim, J. E., & Hofmeister, H. (2001). Couples' work/retirement transitions, gender, and marital quality. *Social Psychology Quarterly, 64,* 55–71.

Moen, P., Robison, J., & Fields, V. (1994). Women's work and caregiving roles: A life course approach. *Journal of Gerontology: Social Sciences, 49,* S176-S186.

National Alliance for Caregiving and American Association of Retired Persons (NAC/AARP). (1997). *Family caregiving in the U.S.—Findings from a national survey.* Bethesda, MD: Author.

National Family Caregivers Association. (1997). Member survey 1997: A profile of caregivers. www.nfcacares.org/survey.html.

Neal, M. B., Ingersoll-Dayton, B., & Starrels, M. E. (1997). Gender and relationship differences in caregiving patterns and consequences among employed caregivers. *Gerontologist, 37,* 804–816.

Neumark, D. B., & McLennan, M. (1995). Sex discrimination and women's labor market outcomes. *Journal of Human Resources, 30,* 713–740.

O'Grady-LeShane, R., & Williamson, J. B. (1992). Family provisions in old-age pensions: Twenty industrial nations. In M. Szinovacz, D. J. Ekerdt, & B. H. Vinick (Eds.), *Families and retirement* (pp. 64–77). Newbury Park, CA: Sage.

O'Rand, A. M. (1996). The precious and the precocious: Understanding cumulative disadvantage and cumulative advantage. *The Gerontologist, 36,* 230–238.

O'Rand, A. M. (2001). Perpetuating women's disadvantage: Trends in us private pensions. In J. Ginn, D. Street, & S. Arber (Eds.), *Women, work and pensions: International issues and prospects* (pp. 142–157). Buckingham: Open University Press.

O'Rand, A. M., & Farkas, J. I. (2002). Couples' retirement timing in the United States in the 1990s. *International Journal of Sociology, 32,* 11–29.

O'Rand, A. M., & Henretta, J. C. (1999). *Age and inequality: Diverse pathways through later life.* Boulder, CO: Westview.

Pavalko, E. K., & Artis, J. E. (1997). Women's caregiving and paid work: Causal relationships in late mid-life. *Journal of Gerontology: Social Sciences, 52B,* S1–S10.

Pavalko, E. K., Mossakowski, K., & Hamilton, V. (2003). Does perceived discrimination affect health? Longitudinal relationships between work discrimination and women's physical and emotional health. *Journal of Health and Social Behavior, 44,* 18–33.

Pavalko, E. K., & Smith, B. (1999). The rhythm of work: Health effects of women's work dynamics. *Social Forces, 77,* 1141–1162.

Pavalko, E. K., & Woodbury, S. (2000). Social roles as process: Caregiving careers and women's health. *Journal of Health and Social Behavior, 41,* 91–105.

Perry, E. L., Kulik, C. T., & Bourhis, A. C. (1996). Moderating effect of personal and contextual factors in age discrimination. *Journal of Applied Psychology, 81,* 628–647.

Quadagno, J. (1988). Women's access to pensions and the structure of eligibility rules: Systems of production and reproduction. *Sociological Quarterly, 29,* 541–558.

Rexroat, C. (1992). Changes in the employment continuity of succeeding cohorts of young women. *Work and Occupations, 19,* 18–34.

Robison, J., Moen, P., & Dempster-McClain, D. (1995). Women's caregiving: Changing profiles and pathways. *Journal of Gerontology: Social Sciences, 50B,* S362–S373.

Rosenfeld, R. (1992). Job mobility and career processes. *Annual Review of Sociology, 18,* 39–61.

Ruhm, C. (1998). The economic consequences of parental leave mandates: Lessons from Europe. *Quarterly Journal of Economics, 113*, 285–317.

Schaie, K. W., & Schooler, C. (1998). *The impact of work on older workers.* New York: Springer.

Scharlach, A. E., & Boyd, S. L. (1989). Caregiving and employment: Results of an employee survey. *The Gerontologist, 29*, 382–387.

Schulz, R., O'Brien, A. T., Bookwala, J., & Fleissner, K. (1995). Psychiatric and physical morbidity effects of dementia caregiving: Prevalence, correlates, and causes. *Gerontologist, 35*(6), 771–791.

Schulz, R., Visintainer, P., & Williamson, G. M. (1990). Psychiatric and physical morbidity effects of caregiving. *Journal of Gerontology: Psychological Sciences, 45*(5), P181–P191.

Sigelman, L., & Sigelman, C. K. (1982). Sexism, racism, and ageism in voting behavior: An experimental analysis. *Social Psychology Quarterly, 45*(4), 263–269.

Spillman, B. C., & Pezzin, L. E. (2000). Potential and active family caregivers: Changing networks and the "sandwich generation." *Milbank Quarterly, 78*(3), 347–374.

Spitze, G., Logan, J. R., Joseph, G., & Lee, E. (1994). Middle generation roles and the well-being of men and women. *Journal of Gerontology, Social Sciences, 49*(3), S107-S116.

Staudinger, U. M., & Bluck, S. (2001). A view on midlife development from life-span theory. In M. E. Lachman (Ed.), *Handbook of midlife development* (pp. 3–39). New York: Wiley.

Stone, R., Cafferata, G., & Sangl, J. (1987). Caregivers of the frail elderly: A national profile. *The Gerontologist, 27*(5), 616–626.

Street, D., & Wilmoth, J. (2001). Social insecurity? Women and pensions in the U.S. In J. Ginn, D. Street, & S. Arber (Eds.), *Women, work and pensions: International issues and prospects* (pp. 120–141). Buckingham: Open University Press.

Szinovacz, M., & Ekerdt, D. J. (1995). Families and retirement. In V. Bedford & R. Blieszner (Eds.), *Handbook on aging and the family* (pp. 375–400). New York: Academic Press.

Thoits, P. A., & Hewitt, L. N. (2001). Volunteer work and well-being. *Journal of Health and Social Behavior, 42*(2), 115–131.

U.S. Bureau of Labor Statistics. (2002). *Employee benefits in private industry, 2000.* Washington, DC: United States Department of Labor.

Waldfogel, J. (2001). Family and medical leave: Evidence from the 2000 surveys. *Monthly Labor Review, 124*(9), 17–23.

Waldron, I., & Jacobs, J. A. (1988). Effects of labor force participation on women's health: New evidence from a longitudinal study. *Journal of Occupational Medicine, 30*(12), 977–983.

Walker, A. J., Pratt, C. C., & Eddy, L. (1995). Informal caregiving to aging family members: A critical review. *Family Relations, 44*(4), 402–411.

Warr, P. (1998). Age, work and mental health. In K. W. Schaie & C. Schooler (Eds.), *The impact of work on older workers* (pp. 252–298). New York: Springer.

Willson, A. E., & Hardy, M. A. (2002). Racial disparities in income security for a cohort of aging American women. *Social Forces, 80*(4), 1283–1306.

Wolf, D. A., & Soldo, B. J. (1994). Married women's allocation of time to employment and care of elderly parents. *The Journal of Human Resources, 29*(4), 1259–1276.

PART VI

Occupations,
Workplace Settings,
and Health of Families

26

The Impact
of Occupational Injuries
and Illnesses on Families

Allard E. Dembe

University of Massachusetts Medical School

Job-related injury and illness is a common source of disability and hardship among the U.S. adult population. Each year more than 5 million Americans report workplace injuries and illnesses (Bureau of Labor Statistics, 2002). The annual direct and indirect costs of these conditions are estimated at $155 billion, far exceeding the costs associated with AIDS and Alzheimer's disease and roughly comparable to costs for cancer and coronary heart disease (CHD) in the United States (Leigh, Markowitz, Fahs, & Landrigan, 2000). Medical care and wage-replacement benefits for workplace injuries and illnesses are generally provided under state-regulated workers' compensation insurance plans, which cover 98% of the American workforce (Thompson, Reno, Mont, Burton, & Thomason, 2002). However, authorities believe that many occupational injuries and illnesses are not reported to or accepted by workers' compensation insurers, and that workers' compensation claims data, therefore, underestimate the true extent of the problem (Azaroff, Levenstein, & Wegman, 2002).

Numerous studies have documented the effects of occupational injuries and illnesses on workers. Some of the most common effects are physical impairment, functional limitations, wage loss, and restrictions on the worker's ability to perform job duties. Recently researchers have conducted expanded outcomes assessments in this area, vastly enhancing knowledge about the broader social and economic consequences of work-related injuries and illnesses (Dembe, 2001; Keogh, Gucer, Nuwayhid, & Gordon, 2000; Morse, Levenstein, Warren, Dillon, & Warren, 1998; Pransky et al., 2000; Weil, 2001). Evidence has begun to accumulate suggesting that occupational injuries and illnesses, in addition to affecting the injured worker, also have significant repercussions for the worker's family and children. In this chapter, I explore this emerging area of study, review relevant findings, and propose an agenda for future research in this field.

CONSEQUENCES OF INJURIES AND ILLNESSES FOR FAMILIES

Injuries and illnesses to an individual can affect the health and well-being of the individual's family in many ways. The multiple pathways through which injuries or illnesses affect families have not yet been determined fully. However, existing research points to at least five mediating routes—medical care and recovery, psychological and behavioral, functional, economic, and vocational responses—by which a change in health can create adverse repercussions for a spouse, children, parents, and other household members (see e.g., Leske & Jiricka, 1998; Patterson & Garwick, 1994; Stein & Riessman, 1980; Steinglass, 2000).

For example, family members often must adjust to the expanded health care needs of a relative who has sustained a serious medical problem or chronic condition. Family members may need to furnish transportation to the site of care, administer medications and other home health care services, communicate with medical providers and health insurers, and provide other forms of assistance.

It is also common for individuals suffering injuries or illnesses to respond with feelings of anger, depression, stress, and alienation. Some may become violent or suicidal. Others attempt to deal with a serious medical problem by adopting unhealthy behaviors, such as smoking, consumption of alcohol, or use of drugs. Many feel isolated as a result of their condition and subsequent inability to perform customary activities. These responses potentially affect domestic relationships and family function.

Physical impairments resulting from an injury or illness can limit an individual's ability to perform daily functions and restrict capacity to participate in normal activities. This can place a burden on others in the family. A sick or injured mother, for example, may be unable to perform routine functions such as shopping, child care, or housework. The ability to maintain close relationships with family members may be inhibited, as might sexual relations with the person's partner. Children and family members sometimes must as-

TABLE 26.1
Effects of Worker Injury or Illness on Family

Emotional and Affective States	Impaired Relationships	Functional Changes and Domestic Roles	Financial Hardships
Depression	Separation	Family caregiving	Loss of income
Alienation	Divorce	Child-care duties	Increased expenses
Anger	Poor communication	Household chores	Sold belongings
Resentment	Conflict	Work less (or more)	Moved
Stress	Withdrawal	Transportation needs	Borrowed (or lent)
Violence	Less intimacy	Educational change	Assistive devices
Sleep problems	Less family time	Fewer social activities	Lost insurance
Impatience		Home helpers	
Irritability			

sume additional responsibilities to compensate for the individual's reduced functioning.

The most common vocational impact of an injury or sickness is short- or long-term absence from work. Workers who return to the workplace after an injury or illness also encounter various problems, including reduced work hours, diminished productivity, inability to handle regular job responsibilities, and decreased quality of work life. Injured workers are more likely than uninjured workers to experience employment changes, including being laid off, fired, transferred to another job, and retiring, quitting, or dropping out of the labor market. These job transitions can impose pressures on family life, for example, by altering daily schedules, increasing the work responsibilities of other family members, and eliciting changes in the family's health insurance coverage.

Finally, sickness, injuries, and chronic conditions can exert a substantial financial impact on families by reducing employment earnings and potentially increasing legal and medical expenses. The resulting lost income can precipitate a variety of responses in the family, including disposition of assets, additional debt, cutting back on educational or recreational activities, dipping into savings, seeking benefits from welfare or other assistance programs, and finding less costly alternatives for child care and other family needs. Table 26.1 classifies the main effects on families and children that have been noted in the research literature.

SPECIAL ISSUES INVOLVING
OCCUPATIONAL INJURIES AND ILLNESSES

Occupational injuries and illnesses generally have similar effects on families as do other, nonwork-related injuries and chronic conditions, such as cancer and arthritis. Despite these similarities, the evidence suggests there are also differences for families and children living with a relative suffering from a work-related condition that can create special complexities and intensify the difficulties encountered. For example, in cases of occupational injuries and illnesses, families often must contend with an unfriendly workers' compensation system, reluctance by employers and workers' compensation insurers to accept responsibility for the injury, and conflicts involving the need to prove occupational causation (to qualify for benefits). Delays in medical treatment and legal disputes are common. In workers' compensation cases, the employer and insurer often determine which doctors and medical professionals will be involved, thereby complicating the process of accessing care and impeding communications between the family and unfamiliar clinicians. There are few support structures available for families through workers' compensation, and interactions among the family and employers, case managers, and insurance claims administrators are frequently difficult and unsettling.

A work-related disorder is always couched in the larger context of pre-vailing employer–employee relations, and issues of timing for return to work, extent of functional impairment, and recovery of lost wages are often paramount. Along with the standard economic concerns that accompany any family member's illness, occupational disorders have the added dimension of directly relating to employment activities and status, which can raise ques-tions about the injured worker's proficiency and diligence in performing job duties, and introduce concerns about applying for and securing disability and wage-replacement benefits under workers' compensation.

In the case of work-related conditions, the worker's family must confront the sometimes competing demands of the injured individual's need to return to work quickly while also allowing time for that person to regain full health and functional capacity. Workers who delay their return to work run the risk of being labeled as malingerers by the employer, insurer, and others (Dembe & Boden, 2000). The various legal, insurance, compensation, and labor-relations ramifications of these considerations can place additional stress on a family. Table 26.2 summarizes the special considerations that can intensify the effects of a work-related injury or illness on families.

THE SOCIAL CONSEQUENCES OF OCCUPATIONAL INJURIES AND ILLNESSES

Given the variety of workplace influences on health and the wide assortment of illnesses linked to occupational risk factors, the impacts on workers and their families are potentially enormous. Some of the consequences of work-place injuries and illnesses are obvious and have been studied extensively. For example, the time lost from work owing to injury is a major concern of government safety agencies, employers, and workers' compensation insur-

TABLE 26.2
Special Issues Affecting Families of Individuals
With a Work-Related Injury or Illness

Issue	Description
Employment Status	Work-related injuries often jeopardize a worker's continued employment, and thus a family's economic stability. Some employers see workplace accidents and reported work injuries as indicative of poor performance, carelessness, negligence, or malingering.
Medical care	Most state workers' compensation laws allow the employer or its insurer to direct medical care and choose the worker's treating physician. Disputes concerning medical care and choice of physicians are common in workers' compensation and often are litigated. Workers must prove that their condition is caused by work to obtain care under workers' compensation, which also creates delays and disputes in some cases.
Return to work	The employer, insurer, and employer's medical providers can exert pressure on workers to return to work quickly and, in some cases, prematurely. There is generally reduced latitude for an injured worker to remain at home for full recovery, compared with other types of medical conditions.
Income protection and economic losses	In some jurisdictions, the benefits available under workers' compensation are relatively low and do not represent adequate replacement for a family's income compared with what would be obtainable under other forms of disability and unemployment insurance. Generally, workers' compensation benefits are the only type allowed for workers with occupational injuries and illnesses.
Disability and impairment determination	Workers' compensation benefits and continued absence from work often depend on a disability evaluation and quantified rating of impairment. This system of tying benefits to the extent of disability encourages disability behavior and may discourage full resumption of functions and activities by injured family members.
Stress	Disputes, distrust, suspicion, and conflict are particularly common following workplace injuries and illnesses. Dealing with these issues can place additional stress on workers and their families.

ance carriers, who pay benefits for the employees' lost wages. The processes by which workplace injuries and illnesses lead to temporary or permanent physical impairment, limitations in functional ability, and disability among affected workers are key issues for occupational medicine professionals, rehabilitation specialists, and therapists. The legal and economic implications of these processes are extensive, and they affect the worker's eligibility for benefits and return to productive employment.

Because of the significant economic, employment, and legal ramifications, researchers have documented the direct effect of workplace injury on workers' compensation costs and employment outcomes relatively well. For example, recent research has shown that workers injured on the job sustain long-term earnings losses that are not fully recovered through workers' compensation benefits even 10 years after the original injury (Reville, Schoeni, & Martin, 2002).

However, considerably less is known about the indirect impacts of occupational injuries and illnesses on workers' lives and the accompanying ramifications for their families, children, and communities. Through the support of the National Institute for Occupational Safety and Health (NIOSH) and other agencies, a few preliminary investigations have recently been undertaken to identify and assess the broader social and economic consequences of occupational injuries and illnesses (Boden, Biddle, & Spieler, 2001; Dembe, 2001; Whatman et al., 2002). Recent studies have examined such effects as social functioning, general health status, psychological and behavioral reactions, long-term vocational experiences, and changes in personal economic circumstances, in addition to more traditional biological, physical, and clinical parameters (Keller, 2001; Keogh et al., 2000; Morse et al., 1998; Pransky & Himmelstein, 1996; Pransky et al., 2000).

Several studies have collected information from injured workers regarding their perceptions about the process of filing claims for workers' compensation benefits and their interactions with the workers' compensation insurance system (Imershein, Hill, & Reynolds, 1994; MacDonald, 2000; Strunin & Boden, 2000; Sum, 1996). Other studies have examined injured workers' experiences in accessing needed medical care and their satisfaction with the services received (Kyes et al., 1999; Rudolph, Dervin, Cheadle, Maizlish, & Wickizer, 2002). Several investigations are examining social inequalities in occupational health and health services based on workers' race, ethnicity, gender, and socioeconomic status (Dembe, Savageau, Amick, & Banks, 2003; Strunin & Boden, 1997).

EVIDENCE EXAMINING THE IMPACTS OF WORK-RELATED INJURIES AND ILLNESSES ON FAMILIES AND CHILDREN

Few studies directly measure the specific effects of occupational injuries and illnesses on workers' families and children. Most available information infers potential consequences for families from the direct effects experienced by the worker. Most of the studies examining these effects have been qualitative, and few have had suitable comparison groups. As a result, reliable evidence on this topic is limited, and more empirical investigation is needed.

Contemporary research into the effects of illness and injury on family members is grounded in the view of a family as an interconnected system, in which events that occur in the life of individual family members cause changes in the behavior of family members as individuals and as a group. Sachs and Ellenberg (1994) used a systems orientation to describe the various adaptations families made when a family member suffered a workplace injury. Based on case studies and their clinical experience as family therapists, they identified four common reactions: (a) role changes, (b) changes in communications, (c) problems of intimacy, and (d) problems of boundaries. Examples of role changes include other family members working longer hours, assuming household chores, and spending less time supervising children's school and social activities. With respect to communications, they noted increased family conflict and squabbles, particularly surrounding issues of financial security, child care, and return to work. In addition, Sachs and Ellenberg observed that injured workers are often unwilling to discuss sensitive family topics. Intimacy problems were evident in reduced feelings of family cohesiveness, less time for family interaction, and less desire and physical intimacy among adult partners. Finally, boundary issues involve lack of understanding and sympathy across generations and reversals in the caregiving relationships usually experienced between parents and children.

In perhaps the most comprehensive assessment of the social effects of workplace injuries and illnesses, the New Zealand Department of Labor analyzed the effects of 15 serious workplace injuries and illnesses through in-depth interviews of 68 workers, their employers, coworkers, and family members (Whatman et al., 2002). The New Zealand researchers concluded that, "In all [fifteen] cases, the family suffered emotionally, mentally, and financially. Family relationships were affected, mostly negatively" (p. 13). Major family consequences included emotional stress, financial pressures, changes in family relationships, physical and emotional isolation, changes precipitated by family caregiving to the injured worker, and changes in domestic roles and responsibilities. Emotional stress in the family was manifested by injured workers perceiving a lack of support from other family members, family members expressing feelings of guilt about the injured worker's condition, affective changes in family relationships (arguments, irritability, isolation), and increased smoking and substance abuse by children and other family members. Financial pressures included increased medical costs and direct loss of income, transportation costs (e.g., taxis), and costs required for purchasing assistive devices for the home (e.g., orthopedic beds, handrails). The study estimated average nonreimbursed costs per case to be approximately $57,000 (N.Z.). The financial pressures led to various consequences for the families, including lifestyle changes, home sales, disposition of assets (cars, trucks), and moves into smaller residences. Adverse effects on family relationships included numerous cases of separation, divorce, loss of physical intimacy, alienation, and breakdown of the family unit. Many of the family members indicated they had either left work, lost time from work, changed jobs, terminated their education, or gave up recreational activities as a result of their relative's injury. Common changes in domestic roles and responsibilities included family members assuming injured workers' duties for child care and transportation, the hiring of additional home help, and making alternative arrangements for care of elderly parents.

The Australian Industry Commission (1995) obtained similar results in a study that identified specific ways that occupational injuries and illnesses affected injured workers' families and friends. They included a substantial deterioration in living standard for family members, difficulty in social interaction, marital breakups, domestic violence, and feelings of alienation. According to this report, the effects were greater for workers with occupational diseases than for those with occupational injuries. The Commission also attempted to estimate indirect and direct costs associated with workplace injuries and illnesses. While noting that the tangible indirect costs related to "loss of leisure opportunities and general decline in the quality of life of the worker and family, reduced social interaction and social status, and losses due to family members nursing the injured worker," they concluded that the magnitude of those losses was "not estimable" (Australian Industry Commission, 1995, Appendix C, p. 112).

In another qualitative study, Strunin and Boden (1997) conducted ethnographic interviews with 60 injured workers in Wisconsin who had been out of work for more than 1 month. About one fourth of these workers (27%) reported that they could not have sex as a result of their injury, and 10% had difficulty attending their children's events (e.g., because of problems in prolonged sitting). Several had trouble sleeping or getting up in the morning. Frequently mentioned family effects included diminished ability to perform home responsibilities, decreased patience with children and spouses because of pain, and complaints about the quality of housework or cooking done by others when the injured worker could no longer do it. Most injured men reported difficulty mowing the lawn or shoveling snow, and several had problems doing yard work or gardening. One third of the injured workers reported some difficulty performing other chores, including shopping and taking out garbage. Men were likely to report psychological reactions (e.g., depression, anger) related to perceived loss of the masculine role, reduced independence, and the need to hire people to take care of their houses.

A survey of injured workers with permanent impairments conducted by the Texas Workers' Compensation Research Center (1995) found that 83% of the subjects encountered a significant family-related hardship as the result of their injury. Identified hardships included moving in with relatives (reported by 40% of respondents), borrowing money (53%), depleting savings (53%), and being fired (27%). About three fourths (72%) of the injured workers needed some form of financial assistance in addition to workers' compensation to respond to the injury and its aftermath. The most common source of financial assistance was friends and relatives (31%), followed by food stamps (19%) and Social Security disability benefits (15%).

A case-control study in Connecticut found that, compared with uninjured persons of working age, individuals who had suffered a work-related upper extremity disorder were more likely to have been divorced recently (OR = 1.91, 95% CI: 1.01–3.58), moved for financial reasons (OR = 2.41, 95% CI: 1.20–4.86), sold a home (OR = 3.44, 95% CI: 1.14–10.35) or car (OR = 2.45, 95% CI: 1.04–5.74), experience stress at home (OR = 1.31, CI: 0.95–1.82), and lost their health insurance (OR = 1.91, 95% CI: 0.99–3.71; Morse et al., 1998). About 24% of the injured workers in this study reported difficulty performing child-care activities compared with less than 4% of the controls (OR = 8.2, 85% CI: 4.9–13.8). More than one half of the injured individuals reported needing to limit home activities as a result of their injury.

A similar survey of workers in Maryland who had suffered work-related upper extremity cumulative trauma disorders found that 11 to 46 months after initially reporting their injury (average of 28 months), a sizable proportion still had difficulty performing various household activities, including lifting a child over a crib rail (53.7%), mopping floors (51.3%), cooking at a stove top (27.2%), and carrying a small bag of groceries (43.8%; Keogh et al., 2000). Almost one half (47.9%) of the injured workers reported family problems as the result of their condition; 10.9% had separated from their spouse or partner, 15.6% could no longer afford to maintain a car, 5.6% had moved to a less expensive residence, 31.9% had borrowed money from family and friends, and 36% had been contacted by collection agencies. About one third of the respondents (31%) reported symptoms suggestive of clinical depression. Most (63.9%) said that their condition interfered with performing home and recreational activities, and 53.3% had problems sleeping. About 38% of respondents indicated they had been laid off, fired, or quit the job they had held at the time of their injury. However, interestingly, the injured workers reported that the effect of their condition was felt more at home than on the job.

Dawson (1994) interviewed 45 members of a Pennsylvania support group for injured workers with contested workers' compensation claims about their experience obtaining compensation and medical care for their injuries. Respondents reported a variety of consequences for their spouses, families, relatives, and communities, including an inability to participate in family activities, loss of sex life, divorce, family financial pressures, and emotional stress related to feelings of depression, lowered self-esteem, frustration, and anger. Seven (15.5%) of the injured workers reported that their children's educational plans had been disrupted as a result of their injury and the workers' compensation disputes. About two thirds of the injured workers had been forced to sell personal items and family assets, including autos, businesses, and residences. Forty percent reported suicidal feelings at some point following their injury, and almost one third reported needing assistance from public and private social services for themselves or their family members.

Findings such as these are not unusual. Feuerstein, Sult, and Houle (1985) documented family conflict and dysfunction among individuals with chronic low back pain. Data from the National Longitudinal Survey indicate that people experiencing a workplace injury or illness are 25% more likely to be divorced than other working-age adults (Dembe, Savageau, Erickson, & Banks, 2002). Workers with occupational musculoskeletal injuries participating in specially designed support groups in Canada reported a variety of effects on family function, including problems sleeping and performing common household tasks. They also expressed feelings of frustration, anger, and depression. The loss of independence after their injury and the deterioration in family relations emerged as significant issues among the support group participants (Mignone & Guidotti, 1999). Among a sample of New Hampshire workers with work-related upper extremity and lower back injuries, 33.7% dipped into savings, 33.4% had problems paying bills, 28.4% had to borrow money, and 14.8% sold personal belongings. These social effects were much more widespread among workers with injuries that caused at least 1 week of missed work (Pransky et al., 2000). Hétu, Lalonde, and Getty (1987) found that family members of workers with occupational noise-induced hearing loss experienced substantial disruption in family function and communications. Family members were often irritated at being asked to repeat statements, annoyed with the high volume used by the worker for listening to TV and radio and the loud voice used by the worker, and reported problems stemming from the worker's need to have a quiet period after returning home from the noisy work environment.

The preceding summary of available research illustrates some of the ways that occupational injuries and illnesses can affect the families and children of the injured worker. Research is still limited, however, and the available information often derives from relatively unstructured qualitative observations rather than systematic analytical studies. This synopsis has focused on the secondary effects to family members (e.g., spouse, children, parents) of a worker's injury. It has not covered more direct effects of occupational injuries on families, such as occupational injuries to working children; illness or injury to family members from indirect exposure to occupational toxins, as might occur from pesticide exposure to children of farmers or as the result of workers inadvertently bringing lead, mercury, or other workplace contaminants into the home; workplace reproductive hazards; or special occupational health issues involving working women, such as their heightened vulnerability to workplace violence.

CONCLUSION AND POLICY IMPLICATIONS

I have described available evidence suggesting that occupational injuries and illnesses have significant impacts on the families and children of affected workers. These effects are not isolated, but rather occur in a broader context of social, economic, and community-based influences on health and family function. The effects described in this chapter are manifestations of the deep connections between individuals and their work, and they exemplify one way that employment can affect the health of populations. Family reactions to a relative's work-related condition are inevitably colored by special employment-related considerations, including workers' compensation claims, the availability of wage replacement benefits, pressures to resume work, and the employer's relationship to the affected worker. These factors potentially can intensify the consequences of the worker's injury or illness for the family.

These observations help illustrate the significant role played by occupation as a social determinant of health and disease. As evidence mounts about the contribution of employment experiences in the etiology of many common ailments, it is likely that the definition of an *occupational disorder* will continue to evolve and expand (Dembe, 1996; Frank & Maetzel, 2000; Maetzel, Makela, Hawker, & Bombardier, 1997; Shainblum, Sullivan, & Frank, 2000). For example, evidence has accumulated in recent years that workplace hazards may contribute to the risk of contracting a variety of common medical ailments, including cardiovascular disease, arthritis, diabetes, and asthma (Belkic, Schnall, Landsbergis, & Baker, 2000; Cooper, 1995; Johnson et al., 2000; Rahman, Tondel, Ahmad, Axelson, 1998; Schouten, de Bie, & Swaen, 2002). Knowledge about the diversity of job-related influences on health—including the organization of work, psychosocial aspects of employment, and workplace-based social support—will grow as additional studies in this area are completed. These developments will serve to reinforce and strengthen our understanding of the significant influence of employment and the direct and indirect repercussions of work-related injuries for affected workers and their families.

Additional research is critical to understanding and measuring these effects, especially well-designed studies that can better evaluate the social consequences of occupational injuries and illnesses. Measures of the effects on the injured workers' families and their associated costs should be included more frequently in outcome studies involving individuals with work-related conditions. Studies are needed that systematically assess the nature and extent of these effects by identifying appropriate comparison groups and using standardized instruments for collecting data on family effects. Adequate study populations are required that represent a broad spectrum of ages, medical conditions, residences, and types of employment. Questions about the incidence of occupational injuries and illnesses and other employment-related factors should be routinely included in studies of family function and children's health. Differences in family effects among subpopulations of workers with differing sociodemographic characteristics should also be assessed. Investigations in this field must account for the complex interplay between occupational determinants and other social, behavioral, economic, and environmental factors. Some key areas for additional research on workers with occupational injuries and illnesses include the extent and nature of family caregiving that is provided; the effect on the educational, vocational, and recreational activities of children; alcohol and substance use among family members; the influence of workers' compensation system characteristics on families; and the communication experiences of family members with employers and workers' compensation insurers.

The ultimate objective of these research efforts should be to develop effective strategies for mitigating the adverse consequences of a workplace injury or illnesses. Potential strategies might include: (a) counseling for the injured worker, children, and other family members regarding possible coping mechanisms and the pressures created by the family member's affliction; (b) improved methods for ensuring effective communication among the employer, medical providers, the injured worker, and family members; (c) information for family members on how to provide needed support and suggested adaptive techniques, including technical advice on physical accommodations and assistive devices for the home; (d) medical treatment for psychological symptoms in the patient (e.g., depression) and, when appropriate, for affected family members; (e) appropriate medication and psychological therapy to manage the injured worker's pain and disability; (f) help for patients and their families in applying for appropriate social benefits (e.g., unemployment) to offset financial and physical losses; and (g) policy changes to allow workers' compensation insurance to pay for counseling and other services for affected family members (list adapted, in part, from Gatchel, Adams, Polatin, & Kishino, 2002).

Implementing these strategies requires a coordinated effort among employers, medical providers, insurers, and community-based support systems. Federal agencies, including NIOSH and the National Institute of Child Health and Human Development, should be encouraged to take the lead on developing plans to move forward in these areas. Cooperation and participation from state workers' compensation agencies and from labor and employer organizations should be solicited. Ultimately, the burdens created by occupational injuries and illnesses will always be borne primarily by the affected workers and their families, but additional research and well-conceived intervention strategies will enable us to plan more effectively for these occurrences and ensure that the appropriate supportive mechanisms are in place.

REFERENCES

Australian Industry Commission. (1995, September). *Work, health, and safety: An inquiry into occupational health and safety* (Report No. 47). Canberra: Australian Government Publishing Service.

Azaroff, L. S., Levenstein, C., & Wegman, D. H. (2002). Occupational injury and illness surveillance: Conceptual filters explain underreporting. *American Journal of Public Health, 92*(9), 1421–1429.

Belkic, K., Schnall, P., Landsbergis, P., & Baker, D. (2000). The workplace and cardiovascular health: Conclusions and thoughts for a future agenda. *Occupational Medicine, 15*(1), 307–321.

Boden, L., Biddle, E., & Spieler, E. (2001). Social and economic impacts of workplace illness and injury: Current and future directions for research. *American Journal of Industrial Medicine, 40,* 398–402.

Bureau of Labor Statistics, U.S. Department of Labor Statistics. (2002). *Survey of occupational injuries and illnesses 2001.* Washington, DC: Government Printing Office.

Cooper, C. (1995). Occupational activity and the risk of osteoarthritis. *Journal of Rheumatology, 22*(Suppl. 43), 10–12.

Dawson, S. (1994). Workers' compensation in Pennsylvania: The effects of delayed contested cases. *Journal of Health Social Policy, 6*(1), 87–100.

Dembe, A. (1996). *Occupation and disease: How social factors affect the conception of work-related disorders.* New Haven, CT: Yale University Press.

Dembe, A. (2001). The social consequences of occupational injuries and illnesses. *American Journal of Industrial Medicine, 40*(4), 403–417.

Dembe, A., & Boden, L. (2000). Moral hazard: A question of morality? *New Solutions, 10*(3), 257–279.

Dembe, A., Savageau, J., Amick, B., & Banks, S. (2003). *Racial and ethnic variations in office-based medical care for work-related injuries and illnesses* (Working paper). Worcester: UMass Center for Health Policy and Research.

Dembe, A., Savageau, J., Erickson, J., & Banks, S. (2002, June). *Social inequalities in occupational health and health care: Preliminary results from the National Longitudinal Survey of Youth, 1998.* Poster presentation at the annual meeting of the Academy of Health Policy and Health Services Research, Washington, DC.

Feurerstein, M., Sult, S., & Houle, M. (1985). Environmental stressors and chronic low back pain: Life events, family and work environment. *Pain, 22,* 295–307.

Frank, J., & Maetzel, A. (2000). Determining occupational disorder: Can this camel carry more straw? In T. Sullivan (Ed.), *Injury and the new world of work* (pp. 265–283). Vancouver: UBC Press.

Gatchel, R., Adams, L., Polatin, P., & Kishino, N. (2002). Secondary loss and pain-associated disability: Theoretical overview and treatment implications. *Journal of Occupational Rehabilitation, 12*(2), 99–110.

Hétu, R., Lalonde, M., & Getty, L. (1987). Psychological disadvantages associated with occupational hearing loss as experienced in the family. *Audiology, 26,* 141–152.

Imershein, A., Hill, A., & Reynolds, A. (1994). The workers' compensation system as a quality of life problem for workers' compensation claimants. *Advanced Medical Sociology, 5,* 181–200.

Johnson, A., Dimich-Ward, H., Manfreda, J., Becklake, M. R., Ernst, P., Sears, M. R., et al. (2000). Occupational asthma in adults in six Canadian communities. *American Journal of Respiratory and Critical Care Medicine, 162,* 2058–2062.

Keller, S. D. (2001). Quantifying social consequences of occupational injuries and illnesses: State of the art and research agenda. *American Journal of Industrial Medicine, 40,* 438–451.

Keogh, J., Gucer, P., Nuwayhid, I., & Gordon, J. (2000). The impact of occupational injury on injured worker and family: Outcomes of upper extremity cumulative trauma disorders in Maryland workers. *American Journal of Industrial Medicine*, 38, 1–9.

Kyes, K. B., Wickizer, T. M., Franklin, G., Cain, K., Cheadle, A., Madden, C., et al. (1999). Evaluation of the Washington state workers' compensation managed care pilot program: Medical outcomes and patient satisfaction. *Medical Care*, 37(10), 972–981.

Leigh, J., Markowitz, S., Fahs, M., & Landrigan, P. (2000). *Costs of occupational injuries & illnesses*. Ann Arbor: University of Michigan Press.

Leske, J., & Jiricka, M. (1998). Impact of family demands and family strengths and capabilities on family well-being and adaptation after critical injury. *American Journal of Critical Care*, 7(5), 383–392.

MacDonald, C. (2000). Evaluating work comp system from injured workers' perspective. *Compact*, 2000, 12–16.

Maetzel, A., Makela, M., Hawker, G., & Bombardier, C. (1997). Osteoarthritis of the hip and knee and mechanical occupational exposure: A systematic overview of the evidence. *Journal of Rheumatology*, 24, 1599–1607.

Mignone, J., & Guidotti, T. L. (1999). Support groups for injured workers: Process and outcomes. *Journal of Occupational and Environmental Medicine*, 41(12), 1059–1064.

Morse, T., Levenstein, C., Warren, A., Dillon, C., & Warren, N. (1998). The economic and social consequences of work-related musculoskeletal disorders: The Connecticut upper-extremity surveillance project (CUSP). *International Journal of Occupational and Environmental Health*, 4, 209–216.

Patterson, J., & Garwick, A. (1994). The impact of chronic illness on families: A family systems perspective. *Annals of Behavioral Medicine*, 16(2), 131–142.

Pransky, G., Benjamin, K., Hill-Fotouhi, C., Himmelstein, J., Fletcher, K. E., Katz, J. N., et al. (2000). Outcomes in work-related upper extremity and low back injuries: Results of a retrospective study. *American Journal of Industrial Medicine*, 37(4), 400–409.

Pransky, G., & Himmelstein, J. (1996). Outcomes research: Implications for occupational health. *American Journal of Industrial Medicine*, 29(6), 573–583.

Rahman, M., Tondel, M., Ahmad, S. A., & Axelson, O. (1998). Diabetes mellitus associated with arsenic exposure in Bangladesh. *American Journal of Epidemiology*, 148(2), 198–203.

Reville, R, Schoeni, R., & Martin, C. (2002). *Trends in earnings loss from disabling workplace injuries in California*. Santa Monica, CA: RAND Institute on Civil Justice.

Rudolph, L., Dervin, K., Cheadle, A., Maizlish, N., & Wickizer, T. (2002). What do injured workers think about their medical care and outcomes after work injury. *Journal of Occupational and Environmental Medicine*, 44(5), 425–434.

Sachs, P., & Ellenberg, D. (1994). The family system and adaptation to an injured worker. *American Journal of Family Therapy*, 22(3), 263–272.

Schouten, J., de Bie, R., & Swaen, G. (2002). An update on the relationship between occupational factors and osteoarthritis of the hip and knee. *Current Opinion in Rheumatology*, 14, 89–92.

Shainblum, E., Sullivan, T., & Frank, J. (2000). Multicausality, non-traditional injury, and the future of workers' compensation. In M. Gunderson & D. Hyatt (Eds.), *Workers' compensation: Foundations for reform* (pp. 58–95). Toronto: University of Toronto Press.

Stein, R., & Riessman, C. (1980). The development of an Impact-on-Family Scale: Preliminary findings. *Medical Care*, 18(4), 465–472.

Steinglass, P. (2000). Family processes and chronic illness. In L. Baider, C. Cooper, & A. K. De-Nour (Eds.), *Cancer and the family* (2nd ed., pp. 3–16). New York: Wiley.

Strunin, L., & Boden, L. (1997, October). *The human costs of occupational injuries*. Presentation at the National Occupational Injury Research Symposium, Morgantown, WV.

Strunin, L., & Boden, L. (2000). Paths of reentry: Employment experiences of injured workers. *American Journal of Industrial Medicine, 38,* 373–384.

Sum, J. (1996). *Navigating the California workers' compensation system: The injured worker's experience.* San Francisco: Commission on Health and Safety and Workers' Compensation.

Texas Workers' Compensation Research Center. (1995). Economic outcomes of injured workers with permanent impairments. *The Research Review, 27*(3), 1–4.

Thompson, C., Reno, V., Mont, D., Burton, Jr., J., & Thomason, T. (2002). Workers' compensation coverage. *Workers' Compensation Policy Review, 2,* 13–18.

Weil, D. (2001). Valuing the economic consequences of work injury and illness: A comparison of methods and findings. *American Journal of Industrial Medicine, 40*(4), 418–437.

Whatman, R., Adams, M., Burton, J., Butcher, F., Graham, S., McLeod, A., et al. (2002). *Aftermath: The social and economic consequences of workplace injury and illness.* Wellington: New Zealand Department of Labour.

27

Labor Markets and Health: A Social Epidemiological View

Benjamin C. Amick III

The University of Texas, Houston

Cam Mustard

The University of Toronto

LABOR MARKETS AND HEALTH: A SOCIAL EPIDEMIOLOGICAL PERSPECTIVE

Other chapters in this volume demonstrate the strong theoretical and substantive contributions of sociology, economics, psychology, and anthropology to our understanding of the workplace–workforce mismatch or work-family conflict. As the chapters also demonstrate, however, there is little epidemiological research. Consequently, the fields' strengths have not been integrated within epidemiology, whose focus is assessing exposure, defining health outcomes, and understanding the causes of illnesses, injuries, and diseases. Integrating epidemiological design concepts and measurement issues could help develop effective interventions that reduce illness, injury, and disease and improve health.

In this chapter, we bring together the perspectives of social epidemiology and recent developments in work and health research. Our goals are twofold: (a) to place work and health research in a broader social epidemiological framework, and (b) to provide a more complete explication of relevant

413

labor market exposures and its measurement over the working life course. In achieving these goals, we elaborate a more comprehensive framework to stimulate new research questions and analytic strategies for addressing the workforce–workplace mismatch. Research synthesis has been hindered by a lack of organizing frames. Therefore, a second goal is to encourage a common language for researchers collectively engaged in research on work, family, and health.

We first briefly review the advantages of a social epidemiological perspective and discuss the need for a new labor markets and health framework. We then briefly describe the labor markets and health framework. Finally, we review major working life course research themes and apply them to the labor markets and health framework.

WHY A SOCIAL EPIDEMIOLOGICAL PERSPECTIVE?

Although debate persists on the need to establish a social epidemiological perspective (Kaufman, 2001; Zielhuis & Kiemeney, 2001), all agree on its intent—to explore how sociocultural phenomena affect disease and health (Martikainen, Bartley, & Lahelma, 2002). The perspective offers the opportunity to reexamine common social exposure models (such as socioeconomic status [SES]) used in epidemiology in light of recent theoretical advances in the social sciences, perhaps leading to an integration of social science and epidemiology and an elaboration of more complex exposure and etiological models.

Social epidemiology is impelled forward by two empirical observations. First, with the exception of breast cancer, all injuries, illnesses, and diseases are more prevalent for people lower in the social hierarchy (Lynch & Kaplan, 2000). Second, the social gradient in health means that each step down the social hierarchy is associated with greater risk, and, conversely, each step up the hierarchy is associated with less risk. The Whitehall studies of the British Civil Service clearly illustrate the social gradient (Marmot, Bosma, Hemingway, Brunner, & Stansfeld, 1997). Figure 27.1 shows the different cardiovascular disease incidence rates between those at the top of the Whitehall civil service (e.g., administration or professional positions) and those farther down the social hierarchy (e.g., clerical positions). Note the relative or gradient effect; no matter what position one selects in the British Civil Service, those in jobs below it in ranking have poorer health and those above it have better health. The figure also illustrates that the contribution of traditional biomedical risk factors fails to account for the gradient.

A social epidemiological perspective presents several research challenges. One challenge is to clearly define social and psychosocial exposures. *Psycho-*

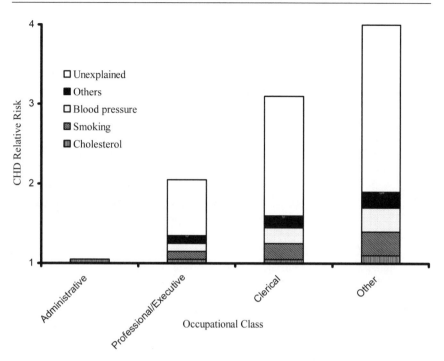

FIG. 27.1.   The social gradient in health as illustrated by Whitehall research
(Source: Rose and Marmot, 1981).

social exposure is a property of individuals, whereas *social exposure* is a property of aggregates of individuals, sociostructural elements of a society, social
institutions within a society, or societies per se. Psychosocial epidemiology
has demonstrated the significance of many exposures (e.g., social support,
anger/hostility, perceived stress, depression) in disease. These risk factors,
along with biomedical risk factors, must be considered to understand the risk
attributable to social factors in disease etiology.

A second challenge is to develop cross-level explanations to guide research. Cross-level explanations refer to theoretical or conceptual account-
ings for why and how social conditions affect individual attitudes, behaviors,
physiological patterns, and health. Cross-level explanations fall under two
types. Linear explanations (e.g., that socioeconomic position or social class
determines different work exposures, which create health disparities) are
causal, suggesting that social conditions affect more traditional risk factors
(e.g., high blood pressure for heart disease), which in turn affect health. The
second type is a contextual explanation; for example, local sociocultural contexts established by organizations (e.g., organizational downsizing or culture)
or the regional labor markets (e.g., job opportunities) moderate how work

exposures affect health. These cross-level explanations are not the same and imply different research designs and analytic approaches. Both require the researcher to consider how etiological processes are influenced by the social phenomenon under study. Consequently, a social epidemiological perspective should attend to the psychosocial, cognitive, perceptual, behavioral, biomechanical, and physiological pathways by which the social environment "gets under the skin" (Mustard, Lavis, & Ostry, 2005).

Many researchers focus on one part of the labor market experiences and health puzzle. Studies have "drilled down" to understand, for example, the role of unemployment, psychosocial work conditions (e.g., work stress), the social gradient, the organization, the interplay of the individual personality characteristics with work states, or ergonomic conditions in disease etiology. Few have considered a more integrative perspective that would perhaps lead to new questions or might challenge measurement and research design approaches. Davis' (2002) cautionary note to breast cancer researchers and policymakers could be considered as a point of departure: "Breast cancer research is at a crossroads that may not be apparent to those in the thick of it. The millions allocated to research have produced what one editor of the *Lancet* describes as a glut of the same old studies. Different questions must be asked to break the logjam" (p. 22).

THE LABOR MARKETS AND HEALTH FRAMEWORK

The labor markets and health framework focuses on the adult working life course and the social institutions shaping individual labor market activities. The framework is designed to redirect social epidemiological research toward a focus on labor market experiences and the social status hierarchy, and to assign as a research object those social actors (e.g., employers, trade unions, and government) who shape an individual's labor market experiences (e.g., through organizational structure), rather than considering them passive receivers of scientific information. The framework, described by Amick and Lavis (2000), has four features. First, it integrates experiences related to the availability of work and the nature of work into the same model, focusing research on cumulative labor market experiences. The second feature is that the framework focuses research on the cumulative health effects of labor market experiences and the reciprocal effects of health and these experiences. Combined, the first two features establish a working life course perspective. The third feature is that it highlights the deeper social structuring of labor market experiences and the working life course, and the potential influence of social status hierarchies on the relation between labor market experiences and health. Finally, the framework recognizes employers, governments, and other social institutions as entities whose practices and policies directly affect labor market experiences and the working life course, thus making practice and policy interventions suitable subjects for social epidemiological research.

Labor Market Experiences

Labor market experiences relate to both the availability and nature of work (Amick & Lavis, 2000; Mustard et al., 2005). In the current understanding, these experiences are related to the risk of injury and illness in occupational settings.

Table 27.1 lists six labor market states related to the availability of work. Three are underwork variants (either discouraged, unemployed, or underemployed). The fourth is a fear of those states, and the fifth is overwork. Discouraged workers have ceased looking for work because it is unavailable, unemployed workers are still looking for work, whereas underemployed workers work less than full time because more work is unavailable. These labor market states are modified by time to create labor market experiences that increase morbidity and mortality risk (Mustard et al., 2005).

TABLE 27.1
Labor Market Experiences Related to the Nature and Availability of Work*

	Availability of Work	
Labor Market States	Short Term and/or Cyclical	Long Term and/or Structural
Discouraged worker	Lack of work	Lack of skills
Unemployed	Temporary layoff	Permanent job loss
Underemployed	Forced work-sharing	Involuntary part-time employment
Fear of unemployment	Job insecurity	Employability insecurity
Fully employed		
Overemployed/overworked	Temporary work hour increase	Permanent work hour increase
	Nature of Work	
	Single Point in Time	Over Time
Single work characteristic	Repetitive work	Increasing job demands
Multiple characteristics	High job demands, low job control	Cumulative job strain
Job position within firm or society	Low employment grade	Lack of career mobility

*The table is adapted from Amick and Lavis (2000).

The nature of work encompasses the job characteristics within the firm (Table 27.1). Only by examining labor market experiences over time can working life course experiences be related to health through, for example, cumulative exposure models. The labor markets and health framework provides an opportunity to describe what Elder, George, and Shanahan (1996) termed "linked lives as convoys of support and stress" (p. 270). To understand how lives are shaped as convoys requires a framework that considers the social structures and processes shaping labor market experiences.

The Social Context

Contextual factors profoundly shape an individual's labor market experiences and alter the relation between labor market experiences and health (Amick & Lavis, 2000). In the context of psychosocial work exposure research, Söderfeldt et al. (1997) found a contextual organizational effect above and beyond the individual exposure-health relationship. Labor market experiences arise from conditions created by firm-level organizational and human resource decisions. Trade unions and labor market intermediaries (e.g., community colleges and community-based nonprofit employment programs) also shape labor market experiences. Furthermore, the relation between labor market conditions and health is potentially affected by firm- and government-level actions. Government policies (e.g., the Americans with Disabilities Act) affect the injured worker's return to work (Burkhauser & Daly, 1996). Beland, Birch, and Stoddart (2002) found that the relation between unemployment and self-reported health did not vary if the experience were shared by others (i.e., the local unemployment rate was high). This finding in Canada can be contrasted with research by Turner (1995) in the United States, who found a contextual effect. The lack of consistent effects across studies could be because of different Social Security and health care systems. Furthermore, these social actors influence how labor market experiences are distributed within a society. For example, firm- and government-level actions create unique labor market experiences for particular groups (e.g., women and African Americans) that can have health consequences.

LABOR MARKETS AND HEALTH:
A SOCIAL EPIDEMIOLOGICAL FRAMING

The Need to Consider a Working
Life Course Perspective

Epidemiological research on the health effects of paid work during adult life is fragmented. Research on the health consequences of unemployment remains unconnected to working conditions and health research (Mustard et al., 2005). An opportunity exists for integrating research on the nature of work (e.g., work stress and ergonomics) and the availability of work (e.g., unemployment and job security) into a coherent working life course perspective. A working life course perspective requires a theoretical and methodological shift. It challenges the researcher to consider exposure models that include a time dimension, explicit statements about when etiological mechanisms act during an exposure period, and, most important, design and analytic problems associated with interrupted careers. Although we do not discuss them here, the same issues and opportunities occur in family and work-family conflict research.

Multiple job transitions create a challenge in cumulating working life course exposure. A person with a high school education experiences on average nine major job changes throughout his or her career (Sennett, 1998). Between 10 and 20 million American workers participate in the contingent economy (Kalleberg et al., 1997). The nature of work may vary greatly depending on the job, and periods of unemployment may be interspersed among these various jobs. Research must jointly consider the nature and availability of work when modeling working life course exposures.

Modeling lifetime or cumulative psychosocial exposures related to the nature of work presents a methodological challenge. It requires data spanning an individual's career at those points that affect pathological processes. It also requires extensive biological data to model dose burden. A common practice in occupational epidemiology is to intensely study an exposure to understand how it affects biological processes that determine pathology (Checkoway, Pearce, & Kriebel, 2004). Yet unlike classical occupational exposures (e.g., radiation) with more readily observable dose burdens, the mental, neurohormonal, neuroimmunological, biomechanical, or behavioral processes associated with labor market experiences are complex, influenced by psychosocial, environmental, and individual factors.

An added complication is the controversy surrounding whether valid and reliable exposure assessment can be attained with worker self-report, observer rating, or some physical measurement (Spieholz, Silverstein, Morgan, Checkoway, & Kaufman, 2001). The debate over measuring psychosocial work exposure has been extensively reviewed elsewhere (Kasl, 1998). There are no commonly agreed-on exposure definitions, which leads to a wide range of measures limiting comparability across studies and research synthesis. When generic subjective exposures are assessed (e.g., the Karasek et al. [1998] job strain exposures), specific stressors unique to a particular occupation, job, industry, or work environment are missed. This may lead to risk underestimation or biased risk assessment if workers are misclassified in terms of overall exposure. Cumulated over time, these biases can severely limit the validity of risk estimates.

Further complicating exposure measurement is a lack of research on the cognitive processes involved in answering generic psychosocial or physical work exposure questions (Mathiowetz, 1994; Sudman, Bradburn, & Schwartz, 1996). For example, little is known about whether physical workload influences how a worker answers psychological job demand questions about hard work, fast work, or excessive work. Physical workload, as measured by energy expenditure, predicts psychosocial exposure (Josephson et al., 1999).

Numerous researchers have sought to develop objective psychosocial exposure measures to address self-reported exposure problems. The dominant strategy has been to develop a job exposure matrix (Schwartz, Pieper, & Karasek, 1988) using self-report data from other sources and linking it to individual health data through an occupation code. This exposure imputation procedure has the advantage of separating the exposure assessment from the individual, but valuable within-occupation variation is often missing. Health researchers have used matrixes developed using expert rater systems such as the Position Analysis Questionnaire (Murphy, 1991) or the Dictionary of Occupational Titles (Moore & Hayward, 1990). Alternatively, trained raters have assessed psychosocial exposures (Greiner, Krause, Ragland, & Fisher, 1998). The rater approach assumes psychosocial exposures are observables that can be validly and reliably assessed. Preliminary results are mixed, suggesting strong (House, 1980) and weak (Greiner et al., 1998) correspondence between observer-rated and self-reported psychosocial exposure measures. A variant of the expert rater approach uses supervisors to assess psychosocial job exposures (Bosma et al., 1997). Too few studies exist to assess whether observation of psychosocial work conditions is possible and whether it is commensurate or complementary to self-reported exposure assessment.

Unique problems modeling working life course exposures are illustrated by reviewing the three types of data censoring: left, right, and mid-censoring. Mid-censoring characterizes many careers in which people are not working for periods of time. A person who has taken time off for children, a person laid off from a job and looking for work, or a person out on a series of long-term disability claims owing to a back injury all have working life courses that involve multiple job transitions. To create virtuous working life courses for these three circumstances requires different occupational health, public health, and social interventions. For example, if targeting social policies is a goal, then appropriate responses would be child care, job retraining, or disability management, respectively. The conceptual and methodological challenge is to model the transitions embedded in interrupted labor market careers and understand the reasons for each transition and relative contribution of each to disease. Unless this is accomplished, understanding which types of policy are relevant remains unreachable.

A left-censoring problem occurs when a cohort is established at a point in calendar time, not work time. Important exposures may have already occurred. This problem results in unknown variability about when a work exposure started. Consider the following example. A study begins in 1970 and follows subjects until death, observing an individual's mortality in the fifth year of follow-up. However, the person has been working for 20 years. Lifetime work exposure might be misspecified, and the exposure effect may show up as an age-related risk or not show up at all. Ideally, one would measure the individual's full work history, including the period prior to cohort inception.

A problem when modeling lifetime or cumulative exposure is determining how much follow-up time is necessary for situations with long latency before health is affected. Should the exposure that is assessed early in the cohort study be carried forward? If so, for how long? What about the role of unemployment (i.e., the gaps in exposure)? For how long after retirement is the work exposure relevant before the aging process overwhelms the exposure risk? McDonough, Duncan, Williams, and House (1997) followed people for 5 years after exposure to economic conditions to ascertain health transitions.

A final conceptual challenge is that working must be understood in the context of many other life transitions. Retiring early may have different health implications than retiring late. Working in a unionized company has implications for job and employability security that may affect psychosocial job experiences. Women may have a different view of paid work than men because of the competing demands of unpaid work (Moen, Robinson, & Fields, 1994). In addition, the social context created by the regional labor market can change the event's significance. Amick and Lavis (2000) showed that individuals who are unemployed in an area with low unemployment are at higher risk of death compared with those who are unemployed in a high unemployment area.

The Need to Place the Working Life Course in Social Context

The negative health risks of labor market experiences often appear to cluster around position in the occupational structure as one indicator of social status or social class (Johnson & Hall, 1995). Several cohort studies have documented the emergence of an occupational status gradient in health (cf. Mustard, Vermeulen, & Lavis, 2003). These studies suggest that the social sorting processes of individuals into jobs by education, age, gender, or race and ethnicity create an inequitable risk distribution leading to health inequalities. Social stratification within the society's opportunity structure is a fundamental cause of health inequalities, and work is but one pathway whereby the process of stratification affects health. Therefore, prevention efforts should focus on changing sorting processes or opportunities, rather than labor market experiences per se.

Sorting may create an exposure gradient. Johnson and Hall (1995) contended that, as a consequence of the unequal power distribution within society, manual and nonmanual labor classes have unique exposures. Manual workers are more likely to be exposed to environmental and physical job hazards as well as psychosocial job hazards. A retrospective case-control study of nonfatal myocardial infarction in men found psychosocial job strain (i.e., high psychological job demands and low job control) was a risk factor only for manual workers (Hallquist, Diderichsen, Theorell, Reuterwall, & Ahlbom, 1998). If the effect of job strain on health is modified by class position, this suggests a more complex set of processes than a simple pathway where class determines exposure. The unequal distribution of power is thus the focus of intervention and, in many countries, has been addressed through trade unions, where workers can exercise collective control over working conditions through their trade union membership (Johnson & Hall, 1995).

One study illustrates the importance of keeping social class separate from labor market exposures. Bartley and Plewis (2002) combined social class with unemployment status to create a combined measure of "accumulated labor market disadvantage." A person accumulated disadvantage by being in a low class in 1971, 1981, or 1991 or being unemployed in each of the same 3 years; the most disadvantaged are given a score of six. Although this accumulated disadvantage was related to long-standing illness in the United Kingdom, it is unclear whether class operates synergistically with unemployment status or unemployment mediates the relation between social class and long-standing illness. Here it is difficult to conclude the unequal distribution of power is the fundamental cause.

As described earlier, the Whitehall study shows that a linear relation between job class and the incidence of coronary heart disease (CHD) cannot be explained by the unequal distribution of traditional behavioral and biological risk factors such as smoking, high blood pressure, and cholesterol (Rose & Marmot, 1981). However, Fig. 27.2 shows how the unequal distribution of job control, with those in higher classes having more control, affects the relation between CHD incidence and social class when psychosocial work conditions are considered. Job control, or the differing ability to influence how and what one does during the workday, accounts for much of the health difference between British civil servants in different positions in the organization. These findings are not unexpected given that, as a bureaucracy, Whitehall is an efficient structure for controlling and coordinating activities. Chandler (1984) described bureaucratic growth as creating new organizational levels to minimize the span of control of the level below and to maintain the opportunity for coordination among even smaller numbers of individuals at higher levels. Thus, the Whitehall social status gradient in health emerges

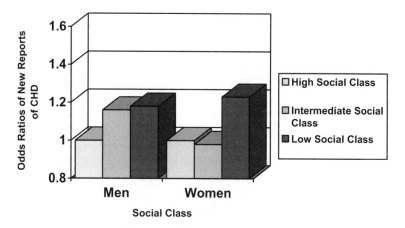

FIG. 27.2.   The relationship between social class and coronary heart disease (CHD) incidence in the Whitehall study of British civil servants by gender after adjusting for work conditions (Source: Marmot et al., 1997).

from an organizational structure designed to maintain power through control and coordination. From a prevention perspective, this argues for attending to structural determinants at the organizational level.

LIFE COURSE RESEARCH APPLICATIONS TO LABOR MARKETS AND HEALTH

Most research simplifies the complexity of working life by focusing on either the availability or nature of work. Often research focuses on baseline exposures obtained from a worker sample representative of all workers, thereby mixing baseline measures obtained from older workers with those obtained from younger workers. To facilitate a shift in thinking, we discuss four life course research themes: (a) individual lives are shaped by their historical time and place; (b) each individual can exert personal agency, but this agency is often moderated by social constraints; (c) there is a social timing to the life course; and (d) there is an interdependence of lives (Elder et al., 1996). These themes are discussed next in the context of labor markets and health research.

The Importance of Time and Place

Labor market experiences may take on different meanings depending on the time and place in which they occur. Today fewer employers are providing health care benefits, and, with health care costs rising, workers are choosing not to seek care. Assuming access to care is fundamental to health, it follows that studying worker health in the post-1990s period is far different from that in the 1980s. Similarly, a worker unemployed in the United States has different government supports compared with those in many European countries (Amick & Lavis, 2000) and Canada (Beland et al., 2002). This is a challenge for research synthesis using single-country studies and encourages the development of cross-national research projects.

The concept of time can challenge our thinking in other ways. People experience multiple labor market exposures of different intensity and duration. One challenge is cumulating these experiences at the individual level. Grzywacz and Dooley (2003) attempted to cumulate labor market experiences into a continuum ranging from unemployed to optimal job (both economically and psychologically optimal). Although they observed modest relations with self-reported health, there are still too few data to validate an approach where a measurement continuum is assumed to exist between job availability and the nature of work given that a job transition per se can also affect health (Metcalfe et al., 2003). Similarly, the frequency of unemployment spells between the ages of 20 and 30 is strongly related to subsequent mental health disorders and declines in perceived health (Power, Matthews, & Manor, 1998). Other nonwork-related transitions (e.g., from being healthy to having an illness or injury, or from being single to being married) can also affect health and should be included in any working life course study. This time-based complexity suggests new questions and demands new analytic approaches.

Amick et al. (2002) cumulated working life exposures in a study using 25 years of labor market exposure information. The study examined the relationship between lifetime exposure to a working condition and mortality after adjusting for a range of other significant predictors of mortality, including income, health status, other labor market experiences (i.e., unemployment), and transitions (i.e., retirement). People who spent the majority of their working life in low-control jobs were at a 50% increased risk of dying (OR 1.5, CI 1.18–1.91) compared with those who spent their working life in a high-control job (see Fig. 27.3). The effect persists for those working in the medium- to low-exposure group, but diminishes beyond that. The result suggests that providing people with a modicum of control through career growth can significantly reduce the risk of dying. Control in a job reduced the increased risk to 43% per 10 years after exposure (OR 1.43, CI 1.13–1.81). In other words, 10 years after retirees stopped working, and even after accounting for a range of important early mortality risk factors, those who spent their working lives in low-control jobs were at an increased risk of mortality.

Few studies have had the data to examine alternative psychosocial exposure models. Most prospective research captures baseline exposure and determines how well baseline exposure status predicts the incidence of events, whereas others measure average exposure (Hall, 1991), first or last exposure (Moore

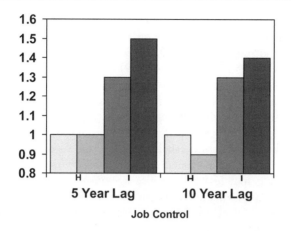

FIG. 27.3.   The relationship between job control and
mortality in the panel study of income dynamics after 25
years of follow-up (Model adjusted for age, race, gender,
year, family income, family size, retirement, unemployment, and baseline disability. Source: Amick et al.,
2002).

& Hayward, 1990), or short-term changes in exposure status (Theorell et
al., 1998). These approaches suffer from what is termed a *slice of life* cohort
effect, where left censoring truncates work histories, thereby biasing baseline exposure measures (Checkoway et al., 2004). To resolve this problem,
Johnson, Stewart, Hall, Fredlund, and Theorell (1996) matched individuals
in 5-year exposure periods with unexposed individuals working equal numbers of years. They then followed these individuals through an event using
a nested case-control prospective study design. Part of the difficulty in the
field is the lack of underlying dose-burden formulations (Checkoway et al.,
2004). Further conceptual refinements will require disease- or illness-specific
exposure formulations.

Human Agency and Its Constraints

People are planners and make decisions throughout their lives, especially as
adults, to construct their life course. Not everyone has the opportunity to
make the same decision owing to social constraints, and these are often taken
into account in the planning. For example, individuals are constrained about
job choice because of their education or constrained by health care benefits
or lack thereof. Furthermore, health can constrain what individuals can do or
want to do in the labor market. Therefore, a working life course perspective
should consider the role of human agency and the important social constraints
that influence life.

Consider workers undergoing carpal tunnel surgery (CTS) who were studied to determine the predictors of their return to work (Katz et al., 2005). Workers who had improved self-efficacy were more likely to be working 12 months later (OR 0.32, 95% CI 0.11–0.91). *Self-efficacy* is defined as one's self-reported ability to manage one's pain and to function well in the job given one's health. Self-efficacy is determined by individual characteristics (such as mental health), characteristics of the physician–patient interaction (such as developing a program to return to work with modified duties), and worker–workplace interaction (such as supervisor support). The return to employment is an important transition for workers with injuries or illnesses. Otherwise workers may leave the labor force with a disability status and potentially become disconnected from the labor market.

Four organizational characteristics considered important in shaping the return to work begin to expand our conceptualization of important workplace enablers or constraints. A firm's people-oriented culture (OR 1.86, p = .006), safety climate (OR 1.59, p = .03), disability management programs (OR 2.24, p = .02), and ergonomics practices (OR 1.77, p = .002) all significantly predicted 6-month return to work in the CTS study cohort described earlier (Amick et al., 2000). Similarly, Zohar (2000) showed how safety policies affect injury risk. In a large manufacturing business, injury risk varied by work unit, and this variability was driven by how supervisors and work groups informally implemented the organizational policies and programs. Common individual protective and risk factors are embedded in a social context with a specific local social structure that may determine the risk factor distribution or modify the effect of individual risk factors on disease outcomes. These structural constraints (i.e., the organizational controls described earlier) often go unmeasured in risk behavior research. The possibility to modify organizational conditions rather than individual behaviors offers the opportunity to improve population health.

Poor health is a potential constraint on employment and may be associated with leaving the workforce (McDonough & Amick, 2001). The problem of health selection is both a methodological and substantive concern. Health selection into work occurs when socioeconomic opportunities are constrained by a person's health. Health is an intervening variable in the relation between work exposure and morbidity and mortality. It is highly probable that certain jobs at different life stages contribute to a person's health, and health contributes to changing jobs and new exposures. Analyses that do not consider past work exposures among the unemployed and their health consequences underestimate work effects and overestimate unemployment effects.

Health selection is also a problem when using retrospective recall of job history to ascertain working life exposures. For example, Metcalfe et al. (2003) used a single question to ascertain job changes during a person's working life. They used these job change histories to construct exposure measures, but they had no information on prior health and whether changes in health caused a worker to change jobs. Again risk estimates are potentially biased. More precise risk estimation requires understanding the cumulative effects of work on health and the constraints of health on work.

Most cohort studies of psychosocial work exposure do not consider health as an intermediate variable affecting and affected by exposure (Robbins, 1986). This can lead to problems in interpreting significant risks. A study by Rogers and Carrigan (1995) that linked the National Health Interview Survey to the National Death Index found that workers who were classified as changing from an occupational status to low status during their working life were at an increased risk of mortality. However, because the researchers were unable to examine the factors that determine the shift from high to low status, it could be that health was acting as an intermediate variable. Amick and Lavis (2000) showed that the relationship between the underuse of skills and mortality is potentially mediated by health for older African-American workers. Health led older African Americans (but not other workers) to move to jobs where skills were underused. Chandola, Bartley, Sacker, Jenkinson, and Marmot (2003) found no effect of physical or mental health on movement of Whitehall civil servants across job grades during a 20-year period. Without considering health's effect on labor market experiences, research can inappropriately conclude that a relationship exists when it does not, whereas knowing the health selection biases strengthens the conclusions.

Social Timing to the Life Course

Social timing implies an appropriate time or age for specific events, such as marriage or retirement. Inappropriate timing may signal the occurrence of a health event. For example, in the Panel Study of Income Dynamics, the relation between retirement and mortality varies by age (Amick et al., 2002). Retirement at a young age markedly increases the mortality risk, which implies that poor health may be one factor leading to retirement and early death. However, it is equally plausible that leaving a significant adult social role early in life could lead to health problems. As a person ages, retirement becomes a more accepted social transition.

It may be that certain risk factor effects on health are more age graded than others, and some inconsistencies in research findings may be the result of how meaning changes. For example, in a study of the relation between health and unemployment, a shift from good to poor (self-rated) health had a significant effect on the likelihood of a man leaving the workforce between the ages of 25 and 39, but not between the ages of 40 and 61 (McDonough & Amick, 2001). This age-graded relationship suggests health changes have a different meaning at different life stages. Social timing suggests that social context and meaning may change over the life course. This suggests the need to move away from absolute principles in risk factor research that imply a fixed set of universal risk factors, which are inevitably associated with a fixed set of consequences.

Interdependence of Lives

Living in a socially integrated community promotes health. Social support from a spouse or supervisor can increase functional health (Berkman & Glass, 2000). Similarly, what parents do affects children's developmental health and well-being (Meneghan, 1991). Linked lives not only convey positive benefits, but also negative consequences. Living in a neighborhood with high rates of violence increases the risk of experiencing violence (Sampson & Raudenbusch, 1999). Work, and how it is structured, can affect the interconnectedness of parents and children and both parent and child health.

For example, using the National Longitudinal Survey of Youth, Menaghan (1991) investigated how parental work environments affect children's development. In one analysis, children's negative emotions were predicted by parental work characteristics such as low complexity of mothers' work and low complexity of spouse's occupation, as well as household and personal characteristics. Jobs with little complexity offer few opportunities for workers to engage in intellectual activities such as working with data or ideas. These jobs also provide few opportunities to make decisions (i.e., job control). Consequently, work affects how parents engage and interact with their children. The intergenerational transmission of work's negative consequences implies that appropriately structured workplaces may have a salubrious or negative effect on child development.

CONCLUSION

We have presented a social epidemiological perspective of work, and particularly the importance of social status and labor market characteristics to health. The social epidemiological perspective provides a unique opportunity to better integrate social science into epidemiological inquiry. We illustrate this by suggesting how life course research can raise new challenges and suggest new directions in epidemiological research. By way of synthesis, we offer a model with two explanatory axes: a socioecologic dimension and a time dimension.

Along the socioecologic dimension are the separate, but interdependent, risk factors at the individual and social levels. At one end of the continuum individual-level research is conducted, whereas at the other end is cross-level research. In addition, the social clustering of risk as a consequence of the socioecologic conditions is contrasted with an individual-level formulation where each risk is examined independently. The term *habitas* can be used to denote a social embedding of the risk clustering (Johnson & Hall, 1995).

The time axis represents a commingling of conceptual and methodological perspectives. At one end are the slice of life studies with censoring problems that arise when relationhips between exposure and health relationships are assessed using a sample of younger and older workers. Also at this end are exposures assessed at a single point in time compared with multiple points of exposure (noted at the other end of the axis). The life course perspective is another element of the time dimension, and it acknowledges the importance not only of cumulating risk, but also of considering the role of health as an intervening variable, as well as the importance of other life course transitions.

ACKNOWLEDGMENTS

This chapter was supported by funds from the Texas Program for Society and Health at the James A. Baker III Institute for Public Policy at Rice University and travel funds from the Institute for Work and Health, Toronto, Canada. An expanded version of this chapter is available from the Institute for Work and Health as a working paper.

REFERENCES

Amick B. C., III, & Lavis, J. N. (2000). Labor markets and health: A framework and set of applications. In A. Tarlov & R. St. Peter (Eds.), *Society and population health* (pp. 178–210). New York: The New Press.

Amick B. C., III, McDonough, P., Chang, H., Rogers, W. H., Pieper, C. F., & Duncan, G. (2002). Relationship between all-cause mortality and cumulative working life course psychosocial and physical exposures in the United States labor market from 1968 to 1992. *Psychosomatic Medicine, 64*, 370–381.

Amick, B. C., III, Habeck, R. V., Hunt, A., Fossel, A. H., Chapin, A., Keller, R. B., et al. (2000). Measuring the impact of organizational behaviors on work disability prevention and management. *Journal of Occupational Rehabilitation, 10*, 21–38.

Bartley, M., & Plewis, I. (2002). Accumulated labor market disadvantage and limiting long-term illness: Data from 1971–1991 Office of National Statistics Longitudinal Study. *International Journal of Epidemiology, 31*, 336–341.

Beland, F., Birch, S., & Stoddart, G. (2002). Unemployment and health: Contextual-level influences on the production of health in populations. *Social Science & Medicine, 55*, 2033–2052.

Berkman, L., & Glass, T. (2000). Social integration, social networks, social support and health. In L. F. Berkman & I. Kawachi (Eds.), *Social epidemiology* (pp. 137–174). Oxford, England: Oxford University Press.

Bosma, H., Marmot, M. G., Hemingway, H., Nicholson, A., Brunner, E. J., & Stansfeld, S. (1997). Low job control and risk of coronary heart disease in the Whitehall II (prospective cohort) study. *British Medical Journal, 314*, 558–565.

Burkhauser, R. V., & Daly, M. C. (1996). Employment and economic well-being following the onset of a disability. In J. L. Mashaw, V. Reno, R. V. Burkhauser, & M. Berkowitz (Eds.), *Disability, work and cash benefits* (pp. 263–289). Kalamazoo, MI: W.E. Upjohn Institute for Employment Research.

Chandler, A. (1984). The emergence of managerial capitalism. *Business History Review, 58*, 473–503.

Chandola, T., Bartley, M., Sacker, A., Jenkinson, C., & Marmot, M. (2003). Health selection in the Whitehall II study, UK. *Social Science & Medicine, 56*, 2059–2072.

Checkoway, H., Pearce, N., & Kriebel, D. (2004). *Research methods in occupational epidemiology* (2nd ed.). New York: Oxford University Press.

Davis, D. (2002). *When smoke ran like water: Tales against environmental deception and the battle against pollution.* New York: Basic Books.

Elder, G. H., George, L. K., & Shanahan, M. J. (1996). Psychosocial stress over the life course. In H. Kaplan (Ed.), *Psychosocial stress* (pp. 247–292). New York: Academic Press.

Greiner, B., Krause, N., Ragland, D. R., & Fisher J. (1998). Objective stress factors, accidents, and absenteeism in transit operators: A theoretical framework and empirical evidence. *Journal of Occupational Health Psychology, 3*, 130–146.

Grzywacz, J., & Dooley, D. (2003). "Good jobs" to "Bad jobs": Replicated evidence of an employment continuum from two large surveys. *Social Science & Medicine, 56*, 1749–1760.

Hall, E. (1991). Gender, work control, and stress: A theoretical discussion and empirical test. In J. V. Johnson & G. Johansson (Eds.), *The psychosocial work environment: Work organization, democratization and health* (pp. 89–108). Amityville, NY: Baywood.

Hallquist, J., Diderichsen, F., Theorell, T., Reuterwall, C., & Ahlbom, A. (1998). Is the effect of job strain on myocardial infarction risk due to interaction between high psychological demands and low decision latitude? Results from Stockholm Heart Epidmeiology Program (SHEP). *Social Science and Medicine, 46*, 1405–1415.

House, J. S. (1980). *Occupational stress and the mental and physical health of factory workers.* Ann Arbor, MI: The University of Michigan.

Johnson, J. V., & Hall, E. (1995). Class, work and health. In B. C. Amick III, S. Levine, A. R. Tarlov, & D.C. Walsh (Eds.), *Society & health* (pp. 247–271). New York: Oxford University Press.

Johnson, J. V., Stewart, W., Hall, E. M., Fredlund, P., & Theorell, T. (1996). Long-term psychosocial work environment and cardiovascular mortality among Swedish men. *American Journal of Public Health, 86*, 324–331.

Josephson, M., Pernold, G., Ahlberg-Hulten, G., Harenstam, A., Theorell, T., Vingard, E., et al. (1999). Differences in the association between psychosocial work conditions and physical work load in female- and male-dominated occupations. *American Industrial Hygiene Association Journal, 60*, 673–678.

Kalleberg, A. L., Rasell, E., Hudson, K., Webster, D., Reskin, B. F., & Cassirer, N. (1997). *Nonstandard work, substandard jobs: Flexible work arrangements in the U.S.* Washington, DC: Economic Policy Institute.

Karasek, R., Brisson, C., Kawakami, N., Bongers, P., Houtman, I., & Amick, B. (1998). The job content questionnaire (JCQ): An instrument for internationally comparative assessments of psychosocial job characteristics. *Journal of Occupational Health Psychology, 3*, 322–355.

Kasl, S. V. (1998). Measuring job stressors and studying the health impact of the work environment: An epidemiologic commentary. *Journal of Occupational Health Psychology, 3*, 390–401.

Katz, J. N., Amick, B. C., III, Keller, R., Fossel, A. H., Ossmann, J., Soucie, V., et al. (2005). Determinants of work disability following surgery for carpal tunnel syndrome. *American Journal of Industrial Medicine, 47*, 120–130.

Kaufman, J. S. (2001). Commentary: Social epidemiology? Way! *International Journal of Epidemiology, 30*, 48–49.

Lynch, J., & Kaplan, G. (2000). Socioeconomic position. In L. F. Berkman & I. Kawachi (Eds.), *Social epidemiology* (pp. 13–36). Oxford: Oxford University Press.

Marmot, M. G., Bosma, H., Hemingway, H., Brunner, E., & Stansfeld, S. (1997). Contribution of job control and other risk factors to social variations in coronary heart disease incidence. *Lancet*, *350*, 235–239.

Martikainen, P., Bartley, M., & Lahelma, E. (2002). Psychosocial determinants of health in social epidemiology. *International Journal of Epidemiology*, *31*, 1091–1093.

Mathiowetz, N. A. (1994, March). *Autobiographical memory and the validity of survey data: Implications for the design of the Panel Study of Income Dynamics* (PSID Working Paper). Ann Arbor, MI: Institute for Social Research.

McDonough, P., & Amick III, B. C. (2001). The social context of health selection: A longitudinal study of health and employment. *Social Science & Medicine*, *53*, 135–145.

McDonough, P., Duncan, G. J., Williams, D., & House, J. (1997). Income dynamics and mortality. *American Journal of Public Health*, *87*, 1476–1483.

Meneghan, E. (1991). Work experiences and family interaction processes: The long arm of the job? *Annual Review of Sociology*, *17*, 419–444.

Metcalfe, C., Davey Smith, G., Sterne, J. A. C., Heslop, P., Macleod, J., & Hart, C. (2003). Frequent job change and associated health. *Social Science & Medicine*, *56*, 1–15.

Moen, P., Robinson, J., & Fields, V. (1994). Women's work and caregiving roles: A life course approach. *Journal of Gerontology*, *49*, S176–S186.

Moore, D. E., & Hayward, M. D. (1990). Occupational careers and mortality of elderly men. *Demography*, *27*, 31–53.

Murphy, L. R. (1991). Job dimensions associated with severe disability due to cardiovascular disease. *Journal of Clinical Epidemiology*, *44*, 155–166.

Mustard, C. A., Vermeulen, M., & Lavis, J. N. (2003). Is position in the occupational hierarchy a determinant of decline in perceived health status? *Social Science & Medicine*, *57*, 2291–2303.

Mustard, C. A., Lavis, J., & Ostry A. (2005). New evidence and enhanced understandings: Labour market experiences and health. In J. Heymann, C. Hertzman, M. Barer, & R. Evans (Eds.), *Creating healthier societies: From analysis to action* (pp. 421–495). New York: Oxford University Press.

Power, C., Matthews, S., & Manor, O. (1998). Inequalities in self-rated health: Explanations from different stages of life. *The Lancet*, *351*, 1009–1014.

Robbins, J. M. (1986). A new approach to causal inference in mortality studies with extended exposure periods—application to control the health worker survivor effect. *Math Model*, *7*, 1393–1512.

Rogers, R. G., & Carrigan, J. A. (1995). *Occupational status and mortality* (Working Paper 95-2). Boulder, CO: University of Colorado.

Rose, G., & Marmot, M. (1981). Social class and coronary heart disease. *British Heart Journal*, *45*,13–19.

Sampson, R. J., & Raudenbush, S. W. (1999). Systematic social observation of public spaces: A new look at disorder in urban neighborhoods. *American Journal of Sociology*, *105*, 603–651.

Schwartz, J. E., Pieper, C. F., & Karasek, R. A. (1988). A procedure for linking psychosocial job characteristics data to health surveys. *American Journal of Public Health*, *78*, 904–909.

Sennett, R. (1998). The corrosion of character: *The personal consequences of work in the new capitalism*. New York: Norton.

Söderfeldt, B., Söderfeldt, M., Jones, K., O'Camp, P., Muntaner, C., Ohlson, C. G., et al. (1997). Does organization matter? A multilevel analysis of the demand-control model applied to human services. *Social Science & Medicine*, *44*, 527–534.

Spielholz, P., Silverstein, B., Morgan, M., Checkoway, H., & Kaufman, J. (2001). Comparison of self-report, video observation and direct methods for upper extremity musculoskeletal disorder physical risk factors. *Ergonomics*, *44*, 588–613.

Sudman, S., Bradburn, N., & Schwartz, N. (1996). *Thinking about answers: The application of cognitive processes to survey methodology*. San Francisco: Jossey-Bass.

Theorell, T., Tsutsumi, A., Hallquist, J., Rueterwall, C., Hogstedt, C., Fredlund, P., et al. (1998). Decision latitude, job strain and myocardial infarction: A study of working men in Stockholm. *American Journal of Public Health, 88,* 382–388.

Turner, J. B. (1995). Economic context and the health effects of unemployment. *Journal of Health and Social Behavior, 36,* 213–229.

Zielhuis, G. A., & Kiemeney, L. A. (2001). Social epidemiology? No way. *International Journal of Epidemiology, 30,* 43–44.

Zohar, D. (2000). A group-level model of safety climate: Testing the effect of group climate on microaccidents in manufacturing jobs. *Journal of Applied Psychology, 85,* 587–596.

28

A Systematic Approach to the Assessment of the Psychological Work Environment and the Associations With Family-Work Conflict

Tage S. Kristensen
Lars Smith-Hansen
Nicole Jansen
National Institute of Occupational Health, Copenhagen

The psychosocial work environment is considered to be one of the most important work environment issues in contemporary and future societies. Typically psychosocial factors at work include demands at work, work organization, content of work, leadership, and interpersonal relations at the worksite. These factors may have harmful as well as beneficial effects for the employees. A large proportion of employees in the industrialized world report being exposed to negative psychosocial factors at work, and the consequences are significant for the workers, workplaces, and society. Among these consequences are musculoskeletal disorders, cardiovascular diseases, mental disorders, stress, burnout, reduced quality of life, sickness absence, labor turnover, decreased motivation and productivity, and work-family conflict.

We focus here on work-family conflict—a situation in which fulfilling the roles in one of the two domains (family or work) is in conflict with fulfilling the roles in the other because of limited time or energy. It is vital to identify the factors at work that increase the likelihood of work-family conflict.

One method of identifying these factors is to use validated, standardized questionnaires. We offer such a tool in this chapter—the Copenhagen Psychosocial Questionnaire (COPSOQ). We also illustrate the connection between work environment factors and work-family conflict by presenting results from three different studies: the Danish Psychosocial Work Environment Study, the Danish SARA study, and the Dutch Maastricht Cohort Study on Fatigue.

THE COPENHAGEN PSYCHOSOCIAL QUESTIONNAIRE

The Copenhagen Psychosocial Questionnaire is, to be precise, not one, but three questionnaires: a long version for research use, a midsize version to be used by work environment professionals, and a short version for the workplaces. By offering a three-level instrument, we hoped to achieve the following objectives:

- To develop valid and relevant instruments for assessing psychosocial factors at work;
- To make national and international comparisons possible;
- To improve evaluations of interventions;
- To facilitate surveillance and benchmarking;
- To improve the communication among workplaces, work environment professionals, and researchers; and
- To make it easier to operationalize and understand difficult concepts and theories.

Sample

The development of COPSOQ was based on responses to standardized questionnaires from a representative sample of 1,858 working Danes between ages 20 and 60 (49% women; response rate 62%). In Denmark and other European countries, response rates in large population surveys have been declining during the last decades, which is regrettable. The Central Person Register provided names and addresses. Socioeconomic status (SES) and psychosocial work environment results are found in Kristensen, Borg, and Hannerz (2002). The respondents were classified according to job title using the International Standard Classification of Occupations (ISCO) and with regard to SES. The classifications are: (a) white-collar workers with managerial positions, (b) other white-collar workers, (c) skilled blue-collar workers, and (d) semi- and unskilled blue-collar workers.

Selection of Questions for the Test Questionnaire

Before we began to construct our test questionnaire, we collected and reviewed several international and Danish questionnaires in the field. We selected items and scales based on the following objectives:

Comprehensiveness: We wanted our questionnaire to be comprehensive —that is, to get "all the way around" the psychosocial work environment without any clear gaps. We considered several well-known questionnaires, such as the Job Content questionnaire and the Effort-Reward Imbalance questionnaire to be much too narrow given that they only include a limited number of psychosocial factors.

Relevance: We wanted our questionnaire to be relevant for modern workplaces in human service work and information work, as well as more traditional sectors such as industry and transportation. To achieve this, we looked for questions on emotional demands, cognitive demands, and different aspects of interpersonal relationships at work.

Appreciative approach: Furthermore, we did not want the questionnaire to be exclusively "problem oriented," but also to include more positive and appreciative aspects, such as commitment, social community, feedback, and support.

Theoretical background: Our theoretical background is general stress theory with a strong emphasis on a democratic and participative approach combined with a methodological orientation based on standardized questionnaires and epidemiological methodology (Cox, 1993; Johnson & Johansson, 1991; Karasek & Theorell, 1990; Kompier, Geurts, Gründemann, Vink, & Smulders, 1998; Levi, 1981; Marmot & Wilkinson, 1999).

Empowerment: Our goals included developing two user-friendly, high-quality questionnaires: a midsize version for work environment professionals and a short version for the workplaces. By doing this, we wanted to emphasize that nonexperts are able to work with complicated work environment issues such as psychosocial work environment factors.

Among the reviewed questionnaires, only the QPS-Nordic (Dallner et al., 2000) was close to meeting our needs. This is a modern, comprehensive, and well-validated questionnaire, but it also missed several dimensions, such as emotional and cognitive demands, meaning of work, job insecurity, job satisfaction, stress, and health.

With regard to the individual questions, we preferred straightforward and simple questions phrased in normal language and formulated as real questions, not statements such as, "I get sufficient support from my superior." For similar reasons, we also avoided response categories such as *agree* or *strongly disagree*. For most of the questions, we preferred five response options as a way to increase precision and reliability and provide a reasonable range of choices for the respondents. For most questions, we used either intensity (from *to a very large extent* to *to a very small extent*) or frequency (from *always* to *never or hardly ever*). The final version included 165 questions (including 20 new questions formed by us) intended to capture 31 psychosocial dimensions. In addition, we included 13 questions on background; 10 questions on bullying, harassment, and violence; 8 questions on family-work issues; and 1 question on tobacco use.

Constructing the Three Questionnaires

The focus of the COPSOQ is the scales measuring psychosocial factors at work. The questions on violence, harassment, bullying, and work-family conflict are optional. All the scales are from 0 to 100, with high values representing a high level of the concept being measured. In other words, high values on the mental health scale mean good mental health, whereas high values on the somatic stress scale indicate high stress levels. We constructed all scales as simple averages with equal weights to the items and equal intervals between response options. In most cases, we provided five response options (such as *always, often, sometimes, seldom,* and *never/hardly ever*), which means that the five options were scored 100, 75, 50, 25, and 0.

The Long Questionnaire

In constructing the scales for the long questionnaire, we used factor analyses and analyses of internal reliability. In the factor analyses, we discovered that some of the items belonged in other scales and some items could not be used at all in the questionnaire. With regard to the internal reliability, we analyzed interitem correlations and item correlations with the whole scale. (Rules of thumb were that interitem correlations should be between 0.20 and 0.70, and correlations with the total scale should be above 0.40.) Furthermore, we inspected the response distribution of the items. Our guiding principle was to avoid floor or ceiling effects and items with more than 5% missing. Our theoretical point of departure was the scales we had constructed according to our hypotheses based on earlier research. The factor analyses and our inspection of the items forced us to change most of these scales. In fact only four of our original scales survived in the intended form. The two short-form 36 (SF-36) scales on mental health and vitality (Ware, Snow, Kosinski, & Gandek, 1993) could not be confirmed as separate dimensions in our factor analyses, and they correlate highly ($r = .73$). However, we decided to keep the SF-36 and stress profile scales (Setterlind & Larson, 1995) unchanged in our long questionnaire to facilitate comparisons with other researchers. We ended up with 30 scales based on 141 questions (see Table 28.1).

The Midsize Questionnaire

The next step was to create the midsize questionnaire. We reduced the number of items in two ways. First, we excluded the four individual-level scales on coping and sense of coherence given that the midsize questionnaire was to be used in evaluating workplaces and jobs, not individuals. Second, we reduced the length of all the longer scales to a maximum of four items (with two exceptions: the two five-item scales from the SF-36). Our analyses show that we were able to keep 85% to 96% of the original variation of the longer scales after the reduction. The midsize questionnaire consists of 95 questions forming 26 scales (see Table 28.1).

Our next step was to develop a user-friendly software system for the midsize questionnaire. The system transformed all the scales into adjusted scales with a median value of 50 points in our national database. Furthermore, 60 points corresponds to the 60th percentile, 90 points to the 90th percentile, and so forth. In the graphics of the software presentation program, all bars between 40 and 60 are yellow, bars above 60 are green, and bars below 40 are red. For the six scales in which high values are bad (quantitative demands, emotional demands, demands for hiding emotions, sensorial demands, job insecurity, and role conflicts), the red and green colors are reversed. This program makes it simple for the professionals to spot the problem areas (red) and resource areas (green). To avoid statistical uncertainty, we recommend that average values for groups below 20 persons be treated with caution. This means that all comparisons using this software program are against the Danish national averages. If other normative levels are required, the program must be changed accordingly.

The Short Questionnaire

To construct the short questionnaire, we entered all the 18 work environment scales (the top 18 scales of Table 28.1) in a new factor analysis. This time three main clusters of scales emerged: (a) demands at work, including quantitative, cognitive, emotional, sensory, and demands for hiding emotions; (b) influence and possibilities for development; and (c) interpersonal relations and leadership. We used items from the midsize questionnaire that

TABLE 28.1
Scales, Number of Questions, and Cronbach's Alphas
for the Three COPSOQ Questionnaires

Scale	Research Questionnaire		Middle Questionnaire		Short Questionnaire	
	Number of questions	Cronbach's α	Number of questions	Cronbach's α	Number of questions	Cronbach's α
Quantitative demands	7	0.80	4	0.65	3	
Cognitive demands	8	0.86	4	0.78		
Emotional demands	3	0.87	3	(0.87)	2	
Demands for hiding emotions	2	0.59	2	(0.59)	1	6 0.68
Sensory demands	5	0.70	4	0.66		
Influence at work	10	0.83	4	0.73	3	
Possibilities for development	7	0.82	4	0.75	2	
Degree of freedom at work	4	0.68	4	(0.68)	1	10 0.78
Meaning of work	3	0.77	3	(0.77)	2	
Commitment to the workplace	4	0.74	4	(0.74)	2	
Predictability	2	0.78	2	(0.78)	2	
Role clarity	4	0.77	4	(0.77)		
Role conflicts	4	0.72	4	(0.72)		
Quality of leadership	8	0.93	4	0.87	2	
Social support	4	0.74	4	(0.74)	2	10 0.81
Feedback at work	2	0.64	2	(0.64)	2	
Social relations	2	0.65	2	(0.65)		
Sense of community	3	0.80	3	(0.80)	2	
Insecurity at work	4	0.61	4	(0.61)	4	(0.61)
Job satisfaction	7	0.84	4	0.75	4	(0.75)
General health	5	0.75	5	(0.75)	1	—
Mental health	5	0.80	5	(0.80)	5	(0.80)
Vitality	4	0.80	4	(0.80)	4	(0.80)
Behavioral stress	8	0.79	4	0.65		
Somatic stress	7	0.76	4	0.62		
Cognitive stress	4	0.85	4	0.85		
Sense of coherence	9	0.71				
Problem-focused coping	2	0.75				
Selective coping	2	0.61				
Resigning coping	2	0.66				
Number of questions	141		95		44	
Number of scales	30		26		8	

N = 1,603–1,850 for the different scales.

represent these three main dimensions of work. We made this selection on a theoretical basis; it was not guided by statistical procedures. Furthermore, we chose to reduce the number of items by excluding the three stress scales and by using just one item to assess general health. In this way, the short questionnaire ended up consisting of 44 questions forming eight scales (see Table 28.1).

In the user-friendly version of the short questionnaire, we gave all the response options values ranging from 0 to 4. In this way, the respondent or someone else at the workplace can sum the scores for the eight dimensions. For example, the scale on interpersonal relations and leadership ranges from 0 (*very poor*) to 40 (*extremely good*). The average for Denmark is 24 points, and average points for a worksite or department above 27 or below 21, respectively, are considered *very good* and *very bad*, respectively.

RESULTS FROM THE COPENHAGEN PSYCHOSOCIAL QUESTIONNAIRE

Overview of the COPSOQ

Table 28.1 provides an overview of COPSOQ. The first five of the work environment scales span several different job demands: quantitative, cognitive, emotional, sensory, and demands for hiding emotions. This differentiation of demands is a novel feature of the COPSOQ. Most other psychosocial questionnaires have included one, loosely defined job-demand scale. The next five dimensions are related to influence and possibilities for development. These dimensions are specifically job related and can be heavily influenced by decisions regarding the hierarchical structure of the worksite, the division of labor among employees, and the content of the individual jobs. The third group of variables is related to interpersonal relations and leadership. The main feature of these factors is that identical worksites with the same structure and the same production may score differently on these dimensions. This is because these work environment factors are extremely dependent on the quality of the social relations within the group of colleagues and leaders working together. We all know how destructive one or two hostile and aggressive persons can be in a group or what a difference a new leader can make. For these factors, the saying "we are each other's environment" applies perfectly.

The next two items are job insecurity and satisfaction, and they are followed by several health and well-being factors. The first three (general health, mental health, and vitality) are from the SF-36 questionnaire, while the next three (behavioral, somatic, and cognitive stress) are from the Setterlind Stress Profile. Finally, the long questionnaire comprises a scale on sense of coherence and three very short scales on individual coping styles.

Examples of Analyses Based on the COPSOQ

Although the two shorter versions are developed for practical use at the work-sites, the long version can be applied in research to develop knowledge and understanding of the psychosocial work environment. We present a few selected results from the national study to demonstrate the potential of the COPSOQ.

Figure 28.1 shows the distribution of jobs along the dimension of influence at work. This dimension is one that is key to health, well-being, absence from work, and several other factors, such as work-family conflict. The figure shows marked variation. The low-influence jobs employ workers in the food industry, office clerks, drivers, and cleaners. It is well established that these jobs lend themselves to high risk for absence and turnover, disease risks, and low job satisfaction (Johnson & Johansson, 1991; Karasek & Theorell, 1990). The jobs with high influence are directors and leaders, but also—somewhat surprisingly—several jobs related to teaching and child day care.

Analyses of the distribution of jobs along psychosocial factors (influence, meaning, support, predictability, and demands) show a rather clear picture, with drivers, cleaners, and food industry workers as the *national high-risk occupations*. The best psychosocial working conditions are found among directors, leaders, and kindergarten teachers. Looking at industries, the best working conditions are found in the pharmaceutical industry, the electronics industry, and in day care. The worst conditions are found in transportation, cleaning, and slaughterhouses.

These national results have been used by the Danish minister of labor and the Danish labor inspection as the basis for the national plan for improving the psychosocial work environment. The goal is to improve the psychosocial work environment to a certain level by 2005, and the COPSOQ scales are to be used to evaluate any progress made.

Figure 28.2 shows the distribution of socioeconomic groups in a model of the information society. Modern society is increasingly characterized by fast change combined with extensive use of information technology. In such a society, those with high cognitive demands and high possibilities for development will be able to cope with the challenges of the changing work life. Figure 28.2 shows that worker social class I (white-collar workers with managerial positions) is clearly situated in the quadrant with high cognitive demands and high possibilities for development. This is the quadrant of *development and growth*. Social class IV (unskilled workers) is in the opposite quadrant of *stagnation and passivity*. This is a highly unfavorable situation, and distribution suggests that the cleavage in the Danish society is between the unskilled workers and the three other social classes. People with jobs in the *stagnation and passivity* quadrant tend to feel isolated from the rest of the society, which is characterized by computers, Internet, cell phones, and globalization. The

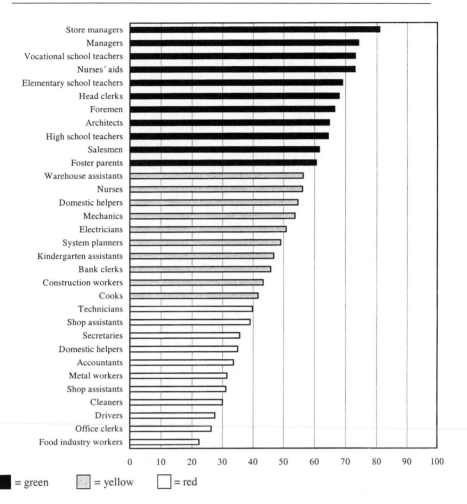

FIG. 28.1. The distribution of jobs by how much influence workers believe they have at work in the Danish labor market. Green = falls above the 60th percentile (i.e., "resource" areas); yellow = falls between the 40th and 60th percentile; red = falls below the 40th percentile (i.e., "problem" areas).

result can be aggressive behavior, hostility, passivity, low participation in the civil society, and so forth.

These examples illustrate how a comprehensive questionnaire such as the COPSOQ can be used to pinpoint high-risk groups, groups with specific work environment problems, or groups with low involvement and poor possibilities in the modern information society. We now turn to the issue of work-family conflict.

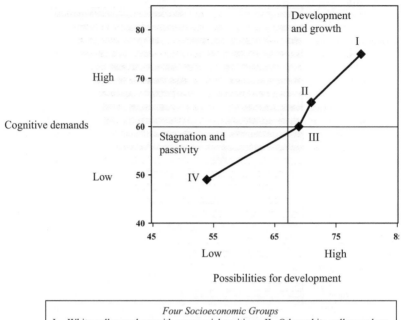

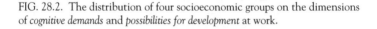

Possibilities for development

Four Socioeconomic Groups
I. White-collar workers with managerial positions; II. Other white-collar workers III. Skilled blue-collar workers; IV. Semi- and unskilled blue-collar workers.

FIG. 28.2. The distribution of four socioeconomic groups on the dimensions of *cognitive demands* and *possibilities for development* at work.

WORK-FAMILY CONFLICT

Definition and Measurement of Work-Family Conflict

Work-family conflict has been measured in many different ways, but rarely defined. In our research, we view work-family conflict as a rather new phenomenon in modern industrial societies. As noted before, we define it as a situation in which fulfilling the roles in one of the two domains conflicts with fulfilling the roles in the other. We consider there to be three necessary conditions for work-family conflict to exist in the modern sense of this concept: (a) Division between family and work: Family members work outside the family for a wage; (b) High participation rate of women at the labor market: Women have dual roles; and (c) High value placed on family roles by both parents in the family: Men and women want to be good parents for their children and good spouses for their partners.

Furthermore, we distinguish between work-family interference, on the one hand, and genuine work-family conflict, on the other. There has always been interference between the two domains, but the specific feature about modern work-family conflict is the potential conflict between work and family with respect to the time and energy of the parents. A clear illustration of this conflict was given by a participant in one of our studies: "I always leave my job too early, only to discover that I always get home too late."

In our basic test questionnaire for the COPSOQ, we measured work-family conflict with three different questions:

1. General conflict: "Is there sometimes a conflict between your work and your private life, which makes you want to be both places at the same time?" (Yes, often; yes, regularly; seldom; no, never.)

2. Energy conflict: "Do you feel that your work demands so much of your energy that it affects your private life?" (Yes, definitely; yes, to a certain degree; yes, but not much; no, not at all.)

3. Time conflict: "Do you have sufficient time at home and with your family?" (To a great extent; to some extent; somewhat; not very much; to a very small extent.)

Work-Family Conflict in the COPSOQ Database

According to our general theory about work and family, we would expect work-family conflict to be more common among employees in jobs with high demands (quantitative and emotional), low influence, low predictability, low degrees of freedom, high role conflicts, low social support, and poor leadership. In Table 28.2, we tested these assumptions with multivariate linear regression analyses of the cross-sectional COPSOQ database. These analyses show clear associations between a number of the psychosocial work environment variables and the three work-family conflict items. We found statistically significant associations with work-family conflict for all three dimensions described earlier. The strongest and most consistent associations are seen for quantitative and emotional demands. Contrary to our expectations, we found no independent associations for predictability, role conflicts, and social support.

It is well known that associations found in cross-sectional questionnaires do not necessarily reflect causality. We see our results as being more descriptive; persons who perceive work-family conflicts also tend to experience more psychosocial work environment stressors, such as high demands, low influence, low meaning, low role clarity, and low quality of leadership. These persons face a double strain, and we view them as clear candidates for (future) stress, ill health, absence, and turnover.

TABLE 28.2
Associations (as Indicated by p) Between Work Environment
Variables and Three Indicators of Work-Family Conflict

	General Conflict	Energy Conflict	Time Conflict
	p	p	p
Quantitative demands	***	***	***
Cognitive demands	*		
Emotional demands	***	***	***
Demands for hiding emotions		*	
Influence at work		**	
Possibilities for development		**	
Degrees of freedom at work	***		
Meaning of work	**		**
Commitment to the workplace		**	
Role clarity			**
Quality of leadership		***	***
Sense of community	*	**	

Note. Multivariate analyses included all 18 work environment dimensions of COPSOQ as independent variables. Nonsignificant associations were: sensory demands, predictability, role conflicts, social support, feedback, and social relations.
  *$p \leq 0.05$; **$p \leq 0.01$; ***$p \leq 0.001$.

Testing a Full Model for Work-Family Conflict in the SARA Study

In another study at NIOH, Copenhagen (the SARA study of 3,010 employees; see Nielsen, Kristensen, & Smith-Hansen, 2002), we tested a more fully developed model of work-family conflict. This model is shown in Figure 28.3. According to the model, work-family conflict depends on a number of factors in both the family and at work. Furthermore, the health and well-being of the workers depend on factors in the family, at work, and the level of work-family conflict. All five of these associations can go in both directions. For example, work-family conflict can result in changes of working hours at the job or in a shift to a new job as a way to reduce work-family conflict. Even the anticipation of work-family conflict can influence behavior. For example, people may avoid having (more) children to prevent future work-family conflict.

Table 28.3 illustrates Arrow 1 in Fig. 28.3: the association between family structure and family-work conflict. Clearly couples with young children and single parents with children experience work-family conflict more often than the other groups in the study. The fact that single parents do not have even higher levels of work-family conflict can be explained by the somewhat higher prevalence of part-time work within this group (40% work part time compared with 30% in the full sample).

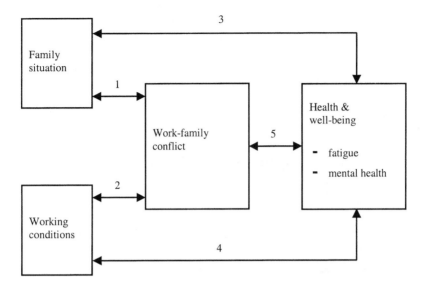

FIG. 28.3. Basic model for work-family conflict.

TABLE 28.3
Proportion Reporting Work-Family Conflict
Among Respondents in Different Family Structures

Family Structure	Energy Conflict (%)	General Conflict (%)
Single without children	31.7	9.2
Couple without children	38.9	13.8
Couple with older children (7+ years)	46.2	20.8
Couple with young children (0–6 years)	53.2	31.8
Single with any children	51.9	27.0
Total	43.2	19.3

Note. Results from the SARA study of 3,010 employees.

Arrow 2 in Fig. 28.3 is illustrated in Fig. 28.4. In this illustration of the model, we focus on the strongest work environment predictor of work-family conflict: quantitative job demands. There are clear associations between job demands and the prevalence of work-family conflict. It should be noted that both factors are self-reported, which creates common method variance. Nevertheless, Fig. 28.4 shows that people who experience high job demands also tend to experience high levels of work-family conflict.

The associations between family structure and the two measures of well-being (Arrow 3) are rather weak. Persons with the best health are those who have partners, whereas those who live alone have poorer health. This confirms a well-documented association in the family and social network research. The clearest result is that parents living alone with their child(ren) are more tired than the other respondents in the study (data not shown).

Figure 28.5 illustrates Arrow 4 in Fig. 28.3. We see that quantitative job demands are clearly related to mental health as well as vitality. In particular, the association with vitality is clear and highly significant.

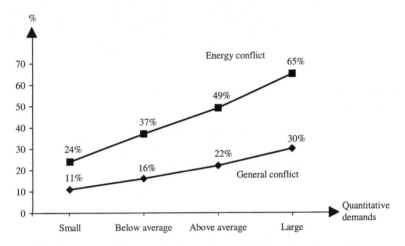

FIG. 28.4. Associations between quantitative job demands and two indicators of work-family conflict in the SARA study.

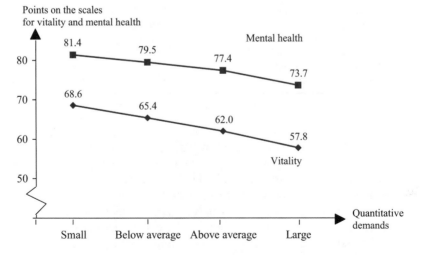

FIG. 28.5. Associations between job demands and two measures of well-being: vitality and mental health (SARA study).

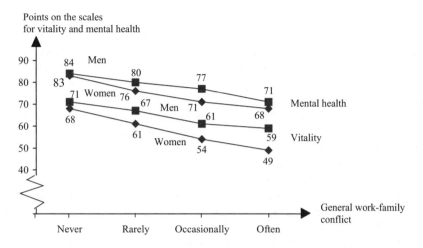

FIG. 28.6. Associations between the degree of perceived work-family conflict and two measures of well-being: vitality and mental health (SARA study).

Finally, Arrow 5 is illustrated in Fig. 28.6. This figure shows the association between the occurrence of general work-family conflict and the two measures of mental health and well-being. The gradients are clear for both genders, and the association with vitality is most pronounced for women. A common interpretation arising from all the measures is that those who are most tired often report work-family conflict, and work-family conflict may lead to fatigue.

A Dutch Longitudinal Study of Work-Family Conflict: The Maastricht Cohort Study on Fatigue

The Maastricht Cohort Study on Fatigue at Work examines the significance of psychosocial work environmental factors for work-family conflict. The study is longitudinal in design and involves a large cohort of 12,095 employees (Jansen, Kant, Kristensen, & Nijhuis, 2003; Jansen, Kant, Nijhuis, Swaen, & Kristensen, 2003). This study adds to the picture already suggested before by offering a glimpse of dynamic (1-year) changes in work, family, work-family conflict, and fatigue, rather than a point-in-time view. Furthermore, the study was able to measure some of the dimensions with higher precision and specificity than in the COPSOQ. For instance, they were able to measure different aspects of quantitative demands, such as overtime, normal working hours, shift work, and commuting time. With regard to risk factors for work-family conflict, the study came to several conclusions for men and women. First, demand issues that created risk were psychological demands, physical demands, overtime work, shift work, and long commutes. Second, dimensions related to the organization of work that posed risk were low influence at work and being unable to take a day off when desired. Third, interpersonal relations and leadership domains that led to risk included conflicts at work, low social support, and low predictability (not knowing one's schedule 1 month in advance). The Maastricht Study does not use the same dimensions as the COPSOQ, but the general picture is similar, which underscores the significance of including the psychosocial work environment factors in studies of work-family conflict.

The Maastricht Study also demonstrated the reciprocal nature of many of the associations studied. For instance, fatigue seems to be both a risk factor for work-family conflict and a consequence of work-family conflict. Also this study showed that persons with work-family conflict were more likely to have reduced working hours at follow-up than persons who did not experience work-family conflict. This tendency was strongest among women. Results of this type show how complicated it is to study work-family conflict; working long hours is a risk factor for work-family conflict, but work-family conflict is a risk factor for shorter working hours. Feedback loops such as these tend to mask many of the associations between working conditions and work-family conflict. The results also suggest why the prevalence of work-family conflict is similar for men and women: Women have a higher workload in the family, but they are able to reduce their occupational workload to reduce the overall demands of work and family.

DISCUSSION AND PERSPECTIVES

In this chapter, we presented research results from Denmark and the Netherlands supporting the view that psychosocial factors at work play a key role in work-family conflict. The research examined three factors that might influence work-family conflict: demands at work, degree of influence at work and the possibility for career development, and interpersonal relations and leadership quality. We summarize the findings for each.

Demands at Work

Demands seem to increase the risk of work-family conflict in two ways— through time conflict and conflict of energy. For instance, overtime takes more of the person's time and, at the same time, results in more fatigue. Shift work interferes directly with the rhythm of the family, and emotional demands may drain the worker of the mental resources needed to cope with the problems of children and marriage.

Influence and Possibilities for Career Development

Among the dimensions related to the organization and content of work, we found evidence for the significance of influence at work, degree of freedom (with respect to working time, breaks, vacation), and several other factors. These dimensions are important because they enable the worker to control working hours, which again makes it easier to cope with family demands. A high level of influence at work also enables the worker to cope better with his or her own fatigue so that chronic fatigue is avoided.

Interpersonal Relations and Leadership

The third dimension involves the relations between colleagues and supervisors. We found that factors such as role clarity, quality of leadership, social support, and conflicts at work were related to work-family conflict. These results underscore that colleagues may be able to help and support one another in many ways that could reduce work-family conflict. Also good leadership providing predictability of future working hours, role clarity, and social support may be a key factor.

It should be pointed out that work-family conflict is not a symmetrical conflict: Work tends to have a greater degree of influence than the family. The individual worker has much less power at the workplace than in the family, and the negative sanctions for not complying with workplace rules or expectations are often quite substantial. Many workplaces see themselves as family friendly, but this may be more lip service than everyday practice (Hochschild, 1997). Furthermore, the employees may feel more valued, competent, and successful at work than in the family, which further adds to the imbalance between work and family (Hochschild, 1997). When "work becomes home and home becomes work," the family and its members tend to be the losers.

The likelihood of this outcome is strengthened by the tendency toward work without limits in the modern organizations. Limits of space and time tend to disappear, which means that work invades leisure time, intended to be used with the family. The workplace becomes ubiquitous, with laptops, cell phones, and e-mail allowing the employee to work everywhere and be reached by the workplace even at the beach or in the bedroom.

The key to reducing work-family conflict lies in the labor market in general and in the individual workplaces in particular. Improvements to the psychosocial work environment along the lines suggested in this chapter should certainly be considered in any attempt to reduce work-family conflict. Reliable and valid questionnaires are necessary for making systematic assessments and improvement to the psychosocial work environment. We believe the COPSOQ has been very useful in this respect. National versions of the COPSOQ have been or are being developed in Spain, Sweden, Norway, Germany, Belgium, Turkey, and Brazil, which makes international collaboration and comparisons possible.

REFERENCES

Cox, T. (1993). *Stress research and stress management: Putting theory to work*. Sudbury, UK: HSE Books.

Dallner, M., Elo, A.-L., Gamberale, F., Hottinen, V., Knardahl, S., Lindström, K., Skogstad, A., & Ørhede, E. (2000). *Validation of the General Nordic Questionnaire (QPSNordic) for psychological and social factors at work* (Nord 2000:12). Copenhagen: Nordic Council of Ministers.

Hochschild, A. (1997). *The time bind. When work becomes home and home becomes work*. New York: Metropolitan Books.

Jansen, N. W. H., Kant, I. J., Kristensen, T. S., & Nijhuis, F. J. N. (2003). Antecedents and consequences of work-family conflict: A prospective cohort study. *Journal of Occupational and Environmental Medicine, 45*, 479–491.

Jansen, N. W. H., Kant, I., Nijhuis, F. J. N, Swaen, G. M. H., & Kristensen, T. S. (2003). *Impact of working time arrangements on work-home interference among Dutch employees*. Manuscript submitted for publication.

Johnson, J. V., & Johansson, G. (Eds.). (1991). *The psychosocial work environment: Work organization, democratization and health*. Amityville: Baywood.

Karasek, R., & Theorell, T. (1990). *Healthy work. Stress, productivity, and the reconstruction of working life*. New York: Basic Books.

Kompier, M. A. J., Geurts, S. A. E., Gründemann, R. W. M., Vink, P., & Smulders, P. G. W. (1998). Cases in stress prevention: The success of a participative and stepwise approach. *Stress Medicine, 14*, 155–168.

Kristensen, T. S., Borg, V., & Hannerz, H. (2002). Socioeconomic status and psychosocial work environment: Results from a Danish national study. *Scandinavian Journal of Public Health, 30*, 41–48.

Levi, L. (1981). *Preventing work stress*. Reading, MA: Addison-Wesley.

Marmot, M., & Wilkinson, R. G. (Eds.). (1999). *Social determinants of health*. Oxford: Oxford University Press.

Nielsen, M. L., Kristensen, T. S., & Smith-Hansen, L. (2002). The Intervention Project on Absence and Well-being (IPAW): Design and results from the baseline of a 5-year study. *Work & Stress, 16*, 191–206.

Setterlind, S., & Larson, G. (1995). The Stress Profile: A psychosocial approach to measuring stress. *Stress Medicine, 11*, 85–92.

Ware, J. E., Snow, K. K., Kosinski, M., & Gandek, B. (1993). *SF-36 health survey. Manual and interpretation guide*. Boston: The Health Institute, New England Medical Center.

PART VII

Low-Income Families
and Work, Care, Health,
and Well-Being

29

Work in the Working Class: Challenges Facing Families

Maureen Perry-Jenkins

University of Massachusetts Amherst

Vinnie Caritino and his wife, Donna, were high school sweethearts and have been married just over a year. Both have lived in their hometown of Springville, Massachusetts, their entire lives. Vinnie works full time at a paper-making plant in town, and Donna is an express mail delivery worker. Vinnie works rotating shifts that alternate between 7 A.M. to 3 P.M., 3 P.M. to 11 P.M., and 11 P.M. to 7 A.M. every 2 weeks. Donna works a 6 A.M. to 2 P.M. shift. Both make more than the current state minimum wage of $6.75 an hour; Vinnie's hourly rate is $8.75 for his 7 to 3 shift and $9.50 for nonday shifts. Donna makes a flat $10.00 an hour. Their combined gross family income is $38,729. After taxes, they bring home about $28,275 yearly or about $543 per week. They rent a small ranch house, have two cars ("one on its last legs," according to Donna), and by their own account "are making it." The most exciting news for the Caritinos is they are expecting their first child in fewer than 2 months.

In this chapter, I explore how working-class families like Vinnie and Donna face the challenges of work and family life as they become new parents and juggle the demands of two jobs. To foreshadow the story, as the data from the Work and Family Transitions Project (WFTP) and that of other researchers illustrate, it is impossible to characterize the working-class experience in any typical or monolithic way. As with any attempt to group individuals by a specific criterion, be it race, ethnicity, gender, or social class, there is often more variability within groups than between groups. However, an important aim of this chapter is to highlight some of the challenges facing low-wage workers—those with low levels of education who are working in unskilled or semiskilled jobs trying to manage the demands of work and family life. Looking within the lives of working-class families, rather than comparing them with families in other classes, uncovers unique work and family issues and themes in working-class families.

The primary goals of this chapter are threefold. First, I address theoretical and methodological issues that have both hindered and challenged an understanding of social class as it influences work and family. Second, I highlight specific research that points to ways in which social class shapes work-family links, and I discuss shortcomings in our current knowledge base. Finally, I offer implications for research and workplace policies and interventions in light of the unique challenges and life circumstances of working-class individuals and their families.

THEORETICAL AND METHODOLOGICAL ISSUES: WHAT IS SOCIAL CLASS?

The complex and thorny concept of social class deserves attention. One of the great debates in sociology centers on the concept of social class (Bornstein & Bradley, 2003; Wright, 1997). Researchers differ on whether social class is a discrete or continuous variable, whether it is a one- or multidimensional concept, whether it is constructed in one's community or in society at large, whether it is a subjective or objective phenomenon, and what component of socioeconomic status (SES) is most salient (Hoffman, 2003). Nevertheless, Wright (1997) proposed that, in conceptualizing class, it is useful to think of individuals as situated within locations in the class structure—locations that are defined along two dimensions: relationship to authority and possession of skills or expertise. The working class, who Wright contended compose the largest component of workers in the United States, are located in jobs with little to no authority and requiring little (semiskilled) to no skill. Gilbert and Kahl (1993), although acknowledging that class is a moving target, with individuals and families regularly moving across status levels in response to economic surges and downturns, proposed that working-class employees compose about 30% to 35% of the U.S. workforce. They distinguished between working class and working poor primarily based on education, with working-class employees typically holding a high school degree and the working poor usually having some high school education, but no degree. Working-class workers hold jobs such as machine operators, craftspeople, clerical workers, and sales workers; the working poor are most often service workers, laborers, or low-paid operators and clericals. Catanzarite (2002) pointed to the rise of *brown-collar* occupations, especially among recent immigrant Latinos. Brown-collar jobs are poorly paid, irregular occupations often in service industries or agriculture. This research reminds us that social class statuses are not randomly distributed by gender, race, and ethnicity—a fact that must remain at the forefront of any discussion that addresses links between social class and family life.

It would be inaccurate to suggest that social class is about income alone. Many have posited that the most important aspects of social class are those factors that shape one's social reality and values (Kohn, 1979; Rubin, 1994; Wright, 1997). As Kohn (1979) stated, social class remains compelling to social scientists

> because it captures the reality that the intricate interplay of all these variables (i.e., income, education, occupation) creates different levels of the social order. Members of different social classes, by virtue of enjoying (or suffering) different conditions of life come to see the world differently—to develop different conceptions of social reality, different aspirations and hopes and fears, different conceptions of the desirable. (p. 48)

For many social scientists, social class serves as a proxy for shared values. In fact our interests often lie in the cultural norms and ideologies that represent a social class status—norms that come to shape experiences and goals related to work and family life.

Perplexing methodological issues arise in measuring social class. What components of class are most important: income, education, occupation, or some combination of the three? Although the Hollingshead Four-Factor Index of Social Status (Hollingshead, 1975) is the most widely cited index of SES (Bornstein, Hahn, Suwalsky, & Haynes, 2003), some scholars argue that, "developmental research is ill-served by an aggregated, simplified, or superficial treatment of SES" (Duncan & Magnuson, 2003, p. 83). Duncan and Magnuson found that the three primary indicators of class (i.e., income, education, occupation) function differently depending on the population under study, the developmental age of children, and the outcomes examined. They suggested that researchers assess all three indicators independently given that each represents a distinct theoretical construct, and this approach allows researchers to examine independent, additive, and interactive effects of the factors.

Yet another methodological challenge concerns the appropriate unit of analysis. For a two-income family, do we assess class at the individual or dyadic level? With the goal of developing a universal method of assessing social class, Hauser (1994) recommended that, "it is better to focus on the characteristics of one adult in the household, a head of household, householder, or principal earner, who may be male or female, and to ascertain the educational attainment, labor force status and occupational position of that person" (p. 1542).

What do we do, however, if there are two primary breadwinners in a family, which is often the case in working-class families, where wives may contribute between 40% and 50% of the family income? Moreover, studies have revealed that the combination of class statuses within a family (such as a middle-class wife married to a working-class husband) is related to different family processes in family work and marital conflict (Perry-Jenkins & Folk, 1994). Wright (1997), questioning the conventional view that the class of a woman is derived from the class of her husband, proposed that if both individuals have direct relations to the means of production, a combination of direct and mediated class locations arises that holds implications for family life. Thus, it is critical in two-parent households to assess the class of both partners to understand the potential implications of social class for family life.

THEORIZING ABOUT WORK AND FAMILY ISSUES: THE IMPORTANCE OF CONTEXT

Research has proposed numerous theories to explain how work conditions are related to workers' mental and physical health and family relationships. These theoretical perspectives have arisen from a variety of disciplines, such as developmental psychology, sociology, social psychology, health psychology, economics and labor studies, to name just a few (Perry-Jenkins, Repetti, & Crouter, 2000). What has been missing from much of the theoretical research on the work-family interface is attention to the role of sociocultural contexts as they shape work-family processes. From an ecological perspective, Bronfenbrenner (1986) proposed that we should not only attend to aspects of social context, such as race, class, gender, and family structure, but also to the idea that family processes may differ within contexts and ultimately hold different consequences for human development.

A common strategy in much of the empirical research on work-family relations is to control for factors such as race, income, education, or occupational status with the aim of elucidating some pure process linking aspects of work to some feature of adults' or children's mental health or development. There are two key flaws with this conceptual and statistical approach. First, it neglects how work and family links may differ within sociocultural niches. A paucity of studies explores how aspects of race and ethnicity, social class, and gender (e.g., same-sex households) affect the type of work-family processes within families. Second, although it may be possible to control for key demographic variables in analyses, it is not quite so easy in the real world. Far more interesting questions arise when we explore work and family interrelations within their social, economic, and cultural contexts.

In our empirical attempt to look within the context of social class using the National Survey of Families and Household (Perry-Jenkins & Folk, 1994), my colleagues and I addressed some well-worn questions in work-family research on how the division of labor and perceptions of its fairness are related to marital quality, but we added a slight twist. We examined these relations in four types of dual-earner couples defined by social class typologies: (a) both spouses are working class, (b) both spouses are middle class, (c) husband is working class and wife is middle class, and (d) husband is middle class and wife is working class. Findings reveal that relations between the division of household labor, perceptions of equity, and marital conflict differed across groups. For middle-class wives, perceptions of equity had the strongest effect on marital conflict—with less equity being related to more conflict—while the actual division of labor was unrelated to marital conflict for this group. In contrast, for working-class wives, the more tasks they performed, the less marital conflict they reported, and equity was unrelated to marital quality. In addition, the findings also suggest that the combination of a husband and wife's class leads to different sets of relations among variables. For example, working-class wives with middle-class husbands did not equate equity with a more equal division of household chores, whereas working-class wives with working-class husbands did link equity to a more equal division of labor. Had we controlled for social class in these analyses, we would have masked differences that emerged across groups.

Bornstein and Bradley (2003) presented compelling evidence of the powerful and direct effects of social class on parenting styles, parents' mental health, and child outcomes. Even more interesting are studies that examine mediator models, whereby social class is related to parenting style or stimulates components of home life that, in turn, predict children's academic and social development (Bradley & Corwyn, 2003; Leventhal & Brooks-Gunn, 2003). Although these studies provide insight into the powerful effects of income, education, and job status, far less is known about the nature of working- and middle-class jobs as potential contexts for human development. Specifically, what is it about occupations that matter for workers and their families?

Kohn (1979) was among the first to describe how one's job experiences, specifically occupational self-direction, could influence one's values and goals on childrearing. According to Kohn, self-direction is characterized by high levels of job autonomy, low levels of supervision, and complex work tasks—dimensions of work most often found in middle- or upper middle-class jobs. In contrast, blue-collar workers are more likely to be employed in jobs that are routinized, highly supervised, and have little autonomy. Kohn found that fathers holding jobs where self-direction is valued were more likely to value these traits in their children, whereas fathers in jobs where conformity was required valued obedience and conformity in their children. More recently, Menaghan and Parcel (1995) elucidated similar processes for employed mothers; they linked occupational self-direction to more stimulating home environments and enhanced reading scores in children (Parcel & Menaghan, 1994).

Much is learned when we look past income and occupational status to understand how experiences of the job shape values and beliefs. On a cautionary note, we must take care not to accept, at face value, social approaches that compare working- and middle-class occupations (Bronfenbrenner & Crouter, 1982). Simplistic comparisons might lead us to conclude that working-class jobs are mundane, routinized, and highly supervised, whereas middle-class occupations have high autonomy, low supervision, and complex tasks. On average, these differences may emerge; however, many blue-collar workers find their jobs fulfilling and challenging, just as many white-collar workers evaluate their work as routinized and highly controlled. An aim of the following section is to highlight unique work and family issues with which working-class families deal every day and, in so doing, reveal the range of experiences and emotions that surround their decisions about how best to manage work and family life.

WORK AND FAMILY CHALLENGES OF WORKING-CLASS FAMILIES: A LOOK AT THE RESEARCH

I now turn to a review of current research and supplement these studies with new findings from an ongoing, longitudinal study—the WFTP. The goal of the WFTP is to examine how working-class, dual-earner couples experience the transition to parenthood while holding down full-time jobs. I highlight major themes unique to these families while also addressing issues of within-group variability.

The Work and Family Transitions Project

The WFTP gathered data from 153 working-class, dual-earner couples experiencing the transition to parenthood for the first time. The study recruited heterosexual couples in their third trimester of pregnancy from various prenatal classes at hospitals in western New England. Both members of couples in the study were either married or cohabiting (for at least 1 year) at the time of inclusion in the study, were *working class* (defined by restricting educational level to an associate's degree or less), were expecting their first child, were employed full time (32+ hours per week) prior to the baby's birth, and planned to return to full-time work within 6 months of the baby's birth.

Hospital data in the study region indicated that between 75% and 85% of first-time parents attended prenatal classes. Of those not attending classes, nearly 80% were single mothers and did not fit the criteria for inclusion in the study. Thus, we had access to a fairly representative sample of first-time new parents.

Trained graduate students described the study at the beginning of each prenatal class. At that time, all parents filled out a short demographic form with basic information on age, marital status, income, type of job, work hours, and intent to return to work after the baby's birth. Expectant parents also indicated whether they would be willing to have study members contact them to describe the project in more detail, and, if so, they provided contact information. Thus, the study was able to compare a sample of first-time parents with the broader population of first-time parents in the area. The present sample, as expected, was significantly less educated, had lower incomes, and worked more hours than the full sample of new parents.

Both partners participated in four interviews across the transition to parenthood and completed one mail survey. They were interviewed (a) during the couples' third trimester of pregnancy; (b) approximately 1 month after the baby's birth, but before the mother had returned to full-time employment; (c) 1 month after the mother's return to full-time employment (15 weeks postpartum on average); (d) 6 months postpartum through a mail survey; and (e) 1 year later in a follow-up interview. At Phases 1, 2, 3, and 5, researchers conducted interviews separately with both partners in their homes, and the interviews were between 2 and 3 hours. To ensure privacy, researchers interviewed mothers and fathers in different rooms out of hearing distance from each other. For the purpose of this study, respondents completed a series of standardized questionnaires as well as open-ended questions that delved into areas such as work, psychological well-being, the marital-partner relationship, social support, gender roles, and child development.

The age of participants ranged from 19 to 41. Despite the large range, the mean and median ages for men and women were virtually the same. Men's mean age at the time of their partner's pregnancy was 29.1 (median 28.7), and women's average age was 27.8 (median 27.5). Nearly 80% (79.7%) of the couples were married, and the average length of relationship was 3.3 years. Cohabiting couples had been living together an average of 2.1 years. A high percentage of those who participated were White (92.2% of women, 90.6% of men), with only 1.5% representing African Americans, 1% Latino women, 3% Latino men, and 5% not reporting race or ethnicity. Over the years, we made an intense effort to increase our enrollment of minority families. We partnered with the Women, Infants, and Children (WIC) program and two prenatal clinics in neighboring communities. With the help of our colleagues in the community, we soon came to realize a critical flaw in the original study design that served to eliminate many minority families. Specifically, the study was designed around a life course pattern that included finishing school, getting a job, getting married, and having children, in that order. The bias in these assumptions (i.e., White, middle-class bias) excluded a majority of African-American families given the recent demographic data indicating the majority of African-American women become first-time parents as single mothers. In addition, demographic data on the large Puerto Rican community in a nearby town indicated that the majority of employed women in this group did not return to work after the birth of their baby. Thus, they did not meet the criteria of having to return to work soon after the baby's birth. In an effort to correct for these shortcomings, a new continuation study is currently underway that explores the transition to parenthood for employed African-American and White single mothers.

Given the restricted sampling criteria, educational attainment ranged considerably. For instance, the highest degree was a high school diploma or GED, held by 16% of women and 22.5% of men. A majority of the sample (44.8% of women and 63.4% of men) had some type of additional schooling or vocational training after high school (e.g., beautician's school, refrigeration mechanic training, truck driving). However, only 31% of women and 14.1% of men held a 1- or 2-year associate's degree. None of the parents had a college degree.

Individually reported income ranged from $7,000 to $54,000 annually for men and from $6,000 to $60,000 for women. Median salaries were $27,000 and $22,000 for men and women, respectively, and the median family income was $47,000. In addition, more respondents (52.7% of women and 68.9% of men) fell into the middle-income category ($20,000–$40,000) than any of the other categories. Thirty-five percent of women and 18% of men earned less than $20,000 annually, and only 7.9% of women and 13.1% of men earned $40,000 or more in the past year. Thus, in most cases, the loss of one partner's income would move many of the families close to or below the poverty line. The most common types of jobs held by men were factory workers, truck drivers, and food service workers. Women were employed most often as food service workers, factory workers, and beauticians. Using these findings from the WFTP, as well as other studies, I address specific and unique challenges facing working-class employees and their families.

Work Hours, Work Schedules, and Work Preferences

Obtaining accurate data on work hours and schedules is especially challenging with a working-class sample for several reasons. Many working-class occupations, such as service work and agricultural jobs, are subject to seasonal variations, leading to unstable and varied work hours. For example, in our sample of first-time parents, we found that over a year's time, more than one third of the sample changed jobs, and another one third added a second job or dropped a job. Duncan and Magnuson (2003) noted that 25% of people living in poverty 1 year have incomes above the poverty level the next year.

Work hours are not stable, and much could be learned from studying the effects on parents and their children of continual movement into and out of the workforce.

Second, as we inquired about work schedules and work hours in our home interviews with couples, we often found discrepancies in spousal reports. In exploring these discrepancies, we found that husbands, especially in the first interview, were extremely hesitant to report under-the-table income for fear that the information would be reported to the Internal Revenue Service (IRS). As we learned about this problem, we prefaced our discussions about income and work hours with a reminder that their responses were confidential and would not be shared with outside sources. By the 1-year follow-up interview, far more husbands reported working multiple jobs that were not on the books; thus, their work hours increased, on average, by 15% to 20% from the first interview. It is reasonable to conclude that these same measurement issues are at work in national workforce data sets; therefore, estimates of work hours for low-income workers may be significantly deflated. As we learned from Vinnie, the husband introduced at the beginning of this chapter, under-the-table work was vital to keeping the family financially solvent: "The money I make nights and weekends, when I help my brother-in-law with his moving jobs, is what keeps our heads above water. We use that money to cover the unexpected things like wedding gifts or holidays . . . and it lets us go out once in a while."

As Presser's work highlighted, shift work is far more common in working-class occupations (Presser & Cox, 1997), with blue-collar employees more likely to work nonday or rotating shifts than middle- and upper middle-class employees. Shift work is most common among workers in service occupations, such as protective services (49%), which includes police, firefighters, guards, and food services (40.4%) and among those employed as operators, fabricators, and laborers (25.4%; U.S. Bureau of Labor Statistics, 2001). Moreover, shift work has been linked to greater marital instability (Presser, 2000), lower marital quality, and increased depression during the first year of parenthood (Perry-Jenkins, Goldberg, Pierce, & Haley, 2002). Yet many new parents in our sample view alternating shifts as an ideal way to maintain exclusive parental care and to save on the high costs of child care. The research thus far has not elucidated the processes whereby shift work affects marriages and well-being. We need studies that explore the variability within shift work couples—why some cope well and others do not—and that examine the specific factors that link job schedules to aspects of married life and personal well-being.

Work preferences have consistently linked paid employment to maternal mental health. Mothers who prefer to be employed report significantly higher well-being than those who would prefer not to work (Steil, 1997). The few studies that have addressed class differences in work preferences find that women in higher status jobs emphasize the centrality of paid employment in their lives (Steil, 1997). In a recent study of 300 career women ages 35 to 49, 87% reported that they were considering job changes to accommodate their family life, but the majority did not want to relinquish their careers, only modify them (Morris, 1995).

Women in blue-collar occupations are more likely to work because of economic necessity and usually contribute a more significant proportion of the family income than their white-collar counterparts (Steil, 1997). Nevertheless, these results should not suggest that women in working-class occupations are not committed to their jobs. In fact one study found a stronger, positive relation between paid work and well-being for blue-collar than white-collar female workers (Warr & Parry, 1982). In addition, several studies indicate that working-class mothers would work even if they did not need the money (Ferree, 1976; Malson, 1983).

In the WFTP sample, 88.9% of women and 81% of men prior to the baby's birth preferred that the women be employed. By the baby's first birthday, 49% of mothers preferred to be employed, and 58% of fathers preferred their wives to work. When asked why they were employed, nearly 90% of working mothers said the primary reason was financial—they needed the money. As we probed further, however, and asked, "So, if money were not an issue, then you would not work outside of the home at all?", 61% of mothers indicated that they would still work even if they did not need the money. The reasons they cited for working included enjoying the job, a sense of accomplishment, seeing other adults, and being bored at home. Thus, contrary to some stereotypical notions of working-class jobs being mundane and boring, a significant percentage of mothers in our study found satisfaction in their work. In fact the mother in our sample who reported the highest job satisfaction and commitment ratings worked in a meat-packing plant on the 3 to 11 shift.

Missing from this more general discussion of work preferences is the question of how a family's life stage may affect how workers feel about their jobs. Studies tend to highlight the pressure-filled days of life with young children, two jobs, and heavy time demands. A different story may emerge as children enter school and become more independent, and as parents gain more control both at home and at work.

Workplace Policies and Supports

In 1993, Congress passed the landmark legislation, the Family and Medical Leave Act (FMLA). The Act allows for 12 weeks of unpaid leave with job protection for employees having or adopting children; for the care of an ill child, spouse, or parent; or to address one's own health issue. Of course the critical word in this legislation for working-class families is *unpaid*. Findings show that women, parents, those with little income, and African Americans are particularly likely to perceive a need for job leaves, yet it is married (not single) women and Whites who are most likely to take leaves (Gerstel & McGonagle, 1999). Estes and Glass (1996) argued that this type of legislation represents "an emerging class cleavage" in work and family legislation. Moreover, according to the U.S. Department of Labor, the FMLA excludes approximately 90% of employers, and Ruhm (chap. 21, this volume) estimates that approximately one half of all workers are covered by the law (because it applies only to workplaces with 50 or more employees and is of little assistance to part-time, seasonal, or temporary workers). Although the FMLA guarantees most employees their job at the same pay and equal position, one's work schedule is not guaranteed. Donna, the express mail delivery worker introduced at the beginning of the chapter, learned this the hard way. Donna had 10 weeks of leave after her son's birth, and she pieced together a paid leave package by using sick, vacation, and personal time. She planned to return to her job on the 6 A.M. to 2 P.M. shift and had arranged child care with varied family members to provide care on different days. Two days before she was to return to the job, she was informed that her new shift would be from 11 A.M. to 7 P.M., starting the next day. As she said, "Well you can imagine. I burst into tears, it was hard enough going back in the first place, but 11–7, how was I going to manage that? I was ready to quit but what could I do. We needed the job."

Within a month, Donna had another run in with her supervisor. She requested that during her midday break she be allowed to return to the office to pump her breast milk. He turned down the request. Therefore, at 3:00 P.M. every day, Donna parked her truck on the side of the road, slipped into the back cab, and pumped her milk for 20 minutes. She summed up her experience with her boss in these words: "He is a guy, he just doesn't get it."

Ten percent of the mothers in the WFTP sample had a fully paid leave, 51% had a partially paid leave, and 38% had an unpaid leave. At first glance, these numbers look quite promising. However, we asked the mothers to document, week by week, the type of pay they were receiving. Of the 61% that had at least some paid leave, only 16% had paid parental leave. The majority used vacation time, sick time, and personal days to pay for their leave. The hidden cost of this strategy emerged when we visited parents after they had returned to work. Infants often get ill, especially those in child-care arrangements who are exposed to other children. Many parents, especially mothers, had already used all of their sick, vacation, and personal time. We began hearing stories about getting written up by supervisors for unexcused absences, being docked pay, and getting warnings. Donna also had this problem because she had used up all her discretionary time when her baby was born; when he became ill, she had no choice but to stay home without pay. By the 1-year follow-up, Donna had three warnings in her file and was worried about job security.

Mandatory overtime is another issue that arose as a problem for many of the new parents in the WFTP. Mandatory overtime hours are those above the standard work week (usually 40 hours) that the employer makes compulsory with the threat of job loss or the threat of other reprisals such as demotions, assignment to unattractive work shifts or tasks, and loss of a day's or multiple days' pay. Based on the Fair Labor Standards Act of 1938, there are no limits on overtime, but an overtime premium must be paid. Although many of our new parents welcomed overtime pay, the random nature and timing of mandatory overtime created problems. One mother in the sample worked in a manufacturing plant and would often be told halfway through a shift that she must work overtime. This meant she had to make alternative arrangements to pick up her child from child care. Not surprisingly, mandatory overtime occurs most often in highly supervised, low control occupations. Time-use data clearly indicate that upper middle-class workers often put in long work hours. However, the critical distinction is level of control. When the worker is his or her own boss, time crunches can be planned, and some flexibility is built in. For example, a lawyer might run out to do an errand or run home for a quick meal with the family and return to finish a task later in the evening. Mandatory overtime at lower level jobs is most often at the supervisor's discretion.

A related and especially salient policy issue for working-class employees is health insurance. Approximately 38.7 million people, or an estimated 14% of the U.S. population, were without health insurance coverage during the entire year in 2000. Despite the slight declines in the uninsured between 2001 and 2002, overall rates of uninsured individuals, especially children, skyrocketed during the 1990s. In our sample of new parents, the majority of women (85%) and men (88%) reported having insurance coverage, but for a significant number their insurance did not extend to family members. For one fourth of the couples in the sample, one spouse was insured and the other was not, and of that group 65% had only individual coverage.

This issue of coverage becomes more central with the birth of a child. For example, Jillian worked at a privately owned grocery store where all the male employees with children had family coverage. She assumed when her child was born that she, too, would gain coverage for her child. Instead her boss' response was, "It is the man's job to provide health coverage for his family, not yours." Although Jillian knew this policy was not legal, she felt she could not risk pushing the issue further and creating a hostile work environemnt, nor could she afford to drag it into court. However, we heard stories about supervisors who allowed workers to stay at home with sick children and not report it as a sick day, and one story where a supervisor's wife provided child care for an employee when the child was sick. These examples highlight a recurring theme during interviews—the idiosynchratic nature of workplace policies and benefits. It appeared, for better and for worse, that workplace policies were in the hands of supervisors who could decide how best to dole them out.

As we asked new parents about their workplace policies and benefits, the social class bias implicit in our measure of workplace supports became painfully obvious. For example, we asked about flextime, job sharing, options to work at home, part-time pay with full-time benefits, paid parental leave, child-care reimbursements, referral services, onsite care, and dependent care assistance plans. We spent many a project meeting wondering whether we should even continue to ask these questions given that the majority of the participants found the questions either extremely humorous or completely infuriating. Fewer than 5% of all parents reported having any form of child-care reimbursement, referral services, or onsite care. Although 24% reported having a dependent care assistance plan at work (a policy that allows for employees to pay for child care with pretax dollars), only 2% reported using this benefit despite that it could save them between 25% and 33% of child-care costs. Questions regarding transfers, job counseling, and multiple benefit options were most often met with nonapplicable responses from parents. Thirteen percent had the option to work at home when needed, 19% reported that employees could work part time and receive full-time benefits, and 4% reported job-sharing opportunities. In short, it appears that few family-friendly policies have reached the factory floors or restaurant kitchens of working-class employees.

Finally, child care, especially infant care, was a concern for all the new parents in the sample. Several studies have revealed that working-class families have lower quality care arrangements than either poor or high-income families (Phillips, Voran, Kisker, Howes, & Whitebook, 1994). As Philips and colleagues found, "the most intriguing finding with respect to class equity, however, is the curvilinear relationship that was revealed between quality and family income. The most uniformly poor quality care . . . was found predominantly in middle-class centers (defined as families with incomes ranging from $15,000 to 40,000)" (p. 489). This occurs primarily because poor and very low-income families often have the option to use subsidized child care, and middle-class families can afford higher quality arrangements. Working-class families earn too much to receive child-care subsidies or supports, but too little to afford the high costs of child care. For infant care, research indicates that parents prefer, and most often use, relative care.

In our sample, 20% used parent care exclusively by working alternating shifts; 47% used relative care either in or out of the home; another 19% used family day-care arrangments; 13% had multiple care arrangements blending a mixture of relative, parental, and family day care; and fewer than 2% (one family) used a day-care center. Parents expressed a fear of strangers caring for their babies: "There are a lot of strange people around these days. It's kind of hard to trust people with kids," said one mother; "You know, those *48 Hours* (television show) horror stories . . . ," said another; and "Abuse is my biggest concern . . . there's always a risk." Beyond safety, an additional benefit of relative care is its low cost; many relatives charged nothing or nominal fees for their services. Although many parents were grateful for relative care, it often came with nonmonetary costs. As one mother noted, "It is hard to have your mother watching your every move, especially when you want to do some thing differently than how you were raised."

Family Values and Family Behavior

More than 40 years ago, Komarovsky (1962), in her classic book, *Blue Collar Marriage*, demonstrated how values about work and family life—providing and mothering—were clearly delineated in the working-class families of the 1960s. More recently, studies have refuted the idea that working-class families divide household tasks strictly along gender lines and that employed working-class women are only employed for financial reasons (Ferree, 1987; Rubin, 1994; Ybarra, 1982). Ybarra (1982) found that in working-class, Chicano families, wives' employment was correlated with more egalitarian family roles. In addition, Ybarra found that the majority of these working-class women preferred to be employed. Thompson and Walker (1989) suggested that class realities lead working-class families to more equitably divide up paid and unpaid work.

Some of the most interesting results from our research are those that counter our hypotheses about work and family life. Such was the case for the relation between the division of household and child-care tasks and new mothers' mental health (Goldberg & Perry-Jenkins, 2004). We believed that as fathers performed more child-care tasks, mothers would see the division of labor as more fair and report lower depression. In fact analyses reveal that the more child-care tasks fathers performed, the more depressed new mothers became. Further scrutiny revealed that the mothers with more traditional ideology were significantly more depressed when fathers cared for children than their egalitarian counterparts. Thus, a significant subgroup of the WFTP sample, although working full time, held traditional notions of their role as new mothers. They expected to be performing more child care than they actually were; for these new mothers, things were not as they should be. An interview with Melissa brought this issue to light. Melissa worked 8 A.M. to 4 P.M. in shipping at a candle factory Monday through Friday. Her husband, Josh, worked the 3 P.M. to 11 P.M. shift as a bus driver and, thus, assumed primary care for their son, Ryan, during the day. As Melissa began to fill out the child-care questionnaire after she had been back at work for more than 1 month, she dropped her head into her hands and started to quietly sob, "Don't get me wrong, Josh is a great Dad. He is home all day and takes care of Ryan really well. Then I get home at 4:00 and the baby is tired and whiney and almost ready for bed. Then last night he woke up, I think he is beginning to get his first tooth and all he wanted was Daddy, not me. That hurt. That is not how it should be." The question of whether there are cultural norms within class levels that shape the ways in which work and family life are experienced is an intriguing one and deserving of further inquiry.

LESSONS LEARNED FROM WORKING-CLASS FAMILIES

The Research Perspective: Future Directions

The field shows several promising directions for future research. First, a more ecologically valid approach to examining the effects of work on family's mental and physical health and family functioning would better emphasize the diversity of contexts that can shape these relations. For example, the research on gender and race effects on occupational characteristics suggests that both influence occupational attainment and earnings differently. With respect to earnings, gender effects are more discernible than race effects: Women earn less than men, although African-American men earn less than White men. In contrast, occupational prestige is influenced by both race and gender, with 13% of White women in high-prestige jobs and only 10% of African-American women and 9% of African-American men in high-prestige jobs (Xu & Leffler, 1996). These differences in income and job prestige, which arise as a function of race and gender, are likely to influence how families cope with work-family issues. Moreover, the research on working-class occupations suggests that, on average, workers in lower level jobs have less autonomy and control on the job and fewer supportive workplace policies—again conditions that have consequences for workers' ability to manage work and family life. In short, gender, race, and class matter, and "they matter because they structure interactions, opportunities, consciousness, ideology and the forms of resistance that characterize American life" (Anderson, 1996, p. ix). Looking within the contexts of race and class will enable the field to outline those common and unique factors, both at work and at home, that affect how parents and children in these different contexts fare in terms of their mental health and family relationships.

Second, the field should determine how factors such as class, race, and family structure influence development through proximal processes. As O'Connor and Rutter (1996) pointed out, "the link between culture and proximal processes must go beyond demonstrating group mean differences to include information on how key features are perceived differently in different groups. . . . It is equally necessary to consider variability within cultural groups" (p. 787). Several researchers have addressed the question of how individuals and families adapt to high-stress situations by focusing on risk and protective factors (Garmezy, Masten, & Tellegen, 1984; Rutter, 1987). Patterson (1986) showed that increased risks and stressors, including daily hassles and crises within the family, can significantly affect microsocial processes that make up social interactions. The field must learn more about these microsocial processes that result from stressful work conditions (e.g., forced overtime, low autonomy, nonday shifts) to develop targeted and effective interventions.

Third, Cowan (1991) proposed that individuals' interpretations of their situations are as important as the more objective nature of the demands and resources available in high-stress environments. Thus, in addition to assessing the demands on working parents such as lack of time, highly routinized jobs, and inadequate income, as well as possible resources such as supportive employers and good child care, research should also examine how parents appraise their situations. By including data on both the demands and resources available to new parents and their more subjective assessments of these factors, the field will learn far more than looking at either factor alone.

Finally, as mentioned earlier, work-family issues change over the life course. The stress of combining work with the demands of rearing infants and children is quite different from the financial stress facing parents of college-age children and different again from retirement concerns. Just as family demands and resources change over time, so do work demands change as employees gain seniority. Research is lacking on the work and family issues facing working-class families across the life course.

The Policy Perspective: Future Directions

Many of the family-friendly policies discussed in the work-family research are not well suited to the nature of working-class jobs. Flextime is hardly an option when one's job requires running a machine continually or serving the public. Onsite child care or a reserved slot in a child-care center is also a benefit that is likely to go unused by many working-class employees.

Paid family leave would make a difference for working-class families given that unpaid leave time is simply not realistic for low-income families. In addition, the problem of mandatory overtime must be addressed. Current legislation has now limited the amount of mandatory overtime that nurses and health professionals can do. Multiple lawsuits are now pending, pointing to sleep deprivation and long work hours as threats to workplace safety in many other occupations.

In many workplaces, two-tier policy systems remain that distinguish policies for hourly and salary workers, as if the family needs and work demands for white-collar employees are more important than those at lower levels. Work-family issues are likely to differ for groups of workers in different occupations.

Thus, effective work-family policies will need to be sensitive to the range of issues that occur across the SES spectrum. Given the variability in issues that workers must deal with across jobs and class, it is likely that, in general, policy changes at the level of the workplace will be far more effective than federal-level initiatives. Employers and employees understand the nature of their work, and they are best equipped to design and implement policies and changes that will support workers.

As a case in point, one father in the WFTP described his role on a work team that consisted of line workers from the factory floor, human resource personnel, and company administrators. The team's goal was to identify key stressors in the work and family lives of employees and propose realistic policies and changes to address these issues. So far they have instituted two policies. Workers now have specific weeks when they could be on call for mandatory overtime. The policy allows at least some degree of advanced planning for workers. Workers' break time on the afternoon shift has also been moved from 2:45 to 3:15 so parents can call their children who just got home from school. These changes are small and may seem like temporary fixes covering much deeper issues, but for those involved in the decision-making process the changes meant everything.

Perhaps the myth that America is a classless society—a myth that runs deep—is what keeps us from addressing what Sennett and Cobb (1993) called "the hidden injuries of class." Gilbert and Kahl (1993) suggested we have always been a society in which social class predicts our life chances. "On the night in 1912 when the *Titanic* sank on her maiden voyage across the Atlantic, social class proved to be the key determinant of who survived and who perished. Among the women (who were given priority over men for places in the life boats) 3% of the first class passengers drowned, compared to 16% of the second class passengers, and 45% of the third class passengers" (Lord, 1955, p. 107; cited in Hollingshead & Redlich, 1958, p. 6). Would the same thing happen today? Researchers and policymakers must reckon with the inequities that exist in our economic structures, our work opportunity systems, and our workplaces and create responsive policies and interventions that equalize life chances for all members of society.

ACKNOWLEDGMENTS

This research is supported by a grant from the National Institute of Mental Health (R01-MH56777). I gratefully acknowledge the invaluable assistance of Courtney Pierce, Abbie Goldberg, Betsy Turner, Karen Meteyer, Heather Haley, William Tobin, and all of our hard-working staff, past and present, for their work on all aspects of this research project.

REFERENCES

Anderson, M. L. (1996). Foreword. In E. Chow, D. Wilkinson, & M. Baca Zinn (Eds.), *Race, class, & gender: Common bonds, different voices* (pp. i–ii). Thousand Oaks, CA: Sage.

Bornstein, M. H., & Bradley, R. H. (2003). *Socioeconomic status, parenting, and child development.* Mahwah, NJ: Lawrence Erlbaum Associates.

Bornstein, M. H., Hahn, C., Suwalsky, J. T. D., & Haynes, O. M. (2003). Socioeconomic status, parenting, and child development: The Hollinghead four-factor index of social status and the socioeconomic index of occupations. In M. H. Bornstein & R. H. Bradley (Eds.), *Socioeconomic status, parenting and child development* (pp. 83–106). Mahwah, NJ: Lawrence Erlbaum Associates.

Bradley, R. H., & Corwyn, R. F. (2003). Age and ethnic variations in family process mediators of SES. In M. H. Bornstein & R. H. Bradley (Eds.), *Socioeconomic status, parenting and child development* (pp. 83–106). Mahwah, NJ: Lawrence Erlbaum Associates.

Bronfenbrenner, U. (1986). Ecology of the family as a context for human development: Research perspectives. *Developmental Psychology, 22,* 723–742.

Bronfenbrenner, U., & Crouter, A. C. (1982). Work and family through time and space. In S. Kamerman & C. Hayes (Eds.), *Families that work: Children in a changing society* (pp. 39–83). Washington, DC: National Academy of Sciences.

Catanzarite, L. (2002). Dynamics of segregation and earnings in brown-collar occupations. *Work and Occupations, 29,* 300–346.

Cowan, P. A. (1991). Individual and family life transitions: A proposal for a new definition. In P. A. Cowan & M. Hetherington (Eds.), *Family transitions* (pp. 3–30). Hillsdale, NJ: Lawrence Erlbaum Associates.

Duncan, G. J., & Magnuson, K. A. (2003). Off with Hollingshead: Socioeconomic resources, parenting and child development. In M. H. Bornstein & R. H. Bradley (Eds.) *Socioeconomic status, parenting and child development* (pp. 83–106). Mahwah, NJ: Lawrence Erlbaum Associates.

Estes, S. B., & Glass, J. L. (1996). Job changes following childbirth: Are women trading compensation for family-responsive work conditions? *Work and Occupations, 23,* 405–436.

Ferree, M. M. (1976). Working-class jobs: Housework and paid work as sources of satisfaction. *Social Problems, 22,* 431–441.

Ferree, M. M. (1987). Family and jobs for working-class women: Gender and class systems seen from below. In N. Gerstel & H. E. Gros (Eds.), *Families and work* (pp. 289–301). Philadelphia, PA: Temple University Press.

Garmezy, N., Masten, A. S., & Tellegen, A. (1984). The study of stress and competence in children: A building block for developmental psychopathology. *Child Development, 55,* 97–111.

Gerstel, N., & McGonagle, K. (1999). Job leaves and the limits of the Family and Medical Leave Act: The effects of gender, race, and family. *Journal of Work and Occupations, 26*(4), 510–534.

Gilbert, D., & Kahl, J. A. (1993). *The American class structure: A new synthesis.* Belmont, CA: Wadsworth.

Goldberg, A., & Perry-Jenkins, M. (2004). The division of labor and working-class women's well-being across the transition to parenthood. *Journal of Family Pscyhology, 18,* 225–236.

Hauser, R. M. (1994). Measuring socioeconomic status in studies of child development. *Child Development, 65,* 1541–1545.

Hoffman, L. W. (2003). Methodological issues in studies of SES, parenting, and child development. In M. H. Bornstein & R. H. Bradley (Eds.), *Socioeconomic status, parenting, and child development* (pp. 125–144). Hillsdale, NJ: Lawrence Erlbaum Associates.

Hollingshead, A. B. (1975). *The four-factor index social status*. Unpublished manuscript, Yale University, New Haven, CT.

Hollingshead, A. B., & Redlich, F. (1958). *Social class and mental illness: A community study*. New York: Wiley.

Kohn, M. L. (1979). The effects of social class on parental values and practices. In D. Reiss, & H. A. Hoffman (Eds.), *The American family* (pp. 45–68). New York: Plenum.

Komarovsky, M. (1962). *Blue-collar marriage*. New York: Vintage Books.

Leventhal, T., & Brooks-Gunn, J. (2003). Moving on up: Neighborhood effects on children and families. In M. H. Bornstein & R. H. Bradley (Eds.) *Socioeconomic status, parenting and child development* (pp. 83–106). Mahwah, NJ: Lawrence Erlbaum Associates.

Malson, M. R. (1983). Black women's sex roles: The social context for a new ideology. *Journal of Social Issues, 39*, 101–113.

Menaghan, E. G., & Parcel, T. L. (1995). Social sources of change in children's home environment: The effects of parental occupational experiences and family conditions. *Journal of Marriage and the Family, 57*, 69–84.

Morris, B. (1995, September). Executive women confront midlife crisis. *Fortune*, pp. 60–86.

O'Connor, T. G., & Rutter, M. (1996). Risk mechanisms in development: Some conceptual and methodological considerations. *Developmental Psychology, 32*, 787–795.

Parcel, T. L., & Menaghan, E. G. (1994). *Parents' jobs and children's lives*. New York: Aldine de Gruyter.

Patterson, G. R. (1986). Performance models for antisocial boys. *American Psychologist, 41*, 434–444.

Perry-Jenkins, M., & Folk, K. (1994). Class, couples and conflict: Effects of the division of labor on assessments of marriage in dual-earner families. *Journal of Marriage and the Family, 56*, 165–180.

Perry-Jenkins, M., Goldberg, A., Pierce, C., & Haley, H. L. (2002). *Employment schedules and transition to parenthood: Implications for mental health and marriage*. Manuscript submitted for publication.

Perry-Jenkins, M., Repetti, R., & Crouter, A.C. (2000). Work and family in the 1990s. *Journal of Marriage and Family, 62*, 27–63.

Phillips, D. A., Voran, M., Kisker, E., Howes, C., & Whitebook, M. (1994). Child care for children in poverty: Opportunity or inequity. *Child Development, 65*, 472–492.

Presser, H. B. (2000). Nonstandard work schedules and marital instability. *Journal of Marriage and Family, 62*, 93–110.

Presser, H. B., & Cox, A. G. (1997). The work schedules of low-educated American women and welfare reform. *Monthly Labor Review, 120*, 25–34.

Rubin, L. B. (1994). *Families on the fault line*. New York: HarperCollins.

Rutter, M. (1987). Psychosocial resilience and protective factors. *American Journal of Orthopsychiatry, 57*, 316–332.

Sennett, R., & Cobb, J. (1993). *The hidden injuries of class*. New York: W. W. Norton.

Steil, J. M. (1997). *Marital equality: Its relationship to the well-being of husbands and wives*. Thousand Oaks, CA: Sage.

Thompson, L., & Walker, A. J. (1989). Gender and families: Women and men in marriage, work, and parenthood. *Journal of Marriage and Family, 51*, 845–871.

U.S. Bureau of Labor Statistics, U.S. Department of Labor. (2001). *Employment characteristics of families in 2001. Current Population Survey*. Washington, DC: U.S. Government Printing Office.

Warr, P., & Parry, G. (1982). Paid employment and women's psychological well-being. *Psychological Bulletin, 91*, 498–516.

Wright, E. O. (1997). *Class counts: Comparative studies in class analysis*. New York: Cambridge University Press.

Xu, W., & Leffler, A. (1996). Gender and race effects on occupational prestige, segregation, and earnings. In E. Chow, D. Wilkinson, & M. Baca Zinn (Eds.), *Race, class, and gender: Common bonds, different voices* (pp. 107–124). Thousand Oaks, CA: Sage.

Ybarra, L. (1982). When wives work: The impact on the Chicano family. *Journal of Marriage and the Family, 44,* 169–178.

30

Nonstandard Work and Child-Care Needs of Low-Income Parents

Julia R. Henly
Susan Lambert
University of Chicago

Work-family scholars have long expressed concern for workers with limited education and income. However, only recently have they focused attention on the dilemmas of parents in low-skilled jobs (e.g., Booth, Crouter, & Shanahan, 1999; Dodson, Manuel, & Bravo, 2002; Heymann, 2000; Lambert, 1999). Although these scholars have begun to detail the ways in which low-income parents cope with the dual responsibilities of paid work and parenting, they have paid less attention to how employers structure low-skilled jobs and how workplace practices affect family life. Another arena of study, welfare policy research, has begun to attend to the work side of the welfare-to-work transition (e.g., Holzer, 1990) and the implications of employment characteristics such as earnings, work intensity, and welfare-work combinations for parenting and child well-being (e.g., Chase-Landsdale et al., 2003; Dunifon, Kalil, & Danziger, 2003; Heymann, 2000). With a few notable exceptions (e.g., Dodson et al., 2002; Newman, 1999), however, this research relies on relatively crude job-related measures and, thus, offers limited understanding of variations in employer practices that may matter for parents in different kinds of low-skilled jobs. If we are to improve low-skilled jobs, it seems critical to develop an understanding about work that goes beyond conventional indicators, such as hours, wages, and occupation, and that goes beyond industry and firm-level characteristics, such as churning rates, to reveal how the complexities of work are implemented in daily employer practice.

In this chapter, we hope to advance our knowledge of low-skilled jobs and their implications for family life, especially child caregiving. Our focus is on the policies and practices that define the nature of the employment experience and shape the child-care needs of working parents. We begin with a brief overview of low-skilled jobs in today's economy, paying particular attention to how lesser studied, but increasingly common, aspects of jobs, especially nonstandard employment status and work schedules, can pose significant challenges to managing work and family. We employ data from two linked studies to trace the relation between nonstandard employer practices and workers' child-care arrangements.

WHAT WE KNOW
ABOUT LOW-SKILLED JOBS

Jobs requiring few credentials and limited education seldom provide incomes that exceed the poverty line (Blank, 1997; Danziger & Gottschalk, 1995). This is true even when the jobs are full time (Acs, Phillips, & McKenzie, 2001; Appelbaum, Bernhardt, & Murnane, 2003) and are filled by workers with significant employment histories (Gladden & Taber, 1998). Moreover, only a small proportion of low-skilled jobs provides benefits, such as health insurance, paid sick leave, and family-responsive policies such as flextime (Currie & Yelowitz, 2000; Gerstel & McGonagle, 1999; Glass & Estes, 1997).

The wage gains in compensation made during the tight labor market of the 1990s were modest at best. During the 1990s, male high school graduates recovered about one third of the steep decline in wages during the previous 20 years, whereas the wages of female high school graduates remained stable (but low) during both economic periods (Appelbaum et al., 2003). Even during this tight labor market, "29 percent of working families with children under twelve had incomes lower than the basic family budget for their communities" (Appelbaum et al., 2003, p. 1)

Low-wage jobs are disproportionately found in growth sectors of the low-skilled economy, such as the service sector (Bernstein & Gittleman, 2003). Thus, low-skilled workers are increasingly at risk of poverty. A sizable number of low-wage workers, especially low-income parents with limited education, cycle into and out of poor-quality jobs in the least promising sectors (Meyer & Cancian, 1998; Carnevale & Rose, 2001; Johnson & Corcoran, 2003; Pavetti & Acs, 2001).

Nonstandard Employment

Increasingly, low-skilled jobs have nonstandard features—characteristics that may be directly linked to poor compensation practices and employment outcomes. One dimension of nonstandard work is the employment status of workers, such as temporary, contingent, or part time. Such workers are often excluded from employee protections and opportunities, such as health benefits and training, that may be available to regular, full-time workers in the same workplace (Kalleberg & Schmidt, 1996; Tilly, 1996). Recent case studies of low-wage jobs document the reasons employers rely on nonstandard employment (Appelbaum et al., 2003). Left unaddressed, however, is the relation between nonstandard status jobs and family life. For example, it may be that the ambiguity of working a nonstandard status job makes family budgeting particularly difficult, detracts from family members' sense of security and well-being, and, as discussed next, creates enormous challenges for arranging reliable, high-quality child care.

A second dimension of nonstandard work concerns job schedules. Presser (2003) found that "two-fifths of all employed Americans work mostly at nonstandard times—in the evening, at night, on a rotating shift, or during the weekend" (p. 1). This proportion is even higher for low-skilled workers. During the past two decades, Presser (1986, 1995, 2000, 2003) and her colleagues (e.g., Presser & Cain, 1983; Presser & Cox, 1997) examined the connection between nonstandard schedules and family life and found links between nonstandard schedules and marital discord and instability for couples with children (Presser, 2000, 2003; Staines & Pleck, 1984). Researchers have also found links between nonstandard schedules and poor educational outcomes and problem behaviors for children (Heymann, 2000). The evidence is equivocal that nonstandard schedules have negative implications for parent–child interactions (e.g., eating meals together, assisting with homework), with Presser (2003) concluding that the specific relationship between nonstandard schedules and parent–child interactions depends on "contingencies relating to which parent, which shift, marital status, whether both spouses are employed (among the married) and whether the family has children age five to thirteen only" (p. 173).

Some parents (especially some dual-earner couples) seek jobs with nonstandard schedules as a way to share caregiving and avoid nonparental child care. The majority of low-skilled, unmarried mothers, however, report labor market rather than caregiving reasons for working nonstandard hours (Presser, 2003; Presser & Cox, 1997), which raises the question of how these workers care for their children during working hours. With rare exception, the formal child-care sector does not accommodate nonstandard schedules. Child-care centers and preschools serve children during prearranged weekday, daytime hours; although family child care programs have more flexible daytime hours, they are rarely open weekends or late evenings. Given these constraints, it is not surprising that parents who work nonstandard schedules disproportionately use informal caregivers, especially relative caregivers and shared parental care arrangements (Casper & O'Connell, 1998; Han, 2004; Presser, 2003; Presser & Cox, 1997) and are more likely to use multiple-child care arrangements (Presser, 2003). Left unexplored in the work–child-care research is how low-income parents negotiate and manage these caregiving arrangements and how the quality and stability of the care they secure is shaped by their nonstandard scheduling practices.

The two elements of nonstandard work discussed earlier are typically studied separately and with different approaches. Researchers investigating employment status tend to focus on the organizational or job level, detailing the percentage of jobs in different industries that are not "regular, full-time" (Herzenberg, Alic, & Wial, 1998; Tilly, 1996). These studies provide important information on the shifting nature of employment, but offer little on how employment status affects day-to-day workplace practices or how it matters in the lives of workers and their families. Similarly, studies investigating nonstandard schedules (Presser, 2003) focus mainly on the association between nonstandard schedules and well-being. This research provides little systematic analysis of how employers implement nonstandard schedules, the organizational conditions and workplace dynamics that shape these practices, or the ripple effect that nonstandard scheduling might have in other contexts, such as child-care markets and informal networks of support. In the research reported here, we employ data at the organizational, job, and individual levels to examine how nonstandard status and scheduling unfold on the job and shape the child-care strategies of low-income working mothers.

DESCRIPTION OF LINKED STUDIES

We draw on research from two linked studies underway at the University of Chicago. The Study of Organizational Stratification (SOS) examines low-skilled jobs in four key sectors of Chicago's urban economy: retail, hospitality, shipping and transportation, and financial services. The Study of Work-Child Care Fit (SWCCF) examines hourly, nonmanagement jobs held by women with young children in the retail firms studied in the SOS. Thus, although the unit of analysis of SOS is the job, SWCCF's focus is the worker. Moreover, although SOS examines a range of jobs across four industrial sectors, SWCCF concentrates on working mothers within the retail sector.

The Study of Organizational Stratification

The SOS examines how opportunities for mobility, work-life balance, skill development, and adequate compensation are distributed internally by employers and across and within industries. It is part of the Project on the Public

Economy of Work, which is examining the everyday practices of key institutions involved in welfare reform (public agencies, labor market intermediaries, private employers).

We use a comparative organizational analysis that combines multiple sources of data (administrative, interview, observation) to better understand variations (across jobs, workplaces, and industries) in employer policies and daily employer practices. The three welfare agencies in Chicago we chose for in-depth case study offer variation on client characteristics and access to jobs; the initial employers selected had hired someone who is or was a public aid client of one of the three welfare offices. We have expanded our data collection to include additional retailers to link our organizational-level analysis with data from workers and their child-care providers collected through the SWCCF.

We have detailed data on approximately 84 low-skilled jobs housed in 22 workplaces in the Chicago area. We targeted industries with large numbers of low-skilled jobs (requiring, at most, a high school education): hospitality (seven hotel and catering employers), transportation (three airlines and package delivery services), retail (10 stores and distribution centers), and financial services (two banks). We combine information from interviews and public sources to identify firms' local competitors, constructing matched comparisons within each industry. All the employers are what one would call *major employers*.

Our primary source of information is a semistructured interview conducted with human resource (HR) professionals. We interview HR staff closest to actual employment practices—that is, those responsible for hiring and who know, or have the data for us to calculate, turnover and take-up rates. We supplement information from the interview protocol with data gathered from organizational records, observations at job sites, and, in some workplaces, participant observation.

We gathered information on the overall structure of firms' internal labor markets—specifically, job ladders, training and education availability, compensation packages, turnover, and use of temporary and other nonstandard workers. We also collected detailed information on four specific low-skilled jobs (all entry-level positions requiring no more than a high school diploma): (a) a low-skilled job viewed as core to firm success, (b) a low-skilled noncore job viewed as relatively unimportant to the firm's success, (c) a low-skilled job for comparison across all workplaces (an entry-level clerical position), and (d) a low-skilled job known to be filled by a person on public aid. For each job, we gathered detailed data on whether a particular opportunity (for health insurance, training, etc.) available in the company is extended to workers in the target job, both in policy (e.g., does the compensation package for the job include employer-sponsored health insurance?) and in practice (e.g., the proportion of workers in that job currently eligible for coverage and currently covered). Most of the time, we were able to work with company representatives to secure detailed information on our target jobs—that is, the specific proportion of workers who are benefiting from a policy. When this was impossible, we asked company representatives to rate the target jobs—for example, to indicate whether "most, many, or few workers" leave the job during the year or whether "all, many, or a few workers" in the (target) job are currently enrolled in health insurance. The extent to which we were able to obtain detailed proportions versus general ratings does not vary by industry or job type. Further methodological details are found in Lambert and Haley-Lock (2004) and Lambert and Waxman (2005). In summary, the data allow us to examine the extent to which opportunities in today's major corporations trickle down to lower organizational levels and, if so, for which types of jobs.

The Study of Work-Child Care Fit (SWCCF)

The SWCCF examines how retail workplace practices shape employees' child-care needs and investigates the child-care strategies used by low-income mothers to manage work and caregiving responsibilities.

In an effort to understand the varied experiences within and across workplace settings while still exercising some control over industry-specific variation, SWCCF focuses exclusively on the retail sector. Given the exploratory nature of the study and its aim to uncover informal practices and strategies relevant to working mothers' daily lives, we employed a qualitative research design (Emerson, 1983). The data consist of interviews with 54 hourly, nonmanagement retail employees. (For a subset of 30, their primary child care providers were also interviewed. Here we draw on data from the 54 retail employees only.) All retail employees are mothers of young children, 90% age 5 or younger. They are employed by one of six retail sites participating in SOS (four retail stores, two retail distribution centers).

We recruited participants working day, evening, and night shifts to complete a self-administered screening tool that determined study eligibility, as well as more detailed demographic, job, and child-care items to guide the selection of the employee sample. From a final group of 218 employees, we purposively selected a convenience sample of 8 to 10 eligible employees from each site (54 women). We designed the selection criteria to ensure that the sample represented a range of occupations, job characteristics, and child-care types. However, the sample was not designed to be statistically representative of the broader population of workers employed in the six sites. By pursuing such a research design, we sacrifice generalizability, but maximize our ability to observe a varied set of experiences in great detail.

The 54 women interviewed were employed in five primary occupational categories: 15 manual labor, 11 customer service or clerical, 11 cashier, 10 sales, and 7 miscellaneous occupations. Pay ranged from $7 to $14 per hour.

Wages vary by occupation and firm as well as employee seniority. Although all paid above the minimum wage, the majority of jobs were part time or subject to frequent hour reductions. Employees' primary child-care arrangements included informal family, friend, and neighbor caregivers (28 employees used this form of care), licensed and unlicensed family child-care homes (care provided to a group of children in the provider's home; 14 employees chose this), and centers or preschools (used by 12 employees). As discussed later, the workers often supplemented these primary arrangements with other arrangements in both the formal and informal sectors.

We collected data using semistructured, in-depth interviews about 90 minutes in length (audiotaped and transcribed). We focused on three topics: child care, work, and informal support. Child care includes information about the types, range, management of arrangements, monetary and nonmonetary payment schedules, and the supports other than child care received from providers. Job information includes job history within and outside the firm, job characteristics (wages, benefits, hours), employer practices regarding scheduling and organizing work tasks, and workplace relationships and supports. Finally, information on informal support includes structural network properties, support provided and received, and the interpersonal dynamics involved in accessing support. We report preliminary findings to illustrate the child-care experiences of participants whose jobs represent the kinds of status ambiguity and scheduling instability addressed in this chapter.

AMBIGUOUS EMPLOYMENT STATUS

Drawing from the SOS analysis, we begin by detailing employer practices regarding employment status, highlighting similarities and differences among employers. We then trace how practices related to employment status can surface in the challenges workers face securing child care, concentrating on the experiences of nonmanagement retail workers with young children as analyzed in SWCCF. We also examine employers' scheduling practices and, in turn, the challenges they create for mothers in retail jobs.

Employment status is conventionally understood as an either–or condition: one either holds a job or does not, one either works part time or full time, or one is either a permanent employee or temporary. Our data suggest that at the lower levels of organizations, these basic characteristics of employment can be quite ambiguous. As discussed next, we find that one's status on paper may not be indicative of the number of hours worked or even whether an employee is working at all. This ambiguity in the meaning of employment has implications for the field's understanding of such important labor market indicators as turnover rates and individual labor force participation.

Part- or Full-Time Status May Not Correspond to Hours Worked

All companies we studied had policies distinguishing part- and full-time jobs determined at the time of hiring and based on the number of weekly work hours expected. In practice, however, employment status often bore little resemblance to the number of hours worked. Employers reported that part-time jobs regularly required employees to work beyond part-time "limits," and full-time jobs regularly involved less than full-time hours. For example, in the financial services sector, one of the targeted jobs regularly required 35 or more hours per week, and yet 80% of these jobs were categorized as part time. Across the sectors, we found that once a job was assigned a status, it was difficult to change it regardless of the number of hours an employee worked.

Our data suggest that part-time/full-time status primarily functions to define employees' access to benefits and, in some cases, education. For example, although several companies extended health insurance to part-time workers, the plans were prorated according to status (rather than hours worked) and required hefty employee contributions. Moreover, employers often excluded workers in part-time jobs from formal skill development and training opportunities. Some companies avoided categorizing professional jobs as part time, instead labeling professionals who voluntarily worked reduced hours as *reduced compensation professionals*. Unlike workers in part-time jobs, these professionals were often eligible for full benefits and education supports. In summary, employment status may be a meaningful occupational characteristic because it can signal access to benefits and formal work supports. However, the labels can be deceptive because part- or full-time status does not reliably reflect work hours.

Holding a Job May Not Mean Working

A second source of ambiguity concerns the question of whether a worker is employed or not employed. Although the employers we studied reported that official layoffs were uncommon, none of the employers guaranteed a minimum number of hours to their nonexempt employees. Instead of relying on formal layoffs, employers practiced a policy of workload adjustments or workloading in some lower level jobs.

Across industries, all employers reported lowering and even eliminating hours owing to "business conditions," resulting at its extreme in lengthy employment gaps for workers who remained officially employed by the company. For example, a catalog business did not give its order pickers work hours for several months during the winter, hotels routinely placed housekeepers on furlough during nonpeak seasons, and retailers instituted on-call policies during unpredictable business cycles.

The full implications of working no hours while still being officially employed rest on how employers implement workload adjustments. Some companies allowed workers to volunteer for furlough, whereas others assigned it based on employment status or seniority. Some extended seniority and benefits during times of furlough, whereas others did not. As one HR person at a catering company explained, "Instead of laying people off, we keep them on payroll so that they continue to be covered by insurance and to gain seniority—they just don't get any hours," or any pay.

Holding a job without working places workers in an ambiguous position. It is unclear whether such a worker is employed or not, and these workers are faced with the hard choice of deciding whether they might be better off in the long run if they attempt to secure a new job or if they hold on to a "no-time job" with the hope of securing seniority, benefits, and, eventually, some income.

"Voluntary" Terminations May Be Involuntary

Our research, as does others' (e.g., Holzer, 1990; Tilly, 1996), documents considerable job instability among many low-skilled jobs. For example, of the 60 jobs for which we have specific turnover data, annual turnover rates ranged from 0% to 500%. Half the jobs had annual turnover rates exceeding 50% (i.e., half became vacant during the year), and one third had turnover rates that exceeded 80%. We found the highest annual turnover rates in the transportation industry among package handlers (500%), where the average length of a job was 16 weeks for one employer and only 5 to 6 weeks for another. The average tenure of sales clerks in retail was 6 months to 1 year, with little variation among employers. Housekeepers in the hospitality industry had the longest average job tenure, ranging from 1.5 to 7 years. Entry-level clerical jobs had the lowest rates of annual turnover across industries and employers, ranging from 0% to 10%.

The substantial variation in turnover among low-skilled jobs within employers is especially striking. For example, where package handling saw a 500% turnover rate, the rate for entry-level administrative jobs in the same company requiring comparable employee qualifications was at most 10%. In a hotel with a 44% turnover rate among housekeepers, food preparation jobs saw 10% turnover. This variation both within and between firms suggests that job instability may stem from characteristics of jobs rather than workers.

Indeed the organizational research documents how employers structure turnover to avoid formal layoffs and firings (Doeringer & Piore, 1985; Pfeffer & Cohen, 1984). Some jobs in spot labor markets are designed to enable a tight link between consumer demand and labor costs (Jacobs, 1994). The employers in our study used a variety of methods to ensure a tight link between labor costs and consumer demand, largely passing fluctuations in demand onto workers through workloading and furloughing (Lambert & Haley-Lock, 2004; Lambert & Waxman, 2005). Yet rather than discussing turnover as inherent to the job, employers viewed it as primarily employee initiated and voluntary. A common refrain from human resource representatives was that "people just stop coming to work." Few companies reported terminations for poor job performance even in high-turnover jobs. However, given employer practices on workload adjustments, we argue that explaining exits as voluntary is insufficient and even misleading.

The extent to which employers structure turnover into jobs has implications for workers' income and benefits. Because many companies have a standard 90-day waiting period for benefits, only a small percentage of workers in high-turnover jobs ever become eligible. For example, in one retail firm, we estimated that 75% of lower level employees were covered by health insurance, with the exception of cashiers, who were said to rarely qualify because of their high turnover (at least 100%). For most of the employers we studied who offered universal health coverage, at least one job in the company had low levels of participation because of job holders' limited tenure.

Clearly, turnover is not simply a worker characteristic. One's probability of retention is discernibly different in a job with a 200% than one with a 10% annual turnover rate. Some jobs provide job security and the rewards of seniority; others do not no matter how well workers perform them. Thus, although turnover might look voluntary, it may instead be a matter of employer practice.

Implications of Ambiguous Employment Status for Child Care

The ambiguous nature of employment in low-skilled jobs can translate into ambiguity in child-care needs for workers. When full- or part-time status does not correspond to hours worked, the amount of child care needed becomes uncertain. Moreover, caregiving needs can change drastically with the fits and starts of employment, whether owing to interruptions in the same job or to job turnover. Although child care may be unnecessary during unemployment, it will be necessary again when work resumes, perhaps with a different configuration of hours and days.

As noted, such ambiguity creates child-care scheduling demands that are not easily accommodated by centers and preschools. Moreover, although parents may need less child care when work hours have been reduced, child-care providers may require full payment regardless of whether the allotted hours are used. From the providers' perspective, reliable attendance and payment are justifiable on business and child development grounds. Workload reductions in our study presented some SWCCF workers with the difficult choice of holding on to a child-care slot until work hours increased again or giving up the slot and searching for a new arrangement that better fit their current work needs.

The ambiguity of employment status also has implications for policies designed to assist low-income parents with child care. Eligibility for child-care subsidies is linked to employment status in most states. For example, Illinois grants 6-month part-time and full-time subsidies, with eligibility determined by work effort as reported on the two most recent pay stubs. Workers deemed part-time based on their recent work effort receive part-time subsidies for 6 months. When past work hours differ from those to be worked in the next 6-month period, workers may experience a mismatch between subsidy level and child-care need. In other words, the subsidy system is not sensitive to temporary changes in work.[1]

SCHEDULE INSTABILITY

In this section, we examine the scheduling practices of employers. In particular, we look beyond traditional definitions of nonstandard days and hours to less-studied scheduling features: just-in-time scheduling, fluctuating hours, and shifting schedules. We then consider the implications of these scheduling practices for child-care arrangements.

Just-in-Time Scheduling

The practice of passing fluctuations in consumer demand directly to employees is evident in the scheduling practices of employers. Some employers rely on just-in-time strategies to minimize short-term labor costs. For example, one retailer has a policy of determining staffing levels based on the preceding week's sales broken down by hour. Sales associates are given 2 days' advance notification of their schedules, and the number of associates on the floor at any particular time is a function of the previous week's business. Other employers tightly link demand to labor by regularly sending workers home early from a shift when customer or work demand is low or requiring employees to work on a call-in basis.

Fluctuating Hours: From Overtime to Down Time

Given that employers adjust hours with fluctuating demand, the number of hours jobs require can vary from season to season, from week to week, and even from day to day. For example, one hotel expected its housekeepers to

---

[1] Eligibility for Illinois child-care subsidies can be altered during the 6-month period by submitting additional documentation. However, changes to the subsidy are not immediate, and there can be delays in processing and payment (Action for Children, personal communication).

work 6 days a week, 10 hours a day in the summer, with few, if any, hours scheduled during the winter. In the airline catering business, hours varied week to week. Workers were expected to work overtime during busy weeks and were routinely sent home early during slow periods. Moreover, in some jobs, the length of time worked on any given day varied even when weekly schedules were relatively fixed. For example, lock-box jobs in one bank required workers to process all daily transactions before a shift ended. As a result, a shift could range from 6 to 10 hours depending on the quantity of mail received that day.

Shifting Days and Shifting Shifts

Many of the firms participating in SOS employed workers 24 hours a day, 7 days a week. Thus, an employee's work week could involve several different constellations of days and shifts; the exact type of change varying by job and employer. For example, in some jobs, employers hired workers for a set number of days each week. However, the specific days that were worked could change from week to week. As a result, employees prepared to work up to 7 days a week, when in reality they would only work 3 or 4 days.

The shifts that employees were required to work could also vary throughout the week or, in a few jobs, annually. For example, some retail stores required sales associates and cashiers to work a mix of daytime and weekend or evening shifts. In other jobs, employees worked a fixed shift (e.g., overnight workers at one retail store always started at 11 P.M.). However, workers in these fixed-time shift jobs were regularly at risk of being moved, involuntarily, from one shift to another depending on seniority, job vacancies, or work demands.

Implications of Scheduling Instability for Child Care

Work schedules are essential to understanding child-care arrangements because schedules define the hours that care may be required. This rather obvious point, however, masks the significance of scheduling practices in understanding the complex arrangements parents negotiate and the web of individuals involved in carrying out arrangements.

Just-in-Case and Last-Minute Child Care. Just-in-time scheduling and fluctuations in hours, days, and shifts either require that providers have unusually open and flexible schedules or that parents engage in child-care packaging strategies that involve a patchwork of care arrangements and support both within and outside of the formal child-care sector.

Work schedules that were determined with limited lead time or that required on-call staffing proved particularly difficult for SWCCF participants.

When faced with last-minute scheduling practices, some workers planned for possible work shifts by arranging tentative child care. In this case, parents asked caregivers to be available just in case. A more common approach was to attempt to secure care at the last minute. In this way, workers held their child-care providers to the same scheduling demands they faced.

Regardless of whether women sought just-in-case or last-minute care, they typically used informal caregivers to cover unpredictable work hours. Employees using center and preschool care and family child-care homes typically reported that these arrangements required consistent scheduling and advance notice for changes in care. However, the ability of family, friends, and neighbors (informal care) to reliably help with these last-minute arrangements varied. Even when informal caregivers provided significant support, the process of arranging care was hectic, stressful, and sometimes inadequate. For example, one sales associate in a retail store described securing weekend care as "always a problem." Given only 2 or 3 days' notice, she was forced to rely on a range of providers—her cousin, sister, or mother—with varied success. In her words, "usually they don't want to watch him for me, so at times I have to call off [of work] because I have no one to watch him."

Supplemental Arrangements. Although almost all of the SWCCF participants were able to identify a primary child-care arrangement, a closer look at their child-care strategies revealed multiple formal and informal arrangements. Sixty percent relied on a regular secondary arrangement in addition to their primary caregiver. In addition, irregular multiple arrangements were almost universal in the sample. In fact participants reported up to four different child-care arrangements, and every participant who used a center or preschool arrangement also reported at least one other auxiliary arrangement. Supplemental arrangements were often with family, friends, and neighbors, and parents did not always view these auxiliary caregiving arrangements as child-care providers per se. They were instead considered family or friends who offered informal assistance, often, but not always, without monetary compensation. Moreover, we find that those participants who identified a primary arrangement as *relative care* or *informal care* sometimes used the term to connote a variety of arrangements with different informal caregivers.

We find that supplemental arrangements are linked to four different types of employer practices: upward fluctuating hours, multiple shifts and days, fluctuating shift durations, and shifts that either begin earlier or end later than standard child-care hours. For example, workers whose hours fluctuated upward, such as during the fourth-quarter holiday season in retail, reported needing child care beyond that provided by a primary caregiver. For some SWCCF participants, their primary providers—especially when they were relatives—were able to expand their caregiving to accommodate increased work hours. In fact during especially busy seasons of the year, some SWCCF participants reported taking their children to a relative's house to stay for several days at a time. However, extensive care from a single provider was less common than reliance on second and third providers during periods when hours fluctuated.

The employer practice of scheduling workers across multiple shifts and days also increased the use of supplemental arrangements. For example, a retail sales clerk was scheduled to work two shifts during the week: from 11 A.M. to 5 P.M., and on Friday from 4 P.M. to 9 P.M. She also worked a Saturday daytime shift from 10 A.M. to 5 P.M. As a result, she needed care that started as early as 9 A.M. (to account for commute time) and that ended as late as 10 P.M. She reported relying on her mother—her primary caregiver—and her son's paternal grandmother, her sister, and her boyfriend to accommodate the week's shifts.

The women also relied on supplemental arrangements when their shifts fluctuated in duration. Centers and preschools, and many licensed family child-care homes, do not appear to accommodate fluctuating shift duration, especially when unexpected. When primary providers could not tolerate late child pickups, participants reported arranging just-in-case or routine auxiliary caregivers who would care for the child during the hours after a primary arrangement ended and before the mother's shift ended. These arrangements were typically with relatives, friends, or the child's father, and they were often orchestrated during the work shift.

Finally, women used supplemental arrangements to accommodate shift times that began earlier or ended later than conventional daytime hours. For example, a common day shift at a large building supply store began at 6 A.M. and ended at 3 P.M., and distribution center workers worked shifts from 5 A.M. to 2 P.M. We find that women used relatives, especially grandmothers, as supplemental caregivers to accommodate these shifts. For example, a distribution center worker reported that, to be at work by 5 A.M., she dropped off her child at her mother's home at 4 A.M. Her mother dressed and fed the child in the morning and dropped her at the primary arrangement, a child-care center, by 9 A.M. In addition to accommodating early morning routines, women used supplemental caregivers to retrieve children from primary arrangements in the early evening and care for them (including feeding, bathing, and carrying out bedtime routines) until the employee finished a late day or evening shift. Some participants reported that they would feel uncomfortable relinquishing these intimate child routines to nonrelative providers.

The extensive use of multiple arrangements in our sample of nonstandard workers is greater than survey research would suggest (Presser, 2003). Although this might imply a peculiarity of our sample, it may instead reveal that the prevalence of multiple arrangements is underreported in surveys. After all, in many cases we only learned of supplemental arrangements after probing about specific situations (e.g., how the women handled windows of time before and after work or how they handled fluctuating work hours). Moreover, women did not always view caregivers as child-care providers, and participants sometimes used a generic term like *informal care* to signify a patchwork of multiple informal arrangements. It is unknown whether survey responses are biased as a result of such differences in meaning.

Workplace Accommodations to Scheduling Instability. Given limited formal attention to caregiving needs in the lower level jobs we studied, informal supports in the workplace—byproducts of the social relationships developed between employees and their supervisors and coworkers—can be critical determinants of a job's influence on child-care arrangements. For example, several SWCCF participants reported that coworker relationships sometimes eased work–child-care conflicts and disruptions. In some sites, coworkers swapped shifts, and completed unfinished work, enabling parents to leave on time or early, and they sometimes covered up child-related disruptions at work when they did occur. Supervisor relationships could also ease work and child-care demands. For example, several SWCCF participants described positive supervisory relationships that softened harsh scheduling practices, resulted in supervisors ignoring or excusing absences and tardiness because of child-care reasons, and facilitated transfers to other positions perceived as more family-friendly. Overall, our findings suggest that these kinds of informal supervisory relationships were quite important to work-child care management. However, this level of cooperation at the workplace varied greatly. Just as supervisors could be sources of support, they could also be sources of conflict that exacerbated already difficult scheduling.

CONCLUSION

Our goal in this chapter has been to develop two increasingly important dimensions of work in today's economy—nonstandard employment status and nonstandard work schedules. Our examination of organizational, job-specific, and individual-level data has allowed us to appraise how employers implement and low-income working mothers experience nonstandard employment policies and practices. By doing so, we hope to contribute to the growing scholarship on the nature and consequences of nonstandard work, especially as it concerns low-income families.

Nonstandard employment status and scheduling are becoming standard features of jobs at the lower ranks of organizations. We selected workplaces and workers to provide insight on variations in employer practices and worker experiences in these jobs. Thus, we cannot say for what portion of low-skilled jobs and workers our findings apply. Rather than addressing the question of prevalence, our studies contribute information on the specific mechanisms (e.g., employer practices) that create ambiguity and instability and how these mechanisms, in turn, can lead to different child-care demands among working parents. The findings presented here are preliminary, and the specific links between employer practices and child-care strategies will undergo additional scrutiny in future analyses with these data.

Our studies suggest at least two avenues for future research. First, quantitative studies with representative samples of firms and workers are necessary to determine the extent to which ambiguity and instability are characteristic of jobs in today's workplaces regardless of the labels used to formally classify them. Such analyses would likely involve collecting new data because we are unaware of existing large-scale data sets that tap the nuanced employment practices and worker experiences our studies suggest are important to advancing knowledge on nonstandard status and scheduling. Research should not abandon case studies and qualitative investigations, however, because they provide an entrée into context-specific dynamics that are difficult to capture, and often impractical to assess, using survey approaches. Our findings also suggest that it would be fruitful to pursue a second avenue of workplace-based experimental research to directly examine the causal relationships between mechanisms and outcomes suggested by the in-depth accounts of our research. Specifically, experimental studies that manipulate employer practices around nonstandard status and scheduling, tracing their effects on a range of job-, worker-, and family-level outcomes, could produce critical new insights with relevance for the academic and practice communities.

Regarding the practical implications of our current research, our analyses suggest that ambiguity and instability at work must be tackled head on if we are to promote the well-being of lower skilled workers and their families. We certainly laud efforts to craft child-care policy to accommodate the needs of working parents, especially those disadvantaged by economic circumstances and inflexible jobs. Indeed, elsewhere Henly and Bromer (2002) urged family child-care programs, centers, and preschools to attend to parental job characteristics and consider incorporating family support functions when designing services (Bromer & Henly, 2004). As one reviewer of this chapter noted, the child-care field is far from understanding the complexity of the child-care challenges facing low-income working mothers. Even so, without addressing the nature of jobs, extending child-care program hours, reducing cost, adding services, and increasing the availability of child care will be insufficient to solve the economic or caregiving difficulties faced by parents in low-skilled jobs. Nor does this approach directly address the developmental needs of children. Although complex packages of care have the potential to positively support the multiple needs of children, the patterns of shifting schedules and changing arrangements described by many of our study participants signaled a rather chaotic and potentially unfavorable environment for children (Henly, 2004).

Improving the plight of workers in low-skilled jobs may then require changing employer practices. This does not negate the important role that social policy can and should play in the lives of families (Lambert & Kossek, 2005). Part of the reason employer practices are so integral to family well-being in the United States is because, when compared with other industrialized nations, the United States provides limited support for caregiving and everyday family responsibilities (Lewis & Smithson, 2001; Meyers & Gornick, 2001). If the government readily provided health care benefits, high-quality child care at a reasonable cost, and income assistance to smooth fluctuations in earnings, the deleterious consequences of the employer practices we highlight would be more modest.

Yet even with generous supports from government, employer practices will continue to largely define the conditions under which workers are incorporated into the labor market. For example, even within legal limits on work hours and wages, employers have significant latitude in how they arrange work and design jobs, as they should. To be effective and fair, even the strictest employment laws and policies require the active and willing participation of employers (Lambert & Haley-Lock, 2004). Thus, under any circumstances, employer practices will be critical to distributing resources and rights to workers. Moreover, the decisions employers make are passed onto a web of individuals and institutions, including child-care providers, teachers, spouses, friends, and, of course, children. Developmentalists tell us how family time and family routines benefit children and the individual and social costs to underinvesting in family supervision, monitoring, and high-quality caregiving. Yet workplace practices in the low-skilled jobs we studied make it difficult for parents to spend time with their children or provide the resources children need to thrive. Thus, for these reasons, it is critical that we identify, develop, and disseminate employer practices that can meet the needs of business without sacrificing the well-being of families.

ACKNOWLEDGMENTS

The authors wish to thank Juliet Bromer, Anna Haley-Lock, and Elaine Waxman for their input on the studies and ideas developed in this chapter. The Study on Work–Child Care Fit, reviewed in this chapter, is supported by a research grant from U.S. Department of Health and Human Services in collaboration with the Joint Center for Poverty Research, and by additional funds from the McCormick-Tribune Center for Early Childhood Research and the Louise R. Bowler Faculty Research Award, School of Social Service Administration. The Project on the Public Economy of Work, also reviewed here, is supported by grants from the Ford Foundation, the National Science Foundation, and the Soros' Open Society Institute.

REFERENCES

Acs, G., Phillips, K., & McKenzie, D. (2001). Playing by the rule, but losing the game: Americans in low-income working families. In R. Kazis & M. S. Miller (Eds.), *Low-wage workers in the new economy.* Washington, DC: The Urban Institute Press.

Appelbaum, E., Bernhardt, A., & Murnane, R. (2003). Low-wage America: An overview. In E. Appelbaum, A. Bernhardt, & R. Murnane (Eds.), *Low-wage America* (pp. 1–29). New York: Russell Sage Foundation.

Bernstein, J., & Gittleman, M. (2003, November/December). Exploring low-wage labor with the National Compensation Survey. *Monthly Labor Review,* pp. 3–12.

Blank, R. M. (1997). *It takes a nation: A new agenda for fighting poverty.* New York: Russell Sage Foundation.

Booth, A., Crouter, A., & Shanahan, M. (Eds.). (1999). *Transitions to adulthood in a changing economy: No work, no family no future?* Westport, CT: Greenwood.

Bromer, J., & Henly, J. R. (2004). Child care as family support? Caregiving practices across child care provider types. *Children and Youth Services Review, 26*(10), 941–964.

Carnevale, A., & Rose, S. (2001). Low-earners: Who are they? Do they have a way out? In R. Kazis & M. S. Miller (Eds.), *Low-wage workers in the new economy* (pp. 45–66). Washington, DC: The Urban Institute Press.

Casper, L. M., & O'Connell, M. (1998). Work, income, the economy, and married fathers as child-care providers. *Demography, 35,* 243–250.

Chase-Landsdale, P. L., Moffitt, R., Lohman, B., Cherlin, A., Coley, R. L., Pittman, L., Roff, & Votruba-Drzal, E. (2003). Mothers' transitions from welfare to work and the well-being of preschoolers and adolescents. *Science, 299,* 1548–1552.

Currie, J., & Yelowitz, A. (2000). Health insurance and less skilled workers. In D. Card & R. Blank (Eds.), *Finding jobs* (pp. 233–261). New York: Russell Sage Foundation.

Danziger, S. H., & Gottschalk, P. (1995). *America unequal.* Cambridge, MA: Harvard University Press.

Dodson, L., Manuel, T., & Bravo, E. (2002). *Keeping jobs and raising families in low-income America: It just doesn't work. A report of the Across the Boundaries Project.* Radcliffe Public Policy Center and 9to5 National Association of Working Women. Radcliffe Institute for Advanced Study, Harvard University.

Doeringer, P., & Piore, M. (1985). *Internal labor markets and manpower analysis,* New York: M. E. Sharpe.

Dunifon, R., Kalil, A., & Danziger, S. K. (2003). Does maternal employment mandated by welfare reform affect parenting behavior? *Children & Youth Services Review, 25,* 55–82.

Emerson, R. M. (1983). *Contemporary field research.* Boston: Little, Brown.

Gerstel, N., & McGonagle, K. (1999). Job leaves and the limits of the Family and Medical Leave Act: The effects of gender, race, and family. *Work and Occupations, 26,* 510–534.

Gladden, T., & Taber, C. (1998). Wage progression among less skilled workers. In D. Card & R. Blank (Eds.), *Finding jobs* (pp. 160–192). New York: Russell Sage Foundation.

Glass, J., & Estes, S. (1997). The family responsive workplace. *Annual Review of Sociology, 23,* 289–313.

Han, W. J. (2004). Nonstandard work schedules and child care decisions: Evidence from the NICHD Study of Early Child Care. *Early Childhood Research Quarterly, 19,* 231–256.

Henly, J. R. (2004, October). *Nonstandard work and family life: Themes from a qualitative study of low-income mothers employed in the retail sector.* Paper presented at the 26th annual meeting of the Association for Public Policy Analysis and Management, Atlanta, GA.

Henly, J. R., & Bromer, J. (2002, October). *The role of job characteristics in shaping the child care needs of entry-level workers with young children.* Paper presented at the 24th annual meetings of the Association for Public Policy Analysis and Management, Dallas, TX.

Herzenberg, S., Alic, J., & Wial, H. (1998) *New rules for a new economy*. Ithaca, NY: Cornell University Press.

Heymann, J. (2000). *The widening gap*. New York: Basic Books.

Holzer, H. (1990). *A future of lousy jobs? The changing structure of U.S. wages*. Washington, DC: The Brookings Institute.

Jacobs, D. (1994). Organizational theory and dualism: Some sociological determinants of spot and internal labor markets. *Research in Social Stratification and Mobility, 13*, 203–235.

Johnson, R., & Corcoran, M. (2003). The road to economic self-sufficiency: Job quality and job transition patterns after welfare reform. *Journal of Policy Analysis and Management, 22*, 615–639.

Kalleberg, A., & Schmidt, K. (1996). Contingent employment in organizations. In D. Kalleberg, P. M. Knoke, & J. Spaeth (Eds.), *Organizations in America* (pp. 253–275). Thousand Oaks, CA: Sage.

Lambert, S. (1999). Lower-wage workers and the new realities of work and family. *Annals of the American Academy of Political and Social Sciences, 562*, 174–190.

Lambert, S., & Haley-Lock, A. (2004). The organizational stratification of opportunities for work–life balance: Addressing issues of equality and social justice in the workplace. *Community, Work, and Family, 7*(2), 181–197.

Lambert, S., & Kossek, E. (2005). Future frontiers: Enduring challenges and established assumptions in the work–life field. In E. E. Kossek & S. J. Lambert (Eds.), *Work and life integration: Organizational, cultural, and individual perspectives* (pp. 513–532). Mahwah, NJ: Lawrence Erlbaum Associates.

Lambert, S., & Waxman, E. (2005). Organizational stratification: Distributing opportunities for work–life balance. In E. E. Kossek & S. J. Lambert (Eds.), *Work and life integration: Organizational, cultural, and individual perspectives* (pp. 103–126). Mahwah, NJ: Lawrence Erlbaum Associates.

Lewis, S., & Smithson, J. (2001). Sense of entitlement to support for the reconciliation of employment and family life. *Human Relations, 54*, 1433–1481.

Meyer, D. R., & Cancian, M. (1998). Economic well-being following an exit from aid to families with dependent children. *Journal of Marriage and the Family, 60*, 479–492.

Meyers, M., & Gornick, J. (2001). Gendering welfare state variation: Income transfers, employment support, and family poverty. In N. Hirschmann & U. Liebert (Eds.), *Women & welfare: Theory and practice in the United States and Europe*. New Brunswick, NJ: Rutgers University Press.

Newman, K. (1999). *No shame in my game: The working poor in the inner city*. New York: Russell Sage Foundation.

Pavetti, L. A., & Acs, G. (2001). Moving up, moving out, or going nowhere? A study of the employment patterns of young women and the implications for welfare mothers. *Journal of Policy Analysis and Management, 20*, 721–736.

Pfeffer, J., & Cohen, Y. (1984). Determinants of internal labor markets in organizations. *Administrative Science Quarterly, 29*, 550–572.

Presser, H. B. (1986). Shift work among American women and child care. *Journal of Marriage and the Family, 48*, 551–563.

Presser, H. B. (1995). Job, family, and gender: Determinants of nonstandard work schedules among employed Americans in 1991. *Demography, 32*, 577–598.

Presser, H. B. (2000). Nonstandard work schedules and marital instability. *Journal of Marriage and the Family, 62*, 93–110.

Presser, H. B. (2003). *Working in a 24/7 Economy: Challenges for American Families*. New York: Russell Sage Foundation.

Presser, H. B., & Cain, V. S. (1983). Shift work among dual-earner couples with children. *Science, 219*, 876–879.

Presser, H. B., & Cox, A. G. (1997). The work schedules of low-educated American women and welfare reform. *Monthly Labor Review, 120,* 25–34.

Staines, G. L., & Pleck, J. H. (1984). Nonstandard work schedules and family life. *Journal of Applied Psychology, 69,* 515–523.

Tilly, C. (1996). *Half a job: Bad and good part-time jobs in a changing labor market.* Philadelphia: Temple University Press.

31

Health and Mothers' Employment in Low-Income Families

Linda M. Burton

The Pennsylvania State University

Laura Lein

The University of Texas at Austin

Amy Kolak

The University of Michigan

The passage of the Personal Responsibility and Work Opportunity Reconciliation Act (PRWORA), and with it the implementation of the Temporary Assistance for Needy Families (TANF) program in 1996, directed scholarly, policy, and public attention to the work lives of low-income mothers (Albelda & Withorn, 2002; Cancian, Haverman, Meyer, & Wolfe, 2000; Ehrenreich, 2001; Henly, 2002; Kingfisher, 1996; Mink, 2002; Newman, 2001). PRWORA limits the time that families can receive cash public assistance (now called TANF) and requires beneficiaries, typically the mothers of young children, to enter the workforce or become more work-ready. While there is some variability by state in how the TANF work requirement is enforced, many have argued that the health of TANF eligible mothers and their children has not been at center stage in the political debate on moving

493

families from welfare to work (Burton et al., 2002; Earle & Heymann, 2002; Heymann & Earle, 1999; Olson & Pavetti, 1997). Health care providers, in particular, have cautioned policymakers to strongly consider the relationship between work and health, noting that if the work requirements of welfare reform further exacerbate the physical, mental, and financial vulnerabilities of America's poor, health care providers will be the inundated "inheritors of a failed policy," with low-income families losing substantially more ground in family health and economic security from parental unemployment (Chavkin, Wise, & Romero, 2002).

Both mother and child health affect and are affected by maternal employment, and low-income families may be particularly vulnerable to such effects (Burton, Skinner, Matthews, & Lachicotte, 2002; Earle & Heymann, 2002; Heymann & Earle, 1999; Olson & Pavetti, 1997). A comprehensive understanding of the role that family health plays in the economic security of low-income families is critical to the current policy discourse on welfare reform and maternal employment. Family health is an inclusive concept that refers to the physical and mental co-morbidity among multiple household members (e.g., mother, father, and children), rather than the physical *or* mental health status of just the mother *or* her children (Burton et al., 2003b; Heymann, 2000). The limited number of studies addressing co-morbidity within the family suggests that poor family health prevents sustained employment among low-income women (Danziger et al., 2000; Jayakody, Danzinger, & Pollack, 2000; National Resource Council, 1991; Repetti, Matthews, & Waldron, 1989). Tentative evidence suggests that women who are primary caregivers for multiple dependent family members in poor health are more likely to give up their jobs (National Research Council, 2001).

Drawing on in-depth ethnographic data from 256 economically disadvantaged families that participated in *Welfare, Children, and Families: A Three-City Study*, we examine the relationship between family health and the employment experiences of low-income mothers. We address two questions: What is the prevalence of co-morbid physical and mental illnesses in low-income families? How does family health interact with the employment experiences of low-income mothers? These issues are discussed in the contexts of welfare reform, the low-wage labor job market, and the health experiences of families who are *living poor*.

EMPLOYMENT AND HEALTH IN LOW-INCOME FAMILIES

Our exploration of work and health in low-income families integrates two lines of research—one examining the tenuous jobs held by low-income women (Kalleberg, Reskin, & Hudson, 2000; Lambert, Waxman, & Haley-Lock, 2002; Piven, 2001; Wilson, 1987, 2000), and another chronicling the compromised health of America's poor, particularly minority women (Geronimus, 1996; Heymann, 2000; Link & Phelan, 1996; Maret, 1982; National Research Council, 2001; Repetti et al., 1989; Williams, 2001; Williams & Collins, 1995). Although other factors such as social support, child-care options, and availability of transportation affect mothers' employment (Edin & Lein, 1997; Garey, 1999; Henly & Lyons, 2000; Lane, Mikelson, Sharkey, & Wissoker, 2001), this chapter focuses on family health and mothers' employment—a relatively understudied issue (Burton et al., 2003b; Heymann, 2000). Burdened by complex family health problems, including the care of children and relatives with physical and mental illnesses, and often neglecting their own health, mothers' abilities to find and sustain employment often come tumbling down.

Employment and America's Poor Families

Most families, and certainly most low-income families, expect to support themselves and their households with jobs. Yet job security, regular wages and hours, and the benefits associated with employment in a regular full-time job are increasingly elusive for low-income mothers, as they are for many other employees (Kalleberg et al., 2000; Wagner, Herr, Chang, & Brooks, 1998). The increase in short-term jobs with irregular hours affects the regularity and dependability of paid work for low-income, single mothers (Lambert et al., 2002). Moreover, public welfare for impoverished families in the United States is diminishing while the resources available to them through employment are also declining (Bernstein, 2002; Mink, 2002; Piven, Acker, Hallock, & Morgan, 2002).

The same job may often require changes in numbers of hours and shifts worked (Ehrenreich, 2001; Newman, 2001). Income from jobs in tourism, fast food, and the health care sector varies seasonally, weekly, and, for some workers, daily. As others in this volume have noted, the rotating shifts and different daily or weekly hours (Kalleberg et al., 2000) leave mothers unable to plan ahead for their transportation, child-care, and other needs (Henly & Lyons, 2000).

Women often leave or are fired from jobs that offer them no options when either they or their children are ill; when they have to deal with welfare offices for benefit recertification for benefits such as Medicaid and child-care subsidies; and when they must meet their responsibilities for other dependent family members (often very young or very old) who became ill or disabled. Low-wage working mothers commonly lack such benefits as health insurance, paid vacations, personal or sick days—let alone retirement benefits for after they age out of the labor force (Schexnayder et al., 2002).

Many of the problems faced by low-income single mothers are based in the labor force as much as in the structure of the welfare system (Edin & Lein, 1997; Newman, 1999; Piven, 2001). The irregular patterns of employment and the strategies and resources women use to cope with their work-welfare environment (Burton, Benjamin, Hurt, Woodruff, & Kolak, 2003a; King-fisher, 1996) affect household budgets (Edin & Lein, 1997; Renwick, 1998) and thus their ability to care for their families. Mothers' work experiences detailed in the *Three-City Study* ethnographic component fell into one of five patterns: (a) single jobs of continuous duration sustained by only a few mothers in the study, (b) near continuous employment through multiple job spells, (c) underemployment, (d) churning in and out of employment, and (e) unemployment (Lein, Benjamin, McManus, & Roy, 2002). This chaotic pattern of employment interacts closely with the health issues faced by mothers and their children, as well as with their access to health insurance (Angel, Lein, Henrici, & Leventhal, 2001; Burton et al., 2003b; Cunningham & Park, 2003; Institute of Medicine, 2002). In particular, the departure from welfare combined with the low-wage jobs leaves families without Medicaid (although that situation is improving slightly; Loprest, 2003) or employer-assisted health insurance.

Health in Low-Income Families

Low-income populations are more likely to suffer from substantial physical and mental health problems (Blackwell, Hayward, & Crimmins, 2001; Burton & Whitfield, 2003; Geronimus, 1996; Heymann, 2000; Williams & Collins, 1995) than better-off families, resulting in marked health disparities among different groups (National Research Council, 2001). Health disparities among America's poor are evident in higher deaths rates (particularly for low-income racial and ethnic minorities) from coronary heart disease, cancer, diabetes, and injury (Williams, 2001). Health disparities during early childhood are evident in higher rates of infectious diseases such as measles, rubella, tetanus, and tuberculosis (Vega & Amaro, 1994). These disparities are often attributed to inequalities in health care and education between America's *haves* and *have nots*, the cumulative effects of stress and racism on poor families' health, and hazardous working conditions in low-wage jobs (Gee, 2002; Marks & Choi, 2002; National Research Council, 2001). In the context of these disparities, low-income women are frequently unable to sustain employment because of poor health (Danziger et al., 2000; Jayakody, Danziger, & Pollack, 2000; National Resource Council, 2001; Repetti et al., 1989) or because of their responsibilities for family members in poor health (National Research Council, 2001).

THE *THREE-CITY STUDY* ETHNOGRAPHY

The data on family health and mothers' employment experiences featured in this chapter are from the ethnographic component of a larger research project, *Welfare, Children and Families: A Three-City Study*. The study was carried out over 4 years in Boston, Chicago, and San Antonio to monitor the consequences of welfare reform for the well-being of children and families. The study comprises three interrelated components: (a) a longitudinal in-person survey of approximately 2,400 families in low-income neighborhoods with children ages 0 to 4 and 10 to 14, about 40% of whom were receiving cash welfare payments when they were first interviewed in 1999; (b) an embedded developmental study of a subsample of about 630 children ages 2 to 4 in 1999 and their caregivers; and (c) an ethnographic study of 256 families residing in the same neighborhoods as the survey families, recruited according to the same family income criteria, and who were followed intensively until the project ended in August 2003. African-American, Hispanic, and non-Hispanic White families are represented in all three components and in all three cities. A detailed description of the *Three-City Study* and a series of reports are available at http://www.jhu.edu/~welfare.

All families that participated in the ethnography (*N* = 256 families) had household incomes at or below 200% of the federal poverty line. Table 31.1 shows that the demographic characteristics of the ethnographic sample are in many ways comparable to those in the survey sample in the *Three-City Study*. The largest group of ethnography participants (42%) was Latino or Hispanic (e.g., Puerto Ricans, Mexican Americans, and Central Americans). Of the remaining participants, 38% were African American and 20% were non-Hispanic White.

More than one half of the mothers were age 29 or younger, and a majority of the respondents had a high school diploma or a GED or attended trade school or college. Nearly one half (49%) of the families were receiving welfare (TANF) when they entered the study; one third of these, in compliance with welfare regulations, were also working. Fifty-one percent of the sample was not receiving welfare (TANF) benefits, and the primary earner in the household was either working in a low-wage job or was unemployed. The 256 primary caregivers identified 685 children in their households. Fifty-three percent of the children were ages 4 or younger; 47% were elementary school age or adolescents. One fourth of the primary caregivers were responsible for one child, and 27%, 25%, and 23% for two, three, and four or more children, respectively. The majority (56%) of primary caregivers were unmarried and did not have a partner (e.g., boyfriend) living with them, another 17% were not married but were cohabiting with a partner, 17% were married and living with their spouse, and 10% were married or separated and their spouse was not living in the home.

Between June 1999 and December 2000, the study recruited families at formal child-care settings, Women, Infants, and Children (WIC) offices, local welfare offices, neighborhood community centers, churches, and other public assistance agencies, as well as in less formal neighborhood settings. Of the

TABLE 31.1
Sample Characteristics, Ethnography (N = 256 Families), and Survey (N = 2,402)

Characteristic	Ethnography		Survey*	
	N	%	N	%
City				
Boston	71	28	926	39
Chicago	95	37	762	32
San Antonio	90	35	714	30
Ethnicity/Race				
African American	98	38	1,009	43
Latino/Hispanic	108	42	1,137	48
Non-Hispanic White	50	20	209	9
Ages of primary caregivers				
15–19	21	8	122	5
20–24	67	26	412	17
25–29	62	24	464	19
30–34	36	14	466	19
35–39	35	14	419	17
40+	35	14	517	22
Education				
Less than high school	110	43	843	35
Completed high school or GED	67	26	567	24
College or trade school	79	31	986	41
TANF Status				
TANF	125	49	894	37
Non-TANF	131	51	1,499	63
TANF/Work Status				
TANF/Working	40	16	170	7
TANF/Not Working	85	33	688	30
Non-TANF/Working	64	25	658	28
Non-TANF/Not Working	67	26	814	35
No. of children for whom primary caregiver is responsible				
1	64	25	530	22
2	70	27	775	32
3	63	25	570	24
> 4	59	23	526	22
Children's ages				
< 2	190	28	769	12
2–4	174	25	1,214	19
5–9	205	30	1,712	27
10–14	88	13	1,931	31
15–18	28	4	609	10
Total	685		6,235	
Marital status/living arrangements**				
Not married, not cohabiting	142	56	1,642	69
Married, spouse in home	42	17	324	14
Married, spouse not in home/separated	24	10	276	12
Cohabiting (any marital status)	43	17	151	6

*Percentages may not sum to 100 because of rounding. **There are missing data for five cases in the marital status and living arrangements category.

256 families in the ethnography, we recruited 44 specifically because they had a child under age 9 with a moderate or severe disability. We recruited families of children whose disabilities might make a difference in their caregivers' ability to work or otherwise comply with TANF requirements. We purposively included a broad range of disabilities to represent children with different needs and present the different issues these families face (e.g., autism—high impact behavioral issues; Down syndrome—significant cognitive delays and possible health problems; spina bifida—high impact medical problems; and cerebral palsy—physical and perhaps cognitive delays). Medical diagnoses of these children include cerebral palsy, Down syndrome, seizure disorder, severe Attention Deficit-Hyperactivity Disorder (ADHD), significant developmental delays, visual and hearing impairments, spina bifida, Pervasive Developmental Disorder, autism, chondrodysplasia punetata, various syndromes (e.g., Kartagener syndrome, Angelman syndrome, and Cri-du-chat syndrome), severe asthma, and other involved medical conditions (e.g., congenital heart problems, brain damage, lung disease) that resulted in developmental delay and disability (Skinner, Slattery, Lachicotte, Cherlin, & Burton, 2002). We include this purposive subsample here because the 44 participants are similar on health and employment issues to the sample of 212 families recruited for the overall ethnography. In fact similar health problems were prevalent in the families we studied even when they were not purposively recruited for health conditions.

The ethnography employed a method of structured discovery in which in-depth interviews and observations focused on specific topics, but allowed flexibility to capture unexpected findings and relationships among topics (Burton et al., 2001; Winston et al., 1999). The interviews addressed health and health access; experiences with TANF and other public assistance programs; education, work experiences, and future plans; family economics; child development, parenting, and intimate relationships; support networks; family routines; and home and neighborhood environments. Ethnographers also engaged in participant observation, accompanying the mother and her children to the welfare office, doctor, hospital, clinic, or workplace, and noting both context and interactions. Ethnographers met with each family once or twice each month, on average, for 12 to 18 months, with follow-up interviews at 6 months and 1 year after the 18-month intensive period. Researchers coded interview transcripts, field notes, and other documents for entry into a qualitative data management (QDM) software application and summarized into a case profile for each family. The QDM program and case profiles enabled counts across the entire sample of ethnographic families as well as detailed analyses of individual cases.

Using profiles developed on each family and the QDM software, the research team assessed each family's health status and the mothers' employment histories. The team then constructed tables with health and employment information for each of the 256 families in the sample. Data on each family were cross-checked through an iterative process; researchers compared information from family profiles with information available from the data collection team, information from the data processing team (the QDAs), and information that had been coded into the QDM software.

Measuring Health

In the ethnography, we asked mothers to describe any illnesses affecting them and their children that had been diagnosed by a physician or mental health professional. In some cases, mothers and children were receiving medical care, but physicians or mental health professionals had not yet rendered a definitive diagnosis. In these instances, we asked the primary caregiver to tell us what the doctor was treating them for, acknowledging that it was a temporary diagnosis.

Many caregivers were quite detailed in delineating their health problems because they were applying for Supplemental Security Income (SSI) for themselves or children. Such applications require a physician's report and exact descriptions of disabling ailments. Others were less exact in reporting health problems. Some had more immediate concerns, and as one young primary caregiver who had "some form of cancer" indicated, "I don't want to deal with it yet." Others did not acknowledge their children's disabilities or overt behavioral problems because they did not want other family members, their churches, or schools labeling their children as *slow, crazy, dumb, wild, sickly,* or *uncontrollable*. Still others did not understand the diagnoses from physicians or mental health professionals because, as one mother said, it "wasn't explained in a way that I could understand." Finally, some participants used cultural terms to describe their mental and physical ailments, such as *nerviosa*, which encompasses anxiety, panic attacks, and depression; *getting in a mood*, which in some families is synonymous with mild schizophrenia, paranoia, and anxiety disorders; *sugar*, which implies diabetes; and *water*, which in one neighborhood setting meant hypertension characterized by water retention and extremely swollen hands, wrists, ankles, and feet.

Gathering precise health data on the families involved considerable effort and was only achieved after months of in-depth discussion, observation, and verification of illnesses by the primary caregivers. Although the families experienced numerous episodes of short-term illnesses, this analysis focuses specifically on the major health problems the families experienced as defined by the National Center for Chronic Disease Prevention and Health Promotion (Centers for Disease Control, 2000), the Surgeon General's Call to Action to Prevent and Decrease Overweight and Obesity (U.S. Dept. of Health and Human Services, 2001), and recent National Institutes of Health reports that outline principal population health concerns, including diseases of the nervous, endocrine, metabolic, circulatory, and respiratory systems (National Research Council, 2001).

The most common physical ailments mothers reported were severe obesity, hepatitis, hypertension, cancer, arthritic conditions, cardiovascular disease, and diabetes; for their children, they reported diabetes, severe asthma, seizures, and lead poisoning. Chronic dental problems, such as *brown teeth* and advanced gum disease, were also common for adults and children, particularly in San Antonio.

Most (87%, N = 256 mothers) of the mothers reported mental health problems based on a diagnosis from a mental health professional (e.g., psychiatrist). Mothers most frequently reported experiences with depression, anxiety, posttraumatic stress disorder (PTSD), and chronic stress, and for their children, ADHD, autism, anxiety, and depression. Recent reports on mental health issues in low-income populations corroborate our findings (Beardslee, Versage, & Gladstone, 1998; Chandler & Meisel, 2000; Danziger et al., 2000; Fergusson, Horwood, & Lynsky, 1993; Garrison, Addy, Jackson, McKeown, & Waller, 1992; Jayakody et al., 2000; Kessler & Zhoa, 1999; Lennon, Blome, & English, 2002), as well as referral to the *DSM–IV* listing of conditions (American Psychiatric Association, 1994).

The Prevalence of Health Problems in Families

Our study of health problems focuses on the family as the principal unit of analysis. Families are defined as the primary caregiver(s) and the children for whom the caregiver is responsible. The decision to examine health as a family issue rather than just the parents or the children was based on the presence of multiple health problems among families in the ethnography. The health problems of mothers and fathers and their children were integrally linked and could not be discussed as separate issues. The chronic health conditions of children—as well as other family members—proved as problematic to sustaining work as did a caregiver's own health problems.

Family health profiles fell into four categories (N = 256 families):

1. Concurrent family health problems (63%), where two or more members had chronic physical and mental health conditions;

2. Primary caregiver health problems only (15%), where only the primary caregiver had one or more chronic conditions;

3. Child health problems only (9%), where a child was the only family member with one or more chronic conditions; and

4. No reported family health problems (13%), where no one in the family reported chronic conditions.

Families experiencing concurrent illnesses usually included a mother who had multiple health conditions; 78% of the mothers in the sample reported multiple physical illnesses or a combination of physical and mental illnesses, often depression. For example, Earlene, a 45-year-old primary caregiver of two grandchildren, had hepatitis C, high blood pressure, and vision problems, as well as constant stomach pain and arthritis in her knees. She also suffered depression and anxiety and had not left her house during the preceding year. Shortly after we met her, Earlene checked herself into a mental hospital because she was so depressed that she "felt like the walls in her house were closing in on her." One of her daughters took care of the grandchildren while she was in the hospital. Earlene continued to take numerous daily medications for her mental and physical health conditions.

As noted in Table 31.1, the mothers in the sample were relatively young, with approximately 83% ages 39 or younger. The young ages of the primary caregivers, coupled with the high incidence of multiple chronic physical and mental illnesses, made them justifiably fearful for their middle and later years. Females with severe chronic physical and mental health problems early in life are likely to have exacerbated health problems as they approach midlife and old age (Blackwell et al., 2001; Burton & Whitfield, 2003; Geronimus, 1996; National Research Council, 2001). Lupe, a 21-year-old mother of two, was aware of the problems associated with poor health at a young age. She noted:

> Me and my mom talk about how many problems I've had. I'm only 21 and I've had all these problems [asthma, gynecological tumors, and depression] and I worry about in coming years what's going to happen. There are women out there in their 30s having hysterectomies. Is that going to be me?

One third of the mothers saw their health problems reflected in their mothers' lives. Most of these respondents' mothers were disabled or had died of cardiovascular disease, stokes, or cancer before the age of 55. Like their daughters and grandchildren, these women had lengthy histories of infectious and chronic illnesses dating back to their childhoods.

Mothers' Health, Employment, and Caring for Others

Mothers in the study often neglected their own physical and mental health needs to meet the economic and health care needs of their children and other family members. Although most mothers received some support from their spouses, partners, or the fathers of their children, nearly all the women in the study often put symptoms of their illnesses out of their minds and postponed both regular checkups and treatment because being sick interfered with both care for their children and older family members and keeping their jobs. For example, some mothers refused to take medication prescribed for hypertension because they feared it would keep them from being alert enough to care for their young children. Rena, a 25-year-old single mother of three children under age 10, was diagnosed with clinical depression. Lacking a car, she commuted by bus for several hours every day to a third-shift job, on the way delivering and picking up her children from school and child care at her mother's house. Absorbed as she was in the care for her 10-year-old autistic child and her two younger children with asthma, Rena had, as she said, "little time to be depressed." She also had to defend herself from her occasionally violent live-in partner. Rena refused her depression medication even though some days she found it difficult to get out of bed. She could not always afford the medication and worried about side effects. Rena was often overwhelmed, as reflected in her self-care. She went to the doctor only when she felt chest pain, she could not breathe, or she was in intense pain. Otherwise she avoided it because she

> could spend $5.00 looking on the wall at Walgreen's [buying over-the-counter remedies to self-medicate] as opposed to a $20 co-pay for a visit to the doctor. . . . With working, the kids, and cleaning you don't have time to stop and listen to your body, even when there are warning signs of a problem . . . you just "do" until you can just sit in a chair and nod off.

Francine, a 30-year-old mother of three children ages 4, 6, and 8, also had too many other responsibilities to focus on her own health. In her youth, she was hospitalized every year with pneumonia until her freshman year of high school. When Francine joined the ethnographic study, she had just received a "temporary diagnosis of stomach cancer," but Francine did not return to the doctor until the pain was unbearable and she "didn't have other folks to take care of." Her 6-year-old asthmatic son required constant attention. Francine's mother had suffered a recent stroke and heart attack. Francine, like many of the mothers in the study, was her own mother's primary caregiver. With no alternatives for caring for her mother or children, Francine had no time to treat her own medical conditions.

Some mothers, such as Camille, completely discounted their serious illnesses. Camille had been diagnosed and treated with a form of cervical cancer 6 years ago, but the cancer did not stay in remission. Camille noted that, "My doctor says it is eating up my stomach but not spreading yet. Some days I am fine with it, but other times it hurts so bad I just lay down and cry." Despite these problems, "someone has to make me go to the doctor" because her health care providers wanted to hospitalize her. Camille believed nothing could really help her, and she did not agree that she was terminally ill either. She reported that she might be pregnant; she was planning her wedding. Camille believed that, despite the cancer, she would always be able to take care of her children.

Not only did family health problems force mothers to delay their own treatment, but the health of their dependents, including children and elderly relatives, could interfere with work and providing for their family's needs. For example, mothers who reported losing or resigning from full-time jobs ($N =$ 50) frequently cited family health-related responsibilities as a barrier to work. They resigned from or lost their jobs when they missed work to provide care or get others to medical appointments. Mothers responsible for children with mental illnesses such as depression, ADHD, and suicidal ideation were likely to leave work early to manage a medical crisis with their children or take extended time off work when their children were hospitalized or when they could not find sick child care. Denise, a single mother of eight boys, lost at least three jobs during the course of the study when she missed several weeks of work caring for one of her children who had rheumatic fever and heart problems that required frequent hospitalization. Eventually, 68% of the full-time working mothers lost their jobs trying to address their children's health needs while forgoing health care for themselves. As Gina says:

> I worry a lot about how I'm going to cover myself when my kids get sick and I'm going to have to miss work. It's happened before where just one of us would get sick and it just affects our whole life. Our whole life can fall apart like that. I just pray that my children don't get too sick. If I have to make a choice whether I'm going to stay home and take care of my sick kids, or go to work, I'm going to stay home.

Other caregivers of young children faced similar problems, including the grandmothers who were often called on to help. Beatrice, the grandmother and custodial guardian of three grandsons, could not keep a job because she was too busy attending to Malcolm, who was 9 years old and had sickle cell anemia. Beatrice owned a beauty salon, and she often closed it to attend to Malcolm's needs. Putting her family's health needs ahead of financial needs and her own health was not new for Beatrice. She found it difficult to keep a job when rearing her own children because her son had kidney disease. When she faced financial difficulties, she sold her kitchen appliances to a pawnshop.

> Health care for myself is like, I refuse. I try and use my mind in a positive way. My mind tells me that no matter what sickness I have, it's not going to last more than seven days. So deal with it! Even if I am sick, I get up, I walk around with it, because if I get into bed, it's going to last me longer . . . I just refuse it!

The precarious nature of work among the women, especially those whose work histories were characterized by chronic underemployment, poor health, and lack of health insurance, eventually took its toll on all of the mothers and their children. Periodically, the women in these situations were unable to simultaneously juggle their work and health conditions, with a disruption in one area causing, as one mother said, "the walls to come tumbling down."

POLICY RECOMMENDATIONS

The lives of the women in the *Three-City Study* ethnography substantiate a comment by Abraham (1993) that, "When people are poor, they become sick easily. When people are sick, their families quickly become poorer" (p. x). It is imperative that health policies work to improve access to health care for families, and that labor force policy acknowledge family health needs. Neither health nor labor force policy alone, however, can overcome the barriers the mothers in this study faced as they struggled to keep their jobs while working irregular hours and suffering medical conditions often without health insurance.

Family Health and Access to Health Care Services

In 87% of the families in the ethnography, at least one adult or child had both physical and mental health problems. Policymakers must develop and expand health programs for the poor to include attention to physical and mental health care for both children and their caregivers. Mothers in this study indicated that having physical and mental health problems was a prominent and persistent impediment to achieving economic security through employment. Policy must recognize that:

- The high incidence of chronic physical and mental health problems experienced by mothers and their children at very young ages requires improved programs that prevent, identify, treat, and cure illnesses that continue to have cumulative debilitating effects on the lives of poor children and their caregivers.
- Mothers need access to health care providers and health agencies that are accessible to them as workers. Medical facilities accepting Medicaid should provide evening and weekend hours to accommodate families with school and work constraints.
- Mothers without other health insurance need access to Medicaid or other public insurance for themselves as well as their children.

Workforce Policies

In addition to needing regular, better paid employment, mothers such as those in our study need workplace accommodations for their health problems, including:

- sick days and personal days that allow mothers to retain their jobs while dealing with their periodic responsibilities for ill children and other dependents with health needs;

- information about the kinds of health insurance available to them, their eligibility, and the process of applying;
- assistance from workplace supervisors or human resources staff concerning what they can expect from their employers and information on public services eligibility; and
- access to health screening and information about problems (services that could be provided at the workplace) given that the women were often unable to find the time, travel resources, and money for routine health checkups.

ACKNOWLEDGMENTS

We gratefully acknowledge the funders of the ethnographic component of *Welfare, Children, and Families: A Three-City Study*, including: The National Institute of Child Health and Human Development; Assistant Secretary for Planning and Evaluation; U.S. Department of Health and Human Services; Social Security Administration; The Henry J. Kaiser Family Foundation; The Robert Wood Johnson Foundation; The W. K. Kellogg Foundation; The John D. and Catherine T. MacArthur Foundation; The Hogg Foundation for Mental Health; and The Kronkosky Charitable Foundation. We extend special thanks to our 210-member ethnographic team (see project Web site www .jhu.edu/~welfare) and, particularly, the Penn State team, which provided the infrastructure, organization, and data management for the multisite ethnography. Most important, we thank the families that have graciously participated in the project and have given us access to their lives. Where specific examples are used in this chapter, families have been assigned pseudonyms.

REFERENCES

Abraham, L. K. (1993). *Mama might be better off dead*. Chicago: University of Chicago Press.

Albelda, R., & Withorn, A. (2002). *Lost ground: Welfare reform, poverty, and beyond*. Boston: South End Press.

American Psychiatric Association. (1994). *Diagnostic and statistical manual of mental disorders*, 4th ed. (*DSM–IV*). Washington, DC: Author.

Angel, R., Lein, L., Henrici, J., & Leventhal, E. (2001). *Health insurance coverage for children and their caregivers in low-income urban neighborhoods* (Welfare, Children, and Families, Policy Brief 01-2). Baltimore, MD: Johns Hopkins University Press.

Beardslee, W. R., Versage, E. M., & Gladstone, T. R. G. (1998). Children of affectively ill parents: A review of the past 10 years. *Journal of the American Academy of Child & Adolescent Psychiatry, 37,* 1134–1141.

Bernstein, J. (2002, October). *How has the availability, content, and stability of the jobs available for the working poor changed in recent decades? How do work circumstances for low-income families vary as a function of gender, family structure, race, ethnicity, and geography? What implication do these changes have for the widening inequality between the haves and have-nots?* Paper presented at the National Symposium for Family Issues entitled "Work-Family Challenges for Low-Income Parents and their Children," sponsored by the Pennsylvania State University and the National Institute of Child Health and Human Development, University Park, PA.

Blackwell, D. L., Hayward, M. D., & Crimmins, E. M. (2001). Does childhood health affect chronic morbidity in later life? *Social Science and Medicine, 52,* 1269–1284.

Burton, L. M., Jarrett, R., Lein, L., Matthews, S., Quane, J., Skinner, D., et al. (2001, April). *Structured discovery: Ethnography, welfare reform, and the assessment of neighborhoods, families, and children.* Paper presented at the biennial meeting of the Society for Research in Child Development, Minneapolis, MN.

Burton, L. M., Benjamin, A., Hurt, T., Woodruff, S. L., & Kolak, A. (2003a). *An ethnographic study of low-income non-entrants to TANF: Welfare experiences, diversions, and making ends meet.* The Office of the Assistant Secretary for Planning and Evaluation, U.S. Department of Health and Human Services.

Burton, L. M., Skinner, D., Matthews, S., & Lachicotte, W. (2002). *Family health, economic security, and welfare reform.* Paper presented at the annual meeting of the American Sociological Association, Chicago, IL.

Burton, L. M., Tubbs, C., Odoms, A. M., Oh, H. J., Mello, Z. R., & Cherlin, A. (2003b). *Welfare reform, poverty, and health: Ethnographic perspectives on health status and health insurance coverage in low-income families.* Washington, DC: The Kaiser Commission on Medicaid and the Uninsured.

Burton, L. M., & Whitfield, K. E. (2003). "Weathering" toward poorer health in later life: Co-morbidity in low-income families urban families. *Public Policy and Aging Report, 13*(3), 13–18.

Cancian, M., Haverman, R., Meyer, D., & Wolfe, B. (2000). *Before and after TANF: The economic well-being of women leaving welfare.* Madison, WI: Institute for Research on Poverty.

Centers for Disease Control. (2002). *Chronic disease prevention.* http//www.cdc.gov/nccdphp/about.htm.

Chandler, D., & Meisel, J. (2000). *The calworks project: The prevalence of mental health, alcohol and other drug and domestic violence issues among calworks participants in Kern and Stanislaus counties.* Sacramento, CA: California Institute of Mental Health.

Chavkin, W., Wise, P. H., & Romero, D. (2002). Welfare, women, and children: It's time for doctors to speak out. *Journal of American Medical Women's Association, 57,* 3–4.

Cunningham, P. J., & Park, M. H. (2003). *Recent trends in children's health insurance: No gains for low-income children* (Issue Brief No. 29). Washington, DC: Center for Studying Health System Change.

Danziger, S., Corcoran, M., Danziger, S., Heflin, C., Kalil, A., Levine, J. et al. (2000). *Barriers to employment of welfare recipients.* Available at: http://www.ssw.umich.edu/poverty/pubs.html.

Earle, A., & Heymann, J. (2002). What causes job loss among former welfare recipients: The role of family health problems. *Journal of American Medical Women's Association, 57,* 5–10.

Edin, K., & Lein, L. (1997). *Making ends meet.* New York: Russell Sage Foundation.

Ehrenreich, B. (2001). *Nickel and dimed: On (not) getting by in America.* New York: Metropolitan Books.

Fergusson, D. M., Horwood, L. J., & Lynsky, M. T. (1993). Prevalence and comorbidity of DSM–III–R diagnoses in a birth cohort of 15 year olds. *Journal of the American Academy of Child and Adolescent Psychiatry, 32,* 1127–1134.

Garey, A. (1999). *Weaving work and motherhood.* Philadelphia: Temple University Press.

Garrison, C. Z., Addy, C. L., Jackson, K. L., McKeown, R. E., & Waller, J. L. (1992). Major depressive disorder and dysthymia in young adolescents. *American Journal of Epidemiology, 135,* 792–802.

Gee, G. C. (2002). A multilevel analysis of the relationship between institutional and individual racial discrimination and health status. *American Journal of Public Health, 92*, 615–623.

Geronimus, A. T. (1996). Black/white differences in the relationship of maternal age to birthweight: A population-based test of the weathering hypothesis. *Social Science and Medicine, 42*, 589–597.

Henly, J. R. (2002). Informal support networks and the maintenance of low-wage jobs. In F. Munger (Ed.), *Laboring below the line*. New York: Russell Sage.

Henly, J. R., & Lyons, S. (2000). The negotiations of child care and employment demands among low-income parents. *Journal of Social Issues, 56*, 683–705.

Heymann, J. (2000). *The widening gap: Why America's working families are in jeopardy and what can be done about it*. New York: Basic Books.

Heymann, S., & Earle, A. (1999). The impact of welfare reform on parents' ability to care for their children's health. *American Journal of Public Health, 89*, 502–526.

Institute of Medicine. (2002). *Health insurance is a family matter*. Washington, DC: National Academies Press.

Jayakody, R., Danziger, S., & Pollack, H. (2000). Welfare reform, substance use, and mental health. *Journal of Health, Politics, Policy, and Law, 25*, 623–652.

Kalleberg, A., Reskin, B., & Hudson, K. (2000). Bad jobs in America: Standard and nonstandard employment relations and job quality in the United States. *American Sociological Review, 65*, 256–278.

Kessler, R. C., & Zhoa, S. (1999). Overview of descriptive epidemiology of mental disorders. In C. Aneshensel & J. Phelan (Eds.), *Handbook of the sociology of mental health* (pp. 26–57). New York: Kluwer/Academic Plenum.

Kingfisher, C. (1996). *Women in the American welfare trap*. Philadelphia: University of Pennsylvania Press.

Lambert, S., Waxman, E., & Haley-Lock, A. (2002). *Against the odds: A study of instability in lower-skilled jobs* (Working paper, Project on the Public Economy of Work). Chicago: University of Chicago Press.

Lane, J., Mikelson, K. S., Sharkey, P. T., & Wissoker, D. (2001). *Low-income and low-skilled workers' involvement in nonstandard employment: Final Report*. Washington, DC: U.S. Department of Health and Human Resources/ASPE.

Lein, L., Benjamin, A., McManus, M., & Roy, K. (2002, August). *Economic roulette: When is a job not a job?* Paper presented at the annual meeting of the American Sociological Association, Chicago, IL.

Lennon, M. C., Blome, J., & English, K. (2002). Depression among women on welfare: A review of the literature. *Journal of American Medical Women's Association, 57*, 27–32.

Link, B. G., & Phelan, J. C. (1996). Editorial: Understanding sociodemographic differences in health—the role of fundamental social causes. *American Journal of Public Health, 86*, 471–473.

Loprest, P. (2003). *Use of government benefits increases among families leaving welfare. Snapshots of America's families*. Washington, DC: The Urban Institute.

Maret, E. G. (1982). How women's health affects labor force attachment. *Monthly Labor Review, 105*, 56–58.

Marks, N. F., & Choi, H. (2002). Social inequalities, psychological well-being, and health: Longitudinal evidence from a U.S. national study. *Research in the Sociology of Health Care, 20*, 79–106.

Mink, G. (2002). Valuing women's work. In G. Delgado (Ed.), *From poverty to punishment: How welfare reform punishes the poor*. Oakland, CA: Applied Research Center.

National Research Council. (2001). *New horizons in health: An integrative approach*. Committee on Future Directions for Behavioral and Social Sciences Research at the National Institutes of Health, Singer, B. H., & Ryff, C. D. (Eds). Washington, DC: National Academy Press.

Newman, K. S. (1999). *No shame in my game: The working poor in the inner city.* New York: Alfred A. Knopf, Russell Sage Foundation.

Newman, K. S. (2001). Hard times on 125th street: Harlem's poor confront welfare reform. *American Anthropologist, 103*(3), 762–778.

Olson, K., & Pavetti, L. (1997). *Personal and family challenges to the successful transition from welfare to work.* Washington, DC: The Urban Institute.

Piven, F. F. (2001). Welfare reform and the economic and cultural reconstruction of low wage labor markets. In J. Goode & J. Maskovsky (Eds.), *The new poverty studies: The ethnography of power, politics, and impoverished people in the United States* (pp. 135–151). New York: New York University Press.

Piven, F. F., Acker, J., Hallock, M., & Morgen, S. (2002). *Work, welfare and politics: Confronting poverty in the wake of welfare reform.* Eugene, OR: University of Oregon Press.

Renwick, T. J. (1998). *Poverty and single parent families: A study of minimal subsistence household budgets.* New York: Garland.

Repetti, R. K., Matthews, K., & Waldron, I. (1989). Employment and women's health: Effects of paid employment on women's mental and physical health. *American Psychologist, 44*(11), 1394–1401.

Schexnayder, D., Lein, L., Douglas, K., Dominguez, D., Schroeder, D., & Richards, F. (2002, January). *Texas families in transitions/surviving without TANF: An analysis of families diverted from or leaving TANF.* Ray Marshall Center for the Study of Human Resources and Center for Social Work Research, University of Texas at Austin.

Skinner, D., Slattery, E., Lachicotte, W., Cherlin, A., & Burton, L. M. (2002). *Disability, health coverage, and welfare reform.* Washington, DC: The Kaiser Commission on Medicaid and the Uninsured.

U.S. Department of Health and Human Services. (2001). The Surgeon General's call to action to prevent and decrease overweight and obesity. http://www.surgeongeneral.gov/topics/obesity/.

Vega, W. A., & Amaro, H. (1994). Latino outlook: Good health, uncertain prognosis. *Annual Review of Public Health, 15,* 39–47.

Wagner, S., Herr, T., Chang, C., & Brooks, D. (1998). *Five years of welfare: Too long? Too short? Lessons from project match's longitudinal tracking data.* Chicago: Project Match/Erikson Institute.

Williams, D. R. (2001). Racial variations in adult health status: Patterns, paradoxes, and prospects. In N. Smelser, W. J. Wilson, & F. Mitchell (Eds.), *America becoming: Racial trends and their consequences.* Washington, DC: National Academy of Sciences Press.

Williams, D. R., & Collins, C. (1995). U.S. socioeconomic and racial differences in health: Patterns and explanations. *Annual Review of Sociology, 29,* 349–386.

Wilson, W. J. (1987). *The truly disadvantaged: The inner city, the underclass, and public policy.* Chicago: University of Chicago Press.

Wilson, W. J. (2000). *When work disappears.* New York: Alfred Knopf.

Winston, P., Angel, R. J., Burton, L. M., Chase-Lansdale, P. L., Cherlin, A. J., Moffitt, R. A., & Wilson, W. J. (1999). *Welfare, children, and families: Overview and design.* Baltimore: Johns Hopkins University Press.

32

Global Transformations in Work and Family

Jody Heymann
Stephanie Simmons
Alison Earle
Harvard University

If you placed a pin on a world map for every study that has been conducted on working families, North America and Europe would be so littered with markers that there would be little room left to place any more. Although the clustering of markers in North America and Europe would hide critical disparities in the research evidence base—including gaps our research group and others have worked hard to help fill—created by the far greater number of studies on middle-class and professional families than on those living in poverty (Dodson & Bravo, 2004; Earle & Heymann, 2002; Heymann, 2000a, 2000b; Heymann & Earle, 1998, 1999, 2000), the map would accurately represent the dramatic differences in the amount of research conducted in industrialized and developing nations. Nowhere near as many studies have been conducted in the advanced economies of Asia and the Pacific as in North America and Europe, and there is a stark absence of evidence on the conditions working families face in developing economies in Asia, Latin America and Africa.

The limited attention that has been paid to conditions faced by working families in Latin America, Africa, and Asia to date is not a reflection of there being any less necessity to address the problems adults are facing as they seek to care for their families while sustaining an income in these regions. In fact, the problems working families face in poor countries are exacerbated by resource limitations. Moreover, the same demographic transformations that have brought work and family issues into the spotlight in North America and Europe are occurring globally.

The Project on Global Working Families (www.globalworkingfamilies. org), founded and directed by Heymann and built together with Earle, Simmons, and others, is the first program devoted to understanding and improving the relation between working conditions and family health and well-being globally. The project currently involves research in North America, Europe, Latin America, Africa, and Asia. The project has mapped global demographic changes in more than 170 countries, analyzed data from more than 55,000 closed-ended surveys in six countries in five regions, conducted and analyzed more than 1,000 in-depth interviews in six countries in five regions, and examined public policies in 168 countries.

This chapter summarizes findings from the in-depth interviews conducted by the Project on Global Working Families and places this volume's themes in a global context. We first briefly describe global demographic transformations before reviewing the primary data that the Project has collected and highlighting key findings. We next explore commonalities and disparities in the experiences of working families across countries in working conditions, availability to care for and be with children, and consequences for children's health and development. We discuss the policy issues raised by these findings and briefly introduce early findings from the project's study on the wide range of policy approaches currently underway in nations around the globe.

GLOBAL DEMOGRAPHIC TRANSFORMATIONS

Transformations in Labor Force Composition

Throughout human history, both mothers and fathers, in addition to rearing children, have been engaged in productive activity. In recent history, what has changed markedly is not that fathers and mothers work at multiple tasks, but that the location and nature of the work have changed. In North America and Europe between the mid-1800s and the end of the 1900s, dramatic transformations occurred in men's and women's labor. Men entered the wage and salary labor force in large numbers between 1830 and 1930; women entered the wage and salary labor force in similarly large numbers, but twice as fast in the second half of the 20th century (Hernandez, 1998; Hernandez

& Myers, 1993). Following on the heels of men's entry into the industrial and post-industrial labor force, the entry of the majority of women completed the transformation in how families came to meet their caregiving needs in these regions. Parents were increasingly working for pay away from their home and the children and adults for whom they were caring. Moreover, their work hours and conditions fell decreasingly under their own control and were increasingly dictated by supervisors and managers.

Similar transformations occurred in Latin America, Africa, and Asia during the 20th century. Although in many countries men and single women were the first to enter the formal labor force, married women also entered the labor force beginning in the latter half of the 20th century, taking them away from their families during the day. Between 1960 and 2000, the percentage of the labor force composed of women increased from 26% to 38% in the Caribbean, from 16% to 33% in Central America, from 17% to 25% in the Middle East, from 23% to 31% in North Africa, from 27% to 43% in Oceania, and from 21% to 35% in South America.

These changes in the nature and location of work brought with them both opportunities and risks. Most family members who worked the industrial and postindustrial labor force did so in an effort to improve incomes or at least to keep from falling into the pit of declining living standards. Moreover, the entry of more women into the wage and salary workforce created a real opportunity to address gender inequalities. Nevertheless, although these transformations offer hope that it is possible to address long-term gender inequities, such changes will only occur if the need to balance work responsibilities, childrearing, and family care is addressed. Without addressing these fundamental issues, the transformations in the labor force may instead simply mold gender and class inequalities into a new form.

Urbanization Trends

Accompanying changes in the labor force are marked changes in urbanization. Only 18% of the world's population lived in urban areas at the beginning of the 20th century. By the century's end, nearly one half of the world's population was urban (Brockerhoff, 2000; McNeill, 2000). The United Nations estimates that by the year 2030 more than 60% of the developing world's population will live in cities (United Nations Population Division, 2003). The urbanization of countries varies more than trends in the labor force participation of women. Some regions are still mostly rural, whereas others are quite urban. From 1950 to 2000, the percentage of the population living in urban areas increased from 15% to 37% in Africa, from 17% to 37% in Asia, from 51% to 73% in Europe, from 42% to 76% in Latin America and the Caribbean, from 64% to 79% in North America, and from 61% to 73% in

Oceania (United Nations Population Division, 2003). High variability can be found within some regions, such as East Asia, where national rates vary from 16% in Cambodia to 100% in Singapore. However, despite the individual variances, the overall trend worldwide is toward increasing urbanization.

Urbanization plays a key role in the changes that are occurring in community, work, and family life for several reasons. When individuals migrate to urban areas, they often move away from extended family (Aja, 2001; Bolak, 1997; Holmes-Eber, 1997). Even when extended families migrate together to urban areas, the available housing often restricts the ability of large, extended families to reside in one location. To subsist, families living in urban areas often require that many adults be in the paid workforce, and informal as well as formal work in urban areas is often designed in ways that make it hazardous, if not impossible, for children and other dependents to accompany adults to work even if the employer were to allow it.

Effect on Children and Families

The twin trends of urbanization and rising paid labor force participation in most of the world's developing regions mean that fewer adults are near their children or other family members during the workday. Even in rural areas, the transformation of the agricultural economy is pulling the spheres of work and home apart and dramatically changing how children and other family members are cared for.

As a result of these demographic changes, working families in the developing world are now facing work-family challenges similar to those faced by families in industrialized countries, but with two important differences: They are doing so with significantly higher caregiving burdens and far fewer resources. Age-dependency ratios—the ratio of children and elderly to working-age adults—tend to be 50% to 100% higher in the developing world than in industrialized countries (World Bank, 2002). In addition, illness rates for both common and serious diseases are higher in the developing world, further adding to the caregiving responsibilities of working adults.

Not only do working adults in the developing world bear greater caregiving burdens, but they also have far fewer resources to help them meet family needs. Family incomes are far lower, and most governments invest less in social services than those in Europe and North America—not just in absolute dollars, but also as a percentage of total public expenditures (World Bank, 2000). Part of the reason for this is that governments of developing countries face far higher debt burdens (United Nations Development Program, 2000).

What do these trends and transformations mean for the well-being of families globally? Our research suggests that the effects of the transformations in labor force participation and urbanization on child and adult health and on inequalities are critically influenced by working and social conditions (Heymann, 2000a, 2000b, 2002a, 2002b, 2003; Heymann & Earle, 1998, 1999, 2000, 2001; Heymann, Earle, & Egleston, 1996; Heymann, Fischer, & Engelman, 2003; Heymann, Toomey, & Furstenberg, 1999).

IN-DEPTH INTERVIEW STUDIES: EXPERIENCES OF WORKING PARENTS AND THEIR CHILDREN IN FIVE REGIONS

The Project on Global Working Families has interviewed working families, teachers, child-care providers, health care providers, and employers in a wide variety of global settings to examine the experiences of working adults and their families across social class, occupation, ethnicity, region, and economic and public policy contexts. The project developed semistructured, open-ended interview instruments to study the complex mechanisms by which families' work and social conditions affect children's health and development in a diverse group of nations.

Between 1996 and 2003, the Project on Global Working Families conducted more than 1,000 in-depth interviews in Mexico, Botswana, Vietnam, the United States, Russia, and Honduras. Working parents were interviewed in all six countries. We also interviewed child-care providers in Mexico, Botswana, Vietnam, Honduras, and the United States, and health care providers in Mexico, Botswana, Vietnam, and Honduras. Study sites were selected in each country to elicit the experiences of low- and middle-income parents using public services. In all countries where parents attending clinics were recruited for the study, the project took care to include a large number of clinics that served healthy and sick populations (including preventive pediatric, obstetric-gynecologic, and adult care).

In Botswana, the Project recruited participants in government health clinics in Gaborone, Lobatse, and Molepolole. The selected sites included a large, urban, public hospital that provided outpatient care to poor and middle-class families, a health facility that served a wide range of residents living in a small town, and a government-run medical center that served as a main referral center for the approximately 30 area clinics and outlying health posts in a rural area. The response rate in Botswana among parents was 96%.

In Vietnam, to obtain a sample of working parents in the Ho Chi Minh City area with a wide range of economic and living situations, the project team conducted and analyzed interviews from three sites. The sites included a large hospital for children, which serves both urban residents and residents from surrounding rural areas; a government-owned general hospital serving a population with diverse economic backgrounds; and the largest public teaching obstetrics and gynecology hospital. The response rate was 77% for the sample of mothers and 89% for the sample of fathers.

In Mexico, working caregivers visiting clinics in Mexico City and San Cristobal de las Casas, Chiapas, were invited to participate. The study included clinics from three sectors: public health, social security (IMSS), and insurance for state workers (ISSTE). Clinics were chosen to ensure variation in occupation, socioeconomic status (SES), family structure, and ethnicity. The sample included clinics serving public- and private-sector workers, low- and middle-income families, and indigenous and Latino populations. The overall response rate among parents was 87%.

In the United States, we conducted interviews at cities' public health clinics and in public housing projects. Of the parents from the public clinic invited to participate, 82% agreed to do so; of those, 95% completed both a closed-item survey and an in-depth semistructured interview.

We supplemented these studies with focused studies in Honduras and Russia. The project team conducted interviews in Honduras to examine the experience of working families in the long-term aftermath of natural disasters—in this case, Hurricane Mitch. Participants were recruited at shelters, in people's homes, medical clinics, and public day-care centers in the capital, Tegucigalpa, and in the rural towns of Sabana Grande, Monte Grande, Adurasta, San Lorenzo, Luare Abajo, Rosario, and El Chiflón. We conducted interviews and focus groups at the Russian Center for Public Opinion and Market Research (VCIOM) in Moscow to learn how the political, economic, and social transitions of the past decade have affected adults' abilities to get and keep jobs while caring for children and adult family members in need.

Disparities and Commonalities in Experiences

Despite the differences among the studied countries, we found striking commonalities across the interviews. While social and economic conditions influence the specific nature and details of conditions in each country, this research suggests that there are patterns in the experiences of working parents and their children which are common across cultures. We found, for example, that working parents living in poverty share many of the same concerns as other parents, even when dealing with crises, such as the aftermath of a natural disaster in Honduras or the AIDS epidemic in Botswana, or in adjusting to broad social transformations, such as economic liberalization in Russia or rapid industrialization in Vietnam. Working parents in all countries worried about the quality of their children's care when they were at work, their children's health, and how to help their children with schoolwork in the limited time available. The same workplace problems were raised in interviews from all countries: long hours, lack of paid leave, inflexibility, and evening and night shifts. In every country, we found examples of parents who, because of poor working conditions and inadequate supports, had to leave their children alone or in substandard care while they worked. In many cases, the similarities in the stories and experiences are so strong that the quotes from different countries on these topics are nearly indistinguishable after country identifiers are removed.

The Effects of Working Conditions on Children's Health and Educational Outcomes

Past studies primarily from industrialized countries have shown the importance to childhood outcomes of parental involvement in children's education and development (Callahan, Rademacher, & Hildreth, 1998; Fehrmann, Keith, & Reimers, 1987; Griffith, 1996; Iverson, Brownlee, & Walberg, 1981; Keith et al., 1993; Stevenson & Baker, 1987; van der Werf, Creemers, & Guldemond, 2001; World Bank, 1995) and health care (Bowlby, 1964; Coreil, Augustin, Halsey, & Holt, 1994; Kristensson-Hallstron, Elander, & Malmfors, 1997; Mahaffy, 1965; Palmer, 1993; Robertson, 1970; Streatfield & Singarimbun, 1988; Taylor & O'Connor, 1989; Van der Schyff, 1979). In our studies, parents in every country recognized the importance of their involvement in their children's education, but working conditions often made it impossible to help their children with their homework or meet with teachers, and they expressed concern that their children's school performance was suffering. Similarly, parents' poor working conditions—such as facing penalties for taking any time off work—often prevented them from providing the most basic level of health care, including taking their children to the doctor when they fell ill. The conflict between work and caregiving had marked consequences for children's education and health.

Lack of Child Care and Its Effects on Education and Development

Unaffordable and inaccessible child care left too many parents with no choice but to delegate caregiving to older children, especially girls. This was particularly true in poor and single-parent households. Parents expressed deep concern about having to take older children out of school to provide care for younger siblings, cousins, and other children in the family, knowing that their short- and long-term educational opportunities were being put at risk. Kereng (the names have been changed to protect confidentiality), a mother of four in Botswana, knew that asking her older daughter to help with the housework and care for her younger siblings, including one with severe cerebral palsy, was impeding her studies. However, Kereng had no other options. She worked long hours as a maid and could not afford to hire help. "The problem is with the older one. When she comes to my work, I give her the keys and tell her, 'Do a, b, and c when you get home.' I think this is affecting her school work. It's just too much for a kid of her age to do. But I have no choice."

In Vietnam, Anh Dao had been relying on her 13-year-old daughter to care for her two younger children for years. She, too, worried about the effect this additional burden was having on her daughter, but her income as a hired laborer made any other option unrealistic. "I have pity for her. . . . Inside the home there are a lot of tasks. My eldest daughter did everything. She cooked, washed the clothes, wiped the floors." The impact was not limited to daughters. In Russia, Faina's schedule at a manufacturing plant meant that her son had been responsible for his younger sister since he was 10. "The son is one hour late for his classes, unfortunately. He does have such problems: sometimes he is late, sometimes he fails to go school that particular day. He is responsible for his sister."

The effect on older children's education and welfare of having to provide care for younger family members was seen in Central and South America, as well as in Africa and Asia. In Mexico, Petra's oldest daughter filled in for her, caring for her four younger siblings when Petra was at work doing laundry in other people's homes.

> So the girl cares for her brothers and sisters when I go out . . . to earn money. I go out to wash and they stay in the house. She gives them breakfast, cares for them, bathes them, puts their little clothes on. The girl. That's what my daughter does. . . . I tell them not to leave and they stay in the house and I bring them food. That's what I have done. Yeah, I leave them home alone because there's no other way. I don't have anyone to lend me a hand.

In Honduras, 10-year-old Ramon cared for five younger siblings in a temporary shelter for victims of Hurricane Mitch. His parents worked long hours every day, struggling to earn enough to rebuild the family home. Ramon had already been held back in school because of the months he missed while caring for his siblings.

Insufficient Parental Availability

Even when children had adult care providers, parents also often felt they had inadequate time with their children. For many parents, the long hours required to make a living meant that they could not be as involved as they would have liked in their children's education and development. In the worst cases, parents' work demands meant they rarely saw their children awake. Felicia, a Mexican mother of two who worked as an administrator, expressed a common regret that she was missing her daughters' childhood:

> When I come home and they're sleeping I start crying. Because I feel like I'm wasting the best years of my daughters' lives. . . . They are going to grow up and

they are going to leave. And they are going to make their own lives and pass through my hands like a bird that has flown.

Bame, a mother of three who works as an administrative supervisor in Botswana, also desperately wanted to spend more time with her children. As a single mother, the pressure on her to both earn enough to meet her family's basic needs and provide all caregiving was immense:

> Mostly, I'd love to be with my children, to talk with them, to laugh with them. I'd like to hear about their daily life and I'd like it if I could have spent more time with my daughter, hearing about her progress at school. I can't do that to my satisfaction. I've not had time with my other son, either—I don't have time to sit and talk with him.

Luis, a low-income, single parent living in the United States, had few extended family members he could call on to help him when he had to work overtime and nights to make ends meet. He had little time regularly with his children—8-year-old Carlos and 5-year-old Yolanda—and even less ability to take time off from his job as a security guard to meet unpredictable needs. He wanted to visit his children's school regularly, but could not afford to do so when each visit meant losing time from work, losing income, and having more trouble paying the bills. On most days, he saw his children for less than 1 hour.

In all countries we studied, we found working parents who face conflicts between work and being involved with their children's education. Two thirds of respondents mentioned barriers that prevented them from being as involved as they would like to be. (Percentages cited in this section represent the percentage of working parents interviewed on the subject in the representative samples in Mexico, Botswana, and Vietnam.) Work that prevented parents from being available to school-age children in the evenings—because of the long hours, evening shifts, or fatigue—limited the help children received with homework and developmental issues. Because Akayeng, a cook and mother of a 10-year-old in Botswana, often had to work the night shift, her son was already asleep when she got home. "Sometimes when I wake up in the morning, he comes to me and says, 'I have this homework.' So that's the major problem. . . . Maybe because I'm away all the time, he hasn't done much with school." In Vietnam, Le Thu's long hours similarly interfered with her intentions to help her child with his schoolwork:

> Teaching my child, I'm too tired. There's the economic part of it, and then there's the influence of my work. So I'm exhausted and I can't make it a reality; I can't teach my child in a complete way. I really want to, but I can't.

Thatayone, a father of three in Botswana who worked long hours as a clothing salesman, worried that his children would make poor choices because he lacked time to spend with them. He said, "I do not have enough time to spend with them at home and to guide them." In Honduras, Laura echoed, "Children aren't raised well when one has to work all the time." In Mexico, Violeta was asked by her 4-year-old, "Mom, where do you live? You leave in the morning when we are still asleep and you come back when we are asleep again."

Health Risks to Children Due to Parents' Working Conditions

Across countries, children's health also suffered when parents had to work long hours with little flexibility or leave. Again the greatest burden fell on poor households. Among poor respondents, 60% reported difficulties caring for children when they were sick because of work responsibilities, whereas 48% of nonpoor respondents reported such difficulty.

Many respondents spoke of difficulty getting leave to care for their sick or injured children. Viktoriya, a Russian mother, was rearing two boys while working as a dispatcher. "My child is sick and I would be happy to stay home, but I need money. I cannot take even one day in a week, because I am afraid that I will be fired." In Botswana, Bame was told by her supervisor, "Madam, it's either you work for your children or you work for this company. You have to decide whether you still want to work or whether you want to nurse your child." Needing income to provide the basic necessities for her family, she felt she had no choice but to leave her sick child home alone. Many American working parents we interviewed had faced similar decisions. Elizabeth, a mother of three, described her experience: "I was a secretary at a bank and I lost it because of [my daughter] being so sick with asthma I was out so much. . . . It was a choice, either the job or my child, and I picked my child."

Viktoriya, Bame, and Elizabeth were far from alone in having to make the untenable choice between keeping a desperately needed job and leaving a sick child in inadequate care. Silvia, a Mexican single mother of three and a cleaner, explained why she had to leave her 9-year-old son with his 12-year-old sister. "What else can I do . . . if I care for him I lose my job. So I can't care for him. So he has to stay here. They care for each other." In Botswana, Neo faced the same choice between her child's health and her work as a cleaner. Her 10-year-old daughter had epilepsy, but Neo had to leave her alone:

> Sometimes when I'm not there and she's alone and when I get home, I see that she's had her fits . . . she doesn't look well. Sometimes she looks like she's very tired. I'll ask her, "What happened?" and she'll say, "I've been falling down." Sometimes she'll be walking on the road and she'll just fall down. People who are walking by will pick her up and take her home.

While time to care for sick children is critical, parents also play an essential role in the preventive health care of their children. The leading killers of children and youth worldwide include vaccine-preventable diseases, diarrhea, respiratory infections, perinatal problems, and accidents and injuries (United Nations Children's Fund, 2001). Parents' potential role in preventing these is enormous. In our interviews, however, parents were often unable to leave work to take their children to preventive health care visits or to ensure children were cared for in environments where the chances of illness and injury were reduced. In the United States, Sofia feared she would lose her job if she took time off, so she would only ask for leave if her children were seriously ill. "I'm afraid to take days off . . . if [the kids are] really bad, I call the doctor's and schedule an appointment to see them. But I always try to do it at the end of work so I don't miss too much." Elena, a mother of two who worked as a courier in Russia, saw her children's health deteriorate when she could not take them for recommended treatments. "[Their] health isn't that good, due to . . . not always doing the prescribed procedures, for example, the child needs to be brought to physiotherapy. . . . Sometimes you really can't make it, so you don't bring them." In Botswana, Tshwanelo, a court reporter, sometimes put off taking her son to the doctor because of fear of repercussions at work. "Some supervisors are difficult. When you ask for time off, they feel like you are imposing on them. It is very difficult to ask for permission."

When parents had to leave their children alone or in the care of other children, serious accidents often occurred. Although the nature of the accidents varied with the countries' levels of development, children experienced serious accidents and injuries in every country we studied. In the United States, Carolyn, a school social worker, faced a gap in care when her children were home alone after school.

> [My children] had about 20 minutes to be here alone until I came home. During that 20 minutes, there was an accident that happened. There's some glass doors that go between here and the living room. They were fooling around together. Cassie tried to lock Troy out, and he pushed against the glass door. There must have been a fissure in the glass or something, but it broke and his arm went right through. He really cut himself.

Lan, a Vietnamese agricultural worker with two sons, ages 11 and 6, reported that her 6-year-old son had fallen into a well while playing with neighborhood children while she was at work. Another time her children had been "so happily playing with one another that they just ran out of the house really fast, and one child was struck by a vehicle." He was hospitalized for several days. Thatayaone, a father in Botswana, feared for his son's safety while he was home alone, and his fears had recently been realized when his son was hit by a car. "He was trying to go to the other side of the road. . . . A transport car, a taxi, ran over him, and we were informed that he got in a car accident. By the time they informed us he was already in so much pain he couldn't stand it."

In Honduras, Eva was rearing her five children, ages 4 to 14, on the meager earnings she made washing and ironing the clothes of several families. Her children had suffered numerous injuries while home alone. Her daughters had been left with her son (age 14) when one of the preschool girls climbed a ladder, fell, and fractured her skull. When her son was 7 and was caring for his 3-year-old sister, they went off alone to buy some food. Her daughter had a serious fall off one of the hillsides and broke her leg. Another time a daughter cut the tip off her finger as she tried to cook. She sliced all the way through the nerves.

In Botswana, fires and burns were common when children were left alone, as they tried to cook for themselves and their siblings. Nunuko, a maid and a mother of seven, lost everything when her children tried to cook while she was at work.

> They were cooking . . . using the gas stove. I think they switched one button on but didn't light the stove. I can't say what happened, but whatever they did, the whole house was in flames. Everything was burned out. We didn't take a single item out of the house and when I got back from work, I found that what used to be a house was now in ashes.

Lebogang, mother of two in Botswana who worked at a dry cleaner's, was at work when her daughter was severely burned. "When they come back from school, they are alone and I am not there. It was cold that day and they were trying to warm themselves at the fire. Somehow, she fell in the fire and got burned. . . . I found her when I knocked off . . . there were no combis to take me to the hospital."

POLICY ISSUES RAISED BY EXPERIENCES OF WORKING FAMILIES

Our research suggests that working parents worldwide face many of the same challenges. Common themes run through the interviews: Parents need more time to spend with their children, they need to be able to care for their children when they are sick, and they need to ensure their children are succeeding in school. Working parents need more flexibility at work so they can take their children to the doctor for acute illnesses or checkups or so they can meet with their child's teacher. They need access to paid leave when their children are ill so they do not have to leave them alone or in the care of other children.

In meeting these challenges, many working adults face two fundamental problems—discrimination in caring for their families and lack of decent working conditions—which lead to profound economic disadvantages and can have devastating effects on the health and welfare of their families. In terms of fundamental working conditions, many of the worst experiences that we documented could have been avoided if working adults had had decent conditions and simple services, including leave to care for newborn infants and newly adopted children; leave to meet the health needs of all age children and dependent adults; working hours and schedules that allow adults to succeed at work while still caring for family members; wages that are adequate so the total number of hours adults have to work to survive and exit poverty do not preculde them from caring for their families and themselves; and affordable, quality child and elder care which recognizes that in the current global economy, it is not feasible for many men and women to provide care solely by themselves.

How have societies responded to the dramatic changes in the location and nature of work and family caregiving, and what is the effect of these changes on the health and well-being of children? There are at least two important components to understanding how both individual nations and the global community have responded to the historic transformations that have occurred. First, it is important to examine the changes in public policy, both at the level of international agreements and national law. Second, it is critical to analyze whether these public policy changes have been effectively implemented. We are developing a global Work, Family, and Equity Index to answer these questions.

The first step in developing this Index has been to examine international and national policy. The policies covered in the Index address the full spectrum of working families' needs, including those described in our qualitative research: parental availability on a routine basis, parental availability to care for sick children, and parental availability to address children's educational and developmental needs. There are important findings from the first phase of the Work, Family and Equity Index in two areas. First, it is clear from a review of a wide range of international conventions that it is possible to reach widespread global agreement on many of the working conditions and services that are needed, even in a context of important cultural, economic, social, and political differences. Second, there have been valuable advances in legislative policy in several areas that are reviewed below.

Although there are many weak points in key policy areas, there are successes as well. Much attention has been paid to the successes of northern European countries in the area of work-family policy. While analyzing these advances is important, it is equally critical to examine the steps that poorer countries and those in other parts of the world have taken to improve conditions. Successes and failures can be found in every region of the world and at every economic level.

Maternity protection was one of the first labor standards adopted by the International Labor Organization (ILO) in 1919. The importance of paid maternity leave was reiterated by the current ILO Convention on Maternity

Protection (No. 183 of 2000), the United Nations Convention on the Elimination of All Forms of Discrimination Against Women (CEDAW), and the International Covenant on Economic, Social, and Cultural Rights (ICESCR). Globally, progress has been made on maternity leave. One hundred sixty-three countries have guaranteed paid leave for women surrounding childbirth.

Rights related to work are also included in the fundamental United Nations Human Rights Accords. The Universal Declaration of Human Rights—accepted, in theory, by 171 countries—specifies the right to reasonable limitation of working hours and paid leave. ILO Convention 132, the Holidays with Pay Convention, provides for paid annual holidays of at least 3 weeks. At least 96 countries, in all geographic regions and at all economic levels, have laws mandating paid annual leave. At least 84 countries have laws that fix the maximum length of the work week, either by setting upper limits for the total number of weekly hours or the amount of overtime that can be worked in a certain period. At least 98 countries require employers to provide a mandatory day of rest—a period of at least 24 hours off each week.

Although certain policy areas critical to the well-being of working families have been addressed globally, many others have not. Most countries do not guarantee paid leave to care for sick children and adult family members, or for children's educational needs. Most countries do not guarantee child care for children under age 3 or provide enough paid leave for parents to care for them themselves. In addition, we found that less than one half of all countries have antidiscrimination legislation protecting older adults and the disabled. Ensuring these basic conditions should be a priority for employers, governments, and international organizations. They are essential to addressing poverty and long-term gender and class inequalities.

There is significant variance across countries in terms of the amount of enforcement of legislation. While it may be argued that without enforcement legislation and policies will have limited effects, having protective legislation in place is a necessary first step toward improving working conditions. Single firms may develop improved workplace policies on their own initiative, but their voluntary efforts are unlikely to result in universal coverage for employees. Even when benefits to society would be significant, firms have little incentive to improve working conditions and benefits. In fact, there is often a disincentive if the company must bear the cost while its competitors may choose not to provide any coverage. Legislation is thus necessary to increase the likelihood of implementation even if the policy is not fully enforced. At a minimum, having legislation in place can support workers' demands for better treatment.

To date, basic workplace standards that allow workers to care well for their families have not been met for a majority of the world's population. Many of the most critical standards, however, have been recognized across nations, political systems, economic conditions, and cultures through international agreements and, in particular, in a series of United Nations declarations and treaties and ILO standards. Although these international agreements provide a critical first step, this impressive list of conventions contrasts starkly with the conditions many workers with family responsibilities are facing worldwide, as documented by our research. The international agreements demonstrate that consensus can be reached across wide-ranging political, economic, social, and cultural contexts. However, the frequently devastating conditions families face will only change when the conventions are translated into meaningful legislation that is enforced, when policies are fully implemented and followed, and when quality programs and services are affordable and accessible to all.

CONCLUSION

In summary, dramatic transformations in the nature and location of work, the composition of the labor force, the extent of urban residency, and the availability of extended family have transpired globally. Although some of these transformations have the potential to improve standards of living and equity, the potential will only be realized if the marked gender and class disparities in opportunities to succeed at work while rearing children are addressed. None of these transformations is limited geographically to western or northern countries or economically to advanced economies. They affect all developing and industrialized economies in Asia, Latin America, Africa, and Oceania, as well as North America and Europe. As a result, the dilemmas facing working parents and their children have become truly global.

The Project on Global Working Families has carried out the first studies to conduct parallel, in-depth interviews of working parents in five regions around the world. While historical and socioeconomic differences affect the experiences of working parents and their children in relevant ways across the countries studied, more striking than the differences are the vast commonalities in the families' experiences. In all five regions, parents reported significant effects on children's health and development when parents worked extended hours or shifts; when lack of leave and inflexibility at work forced them to choose between addressing their children's health and developmental needs and keeping their jobs; when the lack of adequate child care led to serious accidents and injuries; and when the unavailability of adult care meant that young children had to be pulled out of school to care for preschool siblings.

If it is clear that the challenges are global, it is equally clear that the policy and program solutions need to be global. Countries today vary widely in their approaches to the issues. The Project on Global Working Families is currently examining the policy and program response in various nations to the needs of working families. The early findings are illuminating both with regard to how much has been accomplished to date and how much remains to be done. Most countries currently regulate overtime hours, but far fewer nations have policies that address mandatory evening and night shifts, which particularly affect the ability of parents to spend time with school-age children. Some countries have excellent policies to ensure that working parents can take leave from work to care for sick children, but many countries have no policies that address preventive health needs, and even fewer have policies to address the educational and developmental needs of children. Labor codes that address the needs of working parents and their children are only the first step. Ensuring implementation in the formal sector and extending coverage to jobs in the informal sector are critical components to any truly effective solution.

Individual nations clearly can take, and have taken, important steps to improve the lives of working parents and their children. Yet in the context of global economic competition, it is becoming increasingly difficult for individual nations to act alone and increasingly important to address the needs of working families globally.

REFERENCES

Aja, E. (2001). Urbanization imperatives in Africa: Nigerian experience. *Philosophy & Social Action, 27*, 13–22.

Bolak, H. C. (1997). Marital power dynamics: Women providers and working-class households in Istanbul. In J. Gugler (Ed.), *Cities in the developing world: Issues, theory, and policy* (pp. 218–247). Oxford and New York: Oxford University Press.

Bowlby, J. (1964). *Child care and the growth of love*. London: Pelican.

Brockerhoff, M. P. (2000). An urbanizing world. *Population Bulletin, 55*, 3–44.

Callahan, K., Rademacher, J., & Hildreth, B. (1998). The effect of parent participation in strategies to improve the homework performance of students who are at risk. *Remedial and Special Education, 19*, 131–141.

Coreil, J., Augustin, A., Halsey, N. A., & Holt, E. (1994). Social and psychological costs of preventive child health services in Haiti. *Social Science and Medicine, 38*, 231–238.

Dodson, L., & Bravo, E. (in press). When there is no time or money: Work, family, and community lives of low-income families. In J. Heymann & C. Beem (Eds.), *Societal crossroads: Striving for democracy and equality in an era of working families*. New York: The New Press.

Earle, A., & Heymann, S. J. (2002). What causes job loss among former welfare recipients? The role of family health problems. *Journal of the American Medical Women's Association, 57*, 5–10.

Fehrmann, P., Keith, T., & Reimers, T. (1987). Home influences on school learning: Direct and indirect effects of parental involvement on high school grades. *Journal of Educational Research, 80*, 330–337.

Griffith, J. (1996). Relation of parental involvement, empowerment, and school traits to student academic performance. *Journal of Educational Research, 90*, 33–41.

Hernandez, D. (1998). Children's changing access to resources: A historical perspective. In K. Hansen & A. Garey (Eds.), *Families in the U.S.: Kinship and domestic politics* (pp. 201–215). Philadelphia, PA: Temple University Press.

Hernandez, D., & Myers, D. (1993). *America's children: Resources from family, government, and the economy*. New York: Russell Sage Foundation.

Heymann, S. J. (2000a). What happens during and after school: Conditions faced by working parents living in poverty and their school-age children. *Journal of Children and Poverty, 6*, 5–20.

Heymann, S. J. (2000b). *The widening gap: Why working families are in jeopardy and what can be done about it*. New York: Basic Books.

Heymann, S. J. (2002a). Low-income parents and the time famine. In S. A. Hewlett, N. Rankin, & C. West (Eds.), *Taking parenting public: The case for a new social movement* (pp. 103–116). Lanham, MD: Rowman & Littlefield.

Heymann, S. J. (2002b, November–December). Social transformations and their implications for the global demand for ECCE. *UNESCO Policy Briefs on Early Childhood, 8*, 1–2.

Heymann, S. J. (2003, June). The impact of AIDS on early childhood care and education. *UNESCO Policy Briefs on Early Childhood, 14*, 1–2.

Heymann, S. J., & Earle, A. (1998). The work family balance: What hurdles are parents leaving welfare likely to confront? *Journal of Policy Analysis and Management, 17*, 312–321.

Heymann, S. J., & Earle, A. (1999). The impact of welfare reform on parents' ability to care for their children's health. *American Journal of Public Health, 89*, 502–505.

Heymann, S. J., & Earle, A. (2000). Low-income parents: How do working conditions affect their opportunity to help school-age children at risk? *American Educational Research Journal, 37*, 833–848.

Heymann, S. J., & Earle, A. (2001). The impact of parental working conditions on school-age children: The case of evening work. *Community, Work and Family, 4*, 305–325.

Heymann, S. J., Earle, A., & Egleston, B. (1996). Parental availability for the care of sick children. *Pediatrics, 98*, 226–230.

Heymann, S. J., Fischer, A., & Engelman, M. (2003). Labor conditions and the health of children, elderly and disabled family members. In S. J. Heymann (Ed.), *Global inequalities at work: Work's impact on the health of individuals, families, and societies* (pp. 75–104). New York: Oxford University Press.

Heymann, S. J., Toomey, S., & Furstenberg, F. (1999). Working parents: What factors are involved in their ability to take time off from work when their children are sick? *Archives of Pediatrics & Adolescent Medicine, 153*, 870–874.

Holmes-Eber, P. (1997). Migration, urbanization, and women's kin networks in Tunis. *Journal of Comparative Family Studies, 28*, 54–73.

Iverson, B., Brownlee, G., & Walberg, H. (1981). Parent-teacher contacts and student learning. *Journal of Educational Research, 74*, 394–396.

Keith, T., Keith, P., Troutman, G., Bickley, P., Trivette, P., & Singh, K. (1993). Does parental involvement affect eighth-grade student achievement? Structural analysis of national data. *School Psychology Review, 22*, 474–476.

Kristensson-Hallstron, I., Elander, G., & Malmfors, G. (1997). Increased parental participation on a pediatric surgical daycare unit. *Journal of Clinical Nursing, 6*, 297–302.

Mahaffy, P. (1965). The effects of hospitalization on children admitted for tonsillectomy and adenoidectomy. *Nursing Review, 14*, 12–19.

McNeill, J. R. (2000). *Something new under the sun: An environmental history of the twentieth-century world*. New York: W. W. Norton & Company.

Palmer, S. J. (1993). Care of sick children by parents: A meaningful role. *Journal of Advanced Nursing, 18*, 185.

Robertson, J. (1970). *Young children in hospital*. London: Tavistock.

Stevenson, D., & Baker, D. (1987). The family-school relation and the child's school performance. *Child Development, 58*, 1348–1357.

Streatfield, K., & Singarimbun, M. (1988). Social factors affecting the use of immunization in Indonesia. *Social Science and Medicine, 27*, 1237–1245.

Taylor, M. R. H., & O'Connor, P. (1989). Resident parents and shorter hospital stay. *Archives of Disease in Childhood, 64*, 274–276.

United Nations Children's Fund (UNICEF). (2001). *The state of the world's children, 2001*. New York: Author.

United Nations Development Program (UNDP). (2000). *Human development report*. New York: Oxford University Press.

United Nations Population Division. (2003). *World Population Prospects: The 2002 Revision Population Database*. Available at: http://esa.un.org/unpp/. Accessed: May 7, 2004.

van der Werf, G., Creemers, B., & Guldemond, H. (2001). Improving parental involvement in primary education in Indonesia: Implementation, effects, and costs. *School Effectiveness & School Improvement, 12*, 447–466.

Van der Schyff, G. (1979). The role of parents during their child's hospitalization. *Australian Nursing Journal, 8*, 57–61.

World Bank. (1995). *Priorities and strategies for education: A World Bank review. Development in practice series*. Washington, DC: Author.

World Bank. (2000). *World development report*. New York: Author.

World Bank. (2002). *World development indicators*. Washington, DC: Author.

PART VIII

Conclusion

33

Forging the Future
in Work, Family, Health,
and Well-Being Research

Lynne M. Casper
National Institute of Child Health and Human Development

Suzanne M. Bianchi
University of Maryland

Rosalind Berkowitz King
National Institute of Child Health and Human Development

Demographic, sociological, technological, and economic changes occurring in the United States in the latter half of the 20th century dramatically altered family life, the nature of work, and the conditions of employment (Christensen 2002, 2005; Sayer, Cohen, & Casper, 2004). The contemporary situation presents new challenges for men and women attempting to balance the ever more complex demands of family and work and for employers attempting to adjust to changes in the economy, the nature of work, and the workforce (see chapter 10 in Casper & Bianchi, 2002). Jobs have shifted from the manufacturing and agricultural sectors to the service sector. Rising rates of divorce and out-of-wedlock childbearing have led to a dramatic increase in the prevalence of single-parent families. Today, nearly two thirds of single parents work.[1] Changes in the economy mean that both adults in many married-couple households must work in order to earn a living wage. As Kathleen Christensen explains in the Foreword to this volume, these changes have created a workforce–workplace mismatch in which work and family obligations are in direct competition for many families.

Given these changes, the challenges of integrating work and family can be daunting. Workers are torn among their roles as parents, spouses, and providers, often feeling pressured for both time and money. Stress caused by this friction often has negative effects on the health of the workers and their families. These stresses have a tendency to spill over to other social and community institutions not designed or sufficiently funded to deal with them—schools, social service agencies, police, courts, and religious institutions. Employers with workers facing difficulties at home suffer the high costs of turnover, absenteeism, and lost investments in human capital.

The chapters in this volume allow us to take stock of where we are, point us in the directions we need to go to further research in this area, and suggest solutions to deal with the work–family dilemma that can ultimately improve the health and well-being of workers, their families, employers, and even communities. Many of the chapters in this volume have provided answers to the question of what contributes to work-family conflict, including the lack of flexibility in work schedules, the need for families and employers to accomplish more with less, and the lack of social and policy supports that could address these conflicts. Some chapters have suggested ways in which work-family dilemmas can affect workers' health and well-being and can overflow to affect other family members and employers. Other chapters have provided us with theoretical lenses with which to examine these problems, and still others have suggested tools for improving the quality of research in this area.

Many important conclusions can be drawn from this volume. First and foremost, it highlights the importance of multidisciplinary work on the topic of work, family, health, and well-being. Scholars are trained in distinct disciplinary traditions, each tending to frame work-family issues in their own disciplinary perspective and each using their field's preferred methodological tool kit for investigating research questions. Because these chapters represent different disciplinary traditions, they illustrate in sharp relief the uniqueness and utility of approaching work, family, health, and well-being from a multidisciplinary perspective. The chapters discussing psychological perspectives point to the importance of understanding the individual in studying work-family conflict. Economists and sociologists view interactions as important whether they occur between spouses, managers and employees, or parents

---

[1] See Sayer, Cohen, and Casper (2004) for an excellent summary of these social, economic, demographic, and policy changes.

and children. Anthropological and sociological perspectives teach us that it is sometimes necessary to examine the complexities of everyday activities as people experience them and the meanings individuals attach to these activities to develop theories to explain social phenomena and individual behaviors. The authors who bring perspectives from business schools, labor and industrial relations, management sciences, and public policy remind us that understanding the workplace—how it is organized, how it operates, and how people operate within it—is essential to understanding how work can lead to work-family conflict, and hence to detrimental health and well-being outcomes of both workers and employers. Epidemiological and health sciences perspectives (a) teach us just how complicated the relations among work, family, and health can be, and (b) map out the pathways through which work and family circumstances can affect health.

Second, the volume also points to the crucial topic areas of work-family research and illustrates how all of them are essential for improving research in the area. For example, scholars who explore the important topic of time allocation within families and the activities of everyday life show us the challenges individuals face in meeting work, family, and life demands and can help pinpoint sources of stress. By contrast, studies that focus on the workplace demonstrate how work conditions, structures, and cultures can contribute to work-family conflict and can point to policies and practices that may alleviate these sources of conflict. Studies that focus on health and well-being outcomes related to work or family inform us of the important health and well-being outcomes that may be affected by work-family conflict. By themselves, each of these areas of research provides important pieces of information, but it is only through combining and synthesizing them that one is able to put all of the pieces together to reveal a holistic image of the work, family, and health puzzle.

Without considering all of these disciplinary perspectives and all of these research topics, work-family scholars run the risk of incorrectly framing important research questions, thereby missing the crucial links among work, family, health, and well-being, or conducting research that answers only part of the question. Research that progresses along disciplinary tracks will undoubtedly contribute new insights into work, family, and health research, but it is unlikely to move us very far down the path of explaining exactly how work-family conflict affects health and well-being and what, if anything, can be done to lessen the sources of conflict and improve health.

Third, the volume underscores the importance of considering the contexts in which people live out their work and family lives. Contextual influences include such factors as race; class; culture; the economy; characteristics of the industry, the employer, the occupation, the worker's family, and the community; and policy at multiple levels, including employer administrative policies and broader local, state, or federal policies. Although disciplines often have their own lexicon for describing contexts and differ in their conceptualizations of just how contexts operate to influence behavior, the vast majority of chapters in this volume emphasize the importance of context in understanding the relations among work, family, health, and well-being.

Contexts are alternately viewed as shaping, delimiting, or influencing people's relationships, decisions, actions, inactions, or behaviors. In examining work and family processes, anthropologists focus mainly on culture; economists tend to stress macroeconomic conditions and the role of constraints in shaping decision making; sociologists stress social stratification by characteristics such as race, class, and education and the influence of socially constructed institutions (e.g., education, family, work); developmental psychologists focus on the family, school, and child care; researchers in disciplines that study organizations including management sciences, industrial-organizational psychology, economics, and sociology stress the culture and organization of the workplace; demographers, epidemiologists, and health scientists are concerned with the demographic context and, increasingly, with social and economic contexts as well; and public policy scholars focus on the law, regulations, and social policies and programs. This list is not meant to be inclusive of all the contexts each discipline views as important, but rather is illustrative of the importance researchers place on context across fields and the broad range of factors they consider to be significant.

If one wants to truly understand the interconnections of work, family, health, and well-being, this volume suggests that a careful consideration of these and other contexts is mandatory. Just listing the various contexts points to the complexity of the theories, conceptual models, and methodologies that would be needed to greatly advance research in the work, family, health, and well-being area. The complexity grows exponentially if one considers that individual factors and multiple levels of contextual factors may act alone or in combination to influence work-family conflict and health outcomes.

Fourth, the volume illustrates the difficulty of establishing causal connections between work and family lives as well as health and well-being outcomes. Researchers who specialize in research design argue that the strongest proof of a causal relationship is obtained through experiments that randomly assign people to receive a treatment (Shadish, Cook, & Campbell, 2002). In studies that examine how work-family conflict affects health and well-being, as in all studies that seek to explain human behavior, a random assignment of individuals to families or jobs is not possible. Thus, researchers generally turn to other less powerful methods such as meta-analyses in which the researchers assemble a body of scientific evidence across studies. As Shadish, Cook, and Campbell (2002) noted, meta-analyses and the utilization of quasi-experimental designs play an important role in attempting to establish causation. Yet they encourage researchers to explore ways to incorporate as many elements of the randomized experiment into their designs as possible.

For example, although randomization across employees is generally not possible for methodological, ethical, or other reasons, randomization across worksites in a firm with multiple locations may be possible. Randomization at the worksite level may even be facilitated by variations in state policy or the opening of a new office.

Standards of evidence to establish causality also differ across disciplines, and the wide range of disciplinary perspectives represented in the volume helps illustrate why causal inferences are hard to come by in work, family, health, and well-being research. If research questions are framed with disciplinary biases that are subsequently explored using methodologies that are favored in that discipline, important explanatory variables or causal processes may not be correctly modeled. When this happens, replication and generalization of research results across studies are nearly impossible. This inability to replicate and generalize findings across studies severely weakens the body of scholarly evidence researchers rely on to establish causality.

Some of the chapters in this volume discuss the thorny issue of determining causal relationships, and some even discuss different ways to improve study designs and analytical techniques to strengthen the evidence for causal relationships. The volume also suggests that we can improve studies by engaging in multidisciplinary research. However, the issue of establishing causality in work, family, and health research, in particular, and research that involves human behavior, in general, is not likely to be resolved any time soon and should be taken seriously if we hope to significantly advance science in this area.

Fifth, the volume reminds us that work and family challenges and health issues vary tremendously across families. Low-income families often have only one adult who must provide income and care for dependent family members. Many of these families are in low-wage jobs that, in addition to providing little income as the label implies, typically do not provide health insurance or other family-friendly benefits and usually do not allow for the flexibility in scheduling that many of these families need to care for their loved ones. In these families, many adults must hold down more than one job to make ends meet. In many low-income families, one or more members of the household—parents, their children, and other family members—suffers from serious chronic health problems. These members require expensive prescription medications, intensive caregiving from relatives, and numerous trips to the doctor's office. The primary earners in these families often miss work to care for other family members or when they are ill themselves. These frequent absences can result in dismissal from the job. Thus, these families are often caught between a rock and hard place, needing enough earnings to provide for the health and well-being of their families and needing enough time to care for family members and themselves. Occupational injuries and substance abuse can also interfere with a family's ability to meet its financial and caregiving obligations.

The volume has also shown us that the work, family, and health challenges that families face vary over the life course. Young families typically have young dependent children who require round-the-clock care and supervision. Midlife families may be sandwiched between the financial and caregiving demands of their children and their parents. Young singles face the bleak prospects of the spiraling costs of higher education, as well as landing and keeping a good job in a market that provides few good entry-level positions. The impact of these challenges often varies by gender and race. Women generally participate more than men in caregiving for children and elderly parents. Further, the greater average family size and greater prevalence of disabling health conditions among minorities compared with Whites mean that the burden of caregiving falls most heavily on minority women.

Challenges also vary over the life courses of children and caregivers. Infants require the provision of specialized food in the form of breast milk or formula and regular well-baby visits to the doctor for preventive health care. Elementary school-age children require parental help with homework to build a solid academic foundation and adult supervision in the hours after school. Adolescents place fewer demands on caregivers in the sense that the adolescents may be able to care for themselves or participate in extracurricular activities during the time when they are not in the classroom. However, they require a delicate balance of supervision and autonomy that an overworked parent may find difficult to achieve. A parent going overboard in the direction of too much freedom may facilitate inappropriate risk-taking, whereas a parent going overboard in the direction of too little freedom may hinder the child's development.

Finally, most chapters called for changes in the workplace and in government policies that would enable people to better integrate the demands of work and family life. As this volume suggests, there is little doubt that Americans are time deprived and stretched to their capacity in dealing with the demands of work and everyday life. These pressures engender negative health and well-being consequences for workers and their families, especially children, and for employers. Empirical research suggests that men, women, and families may have reached the limits in their abilities to adapt their behaviors to accommodate the increasing and often conflicting demands of the workplace and family (Sayer, Cohen, & Casper, 2004). Thus, it is doubtful that individual Americans can change their work and family circumstances enough by themselves to improve their health and well-being.

Many of the chapters in this volume have discussed the lack of government and workplace policies in the United States that could allow for more successful integration of work and family lives. They have also shown that laws governing workplace schedules and providing for a living wage are outdated and have not evolved with the changing workforce and economy. Many employers, particularly small businesses and those who offer low-wage jobs, provide few if any family-friendly and work-life benefits.

However, some impressive progress has been made in larger corporations. *Working Mothers* magazine's list of the "100 Best Companies for Working Mothers" has shone a spotlight on some of the most innovative corporate practices and programs to improve their workers' work and family lives. The list was introduced in 1986 and has spawned intense competition among CEOs to implement change in their workplaces so that they will make the list and become the employer of choice for working mothers. These companies have made many important organizational changes. For example, they have added child-care programs, child-care referral services, and reimbursements. They have also expanded child-care services to include afterschool, vacation, and sick-child care. They have provided adoption aid and support services for parents of teens and 'tweens. They have implemented flexible scheduling and benefits for part-time workers. Many are starting to add elder care services. However, an important caveat is that, although most of these companies are large, together they employ only about 2% of all employees, and thus these benefits are available to only a small proportion of the workforce.

As this volume indicates, it is doubtful that more progress will be made in eliminating work-family conflict and improving health unless more widespread work-family policies are adopted. For public or private provision of such support to be successfully implemented in the United States, a case must be made to a wider audience that the lack of work and family policy is costly to employers or governments, in terms of lack of adequate nurturance of children; lack of necessary investment in the productivity of future workers; increased absenteeism, lower worker productivity, and higher turnover of employees; or increased health costs of current workers that result from work and family stress.

Many of the chapters in this volume suggest that stronger scientific evidence is needed to make this case, and some specifically cited the need for intervention research to fill this gap. The volume identifies policies and practices that are thought to improve health but have not been tested broadly with scientifically rigorous methods. Workplace policies and practices that affect an individual's ability to meet work and family demands with implications for health are many and varied. For the most part, researchers and employers use terms like *workplace policies and practices* to refer to rules governing the time and place in which work is conducted. For example, in an effort to enable workers to better combine work and family responsibilities, employers may introduce policies designed to permit greater flexibility in scheduling of work and allow work in telecommuting centers or at home to reduce commuting time. By contrast, facilitating workers' abilities to better combine work and family responsibilities may also be achieved by providing needed services (e.g., child care, health clinic) onsite or close to the worksite, assisting workers with expenses by administering flexible spending accounts, and making available referral services to outside providers. The authors also suggested that research should consider the feasibility of more radical approaches to work redesign.

Despite the desperate need for research in this area, little research that involves systematic implementation and evaluation of interventions exists. Why? Mainly because conducting high-quality research in the workplace is fraught with roadblocks. Even with a strong research design, the implementation of interventions in the workplace is often difficult, as is the case, for example, when a corporation decides to provide flexible work schedule options to employees, but frontline managers are reluctant to approve—or actively discourage—the use of this benefit. Thus, other factors such as workplace culture are related to important organizational outcomes, but systematic, broad-based research has not been conducted to examine the relative importance of each of these workplace dimensions in predicting positive outcomes. In a rigorous research design in which workers are randomly assigned benefits, ethical issues also arise because some employees will receive benefits while others will not. The tendency for high turnover in upper management affects the ability to conduct workplace interventions; long-term agreements for conducting and completing research are difficult to secure. Employers may also be reluctant to allow research to be conducted in their workplaces because they believe it will disrupt operations, lead to reductions in output, or produce results that call for the implementation of costly interventions. Additionally, researchers, employers, and employees may disagree on which are the most important policies and practices to implement.

Making the case for greater private sector and government involvement in the work and family arena is in its infancy in the United States. This volume suggests that the biggest challenge may be to implement policy that fits the needs of workers at all levels of the socioeconomic spectrum and at all stages of their lives, some of whom need child-care or elder care services, some of whom need health care benefits, some of whom need adequate wages and more and better work hours, others of whom need reductions in work hours, and most of whom need greater flexibility in meeting family demands. The volume points out that, although it is likely that organizational change is one of the answers to workforce–workplace mismatches, effecting this change is complex. It also emphasizes that researchers and policymakers must be mindful of employers' needs to remain competitive in an increasingly global marketplace. Finally, it is important that any work-family policy adopted in the United States build on the progress that has been made toward gender equality in paid and unpaid work and not erode it.

REFERENCES

Casper, L. M., & Bianchi, S. M. (2002). *Continuity and change in the American family*. Thousand Oaks, CA: Sage.

Christensen, K. (2002). *Increasing awareness of the mismatch between the workplace and the changing workforce*. New York: Alfred P. Sloan Foundation Brief.

Christensen, K. (in press). Leadership in action: A work and family agenda for the future. In M. Pitt-Catsouphes, E. Kossek, & S. Sweet (Eds.), *The handbook of work and family: Multidisciplinary perspectives and approaches*. Mahwah, NJ: Lawrence Erlbaum Associates.

Sayer, L. C., Cohen, P. N., & Casper, L. M. (2004). *Women, men, and work*. New York and Washington, DC: Russell Sage Foundation and Population Reference Bureau.

Shadish, W. R., Cook, T. D., & Campbell, D. T. (2002). *Experimental and quasi-experimental designs for generalized causal inference*. Boston, MA: Houghton-Mifflin.

About the Contributors

Benjamin C. Amick III is Associate Professor of Behavioral Sciences and Epidemiology at the University of Texas School of Public Health and Associate Director of the Texas Program for Society and Health at Rice University. His research focuses on how labor market participation influences a person's health status and how health is related to productive activity. He recently published research examining working life course exposures from 1968 through 1992 and their relationship to mortality. Currently he is developing the second edition of the *Society and Health* book.

Jeanine K. Andreassi is a doctoral student in Organizational Behavior & Human Resource Management at Baruch College, City University of New York. She holds an MBA in Organizational Behavior from Baruch College and an AB in psychology and an AB in economics from Lafayette College, where she graduated Magna Cum Laude. Prior to graduate school, she worked in Finance for Prudential Financial and since then has interned in Human Resource capacities at Credit Suisse First Boston and Sirota Consulting. She is currently working with Dr. Cynthia Thompson and Dr. Tammy Allen on a study of the dimensionality of work-life culture, and with Dr. Karen Lyness assessing the organizational correlates of women's advancement. Her current research interests are focused on individual antecedents of work-life conflict.

Lotte Bailyn is T Wilson (1953) Professor of Management at MIT's Sloan School of Management and Co-Director of the Alfred P. Sloan Foundation MIT Workplace Center. From 1997 to 1999 she was Chair of the MIT Faculty, and from 1995 to 1997 she was the Matina S. Horner Distinguished Visiting Professor at Radcliffe's Public Policy Institute. She is the author of *Breaking the Mold: Women, Men, and Time in the New Corporate World* (1993) and co-author of *Relinking Life and Work: Toward a Better Future* (1996) and *Beyond Work-Family Balance: Advancing Gender Equity and Workplace Performance* (2002). She is a Fellow of the American Psychological Association.

Suzanne M. Bianchi is Professor of Sociology and Faculty Associate in the Maryland Population Research Center at the University of Maryland at College Park. She was a University of Maryland 2003–2004 Distinguished Scholar-Teacher. She is a family demographer whose research focuses on time use in the family, women's changing work and family lives, and child well-being and poverty. She is author of numerous articles and four books, including *Continuity and Change in the American Family* (2002) (with Lynne Casper) (winner of the 2002 Otis Dudley Duncan Book Award for Distinguished Scholarship from the Population Section, American Sociological Association). She is also winner of the 2001 Rosabeth Moss Kanter Award for Excellence in Work-Family Research and the 2001 Rueben Hill Award of the National Council on Family Relations. She is a past president of the Population Association of America and past chair of the Family and Population Sections of the American Sociological Association.

Ann Bookman is Executive Director of the Massachusetts Institute of Technology Workplace Center based at the Sloan School of Management and funded by the Alfred P. Sloan Foundation. Bookman has held a variety of teaching, research, and administrative positions in the academy at Holy Cross, Lesley College, Wellesley College, and the Bunting Institute of Radcliffe College. She also worked in government as a presidential appointee during the first term of the Clinton administration. She served as Policy and Research Director of the Women's Bureau at the U.S. Department of Labor, and Executive Director of the bipartisan congressional Commission on Family and Medical Leave. Her edited collection, *Women and the Politics of Empowerment* (1988), features ethnographic case studies of grassroots organizing efforts in workplaces and communities and documents the process of creating social change from the bottom up. Her new book, *Starting In Our Own Backyards: How Working Families Can Build Community and Survive the New Economy* (Routledge, 2004), focuses on the importance of community institutions and community involvement for raising healthy families and creating a strong civil society.

Linda M. Burton is Director of the Center for Human Development and Family Research in Diverse Contexts and Professor of Human Development and Family Studies and Sociology at the Pennsylvania State University. Dr. Burton's research explores the relationship among community contexts, poverty, intergenerational family structures and processes, and developmental outcomes across the life course in ethnic/racial minority populations. She is currently one of six principal investigators involved in an extensive, longitudinal, multisite, multimethod study of the impact of welfare reform on families and children (*Welfare, Children, and Families: A Three City Study*). She directs the ethnographic component of the *Three-City Study*, and is also principal investigator of an ethnographic study of rural poverty, families, and child development (*Family Life Project*).

Lynne M. Casper is Health Scientist Administrator and Demographer in the Demographic and Behavioral Sciences Branch at the National Institute of Child Health and Human Development (NICHD), where she directs the family and fertility research portfolio and the training program in population studies. She is currently building new research initiatives in the areas of work, family, health, and well-being and family change. Dr. Casper is co-recipient of the American Sociological Association's 2002 Otis Dudley Duncan Award for Outstanding Scholarship in Social Demography for her book, with Suzanne Bianchi, *Continuity and Change in the American Family*. She is co-editor of the forthcoming Erlbaum volume *Measurement Issues in Family Research* (with Sandra Hofferth). Dr. Casper has also published extensively in the areas of families and households, cohabitation, fatherhood, child care, voting, and demographic methods. She was awarded Vice President Gore's Hammer Award for her work on fatherhood with the Interagency Forum on Child and Family Statistics and the DHHS Secretary's Award for Distinguished Service for her work on the fatherhood initiative. She currently serves as Secretary Treasurer of the Population Association of America.

Kathleen E. Christensen founded and directs the Workplace, Workforce and Working Families Program at the Alfred P. Sloan Foundation in New York City. Prior to joining the Sloan Foundation in 1994, she was Professor of Psychology at the Graduate School and University Center of City University of New York. Christensen has published extensively on the changing nature of work and its relationship to the family. Her books include: *Contingent Work: American Employment Relations in Transition* (Cornell University Press, 1998); *Turbulence in the American Workplace* (Oxford University Press, 1991); *Women and Home-based Work: The Unspoken Contract* (Henry Holt, 1988). She has been awarded fellowships from the Danforth Foundation, Rockefeller Foundation, Mellon Foundation, and National Institute for Humanities. Christensen serves on the Conference Board's Work Life Leadership Council and received the 2004 inaugural Work-Life Legacy Award from the Families and Work Institute for her significant contributions in founding the work-family field.

Jeanette N. Cleveland is Professor of Industrial & Organizational Psychology at the Pennsylvania State University. Her research interests include personal and contextual variables in performance appraisal, workforce diversity issues, work and family issues, and international human resources. She was consulting editor for *Journal of Organizational Behavior* and has served or is currently serving on the editorial boards of *Journal of Applied Psychology, Personnel Psychology, Journal of Management, Academy of Management Journal, Journal of Vocational Behavior, Human Resource Management Review, Journal of Organizational Behavior*, and *International Journal of Management Reviews*. She is the Co-Editor for the Applied Psychology Series for Lawrence Erlbaum and Associates. She is the author of numerous research articles and books, including *Understanding Performance Appraisal: Social, Organizational and Goal Perspectives* (with K. Murphy) and, most recently, *Women and Men in Organizations: Sex and Gender Issues* (with M. Stockdale and K. Murphy, 2000).

Ann C. Crouter is Professor of Human Development and Director of the Center for Work and Family Research at the Pennsylvania State University. Her research, grounded in the ecological perspective on human development, has focused on the connections among parents' work conditions, family dynamics, and the development of school-age children and adolescents. She has explored these issues in the context of three longitudinal research projects focused on dual-earner families, all funded by NICHD and conducted in collaboration with Susan McHale. Crouter is probably best known for her research on day-to-day processes in dual-earner families, including parental knowledge of offspring's daily experiences and the temporal patterning of parent–adolescent involvement and adolescent activities. Her work has appeared in a variety of journals, including *Child Development, Developmental Psychology, Journal of Marriage and Family, Journal of Family Psychology, Family Relations, Journal of Social Issues, Human Relations*, and *Journal of Early Adolescence*, as well as edited volumes and handbooks.

Janet Currie is Professor of Economics at the University of California–Los Angeles. Her work focuses on the evaluation of a broad array of public policies affecting children, including early intervention, health, and nutrition programs. Professor Currie was recently elected to the Executive Committee of the American Economics Association, and serves on the editorial board of the *Quarterly Journal of Economics*, as well as being an associate editor of the *Journal of Public Economics*. She has also served as an editor of the *Journal of Labor Economics* and as an associate editor of the *Journal of Health Economics*. She was one of the first directors of the National Bureau of Economic Research (NBER) Program on Children and Families, and is a Research Associate of NBER and a Research Fellow at the Institute for the Study of Labor (IZA) as well as being affiliated with the University of Michigan's National Poverty Center. She has also served on several National Academy of Science (NAS) and National Institutes of Health panels including the NAS Committee on Population.

Charles N. Darrah is Professor of Anthropology at San Jose State University. He is a cultural anthropologist whose research has focused on work, families, and technology. He is a co-founder of the Silicon Valley Cultures Project, a long-term anthropological study of the everyday lives of people in a region dominated by high-tech industry and imagery. His 1997 book, *Learning and Work: An Exploration in Industrial Ethnography*, is based on fieldwork conducted on the production floors of two manufacturing plants. He and colleagues J. M. Freeman and J. A. English-Lueck are completing the manuscript for *Busy Bodies: The Impact of Busyness on American Families and What They Are Doing About It*. The book is based on a 2-year ethnographic study of dual-career middle-class families that was supported by the Alfred P. Sloan Foundation.

Allard E. Dembe is Associate Professor of Family Medicine and Community Health at the University of Massachusetts Medical School and Senior Research Scientist at the University of Massachusetts Center for Health Policy and Research. He currently serves as Deputy Director of the Robert Wood Johnson Foundation's Workers' Compensation Health Initiative, and co-directs the doctoral and postdoctoral degree program in Occupational Health Services Research at the Harvard University School of Public Health. Dr. Dembe's professional and scholarly interests include health policy and health services research, occupational safety and health, workers' compensation insurance, disability and employment, and social aspects of work and health. He is the author of numerous articles and monographs, including, *Occupation and Disease: How Social Factors Affect the Conception of Work-Related Disorders* (1996).

Alison Earle is Project Director for the Work, Family, and Democracy Initiative and a lecturer at the Harvard School of Public Health. Dr. Earle's research has focused on how public policies affect the needs of working families in the United States and worldwide. She has conducted extensive analyses of the relationship between work and family health, as well as between parental working conditions and children's development in the United States. She initiated seminal research on the relationship between caregiving and job loss. Alison Earle received her PhD in Public Policy from the Kennedy School of Government at Harvard University, where she received both the Henry A. Murray Dissertation Award and a Kennedy PhD Fellowship Award for her graduate work.

Joyce K. Fletcher is Professor of Management at the Simmons School of Management in Boston, Affiliated Faculty at the Simmons Center for Gender in Organizations, and Senior Research Scholar at the Jean Baker Miller Training Institute at the Wellesley College Centers for Women. Fletcher, whose work on leadership focuses on the interaction of gender and power in the workplace, is a frequent speaker at national and international conferences on the topics of women, power, and leadership, and she is the co-author of a widely read Harvard Business Review article entitled, "A Modest Manifesto for Shattering the Glass Ceiling." She is the author of *Disappearing Acts: Gender, Power and Relational Practice at Work*, a book nominated as one of the year's best management books by the Academy of Management in 2001, and co-author of *Beyond Work Family Balance: Advancing Gender Equity and Workplace Performance*.

Megan Gallagher is a Senior Research Analyst at Child Trends and a Master of Public Policy candidate at the Georgetown Public Policy Institute in Washington, DC. Her research interests focus on income supports for low-income families, including welfare and housing programs. She has also conducted research on the implications of maternal employment for child and family well-being.

Jennifer Glass is Professor of Sociology at the University of Iowa. Her research interests include work and family life, family policy, and organizational innovation and change. Her current research projects focus on the effects of workplace flexibility policies on workers' wage growth over time. Past publications include "Blessing or Curse? Work-Family Policies and Mother's Wage Growth" *Work and Occupations*, 2004; and "Toward a Kinder, Gentler Workplace: Envisioning the Integration of Family and Work," *Contemporary Sociology*, 2000. She is a member of the governing council of the American Sociological Association and is the past chair of the Sex and Gender Section of the ASA.

Fang Gong is a PhD candidate in sociology at Indiana University–Bloomington. Her research interests include medical sociology, mental health of ethnic minorities, life course, and quantitative research methods. She is currently working with Dr. Eliza Pavalko and Dr. Scott Long to examine cohort differences in the effects of employment on women's health.

Julia R. Henly is Assistant Professor in the School of Social Service Administration at the University of Chicago. She is a faculty affiliate of the University of Chicago's Center for Human Potential and Public Policy and a research affiliate of the National Poverty Center at the University of Michigan. Henly studies families in poverty, with particular attention to the work-family management strategies of mothers in low-wage employment. Her work examines how low-income families use both formal policy structures (e.g., welfare policy, child care policy) and informal systems (e.g., social support networks) in their efforts to manage work and family responsibilities and cope with economic hardship. Her articles appear in a variety of journals including *Journal of Marriage and Family, Children and Youth Services Review, American Journal of Community Psychology,* and *Social Work Research,* and she has chapters in several edited volumes on the low-wage labor market. Henly is currently directing the Study of Work-Child Care Fit, a qualitative investigation of low-wage retail workers and their child care providers.

Jody Heymann is Founding Director of the Project on Global Working Families. Heymann has led studies examining the experiences of over 50,000 working families in 8 countries and public policies in over 165 countries. An Associate Professor at the Harvard School of Public Health and Harvard Medical School, Heymann is founding chair of the Initiative on Work, Family, and Democracy. She is the Director of Policy at the Harvard Center for Society and Health. Heymann's recent books include *Unfinished Work: Building Equality and Democracy in an Era of Working Families* (New Press, 2005), *Global Inequalities at Work: Work's Impact on the Health of Individuals, Families, and Societies,* Oxford University Press, 2003; and *The Widening Gap: Why America's Working Families Are in Jeopardy and What Can Be Done About It,* Basic Books, 2000. She has served in an advisory capacity to the United Nations Educational, Scientific and Cultural Organization (UNESCO), the World Health Organization (WHO), the International Labor Organization (ILO), the U.S. Senate Committee on Health, Education, Labor, and Pensions, and the U.S. Centers for Disease Control and Prevention, among other organizations. Heymann received her PhD in Public Policy from Harvard University, where she was selected in a university-wide competition as a merit scholar, and her MD with honors from Harvard Medical School.

Harry J. Holzer is Professor of Public Policy at Georgetown University and a Visiting Fellow at The Urban Institute in Washington, DC. Formerly he was Chief Economist for the U.S. Department of Labor and Professor of Economics at Michigan State University. Holzer's research has focused primarily on the labor market problems of minorities and other disadvantaged groups. His books include *The Black Youth Employment Crisis* (co-edited with Richard Freeman, 1986), *What Employers Want: Job Prospects for Less-Educated Workers* (1996), and *Employers and Welfare Recipients: The Effects of Welfare Reform in the Workplace* (2001).

Nicole Jansen is a Postdoctoral Fellow at the Department of Epidemiology at Maastricht University in the Netherlands. Her research activities focus on risk factors and outcomes of work-family conflict, and on the effectiveness of early treatment of employees with an increased risk of long-term sickness absence. She obtained her MSc degrees in Mental Health Sciences and Biological

Psychology at Maastricht University. Her PhD project was embedded within the large-scale prospective Maastricht Cohort Study on Fatigue at Work, and describes the effects of various aspects of working time arrangements on fatigue-related outcomes and the (in)ability of employees to adequately combine work and family life. She received the Netherlands School of Primary Care Research Scientific Award for the best dissertation of 2003.

Susan Jekielek is a Research Associate at Child Trends in Washington, DC. Her work focuses on parental work characteristics and their implications for families and children. She also studies family structure and relationship quality. She has recently co-authored a research brief, "Marriage from a Child's Perspective: How Does Family Structure Affect Children, and What Can We Do About it?" (with Kristin Moore). Other work, "Lifecourse Effects of Work and Family Circumstances on Children" (with Elizabeth C. Cooksey and Elizabeth G. Menaghan) and "Parental Conflict, Marital Disruption, and Children's Emotional Well-Being," has been published in *Social Forces*.

Robert Kaestner is Professor in the Institute of Government and Public Affairs and the Department of Economics at the University of Illinois at Chicago and a Research Associate of the National Bureau of Economic Research. His areas of research interest are health and labor economics. He has recently published articles on the effects of welfare reform on employment, fertility, and health insurance of low-income women; the effects of Medicaid and private health insurance on infant and child health; whether expansions in Medicaid crowded out private health insurance; the impact of state policies on the timing, place of occurrence, and incidence of abortion; and the effect of unintended pregnancy on infant and child development.

Rosalind Berkowitz King is a Health Scientist Administrator in the Demographic and Behavioral Sciences Branch of the National Institute of Child Health and Human Development, National Institutes of Health. Prior to this position, she was a Postdoctoral Fellow in the Carolina Population Center at the University of North Carolina at Chapel Hill. Her research focuses on adolescent romantic relationships, social aspects of adolescent physical development, and other issues related to union formation and fertility. Her recent publications include, "Subfecundity and Anxiety in a Nationally Representative Sample," *Social Science & Medicine*, 2003; and "Age and College Completion: A Life History Analysis of Women Aged 15–44" (with Jerry A. Jacobs), *Sociology of Education*, 2002.

Amy Kolak is a NICHD postdoctoral trainee in Developmental Psychology at the University of Michigan. She completed her PhD in Human Development and Family Studies at the Pennsylvania State University in August

2004. Her research interests focus on family processes and child development. She is especially interested in how factors inside the family (marital conflict, parenting stress, family health) and factors outside of the family (parental work experiences, other socioeconomic forces) impact both family dynamics and child well-being.

Sanders Korenman is Professor in the School of Public Affairs, Baruch College of the City University of New York and Research Associate of the National Bureau of Economic Research. He was a member of the Board on Children, Youth, and Families of the National Academy of Sciences from 1998 to 2003, and a member of its Committee on Family Work Policies. His previous positions include Assistant Professor of Economics and Public Affairs at Princeton University, Associate Professor of Public Affairs at the University of Minnesota, and Senior Economist for labor, welfare, and education for President Clinton's Council of Economic Advisers.

Ellen Ernst Kossek is Professor of Human Resource Management (HRM) and Organizational Behavior at Michigan State University. She is elected to the Board of Governors of the National Academy of Management and was Chair of the Gender & Diversity in Organizations Division. She is a Fellow of the American Psychological Association and Society of Industrial Organizational Psychology for her contributions to work and family research. She has served on the Wharton Work-Life Roundtable. She has published over 30 articles in refereed journals, and several of these have been nominated for or won Best Paper of the Year awards. She is an editorial board member of four journals and has published four books on human resource management, diversity, or work and family. Her current research (with Mary Dean Lee), funded by the Alfred P. Sloan Foundation, investigates managing professionals in new organizational forms.

Tage S. Kristensen is Professor at the Danish Institute of Occupational Health, Copenhagen, Denmark. He has been working on research in the field of occupational health psychology for more than 25 years. Among the main topics of research are work and health of women, work environment in the slaughterhouse industry, working conditions and the risk of cardiovascular diseases, absence from work, human service work and burnout, work-family conflict, and the overall impact of work on health. He has published more than 100 books and articles on these topics and on methods in psychosocial research, medical sociology, prevention, intervention research, and survey methods in occupational health psychology. He founded the Danish Society of Psychosocial Medicine and is now Chairman of the Committee on Cardiology in Occupational Health under the International Commission of Occupational Health (ICOH).

Susan Lambert is Associate Professor in the School of Social Service Administration at the University of Chicago. Lambert's research focuses on the work side of work-life issues. Her current study of workplaces in Chicago investigates the distinction between organizational policies on paper versus those in practice, shedding light on the extent to which opportunities available in the larger corporation trickle down to lower level jobs and, if so, for which kinds of jobs. Lambert's articles appear in leading journals such as the *Academy of Management Journal*, the *Annals of the American Academy of Political and Social Sciences*, and *Social Service Review*. She and Ellen Kossek are co-editors of a book that outlines and extends the theoretical underpinnings of research on work-life integration (2004).

Arleen A. Leibowitz is Professor of Public Policy in the University of California–Los Angeles School of Public Affairs. She has served on the National Research Council Committee on National Statistic and is a member of the editorial board of the *Journal of Policy Analysis and Management*. Dr. Leibowitz's research centers on investments in human capital and health. She has examined the role of maternal education in investments in children, women's labor supply, the demand for child care, and the effect of maternity leave on new mothers' return to work. Dr. Leibowitz's current research in health examines how public policies such as Medicaid and private policies such as managed care affect the health care obtained by children and adults living with HIV.

Laura Lein is Professor in the School of Social Work and Department of Anthropology, the University of Texas at Austin. She is a social anthropologist whose work has concentrated on the interface between families in poverty and the institutions that serve them. She is the author, with Kathryn Edin, of *Making Ends Meet: How Single Mothers Survive Welfare and Low-Wage Work* (New York: Russell Sage Foundation, 1997). Since then she has begun new work with Edin on low-income, nonresidential fathers. Initial findings from this work have been published in "Talking With Low-Income Fathers" in *Poverty Research News 2000* (with Kathryn Edin, Susan Clampet-Lundquist, and Timothy Nelson). She is a Senior Ethnographer collaborating on "Welfare, Children, and Families: A Three-City Study," with Principal Investigators Ron Angel, Linda Burton, P. Lindsay Chase-Lansdale, Andrew Cherlin, Robert Moffitt, and William Julius Wilson. The project has already released several policy briefs on sanctions and access to health insurance on which Lein is co-author.

Debra A. Major is Associate Professor of Psychology at Old Dominion University. She is former editor of *The Industrial-Organizational Psychologist*, and she serves on the editorial board of *Journal of Organizational Behavior*. Her work has appeared in scholarly journals, including *Health Education Research*, *Human Resource Development Quarterly*, *Human Resource Management Review*, *International Journal of Stress Management*, *Journal of Applied Psychology*, *Journal of Business and Psychology*, *Journal of Occupational Health Psychology*, *Psychology of Women Quarterly*, and *Sex Roles*, as well as numerous edited volumes. Her research with Karyn Bernas was a top 20 finalist for the 2001 Rosabeth Moss Kanter Award for Excellence in Work-Family Research. The National Science Foundation sponsored her multiyear research on inclusive climate and work-family culture in the information technology workplace. Her current research interests are focused on the reciprocal relationship between parents' work lives and children's health.

Susan M. McHale is Professor of Human Development at the Pennsylvania State University. Her research focuses on children's and adolescents' family relationships, roles, and everyday activities; she is especially interested in sibling relationship dynamics and the family conditions and experiences that foster similarities and differences in sisters' and brothers' well-being and development. Together with Ann C. Crouter, she has studied these issues in the context of the Penn State Family Relationships Project, a longitudinal study of families that has been funded by NICHD since 1995. In two studies also funded by NICHD, she and Crouter are working with Penn State colleagues, Drs. Linda M. Burton and Dena P. Swanson, and with Dr. Kimberly A. Updegraff at Arizona State University to study siblings' experiences and family dynamics in samples of African-American and Mexican-American families.

Kristin Moore is President and Senior Scholar of Child Trends. A social psychologist, she has been with Child Trends since 1982, studying trends in child and family well-being, the effects of family structure and social change on children, the determinants and consequences of adolescent parenthood, the effects of welfare and welfare reform on children, and positive development. As a survey researcher, she has worked on the design and analysis of numerous social science surveys. Moore is a member of the Family and Child Well-Being Research Network established by the National Institute of Child Health and Human Development to examine the factors that enhance the development and well-being of children. Network members are selected by peer-review. She has been involved in designing, implementing, and conducting analyses on data from the National Evaluation of Welfare to Work Strategies for more than a decade.

Cam Mustard is a Professor in the Department of Public Health Sciences, Faculty of Medicine, University of Toronto, and President & Scientific Director of the Institute for Work & Health. He is Associate Director and

Fellow of the Population Health Program of the Canadian Institute for Advanced Research and a recipient of a CIHR Scientist award (1998–2003). Dr. Mustard has active research interests in the areas of work environments, labor market experiences and health, the distributional equity of publicly funded health and health care programs in Canada, and the epidemiology of socioeconomic health inequalities across the human life course.

Mary C. Noonan is Assistant Professor of Sociology at the University of Iowa. Noonan's research interests include gender, work, and family issues. Her past research has examined the effect of time spent in housework on men's and women's wages. She is currently examining trends over time in men's and women's employment behavior around the time of childbirth. Another project explores the role that family responsibilities play in explaining the sex-based earnings gap among lawyers.

Eliza Pavalko is Associate Professor and Director of Graduate Studies in the Department of Sociology at Indiana University, Bloomington. Her broad research agenda seeks to understand the pathways people pursue in work, family, and other careers across their adult lives and how these pathways intersect with societal changes. An ongoing project, with Scott Long and Fang Gong, funded by the National Institute on Aging, examines cohort changes in women's work and family careers and the implications of those changes for physical and emotional health. A related project with Gil Gee and Scott Long investigates age and cohort changes in self-reports of age discrimination.

Maureen Perry-Jenkins is Associate Professor of Psychology at the University of Massachusetts Amherst and past director of the Center for the Family at the University of Massachusetts. She has numerous publications in the *Journal of Family Issues*, the *Journal of Marriage and Family*, and the *Journal of Family and Economic Issues* that explore work and family issues for working-class families. Her current research involves a 10-year, longitudinal study funded by the National Institute of Mental Health that examines the transition to parenthood and transition back to paid employment for working-class couples and for African-American and Euro-American single mothers. She examines how these multiple transitions are related to family members' well-being and relationships, and what risk and resilience factors differentially shape how well family members cope.

Harriet B. Presser is Distinguished University Professor in the Department of Sociology at the University of Maryland at College Park. She is past president of the Population Association of America (1989) and served on the Council of the American Sociological Association (1990–1993). She was named George Washington University's 1992 Distinguished Alumni Scholar, having received her BA from there, and was elected Fellow of the American Association for the Advancement of Science in 2002. Her residential fellowships include: the Center for Advanced Study in the Behavioral Sciences at Stanford (1986–1987, 1991–1992, and 2003–2004), the Russell Sage Foundation (1998–1999 and summer 2000), the Rockefeller Foundation's Bellagio Study and Conference Center in Italy (February–March 2000), and the Netherlands Institute for Advanced Study in the Humanities and Social Sciences (1994–1995). Professor Presser's research expertise is in the areas of social demography, focusing on the intersections of gender, work, and family. She also studies population and family policy issues from national and international perspectives. Her recent book is titled *Working in a 24/7 Economy: Challenges for American Families* (Russell Sage Foundation, 2003).

David J. Prottas is a doctoral student at Baruch College in Organizational Behavior & Human Resource Management. He received his AB from Vassar College and his MBA in finance and international business from the University of Chicago. He then spent several decades in the financial service industry, most recently in the investment banking division of Citigroup. His research interests include the structural and process antecedents of corporate culture as well as the differences in motivations, attitudes, and outcomes among people who are organizationally employed and those who work under nontraditional work arrangements. He and Cynthia Thompson recently received a grant to study emerging work arrangements in America.

Sara B. Raley is a PhD student and C. Wright Mills fellow in the Sociology program at the University of Maryland at College Park, specializing in demography and gender, work, and family. For the past 3 years, she has worked as a graduate research assistant for Dr. Suzanne M. Bianchi and has been actively involved with the Maryland Population Research Center at the University of Maryland.

Zakia Redd is a Senior Research Analyst at Child Trends. Her research focuses on how social policies and community programs directed toward low-income families affect children's outcomes. She recently managed a research synthesis exploring how mandatory welfare-to-work programs that were experimentally evaluated affected children's outcomes. She also co-authored a paper investigating how transitions between welfare and work relate to children's outcomes. Other research interests include children's use of time outside of school, youth development programs, social connectedness, and educational outcomes. Publications to which she has contributed have appeared in the *Journal of Social Policy* and *The Future of Children*.

Rena Repetti is Professor of Psychology at the University of California–Los Angeles and a core faculty member in the Sloan Foundation's Center for the Everyday Lives of Families at UCLA. Repetti studies stress and coping processes in the family. Her work points to the importance of family and work social environments for the health and well-being of parents and children, and to the dynamic interplay between an individual's efforts to cope with daily stressors and patterns of family interaction. The findings from her research suggest several processes through which common daily stressors originating at work influence individuals and families. For example, Repetti has shown how stress at work can have both a short- and a long-term negative impact on the father–child relationship. The findings from her studies reinforce a social-ecological perspective on families, one in which members' daily lives outside of the home are intimately intertwined with life within the home.

Christopher J. Ruhm is Jefferson-Pilot Excellence Professor of Economics at the University of North Carolina at Greensboro, Research Associate of the National Bureau of Economic Research, and Research Fellow at the Institute for the Study of Labor. During the 1996 to 1997 academic year, he served as Senior Economist on the President's Council of Economic Advisers. Professor Ruhm has conducted extensive research on the determinants of health and risky behaviors, investments in children, the impact of parental leave policies and mandated employment benefits, causes and effects of job displacements, transition into retirement, and the economic consequences of alcohol and illegal drug policies. He is co-author of *Turbulence in the American Workplace* (1990) and has written more than 45 articles or book chapters. He is currently an Associate Editor of the *European Economic Review* and a member of the American Economics Association, International Health Economics Association, and the Society of Labor Economists.

Barbara Schneider is Professor of Sociology and Human Development at the University of Chicago. She currently directs the Data Research and Development Center and co-directs the Alfred P. Sloan Center on Parents, Children, and Work. Interested in the lives of adolescents and their families and schools, she has written widely on these topics. Her most recent publications include, *The Ambitious Generation: America's Teenagers Motivated but Directionless* (co-authored with David Stevenson) and *Trust in Schools, A Core Resource for Improvement* (co-authored with Anthony Bryk). She and Linda Waite are currently completing a book on the Sloan 500 Family Study, *Working Apart: Dual-Career Families and the Work-Life Balance*, to be published by Cambridge University Press in 2005.

Stephanie Simmons is a member of the Project on Global Working Families at the Harvard School of Public Health. She has analyzed interview data gathered by the Project in Vietnam and Russia and data from the Work, Family, and Equity Index in a wide range of policy areas. Her research interests center on children, families, and education.

Lars Smith-Hansen is a Research Assistant at the Danish National Institute of Occupational Health (NIOH), Copenhagen, Denmark. He received his BA,Techn. Soc. from Department of Environment, Technology, and Social Studies at Roskilde University Center. He is responsible for building up and validating a number of empirical databases at the Psychosocial Department, NIOH. His research activities are focused on measurement of psychosocial factors at work and related consequences. He has published chapters, articles, and papers in this field.

Pamela J. Smock is Associate Professor of Sociology and Research Associate Professor at the Population Studies Center of the Institute for Social Research at the University of Michigan–Ann Arbor. Smock is a family demographer and has published numerous articles on topics relating to family patterns and change, and their implications, in the United States. Recent articles include "Cohabitation in the United States: An Appraisal of Research Themes, Findings, and Implications," *Annual Review of Sociology*; "The Effect of Marriage and Divorce on Women's Economic Well-Being," *American Sociological Review*; and "Swapping Families? Serial Parenting and Economic Support for Children" and "The Wax and Wane of Marriage: Prospects for Marriage in the 21st Century," *Journal of Marriage and Family*.

Ross M. Stolzenberg is Professor of Sociology at the University of Chicago. He is editor of the American Sociological Association's research methods journal, *Sociological Methodology*. Previously, he has held academic posts in university departments and programs in social relations, sociology, population dynamics, and applied statistics (variously) at Harvard University, The Johns Hopkins University, and the University of Illinois at Urbana–Champaign. He has held nonacademic posts as a researcher and consultant at The RAND Corporation and as vice president for research and test development at the Graduate Management Admission Council. Stolzenberg's current research concerns the connection between family and labor market processes in stratification systems and the effects of husbands' and wives' work and other behavior on each other's health. His previous research concerns a wide variety of topics, including labor market phenomena, statistical methods, and health and the causes and consequences of religious participation.

Cynthia A. Thompson is Associate Professor of Management and Organizational Behavior in the Zicklin School of Business at Baruch College, City University of New York. During her recent sabbatical she worked as a Senior Research Associate at the Families and Work Institute, where she co-authored *The 2002 National Study of the Changing Workforce*. Her work has been published in both scholarly and practitioner journals, including *Journal of Applied Psychology*, *Journal of Vocational Behavior*, *Journal of Managerial Issues*, *Journal of Social Behavior and Personality*, *Sex Roles*, *Journal of Management Education*, and *Community, Work and Family*. With co-authors Laura Beauvais and Karen Lyness, her research was nominated for the 1999 Rosabeth Moss Kanter Award for Excellence in Work-Family Research. Her current research interests are focused on the structural antecedents of work-life culture.

Linda J. Waite is Lucy Flower Professor of Sociology and co-Director of the Alfred P. Sloan Center on Parents, Children and Work at the University of Chicago, where she also directs the Center on Aging. Her current research interests include the working family, especially dual-career couples with children. She is also interested in the role of the family at older ages, in the health and functioning of individuals, intergenerational transfers and exchanges, and employment. She has published widely on the family, including an award-winning book with Frances Goldscheider, *New Families, No Families: The Transformation of the American Home*. Her most recent book, *The Case for Marriage: Why Married People are Happier, Healthier, and Better Off Financially*, with Maggie Gallagher, won the 2000 book award from the Coalition for Marriage, Family, and Couples Education. Her most recent book, *Time Together, Time Apart: How Dual-Career Families Manage*, co-edited with Barbara Schneider, is forthcoming, Cambridge University Press.

Jane Waldfogel is Professor of Social Work and Public Affairs at Columbia University School of Social Work. She is also a research associate at the Centre for Analysis of Social Exclusion at the London School of Economics. Waldfogel has written extensively on the impact of public policies on child and family well-being. She is the author of *The Future of Child Protection: How to Break the Cycle of Abuse and Neglect* (1998) and co-editor (with Sheldon Danziger) of *Securing the Future: Investing in Children from Birth to Adulthood* (2000). Her work has also been published in leading academic journals, including *American Economic Review*, *American Sociological Review*, *Child Development*, *Demography*, *Journal of Policy Analysis and Management*, *Journal of Human Resources*, *Journal of Labor Economics*, and *Journal of Population Economics*. Her current research interests include: economic status, public policy, and child neglect; inequality in early childhood care and education; and work-family policies and child and family well-being.

Richard Wertheimer is Vice President for Internal Management and Area Director for Welfare and Poverty at Child Trends in Washington, DC. Wertheimer is an economist with research and policy expertise on children in working poor families; teen and nonmarital fertility; transitions to adult-hood among vulnerable persons; conditions of children and their mothers at the time of birth; child abuse, neglect, and children in foster care; and indicators of child and youth well-being. He is currently serving as principal investigator on projects encompassing many of these areas, including a study of children in working poor families using data from the Current Population Survey (funded by the Foundation for Child Development), a study of vul-nerable youth (funded by the Annie E. Casey and the Hewlett Foundations), a study of children aging out of foster care (funded by the Casey Foundation), and a state-level survey of policies and programs designed to reduce teen and nonmarital fertility.

Martha Zaslow is Vice President for Research and Senior Scholar at Child Trends in Washington, DC. She is also the Area Director for Early Childhood Development. Zaslow's work focuses on the implications of welfare policies for families and children, the development of children in poverty, maternal employment, child care, and improving survey measures of parenting and of children's development. Recent publications include "Impacts on Children in Experimental Evaluations of Welfare-to-Work Programs," *Future of Children* (with K. A. Moore, J. L. Brooks, P. Morris, K. Tout, & Z. Redd), "How Are Children Faring Under Welfare Reform? Emerging Patterns," in A. Weil and K. Feingold (Eds.), *Welfare Reform: The Next Act* (Urban Institute Press, 2002) (with K. A. Moore, K. Tout, J. Scarpa, & S. Vandivere), and "Maternal Depressive Symptoms and Low Literacy as Potential Barriers to Employment in a Sample of Families Receiving Welfare: Are There Two-Generational Im-plications?" *Women and Health* (with Elizabeth C. Hair & Robin M. Dion).

Author Index

239, 344, 346, *358*, 369, 371, *374*, 449, *450*
Hofferth, S. L., 22, 31, 34, *40*, *41*, 61, 65, 192, 193, *200*, 223, 229, 235, *239*, 349, *359*, *360*
Hoffman, C., 381, *390*
Hoffman, L. W., 171, *184*, 261, 263, 277, 286, *294*, 454, *470*
Hofmeister, H., 386, *392*
Hogstedt, C., 425, *432*
Hohmann, N., 280, *294*
Holden, K. C., 354, *358*, 365, *374*
Hollingshead, A. B., 455, 469, *471*
Holmes-Eber, P., 514, *527*
Holt, E., 517, *526*
Holvino, E., 334, 335n, *341*
Holzer, H. J., 84, 85, *95*, 473, 481, *491*
Hong, J., 383, *391*
Hoogstra, L., 74, *79*
Hooker, K., 57, *65*
Hopper, J., 366, *374*
Horton, F., 235, *239*
Horwitz, A. V., 367, *374*
Horwood, L. J., 501, *507*
Hottinen, V., 435, *450*
Hotz, J., 236, *239*
Hotz, V. J., 303, *310*
Houle, M., 406, *409*
House, J. S., 420, 421, *430*, *431*
Houseman, S., 86, 92, 94, *95*
Houtman, I., 419, *430*
Howell-White, S., 367, *374*
Howes, C., 161, *165*, 290, 292, *294*, 295, 465, *471*
Hoynes, H., 308, *310*
Huber, J., 219, 220, 228, 353, *359*
Hudis, P. M., 350, *358*
Hudson, K., 419, *430*, 494, *508*
Huff, J. W., 99, *113*
Huffman, M., 225, *227*
Hug, R., 247, *257*
Hughes, M. E., 363, *374*, *376*
Hunt, A., *429*
Hunt, G. G., 104, *115*
Hunter, D. J., 47, *48*
Hurt, T., 496, *507*
Huselid, M., 99, *113*
Huston, A. C., 270, 276, *277*
Hutchens, R. M., 373, *374*
Hyde, J. S., 176, 179, 180, *181*, 232, 235, *239*, 250, 252, *257*, 321, *324*

Hyle, P. D., 365, *375*
Hyson, R., 193, *198*

I

Ilg, R., 24, *41*
Imershein, A., 402, *409*
Ingersoll-Dayton, B., 381, 382, *391*, *392*
Ingram, P., 124, 127, *131*
Ishii-Kuntz, M., 347, 348, *357*
Iverson, B., 517, *527*
Izraeli, D. N., 174, *184*

J

Jackson, K. L., 501, *507*
Jacobs, D., 481, *491*
Jacobs, J. A., 44, 48, 67, 68, *79*, 351, *358*, 389, *393*
Jacobson, S., 332, *340*
Jacques, R., 332, 335, *340*, *341*
Jaeger, D. A., 284, *293*
Jaffe, A. J., 356, *358*
Jahn, E. W., 119, 121, *131*, *132*
James-Burdumy, S., 235, *240*, 288, *294*
Jamison, R. L., 122, *131*
Jamner, L. D., 247, *257*
Jansen, N. W. H., 447, *450*
Jarrett, R. L., 263, 270, *277*, 499, *507*
Jaskar, K. L., 173, 174, *182*
Jayakody, R., 494, 496, 501, *508*
Jekielek, S. M., 222, 227, 262, 271, 276, *277*
Jenkinson, C., 427, *430*
Jeong, J., 77, *79*
Jeong, S., 236, *240*
Jiricka, M., 398, *410*
Johansen, A., 195, *199*
Johansson, G., 435, 440, *450*
John, D., 344, *359*, *360*, 371, *376*
Johnson, A. A., 128, 129, *130*, 407, *409*
Johnson, J. S., 369, *375*
Johnson, J. V., 421, 422, 428, *430*, 435, 440, *450*
Johnson, N., 160, *165*
Johnson, P., 118, 119, 121, *132*
Johnson, R. W., 384, 385, *391*, 474, *491*
Johnson, S., 161, *164*
Johnston, J., 285, *294*
Johnston, L. D., 61, 66, 366, *373*

Subject Index